JUST WHAT
THE DOCTOR ORDERED

THIS is called The *Special* Diet Cook Book because it supplies recipes and helpful information for special, or corrective, diets.

If your physician had the time to select the tastiest dishes for your special diet, if he had the time to test them, to calculate the calories in some recipes, and to determine the amounts of carbohydrates, protein, fat, sodium and residue in others—and then to write them up for you, he might have prepared this very book. Since he is a physician and not a chef, we have done it for him. This is his book, to help you attain and maintain good health and happiness. NO corrective diet should be undertaken without the guidance of a doctor.

Your own reason for dieting may be that you wish to look better, to wear more attractive clothes, to be more admired. Your doctor's principal concern is with the dangers of obesity, high blood pressure, ulcers, or other conditions where diet is a vital factor in the treatment. The doctor knows that in some cases, a change in diet may be more important than drugs, that diet correction has at times avoided serious surgical operations, and that diet change may even be the means of prolonging life.

Your physician, above all people, knows human frailties—that "the spirit is willing but the flesh is weak." He knows that few of us can long remain loyal to a restricted diet if it is dull and drab. Diets must be interesting, recipes must produce tempting dishes, menus must be inviting. This book gives a variety of delicious foods to brighten restricted meals. If you are on a rigid diet, nothing will afford you greater satisfaction than finding how well you can eat within the limits of your regimen.

Since this is not a general cook book, no attempt has been made to teach the art of cooking. There are many excellent cook books by culinary experts . . . books which supply basic data as well as family recipes. The good standard cook books should serve as a guide to you, as they have to us. What you want from *The Special Diet Cook Book*, we believe, are ideas for making interesting dishes that will fit into your special diet.

It APPEARS TO ME NECESSARY TO EVERY PHYSICIAN . . .

TO STRIVE TO KNOW, IF HE WOULD WISH TO PERFORM HIS

DUTIES, WHAT MAN IS IN RELATION TO THE ARTICLES OF

FOOD AND DRINK, AND TO HIS OCCUPATIONS, AND WHAT ARE

THE EFFECTS OF EACH OF THEM TO EVERY ONE.

—HIPPOCRATES
author of the Hippocratic Oath,
taken by every physician

THE SPECIAL DIET COOK BOOK

BY

MARVIN SMALL

.

INTRODUCTION BY JAMES R. WILSON, M.D.
*Former Secretary, The Council on Foods and
Nutrition, American Medical Association*

Hawthorn Books, Inc. Publishers • NEW YORK

CONTENTS

ILLUSTRATED CHARTS

INTRODUCTION

WITH good reason, the author believes this book can make life easier and happier for those who must follow special diets.

What are special diets—sometimes called corrective or therapeutic diets? Special diets are modified normal diets; modified to meet the special needs of individual patients.

But what is a normal diet? A normal diet consists of a variety of wholesome foods which supply all essential nutrients and sufficient calories to maintain fitness and desirable weight. It meets the recommended dietary allowances of the Food and Nutrition Board of the National Research Council, and conforms to the "Basic Seven" pattern of food planning. Reasonable care in the selection of foods, available in all parts of the United States, will supply all nutrients known to be essential.

This is the first time, as far as I am aware, that a comprehensive special diet cook book and handbook has been compiled for the non-medical reader. Its preparation required much work and a multitude of calculations. The readily-understood charts, the grouping of recipes, and the calorie and other computations make this book useful to those who are on special diets or who must prepare special diet meals for others.

The author's computations are based upon recent standard data. Nevertheless, it must be recognized that certain items of nutritional data are approximations only and are subject to revision as new information becomes available. This is particularly true of the sodium data. Sodium content of natural foods varies considerably, and information concerning representative averages is incomplete as of this date.

It will be noted that trade or brand names of many food items are used because the author believes Americans buy packaged foods according to brand names. Furthermore, he informs me that the recipes were usually tested with the particular brand of product mentioned. It should be pointed out, however, that other brands may often be substituted when of similar composition.

I would like to comment briefly on a few of the special diets and on problems related to them.

Overweight is a world-wide problem. Its dangers have been called particularly to our attention in America and we have every reason to respect the warning. The increased instance of diabetes, coronary heart disease, hypertension (high blood pressure), and other degenerative diseases among those who are overweight appears to be definitely established.

Overweight is due to overeating. Although there may be modifying factors, the overweight person is overweight simply because he has consumed more food than is required by him and has deposited the excess as fat in the body storehouses where it is unsightly, unnecessary and a health hazard. No food in itself is fattening. Food is converted into unsightly fat only when eaten in excess of body needs.

In order to reduce body fat, the total calorie intake of food must be sufficiently low to make it necessary for the individual to use his own stored fat to supply his body's daily need for fuel.

While reducing, it is important not to neglect the intake of proteins or other essential nutrients. The good reducing diet takes care of this matter. Let your doctor tell you if you need to reduce, how much, and how fast; let him guide you in the selection of a diet. Reducing is a problem of nutrition. Don't pin your faith on a pill.

Increasing weight is also a problem of nutrition. When a patient's weight has fallen below its optimum or desirable level because of illness, anxiety, or for other reasons, a high-calorie diet may be an important part of the treatment. Occasionally, increased weight is desired for aesthetic reasons. This may or may not justify the introduction of a high-calorie diet. Here again the personal physician should be consulted. Leanness that comes naturally is usually a blessing and should not be treated as a physical handicap. Underweight due to malnutrition calls for a readjustment of faulty eating habits and may not require necessarily an increase in calories.

After the desired weight results have been obtained by either a high or low-calorie diet, the object should be to return to a normal diet as soon as possible. This does not mean returning to the diet that got the individual into nutritional difficulties in the first place. Therefore, nutritional education is as important to the patient as dieting.

Those on sodium-restricted diets should have medical supervision for a twofold purpose—to avoid trouble and to attain the maximum hoped-for benefits. Only those recipes which contain ingredients on the individual patient's approved list may be used. It is also well to remember that meats, fish, poultry, eggs and milk all contain relatively large amounts of sodium. In the case of a severely restricted diet, these items may have to be used sparingly.

In the case of all conditions requiring special diets, it is essential to have intelligent patient-doctor cooperation. In diabetes it can be the difference between life and death. Items included in bland diets vary widely. This is due to the individual differences between patients and what they can tolerate, and what the physician is trying to accomplish.

And finally, it should be mentioned that there is an important psychological factor in connection with some special diets, especially in the case of calorie-restriction. It is not enough simply to have a special diet recommended—a motive must be found, and the motive must be compelling because special diets, particularly reduction diets, are serious business. Eating is, after all, a legitimate pleasure that has social as well as nutritional significance. This book can help keep eating a pleasure for those on special diets. This is an added reason for the significance of The Special Diet Cook Book.

It is not the purpose of this book to help anyone put himself on a diet. Self-imposed special diets can be dangerous. Rather, it is the author's sole aim to assist the person for whom a special diet has been prescribed, to prepare more attractive meals within the limits of the doctor's recommendation—and at the same time help to insure the success of the diet.

James R. Wilson, M.D.
Former Secretary, Council on Foods and Nutrition,
American Medical Association

ALL IN THE POINT OF VIEW

Every lover of good food has his own pet restaurant situated somewhere off the beaten path. Mine happens to be the Table du Roy, hidden behind the Galeries Lafayette in mid-town Paris.

You seemingly sit forever dawdling over an apéritif, but something in it seems to wilt your will to rush, and you don't mind the wait. Then an iced pail containing *vin de la maison* is set before you, and pretty soon you make the acquaintance of Monsieur George.

He is big in all directions, and round of face. Even his tall chef's hat looks as if it has a balloon in it. He tells you that you must have so-and-so—you cannot quite make out what he is saying, but he presses the fingers of his hand to his lips, smacks them, lifts them to heaven—repeats this a few times—and, of course, you have agreed to the so-and-so, followed by the something-or-other which has also been ordered through the delicate persuasion of M. George.

After another interval, a waiter brings forth an immense platter containing small crocks of various vegetables and herbs. The assistant sets up two alcohol stoves and places a large copper pan over them. Now M. George re-enters the scene, and with a flourish, empties a crock of butter into the waiting pan. He mixes—and no ordinary mixture is this! He empties a crock of mushrooms, a crock of sliced onions, another crock, another, and another, and still another. Gently he blends with a waving motion. Then with a rhymthic sweep of his hand he captures the steaming aroma and brings it to his nostrils. But do not think he is through with his culinary rites. He mixes again, repeats the gesture, and this time is more satisfied. The operation is continued and the aroma wafting repeated. Finally, at just the right point, a pitcher of cream is poured into the mixture and the whatever-it-is has reached its point of perfection. A sauce is finished—and until now you have not even known that it was to be a sauce. The garçon has brought a delicately sautéed filet of real English sole, and the sauce goes over it. You taste it, and all the Thespian gestures of M. George are forgiven. Heaven has come to earth.

You remember how the ecstasy of the occasion made you refuse the dish that followed, roast pigeon served on a sword—anything after that sauce would have been an anticlimax. And when you left, there stood M. George at the door, handsomely tailored in blue, bowing and beaming . . . a little disappointed to see that you have not eaten the pigeon, but understanding. He hands you a numbered medallion that makes you a member of his club and entitles you to a discount on your next visit. Whether you keep it or not makes little difference, you will always preserve the memory of that meal.

No doubt you have similar memories of some occasion. While it may be necessary now, in the interests of your health, to eliminate a number of the foods which you have enjoyed so much in the past, it certainly is not a requirement of even the most austere diet-regimen that eating be robbed of all its pleasure.

Many of the dishes in this book are new, different and exciting, and seek to intrigue you into trying them. Other recipes are plain and simple because all of us enjoy simplicity at least once in a while—and because many simple dishes are useful as a basis for embellishment. In some cases we have achieved this embellishment for you; in others, we hope you will accept the idea involved and use your own imagination—or refer to other cook books—to create variations that appeal to you.

Dieting is greatly a matter of adjustment—take coffee for example. Time and again you hear people say they never could drink coffee without cream or sugar . . . despite the enthusiasm of black-coffee-drinking friends who insist that the only way you can get the real flavor of coffee is to drink it black and without sweetening. Then comes the day when the doctor says "Diet!" and you may *have* to drink your coffee black. If you are like so many thousands of other dieters, you join the ranks of ravers over black coffee, and wonder how you could ever enjoy it otherwise. The day comes when the taste of cream and sugar in coffee makes you positively ill. Yes, dieting is largely a matter of adjusting your point of view, and surprisingly, that adjustment often brings greater enjoyment.

This book should help you adapt yourself to your restricted diet, so that you no longer yearn for the foods you cannot have . . . perhaps even speed the day when you can—if you wish—again eat "everything"—or almost everything.

—M. S.

ACKNOWLEDGMENTS

Thanks are gratefully expressed to:

THE AMERICAN MEDICAL ASSOCIATION, for its cooperation . . . through the invaluable suggestions of Dr. James R. Wilson, and the review of charts and recipes by members of the staff of the Council on Foods and Nutrition—Thomas J. McDermott, Jr., Ruth Larson and Aznif Tarpinian;

DR. EUGENE F. DuBOIS, Emeritus Professor of Physiology, Cornell University, for his review of the Low Calorie Diet introduction;

DR. LEWIS ROBERT WOLBERG, author of "The Psychology of Eating," for the use of his bar graphs;

DR. JOHN E. SILSON, for his editorial assistance;

DR. ELI GOLDSTEIN, Associate Clinical Professor of Medicine, New York Medical College, for his guidance;

SISTER MAUDE BEHRMAN, Dietitian of Lankenau Hospital, Philadelphia, for many recipes and calculations for the Diabetes Diet section;

J. RICHARD CONNELLY and GROFF CONKLIN of the American Diabetes Association for their contribution of recipes and advice;

ANNA DE PLANTER BOWES, Chief, Nutrition Division, Pennsylvania Department of Health, for assistance in many calorie calculations;

HERBERT H. MARKS, Manager, Insurance Medical Statistics, Metropolitan Life Insurance Company, for his assistance with the weight determination charts;

Home Economists EILEEN ANN DUNHAM and FAY BURNETT (General Foods Corporation), MABEL STEGNER (Waring Blendor), ELSPETH BENNETT (Ralston Purina Co.), RACHEL REED (Borden Co.), ALICE KLINE (Abbott Laboratories), ANNE BARNARD (The Nestlé Co.), REGINA FRISBIE (Kellogg Co.), DEBORAH PERSONIUS (Junket Brand Foods), BETH BAILEY McLEAN (Swift & Co.), MONICA CLARK (American Meat Institute), MRS. REIDUN K. SWEENEY (Quaker Oats Co.), ALICE W. BROWN (Campbell Soup Co.), DEMETRIA TAYLOR, and others, for their contribution of recipes.

DR. CLIVE M. McCAY of Cornell University for his recipe for protein bread;

MILTON OKIN for his valuable advice for the Low Fat–Low Cholesterol section; NINA SALAMON for recipe suggestions in that section;

HERBERT M. ALEXANDER for recognizing the need for such a book . . . and making possible its publication;

My wife, DORY, for preparing—and eating—many of the recipes, and for her general encouragement.

Particular thanks go to my son, PETER SMALL, (B.S., University of Chicago) who devoted more than a year to the handling of innumerable details, including the calculation of food values.

THE SPECIAL
DIET
COOK BOOK

HOW TO DETERMINE YOUR DESIRABLE WEIGHT

THERE are about a hundred and fifty million of us in this country and, fortunately, we are not all cast from the same set of molds, not all made with the same cookie-cutters.

One five-foot woman may have tiny hands, slim ankles, and a small frame. Another woman of exactly the same height can be big-boned and have a heavy frame. Certainly these two women are not expected to weigh the same. For this reason, health authorities have wisely made allowances for the type of a person's build in calculating proper weight. They allow also for normal variations in the weight of the individual.

Here are the most up-to-date tables showing desirable weights for men and women. These were prepared by the Metropolitan Life Insurance Company, based on studies of the length of life of many thousands of persons with different builds.

WEIGHT OF VERY SHORT OR TALL PERSONS

No weight tables have been computed for women under 4 feet 11 inches or over 6 feet in height, nor for men less than 5 feet 2 inches or more than 6 feet 3 inches, since these individuals constitute a small proportion of our population and not enough facts are available. A rough estimate can be worked out by following the general scheme of the established tables. Thus, for men 5 feet 1 inch, the figures would be about as follows: Small frame, 113-122 pounds; Medium, 121-130 pounds; and Large, 128-139 pounds.

For women 4 feet 10 inches, the weight range would be: Small frame, 102-109 pounds; Medium frame, 108-116 pounds; Large, 115-125 pounds. By this process you can determine weights down to 4 feet 7 inches for women, and 4 feet 10 inches for men.

WEIGHT OF PEOPLE UNDER 25 YEARS OF AGE

Authoritative weight tables have not been prepared for persons under 25, largely because growth patterns vary so greatly in the late adolescent and early adult period.

The following method is suggested to estimate desirable weights under 25 years of age: Subtract 1 pound for each year of age from the weights given for each height. For example, at age 18 for girls 5 feet 2 inches, the desirable weights would be: Small frame, 103-111 pounds; Medium frame, 110-118 pounds; Large, 117-123 pounds.

At 5 feet 6 inches: Small frame, 116-125 pounds; Medium, 123-133 pounds; Large frame, 131-143. Such a rule might apply down as far as 17 years of age for girls and 19 for boys, but not below.

HEIGHT (with shoes on) Feet Inches	SMALL FRAME	MEDIUM FRAME	LARGE FRAME
4 11	104–111	110–118	117–127
5 0	105–113	112–120	119–129
5 1	107–115	114–122	121–131
5 2	110–118	117–125	124–135
5 3	113–121	120–128	127–138
5 4	116–125	124–132	131–142
5 5	119–128	127–135	133–145
5 6	123–132	130–140	138–150
5 7	126–136	134–144	142–154
5 8	129–139	137–147	145–158
5 9	133–143	141–151	149–162
5 10	136–147	145–155	152–166
5 11	139–150	148–158	155–169

women

HEIGHT (with shoes on) Feet Inches	SMALL FRAME	MEDIUM FRAME	LARGE FRAME
5 2	116–125	124–133	131–142
5 3	119–128	127–136	133–144
5 4	122–132	130–140	137–149
5 5	126–136	134–144	141–153
5 6	129–139	137–147	145–157
5 7	133–143	141–151	149–162
5 8	136–147	145–156	153–166
5 9	140–151	149–160	157–170
5 10	144–155	153–164	161–175
5 11	148–159	157–168	165–180
6 0	152–164	161–173	169–185
6 1	157–169	166–178	174–190
6 2	163–175	171–184	179–196
6 3	168–180	176–189	184–202

men

Height is figured with shoes on, and the weight includes ordinary clothes, but no hat or overcoat. The weights are for people 25 years and over. Despite all beliefs to the contrary, your weight should not change a great deal after the age of 25. *See next page*—How To Tell Your Frame Size.

HOW TO TELL YOUR FRAME SIZE

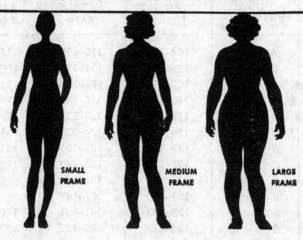

One glance frequently tells the size of a person's bone structure, but more often, there is room for doubt—particularly in overweight people—whose frames are covered with a thick padding of fatty tissue. There are at least six important parts of the body which vary noticeably with skeletal size: the shoulders, chest, pelvis and hips, wrists, knees and ankles. If you are large in just one of these places you might not have a large frame; but if you are large in all six, or even most of them, you fit into the large frame classification. These silhouettes should help you determine the correct size of your frame.

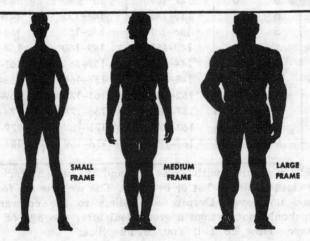

THE LOW CALORIE DIET

Prescribed in weight reduction and weight maintenance

OBESITY, or overweight, is a condition known since ancient days. The word obesity itself first appeared in the English language in the early seventeenth century, derived from the Latin "obesus," which may be translated as "that which has eaten itself fat." Thus the earliest concept of its cause was overeating. Subsequently, with the discovery of the functions of the glands of internal secretion—the thyroid, pituitary, adrenal and sex glands—it was thought that overweight might be caused by disturbances of these glands. Today, doctors know definitely that the basic cause of obesity is the continual eating of more food than the body can burn up. Even if the glands are involved, they are usually only a secondary factor.

Along with this has come the recognition of obesity as a major health problem; that it predisposes its victims to heart disease, high blood pressure, diabetes, arthritis, and other leading causes of disability and death. The human heart is a pump which has to force blood to every part of the body, to keep the tissues supplied with oxygen and energy, and to remove waste products. If a woman gains 20 pounds, she has burdened herself with that much tissue, principally fat, which must be supplied with blood every second of the day and night. This obviously puts an added strain upon the heart, and also upon the lungs, kidneys, and many other organs. The extra weight also increases the burden on the muscles, bones and joints, which can cause backaches, foot troubles, and other pains and discomforts.

This danger is made even greater by the fact that most people begin to put on weight in the middle years of life, producing the so-called "middle age spread." This is precisely the time when they should be thinking of reducing, not increasing, the burden on their hearts and other organs. With increased pounds, they become prone to greater fatigue, mental distress and frustrations, lowered resistance to infection, and a deterioration of personal

17

efficiency, fitness and appearance. Should an operation become necessary, they are definitely poorer risks both directly and through post-operative complications such as thrombosis and embolism. According to actual statistics, there is a greater chance of death from cancer of the liver and gall bladder, kidney disease, appendicitis, hernia, and even accidents, in men and women who are overweight, than in those who are of normal weight. Among people the entire length and breadth of America, obesity is shortening life to a shocking extent—and its correction is imperative.

In this land of abundance, most of us get plenty to eat; and with the existence of shorter working hours and labor-saving devices— vacuum cleaners, washing machines, automobiles—we tend to utilize less of the food that we eat. So the excess becomes fat, and the figure loses its sleek, youthful appearance.

EAT WELL AND WEIGH LESS

Most overweight people would like to keep on eating and still take off weight. It can be done, and without great difficulty. The secret is to dress up the foods that are low in calories, so that they give substantially the same satisfaction as do the high calorie foods. This is not a hardship. But first, one must learn the language of calories, a language anyone can pick up quickly.

A calorie is a unit of measurement, just like an inch or an ounce. An inch measures distance, an ounce measures weight, and a calorie measures the fuel value of foods. Plain water has no food value, and therefore has no calories—it can supply no heat or energy or fat to the body. Cooking oil, on the other hand, is a greatly concentrated source of body fuel, and is among the highest in calories. The calories which are not burned as fuel eventually end up as body fat.

The three forms in which these fuels are found in foods are carbohydrates, proteins and fats. Carbohydrates are the starches and sugars, which constitute the bulk of the calories in grains, vegetables and fruits. Proteins are obtained principally from meat, fish, cheese, poultry and eggs, and also in smaller amounts from beans, whole grains and nuts. Fats are found in almost pure form in butter, oil and shortening, and in variable amounts in meat, nuts and eggs.

While it is possible to become overweight from overeating almost any food, no matter how few calories it may contain, it is

the high calorie foods which are usually the cause of "men running to belly and women to bum," as an old English couplet put
it. You are on the road to successful dieting when you learn how
to satisfy your appetite and appease your hunger with filling, low
calorie foods, instead of concentrated, high calorie foods.

WHY FAT MAKES FAT

Each gram of fat (about ¼ teaspoonful) contains 9 calories,
while each gram of pure protein or carbohydrate contains only 4
calories. An ounce of pure fat contains 255 calories, while an
ounce of pure carbohydrate or protein contains less than half
—113 calories . . . an astounding difference! So your first lesson
is that when you substitute carbohydrate or protein for the
fat in your diet, you cut down the calories. This is particularly
true because fatty foods tend to occur in purer form: for example,
vegetable shortening is almost 100% pure fat, while potatoes contain less than 25% pure carbohydrate. Your doctor would probably not want you to eliminate fat altogether, nor is it feasible
to do so; but it can be reduced considerably.

Broil, bake, boil or steam foods—but do not fry them; use skim
milk instead of whole milk; use low calorie substitutes for butter,
mayonnaise, salad dressing or whipped cream.

The one food form you should not try to skimp on is protein.
This is the material which your body uses to replace the tissues
which wear out in day-to-day living. Carbohydrates, however,
function primarily as a fuel, and when eaten in large amounts,
permit the fats to be deposited on you instead of being burned.

So, the second lesson is to learn to limit the carbohydrate
foods. This can be done by eating those foods which are high
in bulk but low in calories. For example, a good-sized portion of
watermelon may have 20 times the bulk of a tablespoon of sugar,
but contains no more calories. Similarly, a bowl of Puffed Wheat
may have 15 times the satisfying bulk of a tablespoon of flour,
with about the same caloric content. The rest is mainly fiber,
water and air, which add to the volume but not to the calories.

We don't mean for you to try to subsist on watermelon and
Puffed Wheat alone, but we do want to get across the idea that
your stomach is just so big; and if you eat a sufficient amount
at each meal to fill it up, it will help you feel satisfied regardless of
its caloric content. Eat as many of the bulky foods as possible:
clear soups and broths, for example, consist largely of water; celery, asparagus, lettuce and similar vegetables contain a great deal of

non-caloric cellulose; a number of dry cereals are puffed up with air. When you squeeze the juice from an orange, and throw away the pulp, you discard valuable bulk . . . a sliced orange contains exactly the same number of calories as the juice alone, yet it is more filling. So get the most food for your calories, just as you seek to get the most food for your money.

There are many other factors involved in good nutrition! You need a balanced diet; each day you should have adequate protein, leafy green vegetables, citrus fruits and skim milk. A good balanced diet will contain some of the following food groups every day: (1) meat, fish, poultry, eggs; (2) whole grain cereals; (3) fruits, including citrus; (4) vegetables, including the leafy ones and (5) milk (mostly skim milk). A proper selection of these foods will supply all the needed vitamins and minerals. We believe that the charts which follow, and the calorie calculations which appear with each recipe, will enable you to get the most for your calories, and help provide a balanced menu.

EAT DESSERTS

This book gives you a wide variety of dessert recipes to choose from. So often, restricted dieters feel the need of a sweet so much, they go on what doctors call "carbohydrate binges." Don't deny yourself the pleasure of a dessert after a main meal if you have been accustomed to desserts all your life. When you have just about used up your calories on main dishes, you can always fit in a serving of one of the special low calorie gelatin desserts, without exceeding your allotment.

Last, but not least, be sure to see your physician as often as he thinks you should see him. He may want to check your basal metabolism as your weight drops, or to change the diet itself in some way. Even if he only takes a good look at you, he can often tell whether your diet is "agreeing" with you. Don't try to save on doctor's fees when you are on any restricted diet . . . it may cost you more in the end.

SIZE OF SERVINGS

The number of servings shown above each recipe governs the size of the portion to be served the dieter—and it is important that this size be observed faithfully. Members of the family who are on a normal regimen, can of course eat larger portions, and can add potatoes, whipped cream, etc. Where a recipe says "Makes

6 servings" . . . this means 6 *diet servings,* which may be smaller than normal . . . although we have tried to keep all servings just as large as possible, frequently through "padding" of one kind or another.

WHY "TOTAL CALORIES" ARE GIVEN FOR RECIPES

In all cases where recipes call for more than 1 serving, we show the total number of calories in the recipe—as well as the calories for a single diet-serving. Total calories are given to emphasize how important it is to divide the recipe into the stated number of servings. Unless this is done, the value of the calculation is lost.

ADDITIONAL RECIPES IN OTHER DIET SECTIONS

Low calorie dieters will find additional recipes with calculated calories in the Low Sodium and Diabetes sections of this book. These may be used wherever they fit into your diet, and salt may be added to the Low Sodium recipes if desired, without affecting the calorie count.

MEASUREMENTS

All measurements in this cook book are level. "Medium green peppers" refers to the size of the peppers and not to the shade.

WHERE HIGH CALORIE FOODS HAVE BEEN USED

You will occasionally see a high calorie food used in these low calorie recipes. Do not let this disturb you. As long as the calories have been taken into account, and they have been, this is all that matters. The idea is to get a *total* of the most satisfying foods for the least number of calories, and frequently a small piece of butter may be needed to make tasty a low calorie food.

You may read in some reducing article or book that the reducer cannot have bread, rice, corn, olives, or other similar "fattening" foods. This is a rule for those who do not understand calories. Almost any food is permissible in concocting recipes, if used wisely, and if the finished dish remains in low calorie range.

WEIGHT REDUCING FALLACIES—AND THE TRUTH

WHAT SOME PEOPLE BELIEVE	THE TRUTH
Water is fattening.	Water contains no calories and therefore cannot be fattening. This refers to plain water, not to sugar-sweetened soda pop, cola, etc., which are calorific.
Toast is less fattening than untoasted bread.	A slice of bread, whether toasted or untoasted, contains exactly the same number of calories. Toasting does not remove calories.
Dark bread is less fattening than white bread.	Most dark breads have a few less calories than white bread, but some—like Boston brown bread—have more.
Honey is less fattening than sugar.	Even though a pound of sugar contains 30% more calories than a pound of honey, honey is a more concentrated food, and one teaspoonful of honey contains 21 calories, compared with 16 in a teaspoonful of sugar.
Fruit juices are not fattening.	Fruit juices are not low in calories, particularly grape juice and prune juice, which contain about 80 calories in a small glass (4 ounces). Orange juice and grapefruit juice contain about 50 calories in 4 ounces. It is better to eat the fruit itself than drink the juice, because this gives added bulk without extra calories.
In some people, "everything turns into fat."	The only reason some people gain more weight than others who eat exactly the same food, is that they are less active. Frequently, overweight is caused by extra nibbling and extra portions—which are overlooked by those who "enjoy their food."

WEIGHT REDUCING FALLACIES—AND THE TRUTH

WHAT SOME PEOPLE BELIEVE	THE TRUTH
Heart diseases make weight reduction dangerous.	Overweight may shorten the life of a heart sufferer by adding to the heart's burden. Therefore weight reduction is not only desirable, but frequently is vital . . . and is not dangerous when the diet is supervised by a physician.
Meal-skipping is a good way to reduce.	Skipping meals usually increases hunger and results in greater food consumption at the other meals. Eating three less-calorific meals is a more practical method of reducing.
Massage is an aid to weight reduction.	No massage, no steam cabinet or other similar devices, are of any material value in reducing weight.
Exercise helps to reduce weight.	Compared with a proper reduction in food calories, exercise has doubtful value . . . particularly since so much exercise is required to take off a small amount of weight . . . and the exercise whets the appetite for more food. Exercise may even be dangerous to some people, especially those over 40 years of age.
Surgical operations cause a great gain in weight.	The operation causes no weight increase, but inactivity after the operation, coupled with an increase in food during convalescence, often causes a gain. A corrective diet usually will remedy this.
It's natural and healthy to add a few pounds with the years.	Your correct weight at 25 is about what you should weigh for the rest of your life. The Metropolitan Life Insurance Company's records of hundreds of thousands of people explode the idea that you can safely add a few pounds as you grow older. Actually, you will live longer if you stay on the thin side . . . especially after 40.

23

A BASIC "1000 CALORIE" MENU (Approximate)

BREAKFAST	1 MEDIUM ORANGE 1 SOFT-BOILED EGG BLACK COFFEE 1 SLICE WHOLE WHEAT TOAST, VERY LIGHTLY BUTTERED (1/2 teaspoon)
MID-MORNING	1 GLASS SKIM MILK (8-ounces)
LUNCHEON	VEGETABLE BROTH 1 SLICE WHOLE WHEAT BREAD, VERY LIGHTLY BUTTERED TOMATO SALAD (1/2 cup diced tomatoes, large lettuce leaf) 2 tablespoons COTTAGE CHEESE SKIM MILK (8-ounce glass)
DINNER	LEAN MEAT, FISH OR POULTRY (1/4 pound) CARROTS (1/2 cup) STRING BEANS (1/2 cup) SKIM MILK (8-ounce glass) LOW CALORIE GELATIN DESSERT WITH SUGARLESS DESSERT WAFER BLACK COFFEE

APPETIZERS AND SNACKS

TOMATO JUICE COCKTAIL

Makes 1 serving (25 calories).

4 ounces tomato juice
Seasoning as desired: salt, celery salt, onion or garlic salt,
pepper, cayenne, lemon juice, onion juice, Worcestershire sauce, tabasco, etc.

1. Combine juice with desired seasoning or seasonings.

TOMATO JUICE FRAPPÉ

Makes 2 servings (50 calories). Calories in 1 serving: 25.

8 ounces tomato juice   Seasonings as desired

1. Season the tomato juice and pour into freeezing tray of refrigerator. 2. Set cold control for freezing. Freeze to a mush, stirring once. 3. Beat with a fork before serving. Serve at once.

EGGPLANT "CAVIAR"

Makes 12 hors d'oeuvre servings (180 calories). Calories in 1 serving: 15.

1 large eggplant
1 small onion, finely chopped
1 tomato
Salt, pepper, vinegar, oil
Sucaryl or saccharin liquid sweetener

1. Boil or bake eggplant, then peel. If boiled, drain thoroughly; if baked, scoop out inside. 2. Chop eggplant with onion and tomato, adding salt, pepper, vinegar and oil to taste, also a very few drops of non-caloric sweetener. Serve cold.

BROWNED POTATO PEELS

Makes 2 servings (50 calories). Calories in 1 serving: 25.

Peel of large baked potato, which has been well scrubbed before baking
1 teaspoon butter
Salt

1. Cut potato peel into half-inch strips. Butter and salt both sides of strips. 2. Place on cookie sheet in very hot oven (450°F.) until potato strips are nicely browned on both sides.

BEEF TOOTS

Makes 3 servings (148 calories). Calories in 1 serving: 49.

6 thin slices dried beef 2½ inches x 4 inches

6 teaspoons cottage cheese Worcestershire sauce

1. Season cheese with Worcestershire sauce. **2.** Roll the beef into cornucopias and fill with cheese. Fasten with toothpicks.

Variation: SMOKED SALMON TOOTS
Makes 3 servings (140 calories). Calories in 1 serving: 47. Substitute 6 small pieces smoked salmon for the dried beef.

ROLLED HAM

Makes 1 serving (about 50 calories).

1 small thin slice boiled ham   1 spear canned asparagus

1. Roll ham around asparagus and hold together with toothpick.

SHRIMP MOUNDS

Makes 8 servings (480 calories). Calories in 1 serving: 60.

½ pound fresh shrimp
½ tablespoon finely chopped onion
1 teaspoon lemon juice
¼ teaspoon grated lemon rind
5 tablespoons Lowmay or other mayonnaise substitute
½ teaspoon finely chopped celery
½ teaspoon finely chopped green pepper
⅛ teaspoon salt
2 or 3 drops tabasco sauce
Dash of pepper
16 circles of very thin (¼-inch) white bread, size of a half-dollar (1½ inches)
Parsley garnishing

1. Shell the shrimp and remove black intestinal vein before cooking. Cook shrimp and cut into very fine pieces. **2.** Mix all ingredients and pile a heaping teaspoon on each round of bread. Garnish with parsley.

TOMATO AND SHRIMP CANAPÉS

Makes 4 servings (256 calories). Calories in 1 serving: 64.

4 circles of toast
4 thin slices tomato
8 small marinated shrimp
2 teaspoons mayonnaise substitute

1. Place tomato slices on rounds of toast. Top with 2 marinated shrimp on each, and add ½ teaspoon mayonnaise substitute.

CELERY ROOT REMOULADE

Perhaps there are better celery remoulades than that of the Périgordine Restaurant in Paris, but there we first tasted this vervy hors d'oeuvre, and so we—especially Suzie—will always think it the best. The evening was June, the Seine was serene in its bridgy shadows, and the friends were warm and welcoming. But let there be no doubt, the celery remoulade was good—as earthy and spicy and seasoned as an old sailor on the long coastal boats below. We ate it that night as an hors d'oeuvre but on other occasions it was just as right-spot touching as a salad.

Makes 6 servings (216 calories). Calories in 1 serving: 36.

1 large celery root (celeriac)	2 tablespoons vinegar
¼ cup Dijon or other French mustard, if available—otherwise a good American prepared mustard	1½ tablespoons olive oil, preferably French
	½ teaspoon salt
	Cayenne pepper

1. Peel celery root and blanch in salted boiling water for 5 minutes. Drain, and chill in refrigerator. 2. When chilled, cross-slice the celery root into long slender slivers. 3. Beat together the vinegar, mustard, salt, cayenne pepper and olive oil. 4. Immediately before serving give the dressing an extra whipping and pour over the celery root slivers. Keep turning the celery root so that it soaks up as much of the dressing as possible.

GARLIC DIP

490 calories. Calories in 1 tablespoon: 14.

1 pint cottage cheese	2 cloves garlic
¼ to ⅓ cup milk	1 teaspoon salt

1. Whip cottage cheese with milk until smooth and of medium-thick consistency. 2. Crush garlic cloves in salt. Combine garlic, salt 'and cottage cheese and mix thoroughly. 3. Cover and chill in refrigerator for 10 to 12 hours.

DEVILED HAM DIP

774 calories. Calories in 1 tablespoon: 19.

1 can deviled ham (3¾-ounce size)	⅓ to ½ cup milk
1 pint cottage cheese	1 tablespoon grated onion

1. Whip cottage cheese with milk until smooth and of a medium-thick consistency. 2. Stir in grated onion (more if desired) and deviled ham. 3. Blend thoroughly and chill in refrigerator for 10 to 12 hours, to allow flavors to blend.

PICKLED ONIONS

Makes 6 pints (1200 calories). Calories in 3 onions: 20.

4 quarts small white onions
1 quart white vinegar
1 cup salt
1 red sweet pepper, finely chopped

¼ cup sugar
3 tablespoons French's mustard seed
3 tablespoons whole allspice
3 tablespoons peppercorns

1. Make boiling hot brine by dissolving cup of salt in 1½ quarts boiling water. **2.** Peel onions to make perfectly smooth. Cover onions and sweet pepper with boiling hot brine. Leave in brine for 24 hours. **3.** Drain, and soak in fresh water 1 hour. Drain thoroughly. **4.** Mix vinegar, sugar, spices. Boil mixture 1 minute, and pack onions and peppers in hot, sterile jars. **5.** Cover with boiling sirup and seal jars. Cool, and store in cool place.

MARINATED MUSHROOMS

Makes 6 servings (328 calories). Calories in 1 serving: 55.

½ pound small firm mushrooms
Juice of 1 lemon
6 tablespoons vinegar
8 teaspoons olive oil
½ clove garlic, crushed
Small pinch of thyme
Small piece of bay leaf

¼ teaspoon coarsely ground black pepper
¼ teaspoon salt (plus salt for salting boiling water)
Sprig parsley
Few coriander seeds
Chopped chervil or fennel

1. Wash mushrooms and dry quickly. Cut off tough parts of stems. Peel mushrooms and drop into saucepan containing salted water and juice of 1 lemon. Bring to quick boil, then cover and simmer for 8 minutes. **2.** Drain and let cold water run over mushrooms for a second; drain again and place in a bowl. **3.** Make a boiling hot marinade of all other ingredients, except the chopped chervil or fennel. Strain this marinade over the mushrooms and then simmer the marinade and mushrooms together for 5 minutes. **4.** When cold, place in the refrigerator to chill for several hours before serving. Just before serving, dust lightly with the chopped chervil or fennel.

TOMATO CANAPÉS

Makes 4 servings (312 calories). Calories in 1 serving: 78.

4 circles of toast
4 thick slices tomato
1 tablespoon finely chopped green pepper

1 teaspoon butter or margarine
1 strip of bacon
Salt and paprika

1. Place tomato slices on the rounds of toast. **2.** Sprinkle with chopped pepper. Dust with salt and paprika. Dot with butter or margarine. Top each with ¼ strip of bacon. **3.** Broil until tomatoes are soft. Serve at once.

APPLE SNACKS

Makes 4 servings (112 calories). Calories in 1 serving: 28.

1 medium eating apple	4 teaspoons grated American cheese

1. Cut apples crosswise, into slices a little over ¼ inch thick, making about 4 slices. **2.** Sprinkle on a thin layer of grated cheese. **3.** Put under the broiler flame until cheese melts.

STUFFED CELERY

Makes 4 servings (200 calories). Calories in 1 serving: 50.

1 small bunch celery	1 ounce Roquefort cheese
3 rounded tablespoons cottage cheese	1 teaspoon chopped chives or green pepper
1 Souplets or Nestlé vegetable broth tablet	Few drops Worcestershire sauce

1. Prepare celery. Leave smaller stalks whole. Cut larger stalks of celery into 2-inch lengths, make cuts in one end and throw into ice water. **2.** Dissolve Souplets in 2 tablespoons boiling water. Fork in the Roquefort cheese, adding the Worcestershire sauce. **3.** Sprinkle chives or green peppers through cottage cheese and combine cottage cheese with Roquefort mix. Spread finished mixture into celery hollows.

"ON THE WAGON" COCKTAIL

Makes 1 serving (85 calories).

3 ounces clam juice	Slivers of lemon peel
3 ounces tomato juice	Small sprig water cress, parsley or mint
2 cherrystone clams	

1. Vigorously shake juices together with cracked ice (1 ice cube wrapped in towel and pounded with mallet). Use cocktail shaker or Waring Blendor. **2.** Place clams in bottom of 8-ounce glass, pour in shaken juices, add the lemon peel, giving it a twist as you put it into the glass, and garnish with cress, parsley or mint, hooked over edge of glass.

VITAMIN SPREAD

Makes 2 cups of spread (270 calories). Calories in 1 tablespoon: 9.

4 medium carrots
½ green pepper
3 stalks celery
2 tablespoons wheat germ
2 tablespoons chopped nut meats

1 tablespoon horseradish
3 tablespoons Lowmay or other low-calorie mayonnaise substitute
1 teaspoon lemon juice
Salt to taste

1. Grind together very fine the vegetables and wheat germ. 2. Add other ingredients and blend well. Serve on Melba toast or on celery stalks.

CHOPPED LIVER PATÉ

Makes 2 cups—about 12 servings (684 calories). Calories in 1 serving: 57.

1 pound beef liver, sliced
2 Souplets or other vegetable bouillon cubes
1 tablespoon unflavored gelatin (1 envelope Knox's)

2 teaspoons salt
1 teaspoon onion juice
2 teaspoons Worcestershire sauce
Crackers

1. Cook beef liver in 1 cup boiling water to cover until tender, about 10 minutes. Drain well. Remove any tubes or skin. Put cooked liver through food chopper. 2. Dissolve Souplets in boiling water. Soften gelatin in ½ cup cold water, then dissolve over low heat. 3. Combine chopped liver with Souplet broth and dissolved gelatin. Add salt, onion juice and Worcestershire sauce. 4. Mix well. Pour into oiled small loaf pan of 2-cup capacity. 5. Chill until firm. Unmold and cut in slices to serve as first course, or on crackers for hors d'oeuvre. *Note:* Add about 15 calories for each cracker.

TORTILLAS

Throughout Mexico, women kneel before small earthenware ovens and toss cornmeal dough from hand to hand, making tortillas. Tortillas are pancakes, and a lot more—for they serve as bread, forks, spoons and pushers. They are the wrappers for tacos, or Mexican sandwiches, for enchilladas, and other dishes.

Tortillas can be like wet cardboard when soggy, but they are very tasty when fresh and crisp. My wife, who loves Mexico dearly, has tried making tortillas at home, but I see we are now buying canned tortillas put up by Ashley's Inc., of El Paso, Texas. They come 30 in a can and make an excellent low calorie snack.

THE NUMBER OF CALORIES
IN COMMON ALCOHOLIC BEVERAGES

ALE

1 large glass (8 oz.)..100
1 bottle (12 oz.).....148

BEER

1 large glass (8 oz.)..114
1 bottle (12 oz.).....173

BRANDY

1 brandy glass.......75

DAIQUIRI

1 cocktail glass......124

GIN RICKEY or TOM COLLINS

1 highball glass
Rickey 150
Collins 180

HIGHBALL

1 highball glass.....170

LIQUEURS

1 cordial glass—about 70

MANHATTAN

1 cocktail glass 167

MARTINI

1 cocktail glass 147

OLD FASHIONED

1 old fashioned.....183

WHISKEY

1 jigger of Rye......122
(1-1/2 oz.)
1 jigger of Scotch....107
(1-1/2 oz.)

WINE

1 glass red wine......73
1 glass white wine....85

MAIN DISHES

STEAK

Few memories can make an American more dreamy-eyed than the recollection of a steak he once had at a certain restaurant or roadhouse. It may have been the Pen and Pencil or Christ Cella's in New York, The Stock Yards Inn in Chicago or the Columbia in Tampa—the list is long and the steaks are big, thick, dripping with butter, and accompanied by French fried onions and potatoes.

Such gastronomical orgies must now be "just a memory" to the dieter, but a small, boneless tenderloin or sirloin steak, if you can afford it, is good diet fare. It has to be small, not over four by three inches in size and only three-quarters of an inch thick, to keep within 250 calories, which is a reasonable allowance for a meat course, without considering vegetables or salad.

Beth Bailey McLean, Director of Home Economics of Swift & Co., meat packers, says that this is the best way to prepare a thin steak:

"To broil a half-inch to three-quarter-inch steak, we recommend bringing it close to the heating unit, so that it browns before it dries out. Depending on the type of broiler, about two inches would be right. Probably the best suggestion is to use a wire rack set in a pie pan on a broiler rack. About three minutes on each side would be sufficient to make the meat brown outside yet pink inside."

ELECTRIC BROILERS MAKE BETTER BROILED FOODS

Several types of restricted diets call for broiled foods. In the low calorie diet and the low fat diet, broiling is a preferred form of cooking because fats, gravies and sauces are to be avoided. To the bland diet, broiling also brings a required simplicity.

The small household electric broiler is a valuable asset to the dieter. It broils foods even more satisfactorily than outdoor barbecue broiling because juices are not lost and meats are not toughened. It is more convenient than the large stove oven, because it can be used any place where there is a convenient outlet . . . in the kitchen, at the dining table, on the porch or on the lawn. Delicious meals may be broiled using chops, steak, fish, chicken or hamburgers, combined with fruits and vegetables.

What to look for in buying an electric broiler:

1. Be sure the size of the broiler is suited to your family needs. If you know you will only be broiling for one or two, don't get an overly-large broiler. On the other hand, if you expect to be broiling large steaks or several halves of chicken, a small broiler won't do.
2. Open front broilers are becoming more popular, although

closed broilers have advantages too. For dieters, a broiler having several levels is probably best, so that some foods can be broiled close to the heat, while others can be placed further away.

3. Make sure your electric broiler carries the "UL" seal of the Underwriters Laboratories, or is otherwise approved for safety.

4. Get a broiler that is easy to clean and easy to handle.

GRILLED HAMBURGERS

Makes 4 servings (1040 calories). Calories in 1 serving (2 patties): 260.

1¼ pounds lean ground beef round	Salt and pepper

1. Make into 8 patties ½ inch thick and 3 inches in diameter. Do not use salt and pepper at this time but you can mix into meat ½ teaspoon onion salt, ¼ teaspoon garlic salt and 1½ teaspoons Worcestershire sauce, if desired. 2. Preheat griddle or heavy skillet at high heat for 3 minutes. Then reduce heat to low for two minutes. 3. Place patties on griddle. Cook for 2 minutes each side if rare hamburgers are desired, 3 minutes each side for medium done, and 4 minutes each side for well done. Do not press down on patties while cooking. 4. Season with salt and pepper.

Note—Ordinary "lean hamburger meat," made with trimmings, contains about 1450 calories to the pound. Beef ground (or "round cut of beef") contains only 829 calories to the pound and is therefore only about Half as "Fattening."

PEPPERS STUFFED WITH HAM AND RICE

Makes 4 servings (300 calories). Calories in 1 serving: 75.

If served with tomato sauce, add 6 calories for 1 tablespoon of sauce.

4 medium-large green peppers	½ cup cooked rice
¼ cup finely diced boiled ham, no fat	½ small onion, finely chopped
	Salt and pepper

1. Slice off about an inch at the point end of the peppers and remove seeds and membranes from the inside. 2. Parboil peppers 2 minutes, or until almost tender. Drain well. 3. Mix the ham with the boiled rice and chopped onion. Season with salt and pepper. 4. Stuff peppers, place into baking dish with one inch water; bake in moderately hot oven (375°F.) about 30 minutes.

QUICK ITALIAN PIZZAS

Makes 4 servings (440 calories). Calories in 1 serving: 110.

2 English muffins, split in half
4 slices fresh tomato
¼ pound ground beef round
4 thin slices mozzarella cheese (⅛ pound)
½ tablespoon chopped onion

¼ teaspoon chopped garlic
⅛ teaspoon basil
⅛ teaspoon oregano
Pinch of crushed dried red peppers
Salt

1. Lightly toast the split English muffins and place the 4 halves in a baking pan. 2. Place a slice of tomato on top of each muffin half and sprinkle with salt. 3. Combine the ground beef, onion, garlic and ¼ teaspoon salt. Spread this over the tomato. 4. Add the cheese and sprinkle with basil, oregano and dried red pepper. Bake in hot oven (400°F.) for 15 minutes.

JELLIED CHICKEN WITH VEGETABLES

Makes 6 servings (492 calories). Calories in 1 serving: 82.

1 cup sliced chicken
1½ cups chicken stock or canned chicken broth
1 cup vegetables (string beans, peas, carrots, asparagus, etc.)

½ cup pimiento or green pepper
1 tablespoon unflavored gelatin (1 envelope Knox's gelatin)
½ teaspoon salt
Salad greens

1. Soften gelatin in ¼ cup cold water. Add hot chicken broth and stir until dissolved. Add salt, and cool. 2. Dip square mold in cold water and pour in a thin layer of the liquid jelly. Let stiffen slightly and garnish with peppers and other vegetables. 3. Arrange the thickening jelly, chicken slices and vegetables in layers, and chill. Unmold and garnish with salad greens.

CREOLE FRANKFURTERS ON RICE

Makes 6 servings (1608 calories). Calories in 1 serving: 268.

6 frankfurters
½ cup chopped green pepper
½ cup chopped onion
2 cups cooked tomatoes

2 cups cooked rice
3 tablespoons fat
1½ teaspoons salt

1. Brown green pepper and onion in fat. 2. Add rice, tomatoes and salt. Cover and simmer 30 minutes. 3. Place franks on rice and simmer covered another 5 minutes.

BOILED TONGUE

Gives 25 to 35 slices ⅛-inch thick (Calories: about 900 for each pound of tongue). Calories in 1 serving (2 average slices): 160.

How to Cook Fresh Tongue

1. Cover with cold water to which you have added 1½ teaspoons salt for each quart of water. **2.** Bring water to a boil. If desired, add spice and seasonings to cooking water. **3.** Reduce heat and simmer slowly until tender (2½ to 3½ hours for beef tongue, 1 to 1½ hours for calf or pork tongue). Remove the outer skin.

How to Cook Pickled Tongue

1. Cover with cold water. DO NOT add salt to the water. **2.** Bring water to a boil, reduce heat and simmer 2½ to 3½ hours, until tender. Remove the outer skin.

1483776

PAN FRIED LIVER

Makes 6 servings (960 calories). Calories in 1 serving: 160.

1 pound sliced beef or lamb liver	2 tablespoons fat
¼ cup flour	Salt and pepper

1. Dip liver slices in flour. Brown in hot fat. **2.** Season. Cook 10 to 15 minutes over low flame.
Note: For liver and onions, slice into the pan 2 medium onions. This adds about 10 calories for each serving.

BARBECUED LAMB PATTIES

Makes 8 servings (1296 calories). Calories in 1 serving: 162.

1 pound ground lamb	2 tablespoons vinegar
1 tablespoon fat	¾ cup catsup
2 medium onions	1 teaspoon chili powder
2 tablespoons Worcestershire sauce	¼ teaspoon pepper
	2 teaspoons salt

1. Season ground lamb with pepper and 1 teaspoon salt. Shape into 8 patties and brown on both sides in 1 tablespoon hot fat. **2.** To make barbecue sauce, mix onions, Worcestershire sauce, catsup, chili powder and 1 teaspoon salt in ¾ cup of water. **3.** Cover lamb patties with sauce and simmer covered about 45 minutes until piping hot.

KIDNEY STEW

Makes 6 servings (Calories: with pork kidneys—804; with beef kidneys—924). Calories in 1 serving: with pork kidneys—134; with beef kidneys—154.

1 pound pork or beef kidneys	1 teaspoon dry mustard
½ cup sliced onion	1 teaspoon salt
2 tablespoons butter	⅛ teaspoon pepper
2 tablespoons flour	

1. Cut kidneys in half; remove tubes. Cut into cubes and soak 1 hour in cold salt water. **2.** Drain, add fresh cold water, and bring to a boil. Drain again and discard this water. **3.** Add 3 cups cold water, bring to a boil and skim. Add onion and seasonings. Simmer about 1 hour until kidneys are tender. **4.** Brown the flour in the butter and gradually add the kidneys and stock, stirring constantly. **5.** Cook over low flame for about 15 minutes. You may want to add currant jelly, lemon juice or horseradish, but don't forget to increase the calories accordingly.

STEAK TARTARE

Makes 6 servings (1206 calories). Calories in 1 serving: 201.

1 pound lean beef round, finely ground	½ teaspoon black pepper
1 egg	6 pieces thinly sliced bread, with edges trimmed
1 teaspoon scraped onion	Chopped parsley
½ teaspoon salt	

1. Beat egg well and combine with meat, onion, salt and pepper. Mix thoroughly. **2.** Shape into 6 patties. Serve each patty on 1 slice bread, with sprinkle of chopped parsley.

NORWEGIAN JELLIED LAMB CHOPS

Makes 6 servings (1224 calories). Calories in 1 serving: 204.

6 lean rib lamb chops	½ tablespoon vinegar
½ quart meat stock or bouillon	2 whole peppercorns
1 tablespoon unflavored gelatin (1 envelope Knox's)	2 bay leaves

1. Remove excess fat and simmer chops in meat stock until tender. Remove and let the stock cool. **2.** Skim off fat, add bay leaves, peppercorns and vinegar. Bring to a boil. **3.** Remove stock from fire, strain, add gelatin. **4.** Place chops in large serving dish or individual bowls and pour stock over. Chill in refrigerator. Serve cold.

BEEFBURGERS WITH VEGETABLE STUFFING

Makes 4 servings (656 calories). Calories in 1 serving: 164.

4 uncooked hamburger patties, using ½ pound beef round or chuck, 2 tablespoons dry bread crumbs, 1 tablespoon chopped onion, ¼ cup tomato juice, and seasonings

½ cup vegetable broth, made from Souplets or Nestlé tablet

1½ teaspoons flour

FOR VEGETABLE STUFFING:

1½ teaspoons skim milk
1 tablespoon butter or margarine

½ cup mushrooms, finely chopped
¼ cup celery, finely chopped
1 tablespoon onion, finely chopped
¼ teaspoon paprika
1 tablespoon grated carrot
1 tablespoon chopped parsley
1 tablespoon dry fine bread crumbs
⅛ teaspoon salt
Few grains pepper
Few grains rosemary

1. Melt butter in frying pan and sauté mushrooms, celery and onion. Sprinkle with paprika. Cook, covered, over low heat for 10 minutes. 2. Remove from stove and add milk, parsley, carrot, bread crumbs, salt, pepper and rosemary. Mix thoroughly. 3. Place 4 hamburger patties in a baking pan and shape into cups to hold the vegetable stuffing. Insert the stuffing, but do not wash the frying pan. Leave a mound of stuffing above each meat cup. 4. Pour the ½ cup vegetable broth into the stuffing frying pan and bring to a boil. Mix the 1½ teaspoons flour with 1 tablespoon cold water and, when smooth, stir into the boiling broth. Cook for a minute or so, stirring constantly, then pour into baking pan. 5. Bake, uncovered, in moderate oven (350°F.) for 30 minutes, basting twice with sauce in pan.

SWEDISH MEAT CAKES

Makes 4 servings (744 calories). Calories in 1 serving: 186.

¾ pound ground beef round
1 egg
¼ cup cooked carrots
¼ cup cooked turnips
2 tablespoons grated onion

1 tablespoon chopped capers
1 teaspoon horseradish
1 teaspoon salt
⅛ teaspoon pepper

1. Combine ground meat and egg. Mix well. 2. Mash cooked carrots and turnips and add into meat, then add in other ingredients and mix well with hands. 3. Shape into 4 large patties. Chill thoroughly in refrigerator for at least 30 minutes. 4. Preheat broiler and broil meat cakes until brown on both sides.

ABOUT BACON

A slice of bacon, while not filling, can be quite satisfying. When cooked to crispness, and the fat well drained off, one regular slice of bacon contains 30 calories. When used in cooking, where the fat cannot be drained off and is absorbed by the other ingredients, one slice contains 50 calories. And if the fat is partly drained off, the calorie count lies somewhere in between. Here are the correct ways to prepare plain bacon.

PAN FRIED BACON

Place slices of bacon in a cold skillet. Don't overcrowd. Cook slowly, turning to cook evenly. Do not pour off bacon fat during cooking. Drain on paper towel and serve hot.

BROILED BACON

Place bacon slices well apart on broiling rack or wire rack placed in a shallow pan, and broil three inches from heat. Turn once. Drain on paper towel and serve hot.

BAKED BACON

Place bacon slices well apart on wire rack in a shallow baking pan. Bake 10 to 12 minutes, or until brown, in hot oven (400°F.). Drain on paper towel and serve hot.

FRANKFURTER AND BACON SPIRALS

Makes 4 servings (772 calories). Calories in 1 serving: 193.

4 slices bacon	8 ¼-inch slivers of cheddar
4 frankfurters	cheese 1 inch long

1. Inserting point of knife near one end of frankfurter, make a ½-inch-deep cut down the length of the frankfurter, turning it several times as you cut, to form a spiral. **2.** Insert two pieces of cheese into the slit in each frankfurter, wrap each in spiral fashion, with slice of bacon. **3.** Fasten with toothpicks and broil about 5 minutes on each side, 3 inches from heat.

KIDNEY AND BACON GRILL

Makes 4 servings (712 calories). Calories in 1 serving: 178.

4 lamb kidneys	½ cup sifted cracker crumbs
4 slices bacon	Salt and pepper
1 egg, slightly beaten	

1. Cut kidneys in half and remove tubes. Wrap each piece with ½ slice of bacon and fasten with toothpick. **2.** Dip in egg, then in crumbs and place in baking pan. **3.** Bake 20 minutes in hot oven (400°F.). (If you prefer, the bacon and kidneys may be broiled on metal skewers.)

BAKED SWEETBREADS WITH BACON

Makes 4 servings (1184 calories). Calories in 1 serving: 296.

4 slices bacon	1 egg, slightly beaten
1 pound sweetbreads	½ cup crushed cornflakes

1. Cover sweetbreads with water and simmer 20 minutes. 2. Remove from water and cut into 4 pieces. Dip in egg and then roll in cornflake crumbs. 3. Wrap each piece with bacon slice and fasten with toothpicks. 4. Bake in a shallow pan about 20 minutes, or until bacon is done, in hot oven (400°F.).

BACON BROILER LUNCHEON

Makes 4 servings (912 calories). Calories in 1 serving: 228.

12 slices bacon	2 teaspoons butter or
2 cups cooked peas	margarine
4 slices of tomato, ½-inch thick	Salt and pepper

1. Place peas in bottom part of broiler pan, or in shallow baking pan. 2. Place bacon on wire rack or broiler rack, set over the peas. Broil about 3 minutes, 3 inches from heat. 3. Turn bacon, and push slices to one end of rack. Arrange tomato slices on rack and top each with ½ teaspoon butter. Season with salt and pepper. 4. Broil another 3 to 5 minutes, until bacon is done and tomatoes are cooked.

Variation: BACON BROILER FRUIT LUNCHEON
  Total calories: 1000. Calories in 1 serving: 250.
Follow recipe for Bacon Broiler Luncheon, substituting peach halves for the tomato slices.

PEPPERS STUFFED WITH BEEF AND WILD RICE
(or plain rice)

Makes 6 servings (708 calories for wild rice; 816 calories for plain rice). Calories in 1 serving: 118 for wild rice; 136 for plain rice.

2 cups cooked wild rice (or plain rice)	¼ teaspoon salt
6 green peppers	¼ pound chopped lean beef (or lean leftovers)

1. Mix rice, salt and meat. Add small amount of water if rice is very dry. 2. Fill peppers and place in baking dish. Surround peppers with a small amount of hot water. 3. Bake in moderate oven (350°F.) until peppers are tender.

BEEF AND VEAL—250 calorie serving

(Size of one serving containing 250 calories)

ROAST RIBS OF BEEF

3 cooked slices
3" x 2" x 1/4" thick

CHUCK POT ROAST

1 cooked piece,
4" x 1-1/2" x 1" thick

BEEF ROUND

3 cooked pieces,
4" x 1" x 1/4" thick

FLANK STEAK

1 cooked piece,
4" x 2-1/2" x 1/2" thick

PORTERHOUSE STEAK

1 broiled piece,
4" x 2-1/4" x 3/4" thick

SIRLOIN STEAK

1 broiled piece,
4" x 3" x 3/4" thick

**SOUP MEAT
(BEEF SHANK)**

2 cooked pieces, 2-1/2" x
2-1/4" x 5/8" thick

**BEEF OR VEAL STEW
WITH VEGETABLES**

1 cupful

BEEF OR CALF LIVER

3 cooked slices
3" x 2-1/4" x 3/8" thick

BEEF KIDNEY

5 slices,
3" x 2-1/2" x 1/4" thick

BREAST OF VEAL

4 stewed pieces,
2-1/2" x 1-1/4" x 1"

VEAL CUTLET

1 large serving, baked

LAMB, HAM, PORK, AND CHICKEN —250 calorie serving

(Size of one serving containing 250 calories)

LAMB CHOPS	ROAST LEG OF LAMB	FRESH HAM
2 rib chops or 1 large shoulder chop, fried without added fat	3 slices 3" x 2-3/4" x 1/8" thick	2 slices 4" x 2-1/2" x 1/8" thick
SMOKED HAM	**PORK CHOP**	**ROAST LOIN OF PORK**
2 slices, 4" x 2-1/2" x 1/8" thick	1 medium loin chop 3-1/2" x 3" x 5/8" thick	2 slices, 3-1/2" x 3" x 1/4" thick
PORK SPARERIBS	**MEAT LOAF (BEEF and PORK)**	**FRIED CHICKEN (BROILER)**
Meat from 6 average roasted ribs.	1 slice, 4" x 3" x 3/8" thick	1/4 of one chicken
FRIED CHICKEN (FRYER)	**STEWED CHICKEN**	**ROAST CHICKEN or TURKEY**
1/2 breast of one chicken, or 4 small legs	3 slices, 3-1/2" x 2-5/8" x 1/4" thick	3 slices, 3-1/2" x 2-5/8" x 1/4" thick

LUNCHEON MEATS—250 calorie serving

(Size of one serving containing 250 calories)

BACON 5 strips fried and drained.	**BOLOGNA** 4 slices, 4-1/2" diam. x 1/8" thick.	**CHILI CON CARNE** about 2/3 cupful
CORNED BEEF (Canned) 4 slices, 3" x 2-1/4" x 1/4" inch.	**FRANKFURTERS** 2 average cooked franks, 5-1/2" long x 3/4" diam.	**HAMBURGER (Ground beef round only)** 2 small cooked patties, 2 oz. each
HAMBURGER (Butcher's regular ground beef) 1 medium sized cooked patty	**BEEF HASH or CANNED CORNED BEEF HASH** 1 scant cup of cooked hash	**LIVERWURST** 4 slices, 3" diam. x 1/8" thick
LUNCHEON MEAT 3 slices, 1/8" thick	**SALAMI** 2 slices, 3-3/4" diam. x 1/4" thick	**BEEF TONGUE** 5 cooked slices 3" x 2" x 1/8" thick

BEEF, CABBAGE AND TOMATO CASSEROLE

Makes 6 servings (1452 calories). Calories in 1 serving: 242.

1 pound ground beef round
4 cups coarsely shredded cabbage
1 cup soft bread crumbs
2½ cups tomatoes (1 No. 2 can)

1 cup chopped celery
¼ cup chopped onion
2 tablespoons Crisco or other fat
2 teaspoons salt
Few grains pepper

1. Brown the meat in Crisco. Add onion and celery; cook for 5 minutes. **2.** Add tomatoes, salt and pepper. Bring to a boil. **3.** Make 2 alternate layers of cabbage and meat mixture—4 layers in all—and top with bread crumbs. Bake in moderately hot oven (375°F.) for 45 minutes.

FRANKFURTER SKILLET MEAL

Makes 4 servings (1108 calories). Calories in 1 serving: 277.

6 frankfurters
3 medium tomatoes, sliced ½ inch thick
1 large onion, sliced fine

1 green pepper, chopped fine
½ cup grated sharp cheese
½ teaspoon salt

1. Split franks in half lengthwise, then cut into bite-size pieces. **2.** Combine in skillet tomato, onion and chopped green pepper. Put frank pieces over vegetables and cook about 20 minutes over low flame, until vegetables are tender. **3.** Sprinkle cheese over top. Cover and heat 5 minutes more until cheese is melted.

LAMB AND STRING BEANS, ARMENIAN STYLE

Makes 4 servings (1032 calories). Calories in 1 serving: 258.

1 pound string beans
1 cup leftover chopped lamb
3 medium onions, finely chopped

3 tablespoons olive oil
2 tomatoes
¼ cup bouillon
Salt, pepper, nutmeg, clove

1. Heat the oil in a skillet; add the onion and lamb. Stir over a low flame until onion is browned. **2.** "French" the beans (long slivers) and add beans and bouillon. **3.** Cover the skillet and cook until beans are tender, about 15 minutes. **4.** Peel the tomatoes and cut into thick slices. Lay slices over the beans, cover tightly; simmer about 10 minutes more. **5.** Season to taste with salt and pepper, and a dash of nutmeg and clove.

SMALL MEAT BALLS AND MUSHROOMS ON RICE

Makes 4 servings (1152 calories). Calories in 1 serving: 288.

4 portions boiled rice
¾ pound ground beef round
3 cups (½ pound) sliced mushrooms
2 tablespoons butter or margarine
½ of 10½-ounce can Campbell's consommé

¼ cup cooked green peas
1 tablespoon flour
1 tablespoon thick bottled meat sauce
½ teaspoon onion salt
¼ teaspoon celery salt
Paprika

1. Melt butter or margarine in large frying pan. Add mushrooms and sprinkle lightly with paprika. Cook, uncovered, over medium heat for 10 minutes, stirring occasionally. Remove to saucepan. 2. Mix together the ground meat, celery salt, onion salt, meat sauce. Make about 40 very small balls, less than 1 inch big. Brown these in same frying pan in which mushrooms were cooked, turning to brown all sides. Add to mushrooms in saucepan. 3. Make sauce in frying pan using about 2 tablespoonfuls of drippings; add the flour and stir until well blended; then stir in the consommé. Cook until thick and smooth. Stir constantly and scrape up pan scrapings into sauce while stirring. 4. Add the sauce to mushrooms and meat balls. Cover and cook slowly for 5 minutes. 5. Serve on boiled rice and top each serving with few cooked green peas.

PORK SAUSAGE WITH ONIONS

Makes 4 servings (1100 calories). Calories in 1 serving: 275.

½ pound pork sausage meat   2 medium onions, sliced

1. Shape sausage into patties. Place in cold skillet. 2. Cook over low flame until thoroughly done. Pour off fat as it accumulates. 3. Brown onions slowly in a small amount of sausage drippings.

VEAL PARMESAN

Makes 4 servings (888 calories). Calories in 1 serving: 222.

¾ pound lean veal, cut into four ½-inch slices
3 tablespoons butter or margarine
1 clove garlic, chopped

3 tablespoons grated Parmesan cheese
2 teaspoons paprika
Salt and pepper

1. Pound veal until slices become very thin. 2. Heat butter or margarine in heavy skillet, add chopped garlic, then add veal slices. Sprinkle with cheese, paprika, salt and pepper. 3. Cook slowly for 10 to 15 minutes. Turn meat only once during cooking.

BROILED HAM AND ASPARAGUS

Makes 1 serving (180 calories).

1 thin slice boiled ham (lean)	1 slice thin toast
1 serving cooked asparagus	1 tablespoon grated cheese

1. Place boiled ham on the toast and put the cooked asparagus over this. Sprinkle on the grated cheese. 2. Place under the broiler until the cheese melts and bubbles.

BAKED EGGPLANT WITH MEAT STUFFING

Makes 4 servings (724 calories). Calories in 1 serving: 181.

1 medium eggplant (1¼ pounds)	1 tablespoon onion, finely chopped
½ pound ground beef round	1 tablespoon green pepper, finely chopped
½ cup soft bread crumbs	
1 egg, slightly beaten	1 tablespoon chopped parsley
1 tablespoon butter or margarine	½ teaspoon salt
	⅛ teaspoon nutmeg

1. Cut eggplant in half lengthwise and cook in 2 quarts boiling salted water for 10 minutes. Pour off water, then scoop out eggplant pulp, chop up, and save. Leave a shell about ½ inch thick. 2. Sauté chopped onion and chopped pepper in butter for about 5 minutes, until onions are light yellow. 3. Add the meat and continue cooking until meat loses its pink color. Stir constantly. Add chopped eggplant pulp, bread crumbs, chopped parsley, salt and nutmeg. Mix thoroughly. 4. Remove from stove, and, when a little cool, stir in the slightly beaten egg. 5. Fill eggplant shells with this stuffing and place in baking pan, lightly greased, or with spoonful of water. Bake in moderate oven (350°F.) for 45 minutes.

BRAINS IN TOMATO SAUCE

Makes 4 servings (736 calories). Calories in 1 serving: 184.

2 cups cubed cooked brains	2 tablespoons chopped onion
2 cups cooked tomatoes	½ cup chopped celery
2 tablespoons butter or margarine	1 tablespoon flour
	Salt and pepper

1. (To cook brains: Soak in salted water 15 minutes. Cook in simmering water 15 minutes.) 2. Brown onion in butter. Add tomatoes and celery. Cover and simmer about 20 minutes. 3. Add flour and seasonings. Stir until thickened. 4. Cut brains into serving pieces and add to sauce. Simmer until heated through. If served on toast, add 65 calories for each piece of toast.

DUCK IN ORANGE MOLD

Makes 6 servings (840 calories). Calories in 1 serving: 140.

2 cups cooked, skinned, lean duck meat, diced
2 envelopes orange flavor Glow or D-Zerta low-calorie gelatin

1 cup diced orange sections
2 tablespoons lemon juice
Lettuce

1. Place gelatin in 2-quart mixing bowl. Add 1½ cups boiling water and lemon juice. 2. Chill until sirupy. Stir in duck meat and orange sections. 3. Place in 6 lightly oiled individual molds or 1-quart ring mold. Chill until firm. 4. Unmold on lettuce.

CREOLE MEAT LOAF

Makes 6 servings (1584 calories). Calories in 1 serving: 264.

½ cup uncooked farina
1 pound ground round of beef
1 egg, slightly beaten
1 cup condensed tomato soup (1½ cans)

3 tablespoons minced onion
2 teaspoons prepared mustard
¼ teaspoon sage or thyme
1½ teaspoons salt
¼ teaspoon pepper

1. Combine farina, beef, egg and seasonings. 2. Mix together tomato soup and ½ cup water. Save ½ cup of this mixture for basting, and add the rest to meat mixture. 3. Blend lightly and pack into small loaf pan. Bake 50 minutes in moderate oven (350°F.). 4. Baste during baking with the unused ½ cup of tomato soup mixture.

MEAT PATTIES

Makes 6 servings (1332 calories). Calories in 1 serving: 222.

1 pound ground round of beef
⅔ cup soft bread crumbs
⅔ cup Starlac or other skim milk powder
1 egg, beaten slightly

1 small onion, chopped
1 green pepper, chopped
1 teaspoon salt
¼ teaspoon pepper

1. Mix together ground meat, bread crumbs and skim milk powder. 2. Thoroughly mix in egg, onion, pepper, seasonings and ⅔ cup water. Shape into six 3-inch patties. 3. Preheat broiler. Place patties on aluminum foil in broiler pan and broil until brown on both sides and done through.

MEAT BALL AND KIDNEY STEW

Makes 6 servings (1542 calories). Calories in 1 serving: 257.

½ pound ground beef round
1 beef kidney
1 egg, slightly beaten
2 tablespoons butter or margarine
2 tablespoons flour
1 Nestlé bouillon cube or Souplet vegetable broth tablet

½ cup thinly sliced mushrooms
1 bay leaf
½ teaspoon salt
¼ teaspoon onion salt
¼ teaspoon garlic salt
½ teaspoon paprika
⅛ teaspoon pepper

1. Soak the kidney in cold water for 1 hour. Bring 1 quart fresh water to a boil in saucepan and place kidney in this rapidly boiling water. **2.** Reduce heat to low, and simmer kidney for 20 minutes. Remove kidney and place in refrigerator, but do not discard liquid. **3.** Add bay leaf, salt and bouillon cube (or Souplet) to liquid and simmer until stock is reduced to about 2 cups. Remove bay leaf, save stock. **4.** When kidney is cool, slice lengthwise and remove the tubes and white centers. Cut kidney into very thin slices. **5.** Combine ground beef, egg, garlic salt, onion salt and pepper. Mix thoroughly and make into about 16 one-inch balls. **6.** Melt butter in deep skillet and add meat balls, kidneys and thinly sliced mushrooms. Brown thoroughly. Sprinkle flour over meat and continue cooking until meat is well coated. Add the stock slowly, stirring constantly until sauce is thick and smooth. **7.** Cover and cook slowly for 10 minutes. Add paprika and simmer for another minute. Serve at once.

HUNGARIAN GOULASH

Makes 6 servings (1860 calories). Calories in 1 serving: 310.

2 pounds top round of beef, cut
into 1-inch squares
1 cup consommé
1 cup tomato juice
½ medium size green pepper,
diced
2 cloves garlic

3 medium carrots cut in 1-inch
lengths
1 teaspoon paprika
1 teaspoon salt
½ teaspoon pepper
1 bay leaf

1. Use large iron pot and put in all ingredients except carrots. Cover and simmer for 2½ hours. **2.** Add the carrots and simmer another 30 minutes. If necessary add a little more consommé or tomato juice.

HUNGARIAN STUFFED PEPPERS

Makes 4 servings (960 calories). Calories in 1 serving: 240.

4 large green peppers
½ pound ground beef round
2½ cups tomatoes (1 No. 2 can)
2 cups sauerkraut (15-ounce can)
¼ cup white rice

1 tablespoon flour
1 tablespoon butter or margarine
2 tablespoons chopped onion
1 bay leaf
1 teaspoon salt
¼ teaspoon pepper

1. Cut stems off peppers and scrape out seeds. Soak peppers in boiling water 5 minutes; drain. 2. Brown the flour lightly in saucepan on low heat 5 minutes. Add butter and brown together. Stir in tomatoes and add 3 quarts boiling water, sauerkraut, bay leaf, ½ teaspoon salt and ⅛ teaspoon pepper. 3. Combine beef, rice, onion, ½ teaspoon salt, ⅛ teaspoon pepper; mix together thoroughly with a little water. 4. Fill peppers with meat mixture and place stuffed peppers in the sauce, which should cover the peppers. 5. Cover saucepan and cook slowly for about 2 hours.

HOT HAM BANANA ROLLS

Makes 4 servings (860 calories). Calories in 1 serving: 215.

4 thin slices boiled ham
4 firm bananas

1½ tablespoons butter
Prepared mustard

1. Spread mustard lightly on each ham slice. 2. Peel bananas and wrap each in a prepared ham slice. Brush tips of bananas with melted butter. 3. Place into a baking dish greased with the remaining butter. Bake in moderate oven (350°F.) 30 minutes, or until tender.

LIVER WITH BROWN SAUCE

Makes 4 servings (888 calories). Calories in 1 serving: 222.

1 pound calf or beef liver
4 slices lean bacon
1½ cups hot beef stock (2 bouillon cubes in 1½ cups boiling water)

1½ tablespoons flour
1 teaspoon Worcestershire sauce
Salt

1. Cook bacon in frying pan, remove from fat and keep warm. 2. Cut liver in pieces, dredge in flour and brown on each side in hot bacon fat. Place bacon and liver on hot platter. 3. Blend flour with pan fat until nicely browned. Add hot stock, stirring until sauce thickens. 4. Add Worcestershire sauce and salt, if needed. Pour sauce over liver and serve.

BAKED TOMATOES WITH MEAT STUFFING

Makes 4 servings (500 calories). Calories in 1 serving: 125.

4 medium tomatoes
¼ pound ground beef chuck
½ cup soft bread crumbs
1½ teaspoons butter or margarine
2 tablespoons chopped onion
⅛ teaspoon basil
¼ teaspoon Worcestershire sauce
¼ teaspoon salt
Pinch of pepper
Pinch of anise seeds
Paprika

1. Cut off tomato tops, scoop out pulp and save it. Lightly salt and pepper insides of tomatoes. 2. Melt butter or margarine in small frying pan. Add onion and fry over low heat for 5 minutes. Add ground meat and continue cooking for 10 minutes, with heat low, until meat is browned lightly. Stir frequently to keep meat crumbled. 3. Remove meat from stove, crumble bread crumbs very fine and add to the meat. Mix well and add remaining ingredients. Mix well and fill tomatoes with this mixture. 4. Place stuffed tomatoes in shallow baking dish and add hot water to ¼-inch level. Bake in moderately hot oven (375°F.) for 25 minutes. Pulp of tomatoes may be saved for a sauce, vegetable soup, meat loaf, or stewed as an extra vegetable.

FRANKFURTERS AND BEANS CASSEROLE

Makes 6 servings (1992 calories). Calories in 1 serving: 332.

6 frankfurters
3 cups baked beans (in tomato sauce, not molasses)
2 tablespoons melted butter or margarine
1 tablespoon butter or margarine for greasing dish
1 tablespoon molasses
1 teaspoon horseradish

1. Mix beans, molasses and horseradish. Place in a lightly greased 1-quart casserole. 2. Bake about 30 minutes in moderate oven (350°F.). Brush frankfurters with melted butter. 3. Place franks on beans, cover and bake about 10 minutes more.

BRAISED PORK HEARTS

Makes 6 servings (948 calories). Calories in 1 serving: 158.

2 pork hearts
2 medium onions, sliced
3 tablespoons fat
2 tablespoons flour
2 teaspoons salt

1. Trim and quarter pork hearts. Dip in flour and brown with onions in hot fat. 2. Season. When well browned, add ½ cup water and cook covered over low flame 2 hours, or until tender.

VEAL MOUSSE

Makes 6 servings (1452 calories). Calories in 1 serving: 242.

1½ pounds veal	1 large onion, sliced
1 veal knuckle bone	1 small carrot, quartered
2 egg yolks	1 large bay leaf
½ cup chilled and whipped evaporated milk	1¼ teaspoons salt
	6 sprigs parsley
1 tablespoon unflavored gelatin (1 envelope Knox's)	8 peppercorns
	Dash cayenne pepper

1. Cook meat, bone, onion, carrot, bay leaf, parsley, peppercorns, 1 teaspoon salt and 5 cups cold water. Cook until meat is tender; put it through a chopper; strain broth, cool it and remove fat. **2.** Soften gelatin in ¼ cup of the cold broth. **3.** Heat the rest of the broth in a double boiler, beat the egg yolks and pour hot broth over them. Return to boiler and cook until mixture is like custard and coats the back of the stirring spoon. **4.** Add the softened gelatin, stir until dissolved, and combine with the meat, ¼ teaspoon salt, and cayenne. Chill. **5.** When almost setting, fold in the whipped evaporated milk. Turn into a wet mold, and chill.

BEEF BIRDS

Makes 4 servings (1408 calories). Calories in 1 serving: 352.

1½ pounds lean round steak	2 cups canned bouillon or broth made with Souplets vegetable tablets
6 medium mushrooms (leave stems on)	
2 medium onions (slice one)	½ clove garlic
2 medium carrots, sliced	⅛ teaspoon thyme
1 green pepper, chopped	3 sprigs parsley
1 stalk celery (leave top on)	Salt and pepper

1. Cut steak into 4 pieces about 1 inch thick and 4 inches by 3 inches. Pound these until they come down to about half thickness. **2.** Grind up the meat trimmings with one onion, the celery, garlic, mushrooms and parsley. Season with the thyme and salt and pepper. **3.** Spread this ground mixture on the 4 slices of steak, roll very tightly and tie at each end with heavy string. **4.** Place the rolls in baking dish, side by side, and add the bouillon, chopped green pepper, sliced onion and sliced carrots. Cover tightly. **5.** Preheat oven and bake ½ hour in moderate oven (350°F.), then turn over birds and bake another ½ hour. Remove onto warm serving platter; take off strings. Keep birds warm while you make gravy. **6.** Strain the gravy, remove any fat from beef, and press the pulp of vegetables through sieve. Season if necessary. Pour over birds and serve at once.

SWISS STEAK DINNER

Makes 8 servings (2800 calories). Calories in 1 serving: 350.

2½ pounds round steak
1½ cups onions, sliced
1 cup tomato juice, heated
½ cup flour

3 tablespoons fat
1 teaspoon dry mustard
¼ teaspoon pepper
1½ teaspoons salt

1. Mix flour, mustard, salt and pepper. Using a meat pounder or edge of a heavy saucer, pound flour mixture into the steak until all flour is absorbed. **2.** Brown meat in hot fat thoroughly and slowly on both sides. **3.** Pour hot tomato juice over steak and arrange sliced onions on top. **4.** Simmer gently, covered, for 2½ to 3 hours, until tender.

SWEETBREADS EN BROCHETTE

Makes 4 servings (1112 calories). Calories in 1 serving: 278.

4 slices bacon
1 pound sweetbreads
Salt and pepper

1 tablespoon melted butter or margarine

1. Cover sweetbreads with water and simmer 20 minutes. **2.** Cut bacon into 1-inch pieces, and sweetbreads into 1-inch cubes. Season with salt and pepper. **3.** On 4 metal skewers place alternate slices of bacon and sweetbread. Brush with melted butter. **4.** Broil 10 to 15 minutes, about 3 inches from heat, turning to brown evenly.

CHICKEN IN TOMATO ASPIC RING

Makes 8 servings (1000 calories). Calories in 1 serving: 125.

2 cups cubed cooked or canned chicken
4 cups tomato juice
4 Souplets vegetable broth tablets or Nestlé's chicken bouillon cubes
1 bay leaf

4 peppercorns
4 whole cloves
2 tablespoons unflavored gelatin (2 envelopes Knox's)
2 teaspoons sugar
Few sprigs parsley
Salt and pepper to taste

1. Heat tomato juice with Souplets tablets or bouillon cubes, bay leaf, spices and parsley. Cover and simmer 10 minutes. Strain. **2.** Soften gelatin in ¼ cup cold water, add tomato juice mixture and stir until gelatin dissolves. **3.** Add sugar, salt and pepper. Chill until sirupy. Fold in chicken. **4.** Pour into ring mold and chill until firm. **5.** To serve, unmold on salad greens.

FRANKFURTER RICE DINNER

Makes 6 servings (1494 calories). Calories in 1 serving: 249.

6 frankfurters
2 cups cooked rice
1 cup soup stock (or 3 bouillon cubes in 1 cup water)
3 tablespoons flour

2 tablespoons fat
1 tablespoon prepared mustard
1 teaspoon Worcestershire sauce
1 teaspoon salt

1. Simmer franks 5 to 8 minutes in hot water. Heat rice. **2.** To prepare mustard sauce, melt fat and add flour. Brown over low flame. **3.** Add soup stock to sauce and cook until thick. Turn off flame, add salt, mustard and Worcestershire sauce. **4.** Serve franks on rice, covered with sauce.

SPANISH CHICKEN

Makes 4 servings (1000 calories). Calories in 1 serving: 250.

1 young chicken (2 pounds), cut in pieces
2 tomatoes, chopped
1 green pepper, chopped
1 onion, chopped

½ cup capers
1 cup pitted green olives
1 pimiento, chopped
1 teaspoon salt

1. Place all ingredients in pot, with just enough water to cover. **2.** Cover pot and simmer for 1½ hours.

BARBECUED MEAT LOAF INDIVIDUALS

Makes 4 servings (1012 calories). Calories in 1 serving: 253.

1 pound ground beef round
1 egg, slightly beaten
2 tablespoons onion, finely chopped
4 tablespoons dry fine bread crumbs
2 tablespoons horseradish
1 tablespoon chopped parsley

1 teaspoon salt
⅛ teaspoon pepper
1 large ripe tomato
1 teaspoon onion juice
2 tablespoons Worcestershire sauce
½ teaspoon dry mustard
Few drops tabasco

1. Combine beef, egg, chopped onion, bread crumbs, horseradish, parsley, salt and pepper. Mix thoroughly and form into 4 oblong loaves. Place in shallow baking pan. **2.** Chop up the tomato and combine with onion juice, Worcestershire sauce, mustard and tabasco. Heat and then spread over top and sides of each loaf. **3.** Bake in moderate oven (350°F.) for 45 minutes. Once, half way through baking, baste loaves with pan drippings.

CORNED BEEF HASH

Makes 4 servings (992 calories). Calories in 1 serving: 248.

1 pound can corned beef hash   4 slices canned pineapple

1. Chill can of hash. Remove both ends from can and push out contents in one piece. Cut into 4 slices and place on broiler rack. **2.** Broil 3 inches from flame for about 8 minutes. Turn over hash slices and top each patty with slice of pineapple. **3.** Continue broiling until pineapple is heated through and hash is golden brown.

BAKED LIVER LOAF

Makes 4 or 5 servings (1240 calories). Calories in 1 serving: 248 if 5 servings; 310 if 4 servings.

1 pound beef liver	1 egg, slightly beaten
1 onion	1 cup skim milk
1 cup bread crumbs, soft	1 teaspoon salt

1. Cook liver 5 to 10 minutes in salted water which has been brought to a boil. **2.** Grind liver and onion together in a food chopper, add crumbs, egg, milk and salt. Mix well. **3.** Put into baking dish greased with 1 tablespoon shortening. **4.** Set dish in pan of hot water and bake for ½ hour in moderate oven (350°F.).

SAVORY TRIPE

Makes 6 servings (678 calories). Calories in 1 serving: 113.

1 pound fresh or pickled tripe	1 teaspoon vinegar
½ cup sliced onion	1 bay leaf
½ cup diced carrots	1 sprig parsley
2 tablespoons butter or margarine	1 sprig thyme
	½ sprig marjoram
1 tablespoon flour	1 whole clove
1 tablespoon Worcestershire sauce	¼ teaspoon peppercorns
	1 teaspoon salt

1. Cut tripe into servings. If fresh tripe is used, simmer 1 hour in salted water (2 teaspoons salt to each quart of water). *Note:* Precooking is not necessary if pickled tripe is used. **2.** Drain. Prepare sauce by cooking the onion in butter until golden brown. Add flour, chopped herbs, seasonings and carrots. **3.** Stir in 1 cup of water and simmer 25 minutes. Add vinegar. (If pickled tripe is used, do not add any vinegar.) **4.** Place cooked tripe in pan. Strain sauce over tripe. Cover and simmer until tripe is hot.

BEEF AND MUSHROOM INDIVIDUALS

Makes 2 servings (690 calories). Calories in 1 serving: 345.

For Beef Mixture:

¼ cup soft bread crumbs	1 egg, slightly beaten
¼ cup canned tomato sauce	½ tablespoon chopped parsley
½ pound ground beef round	½ teaspoon salt
¼ cup chopped celery or fine-	¼ teaspoon basil
ly grated carrot	⅛ teaspoon pepper

1. Soak bread crumbs in tomato sauce. 2. Mix all other ingredients together, then combine with soaked bread crumbs and mix thoroughly.

For Mushroom Mixture:

¼ pound fresh mushrooms	⅛ teaspoon salt
1 tablespoon butter	⅛ teaspoon paprika
¼ cup onion, finely sliced	⅛ teaspoon marjoram

1. Wash but do not peel mushrooms; slice off and discard ends of stems. Cut into thin slices. 2. Melt butter in a frying pan and sauté mushrooms and onions, with the spices, for about 7 minutes. Use medium-low heat. 3. Lightly grease 2 individual casseroles and place half the mushroom mixture in each. Over this put half the meat mixture. 4. Bake in a moderate oven (350°F.) for 30 to 35 minutes. Serve in casseroles or on warm plates.

HERB FLAVORED MEAT LOAF

(To be served hot, cold, or sliced very thin for cold buffet)

Makes 4 servings (1036 calories). Calories in 1 serving: 259.

1 pound ground beef round	1 clove garlic, finely chopped
1 egg, slightly beaten	1 teaspoon salt
2 tablespoons grated onion	¼ teaspoon oregano
½ cup soft bread crumbs	⅛ teaspoon rosemary
½ cup skim milk	¼ teaspoon basil
2 tablespoons parsley, finely	½ teaspoon paprika
chopped	¼ teaspoon pepper

1. Soak bread crumbs in milk. 2. Combine all ingredients and mix thoroughly. 3. Make into a loaf in loaf pan. Bake for 1 hour in a moderate oven (350°F.). Serve hot or cold. When cold, can be thinly sliced for cold buffet.

SCOTCH STEW

Makes 4 servings (700 calories). Calories in 1 serving: 175.

4 large potatoes
4 medium onions, sliced

2 or 3 slices lean bacon
1 bouillon cube

1. Pare and cube potatoes. Put potatoes and onions into large stew pan. 2. Cut bacon into small pieces and add. 3. Dissolve bouillon cube in 2 cups boiling water and pour over potatoes. 4. Cover and boil gently until onions and potatoes are soft. If necessary, add extra water to make more gravy.

SCRAMBLED BRAINS

Makes 4 servings (976 calories). Calories in 1 serving: 244.

1 veal brain
4 eggs
2 tablespoons milk
1 tablespoon butter or margarine

4 slices toast
2 tablespoons finely chopped parsley
Salt and pepper

1. Soak brain in salted water 15 minutes. Cook in simmering water 15 minutes. 2. Chop brain fine and fry in butter. Stir until browned. 3. Add eggs, beaten with milk. Cook over medium flame, stirring until set. 4. Season and serve on toast, garnished with parsley.

JELLIED VEAL TIMBALES

Makes 8 servings (1168 calories). Calories in 1 serving: 146.

3 cups finely diced cooked veal
4 Souplets vegetable broth tablets
2 tablespoons unflavored gelatin (2 envelopes Knox's gelatin)
3 tablespoons sugar

½ cup vinegar
3 tablespoons lemon juice
¼ cup minced pimiento
¼ cup chopped parsley
1 teaspoon Worcestershire sauce
1 teaspoon salt

1. Soften gelatin in ½ cup cold water. 2. Dissolve Souplets in 2 cups boiling water, add to gelatin and stir until dissolved. 3. Add sugar, vinegar, lemon juice, salt and Worcestershire sauce. Chill until sirupy. 4. Fold in parsley, pimiento and veal. Spoon into custard cups and chill until set. 5. Serve unmolded on salad greens.

SHISH-KABOBS

Makes 4 servings (1360 calories). Calories in 1 serving: 340.

1 pound lamb steak ¾-inch thick
4 slices canned pineapple, water pack
¼ pound mushrooms

1½ tablespoons cooking oil
2 tablespoons minced onion
3 tablespoons lemon juice
½ teaspoon salt

1. Cut lamb into 1-inch squares and marinate for several hours in oil, lemon juice, minced onion and salt. **2.** Drain lamb and alternate on 4 metal skewers with mushroom caps and 1-inch pieces of pineapple. **3.** Broil 4 inches from broiler unit about 12 to 15 minutes, turning several times.

GROUND BEEF AND EGGPLANT

Makes 6 servings (1014 calories). Calories in 1 serving: 169.

1 large eggplant
1 pound ground beef round
¼ cup dry bread crumbs
Salt and pepper

½ tablespoon butter or margarine, to grease baking dish
Lemon juice

1. Peel eggplant. Cut into ¾-inch slices. Sprinkle with lemon juice. **2.** Mix salt and pepper into ground beef. Grease baking dish lightly. **3.** Place sliced eggplant at bottom of baking dish. Cover with a ¼-inch layer of ground beef and sprinkle with bread crumbs. **4.** Repeat layers to make 3 each of eggplant, beef and bread crumbs. Sprinkle bread crumbs over the top and bake in moderately hot oven (375°F.) for about 30 minutes, or until tender.

BANANA MEAT LOAF

Makes 5 servings (1165 calories). Calories in 1 serving: 233.

1 pound ground beef round
¾ cup mashed bananas (not overly ripe)—about 2 medium bananas

1 cup soft bread crumbs
1 tablespoon chopped onion
½ teaspoon dry mustard
¼ teaspoon pepper

1. Combine meat, crumbs, onion, salt and pepper—mix them thoroughly in mixing bowl. **2.** Combine bananas and mustard. Add to meat mixture and mix thoroughly. **3.** Form into a loaf and place in baking dish with 2 tablespoons water, or set on aluminum foil in bottom of baking dish and use no water. **4.** Bake in a moderate oven (350°F.) about 1 hour.

BEEF RING

Makes 5 servings (1800 calories). Calories in 1 serving: 360.

1½ pounds ground beef round (chuck may be used, but if so, add 300 calories to total recipe, 60 calories per serving)
1 egg

⅔ cup skim milk
1½ slices bread
1 medium onion, chopped
2 celery leaves, chopped
3 sprigs parsley, chopped
Dash of sage or thyme

1. Break up bread into crumbs and mix all ingredients well, with your hands. Place in ring pan or loaf pan. 2. Preheat oven and bake at 375°F. for 45 minutes. Serve with tomato, onion and pepper sauce if calorie allowance permits.

LAMB CHOPS NEW ORLEANS

Makes 4 servings (1456 calories). Calories in 1 serving: 364.

4 lamb shoulder chops ½-inch thick (total weight under 1 pound)
1½ cups tomato juice

¼ cup chopped green pepper
¼ cup chopped onion
3 tablespoons fat
Salt and pepper

1. Brown chops in hot fat until golden brown. Season. 2. Add tomato juice, green pepper and onion. 3. Simmer covered 30 minutes or until tender.

HAMBURGER EN BROCHETTE

Makes 4 servings (1480 calories). Calories in 1 serving: 370.

½ pound ground beef round
½ of well beaten egg
½ tablespoon dry fine bread crumbs
⅛ teaspoon salt
¼ teaspoon scraped onion

⅛ teaspoon garlic salt
Few grains pepper
12 canned whole mushrooms
12 ½-inch thick squares of American process cheese

1. Mix all ingredients except mushrooms and cheese. Shape into 16 small patties. 2. Use four 6-inch skewers, allowing 4 hamburgers to each skewer. Thread the skewers with a hamburger, mushroom and piece of cheese, hamburger, etc. Start and end with hamburger, and use 3 mushrooms and 3 pieces of cheese to each skewer. 3. Preheat broiler for 10 minutes at full heat, then adjust broiler to medium heat (425°F.). 4. Place skewers in a shallow pan and set pan on broiler rack so that meat is 3 inches from tip of flame. Broil for 5 minutes, then turn and broil another 5 minutes. 5. Push off skewer, garnish with parsley, and serve at once.

SAVORY VEAL CHOPS

Makes 4 servings (1480 calories). Calories in 1 serving: 370.

4 veal chops, ⅜-inch thick
3 tablespoons fat
3 tablespoons flour
¾ cup fine dry bread crumbs
1 egg, beaten

1 tablespoon dry mustard
1 tablespoon brown sugar
1 teaspoon poultry seasoning
Dash of pepper
2 teaspoons salt

1. Wipe chops with damp cloth. **2.** Mix bread crumbs, mustard, salt, brown sugar, poultry seasoning and pepper. **3.** Dip chops in flour, then in egg diluted with 2 tablespoons water. Roll in bread crumb mixture. **4.** Brown well on both sides in hot fat. Cook over a low flame about 45 minutes, in heavy skillet (if light skillet is used, add ¼ cup hot water).

BROILED CHICKEN AND MUSHROOMS

Makes 4 servings (1552 calories). Calories in 1 serving: 388.

2½ pound broiling chicken
12 large mushrooms
2 tablespoons flour

2 tablespoons butter or
margarine
Salt and pepper

1. Have chicken prepared for broiling, wash and dry. **2.** Brush with butter; dust with flour, salt and pepper. **3.** Place skin side up in broiler, 3 inches from heat. Broil 8 to 10 minutes. **4.** Turn chicken and arrange mushrooms around chicken on pan. Broil 5 to 8 minutes longer or until chicken is cooked through and well browned.

BEEF STEW WITH TOMATO SAUCE

Makes 6 servings (2400 calories). Calories in 1 serving: 400.

2 pounds lean round of beef
2 tablespoons flour
2 tablespoons fat
1 can tomato sauce
2 teaspoons salt

⅛ teaspoon thyme
½ bay leaf
¼ teaspoon pepper
6 medium onions
6 medium carrots

1. Cut meat in stew-size pieces, roll in flour and brown in the fat, in a heavy skillet or saucepan. **2.** Add the tomato sauce, salt, thyme, bay leaf and pepper. Cover tightly and cook over low flame for 1½ hours, or until almost tender. **3.** Clean and add onions and carrots. Cook 30 to 45 minutes longer, until vegetables are tender.

BRAISED LIVER À LA CREOLE

Makes 6 servings (1152 calories). Calories in 1 serving: 192.

1 pound sliced beef liver	2 tablespoons chopped onion
2 cups cooked tomatoes	Small amount of flour
3 tablespoons fat	Salt and pepper

1. Dip liver slices in flour. Brown in hot fat. **2.** Season. Add onion and tomatoes. **3.** Cook covered 15 minutes under low flame. Uncover and cook 15 minutes longer until liver is tender and sauce is thickened.

BRAISED BEEF CUBES

Makes 4 servings (1672 calories). Calories in 1 serving: 418.

2 pounds lean round of beef in 1 ½-inch cubes	1 tablespoon vinegar
1 Nestlé bouillon cube or Souplets vegetable broth tablet	1 bay leaf
	Salt and pepper

1. Place ingredients and 1 cup water in heavy pot with tight fitting cover. **2.** Simmer over lowest possible flame for 2 to 3 hours, or until meat is tender. Add a little water during cooking, if necessary, but there should be hardly any liquid when dish is ready to serve.

BEEF À LA MODE

Makes 8 servings (3440 calories). Calories in 1 serving: 430.

4 pounds lean boneless round of beef	¼ teaspoon oregano
1 cup canned bouillon	¼ teaspoon celery seed
¼ cup wine vinegar, diluted in 1 cup water	1 teaspoon salt
2 large onions, sliced	10 peppercorns, cracked
1 clove garlic, chopped	3 cloves
	2 bay leaves

1. Set beef overnight to marinate in all the rest of the ingredients. **2.** Remove from marinade and dry with paper towels. Quickly brown meat on all sides, using a dry, preheated deep pan or heavy pot. **3.** Add the marinade in which the meat had been marinating. Bring to a boil. **4.** Preheat oven to 450°F. and put in the tightly covered pot. After 10 minutes, turn heat down to 250°F. Cook for 2 to 2½ hours, perhaps more if meat is tough. **5.** When meat is done, put on warm platter, and keep warm while you strain liquid into a bowl; discard the vegetables, and skim off all fat; if necessary, use ice cubes to bring fat to surface, then reheat. Add salt and pepper if needed. **6.** Slice meat and pour gravy over it.

SKINNED LONG ISLAND DUCKLING, BROILED

Makes 6 servings (1890 calories). Calories in 1 serving: 315.

The skin and fat layer beneath the skin usually make duckling a prohibitive meat for the low-calorie diet. But when the skin and fat are removed, the calorie count is decidedly lower. Here is how it is done:

4-pound Long Island Duckling, ready-to-cook weight	1 teaspoon Kitchen Bouquet
	½ teaspoon salt
1 tablespoon lemon juice	½ teaspoon ginger

1. Cut wing tips from duck. With sharp knife score duck skin from neck to vent along center of breast. **2.** Peel back layer of skin and fat with one hand, running knife underneath to help cut connective tissue but keeping flesh intact. **3.** Cut skinned duckling in quarters. Remove wings from breast quarters. These may be broiled or cooked with the giblets and wing tips to make broth. **4.** Place pieces of duckling in a bowl and sprinkle with the lemon juice, kitchen bouquet, salt and ginger. Toss lightly to coat evenly. Let stand half an hour. **5.** Arrange pieces of duckling on rack in preheated broiling compartment, bony side or inside up. Broil 4 to 5 inches from moderate heat for 15 minutes. Turn pieces and continue broiling for another 15 minutes. Serve immediately.

CHILI CON CARNE (WITHOUT BEANS)

Makes 4 servings (1260 calories). Calories in 1 serving: 315.

1 pound ground beef chuck	1 teaspoon paprika
2 tablespoons olive oil	1 teaspoon oregano
½ cup chopped onion	1 teaspoon salt
1 tablespoon chili powder	¼ teaspoon cayenne pepper
1 clove garlic, chopped	

1. Heat olive oil in skillet, add ground beef and brown thoroughly. Takes about 10 minutes. **2.** Add onion and garlic and cook over very low heat for 5 minutes. **3.** Add remaining ingredients and cook slowly, for 15 minutes, stirring occasionally.

TONGUE AND PEAS, SCALLOPED

Makes 4 servings (1300 calories). Calories in 1 serving: 325.

2 cups cooked cubed tongue	4 tablespoons shredded cheddar cheese
1 cup cooked carrots and peas	
2 cups vegetable creamy sauce	

1. Combine tongue, peas and vegetable creamy sauce. **2.** Place mixture in casserole. Top with cheese. **3.** Bake about 30 minutes in moderate oven (350°F.).

120 CALORIE PORTIONS
OF FISH

*size before cooking

ANCHOVIES, canned

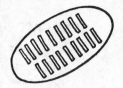

18 thin fillets

BASS, SEA, *

1 serving
3" x 3" x 1"

BLUEFISH, *

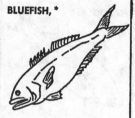

1 serving
3" x 3" x 1"

BUTTERFISH, cooked

1 fish 6-1/2" long
plus 1/2 fish

CAVIAR, canned

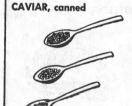

3 tablespoons

CLAMS, *

9 medium clams

CODFISH STEAK, *

1 steak
3" x 5" x 3/4"

CODFISH CAKES

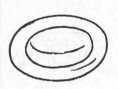

1 fish cake
2-1/2" across

CRAB, canned

1 cup crabmeat

EEL, smoked

1 small serving
(1-1/2 ounces)

120 CALORIE PORTIONS
OF FISH

*size before cooking

FLOUNDER or SOLE *

2 servings, each
4" x 2" x 3/4"

FROGS' LEGS

1 serving
total 6 ounces

HADDOCK, *

1 serving
3" x 3-1/2" x 3/4"

HALIBUT STEAK, *

1 serving
2-1/2" x 2-1/2" x 1"

HERRING, *

1 small fish

LOBSTER, boiled

1 lobster
3/4 to 1 pound

OYSTERS, with juice

1 dozen oysters

PERCH, YELLOW, *

1 large perch

PORGY or SCUP

2 servings, each
3" x 2" x 3/4"

SALMON, canned

3/4 cupful

120 CALORIE PORTIONS OF FISH *size before cooking

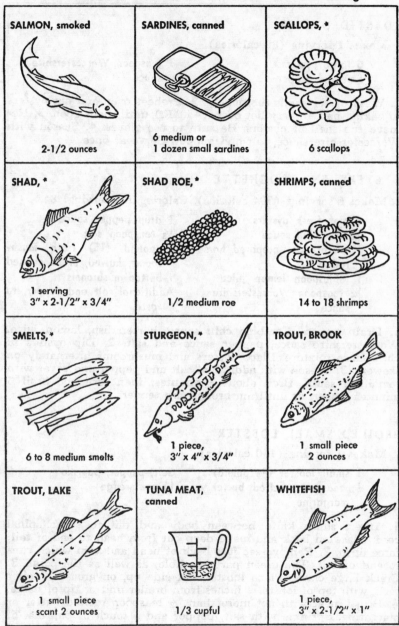

SALMON, smoked 2-1/2 ounces	**SARDINES, canned** 6 medium or 1 dozen small sardines	**SCALLOPS, *** 6 scallops
SHAD, * 1 serving 3" x 2-1/2" x 3/4"	**SHAD ROE, *** 1/2 medium roe	**SHRIMPS, canned** 14 to 18 shrimps
SMELTS, * 6 to 8 medium smelts	**STURGEON, *** 1 piece, 3" x 4" x 3/4"	**TROUT, BROOK** 1 small piece 2 ounces
TROUT, LAKE 1 small piece scant 2 ounces	**TUNA MEAT,** **canned** 1/3 cupful	**WHITEFISH** 1 piece, 3" x 2-1/2" x 1"

ROASTED OYSTER

Makes 1 serving (80 calories).

6 large oysters
Salt and pepper

1 teaspoon Worcestershire
sauce

1. Wash oyster shells thoroughly. **2.** Preheat oven and put oysters in baking pan, in very hot oven (450°F.) until shells open. **3.** Remove top shell of oysters. Be sure to use gloves. **4.** Season with Worcestershire sauce, salt and pepper. Serve at once.

OYSTERS EN BROCHETTE

Makes 6 servings (504 calories). Calories in 1 serving: 84.

1 pint fresh oysters
⅓ cup chili sauce
1½ teaspoons prepared horse-radish
1 tablespoon lemon juice
¼ teaspoon Worcestershire sauce

1 drop pepper sauce
⅛ teaspoon salt
½ pound (15) fresh mush-rooms, halved, or 30 canned button mushrooms
Additional salt and pepper, to taste

1. Drain oysters. Combine chili sauce, horseradish, lemon juice, Worcestershire sauce, pepper sauce and salt. **2.** Dip oysters in chili sauce mixture. Place oysters and mushrooms alternately on skewers. **3.** Season with additional salt and pepper and cover with remaining sauce. Broil about 3 minutes; then turn and broil 3 minutes longer, or until mushrooms are tender.

BROILED SMALL LOBSTER

Makes 1 serving (140 calories).

1 small lobster (¾ pound)
½ teaspoon melted butter or margarine

Salt, pepper, paprika
Lemon wedge

1. Insert sharp knife between body and tail to sever spinal cord. Place on back and make deep cut from head to end of tail; force open. **2.** Remove sac just back of head and vein which runs to end of tail. The green part is edible, as well as the coral. **3.** Crack large claws. Place lobster, cut side up, on greased broiler rack, with top of lobster 2 inches from broiler unit or tip of flame. **4.** Brush meat with not more than ½ teaspoon melted butter or margarine. Sprinkle with salt, pepper and a touch of paprika. **5.** Broil 15 to 20 minutes, or until browned. Turn and broil 5 to 10 minutes. Serve with lemon wedge. No butter sauce!

OYSTERS OR CLAMS ON HALF SHELL

Makes 3 servings (240 calories). Calories in 1 serving: 80.

1 dozen oysters or clams on half shell	Cracked or crushed ice
2 small glasses of cocktail sauce	2 wedges lemon or lime
	Touch of chopped parsley

1. Set cocktail glass in middle of soup plate. Fill plate with ice and arrange 4 oysters or clams fan-wise around the cocktail sauce.

Cocktail Sauce

Makes 3 servings (90 calories). Calories in 1 serving: 30.

3 tablespoons grated horse-radish	3 tablespoons catsup
	Pinch of cayenne
3 drops tabasco or Worcester-shire sauce	Pinch of salt

1. Mix ingredients thoroughly. Chill in refrigerator.

SHRIMP COOKED IN COURT BOUILLON

Makes 4 servings (620 calories). Calories in 1 serving: 155.

1 pound shrimp	1 scallion or small onion, chopped
1 tablespoon vinegar	
1 stalk celery with leaves, chopped	Dash of cayenne pepper or tabasco sauce
1 bay leaf	1 teaspoon salt

1. Boil together 1 cup water and vinegar, celery, scallion and seasonings. Boil 10 minutes, and strain. 2. Prepare shrimp—peel, remove sand and veins, wash. 3. Add shrimp to stock and simmer 5 minutes. Strain shrimp from stock and use for such dishes as shrimp cocktail, casseroles, etc. Reserve stock for use in sauces.

STEAMED CLAMS

Makes 4 servings (640 calories). Calories in 1 serving: 160.

4 dozen soft-shelled clams in shell	Salt and pepper

1. Scrub clams and rinse in cold running water until all sand is removed. 2. Place in large saucepan, add ½ cup hot water, cover and cook slowly 20 minutes, or until shells open. 3. Place clams on hot platter. Season broth with salt and pepper and serve in cups.

No butter sauce with this recipe because the clams are good as they are, accompanied by sips of broth.

SEAFOOD WITH SPAGHETTI

Makes 1 generous serving (150 calories).

8 ounces fresh cod haddock
½ ounce Gluten Spaghetti
Curls
1 clove garlic
1 slice onion

½ cup unseasoned tomato
juice
1 stalk celery
½ teaspoon salt

1. Simmer the fish in a covered saucepan with ½ cup water, ½ teaspoon salt, slice of onion and the stalk of celery about 20 minutes or until tender. **2.** Remove vegetables and flake the fish with a fork. **3.** Put Spaghetti Curls on to boil as directed on the package. **4.** Add the peeled clove of garlic to the tomato juice and bring to a boil. **5.** Remove the garlic and add the tomato juice to the fish and liquid that remains in the pan. **6.** Mix the drained spaghetti with the fish and sauce and serve with grated cheese. (Add 8 calories for each teaspoon of grated cheese.)

FISH MOUSSE

Makes 1 generous serving (100 calories).

4 ounces cold flaked boiled
cod or haddock
1 envelope lemon or lime low-
calorie gelatin (Glow or
D-Zerta)

1 teaspoon onion juice
1 teaspoon lemon juice
1 tablespoon Lowmay or other
mayonnaise substitute
½ teaspoon salt

1. Dissolve gelatin in ½ cup boiling water and chill until sirupy. **2.** Mix other ingredients together and fold into the chilled gelatin. **3.** Pour into ½-pint mold or small bowl and chill until firm. To serve, unmold on salad greens with cole slaw, as a main dish.

HADDOCK PIQUANT

Makes 4 servings (523 calories). Calories in 1 serving: 131.

1 box (1 pound) frozen haddock fillets
2 tablespoons butter, melted
1 tablespoon lemon juice

2 teaspoons minced onion
½ teaspoon salt
⅛ teaspoon pepper
1 tablespoon chopped parsley

1. Thaw fillets as directed on the package. Place in greased shallow baking dish. **2.** Combine butter, lemon juice, onion, salt and pepper. Pour over fish. **3.** Bake in hot oven (400°F.) 25 minutes, or until fish can easily be flaked with a fork. **4.** Sprinkle with parsley. Serve at once.

DANISH CUCUMBER BOATS

Makes 1 serving (about 60 calories).

2 tablespoons flaked fish, shrimp or crabmeat salad made with Lowmay or other mayonnaise substitute

1 small cucumber
1 lettuce leaf

1. Cut thin slice off one side of cucumber and hollow out center. 2. Fill with flaked fish or shellfish salad. 3. Arrange lettuce leaf to look like a sail on the cucumber boat; use a wooden skewer for support.

SCALLOP STEW

Makes 4 servings (868 calories). Calories in 1 serving: 217.

2 cups scallops
1 quart skim milk
2 tablespoons butter or margarine

Salt and pepper
Pinch of mace or nutmeg
Dash of paprika

1. Melt butter, add scallops and cook 5 minutes. Scald the milk and combine with scallops. 2. Add salt and pepper to taste, and mace or nutmeg. Simmer for 3 minutes and serve at once, with dash of paprika.

OYSTER STEW

Makes 4 servings (1308 calories). Calories in 1 serving: 327.

Same ingredients and directions as Scallop Stew above.

OYSTERS ORIENTALE

Makes 4 servings (700 calories). Calories in 1 serving: 175.

2 dozen shucked oysters
6 slices lean bacon
4 firm tomatoes

12 pimiento-stuffed olives
Sprigs of water cress or parsley
Paprika, salt and pepper

1. Cut bacon into 2-inch pieces. Slice tomatoes about ⅜ inch thick. Make sure oysters are free from shell particles. 2. On 12 skewers, arrange bacon, oysters, and tomato slices, with stuffed olive in center. 3. Sprinkle very lightly with salt and pepper. Place skewers in shallow baking dish. 4. Preheat broiler and place baking dish 3 inches below the flame; broil until tomatoes are heated through and bacon is crisp—about 3 minutes. 5. Serve hot on warm plates; sprinkle with paprika and garnish with water cress or parsley.

VEGETABLE STUFFED COD

Makes 4 servings (536 calories). Calories in 1 serving: 134.

1 package frozen codfish (1 pound)
1 carrot
½ green pepper
1 medium onion
1 large stalk celery
1 medium tomato
3 sprigs parsley
1 teaspoon salt
⅛ teaspoon pepper
¼ teaspoon tarragon, dill or dry mustard
1 tablespoon butter or margarine, for greasing baking dish

1. Let fish stand at room temperature to defrost. **2.** Chop all vegetables fine. Season. **3.** Preheat oven at hot (400°F.). **4.** Cut cod in half and put one side of fish, skin down, in lightly greased baking dish. Pile vegetables over this and cover with other piece of cod. Bake about 40 minutes, or until tender.

BAKED TOMATOES STUFFED WITH SHRIMP

Makes 4 servings (544 calories). Calories in 1 serving: 136.

4 large tomatoes
1 tablespoon butter or margarine
1 cup cooked fresh or canned shrimp
1 small onion, minced
¼ cup soft bread crumbs
1 tablespoon chopped parsley or ⅛ teaspoon powdered basil
1½ tablespoons grated cheddar cheese
Salt and pepper

1. Prepare tomatoes by removing centers; sprinkle with salt; turn upside down to drain. **2.** Sauté onion in butter or margarine until tender; then add shrimp, bread crumbs, parsley or basil, and salt and pepper to taste. **3.** Fill tomatoes with mixture and cover with cheese. Bake in moderate oven (350°F.) 15 to 20 minutes.

FISH FILLETS BAKED IN TOMATO SAUCE

Makes 6 servings (flounder 912 calories; sea bass 840 calories). Calories in 1 serving: flounder 152; sea bass 140.

1½ pounds fish fillets (flounder or sea bass)
1 can Campbell's tomato soup
Salt and pepper

1. Heat oven to 375°F. (moderately hot). Arrange fish fillets in baking pan. **2.** Sprinkle with salt and pepper. Mix soup and ¼ cup water; pour over fish. **3.** Bake 25 to 30 minutes.

COD WITH BAKED TOMATOES

Makes 4 servings (680 calories). Calories in 1 serving: 170.

1 box (1 pound) frozen cod fillets
1 medium onion, sliced
2 tablespoons butter (1 melted)

4 tomatoes, halved
Salt, pepper, paprika
4 lemon wedges

1. Thaw cod as directed on the package. Arrange onion slices in greased shallow baking dish. **2.** Place fish on top. Sprinkle with salt, pepper and paprika. Dot with butter. **3.** Bake in hot oven (400°F.) 20 minutes. Remove from oven. **4.** Arrange tomato halves around fish. Brush with melted butter and season with salt and pepper. **5.** Return baking dish to oven and continue baking 20 minutes longer, or until fish can easily be flaked with a fork. Garnish with lemon wedges, if desired.

MUSSELS EN BROCHETTE

Mussels are nearly the lowest in calories among all seafood.

Makes 4 servings (680 calories). Calories in 1 serving: 170.

4 dozen mussels, in closed shells
4 slices lean bacon
8 pimiento-stuffed olives

2 lemons, quartered
½ teaspoon salt
¼ teaspoon paprika
Sprigs of parsley

1. Scrub mussels well; pry open with sharp knife. Remove mussels and take off dark hairy beards. **2.** Season mussels with salt and paprika. Cut bacon in 1-inch pieces. **3.** Place mussels and bacon alternately, on 8 skewers. Arrange a stuffed olive in the middle. **4.** Place skewers in shallow baking pan. Preheat your broiler and set pan 3 inches below the flame. **5.** Broil 2 minutes on each side, until bacon is crisp and brown. Serve hot on warm plates. Garnish with lemon quarters and sprigs of parsley.

ESCALLOPED FISH

Makes 1 serving (179 calories).

2 heaping tablespoons flaked lean fish
1 egg white

1 teaspoon butter
Salt and pepper, to taste

1. Mix ingredients, adding water to moisten. **2.** Place mixture in individual mold. **3.** Set mold in pan of water and bake 30 minutes in moderate oven (350°F.).

WESTERN SALMON

Makes 4 servings (572 calories). Calories in 1 serving: 143.

1 can (3 ounce) pink or red salmon, flaked	2 tablespoons butter
1 can tomato soup	2 teaspoons Worcestershire sauce

1. Remove skin and any bones from salmon; flake in rather large pieces. **2.** Melt butter in frying pan. Add salmon and heat slowly. Pour can of tomato soup over, mix and heat till hot. **3.** Just before removing from fire, stir in Worcestershire sauce. If served on toast, add 65 calories for each slice of toast.

CHOW HAR (Shrimps in Black Bean and Garlic Sauce)

Makes 4 servings (824 calories). Calories in 1 serving: 206.

1 pound shrimps	1 tablespoon cornstarch
2 tablespoons peanut oil	½ teaspoon Ac'cent powder or other brand monosodium glutamate (MSG)
1 small clove garlic, finely chopped	
1 tablespoon Chinese black beans	2 green onions, chopped fine
	Salt and pepper

1. Shell and clean shrimps; remove black vein. **2.** Heat peanut oil in large frying pan until hot and put in shrimps. Cook for 5 minutes. **3.** Wash and mash beans and blend with garlic, cornstarch and Ac'cent in ½ cup water. **4.** Add to shrimps; add green onions. Cook, covered, for 5 minutes. Salt and pepper to taste. Toss and mix thoroughly and serve at once on warm platter.

BROILED FISH DINNER

Makes 4 servings (844 calories). Calories in 1 serving: 211.

4 haddock fillets (1 pound total)	2 tablespoons melted butter or margarine
4 tomatoes	1 tablespoon melted fat
2 medium potatoes, boiled and sliced	Salt and pepper

1. Place a piece of waxed paper in pan. Place fish skin side down on paper. **2.** Brush with melted fat and sprinkle with salt and pepper. **3.** Set broiler pan in broiler oven so that fish is 3 inches from heat. **4.** Cut tomatoes in halves, spread melted butter over each half and sprinkle with salt and pepper. After fish has broiled 10 minutes, place tomatoes and potatoes around fish; broil 10 minutes more.

BARBECUED COD OR HADDOCK

Makes 4 servings (1040 calories). Calories in 1 serving: 260.

2 pounds cod or haddock
1 medium onion, finely
    chopped
1½ tablespoons butter or
    margarine
Juice of ½ lemon
⅓ cup catchup

2 teaspoons vinegar
1 teaspoon honey
¼ teaspoon curry powder or
    turmeric or 1 teaspoon
    Worcestershire sauce
Cayenne pepper, to taste

1. Arrange fish on greased baking dish, skin side down. Sprinkle with salt. **2.** Simmer remaining ingredients together to make a thick sauce. Spread sauce thinly over fish. **3.** Broil 15 to 20 minutes under moderate heat, basting with sauce every few minutes.

FISH CAKES IN BLANKETS

Makes 4 servings (1128 calories). Calories in 1 serving: 282.

1 can (10-ounce) ready codfish
    cakes

4 strips bacon
4 eggs

1. Divide fish cake mixture into 4 equal portions and shape into round cakes. Circle a strip of bacon around each cake and fasten with toothpick. Place in baking pan. **2.** Make a depression in top of each cake, drop egg in each depression. **3.** Bake in hot oven (400°F.) until egg is firm and bacon brown.

BAKED HALIBUT WITH CHEESE SAUCE

Makes 4 servings (1300 calories). Calories in 1 serving: 325.

2 halibut fillets (1½ pounds)
½ teaspoon butter or mar-
    garine
¼ pound grated cheddar
    cheese
1 egg, well beaten

1½ teaspoons salt
¼ teaspoon pepper
¼ teaspoon dry mustard
1 cup skim milk
4 sprigs parsley

1. Put halibut fillets in greased baking pan. Sprinkle with 1 teaspoon of the salt, ⅛ teaspoon of the pepper. **2.** Bake in very hot oven (450°F.) until fish can be flaked with a fork. **3.** Mix grated cheese, beaten egg, the dry mustard, ½ teaspoon salt and ⅛ teaspoon pepper. Scald the milk and slowly stir it into cheese mixture. Then cook this slowly in double boiler until smooth, thick sauce is made. **4.** Place fish on warm platter, pour on cheese sauce and garnish with parsley. Serve at once.

CALORIES IN EGGS

BOILED EGG

1 egg . . . soft, hard or medium—77 calories

FRIED EGG

1 egg...fried in 1 teaspoon butter—110 calories

OMELET, PLAIN

1-egg omelet—120 calories

OMELET, SPANISH

1 egg with 2 tablespoons sauce—165 calories

POACHED EGG

1 medium size egg poached—77 calories

SCRAMBLED EGG

1 egg scrambled with 1 tablespoon milk and 1 teaspoon fat— 120 calories

DRIED WHOLE EGG

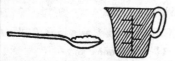

1 tablespoon—41 calories 1 cupful—640 calories

RAW WHOLE EGG

1 medium size (average) egg—77 calories

RAW EGG WHITE

1 average white of egg— 16 calories

RAW EGG YOLK

1 average yolk of egg— 61 calories

EGGS

An egg contains about 77 calories and supplies 6.4 grams of protein. This represents 10% of the entire day's requirement of protein for the average woman and 9% for the average man. Protein has a number of important functions, the chief one (in adults) being to replace the constantly wearing-out tissues of the body.

One egg also supplies the following percentages of the adult daily minimum requirement of vital vitamins and minerals:

Vitamin A	—	11.4%
Vitamin B$_1$	—	4.0%
Vitamin B$_2$	—	8.5%
Vitamin C	—	None
Vitamin D	—	45 units
Niacin	—	.05 mg. (daily requirement not established)
Calcium	—	3.4%
Phosphorus	—	14.0%
Iron	—	11.7%

The egg, symbol of life, is a valuable diet food, as you can see from these figures. Eaten soft- or hard-boiled, coddled, shirred, poached or raw, the calorie content is favorable to the low calorie diet.

SOFT-BOILED EGGS

For one egg, boil 2 cups of water; for each extra egg, add a half cup. When the water has boiled, place the eggs in the pot gently, put on the cover, and turn out the flame. Leave pot on the turned off burner, or back of stove, to keep the water from cooling too fast.

For very soft eggs, leave eggs in the water 5 minutes. For less soft, 8 minutes. If eggs have been taken right out of the refrigerator, cook 1 minute longer—or better yet, use Method No. 2.

HARD-BOILED EGGS

For one egg allow 2 cups boiling water; for each extra egg add half a cup. Place eggs in boiling water gently, cover pot, turn off the flame, and keep the pot on turned-off burner or back of stove, so water does not cool too fast. Leave in eggs 30 to 40 minutes, then drain off water and cover eggs with cold water to prevent discoloration of yolks.

CODDLED EGGS

Place eggs in boiling water, but reduce the heat at once and keep the water just below boiling. Allow 6 minutes for lightly coddled eggs and 8 minutes for firmly coddled.

SHIRRED EGGS

Beat 2 egg whites until very stiff. Heat them into a lightly greased Pyrex dish. Make 2 cavities in the egg whites, not too near the edge. Gently drop in 2 unbroken egg yolks. Place the dish in moderate oven (350°F.) for 10 minutes, or until eggs are set. Season with salt, paprika. Sprinkle on chopped chives, if desired.

Add to each egg's 77 calories, about 10 calories for dish greasing.

POACHED EGGS

Use a skillet or shallow saucepan, and fill two-thirds full of salted water—½ teaspoon of salt to 4 cups of water. A teaspoon of vinegar added to the water keeps the whites from spreading. Bring the water to a boil, then reduce the flame and keep the water just under the boiling point.

Break eggs separately in a saucer and slip each egg gently from the saucer into the water. As the eggs cook, spoon some of the water over the eggs, to cook the tops.

Remove eggs when the whites are firm and a film forms over the yolks. Use a perforated spoon or pancake turner to remove. Sprinkle eggs with paprika or pepper.

POACHED EGGS FRENCH STYLE

Put 3 pints boiling water in a large saucepan; add 1 tablespoon vinegar and 2 teaspoons salt. Stir the boiling water vigorously with large wooden spoon held vertically, until a whirlpool is formed in the center. Have ready one egg broken into a cup and drop this into the water "hole."

Reduce water to a simmer, and cook until the white is set. Lift out with perforated spoon or pancake turner.

VENETIAN EGGS

Makes 4 servings (392 calories). Calories in 1 serving: 98.

3 eggs	1 teaspoon salt
1¼ cups tomatoes (½ No. 2 can)	2 drops Sacrose no-calorie saccharin sweetener
1 tablespoon butter	Small bay leaf
1 tablespoon chopped onion	Few grains paprika

1. Melt butter in skillet, add chopped onion and cook together a few minutes. Add tomatoes, bay leaf, salt, Sacrose, paprika. 2. When hot, pour in eggs. Break up eggs with fork after they start to cook.

TOMATO POACHED EGGS

Makes 4 servings (400 calories). Calories in 1 serving: 100.

4 eggs   Salt
1 can tomato sauce

1. Heat tomato sauce in shallow saucepan. 2. Break the eggs into sauce, sprinkle with salt. 3. Cover pan and simmer over low heat until eggs are firm. Serve with the sauce.

SCRAMBLED EGGS

Makes 1 serving (82 calories).

1 egg   Salt and pepper
1 tablespoon skim milk

1. Use a heavy pan and a low flame. 2. Stir egg and milk together, gently and constantly. Add salt before or after cooking. Add pepper after.

WHIPPED SCRAMBLED EGGS MADE IN DOUBLE BOILER

Makes 1 serving (77 calories).

1 egg   Salt and pepper

1. Season, and whip egg to fluffiness with rotary beater. 2. Pour egg into double boiler top, with water boiling briskly in boiler bottom. 3. Cover boiler and let cook until done, stirring occasionally.

DOWN EAST BAKED EGGS

Makes 4 servings (600 calories). Calories in 1 serving: 150.

4 eggs   ¼ cup soft bread crumbs
2 egg yolks   2 teaspoons chopped chives
2 sardines   2 teaspoons chopped parsley
1 tablespoon melted butter or   Salt and pepper
    margarine

1. Break up sardines well, with fork. Mix egg yolks, bread crumbs, melted butter, sardines, chives, parsley, salt and pepper. 2. Spread mixture in bottom of Pyrex baking dish. Place in very slow oven (250°F.) until set. 3. Carefully drop the whole eggs on top of mixture; do not break yolks. Sprinkle with salt and pepper. 4. Bake in moderate oven (350°F.) 20 to 30 minutes, or until eggs are set. Serve at once.

FOAMY OMELET

Makes 1 serving (132 calories).

1 egg, separated
1½ teaspoons butter or margarine

1 tablespoon skim milk
⅛ teaspoon salt
Few grains pepper

1. Beat egg white to a stiff froth. Beat yolk until light, then add milk, salt and pepper. **2.** Lightly fold beaten yolk into stiff white. **3.** Put butter in hot frying pan; when it bubbles pour in mixture. Shake pan gently so omelet does not stick. Lift up at sides with spatula or knife to see when bottom is done to a delicate brown. **4.** Preheat oven, and set pan in oven a minute, to cook top. When white is set, fold omelet half over, turn out on hot dish, and serve at once.

Variation: FOAMY OMELET WITH CHOPPED PARSLEY

Calories in 1 serving: 133.

Add 1 teaspoon chopped parsley when omelet is cooked, just before folding half over.

Variation: FOAMY OMELET WITH STEWED TOMATOES

Calories in 1 serving: 135.

Add 1 tablespoon stewed tomatoes when milk and seasonings are added, or when omelet is cooked, just before folding half over.

Variation: FOAMY OMELET WITH ASPARAGUS TIPS

Calories in 1 serving: 143.

Warm 3 asparagus tips and add to omelet when cooked, just before folding half over.

Variation: FOAMY OMELET WITH CHOPPED HAM

Calories in 1 serving: 188.

Chop fine 1 tablespoon lean, leftover ham, and add to yolk when milk and seasonings are added, or when omelet is cooked, just before folding half over.

Variation: FOAMY OMELET WITH CHOPPED OYSTERS

Calories in 1 serving: 192.

Chop 2 oysters and add when milk and seasonings are added, or when omelet is cooked, just before folding half over.

BAKED MEAT OMELET

Makes 1 serving (232 calories).

1 egg, separated
1 tablespoon skim milk
1½ teaspoons butter or margarine
⅛ teaspoon salt

Few grains pepper
2 tablespoons finely chopped lean leftover meat or chicken
1½ teaspoons grease for baking dish

1. Prepare foamy omelet according to recipe (see p. 76). **2.** Add the meat when the white is set, just before folding half over. **3.** Put in a small Pyrex dish which has been lightly greased. Set in pan of water and bake until firm.

CHEESE OMELET

Makes 4 servings (760 calories). Calories in 1 serving: 190.

6 eggs
Scant ½ cup grated American or Swiss cheese
Salt and pepper to taste

1 tablespoon butter or margarine
1 teaspoon chopped parsley

1. Beat eggs thoroughly, add 4 tablespoons water, salt and pepper, and blend well. **2.** Stir in cheese. In a heavy frying pan, over a hot flame, heat the butter, without browning it. **3.** Pour in the egg-cheese mixture, and with spatula or fork quickly press the edges back toward the center as soon as they thicken. Repeat until eggs no longer run. **4.** Bring the contents of the pan to the side nearest you and fold the omelet in half. Let it slide to the other side, and have a hot platter ready to receive it. Sprinkle top with chopped parsley.

CHICKEN SOUP OMELET

Makes 4 servings (708 calories). Calories in 1 serving: 177.

1 can chicken soup with noodles or rice (as soup comes, no added water)

5 eggs
1½ tablespoons butter or margarine

1. Beat eggs slightly, just enough to blend whites and yolks. Add soup. **2.** Heat a large heavy frying pan and put in butter. When melted, turn in egg-soup mixture, and reduce heat slightly. **3.** As omelet cooks, lift with a spatula, to let the uncooked part run underneath. **4.** When omelet has a creamy consistency, increase heat to give a quick brown to the bottom. **5.** Fold over omelet and turn out onto hot platter.

CHARCOAL DEALER'S OMELET

Makes 4 servings (572 calories). Calories in 1 serving: 143.

1 cup chopped onions	4 eggs
2 tablespoons butter or margarine	Salt and pepper

1. Sauté chopped onions in butter or shortening, until golden brown. **2.** Remove onions, leave fat in skillet. **3.** Beat eggs, add salt and pepper, and make omelet in same skillet. **4.** Serve omelet with onions on top, or folded in.

SWEDISH SOLOGA OR "SUN EYE"

Makes 1 serving (110 calories).

5 anchovies, boned and finely chopped	1 egg yolk
1 small onion, finely chopped	Sprig of parsley

1. Place finely chopped anchovies in a small ring (about 1½ inches in diameter) on bread-and-butter plate. **2.** Arrange ring of chopped onion, inside the anchovy ring. **3.** Slide the raw egg yolk from a saucer into the center of the ring. Garnish with parsley.

PICNIC EGGS

Makes 4 servings (524 calories). Calories in 1 serving: 131.

4 hard-boiled eggs	Pepper
⅓ cup grated Parmesan cheese	Skim milk
1 teaspoon prepared mustard	

1. Halve the eggs lengthwise. **2.** Remove the yolks and mash. Add the cheese, mustard, few grains of pepper and enough milk to moisten well. **3.** Beat until fluffy and refill the egg whites.

PICKLED EGGS

Makes 3 servings (315 calories). Calories in 1 serving: 105.

3 hard-boiled eggs	½ cup vinegar
2 teaspoons butter or margarine	¼ teaspoon salt
	⅛ teaspoon pepper

1. Slice eggs lengthwise. **2.** Bring other ingredients to a boil and pour over sliced eggs.

CHEESE SOUFFLÉ

Makes 4 servings (680 calories). Calories in 1 serving: 170.

1 tablespoon shortening	⅔ cup skim milk
2 tablespoons flour	2 eggs, separated
⅔ cup grated American cheese	½ teaspoon salt
	Few grains pepper

1. Melt shortening. Stir in flour, salt and pepper. Stir in milk and cook over low heat until mixture thickens. 2. Add grated cheese and stir until melted. 3. Stir mixture into slightly beaten egg yolks. Fold in stiffly beaten egg whites. 4. Pour into a 1-quart, ungreased baking dish. Set dish into pan of hot water and bake in moderately slow oven (325°F.) 1 hour, or until knife, when inserted in center, comes out clean. Serve at once.

Variation: TUNA FISH SOUFFLÉ

Calories the same.

Substitute ⅔ cup flaked or grated tuna fish for the cheese.

Variation: VEGETABLE SOUFFLÉ

Total calories: about 420. Calories in 1 serving: about 105.

Substitute ½ cup strained, cooked or canned carrots, spinach or other vegetable for the cheese.

Variation: TONGUE SOUFFLÉ

Total calories: 620. Calories in 1 serving: 155.

Substitute ½ cup ground or finely cut canned smoked tongue for the cheese.

NEW ENGLAND CLAM OMELET-SOUFFLÉ

Makes 6 servings (990 calories). Calories in 1 serving: 165.

6 eggs, separated	2 teaspoons butter or margarine
1 cup chopped cooked clams	
1 teaspoon salt	⅛ teaspoon pepper

1. Beat egg yolks until light. Add 6 tablespoons water. Add the salt, pepper and clams. 2. Beat egg whites stiffly and fold into yolk mixture. 3. Put butter in skillet and set over low flame. 4. Turn mixture into skillet and cook slowly until bubbles show on top, and omelet is brown underneath. 5. Put in moderately slow oven (325°F.) for 5 minutes, or until omelet is dry on top. Remove from skillet and fold over. Serve immediately.

ASPARAGUS SOUFFLÉ

(Adapted from a recipe of famous Beaumont Inn, on State Highway 35, in Harrodsburg, Kentucky.)

Makes 2 servings (372 calories). Calories in 1 serving: 186.

1 egg, beaten
1½ cups skim milk
1 cup cut-up asparagus
1 tablespoon flour

½ teaspoon saccharin liquid
sweetener
1 tablespoon melted butter
½ teaspoon salt

1. Mix asparagus and flour. **2.** Mix beaten egg and milk. Combine with asparagus mixture, and stir well. **3.** Add saccharin, seasonings and butter, and place in deep baking dish. **4.** Bake in moderate oven (350°F.), stirring occasionally until mixture begins to thicken. Bake until firm, but not long enough to bake dry.

EGG À LA FLORENTINE

Makes 1 serving (160 calories).

½ cup freshly cooked, finely chopped, well-seasoned spinach
½ teaspoon butter or margarine

1½ teaspoons grated cheese
1 egg
Salt and pepper
1 tablespoon thin white sauce

1. Butter individual ramekin or casserole and put in spinach. **2.** Sprinkle with half the grated cheese. **3.** Make a slight hollow in the center and drop egg into the hollow. Dust with salt and pepper. **4.** Cover with the cream sauce and sprinkle on the rest of the grated cheese. **5.** Bake in moderately hot oven (375°F.) 10 to 12 minutes, or until egg is set and top delicately browned.

MEAT-FILLED EGG

Makes 1 serving (150 calories).

1 hard-boiled egg
1 teaspoon buttermilk or tomato juice
⅛ teaspoon dry mustard
Dash of paprika

Salt
2 teaspoons finely chopped cooked tongue or chicken
Bed of parsley, chicory or lettuce

1. Cut shelled egg in half lengthwise. **2.** Remove yolk and rub to a smooth paste, adding buttermilk or tomato juice, chopped meat, mustard, paprika and salt to taste. Mix thoroughly. **3.** Fill whites with mixture and serve on bed of greens.

EGG OPEN SANDWICH

Makes 1 serving (175 calories).

1 hard-boiled egg
¼ teaspoon salt
⅛ teaspoon dry mustard
3 drops vinegar

1 teaspoon butter or olive oil
1 thin slice bread
½ teaspoon chopped water cress or parsley

1. Mince egg very fine (use silver fork). **2.** Add seasonings and butter or olive oil, and blend in thoroughly. **3.** Spread bread with egg mixture, cut in triangles and sprinkle with water cress or parsley.

CREAMED EGG

Makes 1 serving (176 calories).

1 egg
¾ cup skim milk
1 teaspoon butter

¼ teaspoon salt
Few grains pepper

1. In double boiler top, beat egg with fork until light. Add other ingredients. **2.** Set on boiler bottom containing boiling water, and stir with fork several times. **3.** Cover boiler top, and allow to cook until mixture sets like baked custard. Do not stir or allow to cook beyond setting, or it will separate. **4.** Remove by spoonfuls and serve at once. Add more salt and pepper if needed.

EGG NEST

Makes 1 serving (150 calories).

1 egg, separated
½ teaspoon butter

Salt and pepper
1 thin slice toast

1. Beat egg white, with few grains salt, until stiff. **2.** Place on toast in baking dish. Make hollow in the center and put in the butter. **3.** Slip in egg yolk. Bake in moderately hot oven (375°F.) until set. Add pepper.

SUPPER EGGS WITH SCALLIONS

Makes 2 servings (340 calories). Calories in 1 serving: 170.

3 freshly cooked hard-boiled eggs
1 tablespoon melted butter or margarine

2 scallions, thinly sliced, including tops
¼ teaspoon salt
Few grains pepper

1. Slice hot eggs into warm serving dish. Sprinkle on salt and pepper. **2.** Add melted butter and sliced scallions. Serve at once.

VEGETABLE CALORIE CHART

Each box shows amount equal to **50 CALORIES**

ARTICHOKE

French:
1 large bud
Jerusalem:
3 small 1-1/2" wide

ASPARAGUS

1-1/2 cups or
12 stalks cooked

BEANS, Lima

1/3 cup cooked

BEANS, Navy (or Kidney)

scant 1/4 cup cooked

BEANS, Snap, String or Wax

2 cups cooked

BEETS

2/3 cup diced cooked

BEET or TURNIP Greens

1 cup cooked

BROCCOLI

2 medium stalks or
1-1/4 cups, cooked;
or 7 ounces frozen

BRUSSELS SPROUTS

2/3 cup or
about 8 sprouts cooked;
or 3-1/2 ounces frozen

CABBAGE

1-1/4 cups cooked; or 2 cups
raw, shredded;
or 1 large head raw

CARROTS

1 cup diced, cooked; or
full cup raw, shredded;
or 1 large or 2 small raw

CAULIFLOWER

1/2 small head; or
1-2/3 cups cooked;
or 7 ounces frozen

CELERY

15 small inner stalks
raw (8 outer stalks); or
2-1/2 cups diced, raw

CORN

1/2 medium ear; or
1/3 cup canned

VEGETABLE CALORIE CHART Each box shows amount equal to **50 CALORIES**	**CUCUMBER** 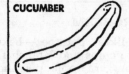 Two, 7 inches long	**EGG PLANT** 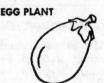 4 slices raw or 1 cup diced, raw
LETTUCE 1 medium head 4-1/2 inches wide	**MUSHROOMS** 30 small or 12 large fresh, or 1-2/3 cups canned	**OKRA** 15 pods 3" long raw or cooked
ONIONS 1 large raw (2-1/2" wide) or 2 or 3 small; 3/4 cup raw, chopped; or 2/3 cup cooked	**PARSNIPS** 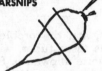 1/3 large raw; or 1/2 cup cooked	**PEAS, Green**  1/2 cup fresh; or 1/3 cup canned; or 2-1/3 oz. frozen
PEPPERS, Green 2-1/2 raw or baked; or 1 cup chopped raw	**POTATOES** 1/2 medium potato (2-1/2 inches wide) baked or boiled	**SPINACH** 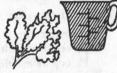 1 cup cooked; or 8-3/4 ounces frozen
SQUASH  Summer: 1-1/2 cups diced and cooked Winter: 1/2 cup baked or boiled	**TOMATOES** Fresh: 1 beefsteak size or 2 small Canned: 1 cupful	**TURNIPS, White** 1-1/4 cup diced, cooked

POTATOES—THE PROBLEM

Almost everybody likes potatoes—baked, boiled, mashed, creamed or fried. Potato chips and French fries now stand beside the hot dog, the hamburger, apple pie and ice cream as basic Americana.

A good source of energy, a good source of the B family of vitamins, potatoes, nevertheless, can hardly be allowed liberally on the calorie-restricted diet without crowding out other, more varied, more filling or more needed foods. A plain little cooked potato contains 85 calories, a medium-size potato 129 calories. And it isn't only the potato that counts, but also the butter, cream or fat that is added. Compare the high calories of a potato with the much lower calories of these filling, vitamin-rich vegetables:

6 stalks fresh asparagus	25 calories
10 small or 4 large mushrooms	16 calories
½ cup beets	34 calories
½ cup shredded cabbage	12 calories
4 stalks celery	22 calories
2 slices eggplant	24 calories

But you love potatoes, and the problem is to help you get an occasional serving of this tasty tuber, without having it take too big a bite out of your calorie allowance. Fried or creamed potatoes should be forgotten completely, until the doctor restores you to a normal diet. But here are a few potato recipes which might be enjoyed during calorie-restricted diet days.

MASHED POTATOES

Makes 6 servings (400 calories). Calories in 1 serving: 66.

3 medium potatoes	Paprika
¼ teaspoon salt	1 tablespoon chopped parsley
½ cup skim milk	or chives

1. Boil potatoes in salted water 20 to 30 minutes. Drain and peel. **2.** Mash at once. Add the milk while mashing. **3.** Beat until fluffy. Sprinkle lightly with paprika. Sprinkle with parsley or chives.

BAKED POTATO WAFERS

Makes 6 servings (400 calories). Calories in 1 serving: 66.

2 large baking potatoes	Salt and pepper
3 teaspoons butter or margarine	1 teaspoon finely chopped parsley

1. Scrub potatoes thoroughly and rub skins with butter—¾ teaspoon to each potato. **2.** Slice potatoes into ¼-inch round slices. Butter skillet with remaining 1½ teaspoons of butter or margarine and lay in slices. Season with salt and pepper. **3.** Cover skillet and bake in moderately hot oven (375°F.) for 20 minutes or until tender. Turn slices to brown on both sides. **4.** Serve garnished with parsley.

REDUCED BAKED POTATO

Makes 2 servings (160 calories). Calories in 1 serving: 80.

1 large flat baking potato   1 teaspoon butter, margarine or salad oil

1. Scrub potato. Cut in half lengthwise. **2.** Scoop out all but ½ inch of the potato, all around. Spread on butter, margarine or oil. **3.** Bake in very hot oven (450°F.) until crisp and brown.

BAKED POTATO STUFFED WITH COTTAGE CHEESE

Makes 6 servings (552 calories). Calories in 1 serving: 92.

3 freshly baked medium potatoes   1 cup cottage cheese
½ cup skim milk   Salt, pepper, paprika

1. Cut baked potatoes in half, lengthwise, and scoop out the potato. **2.** Mash and beat in the skim milk. Then beat in the cottage cheese, and at the same time season with salt and pepper. **3.** Refill the potato shells with mixture, and sprinkle with paprika. **4.** Return to hot oven (400°F.) and bake until top is brown.

DIET POTATO PANCAKE

Makes 4 servings (372 calories). Calories in 1 serving: 93.

3 medium potatoes   1½ teaspoons shortening
1 small onion   Salt and pepper

1. Wash, but do not peel, potatoes. Grate on medium grater. Grate in onion. **2.** In a well-greased skillet, spread potato mixture out to about ¼-inch thickness. Leave whole or separate gently, into small pancakes. **3.** Cook over slow to medium flame until bottom is brown and turn over to brown the other side. Season with salt and pepper and serve hot.

BAKER'S POTATOES

The French custom of sending food to the neighborhood baker to cook in his ever-hot ovens gives these delicious potatoes their name. The original recipe calls for lots of butter on top, but we have to do with less.

Makes 6 servings (780 calories). Calories in 1 serving: 130.

2 pounds potatoes
2 medium onions
1½ teaspoons salt
Pepper
2 teaspoons chopped parsley

Stock, or broth made with Herbox, Nestlé or other bouillon cubes
2 teaspoons butter or margarine

1. Peel and thinly slice the potatoes and onions. **2.** Arrange in a large shallow Pyrex baking dish, to come not much over ½ inch deep. **3.** Sprinkle on the salt generously. Pepper to taste. Sprinkle on the parsley. Spread the top layer lightly but thoroughly with the butter or margarine. **4.** Pour on enough stock to come to almost the top of the potatoes. **5.** Set into hot oven (400°F.) for about 1 hour, until liquid is absorbed and potatoes are soft, with brown crust on top. Serve at the table right from the oven dish.

SUNNY POTATOES

Makes 6 servings (810 calories). Calories in 1 serving: 135.

3 medium-large potatoes
5 medium carrots
1 medium onion
2 tablespoons skim milk

2 tablespoons butter or margarine
Salt and pepper
Sprig of parsley

1. Peel and slice potatoes; clean and dice carrots. Cook together in 1½ inches of water, in tightly covered saucepan, until tender. Press through ricer or coarse sieve. **2.** Dice onion and brown it in butter or margarine. Add to potatoes and carrots. At same time, add in milk, salt and pepper. **3.** Beat well and serve at once, garnished with parsley.

ASPARAGUS MILANAISE

Makes 2 servings (130 calories). Calories in 1 serving: 65.

12 stalks cooked asparagus
2 tablespoons grated Parmesan cheese

1 teaspoon melted butter
2 slivers canned pimiento

1. Place the asparagus on Pyrex serving dish and cover the tips with the grated cheese. **2.** Sprinkle melted butter over the cheese and brown quickly under the broiler. **3.** Garnish with pimiento strips.

MASHED POTATOES

Makes 2 servings (170 calories). Calories in 1 serving: 85.

2 small potatoes
Salt and pepper

2 tablespoons skim milk or
buttermilk

1. Peel and quarter potatoes. Cook until soft, in just enough salted water to cover. Drain. **2.** Mash or rice, then add milk or buttermilk, salt, and pepper.

AMERICANIZED CHOP SUEY

Makes 6 servings (1332 calories). Calories in 1 serving: 222.

½ pound ground beef round
2½ cups tomatoes (1 No. 2 can)
1 cup celery cut into thin strips, about 1 inch long

1 cup onions, finely sliced
2 tablespoons soy sauce
1 cup elbow macaroni
2 tablespoons oil
2½ teaspoons salt

1. Cook macaroni in 2 quarts boiling salted water for 10 minutes. Stir occasionally. Drain and rinse. **2.** Heat oil in skillet, add onions and cook over medium heat for 5 minutes, or until onions are slightly yellow. **3.** Add heat and continue cooking for 10 to 15 minutes or until well browned. Stir frequently. Add tomatoes and 1½ teaspoons salt, cover and cook for 10 minutes. Add celery, cook 5 minutes longer. **4.** Combine meat sauce and macaroni, season with soy sauce and cook slowly 5 minutes.

OYSTER STUFFED MUSHROOMS

Makes 4 servings (708 calories). Calories in 1 serving: 177.

8 large mushrooms
2½ tablespoons butter or margarine
1 cup chopped cooked or canned oysters
1½ cups soft bread crumbs

1 tablespoon finely chopped onion
½ teaspoon Worcestershire sauce
¼ teaspoon salt

1. Clean mushrooms. Remove stems and chop fine. **2.** Combine chopped mushroom stems and minced onion. Sauté together in scant 2 tablespoons butter or margarine for 8 minutes, or until tender. Add oysters, Worcestershire sauce, salt and crumbs. **3.** Stuff mushroom cups with this mixture and place in shallow baking dish. Add 1 tablespoon water. **4.** Dot with remaining butter or margarine and bake in hot oven (400°F.) 25 minutes.

BAKED SQUASH PUDDING

(This recipe is from the newly revised *Pocket Cook Book,* which contains many valuable cooking helps and ideas.)

Makes 4 servings (720 calories). Calories in 1 serving: 180.

1¼ cups cooked Hubbard (winter) squash
2 eggs
⅓ cup firmly packed light brown sugar

¼ cup molasses
¾ cup skim milk
½ teaspoon salt
¼ teaspoon cinnamon

1. If squash is very moist, cook slowly to evaporate some of the liquid. 2. Strain squash and combine with sugar, molasses, salt and cinnamon. 3. Beat eggs and add with milk. Pour into greased baking dish. Bake in moderately slow oven (325°F.) 1 hour 30 minutes.

CONTINENTAL STYLE PEAS AND MUSHROOMS

Makes 4 servings (554 calories). Calories in 1 serving: 138.

2 cups hot, drained peas, fresh or canned
1 cup sliced mushrooms, fresh or canned
2 tablespoons butter or margarine

¼ cup finely chopped onion
¼ teaspoon salt
¼ teaspoon nutmeg
⅛ teaspoon marjoram
Few grains pepper

1. Sauté onion and mushrooms in skillet for about 5 minutes. 2. Add all other ingredients except peas. Blend together, then add the hot peas.

CARROTS AND ASPARAGUS AU GRATIN

Makes 4 servings (224 calories). Calories in 1 serving: 56.

¾ pound cooked asparagus (or 1 No. 300 can)
½ cup broth (made with vegetable bouillon cube)
1½ tablespoons chopped parsley

1½ cups cooked carrots, diced or sliced (or a little over ½ a No. 2 can)
2 tablespoons dry grated cheddar cheese

1. Mix carrots and parsley with the asparagus. 2. Place in shallow baking dish, pour in vegetable broth, and sprinkle with cheese. 3. Bake, uncovered, in moderate oven (350°F.), 20 to 25 minutes.

HARVARD BEETS

Makes 4 servings (168 calories). Calories in 1 serving: 42.

2¼ cups cooked beets (or 1 No. 2 can)
¼ cup cider vinegar

1 tablespoon cornstarch
½ teaspoon salt
6 Sucaryl tablets

1. Dice or slice beets. 2. Mash Sucaryl tablets and dissolve in ¼ cup water. 3. Combine cornstarch, salt, vinegar and dissolved Sucaryl. Cook over low heat until thickened, stirring constantly. 4. Add beets and heat until beets are hot.

CELERY AND BEETS

Makes 4 servings (100 calories). Calories in 1 serving: 25.

1⅓ cups cooked, sliced celery
⅔ cup cooked, sliced beets
Few grains salt

1 teaspoon mixed pickling spice, if extra flavor is desired

1. Mix celery and beets, season, reheat 5 to 10 minutes. 2. If pickling spice is not used, sprinkle with chopped mint.

BEET GREENS WITH BUTTER

Makes 4 servings (249 calories). Calories in 1 serving: 62.

1½ pounds beet greens
Salt and pepper

1½ tablespoons melted butter, margarine or salad oil

1. Remove tough stems and wilted leaves. Wash several times in cold water until all sand is removed. 2. Drain slightly and place in saucepan. 3. Cover and cook 10 to 20 minutes or until tender. Turn greens once during cooking. 4. Add melted butter, margarine or salad oil. Season with salt and pepper.

BEAN STEW

Makes 4 servings (112 calories). Calories in 1 serving: 28.

⅔ cup tomato juice
2 cups 1-inch lengths cooked wax beans
2 tablespoons chopped parsley

½ large green pepper, chopped
Salt and paprika or curry, to taste

1. Heat tomato juice, add pepper, and simmer 5 minutes. 2. Add beans, cover, and simmer 10 minutes. Season to taste. 3. Sprinkle with parsley, serve at once.

LOUISIANA BEANS

Makes 4 servings (88 calories). Calories in 1 serving: 22.

2 cups cooked 1-inch lengths wax beans or string beans
⅓ cup grated carrots

1 canned pimiento
½ bunch water cress, chopped

1. Cut up pimiento into slices. 2. Heat beans, carrots and pimiento in double boiler. 3. Sprinkle vegetables with chopped water cress before serving.

SNAP BEANS WITH MUSHROOMS

Makes 3 servings (189 calories). Calories in 1 serving: 63.

1½ cups cooked sliced snap beans
1½ tablespoons grated Parmesan cheese

½ pound mushrooms
Fresh dried thyme or marjoram, to taste

1. Broil and slice mushrooms, or pan broil sliced mushrooms. 2. Mix mushrooms with beans; blend with chopped thyme or marjoram. Reheat if necessary. 3. Sprinkle with grated cheese before serving.

BAKED BROCCOLI

Makes 4 servings (232 calories). Calories in 1 serving: 58.

1 medium bunch broccoli, cooked
2 tablespoons grated Parmesan cheese

⅔ cup stewed tomatoes
1 scant tablespoon chopped parsley

1. Break up broccoli into flowerets, or chop coarsely. 2. Mix with tomatoes, and pour into baking dish. Cover with cheese and parsley. 3. Bake, uncovered, in moderate oven (350°F.), for 35 to 40 minutes.

HUNGARIAN BRUSSELS SPROUTS

Makes 6 servings (324 calories). Calories in 1 serving: 54.

1½ pounds cooked Brussels sprouts (1 quart)
1 cup stewed tomatoes
1 medium green pepper, chopped

1 bay leaf
1 tablespoon caraway seeds
½ teaspoon paprika
Salt to taste

1. Slice sprouts in half, lengthwise. 2. Heat tomatoes and add all other ingredients except sprouts. Simmer for 5 minutes. 3. Remove bay leaf, add sprouts and heat thoroughly, about 10 minutes.

BOILED CABBAGE WEDGES

Makes 4 servings (80 calories). Calories in 1 serving: 20.

1 small head cabbage
⅔ teaspoon caraway seeds

Salt and pepper

1. Remove wilted leaves. Cut cabbage into eighths. Rinse in cold running water. **2.** Cover with small amount of boiling, well-salted water. Add caraway seeds. **3.** Cover pan and bring to quick boil. Then simmer 15 to 20 minutes until tender. **4.** Drain and season with salt and pepper.

CARROT CASSEROLE

Makes 4 servings (172 calories). Calories in 1 serving: 43.

1 pound carrots (weight includes tops)
1 large tomato

1 cup vegetable broth made
from Souplets tablet
2 teaspoons chopped parsley

1. Remove tops, wash and scrape carrots. Cube or slice carrots. **2.** Place in baking dish and add boiling cup Souplets broth. If necessary to bring liquid to ⅓ depth of carrots, add additional boiling water. **3.** Slice tomato and cover carrots. Place cover on pot and bake in slow or moderately slow oven (300-325°F.) until tender, about 35 minutes. **4.** Uncover and bake for another 5 minutes. **5.** Sprinkle with parsley and serve on warm platter.

KALE WITH APPLE AND TOMATO

Makes 4 servings (180 calories). Calories in 1 serving: 45.

2 cups cooked kale, chopped
1 medium apple

⅓ cup stewed tomato
½ teaspoon salt

1. Shred the apple, do not peel. **2.** Heat the stewed tomato in saucepan, add the kale, shredded apple and salt. **3.** Cover and simmer until tender.

KNOB CELERY (CELERIAC)

Makes 4 servings (180 calories). Calories in 1 serving: 45.

1 pound knob celery (2 small
knobs, or 1 large)
1 teaspoon lemon juice

Scant teaspoon salt
Chopped chives or water cress

1. Wash and scrape knobs. Leave whole if small knobs; if large, slice or dice. **2.** Cover with salted boiling water, cover pot, and simmer until tender, from 15 to 30 minutes. **3.** Drain; sprinkle with lemon juice and chopped greens.

BAKED CAULIFLOWER AU GRATIN

Makes 4 servings (200 calories). Calories in 1 serving: 50.

1 medium head cauliflower
(2 pounds as bought)
⅓ cup tomato juice

4 tablespoons dry grated
cheese
Salt and pepper

1. Wash and cook whole cauliflower. Drain. 2. Place, head up, in baking dish and pour on tomato juice. Sprinkle with cheese, and season. 3. Bake, uncovered, in moderate oven (350°F.) for 25 to 35 minutes.

BROCCOLI WITH CHEESE AND BUTTERMILK

Makes 4 servings (312 calories). Calories in 1 serving: 78.

1 medium bunch broccoli
(1¾ pounds)
⅓ cup buttermilk

⅓ cup dry grated cheese
Sage to taste
Salt to taste

1. Mix all ingredients in double boiler. 2. Cover tightly and heat thoroughly. Serve on warm platter.

VEGETABLE STEW

Makes 4 servings (328 calories). Calories in 1 serving: 82.

4 cups leftover or fresh vegetables—sliced string beans,
diced carrots, peas, shredded
cabbage, etc.
1 medium tomato
4 large sliced mushrooms

1 bouillon cube or vegetable
tablet
½ green pepper, chopped
½ small onion
1 teaspoon chopped parsley

1. Dissolve bouillon cube in 2 cups boiling water. 2. Add vegetables. Season with parsley, salt and pepper. 3. Cook gently till tender.

PANNED CELERY

Makes 4 servings (88 calories). Calories in 1 serving: 22.

1 large bunch celery (about
1½ pounds)
Scant ¼ cup tomato juice

¼ teaspoon salt
Few grains white pepper

1. Wash celery and cut into 1-inch pieces. 2. Heat tomato juice, add celery pieces. Cover pan and simmer 10 to 20 minutes, until tender. Season with salt and pepper.

TOMATO-RICE PILAF

Makes 6 servings (522 calories). Calories in 1 serving: 87.

¾ cup uncooked white rice
4 slices bacon
1 medium onion, finely chopped
1 tablespoon chopped green pepper

6 to 8 okra, sliced
1 No. 2½ can tomatoes
1 tablespoon sugar
1 teaspoon salt
1 tablespoon chopped parsley

1. Cook rice until tender. **2.** Cook bacon, draining off fat thoroughly. Also drain on paper, pressing paper on bacon to absorb excess fat. **3.** Simmer tomatoes, chopped onion, chopped pepper, okra, salt and sugar, for 15 minutes. **4.** Add drained rice to this and simmer 5 minutes longer. **5.** Just before serving, break up bacon into small pieces and mix in pilaf or sprinkle on top. Sprinkle chopped parsley as garnishing.

COOKED RADISHES

Makes 6 servings (90 calories). Calories in 1 serving: 15.

3 bunches radishes
½ teaspoon salt

Pepper
2 teaspoons butter

1. Wash radishes; remove roots and leaves; place in saucepan. **2.** Cover with water, add the salt, and boil, uncovered, 15 to 20 minutes. **3.** Drain, season with pepper, and serve with lump of butter (⅓ teaspoon to each portion).

SOUTHERN FRANCE SQUASH-AND-EGGPLANT

Makes 4 servings (800 calories). Calories in 1 serving: 200.

1 medium zucchini or summer squash
1 medium eggplant
4 tomatoes
3 tablespoons olive oil or salad oil

1 small onion, finely chopped
1 tablespoon chopped parsley
1 clove garlic, finely chopped
1 bay leaf
¼ cup grated Parmesan cheese
Salt and pepper

1. Pare squash if skin is tough. Dice, and cook 10 minutes in boiling water, and drain. Peel and dice eggplant. Cook 10 minutes in boiling water and drain. Peel tomatoes and cut in pieces. **2.** Put oil in saucepan, brown the chopped onion and add all other ingredients except the cheese. Season with salt and pepper. **3.** Cook until vegetables are tender, about 20 minutes. Season again if necessary. **4.** Place in shallow baking dish, sprinkle with cheese and brown under the broiler.

SIMMERED CUCUMBERS

Makes 3 servings (52 calories). Calories in 1 serving: 17..

2 medium cucumbers	2 tablespoons chopped parsley,
⅓ cup tomato juice	dill or chives
¼ teaspoon salt	

1. Peel cucumbers only if skin is tough. Slice cucumbers lengthwise, 3 or 4 slices to each cucumber. 2. Heat tomato juice, add cucumbers and salt. Cover, and simmer until tender. 3. Sprinkle generously with parsley, dill or chives.

SNAP BEANS WITH EGG SAUCE

Makes 4 servings (520 calories). Calories in 1 serving: 130.

1 pound young string beans, wax beans or green beans	2 egg yolks
	1 tablespoon flour
1 cup fresh skim milk or soup stock	1 tablespoon lemon juice
	¼ teaspoon salt
1½ tablespoons butter	⅛ teaspoon paprika

1. Prepare beans and tie loosely into small bunches. 2. Cook, covered, in 1¼ cups boiling water for 20 minutes, or until tender. Drain, untie and place on warm platter. 3. Melt butter and stir in flour until blended. Stir in the skim milk or stock. 4. When sauce is smooth and boiling, remove from the stove and beat in the egg yolks. 5. Over low heat, stir the sauce for a minute more, while eggs thicken. Add the salt, paprika and lemon juice. Pour the sauce down the center of the stack of beans.

SAVORY RICE

Makes 2 servings (290 calories). Calories in 1 serving: 145.

¼ cup uncooked white rice	1 clove garlic, finely minced
1 tablespoon finely chopped onion	¼ teaspoon paprika
	⅛ teaspoon salt
½ tablespoon butter	⅛ teaspoon dried savory
½ tablespoon salad oil	1 chicken bouillon cube or
½ tablespoon finely chopped parsley	package G. Washington's chicken-like broth

1. Wash rice; drain. Heat butter and oil in small skillet. Add onion, garlic and rice. 2. Cook over low flame, uncovered, until rice has browned. Stir often. 3. Stir in the rest of the ingredients, slowly. 4. Cover, and cook for 20 to 25 minutes, or until rice is tender.

BROILED PEPPERS

Makes 4 servings (48 calories). Calories in 1 serving: 12.

2 large green peppers   Salt
2 teaspoons milk

1. Cut peppers in half, remove seeds and white veins. 2. Cut into strips or quarters and broil under medium broiler until edges curl. 3. Moisten with milk and season with salt.

GREEN BEANS AND CELERY

Makes 5 servings (140 calories). Calories in 1 serving: 28.

1½ cups sliced celery   1 box (10 ounces) frozen cut
1 teaspoon salt   green beans*
1⅓ cups boiling water

1. Add celery and salt to boiling water in saucepan. Add frozen green beans and bring again to a boil, separating beans with a fork. 2. Then cook gently 10 to 12 minutes, or until beans are just tender. Drain and season to taste.

*If desired, 1 box (10 ounces) frozen French Style green beans may be used. Cook beans 8 to 10 minutes, or until just tender.

ITALIAN STYLE CABBAGE

Makes 4 servings (260 calories). Calories in 1 serving: 65.

1½ pounds cabbage   1 bay leaf
⅔ cup stewed tomatoes   1 teaspoon lemon juice
⅔ tablespoon caraway seeds,   2 tablespoons Parmesan cheese
  chopped   Salt and pepper

1. Wash, scald and shred cabbage coarsely. 2. Heat tomatoes in skillet, add caraway seeds, bay leaf, lemon juice, salt and pepper. 3. Cover; simmer for 5 minutes, and remove bay leaf. 4. Add cabbage, cover tightly and simmer 10 to 15 minutes, or until tender. Sprinkle with cheese before serving.

PEAS AND CARROTS

Makes 3 servings (156 calories). Calories in 1 serving: 52.

1 cup cooked carrots, diced or   ⅛ teaspoon salt
  sliced   Thyme and white pepper, to
1 cup cooked green peas   taste

1. Place all the ingredients in a deep dish and shake well; do not mix with spoon. 2. Reheat in double boiler if necessary.

ONION

During World War II, one of my associates listened to a lecture by an Army colonel, who declared it was even more noble to add flavor to the field rations of our soldiers than to fight at the front. So I soon found myself in the business of drying and flaking the flavorsome onion, with a vast porcelain-lined tunnel and huge blowers to extract moisture as fast as the onion slices could be fed into the cavernous mouth. It is, I can tell you, an expensive way to learn about a vegetable—any vegetable.

Onions grow extensively in the rich black soil around Middletown, New York, but they grow quietly and considerately. Little did the citizens of this pleasant community know what onions could be like when broiled en masse, hours on end. Even the famed Hambletonian trotting races at nearby Goshen came to a temporary halt. Today these good people (and horses) are grateful that onions are grown but no longer dried in Middletown, and so am I.

Makes 4 servings (200 calories). Calories in 1 serving: 50.

1 pound small white onions   Salt and paprika

1. Peel onions under running water, cut off a thin slice from each end. 2. Barely cover onions with boiling water in a saucepan. Cover and cook for 20 to 30 minutes, or until onions are soft, but not broken. 3. Season with salt and paprika. Serve at once.

BOILED ONIONS WITH BACON AND TOMATO SAUCE

Makes 6 servings (900 calories). Calories in 1 serving: 150.

6 cups small onions   1 can Campbell's tomato soup
5 slices bacon   Dash of pepper

1. Cook onions in boiling salted water 30 to 40 minutes. Drain. 2. Cut bacon into small squares and cook until crisp. Add soup and pepper. 3. Heat onions in sauce. Serve hot.

SAUTÉED MUSHROOMS

Makes 4 servings (260 calories). Calories in 1 serving: 65.

1 pound mushrooms   1 clove garlic
2 tablespoons butter or bacon ½ teaspoon lemon juice
fat   Salt

1. Wash, dry, clean and slice mushrooms. 2. Rub a skillet with garlic and melt the butter. Add the mushrooms and sauté them quickly until done, 4 or 5 minutes. 3. Shake the skillet, or stir mushrooms. When mushrooms are well coated, reduce heat to moderate flame and add the lemon juice and salt.

ONIONS AND APPLES

Makes 3 servings (400 calories). Calories in 1 serving: 133.

1 large yellow onion	2 large cooking apples
1 tablespoon butter or mar-	1 teaspoon brown sugar
garine	Salt, pepper

1. Peel and slice onion. Melt butter in frying pan, add the onion and cook over low heat. Stir or shake pan occasionally to insure even browning. **2.** Wash and core the apples, but do not peel. Quarter and slice apples. **3.** Add apples to onions after onions have been cooking about 10 minutes. Cover, and cook for about 10 minutes more. Season to taste. Add sprinkling of brown sugar just before serving.

Variation: Equal parts onion slices and green pepper rings—1 large onion, 1 large pepper. Pan fry slowly, in 1 tablespoon butter or margarine, until tender and light brown. Stir or shake occasionally.

Makes 3 servings (528 calories). Calories in 1 serving: 176.

HARICOTS VERTS À LA POULETTE

Makes 4 servings (300 calories). Calories in 1 serving: 75.

1 pound string beans (or 1 No.	⅛ cup chopped celery
2½ can small green beans)	1 teaspoon lemon juice
1 egg yolk	¾ teaspoon salt
1 cup sliced onion, finely	¼ teaspoon sugar
chopped	Pepper and paprika
¼ cup skim milk	

1. Prepare beans and cut into 2-inch lengths. Add chopped onion and small amount of water. Cook until tender, and season with salt and sugar. **2.** Beat egg yolk, add the skim milk, lemon juice, a dash of paprika and pepper, and the celery. Pour this over the beans and heat very slowly to avoid curdling.

MINT GLAZED CARROTS

Makes 4 servings (308 calories). Calories in 1 serving: 77.

2½ cups cooked diced carrots	1 tablespoon butter, marga-
(or 1 No. 2 can)	rine or salad oil
2 tablespoons mint jelly	

1. Drain carrots. Add jelly and butter, margarine or salad oil. **2.** Heat slowly, stirring constantly, until jelly is melted and carrots are heated.

CHINESE BOILED RICE

The Chinese say that when properly cooked, rice must absorb all the allotted moisture. Each grain must be dry and evenly textured, no matter how soft it may be.

Makes 4 servings (692 calories). Calories in 1 serving: 173.

    1 cup rice

1. Wash rice; drain. If rice is the long-grained variety, add 1½ to 2 cups cold water, depending on desired softness of rice. If rice is oval-grained, increase water by ½ cup. **2.** Boil over high flame, stirring to prevent sticking. After boiling for 5 minutes, or as soon as most of the free water has been boiled off, reduce flame as low as possible. **3.** Cover, and simmer for 20 minutes if rice is long-grained, or until rice is soft and has lost its shiny, wet appearance. If rice is oval-grained, simmer for 15 minutes, then turn rice over, cover the pot again, and simmer for 15 minutes more.

MINTED GREEN PEAS

Makes 4 servings (320 calories). Calories in 1 serving: 80.

2 cups shelled fresh peas (about 2 pounds unshelled), or 1 No. 1 tall can	1 tablespoon butter or margarine
2 tablespoons chopped fresh mint leaves	¼ teaspoon salt
	Few grains sugar

1. Cook peas in tightly covered saucepan for 5 to 8 minutes, with ½ cup cold water, salt and sugar. Cook at moderate heat (350°F.). If canned peas are used, just heat in their own liquid. **2.** Just before serving, add the butter or margarine, and the chopped mint. Stir, or shake pan to distribute evenly.

SIMPLE SNAP BEAN CASSEROLE

Makes 6 servings (510 calories). Calories in 1 serving: 85.

1 pound string beans, wax beans or green beans	2 medium green peppers, chopped
4 medium white onions, chopped	1½ tablespoons butter or margarine
Salt and paprika	

1. String the beans. Grease a baking dish lightly and place a layer of beans in it. **2.** Dot with butter, then add alternating layers of onions, beans and peppers, ending with a layer of beans. Sprinkle each layer with salt and paprika and dot each layer lightly with butter or margarine. **3.** Cover the dish and bake in a moderate oven (350°F.) for 1¼ hours, or until beans are tender.

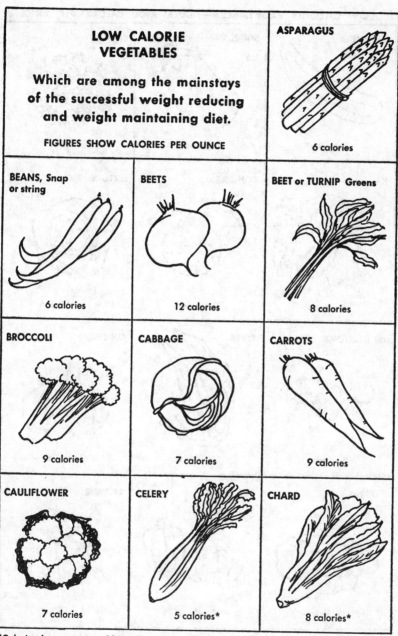

LOW CALORIE VEGETABLES

Which are among the mainstays of the successful weight reducing and weight maintaining diet.

FIGURES SHOW CALORIES PER OUNCE

ASPARAGUS

6 calories

BEANS, Snap or string

6 calories

BEETS

12 calories

BEET or TURNIP Greens

8 calories

BROCCOLI

9 calories

CABBAGE

7 calories

CARROTS

9 calories

CAULIFLOWER

7 calories

CELERY

5 calories*

CHARD

8 calories*

*Calories for raw vegetables. All others are for cooked vegetables without added butter.

99

LOW CALORIE VEGETABLES — FIGURES SHOW CALORIES PER OUNCE

CUCUMBER	EGGPLANT	ENDIVE
5 calories*	7 calories*	5 calories*

KALE	KOHLRABI	LETTUCE
12 calories	9 calories	4 calories*

MUSHROOMS	OKRA	ONIONS
5 calories	10 calories	11 calories

PEPPERS	PUMPKINS	RADISHES
8 calories*	10 calories	6 calories*

*Calories for raw vegetables. All others are for cooked vegetables without added butter.

LOW CALORIE VEGETABLES — FIGURES SHOW CALORIES PER OUNCE

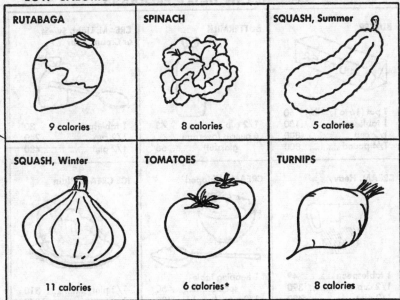

RUTABAGA	SPINACH	SQUASH, Summer
9 calories	8 calories	5 calories

SQUASH, Winter	TOMATOES	TURNIPS
11 calories	6 calories*	8 calories

CALORIES IN FAVORITE FRUITS

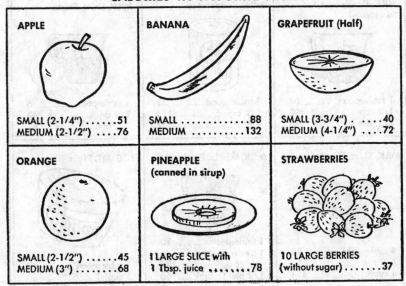

APPLE
SMALL (2-1/4") 51
MEDIUM (2-1/2") 76

BANANA
SMALL 88
MEDIUM 132

GRAPEFRUIT (Half)
SMALL (3-3/4") 40
MEDIUM (4-1/4") 72

ORANGE
SMALL (2-1/2") 45
MEDIUM (3") 68

PINEAPPLE
(canned in sirup)
1 LARGE SLICE with
1 Tbsp. juice 78

STRAWBERRIES
10 LARGE BERRIES
(without sugar) 37

CALORIES IN DAIRY PRODUCTS

BUTTER

1 pat (16 to 1/4 lb.).. 50
1 tablespoon 100
1/2 cup 800
1/4 pound 800

BUTTERMILK

1/2 cup 43
6 ounces (average
    glassful) 66

CREAM, Light, Sweet or Cream, Sour

1 tablespoon 30
1/2 cup 240
1/2 pint 480

CREAM, Heavy

1 tablespoon 49
1/2 cup 390
1/2 pint 780

CREAM, Whipped

1 heaping table-
    spoon 50
1/2 pint (1 cup) 400

ICE CREAM, Plain

1/2 pint 310
1 quart 1240

MILK, Condensed, Sweetened

1 tablespoon 64
1/2 cup 490
1/2 pint 980

MILK, Evaporated

1 tablespoon 22
1/2 cup 173
1 can 567

MILK, Skim, Fresh

1 tablespoon 6
1/2 cup 43
1/2 pint 87

MILK, Skim, Powder

1 tablespoon 28
1/2 cup 217
1 cupful 434

MILK, Whole, Fresh

1 tablespoon 10
1 average glassful
    (6 ounces) 124
1/2 pint (1 cup) 166

YOGURT, Plain

1 tablespoon 10
1 cupful 160

Also see charts "Calories in 1 ounce of Cheese" and "Calories in Eggs"

CALORIES IN ONE OUNCE OF CHEESE

BLUE MOLD CHEESE	CAMEMBERT	CHEDDAR CHEESE
104 calories	85 calories	113 calories

COTTAGE CHEESE (uncreamed)	CREAM CHEESE	GRUYERE CHEESE
27 calories	106 calories	115 calories

LIEDERKRANZ	LIMBURGER	PARMESAN
85 calories	97 calories	112 calories

ROQUEFORT	SWISS CHEESE	VELVEETA
111 calories	105 calories	92 calories

SKIM MILK

Whole milk contains 170 calories to the cup, whereas a cup of skim milk contains only 88 calories.

	A cup of skim milk contains these percentages of your daily minimum requirements	A cup of whole milk contains these percentages of your daily minimum requirements
Protein	13.6%	13.5%
Calcium	29.3%	29.1%
Phosphorus	31.8%	30.2%
Iron	6.0%	5.0%
Vitamin A	none	9.4%
Vitamin B-1	9.2%	11.0%
Vitamin B-2	29.0%	35.4%
Vitamin C	4.0%	5.0%

The only essential difference between skim milk and whole milk is that skim milk has no Vitamin A, and you must get Vitamin A from other foods, or from vitamin supplements.

Skim milk is an important food in the low calorie diet. Many dairies now sell fluid milk already skimmed, but if you cannot purchase skim milk use fresh whole milk (not homogenized milk) and skim it by setting bottle in cold place to allow the cream to settle to the top. Pour off all cream, allow to chill again and remove any additional cream that settles. Powdered skim milk and skim milk tablets are also available.

FLAVOR IDEA: Fresh vanilla bean flavors milk without adding calories. Place bean in glass of milk in refrigerator. (Wash bean in cold water after use and place in next glass of milk or return to corked bottle.)

COTTAGE CHEESE

To obtain genuine low calorie UNCREAMED cottage cheese is sometimes difficult, so here is an easy way to make it yourself. Permit milk to sour in a covered jar kept in a warm place, until the whey separates from the curd. Drain the curd in a bag made of crash toweling. When it is firm to the touch, place it on ice for several hours. Remove it from the bag, put it in a bowl. Work it with a wire whisk until it is smooth and creamy.

COTTAGE CHEESE MADE WITH RENNET TABLET

This recipe makes a low calorie cottage cheese, sweeter in flavor, than if no rennet were used. Its texture will be small, fine-grained. For low sodium diets, omit the salt in step number 6.

¼ Junket rennet tablet	¼ cup buttermilk
1 gallon skim milk	½ teaspoon salt

1. Dissolve Junket rennet tablet by crushing in 2 tablespoons cold water. Combine skim milk and buttermilk and heat to remove chill only (75°F.). **2.** Add only 1 tablespoon of the rennet tablet solution (discard remainder) and stir well. Cover with a towel and let stand at room temperature 16-20 hours or until a smooth, firm curd has formed. **3.** Cut curd in 1½″ squares using a long knife. In order to raise the temperature of the curd add 1 quart lukewarm water (110°F.). **4.** After about 30 minutes add two more quarts of slightly warmer water (120°F.). Heat curd to 120°F., stirring gently every three or four minutes. Hold the curd at this temperature for 40 minutes. Pour off whey. **5.** Wash the remaining curds by adding enough medium cold water (75°F.) to fill the container to about the same level as occupied by the whey drained off it. Gently stir the curd for about 1 minute. Allow it to remain undisturbed for another 5 minutes and then drain again until most of the whey is gone. Follow this with two successive washings of colder water (about 50°F.). **6.** Drain the curd on drain board or in cheesecloth bag until the curd is free from whey. Season with ½ teaspoon salt.

HIGH PROTEIN BREAD

This popular recipe was developed by Dr. Clive McCay of Cornell University.

Total calories: 1275. Calories in 1 slice (⅜-inch thick): 53.

½ package or cake dry yeast	2 teaspoons sugar
2½ cups enriched flour, preferably unbleached	2 teaspoons shortening
	1½ teaspoons salt
3 tablespoons full-fat soy flour	2 teaspoons wheat germ
3½ tablespoons dry skim milk	

1. Dissolve yeast in 1 cup lukewarm water (not hot), about 85°F. **2.** Combine all dry ingredients in mixing bowl. Pour in yeast solution and start mixing. **3.** Add shortening and mix until the dough is smooth. **4.** Place dough in a well-greased bowl, cover and let rise in a warm place (80° to 85°F.) for 1½ hours. **5.** Punch down dough by plunging a fist in the center of it. Fold over edges of dough and turn upside down. Cover and let rise 15 to 20 minutes. **6.** Shape into a loaf and place in greased bread pan (9 x 4 x 3 inches). Cover and let stand about 50 to 60 minutes in a warm place until dough fills the pan. **7.** Bake in hot oven (400°F.) about 35 minutes.

HOW TO MAKE GOOD COFFEE EVERY TIME

Since coffee is the leading American beverage, one would expect this to be a culinary department in which housewives and restaurants excel. Yet coffee-making is a most neglected kitchen skill.

To the person on a low calorie diet, black coffee is important because it contains no calories and gives the satisfaction and stimulation which most dieters require. Those who insist on drinking light or sweetened coffee must depend upon skim milk or saccharin or other non-caloric sweeteners . . . and here too, the coffee must be nothing short of excellent. So, even if you consider yourself a good coffee-maker, read these directions. A uniformly good brew —full-bodied, clear, and with a tempting aroma—is made by following these rules:

1. Measure coffee and water accurately—For good, tasty coffee, use one standard coffee measure (two level measuring tablespoonfuls) of *fresh* coffee to each three-quarters of a measuring cup (six ounces) of fresh, cold water.

2. Make certain the coffeepot is sparkling clean—not just rinsed. Keep a brush handy to scrub out the oils which coat the inside of the coffeepot every time you use it. For best results, always use the right size pot . . . for two cups of coffee, a two-cup pot; for four cups, a four-cup pot. This is important.

3. Never boil coffee—serve it as soon as possible after brewing. If it is necessary to keep your coffee hot for a time, place the pot in a pan of hot water or over very low heat on an asbestos mat. *Drip*—To make good coffee in a drip pot, first bring cold water to a full rolling boil. Measure coffee carefully into the coffee basket, then add the exact amount of boiling water. When the water has dripped through, remove the coffee basket and water container and be sure to stir the hot coffee thoroughly to insure a brew of even strength.

Vacuum—For Silex and other vacuum coffee-makers, measure the cold water into the lower bowl, place over the heat, and while it is reaching the boiling point, insert the filter in the upper bowl. Then measure out the correct amount of finely-ground coffee.

When the water boils, lower the heat and insert the upper bowl. After most of the water has risen into the upper bowl, stir the water and coffee briskly and after two or three minutes, remove the coffee maker from the stove. When all the coffee has returned to the lower bowl, remove the upper section and serve. Never let cloth filters dry once they have been used—keep them in water in the refrigerator between uses. Rinse in clear water, no soap.

Percolator—To get consistently good results with a percolator, first measure cold water accurately into the pot and place it on the stove. When the water boils, remove it from the heat, and then measure the proper amount of coffee into the basket. Cover, return to the heat and allow it to percolate gently for six to eight minutes.

Instant Coffee—The popularity of instant, or ready-made, coffee has grown tremendously in the past few years. For single-cup drinkers, and for those who have difficulty getting uniform flavor in their coffee, the instant style coffee offers a definite advantage.

SOUTHERN STYLE SODA BISCUITS

Makes 32 biscuits (2240 calories). Calories in 1 biscuit: 70.

2 cups sifted all-purpose flour	½ cup sweet milk
¾ teaspoon baking soda	¼ cup (distilled) vinegar
¼ cup shortening	½ teaspoon salt

1. Sift together flour, baking soda and salt. Cut in shortening. **2.** Stir in vinegar and milk. Turn onto floured board and knead lightly. **3.** Roll about ¼ inch thick. Cut biscuits and prick with fork. **4.** Bake on greased baking sheet for 12 to 15 minutes in very hot oven (450°F.).

MUFFINS

Makes 12 muffins (876 calories using water; 954 calories using milk). Calories in 1 muffin: 73 using water; 79½ using milk.

1 egg	can Medical Association
1 cup water or skim milk	Council on Foods and
1½ cups Diet-mix, a prepared mix, accepted by the Ameri-	Nutrition

1. Beat egg and add 1 measured cup milk or water, or a mixture of both. **2.** Stir this into the Diet-mix; pour into lightly greased muffin tin. (Just put a little butter, shortening or fat on your finger or a paper and a rub around tin.) **3.** Bake in a hot oven (400° to 425°F.) for 20 to 30 minutes.

ICED COFFEE SHAKE

Makes 2 servings (60 calories). Calories in 1 serving: 30.

1 cup strong coffee
Small glass (4-ounce) carbonated water

⅔ cup skim milk
1 drop vanilla extract
⅓ cup finely cracked ice

1. Place milk, then coffee, carbonated water and vanilla extract in electric blender or shaker. Then add cracked ice. **2.** Put cover on container and mix until well blended.

HOT COCOA

Makes 1 serving, about 1 cup (85 calories).

2½ tablespoons non-fat dry
milk solids (Starlac or other
skim milk powder)
1 tablespoon cocoa

Dash of cinnamon
¼ teaspoon Sucaryl or saccharin liquid no-calorie sweetener

1. Place ¾ cup water, milk powder, cocoa and cinnamon in glass jar. **2.** Cover tightly and shake until smoothly mixed. **3.** Pour into saucepan and bring to boil. Let simmer about one minute. **4.** Remove from stove and add Sucaryl. Serve immediately.

ORANGE MILK SHAKE

Makes 2 servings (168 calories). Calories in 1 serving: 84.

1 cup skim milk
½ cup fresh or unsweetened
canned orange juice

1 egg white
1 teaspoon grated orange peel
½ cup cracked ice

1. Beat egg white stiff. **2.** Place ingredients in electric blender or shaker. Mix until well blended, ½ minute or more.

PINEAPPLE TEA PUNCH

Makes 1 large serving, or 2 small servings (16 calories). Calories in 1 small serving: 8.

¾ cup cold tea
2 tablespoons pineapple juice
1 tablespoon lemon juice

1 teaspoon liquid saccharin or
other no-calorie sweetener

1. Combine all ingredients and pour over ice cubes in tall glass. **2.** Let stand two or three minutes, then serve.

MINTED TEA

Makes 4 servings (44 calories). Calories in 1 serving: 11.

2 cups hot strong tea
⅓ cup fresh or unsweetened
canned orange juice

Juice of 2 lemons
⅓ teaspoon powdered ginger
2 sprigs fresh mint

1. Bruise the mint. Pour tea over fruit juices and add the mint. **2.** Blend ginger with ⅓ cup hot water; when well mixed add 1 cup cold water. **3.** Mix all ingredients, chill for 1 hour or more.

ORANGE EGG PICK-UP

Makes 6 servings (186 calories). Calories in 1 serving: 31.

1 egg yolk
1 cup fresh or unsweetened
canned orange juice

1 cup carbonated water
Few grains salt
Nutmeg

1. Beat egg yolk. **2.** Mix all ingredients except nutmeg in blender or shaker. Sprinkle nutmeg on top of each glass.

ORANGE COOLER

Makes 3 servings (144 calories). Calories in 1 serving: 48.

1 cup fresh or unsweetened
canned orange juice
1 cup carbonated water

5 teaspoons lemon juice
Cracked ice or ice cubes

1. Mix juices and carbonated water. **2.** Pour over cracked ice or ice cubes, in 3 tall glasses.

APRICOT MILK SHAKE

Makes 2 small servings (146 calories). Calories in 1 serving: 73.

¼ cup drained stewed dried
apricots, unsweetened
3 tablespoons non-fat dry milk
solids (skim milk powder)

1 teaspoon Sacrose or other
no-calorie sweetener
1 teaspoon lemon juice
Ice cubes

1. Place all ingredients with 1 cup cold water in deep bowl. **2.** Beat until smooth with rotary egg beater. **3.** Pour over ice cubes in tall glass and serve immediately.

MILK PUNCH

Makes 1 serving (66 calories).

¾ cup skim milk
¼ cup carbonated water

¼ teaspoon vanilla or almond extract

1. Put milk with flavoring in one glass, carbonated water in another and pour from glass to glass, to make a frothy mixture. Serve at once.

COFFEE MILK SHAKE

Makes 1 serving (84 calories).

1 cup cold black coffee
¼ teaspoon no-calorie sweetener

3 tablespoons non-fat dry milk solids (skim milk powder)
Ice cubes

1. Place all ingredients in glass jar or cocktail shaker. 2. Cover tightly and shake until milk solids are smoothly blended in. 3. Pour over ice cubes. Let stand two or three minutes and then serve.

FRUIT PUNCH

Makes 3 servings (183 calories). Calories in 1 serving: 61.

1 cup fresh or unsweetened canned orange juice
½ cup fresh or unsweetened canned grapefruit juice

1½ cups carbonated water
1 cup finely cracked ice
3 thin lemon slices
Mint leaves

1. Mix juices, carbonated water and ice. 2. Serve with lemon slice hooked over edge of each glass. Garnish with mint leaves.

100 CALORIE PORTIONS
OF CEREALS

(without counting the added milk or sugar calories)

ALL-BRAN
(Kellogg's)

good 1/2 cupful

BRAN FLAKES

3/4 cupful

BABY FOODS, cooked

about 10 tablespoons

CHEERIOS

1 cup plus
2 tablespoons

CORN FLAKES

1-1/4 cups

CORN MEAL,
yellow, enriched,
cooked

1 scant cupful

CREAM OF WHEAT
or FARINA,
cooked

3/4 cupful

WHEAT GERM

1/3 cupful

**RALSTON,
INSTANT**
cooked

scant 3/4 cupful

GRAPE NUTS,
plain

1/4 cupful

100 CALORIE PORTIONS
OF CEREALS

(without counting the added milk or sugar calories)

GRAPE NUTS FLAKES

1 cupful

HOMINY or GRITS, enriched, cooked

1 scant cupful

KIX

1 cupful

MALTEX, cooked

2/3 cupful

OATMEAL or ROLLED OATS, cooked

2/3 cupful

PETTIJOHN'S WHEAT, cooked

2/3 cupful

PEP

1 cupful

MACARONI, cooked

1/2 cupful

EGG NOODLES, cooked

1 cupful

SPAGHETTI, cooked

1/2 cupful

100 CALORIE PORTIONS OF CEREALS

(without counting the added milk or sugar calories)

WHEAT CHEX	**RICE, BROWN, cooked**	**RICE, WHITE, cooked**
1/2 cupful	3/4 cupful	1/2 cupful
RICE, PUFFED	**RICE KRISPIES**	**TAPIOCA**
1 cupful	1 scant cupful	pudding made from 3 tablespoons of dry tapioca
WHEAT, PUFFED	**WHEAT, SHREDDED**	**WHEAT, CRACKED or WHOLE, cooked**
2 cups	1 large biscuit 4" x 2-1/2"	2/3 cupful
WHEATENA, cooked	**CORN SOYA**	**WHEATIES**
2/3 cupful	2/3 cupful	1 cupful

SALADS

V-8 ASPIC

Makes 6 servings (96 calories). Calories in 1 serving: 16.

1 tablespoon unflavored gela-   1½ cups (12-ounce can) V-8
tin (1 envelope Knox's)   or other cocktail vegetable
Frenchette low-calorie dressing   juices

1. Soften gelatin in ¼ cup vegetable juices; set aside. **2.** Heat remaining vegetable juices and add softened gelatin. **3.** Rinse 1 large salad mold or 6 small ones with cold water; pour in aspic and chill until firm. **4.** Serve with Frenchette or other imitation French dressing or a top-knot of Lowmay on crisp lettuce or other salad greens.

HOW TO MAKE OTHER SALADS FROM BASIC V-8 ASPIC RECIPE

1. Combine gelatin, juices and seasonings as directed in basic recipe. **2.** Chill until of the consistency of unbeaten egg white; add not more than 1 cup of any desired drained ingredients. (Additional liquids require additional gelatin.) Be sure you know the number of calories in any added ingredients.

For variety try adding: ¼ cup finely chopped celery, ¼ cup chopped onion, 2 tablespoons chopped green pepper Or, 1 cup large curd cottage cheese and ¼ cup chopped ripe or green olives Or, 1 3-ounce package cream cheese, 1 tablespoon chopped onion and 1 tablespoon chopped parsley Or, 3 hard-cooked eggs, diced, 1 teaspoon prepared mustard and ¼ cup chopped sweet cucumber pickle. *See calorie charts for calories in any added ingredients.*

CAULIFLOWER SALAD

Makes 2 servings (38 calories). Calories in 1 serving: 19.

1 envelope lemon flavor low-   1½ teaspoons green pepper,
calorie gelatin (Glow or   finely cut
D-Zerta)   1 teaspoon vinegar
2 small flowerets cooked cauli-   ¼ teaspoon salt
flower   Dash of pepper
1 teaspoon pimiento, finely cut   Salad greens

1. Dissolve gelatin in ½ cup hot water. Chill. **2.** Combine cauliflower, pepper and pimiento with vinegar and seasonings. Let stand to marinate. **3.** When gelatin is slightly thickened, fold in vegetable mixture. Turn into individual molds. **4.** Chill until firm and unmold on crisp salad greens.

GREEN BEAN–VEGETABLE SALAD

Makes 4 servings (76 calories). Calories in 1 serving: 19.

⅔ cup fresh or canned green beans
⅓ cup grated carrots
⅔ cup shredded cabbage

2 teaspoons chopped green pepper
4 teaspoons Lowmay mayonnaise substitute

1. Combine drained green beans with other vegetables. 2. Chill, and add Lowmay just before serving.

MOLDED RAW VEGETABLE SALAD

Makes 4 five-ounce servings (104 calories). Calories in 1 serving: 26.

1 tablespoon unflavored gelatin (1 envelope Knox's)
1 Souplet
1 tablespoon lemon juice
¼ teaspoon salt

¾ cup finely chopped cabbage
¾ cup shredded raw carrot
½ cup finely chopped celery
Salad greens

1. Soften gelatin in ½ cup cold water, then dissolve over low heat or hot water. 2. Pour 1 cup boiling water over Souplet and let stand until Souplet dissolves. 3. Combine dissolved gelatin and Souplet broth. Add lemon juice and salt. Chill until consistency of egg white. 4. Immediately add and stir in the cabbage, carrot and celery. Pour into individual salad molds. 5. Chill until firm. Serve on crisp salad greens.

TOMATO JELLY WITH VEGETABLES

Makes 6 servings (132 calories). Calories in 1 serving: 22.

¾ cup strained tomatoes
½ cup chopped cabbage
½ cup chopped celery
¼ cup chopped green pepper
¼ cup cooked carrots, cubed
2 tablespoons vinegar

1 tablespoon unflavored gelatin (1 envelope Knox's)
½ teaspoon whole mixed spices
½ teaspoon salt
6 lettuce leaves

1. Bring to a boil ½ cup hot water, and the salt and spices. 2. Soften gelatin in ¼ cup cold water and add to hot liquid. Stir until dissolved. 3. Strain this into the tomatoes and stir in the vinegar. 4. Chill until almost set, then stir in vegetables. Turn into mold and chill until firm. Serve on lettuce.

PEACH CUP SALAD

Makes 6 servings (132 calories). Calories in 1 serving: 22.

6 water-pack canned peach halves
¼ cup celery, finely diced

¼ cup raw apple, finely diced
Chicory or other salad greens

1. Place one peach half on each bed of salad greens. 2. Mix celery and apple. Fill each peach half with one-sixth of this mixture. Chill before serving.

PIMIENTO AND SAUERKRAUT SALAD

Makes 6 servings (138 calories). Calories in 1 serving: 23.

1 cup hot sauerkraut juice
¼ cup cold sauerkraut juice
1 cup cabbage, finely cut
¼ cup pimiento, finely cut
¼ cup celery, finely cut

2 tablespoons lemon juice
1 tablespoon unflavored gelatin (1 envelope Knox's)
6 lettuce leaves

1. Soften gelatin in cold sauerkraut juice. Add hot sauerkraut juice and stir until dissolved. Add lemon juice and cool. 2. When mixture just begins to stiffen, add cut vegetables, mix thoroughly, and pour into mold that has been rinsed in cold water. 3. Chill and serve on lettuce leaf.

MOLDED PEAR SALAD

Makes 4 servings (96 calories). Calories in 1 serving: 24.

2 envelopes raspberry flavor low-calorie gelatin (D-Zerta or Glow)

4 water-pack pear halves
Juice from pear can
4 lettuce leaves

1. Drain fruit juice from pear can and add enough water to make 1 cup. 2. Heat to a gentle boil and add gelatin, stirring until dissolved. 3. Chill until sirupy. Place pears in mold large enough for 4 servings and cover with gelatin. 4. Chill until firm. Cut into 4 equal portions and unmold on lettuce leaf.

CRANBERRY RELISH MOLD

Makes 6 servings (144 calories). Calories in 1 serving: 24.

2 cups cranberries
4 envelopes lemon flavor low-calorie gelatin (D-Zerta or Glow)

1½ to 2 teaspoons Sacrose no-calorie sweetener
2 teaspoons horseradish

1. Put cranberries through food chopper. **2.** Dissolve gelatin in 1 cup hot water. **3.** Add 1 cup cold water and Sacrose. Fold in cranberries and horseradish. **4.** Transfer to mold and chill until firm.

PEAR AND GRAPE SALAD

Makes 4 servings (100 calories). Calories in 1 serving: 25.

⅔ cup water-pack pears, sliced
⅓ cup seedless grapes

2 envelopes lemon flavor low-calorie gelatin (Glow)
Juice from pear can
4 lettuce leaves

1. Drain fruit juice from pear can and add enough boiling water to make 1 cup. **2.** Heat to a gentle boil, add gelatin and stir until dissolved. **3.** Chill until sirupy. Add pears and grapes, pour into 4 individual molds and chill until firm. Unmold on lettuce leaf.

CARROT AND ORANGE SALAD

Makes 6 servings (150 calories). Calories in 1 serving: 25.

1 cup grated raw carrots
½ cup orange juice
1 tablespoon unflavored gelatin (1 envelope Knox's)
1 tablespoon lemon juice

1⅛ teaspoons Sacrose no-calorie sweetener
¼ teaspoon salt
6 lettuce leaves

1. Soften gelatin in ¼ cup cold water. Add salt, Sacrose and 1¼ cups hot water. Stir until dissolved. **2.** Add orange juice and lemon juice, and set aside to stiffen slightly. **3.** Add raw carrots to slightly stiffened gelatin, and pour into individual molds that have been rinsed in cold water. **4.** Chill, and unmold on lettuce leaf.

COLE SLAW

Makes 2 servings (52 calories). Calories in 1 serving: 26.

¼ medium-sized head of green cabbage
2 tablespoons Lowmay mayonnaise substitute

2 tablespoons lemon juice
1 stalk celery
½ teaspoon salt
⅛ teaspoon pepper

1. Shred or grate coarsely the cabbage and celery. **2.** Mix Lowmay and lemon juice and add to vegetables. **3.** Add salt and pepper and mix thoroughly. **4.** Let stand in refrigerator one hour before serving.

BEET SALAD

Makes 6 servings (168 calories). Calories in 1 serving: 28.

1 cup cooked beets, diced
½ cup celery, cut fine
2 tablespoons mild vinegar
1 tablespoon sugar
1 tablespoon finely chopped onion

¼ teaspoon prepared mustard
¼ teaspoon salt
½ envelope Knox's unflavored gelatin
Salad greens

1. Soften gelatin in ¼ cup cold water. Add sugar and ⅔ cup hot water and stir until dissolved. **2.** Add vinegar, salt, mustard and onion, and when it begins to stiffen, stir in beets and celery. **3.** Turn into individual molds which have been dipped in cold water. Serve on lettuce, water cress or romaine.

COLORFUL VEGETABLE SALAD

Makes 1 serving (30 calories).

1 envelope orange flavor low-calorie gelatin (D-Zerta or Glow)
1 tablespoon celery, cut in ½-inch strips
1 tablespoon shredded raw carrots

1 tablespoon raw beets, cut in ½-inch strips
¾ teaspoon vinegar
¼ teaspoon salt
Dash of pepper
Salad greens, carrot strips or celery curls

1. Dissolve gelatin in ½ cup hot water. Chill. **2.** Combine vegetables with vinegar and seasonings; let stand to marinate. **3.** When gelatin is slightly thickened, fold in vegetable mixture. **4.** Turn into individual molds and chill until firm. **5.** Unmold on crisp salad greens. Garnish with carrot strips or celery curls.

SPRING GARDEN SALAD

Makes 4 servings (156 calories). Calories in 1 serving: 39.

1 package lemon flavor low-calorie gelatin
2 tablespoons vinegar
½ cup sliced radishes and 8 small whole radishes

½ teaspoon salt
1 tablespoon finely sliced scallions
½ hard-boiled egg, sliced
Escarole

1. Dissolve gelatin in 1 cup hot water. **2.** Add 1 cup cold water, vinegar, and salt. Chill until slightly thickened. Then fold in radishes and scallions. **3.** Turn into mold. Chill until firm. **4.** Unmold on crisp escarole. Garnish with slices of hard-boiled egg and whole radishes.

SPICED PEACH SALAD

Makes 1 serving (about 30 calories).

1 envelope orange flavor low-calorie gelatin (Glow or D-Zerta)
5 to 6 slices canned, unsweetened peaches, diced
½ teaspoon vinegar

1 small clove
¼-inch stick cinnamon
Dash of salt
Lettuce leaf
Frenchette salad dressing or Lowmay

1. Add spices, salt and vinegar to ½ cup cold water, and bring to a boil. Let simmer very slowly about ½ minute. 2. Strain and dissolve gelatin in hot liquid. 3. Add peaches. Chill. When slightly thickened, stir until peaches are well distributed, and turn into individual molds. 4. Chill until firm. Unmold on lettuce leaf, with 1 teaspoon Lowmay or 3 teaspoons Frenchette.

SPICED GRAPE SALAD

In Spiced Peach Salad recipe substitute raspberry flavor Glow or D-Zerta for the orange flavor gelatin, and 2 rounded tablespoons seeded and halved grapes for the sliced peaches. Cinnamon may be omitted.

PEACH–PEAR SALAD

In Spiced Peach Salad recipe substitute 1 rounded tablespoon diced pears and 2 to 3 slices peaches, diced, for the 5 to 6 slices peaches. Omit cinnamon.

TOMATO ASPIC

Makes 4 servings (148 calories). Calories in 1 serving: 37.

1 tablespoon unflavored gelatin (1 envelope Knox's gelatin)
2 onion slices
1⅞ cups tomato juice

1 tablespoon vinegar
¼ teaspoon salt
½ bay leaf
Few drops tabasco
4 lettuce leaves

1. Add onion, salt, tabasco and bay leaf to tomato juice; simmer for 10 minutes. 2. Soften gelatin in cold water and dissolve in tomato juice mixture. 3. Add vinegar, then strain. Pour into mold which has been rinsed in cold water. 4. Chill until firm and unmold on lettuce. (If desired, serve with Frenchette salad dressing or other French dressing substitute but count those calories extra.)

MINTED HONEYDEW SALAD

Makes 1 serving (30 calories).

1 envelope lime flavor low-calorie gelatin dessert
1 fresh mint leaf

6 medium honeydew melon balls

1. Combine gelatin and mint. **2.** Add ½ cup hot water and stir until dissolved. Let stand 10 minutes; strain. Chill. **3.** When slightly thickened, fold in melon balls. Turn into mold and chill until firm. Unmold.

GRAPEFRUIT AND APPLE SALAD

Makes 1 serving (30 calories).

1 envelope lemon flavor low-calorie gelatin
2 tablespoons diced apple, unpeeled

1 grapefruit section, cut in half
Salad greens

1. Dissolve gelatin in ½ cup boiling water. Chill. **2.** When slightly thickened, fold in fruits. **3.** Turn into individual molds and chill until firm. Unmold on salad greens.

PEPPER CABBAGE

Makes 6 servings (180 calories). Calories in 1 serving: 30.

1 small green pepper, finely chopped
1 small red pepper, finely chopped
3 cups finely shredded cabbage

⅓ to ½ cup vinegar
1 tablespoon sugar (if more sweetening desired, add few drops Sacrose)
1 teaspoon salt

1. Mix cabbage and peppers. **2.** Dissolve sugar and salt in vinegar. Pour over peppers and cabbage.

ASPARAGUS TIP SALAD

Makes 1 serving (28 calories).

4 asparagus spears
1 teaspoon low-calorie mayonnaise substitute

1 green pepper ring
Bed of shredded lettuce

1. Drain the asparagus tips and place inside the green pepper ring. **2.** Set this on bed of shredded lettuce, and put in refrigerator to chill. Serve with teaspoon of Lowmay.

ORANGE-GRAPEFRUIT SALAD

Makes 1 serving (30 calories).

1 envelope orange flavor low-
calorie gelatin
3 sections orange

1½ sections grapefruit
Salad greens

1. Dissolve gelatin in ½ cup boiling water. Chill. 2. Cut orange and grapefruit sections in half and when gelatin is slightly thickened, fold in fruit. 3. Turn into individual molds and chill until firm. 4. Unmold on salad greens.

ZUCCHINI SALAD

Makes 4 servings (128 calories). Calories in 1 serving: 32.

1¼ pounds young zucchini
squash
2½ tablespoons Frenchette
dressing

3 tablespoons chopped parsley
Salt
4 lettuce leaves

1. Cut zucchini crosswise, unpeeled, in pieces 1 inch long. 2. Cook in ½ inch salted boiling water. Cook covered until tender, sometimes only a few minutes. 3. Drain well, and let cool. Place in refrigerator to chill. When cold, mix parsley and dressing through the zucchini. 4. Serve on lettuce leaves.

SIMPLE ONION SALAD

Makes 1 serving (35 calories).

Very thin slices or rings of ½
medium onion—Bermuda,
Italian or Spanish
Lettuce leaf

1½ tablespoons Frenchette
dressing or other low-calorie
French dressing substitute

1. Arrange onion slices on lettuce leaf. Sprinkle on dressing and turn onions to absorb utmost dressing. Add a touch of parsley or mint if you life.

BEETS IN ORANGE JUICE

Makes 6 servings (234 calories). Calories in 1 serving: 39.

2 cups cooked or canned beets,
sliced thin
½ cup orange juice

1 orange rind, grated
1 tablespoon butter

1. Mix ingredients in small pot and heat without boiling.

COLORED CABBAGE SALAD

Makes 2 servings (78 calories). Calories in 1 serving: 39.

1 cup shredded green cabbage
½ cup shredded red cabbage
1 stalk celery, diced

Juice of ¼ lemon
6 tablespoons Buttermilk Herb
Dressing (page 146)

1. Blend all ingredients. **2.** Toss lightly and serve at once.

STUFFED CUCUMBERS ON SOYA CRACKERS

Makes 8 crackers—4 servings (160 calories). Calories in 1 serving: 40.

1 medium cucumber
2 tablespoons cottage cheese
1 tablespoon dry cheddar
cheese
1 tablespoon catsup

2 tablespoons skim milk
1 tablespoon chopped chives
or parsley
8 small soya crackers or halves
of Melba toast

1. Mash the cheeses with the milk and catsup. When soft and well blended, add the chives or parsley. **2.** Peel the cucumber, cut off one end, and core it with a flexible knife. Score the outside of the cucumber lengthwise, with the points of a fork. **3.** Fill the hollowed cucumber with the cheese mixture. **4.** Wrap the cucumber and chill in refrigerator. **5.** When ready to serve, cut into ¼-inch slices and serve on 8 small soya crackers or halves of Melba toast.

HOT COLE SLAW

Makes 6 servings (240 calories). Calories in 1 serving: 40.

3 cups finely shredded cabbage
¼ cup chopped chives

¾ cup freshly made Cooked
Salad Dressing (page 140)

1. Blend all ingredients in glass or enameled mixing bowl. **2.** If cole slaw is not sufficiently hot, heat in double boiler. **3.** Toss lightly and serve at once.

MOLDED COTTAGE CHEESE AND PINEAPPLE SALAD

Makes 6 servings (264 calories). Calories in 1 serving: 44.

½ cup cottage cheese
3 envelopes lemon flavor Glow
low-calorie gelatin
½ cup water-pack pineapple
tidbits or chunks

1 tablespoon chopped green
pepper
1 teaspoon vinegar
6 lettuce leaves

1. Dissolve gelatin in 1½ cups boiling water and chill until it thickens slightly. 2. Blend together all other ingredients and fold into the gelatin mixture. 3. Place into mold that has been dipped into cold water. Chill until firm and unmold onto lettuce.

JELLIED SPINACH RING

Makes 4 servings (180 calories). Calories in 1 serving: 45.

1 box (14 ounces) frozen chopped spinach
1½ cups hot spinach liquid and water
2 chicken bouillon cubes or Souplets vegetable broth tablets

1 tablespoon unflavored gelatin (1 envelope Knox's)
½ teaspoon salt
½ teaspoon grated onion
1½ teaspoons lemon juice
6 lettuce leaves

1. Cook spinach as directed on the package. Drain off spinach liquid into measuring cup and add hot water to make 1½ cups liquid. 2. Dissolve gelatin in ¼ cup cold water in a mixing bowl. 3. Add hot spinach liquid and bouillon cubes to gelatin. Stir until dissolved. 4. Add spinach, salt, onion and lemon juice. Blend. 5. Turn into 1-quart ring mold. Chill until firm. Unmold on crisp lettuce.

Variation: If desired, fill center with 2¾ cups cooked shrimp (1½ pounds). This will add 40 calories to each serving.

COTTAGE CHEESE AND APRICOT SALAD

Makes 6 servings (300 calories). Calories in 1 serving: 50.

1 tablespoon unflavored gelatin (1 envelope Knox's)
6 tablespoons cottage cheese
12 dried apricot halves, cooked without sugar

1 cup of water in which apricots have been cooked, or plain hot water
2 tablespoons lemon juice
6 lettuce leaves

1. Soften gelatin 5 minutes in bowl containing ¼ cup cold water. 2. Add hot liquid and stir until gelatin is dissolved. 3. Place bowl in pan of ice water and stir until mixture begins to thicken, then blend in the apricots. 4. Pour the lemon juice over the cheese and mix thoroughly. Add to the other ingredients. 5. Rinse 6 individual molds in cold water and pour in mixture, making sure there are 2 apricot halves in each mold. 6. Chill until firm and unmold on lettuce leaves.

HOLIDAY PEAR SALAD

Makes 3 servings (132 calories). Calories in 1 serving: 44.

6 water-pack canned pear
halves
1 envelope lime flavor low calorie gelatin

3 lettuce leaves
1 envelope strawberry flavor
low-calorie gelatin (D-Zerta
or Glow)

1. Dissolve lime gelatin in ½ cup boiling water and chill until firm. Dissolve strawberry gelatin in ½ cup boiling water and chill until firm. 2. Arrange 2 pear halves on each crisp lettuce leaf. 3. Put each gelatin separately through a ricer or coarse strainer. On 1 pear half put a spoonful of riced lime gelatin, and on the other pear half put a spoonful of riced strawberry gelatin 4. Chill before serving.

APRICOT–PRUNE–PINEAPPLE SALAD

Makes 3 servings (150 calories). Calories in 1 serving: 50.

9 halves water-pack canned
apricots
3 medium prunes, cooked, unsweetened

¼ cup water-packed pineapple
chunks
3 beds of salad greens

1. Remove pits from prunes and stuff each with large chunk of pineapple. 2. Place stuffed prune in center of bed of salad greens and arrange 3 apricot halves and pieces of pineapple around it. Chill before serving.

SAUERKRAUT SALAD

Makes 6 servings (336 calories). Calories in 1 serving: 56.

2½ cups sauerkraut (1 No. 2
can)
4 tomatoes
1 medium green pepper
2 tablespoons sour cream

2 tablespoons Lowmay or other
mayonnaise substitute
1 teaspoon grated onion
4 radishes
Few sprigs parsley

1. Chill can of sauerkraut in refrigerator overnight, or at least several hours. 2. Drain off sauerkraut juice. Slice radishes thinly. Cut pepper into thin strips. 3. Combine all ingredients except tomatoes in a large bowl. Mix lightly but thoroughly. 4. Cut tomatoes into narrow wedges and arrange 6 of these on each salad plate around a mound of the sauerkraut salad. Place sprigs of parsley between tomato wedges.

GRAPE SALAD

Makes 2 servings (102 calories). Calories in 1 serving: 51.

1 bunch large white or red grapes (¼ pound)
2 lettuce leaves or chicory
3 tablespoons Frenchette low-calorie salad dressing
2 sprigs water cress
Few drops Worcestershire sauce
½ teaspoon horseradish
½ teaspoon sugar

1. Make a special dressing with the Frenchette, Worcestershire sauce, horseradish and sugar. 2. Peel the grapes, remove seeds. 3. Place grapes on chilled lettuce leaves, sprinkle on the dressing, and garnish with sprig of water cress.

CELERY SALAD

Makes 4 servings (180 calories). Calories in 1 serving: 45.

1 small bunch washed celery
1 small banana
Chopped parsley
4 tablespoons Cooked Salad Dressing
4 lettuce leaves

1. Cut celery to bite size. 2. Mash banana and mix with dressing until well blended. Then blend this mixture well with celery. 3. Marinate for an hour or more, stirring occasionally. 4. Sprinkle with parsley and serve on lettuce leaves.

COLD SNAP BEANS SALAD

Makes 1 serving (55 calories).

1 serving cold sliced cooked string beans or butter beans
1 lettuce leaf
2 tablespoons Frenchette or other French dressing substitute

1. Arrange beans appetizingly on lettuce leaf and sprinkle dressing over beans.

BROILED BANANA SALAD

Makes 6 servings (360 calories). Calories in 1 serving: 60.

3 good bananas
2 tablespoons grated cheese— Parmesan, Swiss or cheddar
6 lettuce leaves
Salt
Lemon juice

1. Cut peeled bananas in half lengthwise. Sprinkle with lemon juice. 2. Place in pan, cover with cheese, salt lightly. 3. Broil at medium heat until bananas are brown and soft. 4. Serve hot, next to lettuce leaf on salad plate.

APPLE-CABBAGE SALAD

Makes 6 servings (360 calories). Calories in 1 serving: 60.

3 medium apples, preferably two green cooking apples, one red apple

6 tablespoons Frenchette low-calorie dressing

3 cups shredded cabbage

1 tablespoon prepared horse-radish

6 lettuce leaves

1. Blend horseradish thoroughly with dressing. 2. Dice apples, including peel. 3. Mix apples, cabbage and dressing. Serve on lettuce.

CARROT AND COTTAGE CHEESE SALAD

Makes 1 serving (60 calories).

½ cup grated carrots

1 tablespoon cottage cheese

1 tablespoon Yogurt Dressing, (see page 144)

Chopped onion, to taste

Chopped caraway seeds to taste

Lettuce leaf

1. Place lettuce leaf on plate, with grated carrots in center, in a mound. 2. Blend cheese with the chopped onion and caraway seeds and spread over carrot mound, or make a ball and set on top. 3. Sprinkle dressing over salad, or if Lowmay is used, set on top of cheese and use a touch of parsley or carrot for garnish.

TOMATO ASPIC WITH ARTICHOKE

Makes 4 servings (240 calories). Calories in 1 serving: 60.

1 small can artichoke hearts

1⅓ cups tomato juice (No. 1 can)

1 tablespoon unflavored gela-tin (1 envelope Knox's)

1 tablespoon lemon juice

⅛ teaspoon salt

Few drops Worcestershire sauce

4 lettuce leaves or other salad greens

4 teaspoons mayonnaise sub-stitute

1. Soften gelatin in 3 tablespoons cold tomato juice. Heat ¾ cup tomato juice almost to boiling, add to soften gelatin, and stir until gelatin dissolves. Then add remaining tomato juice. 2. Add lemon juice, salt and Worcestershire sauce. 3. Dip individual molds into cold water, place one artichoke heart in bottom of each mold, and pour over tomato-gelatin mixture. 4. Chill in refrigerator until firm. Unmold and serve on salad greens, with teaspoon mayonnaise substitute atop each.

MAYPOLE SALAD

Makes 4 servings (264 calories). Calories in 1 serving: 61.

½ cup cottage cheese
1 cup water-pack sliced
peaches
1 cup water-pack pears

4 green pepper strips
4 lettuce leaves
Paprika

1. In the center of each lettuce leaf place 2 tablespoons cottage cheese. **2.** Around cottage cheese arrange alternately 4 slices each of peaches and pears, to give maypole effect. Garnish with green pepper strips and dash of paprika.

TOMATO AND ONION SALAD

Makes 2 servings (130 calories). Calories in 1 serving: 65.

1 bunch water cress
2 medium tomatoes, sliced
1 medium onion, sliced

2 tablespoons White Russian
Dressing (page 144)

1. On bed of water cress, alternate slices of tomatoes and onion. **2.** Sprinkle dressing over this, and serve at once. Toss salad at table.

COLE SLAW WITH BACON DRESSING

Makes 6 servings (384 calories). Calories in 1 serving: 64.

1 small head cabbage,
shredded
¼ cup chopped pimiento
1 green pepper, finely chopped
4 slices bacon
1 small onion, finely chopped

¼ cup Lowmay or other
mayonnaise substitute
2 tablespoons vinegar
1 teaspoon sugar
1 teaspoon celery seed
1 teaspoon salt

1. Cut bacon into ½-inch pieces and cook in a heavy skillet with chopped onion. **2.** Stir in Lowmay, vinegar, sugar, celery seed and salt. **3.** Mix the cabbage, pimiento and green pepper in a bowl and pour on the hot dressing. **4.** Blend lightly. May be served hot at once, or chilled and served cold.

PICCALILLI BEETS

Makes 4 servings (240 calories). Calories in 1 serving: 60.

2½ cups cooked diced beets
(or 1 No. 2 can)

2 tablespoons sweet pickle
relish

1. Drain beets, add relish. Heat.

KADOTA FIGS AND SLICED PEACH SALAD

Makes 4 servings (264 calories). Calories in 1 serving: 66.

8 water-pack canned Kadota figs
1 cup water-pack canned sliced peaches
4 lettuce leaves
4 tablespoons Fruit Salad Dressing (page 146)

1. Arrange 3 peach slices in a circle on crisp lettuce leaf. 2. Place 2 figs in the center, and top with 1 tablespoon of Fruit Salad Dressing. Chill and serve.

CANTALOUPE AND BLACKBERRY SALAD

Makes 6 servings (414 calories). Calories in 1 serving: 69.

1 cantaloupe
2 cups washed blackberries
1 grapefruit
3 teaspoons low calorie mayonnaise substitute
6 lettuce leaves

1. Cut flesh of cantaloupe into wedges. Cut out grapefruit segments. 2. On each lettuce leaf make a circle of cantaloupe pieces, alternating with grapefruit segments. Insert blackberries in circle. Top with ½ teaspoon mayonnaise substitute.

FRUIT SALAD

Makes 6 servings (420 calories). Calories in 1 serving: 70.

½ cup water-pack canned pineapple tidbits
½ cup water-pack canned pears
¾ cup Fruit Salad Dressing
½ cup water-pack canned seedless grapes
1 cup water-pack canned freestone peaches
6 lettuce leaves

1. Combine drained pineapple, pears and peaches with the grapes. 2. Moisten with salad dressing. 3. Divide mixture into ½-cup portions. Arrange on crisp lettuce leaves and chill before serving.

BEET AND GRAPEFRUIT SALAD

Makes 4 servings (280 calories). Calories in 1 serving: 70.

4 shredded raw beets
Sections of 1 medium grapefruit
1 small onion, minced
4 tablespoons Buttermilk Herb Dressing
4 lettuce leaves

1. Blend beets, grapefruit, onion and dressing, with folding motion. Toss lightly. 2. Serve on lettuce.

GRAPEFRUIT COLE SLAW

Makes 4 servings (288 calories). Calories in 1 serving: 72.

2 medium grapefruits
½ cup Fruit Salad Dressing

1½ cups finely shredded cabbage

1. Section the grapefruits and mix into cabbage. 2. Pour dressing over mixture and toss lightly.

JELLIED SHRIMP AND VEGETABLE SALAD

Makes 8 servings (688 calories). Calories in 1 serving: 86.

2 cups cooked shrimps
1 cup cooked green peas
½ cup diced celery
1 hard-boiled egg, sliced
1 can Campbell's consommé

1 tablespoon unflavored gelatin soaked in ¼ cup cold water
3 tablespoons lemon juice
½ teaspoon salt

1. Heat consommé; dissolve softened gelatin in it. 2. Add ¾ cup water, salt and lemon juice. Pour small amount of consommé into ring mold and chill until firm. 3. Place layer of shrimps and egg slices onto chilled jelly and pour over enough consommé to cover; chill again. 4. Cut up remaining shrimp and combine with cooked peas, diced celery and consommé. Pour all into ring mold and chill until firm. 5. Serve unmolded on salad greens, with topping of Lowmay low-calorie mayonnaise substitute. Add 2 calories for each piece of lettuce, 15 calories for each tablespoon of Lowmay.

VITAMIN SALAD

Makes 6 servings (330 calories). Calories in 1 serving: 55.

1 package low-calorie fruit-flavored gelatin (Glow or D-Zerta)
1 tablespoon vinegar
1 teaspoon salt
1 cup coarsely chopped raw spinach
½ cup shredded raw carrots

½ cup diced celery
1 teaspoon chopped onion
2 tablespoons chopped mixed pickles
1 cup cottage cheese
⅛ teaspoon grated onion
6 lettuce leaves

1. Dissolve gelatin in 1 cup *hot* water. 2. Add 1 cup cold water, vinegar and salt. Chill until slightly thickened. Then fold in spinach, carrots, celery, chopped onion and pickles. 3. Turn into ring mold. Chill until firm. Unmold on crisp lettuce. 4. Fill center with mixture of cottage cheese and grated onion. Serve with Lowmay or other low-calorie mayonnaise.

BAKED ONION SALAD

Makes 6 servings (330 calories). Calories in 1 serving: 55.

4 large red Bermuda onions	1½ teaspoons salt
2 tablespoons salad oil	⅛ teaspoon pepper
1 tablespoon vinegar	

1. Do not peel onions. Put in pie plate and add ¼ cup water. Bake in moderate oven (350°F.) about 25 minutes. **2.** When cool enough to handle, remove skins. Slice onions, sprinkle with salt, and let stand for 1 hour. **3.** Drain off liquid, which has no use in this recipe. **4.** Beat vinegar, oil and pepper and pour over onions. Serve at once, or chill and serve later.

WILTED LETTUCE SALAD

Makes 4 servings (300 calories). Calories in 1 serving: 75.

3 slices bacon	1½ tablespoons vinegar
⅓ cup chopped ripe olives	1 teaspoon sugar
1 quart (4 cups) bite-size pieces of lettuce	⅛ teaspoon pepper
	¾ teaspoon salt
2 tablespoons chopped onion	

1. Dice bacon and cook slowly until half done. Drain off most of the fat and add onion. **2.** Continue to cook until bacon is crisp; add vinegar, sugar, salt and pepper. Heat to boiling. **3.** Place lettuce in a bowl, add olives. Pour on hot bacon mixture. Toss well.

SEAFOOD IN ASPIC

Makes 4 five-ounce servings (320 calories). Calories in 1 serving: 80.

1 Souplet or other bouillon cube	1 tablespoon lemon juice
1 tablespoon unflavored gelatin (1 envelope Knox's)	½ teaspoon salt
	7-ounce can crab meat
1 cup tomato juice	¼ cup finely diced green pepper
½ teaspoon A-1 sauce or Heinz beefsteak sauce	Salad greens

1. Dissolve Souplet in ½ cup boiling water. Soften gelatin in ¼ cup cold water, then dissolve over low heat. **2.** Combine dissolved gelatin with Souplet broth and add tomato juice, lemon juice, A-1 or Heinz sauce, and salt. **3.** Chill until beginning to thicken. Meanwhile, flake the crab meat, removing any pieces of cartilage. **4.** Combine flaked crab meat with thickened gelatin mixture and stir in green pepper. Pour into lightly oiled molds. **5.** Chill until firm. Serve unmolded on crisp salad greens.

CALIFORNIA CROWN MOLD

Makes 6 servings (768 calories). Calories in 1 serving: 128.

3 cups water-pack canned fruit cocktail, drained
Juice from can of same fruit cocktail

3 envelopes lemon flavor low-calorie gelatin
¼ cup whipping cream

1. To juice of fruit cocktail add boiling water to make 1½ cups. Bring to a gentle boil and dissolve gelatin in it. 2. Chill until slightly thickened. Add 2½ cups of the fruit cocktail to the thickened gelatin. 3. Whip the cream, and fold in. 4. Pour into one large ring mold, or 6 individual ring molds, which have been dipped in cold water. Chill until firm. Unmold and serve with center filled with remaining fruit cocktail.

PEAR SALAD

Makes 4 servings (308 calories). Calories in 1 serving: 77.

4 fresh pears
4 tablespoons cottage cheese

2 tablespoons Yogurt Dressing
Paprika

1. Peel pears, cut in half and core. 2. Fill with cheese and sprinkle with paprika. 3. Drop dressing on pears.

SPINACH AND EGG SALAD

Makes 4 servings (328 calories). Calories in 1 serving: 82.

¾ pound good young spinach
2 small firm tomatoes, sliced

2 hard-boiled eggs, sliced
½ cup Yogurt Dressing

1. Clean spinach and chop finely. 2. Place in salad bowl and toss lightly with dressing. 3. Garnish salad with alternate slices egg and tomato. Serve at once.

PINEAPPLE–TUNA–CELERY SALAD

Makes 6 servings (600 calories). Calories in 1 serving: 100.

1 cup water-pack pineapple chunks or tidbits
1 cup celery, diced
1 cup tuna, flaked
1 tablespoon lemon juice

3 tablespoons Lowmay low-calorie mayonnaise substitute
6 strips of green pepper
6 lettuce leaves

1. Combine well-drained pineapple, celery and tuna. Add lemon juice and Lowmay, mix well and chill. 2. Serve on lettuce leaf, garnished with slice of green pepper.

PRUNE SALAD

Makes 6 servings (480 calories). Calories in 1 serving: 80.

1 cup cooked prunes, cut in small pieces
1 tablespoon unflavored gelatin (1 envelope Knox's)
½ cup cottage cheese
1 tablespoon chopped pickle
1 tablespoon chili sauce
½ teaspoon salt
6 lettuce leaves, or shredded lettuce

1. Soften gelatin in ¼ cup cold water. Add ½ cup hot water and stir until dissolved. 2. Cool, and when mixture begins to have the thickness of egg white, add the salt, chili sauce, cottage cheese, prunes and chopped pickle. 3. Pour into mold that has been rinsed in cold water. Chill, and serve on lettuce leaf or shredded lettuce.

GINGER ALE ASPIC SALAD

Makes 4 servings (320 calories). Calories in 1 serving: 80.

1 tablespoon unflavored gelatin (1 envelope Knox's)
1¾ cups ginger ale
¼ cup lemon juice
¼ cup chopped celery
½ cup seedless grapes
½ cup crushed fresh pineapple
½ cup chopped preserved ginger
4 lettuce leaves

1. Dissolve gelatin in 2 tablespoons cold water and add ¼ cup heated ginger ale. Stir. 2. Stir in lemon juice and remaining ginger ale and chill in refrigerator. 3. When gelatin begins to set, stir in remaining ingredients and pour into 4 individual molds. 4. Chill until hard, unmold on lettuce leaf and serve.

JELLIED APPLESAUCE AND COTTAGE CHEESE SALAD

Makes 6 servings (444 calories). Calories in 1 serving: 74.

1 cup cottage cheese
1 cup skim milk
1 cup unsweetened applesauce
2 tablespoons lemon juice
½ teaspoon lemon flavoring
1 envelope unflavored Knox's gelatin
¼ teaspoon saccharin or Sucaryl liquid sweetener
Salt

1. Soften gelatin in ¼ cup cold water. Place dish over boiling water and stir until gelatin has dissolved. 2. Add cottage cheese, mashed or sieved. Add milk, applesauce, lemon juice, salt, flavoring and sweetener. 3. Turn into mold that has been rinsed in cold water, and chill. When firm, unmold.

PINEAPPLE CHEESE SALAD

Makes 1 serving (90 calories).

1 envelope lemon flavor low-
calorie gelatin
2 tablespoons cooked pineapple, diced

4 tablespoons cottage cheese
½ teaspoon vinegar
¼ teaspoon salt
Lettuce leaf

1. Dissolve gelatin in ½ cup boiling water. Add vinegar and salt.
2. Chill, and when slightly thickened, fold in the cheese and pineapple. Turn into individual mold. 3. Chill until firm. Unmold on
lettuce leaf.

BRAINS AND SWEETBREAD SALAD

Makes 6 servings (552 calories). Calories in 1 serving: 92.

1 cup cubed cooked brains
1 cup cubed cooked sweet-
breads
1 cup diced celery

⅓ cup finely chopped pickles
or olives
¼ cup Frenchette dressing
Salt and pepper
6 lettuce leaves

1. (To cook brains: Soak in salted water 15 minutes. Cook in
simmering water 15 minutes. To cook sweetbreads, do not soak.
Cook in simmering water 25 minutes for beef, 15 to 20 minutes
for veal.) 2. Season brains and sweetbreads. Combine ingredients.
3. Moisten with dressing, toss and chill for ½ hour. Serve on
lettuce.

EGG AND TOMATO SALAD

Makes 4 servings (368 calories). Calories in 1 serving: 92.

1 small head chicory (or other
salad green)
2 medium tomatoes, cut into
wedges or sliced

3 hard-boiled eggs, sliced
5 tablespoons Frenchette or
other low-calorie dressing

1. Tear chicory into small pieces and place in salad bowl. 2. Place
eggs and tomatoes alternately on top. 3. Pour dressing into center
of bowl before serving and toss at table.

CELERY AND EGG SALAD

Makes 4 servings (376 calories). Calories in 1 serving: 94.

2 cups diced celery
3 hard-boiled eggs, chopped

⅔ cup low-calorie French
dressing substitute

1. Mix celery, chopped eggs and dressing.

CHEF'S SALAD

Makes 4 servings (about 400 calories). Calories in 1 serving: about 100.

⅔ cup mixture of slivered, cooked or canned tongue, or ham, chicken or turkey, and Swiss cheese
1 small head chicory
2 small tomatoes

½ Bermuda onion, if desired
1 bunch water cress
Lettuce to line individual salad bowls
8 tablespoons low-calorie French dressing substitute

1. Cut onion in thin crosswise slices and separate into rings. 2. Wash tomatoes and cut in thin wedges. 3. Wash chicory and water cress, separate leaves, drain, and chop coarsely. 4. Combine onion, tomato, chicory, water cress and slivers of meat and cheese. 5. Toss with dressing. Serve on lettuce in individual salad bowls.

JELLIED CRANBERRY SALAD

Makes 2 servings (176 calories). Calories in 1 serving: 88.

2 envelopes lemon flavor Glow low-calorie gelatin
¾ cup homemade cranberry sauce, sweetened with Sacrose or Sucaryl
¼ cup diced celery

Juice of ¼ lemon
2 lettuce leaves or other salad greens
4 teaspoons low calorie mayonnaise substitute

1. Dissolve gelatin according to package directions. 2. Add the lemon juice, celery and cranberry sauce. 3. Pour into 2 individual molds, or 1 serving dish. Chill, and when set, unmold on greens. Serve with 2 teaspoons mayonnaise substitute to each portion.

SEAFOOD SALAD

Makes 1 serving (146 calories).

4 ounces cold boiled fresh cod, haddock, porgy, bass, halibut, flounder (or mixture)
1 teaspoon lemon juice

1 tablespoon Lowmay or other mayonnaise substitute
4 or 5 capers
Large lettuce leaf

1. Break fish into flakes with fork. 2. Add lemon juice, ½ the Lowmay. Salt and pepper. 3. Pile in mound on lettuce and top with rest of Lowmay. 4. Sprinkle with capers and serve.

CHEESE STUFFED LETTUCE

Makes 6 servings (528 calories). Calories in 1 serving: 88.

1 head of lettuce
1 package cream cheese
2 tablespoons Roquefort
2 tablespoons raw carrot,
chopped fine

1 tablespoon green pepper
2 tablespoons raw tomato,
chopped fine
1 teaspoon onion juice
Salt to taste

1. Hollow out the head of lettuce. 2. Blend all remaining ingredients and stuff lettuce. Refrigerate until ready to serve. 3. To serve, cut into 6 wedges.

STUFFED TOMATO SALAD

Makes 6 servings (660 calories). Calories in 1 serving: 110.

6 ripe, firm, medium tomatoes
1½ cups cottage cheese
½ cucumber, diced in ¼-inch
cubes
1 green pepper, finely cut

1 medium onion, finely
chopped
6 teaspoons Lowmay mayon-
naise substitute
6 lettuce leaves

1. Make mixture of cheese, diced cucumber, pepper and onion. 2. Slice off stem end of tomatoes and scoop out centers (reserving them for soup or other use). 3. Fill tomatoes with mixture and top each with teaspoon of Lowmay. Serve on lettuce leaf.

DOUBLE DECKER SALAD

Makes 6 servings (804 calories). Calories in 1 serving: 134.

2 tablespoons unflavored gelatin (2 envelopes Knox's)
1½ cups (12-ounce can) V-8
cocktail vegetable juices
1¼ cups (1 can) Campbell's
condensed cream of celery
soup

1 cup canned tuna fish,
drained
¼ cup diced celery
2 tablespoons mayonnaise substitute
1 teaspoon vinegar
Salad greens

1. Soften 1 envelope of gelatin in ¼ cup cocktail juices. Heat remaining juices and stir in softened gelatin. 2. Pour into a lightly greased 1½-quart mold or loaf pan; chill until firm. 3. Soften other envelope of gelatin in ¼ cup cold water. Heat ¼ of the soup; stir in dissolved gelatin. 4. Blend in remaining soup and rest of ingredients. 5. Pour on top of congealed juice layer; chill until firm. Unmold and serve on crisp greens with mayonnaise substitute.

CRABMEAT AND APPLE SALAD

Makes 4 servings (392 calories). Calories in 1 serving: 98.

2 cups cooked or canned crabmeat
1 large apple (preferably Delicious), diced

4 tablespoons Yogurt Dressing
1 cup shredded lettuce, preferably romaine
Salt and pepper to taste

1. Blend crabmeat and apples with the dressing. Season to taste.
2. Put shredded lettuce in plates and place salad in center. Serve at once.

FRUIT COCKTAIL AND COTTAGE CHEESE SALAD

Makes 4 servings (600 calories). Calories in 1 serving: 150.

2 cups water-pack canned fruit cocktail
1 cup cottage cheese

4 lettuce leaves
4 teaspoons mayonnaise substitute

1. Place 4 tablespoons cottage cheese in a mound, on lettuce leaf.
2. Over this, place ½ cup of drained fruit cocktail. Chill before serving, and top fruit with 1 teaspoon mayonnaise substitute.

LEEK SALAD

Makes 2 servings (200 calories). Calories in 1 serving: 100.

6 boiled leeks
⅓ cup low-calorie French dressing substitute

1 hard-boiled egg, chopped
¼ teaspoon chopped chives
½ teaspoon chopped parsley

1. Chill the white part of the boiled leeks. 2. Mix chopped egg, chives and parsley into the dressing. Serve the dressing over the leeks.

CANDLESTICK SALAD

Makes 1 serving (250 calories).

1 slice fresh pineapple
½ banana
Tiny piece maraschino cherry

1 teaspoon Lowmay or other mayonnaise substitute
Lettuce leaf

1. Core the pineapple slice and place on lettuce leaf. 2. Stand the half banana upright in core-hole of pineapple. 3. Make a cut in tip of banana and insert piece of cherry. 4. Spread the spoonful of Lowmay around base of banana, to cover the joining.

MEAT SALAD

Makes 1 serving (115 calories).

¼ cup finely diced lean left-over meat (lamb, beef, chicken, etc.)
1 teaspoon grated onion
½ teaspoon chopped green pepper
Lettuce leaf

1 tablespoon lemon juice
1 envelope lemon flavor low-calorie gelatin
1 scant teaspoon mayonnaise substitute
¼ teaspoon celery salt

1. Dissolve gelatin in ½ cup scant boiling water. **2.** Add lemon juice, grated onion and celery salt. **3.** Chill until mixture begins to be sirupy. Then fold in diced meat and pepper. **4.** Pour into mold. Chill until firm. Turn out onto lettuce leaf to serve. Top with mayonnaise substitute.

FRESH SALMON SALAD

Makes 6 servings (1500 calories). Calories in 1 serving: 250.

1½ pounds fresh, cooked red salmon
2 medium onions, finely chopped
¼ cup Buttermilk Herb Dressing

½ cup celery, diced
1 bunch water cress
1 medium cucumber, sliced
2 firm medium tomatoes, sliced
Chicory or lettuce

1. Remove skin and bones from fish. Flake fish or cut into small pieces. **2.** Mix fish, celery and onion with the dressing and chill for 1 hour. **3.** Serve on chicory or lettuce, with small tufts of water cress around the salmon and flat of plate garnished with cucumber and tomato slices.

SUNSET SALAD

Makes 2 servings (210 calories). Calories in 1 serving: 105.

3 tablespoons seedless raisins
1 small raw carrot
1 small apple, pared and cored
⅓ cup diced celery
1 tablespoon lemon juice
⅛ teaspoon salt

⅓ teaspoon sugar
Few grains pepper
1½ tablespoons evaporated milk
2 lettuce leaves or other salad greens

1. Put raisins, carrot and apple through medium knife of food chopper. **2.** Add celery, lemon juice, salt, sugar and pepper. Mix well. **3.** Stir in evaporated milk and serve at once on lettuce or salad greens.

WATERMELON SALAD

Makes 2 servings (195 calories). Calories in 1 serving: 98.

1 cup diced watermelon	½ medium cucumber, diced
½ cup shredded lettuce	3 tablespoons Yogurt Dressing
1 medium pear, fresh or water-packed, diced	Paprika
	Mint leaves

1. ALL ingredients must be chilled thoroughly before starting. Chill for at least 2 hours. 2. Put lettuce and cucumber in salad bowl, pour dressing over, and toss gently until well blended. 3. Put melon and pear in center of this, and garnish with paprika and mint leaves. Serve at once.

SHREDDED MEAT SALAD

Makes 4 servings (400 calories). Calories in 1 serving: 100.

½ cup lean meat (chicken, beef or ham), diced	6 tablespoons Cooked Salad Dressing No. 1
2 cups shredded cabbage	Parsley, chopped
2 medium carrots, shredded	Chives or water cress, chopped
1 medium pepper, chopped	

1. Blend vegetables in salad bowl and pour on dressing. Toss lightly. 2. Top with diced meat and sprinkle with garnishings.

MOLDED GRAPEFRUIT AND CARROTS

Makes 8 servings (720 calories). Calories in 1 serving: 90.

2 No. 2 cans unsweetened grapefruit sections and extra unsweetened grapefruit juice to total 3½ cups liquid	1½ cups grated carrots
	½ cup diced celery
	1½ teaspoons Sacrose or other no-calorie liquid sweetener
2 envelopes Knox's unflavored gelatin	½ teaspoon salt
	Salad greens

1. Drain grapefruit sections and measure liquid. Add canned or fresh grapefruit juice to make 3½ cups. 2. Soften gelatin in 1 cup of the grapefruit liquid and heat the remaining 2½ cups. Add heated liquid to softened gelatin. Add Sacrose and salt and let dissolve. Increase seasoning if desired. 3. Chill until mixture is the consistency of egg white. Then fold in the grated carrots, celery and 2 cups of the grapefruit sections. Turn into 6-cup ring mold. Chill until firm. 4. Unmold and garnish with remaining grapefruit sections and salad greens heaped up inside ring.

CHICKEN-TOMATO RING LUNCHEON

Makes 6 servings (660 calories). Calories in 1 serving: 110.

Red Layer:

2 envelopes lemon flavor Glow low-calorie gelatin

1 cup Campbell's tomato soup

1. Dissolve Glow in 1 cup boiling water. Add the soup. 2. Pour into a mold and chill until firm. Then cover with the following:

White Layer:

2 teaspoons Knox's unflavored gelatin softened in 2 table-spoons cold water
1 can Campbell's chicken with rice soup

1 3-ounce package cream cheese
2 tablespoons Lowmay low-calorie mayonnaise substitute

1. Heat soup; add softened gelatin, stirring until dissolved. 2. Cream the cheese and add hot soup mixture a little at a time, stirring steadily, until creamy. Cool. 3. Add Lowmay, pour over red layer and chill until firm.

PEACH SOMBRERO SALAD

Makes 4 servings (576 calories). Calories in 1 serving: 144.

8 canned water-pack peach halves
2 cups cottage cheese
1 canned pimiento

1 green pepper
Salad greens
½ cup French dressing sub-stitute

1. Place salad greens on serving plates. Arrange 2 drained peach halves (round side down) on each plate. 2. Heap cottage cheese in cone shape between peach halves, for crown of "sombrero." 3. Circle the base of the cheese cone with bands cut from pimiento and green pepper. 4. Pour dressing on top and serve.

CRESS, CHEESE AND APPLE SALAD

Makes 1 serving (110 calories).

½ tablespoon water cress, fine-ly chopped
1 medium tart apple, finely chopped

2 tablespoons cottage cheese
1 teaspoon horseradish, pref-erably freshly grated
Lettuce leaf

1. Thoroughly blend cheese with apple and water cress, being careful not to mash. 2. Place on lettuce leaf, sprinkle with horse-radish and serve at once.

JELLIED TONGUE SALAD

Makes 8 servings (1160 calories). Calories in 1 serving: 145.

12 thin slices of tongue
2 tablespoons unflavored gelatin (2 envelopes Knox's)
3 hard-boiled eggs
4 cups chicken or vegetable stock
Juice of 2 lemons

1 medium onion, minced
Strips of pimiento
1½ tablespoons Worcestershire sauce
2 teaspoons salt
8 lettuce leaves

1. Soak gelatin in ½ cup cold water; dissolve in hot stock. 2. Stir in lemon juice, onion, Worcestershire sauce and salt; let stand until mixture begins to jell. 3. Arrange a few tongue slices in bottom of a loaf tin. Cover with jelly, then a layer of sliced egg and pimiento strips. 4. Continue adding layers until ingredients are all used. Chill until firm. 5. To serve, cut in slices with sharp knife and serve on lettuce.

SLICED ONION AND CUCUMBER SALAD

Makes 4 servings (600 calories). Calories in 1 serving: 150.

2 medium cucumbers
2 small white onions

1 recipe Pennsylvania German Salad Dressing

1. Slice onions very thin and slice cucumbers quite thin. 2. Crisp the slices in ice water; drain. Mix in dressing.

BANANA SPLIT LUNCHEON SALAD

Makes 4 servings (900 calories). Calories in 1 serving: 225.

4 ripe medium bananas
4 teaspoons lemon juice
1⅓ cups cottage cheese
2 small oranges
4 lettuce leaves or other salad greens
4 tiny pieces of maraschino cherry

Few blueberries, strawberries, grapes or cubes of red apple with skin left on, for garnishing
6 tablespoons Frenchette or other low-calorie French dressing substitute

1. Peel bananas and cut in half lengthwise. Sprinkle with lemon juice. 2. Place banana halves on salad greens, cut side down. Pile ⅓ cup cottage cheese over the center of each banana and put a piece of cherry on top. 3. Peel oranges and arrange sections, or very thin slices, around cheese. Sprinkle 1½ tablespoons Frenchette dressing over each serving.

HAWAIIAN FRUIT SALAD

Makes 2 servings (500 calories). Calories in 1 serving: 250.

1 whole pineapple
4 sections orange
4 sections grapefruit
2 small bunches seedless, or
  seeded, grapes
1 canned water-pack pear

10 canned water-pack Queen
  Anne cherries
½ medium banana
Juice of ½ lime
2 teaspoons mayonnaise substitute

1. Cut pineapple in half, lengthwise, leaving on leaves. Scoop out most of the fruit and cut it into small pieces. **2.** Cut up other fruits and mix with pineapple. Chill in refrigerator for several hours. Also chill pineapple shells. **3.** Just before serving, drain fruit (holding liquid for other use) and fill pineapple shells. Sprinkle fruit with lime juice, and top with mayonnaise substitute.

HEARTY SALAD PLATE

Makes 2 servings (550 calories). Calories in 1 serving: 275.

1 can (7¾ oz.) pink salmon
⅔ cup cottage cheese
2 portions of any low-calorie
  (about 40 calories per serv-

ing) vegetable salad
2 lettuce leaves or other greens
2 lemon wedges
Salt, pepper and white vinegar

1. Drain off liquid from salmon, remove skin. Season with pepper, and salt if desired. Mash salmon with a little white vinegar, if desired, or leave in chunks. **2.** Place lettuce leaves on 2 plates and arrange on each plate 1 serving salmon, cheese and fresh vegetable salad (lettuce and tomato, cucumber and lettuce, asparagus tips, etc.), or cooked salad (stewed celery, carrots, beets, etc.).

YOGURT PEACH MOLD

Makes 3 servings (306 calories). Calories in 1 serving: 102.

1 tablespoon unflavored gelatin (1 envelope Knox's)
1 egg, separated
1 cup Dannon Yogurt
Few drops almond extract

½ teaspoon liquid Sucaryl or
  other non-caloric sweetening
  solution
½ cup diced water-pack
  peaches

1. Soften gelatin in 2 tablespoons cold water; dissolve over hot water in double boiler. **2.** Beat egg yolk; add yogurt, sweetening solution, almond flavoring and dissolved gelatin; mix well. **3.** Chill until mixture begins to set, beat egg white stiff; fold in with peaches. **4.** Pour into individual molds; chill until set.

DRESSINGS AND SAUCES

BOILED SALAD DRESSING

Makes about 1⅛ cups (18 tablespoons) (216 calories). Calories in 1 tablespoon: 12.

1 teaspoon dry mustard
2 tablespoons flour
¾ teaspoon Sacrose no-calorie sweetener
½ teaspoon salt
Few grains cayenne pepper or ¼ teaspoon paprika
1 egg yolk
¼ cup vinegar
1 tablespoon butter

1. Sift the dry ingredients and dissolve in ½ cup cold water. **2.** Beat the vinegar and egg yolk in double boiler top. Add the water mixture. **3.** Cook over boiling water, stirring constantly, until mixture becomes thick and smooth. Add the butter during cooking. Add the Sacrose toward the end. **4.** Strain, if desired, but not necessary. Chill and serve.

COOKED SALAD DRESSING

Makes about ¾ cup (12 tablespoons) (192 calories). Calories in 1 tablespoon: 16.

½ cup vinegar, preferably wine vinegar
3 egg yolks
½ teaspoon prepared mustard
⅛ teaspoon salt
¼ teaspoon cayenne pepper, if desired, or ⅛ teaspoon cayenne pepper plus ⅛ teaspoon paprika

1. Heat vinegar to boiling. **2.** In double boiler, beat egg yolks and seasonings until thick, then pour hot vinegar slowly over yolks, stirring constantly. **3.** Cook over hot water, stirring constantly until thick. Chill.

ANCHOVY DRESSING

Makes about 1⅛ cups (19 tablespoons) (270 calories). Calories in 1 tablespoon: 14.

1 cup Frenchette dressing or other low-calorie substitute French dressing
3 tablespoons anchovy paste

1. Blend the anchovy paste with the dressing, beating thoroughly.

TWENTY CALORIE DRESSING

Makes about 1¼ cups (20 tablespoons) (400 calories). Calories in 1 tablespoon: 20.

2 tablespoons cornstarch
2 tablespoons salad oil
¼ cup vinegar
¾ teaspoon salt
1½ teaspoons granulated sugar
1 teaspoon prepared horse-radish

1¼ teaspoons prepared mustard
½ teaspoon Worcestershire sauce
½ teaspoon paprika
¼ cup catsup
1 peeled clove garlic

1. Cook cornstarch with ¾ cup water in saucepan, over low heat. Stir constantly for about 5 minutes, until mixture is thick and clear. Remove and cool. 2. Add all ingredients except garlic and beat until smooth and well blended. Add garlic. 3. Store, well covered, in refrigerator. Shake before use.

Note: This dressing is called "Twenty Calorie Dressing," but remember—when you use more than 1 tablespoonful per serving, it's no longer 20 calories.

MUSTARD DRESSING

Makes about 1 cup (16 tablespoons) (352 calories). Calories in 1 tablespoon: 22.

½ cup catsup
2 tablespoons sweetened condensed milk
6 tablespoons prepared mustard

½ tablespoon parsley, finely chopped
½ tablespoon chives, finely chopped
Salt and pepper to taste

1. Beat all ingredients until well blended. 2. Keep in refrigerator. Chill at least 30 minutes before using.

PENNSYLVANIA GERMAN SALAD DRESSING

Makes 1⅛ cup (18 tablespoons) (488 calories). Calories in 1 tablespoon: 27.

½ pint sour cream
1 teaspoon no-calorie liquid sweetener
½ teaspoon dry mustard

¼ teaspoon salt
Few grains celery salt
2 tablespoons white vinegar

1. Whip together all ingredients except vinegar. When thoroughly blended, add the vinegar.

TOWN AND COUNTRY SALAD DRESSING

Town and Country Salad Dressing is really two wonderful dressings in one. Use the same low-calorie ingredients in either. *Stir* them if you want the Country Dressing for slaw, greens, or combination salads. *Whip* them if you want an elegant fluffy Town Dressing for fruit salads.

Makes 8 servings (280 calories). Calories in 1 serving: 35.

SUNKIST TOWN AND COUNTRY DRESSING

½ cup Sunkist lemon juice
½ teaspoon salt
⅛ teaspoon mustard
½ teaspoon Sacrose liquid sweetener

1/16 teaspoon paprika
1 tablespoon cider vinegar
1 small can evaporated milk
3 tablespoons Lowmay mayonnaise substitute

TOWN DRESSING (for fruit salads)

1. Chill milk in bowl or ice tray until crystals form. **2.** Mix salt and spices with Sacrose; add vinegar and lemon juice. **3.** Beat chilled milk very stiff. With beater at low speed, slowly add first mixture. **4.** Fold in Lowmay. Makes one pint (2 cups) whipped dressing.

COUNTRY DRESSING (for slaw, greens, vegetables)

1. Mix salt and spices with Sacrose, then add to Lowmay. **2.** Stir in vinegar and lemon juice, then milk.

SALAD DRESSING WITH CATSUP

Makes about 1¼ cups (20 tablespoons) (400 calories). Calories in 1 tablespoon: 20.

2 teaspoons cornstarch
¼ cup tomato catsup
¼ cup vinegar
2 tablespoons salad oil
1½ teaspoons sugar
1¼ teaspoons prepared mustard

1 peeled clove garlic
1 teaspoon prepared horseradish
¾ teaspoon salt
½ teaspoon paprika
½ teaspoon Worcestershire sauce

1. Place cornstarch in a saucepan with ¾ cup cold water. Cook over low heat, stirring constantly, until clear and thickened, about 5 minutes. **2.** Remove, and cool. Then add all other ingredients except the garlic, and beat until smooth and well blended. Now add the garlic. **3.** Store in covered jar in refrigerator, for use as needed. Shake well before using.

COTTAGE CHEESE DRESSING

Makes 1 cup (16 tablespoons) (304 calories). Calories in 1 tablespoon: 19.

½ cup cottage cheese
¼ cup evaporated milk
3 tablespoons vinegar
1 egg yolk

1 tablespoon sugar
1 teaspoon salt
Dash of pepper

1. Press cheese through a sieve. 2. Moisten with a little of the milk and add the vinegar, salt and pepper. 3. Beat the egg yolk and sugar and add to mixture, then add the remaining milk. 4. Beat until smooth.

YOGURT HERB DRESSING

Makes about 2 cups (600 calories). Calories in 1 tablespoon: 20.

1 jar or container Dannon or other good yogurt
¼ cup celery leaves, finely chopped
¼ cup parsley, minced
¼ cup mayonnaise
3 scallions, thinly sliced

1 tablespoon lemon juice or vinegar
Salt and pepper to taste
1 tablespoon horseradish
1 tablespoon salt
2 teaspoons sugar

1. Combine all ingredients in a bowl. Beat with a fork until well blended. 2. Season as desired with additional lemon juice or vinegar and salt and pepper. 3. Serve with green salads or as a sauce with cold meats or fish.

MAYONNAISE SUBSTITUTE NO. 1

Lowmay—a ready-to-use mayonnaise substitute, approved by the American Medical Association Council on Foods and Nutrition

Calories in 1 teaspoon: 9. Calories in 1 tablespoon: 27.

Variations: HERB MAYONNAISE DRESSING:

Makes 1½ cups. Calories in 1 tablespoon: 23.

To 1 cup Lowmay add ½ tablespoon lemon juice, ¼ teaspoon paprika, ¼ cup finely cut parsley, 1 tablespoon grated onion, 1 tablespoon chopped chives, ⅛ teaspoon curry powder, ½ teaspoon Worcestershire sauce, ¼ cup sour cream.

RUSSIAN DRESSING

Makes 1½ cups. Calories in 1 tablespoon: 21.

Drain ¼ cup chopped green peppers, celery and pimiento. Add to ¼ cup chili sauce and 1 cup Lowmay.

MAYONNAISE SUBSTITUTE NO. 2

Makes about 1 cup (16 tablespoons) (240 calories). Calories in 1 tablespoon: 15.

1 cup yogurt
1 hard-boiled egg, finely
chopped
1 tablespoon lemon juice

¼ teaspoon celery seeds or
curry
¼ teaspoon prepared mustard
½ teaspoon salt

1. Mix all the ingredients thoroughly. 2. Keep in refrigerator. Do not use until chilled for at least ½ hour.

MAYONNAISE SUBSTITUTE NO. 3

Makes about 1⅛ cups (18 tablespoons) (396 calories). Calories in 1 tablespoon: 22.

Yolks of 2 raw eggs
Yolks of 2 hard-boiled eggs
1 cup yogurt
½ teaspoon lemon juice

1 teaspoon chives, finely
chopped
¼ teaspoon salt
Dash of white pepper

1. Finely mash hard-boiled egg yolks and put through coarse sieve. 2. Mix to smooth paste with raw egg yolks. 3. Add remaining ingredients and blend thoroughly. 4. Keep in refrigerator. Chill for at least ½ hour before using.

WHITE RUSSIAN DRESSING

Makes about 1⅛ cups (18 tablespoons) (252 calories). Calories in 1 tablespoon: 14.

1 recipe (about 16 tablespoons)
Mayonnaise Substitute Dressing No. 2
1 tablespoon dill, chopped fine

1 small dill pickle, chopped
fine
1 teaspoon tomato juice

1. Mix all the ingredients thoroughly. 2. Keep in refrigerator. Do not use until chilled for at least ½ hour.

YOGURT DRESSING

Makes about 1¼ cups (20 tablespoons) (180 calories). Calories in 1 tablespoon: 9.

1 cup yogurt
3 tablespoons lemon juice

1 teaspoon salt
¼ teaspoon prepared mustard

1. Mix lemon juice and salt, then blend in mustard. 2. Stir slowly into the yogurt, blending thoroughly. 3. Keep in refrigerator. Chill for at least ½ hour before use.

VARIATIONS ON LOW-CALORIE FRENCHETTE DRESSING

Frenchette dressing is one of the successful low-calorie imitations of French dressing. A teaspoonful of Frenchette dressing contains only 3 calories, a tablespoon 9 calories. Use it "as is" or varied in a dozen or more ways.

Fruit Frenchette Dressing

To ¾ cup (12 teaspoons) Frenchette dressing, add 2 tablespoons each of strained lemon juice and orange juice, ¼ tablespoon Worcestershire or A-1 sauce, 3 teaspoons Dietician sugarless sweetener, ¼ teaspoon prepared mustard and ¼ teaspoon paprika. Beat well and serve very cold. *Calories in 1 tablespoon: 8.*

Honey Dressing

To 1 cup Frenchette dressing add 1 tablespoon each of strained honey, chopped chives, chopped parsley; 1 teaspoon drained, prepared horseradish. Blend thoroughly. Use by the teaspoonful. *Calories in 1 teaspoon: 4.*

Chiffonade Dressing

To 1 cup Frenchette dressing, add 2 finely chopped hard-boiled eggs, 1 tablespoon finely chopped parsley or chervil, 2 tablespoons finely chopped pickled beets, 1 teaspoon grated onion and 1 teaspoon finely chopped green olives. Blend thoroughly. *Calories in 1 tablespoon: 12.*

Parisian Dressing

Thoroughly blend 1 scant teaspoon each of finely chopped parsley, onion, chives, chervil, green pepper and pimiento. Add to 1 cup Frenchette dressing. Stir thoroughly with several ice cubes until mixture thickens. Remove ice and store in refrigerator until needed. *Calories in 1 tablespoon: 9.*

Roquefort Dressing

Crumble 1½ ounces Roquefort cheese with a fork, add to 1 cup Frenchette dressing and blend thoroughly. *Calories in 1 tablespoon: 16.*

Vinaigrette Dressing

To 1 cup Frenchette dressing add 1 teaspoon each of chopped parsley, sweet gherkins, green olives, capers, chives and 1 finely chopped hard-boiled egg. Blend very thoroughly and chill. *Calories in 1 tablespoon: 12.*

Chutney Dressing

To 1 cup Frenchette dressing, add immediately before using, ½ cup of chutney and blend thoroughly. *Calories in 1 tablespoon: 15.*

IMITATION FRENCH DRESSING NO. 2

Makes about 7 tablespoons (112 calories). Calories in 1 tablespoon: 16.

2 tablespoons vinegar	2 tablespoons sugar
2 tablespoons lemon juice	¼ teaspoon salt
1 tablespoon onion, chopped fine	¼ teaspoon mustard
	⅛ teaspoon pepper

1. Mix all ingredients. Keep in refrigerator. Chill at least 30 minutes before use. 2. Shake well and use on salad just before serving. Add water to vinegar if too strong.

BUTTERMILK HERB DRESSING

Makes about 1 cup (16 tablespoons) (96 calories). Calories in 1 tablespoon: 6.

1 cup buttermilk	1 teaspoon water cress
1 teaspoon chives, finely chopped	1 teaspoonful fresh tarragon, finely chopped, or ½ teaspoonful powdered
1 teaspoon fresh chervil, finely chopped, or ½ teaspoonful powdered chervil	¼ teaspoonful dry mustard
	Salt, to taste

1. Mix all ingredients and keep in refrigerator. 2. Chill for at least ½ hour before using.

FRUIT SALAD DRESSING

Makes about ¾ cup (12 tablespoons) (72 calories). Calories in 1 tablespoon: 6.

½ cup orange juice	3 tablespoons lemon juice

(If tarter taste is desired, use more lemon juice and less orange juice, but be sure the juices are unsweetened—preferably use fresh fruit juices.)

¼ teaspoon paprika	Small pinch nutmeg or cinnamon
¼ teaspoon salt	

1. Shake all ingredients in a bottle until well blended. 2. Keep in refrigerator. Chill for at least ½ hour before using. Shake or stir before using.

LOW-CALORIE CATSUP

Makes ½ cup—24 teaspoons (about 100 calories). Calories in 1 teaspoon: 4.

1 cup tomato purée or to-
mato sauce (Hunt's)
1 tablespoon lemon juice
½ teaspoon dry mustard

⅛ teaspoon allspice
1 teaspoon Sacrose or other
liquid saccharin sweetener

1. Place tomato sauce in saucepan. Add lemon juice, mustard and allspice. **2.** Bring to boil. Let simmer over low heat until of desired consistency, about 10 minutes. **3.** Remove from stove and stir in Sacrose. **4.** Use as dressing for cooked vegetables, meat or fish—or add horseradish if diet permits, and use for cocktail sauce on sea foods.

FAMOUS TABASCO SEAFOOD COCKTAIL SAUCE

Makes 4 servings (72 calories). Calories in 1 serving: 18.

¼ teaspoon tabasco sauce
1 tablespoon prepared horseradish
3 tablespoons catsup

1 tablespoon Worcestershire
sauce
1 tablespoon lemon juice
¼ teaspoon salt

1. Mix ingredients.

RED SALAD DRESSING

Makes about 1¼ cups (20 tablespoons) (60 calories). Calories in 1 tablespoon: 3.

1 cup tomato juice
2 tablespoons red wine vinegar
1 clove garlic, cut
½ teaspoon mixed salad herbs

¼ teaspoon dry mustard
½ teaspoon salt
Freshly ground pepper

1. Mix all ingredients well. Let stand for half an hour. **2.** Refrigerate. Shake well before using.

MARINARA SAUCE

Makes about 1 cup (58 calories). Calories in 1 tablespoon: 4.

1 cup tomatoes, fresh or
canned
1 Nestlé bouillon cube

½ clove garlic, finely minced
Pinch of rosemary
Pinch of thyme or oregano

1. Simmer ingredients in ½ cup water over low heat about ½ hour until reduced to a rich sauce.

TOMATO SAUCE

Makes about 1½ cups (63 calories). Calories in 1 tablespoon: 3.

1 cup tomatoes
1 Souplets vegetable broth
tablet
1 onion, finely minced
1 tablespoon lemon juice

1 tablespoon Worcestershire
sauce
1 bay leaf
Saccharin liquid sweetener, salt
and pepper to taste

1. Dissolve Souplets in small amount boiling water. **2.** Simmer all ingredients together for 5 minutes. **3.** Sweeten with saccharin to taste, season with salt and pepper, and store to use as needed.

CREOLE SAUCE

Makes 2¾ cups (176 calories). Calories in 1 tablespoon: 4.

2 cups tomatoes, fresh or
canned
2 tablespoons chopped onion
2 tablespoons minced celery
leaves

2 tablespoons green peppers
2 tablespoons parsley
1 bouillon cube
1 raw carrot, grated
Seasoning

1. Pour tomatoes, onion, peppers, celery leaves and parsley into a saucepan with 1 cup of water. **2.** Add crushed bouillon cube and bring to a boil. Simmer gently ½ hour. **3.** Add grated carrot and season to taste with salt, pepper, tabasco sauce, or powdered red pepper.

VEGETABLE SPAGHETTI SAUCE

Makes 3 servings (100 calories). Calories in 1 serving: 33.

1 Souplets vegetable broth
tablet
4 large mushrooms, sliced
1 green pepper, minced
½ medium tomato, sliced or
cubed

½ medium onion, minced
1 teaspoon butter or vegetable
shortening
¼ clove of garlic
Dash of salt and dry mustard
Paprika, to taste

1. Dissolve Souplets in 1½ cups of boiling water. **2.** Rub pan with clove of garlic and salt; heat butter; add mushrooms, green pepper and onion, and sauté (brown) for about 5 minutes. **3.** Add Souplets dissolved in hot water and tomato; cover and simmer for 15 minutes. Season to taste with paprika and dry mustard.

SWEET AND PUNGENT SAUCE

Makes ½ cup—enough for 2 to 4 servings (30 calories). Calories in 1 tablespoon: 4.

½ cup chicken broth
2 tablespoons vinegar
¼ teaspoon Kitchen Bouquet
(optional)

2 teaspoons cornstarch
1 teaspoon Sacrose no-calorie
sweetener

1. Blend together chicken broth, vinegar, Kitchen Bouquet and cornstarch in saucepan. **2.** Bring to a boil and cook over moderate heat, stirring constantly until sauce thickens, about 1 minute. **3.** Remove from stove and stir in Sacrose. **4.** Serve as sauce with cooked carrots, string beans, poached fish, tongue, eggplant or sea food.

MUSTARD SAUCE

Makes 1 cup (72 calories). Calories in 1 tablespoon: 4½.

2 tablespoons cornstarch
3 tablespoons dry mustard
1 teaspoon Worcestershire
sauce

¼ teaspoon Kitchen Bouquet
2 tablespoons vinegar
1 teaspoon Sacrose no-calorie
sweetener

1. In a small saucepan, combine the cornstarch, mustard, ¼ cup cold water, Worcestershire sauce, Kitchen Bouquet and vinegar; blend until smooth. **2.** Add ¾ cup boiling water and cook, stirring constantly, until sauce thickens and boils. **3.** Remove from stove and add Sacrose. **4.** Use instead of prepared mustard to serve with meat or fish.

BRAZILIAN SAUCE

(This sauce is good over omelets, scrambled eggs, rice, macaroni, noodles and meat or fish cooked in almost any manner.)

Makes almost 2 cups (178 calories). Calories in 1 tablespoon: 6.

1 tablespoon butter
1 cup tomatoes
1 green pepper, minced
1 tablespoon onion, minced

½ cup chopped celery
1 tablespoon Worcestershire
sauce
1 teaspoon salt

1. Mix all ingredients except the Worcestershire sauce and simmer covered for 20 minutes until vegetables are tender. **2.** Add a little hot water if necessary, stirring occasionally. **3.** Add the Worcestershire sauce just before serving.

SAVORY SAUCE

(Good on hot cooked shrimp, gluten noodles or meat loaf)

Makes about 2 cups (345 calories). Calories in 1 tablespoon: 11.

¼ cup finely chopped onion
¼ cup finely chopped green
pepper
2 tablespoons oil or melted
shortening
2 tablespoons flour
1½ cups (12-ounce can) V-8
cocktail vegetable juices

1 tablespoon Worcestershire
sauce
2 teaspoons lemon juice
1 teaspoon paprika
½ teaspoon salt
¼ teaspoon chili powder
Dash of black pepper
Dash of tabasco sauce

1. Cook onion and green pepper until tender in oil in heavy skillet. 2. Remove from heat and stir in flour; blend well. Slowly pour in vegetable juices. 3. Cook, stirring constantly until smooth and thick. Add remaining ingredients; simmer 10 minutes.

TOMATO, ONION AND PEPPER SAUCE

Makes 4 servings (228 calories). Calories in 1 serving: 57.

2 large tomatoes
1 medium onion, chopped
½ medium pepper, finely
chopped

1 tablespoon salad oil
2 tablespoons wine vinegar
Salt and pepper, to taste

1. Peel tomatoes and cut into small pieces and add chopped onion and chopped pepper. 2. Stir in salad oil, vinegar and salt and pepper.

BARBECUE SAUCE

Makes about 3 cups (798 calories). Calories in 1 tablespoon: 17.

1 cup chopped onions
1 cup catsup
1 cup tomatoes, fresh or
canned
1 cup minced celery leaves
2 Souplets vegetable broth
tablets

1 green pepper
2 tablespoons brown sugar
2 tablespoons fat
1 clove garlic, chopped
½ tablespoon dry mustard
Salt, pepper, tabasco or red
pepper

1. Mix garlic and onions. Brown in the fat and add Souplets dissolved in 2 cups of boiling water. 2. Add all other ingredients, bring to a boil and simmer gently about 1 hour until sauce is reduced to about ½ its original volume. 3. Dip meats in this sauce before roasting or broiling, then baste with the sauce while cooking.

SEAFOOD COCKTAIL SAUCE

Makes 6 servings (132 calories). Calories in 1 serving: 22.

2 tablespoons malt vinegar
¼ teaspoon Worcestershire sauce
¼ teaspoon tabasco
3 tablespoons catsup

2 tablespoons grated horse-radish
3 tablespoons chili sauce
Pinch of salt

1. Mix vinegar and salt and stir in Worcestershire sauce. 2. Mix in tabasco and horseradish. 3. Add chili sauce and catsup. Blend.

QUICK TOMATO SAUCE

Makes 1½ cups (270 calories). Calories in 1 tablespoon: 12.

1 can Campbell's tomato soup
1 tablespoon lemon juice or vinegar
1½ teaspoons brown sugar

1 tablespoon Worcestershire sauce or soy sauce
Few grains salt and pepper

1. Combine all ingredients, add ¼ cup hot water, and bring to a boil. Stir until sugar is dissolved.

CREAMY SAUCE

Makes 1⅓ cups (300 calories). Calories in 1 tablespoon: 15.

2 teaspoons butter
¾ tablespoon flour
Scant cup skim milk

Salt, pepper and paprika to taste

1. Melt butter over low heat in a double boiler top. 2. Blend in the flour for 5 to 10 minutes, over low heat. 3. Slowly stir in the milk. Add seasonings. Cook and stir the sauce until smooth. Turn off heat before sauce comes to a boil. Serve at once.

VEGETABLE CREAMY SAUCE

(My daughter Nina's invention, and very good, too!)

Makes 2 servings (138 calories). Calories in 1 serving: 69.

1 tablespoon butter
1 slightly rounded tablespoon flour

½ Souplets vegetable broth tablet
5 drops Worcestershire sauce

1. Melt butter in double boiler top. Blend in the flour for 5 to 10 minutes over low heat. 2. Stir in ¾ cup water gradually, stirring until sauce is smooth. 3. Dissolve the ½ Souplets tablet in a tablespoon of boiling water and add with the Worcestershire sauce. Mix and serve at once.

BARBECUE SAUCE

Makes 6 servings (228 calories). Calories in 1 serving: 38.

1 cup vinegar
½ cup catsup
1 clove garlic
2 tablespoons Worcestershire sauce

1 tablespoon sugar
1 teaspoon dry mustard
½ teaspoon tabasco
1 teaspoon salt

1. Combine all ingredients and simmer 10 minutes. 2. Brush chicken or other meats with the sauce and place in a preheated broiler. 3. Cook until tender, brushing with the sauce and turning every 10 minutes.

APPLE AND HORSERADISH SAUCE

Makes 6 servings (342 calories). Calories in 1 serving: 57.

4 tart medium apples
½ teaspoon sugar

4 tablespoons prepared horse-radish

1. Peel apples and grate into bowl containing horseradish. Blend while grating, to prevent discoloration of apples. 2. Add sugar and blend.

SICILIAN ANCHOVY SAUCE

Makes sauce for 2 servings of spaghetti (150 calories). Calories in 1 serving: 75.

2 dried, salted anchovies
1 teaspoon minced green pepper
½ tablespoon butter or mar-garine

1 teaspoon minced onion
1 Souplets vegetable broth tablet
2 tablespoons minced parsley
4 tablespoons grated cheese

1. Shred anchovies. Add onion and green pepper. Sauté lightly in the butter. 2. Dissolve Souplets in ¼ cup boiling water and add to the sautéed mixture. 3. Simmer gently for a minute or two, to blend. Pour over spaghetti and top with a sprinkling of parsley and cheese.

HORSERADISH BEETS

Makes 4 servings (216 calories). Calories in 1 serving: 54.

2 cups cooked, sliced beets
4 tablespoons grated horse-radish
Lemon juice, to taste

Scant tablespoon chopped parsley or chives
Salt, to taste

1. Mix all ingredients. 2. Reheat if necessary.

HOLLANDAISE SAUCE

Makes 6 servings (432 calories). Calories in 1 serving: 72.

2 egg yolks
3 tablespoons butter
½ teaspoon cornstarch

2 tablespoons lemon juice
¼ teaspoon salt
½ cup boiling water

1. Cream together butter, cornstarch and salt. Place in double boiler over warm (not boiling) water. **2.** Add yolks, one at a time, and stir. **3.** Dilute the lemon juice with ½ cup of boiling water and add to the mixture. Continue stirring. **4.** Bring water in bottom of double boiler to a boil and cook 5 to 8 minutes, until consistency of boiled custard.

PIMIENTO CREAM SAUCE FOR VEGETABLES

Makes ½ cup (80 calories). Calories in 1 tablespoon: 10.

2 tablespoons skim milk
powder (nonfat dry milk
solids)
½ teaspoon cornstarch

1 Souplet or Nestlé bouillon
cube
1 canned pimiento, slivered
Salt and pepper

1. Blend together milk solids and cornstarch in small saucepan. Add ½ cup lukewarm water and stir until smooth. **2.** Add Souplet and bring to boil, stirring constantly. Lower heat and add pimiento. **3.** Let simmer until the Souplet dissolves. Season to taste with salt and pepper. Serve over fresh-cooked vegetables.

Variations: Other sauces may be made simply by substituting other seasonings for the pimiento. For instance, add *2 tablespoons minced parsley,* or *2 teaspoons prepared mustard* or *1 teaspoon paprika.*

CHILI SAUCE

Makes about 2 cups (190 calories). Calories in 1 tablespoon: 6.

3 cups canned tomatoes
¼ cup chopped onions
⅓ cup cider vinegar
1 teaspoon cinnamon
¼ teaspoon allspice

⅛ teaspoon ground cloves
Dash of cayenne pepper
2 drops Sucaryl liquid
1 teaspoon salt
2 teaspoons cornstarch

1. Rub tomatoes through a sieve. Boil tomatoes and vinegar with cornstarch until starch is dissolved. **2.** Add onions and boil until onions are tender. **3.** Add spices and Sucaryl. Boil a few more minutes, mixing thoroughly.

SOUPS

CALORIES IN 1 SERVING OF CAMPBELL'S SOUPS

(After diluting a can of soup with a canful of water, to make
2 servings)

	Calories in each serving
Beef with Bacon	236
Cream of Mushroom	173
Green Pea	166
Scotch Broth	144
Beef	138
Pepper Pot	135
Black Bean	130
Vegetable Beef	129
Ox Tail	115
Cream of Celery	115
Tomato	115
Cream of Chicken	114
Vegetarian Vegetable	105
Vegetable	102
Clam Chowder	99
Cream of Asparagus	96
Chicken Noodle	90
Chicken Gumbo	77
Beef Noodle	75
Chicken with Rice	56
Consommé	46
Bouillon	42

PETITES GARNITURES FOR CONSOMMÉS

On a divided plate or in separate small dishes on a platter, serve minced parsley, chives, paprika, green and red pepper, grated cheese. Let each guest choose his own consommé topping.

Calories for a level teaspoonful: Parsley—½; Chives—2; Paprika—0; Green and red pepper—2; Grated cheddar cheese—8; Grated Parmesan cheese—9.

PARSLEY AND CELERY FOR SOUPS

Calories in 1 teaspoonful: 1. Calories in 1 tablespoonful: 3.

1. Spread out parsley and celery leaves on oven rack or cookie tin.
2. Dry until brittle, in the slowest possible oven. 3. Use crisp and warm for immediate use, and keep in tightly covered jar for future use.

CALORIES IN 1 SERVING OF HEINZ SOUPS

(After diluting a can of soup with a canful of water, to make 2 servings)

	Calories in each serving
Bean with Smoked Pork	202
Cream of Mushroom	158
Vegetable without Meat	130
Vegetable with Beef Stock	126
Cream of Tomato	120
Cream of Green Pea	110
Chicken Noodle	110
Gumbo Creole	104
Cream of Chicken	104
Clam Chowder	104
Beef Noodle	104
Beef with Vegetables	94
Chicken with Rice	60

CHINESE "SOUP FOR THE GODS"

Makes 6 servings (144 calories). Calories in 1 serving: 24.

2 tablespoons soy sauce
1 scallion, coarsely chopped
1 teaspoon salt
1 teaspoon sesame oil, or salad oil

1. Put all ingredients in a soup tureen and pour on 6 cups of boiling water.

CONSOMMÉ WITH CUSTARD

Makes 4 servings (192 calories). Calories in 1 serving: 48.

4 servings clear, fat-skimmed consommé, homemade or canned
1 egg yolk, slightly beaten
1 whole egg, slightly beaten
¼ cup skim milk
Few grains salt and cayenne pepper

1. Mix beaten egg yolk, beaten egg, milk, salt and cayenne. 2. Pour into small (4-inch) shallow pan or baking dish. Set in pan of hot water and bake in moderate oven (350°F.) for 20 minutes, or until set. 3. Cool, and dice or cut into fancy shapes. Heat consommé and add custard just before serving.

JELLIED CHICKEN BOUILLON

Makes 4 servings (56 calories). Calories in 1 serving: 14.

1 tablespoon unflavored gelatin (1 envelope Knox's)	2 cups hot chicken stock (homemade or use Nestlé cubes)
Salt and pepper	
1 tablespoon chopped parsley	

1. Soften gelatin in ¼ cup cold water 5 minutes. 2. Add to hot stock and stir. Add salt and pepper to taste. Add chopped parsley. 3. Chill in refrigerator. When set, break up with fork, or cut into cubes and serve in bouillon cups.

CONSOMMÉ BOUQUETIÈRE

Makes 4 servings (128 calories). Calories in 1 serving: 32.

1 carrot	¼ cup green peas
6 string beans or 1 small white turnip	4 Nestlé chicken flavor bouillon cubes

1. Cut carrot into thin round slices. Cut up beans or cube turnip. Add peas. 2. Cover with 5 cups boiling water and boil gently, uncovered, until tender. 3. Add 4 crushed or softened bouillon cubes. Stir until dissolved, and serve piping hot.

CONSOMMÉ VERMICELLI

Makes 4 servings (148 calories). Calories in 1 serving: 37.

4 Souplets vegetable broth tablets	3 ounces fine vermicelli

1. Dissolve Souplets in 1 quart boiling water. 2. Plunge vermicelli into the soup. Simmer gently 2 to 3 minutes until vermicelli is cooked. 3. Serve with grated cheese.

Note: Add 20 calories for 1 teaspoon grated cheese.

SCALLOP AND RADISH SOUP

Makes 6 servings (402 calories). Calories in 1 serving: 67.

½ pound fresh scallops	1 teaspoon salt
30 radishes	

1. Wash scallops and remove tough side-muscles. Peel radishes. 2. Place whole scallops and radishes in heavy pot with 7 cups water. 3. Cook over low flame 10 minutes, add salt, and continue cooking over low flame 30 minutes more.

CLAM BROTH, HOT OR JELLIED

Makes 4 servings (80 calories). Calories in 1 serving: 20.

1 quart soft-shell clams   Salt and paprika
Celery salt or thyme

1. Scrub clams thoroughly under running water to remove sand.
2. Place in large kettle, add 1 cup water, cover and cook over low
flame for 10 to 20 minutes, until shells pop open. **3.** Pour the
juice through fine strainer or cheesecloth. Add hot water to bring
quantity to 4 cups. Season with salt, and add pinch of celery salt
or thyme. Sprinkle with paprika before serving.

Note: The clams themselves should be eaten too, but without
butter, to maintain low calorie status. Calories in clams: about 200.

Variations: JELLIED CLAM BROTH

Makes 4 servings (112 calories). Calories in 1 serving: 28.

Soften 1 tablespoon unflavored gelatin (1 envelope Knox's) in a
little cold water. Add the hot clam broth, stir until gelatin is dissolved, and set in refrigerator to jell. Serve with chopped parsley
garnishing, and lemon wedge.

HOT CLAM BROTH AND TOMATO JUICE, half and half
Calories in 1 serving (8 ounces): 33.

HOT CLAM BROTH AND V-8 COCKTAIL, half and half
Calories in 1 serving (8 ounces): 30.

"CREAM" OF MUSHROOM SOUP

Makes 4 servings (340 calories). Calories in 1 serving: 85.

1 cup well chopped mushrooms   ½ cup skim milk powder
1 cup Campbell's condensed   Salt and pepper
consommé

1. Blend skim milk powder with 2 cups lukewarm water. **2.** Cook
mushrooms and consommé, covered, until mushrooms are tender.
3. Add to creamy mixture. Season with salt and pepper.

CONSOMMÉ WITH EGG AND SHERRY

Makes 4 servings (340 calories). Calories in 1 serving: 85.

3 cups consommé   1 tablespoon sherry
4 eggs

1. Bring consommé to a boil and add raw, unbeaten eggs. **2.** Add
sherry and beat with rotary beater. Serve at once.

ONION SOUP, CLEAR

Makes 2 servings (32 calories). Calories in 1 serving: 16.

2 vegetable bouillon tablets	2 medium-sized onions
2 cups boiling water	

1. Dissolve vegetable broth tablets in boiling water. 2. Slice in onions and cook until tender.

TOMATO BOUILLON

Makes 1 serving (18 calories).

1 Nestlé chicken bouillon cube   2 tablespoons tomato juice

1. Add bouillon cube and tomato juice to ⅔ cup boiling water. 2. Let simmer for a few minutes and serve.

SWEET PEPPER CONSOMMÉ

Makes 6 servings (144 calories). Calories in 1 serving: 24.

3 medium green or red sweet peppers	1 large onion
2 tomatoes	1 whole clove
	¾ teaspoon salt

1. Quarter the sweet peppers, remove membranes and seeds. Quarter tomatoes and onion. 2. Put all ingredients in a kettle, with 2 quarts boiling water. 3. Cover, and simmer for 1½ hours. Strain and adjust seasoning if necessary. Serve hot or cold.

TUESDAY SOUP

(A Swedish soup, often the main course on Tuesdays)

Makes 6 servings (1012 calories). Calories in 1 serving: 168.

2 cans consommé	3 carrots
2 cups skim milk	2 parsnips
½ cup rice	1 small onion stuck with 1
2 tablespoons butter or	clove
margarine	Salt and pepper

1. Cut cleaned carrots and parsnips into strips. Brown well in butter or margarine. 2. Add consommé and 1 quart cold water. Bring to a boil, add onion with clove and cook for 15 to 20 minutes. 3. Add rice and simmer until rice is tender. Add milk and boil for few minutes longer. Season with salt and pepper.

CREOLE BOUILLABAISSE

Makes 12 portions (1020 calories). Calories in 1 serving: 85.

In Marseilles, France, where bouillabaisse was born, they seem to use an unbelievably large quantity of garlic. We've cut it down a bit here, out of deference to the neighbors, but increase it a little if you like. In Marseilles they also use lobster and a dozen different fish, varying the fish to the season, so act accordingly, making sure you use the leaner fishes, with the lower calories.

4 pounds fish fillets
½ pound mushrooms, thinly
   sliced
2 cups tomato pulp
½ cup California red wine
2 tablespoons butter or
   margarine
2 tablespoons flour

2 large onions, chopped
2 cloves garlic, chopped
1½ teaspoons curry powder
3 bay leaves
8 cloves
1 teaspoon salt
Dash of tabasco sauce

1. Melt butter and sauté onions, garlic and flour until golden brown. 2. Add tomato pulp and 2 cups water, 4 of the cloves, bay leaves, curry powder, tabasco sauce and half the wine. Simmer 30 minutes, then add salt. 3. Simmer the fish fillets 15 minutes in 1½ quarts boiling water, with the remaining 4 cloves and ¼ cup wine. Then add the tomato-wine sauce and the mushrooms and cook 5 minutes. 4. Remove pieces of fish, place on warm platter, pour sauce over fish, and serve.

ITALIAN MINESTRONE SOUP

Makes 4 eight-ounce servings (400 calories). Calories in 1 serving: 100.

1 tablespoon salad oil
1 small clove garlic, minced
¼ cup finely diced onion
½ cup finely diced celery
½ cup finely diced carrots
1 cup finely shredded cabbage

1 cup diced fresh tomatoes
3 Souplets or bouillon cubes
½ cup elbow macaroni
1 cup finely chopped young
   spinach leaves
Salt

1. Place salad oil in saucepan. Add garlic, onion, celery, carrots and cabbage. Let cook over moderate heat for 10 minutes. 2. Add tomatoes, 3 cups hot water and 3 Souplets. Bring to boil and cook until the vegetables are barely tender, about 10 minutes. 3. Meanwhile cook macaroni in boiling, salted water until just tender. Drain well and add to soup. 4. Season to taste with salt. Add chopped spinach and serve immediately.

TOMATO SOUP

Makes 6 servings (660 calories). Calories in 1 serving: 110.

3 cups canned or fresh tomatoes

4 cups beef stock, homemade or made with Nestlé or other bouillon cubes

3 tablespoons raw rice, well washed

3 tablespoons butter or margarine

2 tablespoons finely chopped green pepper

1 onion, finely chopped

3 stalks celery, diced

1 bay leaf

½ teaspoon A-1 sauce or Heinz beefsteak sauce

¼ teaspoon black pepper

1. Sauté chopped onion, green pepper, celery and crushed bay leaf in the butter or margarine, until vegetables are soft, about 10 minutes. 2. Add tomatoes and simmer for 30 minutes. 3. In another saucepan bring beef stock to a boil. Add rice, and cook for 30 minutes, or until rice is just tender. 4. Put tomato mixture through a sieve and add to beef-stock mixture. Check seasoning, and add A-1 sauce, black pepper, and salt to taste. Heat to a boil, and serve.

SCOTCH LEEK SOUP (Cock-a-leekie)

Makes 4 servings (360 calories). Calories in 1 serving: 90.

1 quart chicken broth

½ tablespoon uncooked oatmeal

3 leeks

Salt and pepper

1. Wash and trim the leeks and slice into small pieces. 2. Bring chicken broth to a boil, and sprinkle in the oatmeal and leeks. Season. 3. Simmer until the oatmeal and the leeks are thoroughly tender.

FILIPINO PICADILLO SOUP

Makes 4 servings (800 calories). Calories in 1 serving: 200.

½ pound ground lean meat

3 small potatoes, cubed

1 large tomato, diced

1 medium onion, slices

3 cloves garlic, chopped

½ tablespoon lard

Salt and pepper

1. Sauté garlic in lard, until light brown. 2. Add onion slices and fry 3 minutes. 3. Add tomato, potatoes and meat, and cook on low flame 5 minutes. Season with salt and pepper. 4. Add 4 cups cold water and simmer until done. Serve piping hot.

POULTRY CARCASS SOUP

Makes 4 servings (440 calories). Calories in 1 serving: 110.

Carcass of roast chicken, duck, turkey or goose (leave on remaining bits of meat)
¼ cup uncooked, but washed, rice, barley or vermicelli
1 cup diced celery
5 stalks celery, with leaves
1 onion, sliced
1 carrot, sliced
2 tablespoons chopped parsley
2 tablespoons salt
1 tablespoon A-1, Heinz, or other beefsteak sauce
1½ teaspoons thyme
1 bay leaf
1 teaspoon pepper

1. Place carcass in soup pot. Add 8 cups (2 quarts) water. 2. Add all other ingredients except diced celery, chopped parsley, and barley, rice or vermicelli. 3. Cover pot, bring to a boil and simmer 2 hours. Skim off fat carefully. 4. Take off stove, remove bones, and strain soup through fine strainer. Put back into the soup any bits of meat. 5. Add the diced celery and the ¼ cup of barley, rice or vermicelli. Bring to a boil, and cook over moderate flame 15 to 20 minutes, or until vegetables are tender. Adjust the seasoning if necessary, and serve with sprinkling of chopped parsley.

FISH CHOWDER

Makes 2 eight-ounce servings (210 calories). Calories in 1 serving: 105.

1 teaspoon butter
¼ cup finely diced onion
½ pound lean white fish
1 teaspoon minced parsley
1 Souplet or bouillon cube
¾ cup skim milk
Salt and pepper

1. Place butter in small saucepan. Add onion and let cook about 1 minute. 2. Cut fish in 1-inch cubes and add to onion. Add ¾ cup water, parsley and Souplet. Bring to boil. 3. Let simmer covered over low heat until fish is done, about 5 minutes. 4. Add milk and season to taste with salt and pepper. Heat thoroughly.

MILK BROTH

Makes 1 six-ounce serving (134 calories). If skim milk is used, reduce calories to 74.

¾ cup milk
1 Souplet or other vegetable broth tablet
Dash of pepper

1. Place milk, Souplet and pepper in top of double boiler. Place over boiling water and let heat until Souplet dissolves. 2. Serve immediately for quick luncheon soup, or before bed nightcap.

BARLEY AND VEGETABLE SOUP

Makes 6 servings (576 calories). Calories in 1 serving: 96.

2½ tablespoons barley
½ pound mushrooms
5 large carrots
2½ onions

5 stalks celery, with leaves
1 small potato
Salt and pepper

1. Cook barley in 7½ cups water over moderate flame, for 1 hour. **2.** Clean vegetables and run through food grinder, using fine cutter. After the barley has cooked an hour, add the vegetables to the soup pot, and season with salt and pepper. **3.** Cook over a moderate flame until vegetables are tender, about 15 minutes.

SWEDISH FISH SOUP

Makes 6 servings (840 to 1008 calories). Calories in 1 serving: 140 to 168.

2 to 3 pounds haddock, including head and tail
2 cups skim milk
3 tablespoons flour
2 tablespoons butter or margarine
1 carrot

3 sprigs parsley
Celery tops
1 large bay leaf
8 whole peppercorns
3 cloves
1 teaspoon salt

1. Only remove entrails of fish; use bones, head and tail. **2.** Put fish in soup pot with 2 quarts of cold water. Add vegetables, spices, salt. **3.** Bring to a boil, then simmer for 45 minutes. Strain, but save morsels of fish. **4.** In separate pot, melt butter and add flour, stirring constantly. Add milk and stir to smoothness. **5.** Add the fish broth and pieces of fish. Simmer for a few minutes and season if necessary.

YOGURT BORSCHT

Makes 6 servings (480 calories). Calories in 1 serving: 80.

2½ cups (1 No. 2 can) shredded beets
4½ cups bouillon made from bouillon cubes
6 tablespoons lemon juice

½ teaspoon salt
Few grains pepper
1 cup yogurt (1 container Dannon Yogurt)

1. Combine beets, beet liquor and bouillon; bring to boil. **2.** Simmer 10 minutes; add lemon juice and seasonings. **3.** Serve hot or chilled, topped with a large spoonful of yogurt.

MUSHROOMS AND PORK-SLICE SOUP

Makes 8 servings (824 calories). Calories in 1 serving: 103.

½ pound mushrooms
½ pound lean pork chops,
   boneless
2 tablespoons soy sauce

½ tablespoon cornstarch
½ tablespoon sherry wine
½ teaspoon salt

1. Clean mushrooms and slice thin. **2.** Slice pork very thin, as in Chinese restaurants, and cover with mixture of cornstarch, sherry, and 1 tablespoon of the soy sauce. **3.** Bring 7 cups cold water to a boil, add mushrooms and boil water 1 more minute. Then add salt, remaining soy sauce, and meat. Boil additional 3 minutes and serve soup at once.

CHEESE SOUP

Makes 6 servings (648 calories). Calories in 1 serving: 108.

1 pint skim milk
½ cup chicken broth
1½ tablespoons dark beer or
   ale
½ tablespoon butter
Scant ½ cup flour

⅔ cup grated cheese
½ green pepper, diced
½ carrot, diced
¼ celery stalk, diced
1 slice onion, diced
Few capers

1. Mix milk, chicken broth and ale. Heat over low flame. **2.** Sauté diced vegetables in the butter and add to the heated liquid. **3.** Stir in the flour and cheese, garnish with capers, and serve piping hot.

BAVARIAN CHOWDER

Makes 4 servings (412 calories). Calories in 1 serving: 103.

¼ pound bologna in 1 piece
1½ onions
1 medium potato
½ green pepper
3 stalks celery, with leaves
1 large carrot

¼ small head cabbage
1½ ripe peeled tomatoes (or
   ½ cup canned tomatoes)
1 sprig parsley
Salt and pepper

1. Cut bologna into ½-inch cubes. Boil 3 cups water and add the bologna. Simmer for 15 minutes. **2.** Place all vegetables in a chopping bowl and chop into very small pieces. **3.** Add the vegetables to the bologna after it has simmered about 15 minutes. Season with salt and pepper and cook gently 30 to 45 minutes, or until all vegetables become thoroughly tender.

SCOTCH LAMB AND BARLEY BROTH

Thousands of New Yorkers have for years been enjoying a noon-time bowl of Scotch Broth at the smart little luncheon bar in Lord & Taylor's department store. Aside from apple pie and coffee, Scotch Broth is the only dish served by this eating place every day from the day it opened . . . which attests to the satisfying properties of this meat-and-barley-laden broth.

Makes 6 servings (1824 calories). Calories in 1 serving: 304.

2 pound neck of lamb	1 onion
2 tablespoons barley	2 stalks celery
1 small turnip	2 teaspoons chopped parsley
1 carrot	Salt and pepper

1. Wipe meat, cut into small pieces, and put in saucepan with 2 quarts cold water. 2. Bring to a slow boil, then simmer for 1 hour, skimming well several times. 3. Dice all the vegetables and add to the broth; also add barley, salt and pepper. Continue cooking until vegetables are tender, about 1½ hours longer. 4. Skim again. Sprinkle with chopped parsley just before serving.

CHICKEN SUBGUM SOUP

Makes 4 servings (408 calories). Calories in 1 serving: 102.

½ cup diced cooked chicken	¼ cup bamboo shoots, diced
½ cup diced celery	(if not available fresh or in
¼ cup raw or canned mushrooms, thinly sliced	cans, substitute celery cabbage)
3 water chestnuts, sliced, if available; if not, add 3 small mushrooms, thinly sliced	1 quart chicken stock or canned consommé (1½ cans condensed consommé diluted
½ pimiento, diced	with equal amount of water)

1. Add all the ingredients to chicken stock and boil for 10 minutes.

COLD SHRIMP BISQUE

Makes 4 servings (724 calories). Calories in 1 serving: 181.

½ pound cooked shrimps, chopped	1 tablespoon prepared mustard
½ cucumber, diced	1 tablespoon powdered skim milk
1 quart buttermilk	1 teaspoon sugar
1 tablespoon chopped dill pickle	1 teaspoon salt

1. Mix all ingredients and chill until ready to serve.

ANDALUSIAN COLD SOUP

Makes 6 servings (612 calories). Calories in 1 serving: 102.

2 egg yolks, hard-boiled and chopped fine
2 egg whites, hard-boiled and cut into strips
2 tablespoons olive oil
1 onion chopped fine
1 clove garlic, crushed
Juice of 1 lemon
1½ teaspoons Worcestershire sauce
1 dash tabasco sauce
1 teaspoon dry mustard
1 quart tomato juice
1 green pepper, chopped fine
1 small cucumber, chopped fine
1 lemon, sliced thin
2 pimientos, cut into strips
12 ice cubes
Salt and pepper to taste

1. Work egg yolks and olive oil into a smooth paste in wooden salad bowl. 2. Mix together the chopped onion, garlic, lemon juice, Worcestershire sauce, tabasco sauce, dry mustard and salt and pepper. Add to egg-yolk paste. 3. Work in the tomato juice. 4. Mix separately the chopped green pepper, cucumber, egg whites, lemon slices and pimiento strips. 5. Chill both mixtures for about 3 hours. To serve, divide pepper and cucumber mixture among 6 bowls, place 2 ice cubes in each bowl, and pour in soup.

OYSTER GUMBO

Makes 4 servings (472 calories). Calories in 1 serving: 118.

1 dozen oysters
2 tablespoons flour
2 tablespoons shortening
1 small onion, chopped
2 tablespoons diced celery
1 tablespoon filé powder (ground dried sassafras leaves)
2 tablespoons chopped parsley
1 tablespoon salt
1 teaspoon black pepper
¼ teaspoon thyme
Few drops tabasco sauce or ½ teaspoon Worcestershire sauce
2 bay leaves

1. Melt shortening in small frying pan. Blend in 2 tablespoons flour, then add ¼ cup water, mixing thoroughly. Cook 10 minutes over a low flame, until brown. Stir frequently to keep smooth and scorch-free. 2. Place liquid from the oysters in a large saucepan. Add 6 cups water, and all other ingredients except the oysters and filé powder. 3. Bring to a boil, and blend a little of the mixture into the browned flour. Then turn the flour mixture into the saucepan, bring to a boil again and simmer for 30 minutes. 4. Just before serving, add the oysters and cook for 5 minutes or until the edges of the oysters begin to curl, no longer. 5. Remove from stove, add filé powder and stir briskly. Serve at once. (For non-dieters place a spoonful of cooked rice in the center of the soup plate and float some crumpled bacon on top of the soup.)

CHINESE SOUR SOUP

Makes 8 servings (840 calories). Calories in 1 serving: 105.

½ pound chopped left-over meat or fish, picked over to remove fat, gristle, bones
3 eggs
3 tablespoons vinegar
2 tablespoons cornstarch

3 Souplets vegetable tablets
2 tablespoons La Choy or other soy sauce
1 teaspoon salt
¼ teaspoon black pepper

1. Dissolve vegetable broth tablets in 1 cup boiling water. Add soy sauce and salt. Dissolve cornstarch in 1 cup cold water. **2.** Pour broth mixtures into soup pot and add 5 cups boiling water. Set pot on low flame. **3.** Beat eggs and slowly pour into pot, stirring soup constantly. **4.** Add vinegar, pepper, and meat or fish.

CORN SOUP

Makes 4 servings (496 calories). Calories in 1 serving: 124.

1 cup freshly cooked or canned corn kernels
1 cup tomato juice
2 cups skim milk

1 onion, finely chopped
1 tablespoon butter or margarine
Salt and pepper

1. In a saucepan, sauté the chopped onion in the butter or margarine. Cook 5 minutes, or until onion is soft and golden yellow. **2.** Add tomato juice and milk. Season to taste. Heat to boiling point, then add corn kernels. **3.** Cook soup over very low flame until corn is heated through, but do not let soup boil.

SOUTHERN FRANCE CONSOMMÉ

Makes 4 servings (260 calories). Calories in 1 serving: 65.

1 egg
4 cups well-seasoned consommé (homemade or Campbell's)

About ¼ cup bread crumbs, finely crushed
Pinch of nutmeg

1. While the consommé or broth is on low flame, beat the egg until light, and strings are out. **2.** Pour into measuring cup and add bread crumbs until you have ½ cup in all. **3.** Bring consommé to a rolling boil, add the grated nutmeg, then press the egg-crumb paste through a colander into the boiling consommé. **4.** Boil 2 more minutes, stirring steadily, and serve at once.

MEAT BALL SOUP MEXICAINE

Makes 6 servings (726 calories). Calories in 1 serving: 121.

FOR MEAT BALLS:

¾ pound ground beef round
1 egg, well beaten
¼ cup chopped scallions
1 tablespoon chopped parsley
¼ teaspoon chopped mint

¼ teaspoon marjoram
¼ teaspoon salt
⅛ teaspoon pepper
Flour for dusting

FOR SOUP:

2 beef bouillon cubes
1 egg, well beaten
1 teaspoon salt

1 small bay leaf, crushed
1 cup canned tomatoes

1. Make 1-inch meat balls by combining all meat ball ingredients. Dust with flour. 2. Dissolve bouillon cubes in 4 cups boiling water. Drop in meat balls. 3. Cover and cook slowly for 30 minutes. 4. Add teaspoon salt, crushed bay leaf and cup of tomatoes. Cover and continue slow cooking, for 45 minutes more. 5. Just before serving, stir in the well-beaten egg.

CREOLE GUMBO

Makes 6 servings (1632 calories). Calories in 1 serving: 272.

1½ pounds okra
3 crabs
½ pound fresh shrimp
½ cup lard
1 onion, minced
1 clove garlic, minced

½ tablespoon tomato paste
Small piece of bay leaf
Sprig of thyme
1 tablespoon parsley, chopped fine
Salt and pepper to taste

1. Wash okra and cut into round slices ½ inch thick. 2. Immerse crabs in boiling water for a few seconds. Remove shells and quarter. 3. Put crab *shells* into a pot and cover with 1½ quarts boiling water. Boil for 30 minutes and save this water. 4. While shells are boiling, heat lard in a deep heavy pot, add okra, onion and a little salt and pepper. Cook until okra is browned. 5. Add to okra and onion mixture the tomato paste, garlic and crabs. Brown for 5 minutes. 6. Add water in which shells were cooked and boil the soup 1 hour. 7. Add the shrimp and seasonings, and simmer for 3 hours, stirring occasionally.

LOW-CALORIE GARNISHES FOR SOUPS

Thin slice of lemon
Very thin slice of hard-boiled egg
Thin slice of orange (particularly suited to tomato soup or tomato bouillon)
Small cube of custard
Chopped parsley, water cress, chives, mint or other herbs
A few grains of Puffed Wheat or Puffed Rice
Dietician Brand gluten noodles, soy-gluten macaroni or gluten squares
Popcorn
Grated raw carrot, or other low-calorie vegetable
Diced or grated cooked turnip or other low-calorie vegetable
Pieces of cooked cauliflower, broccoli or 2 or 3 green peas
A few Oysterette crackers
A few corn flakes
Small piece canned pimiento
Small cubes of low-calorie gelatin, particularly lemon flavor.

TUTTI-FRUTTI SOUP

Makes 2 servings (340 calories). Calories in 1 serving: 170.

2 cups canned or fresh fruit cocktail	2 tablespoons lemon juice 1 teaspoon unflavored gelatin

1. Soak gelatin in 2 tablespoons cold water. Melt over hot water. 2. Mix all ingredients in blender until thoroughly blended. 3. Pour into refrigerator tray and chill 1 hour. 4. Remove from refrigerator tray and return to blender for a quick blending before serving.

WATER CRESS SOUP

Makes 4 servings (480 calories). Calories in 1 serving: 120.

1 bunch water cress 2 cups homemade chicken stock or stock made with Nestlé chicken broth cubes 2 tablespoons flour	2 tablespoons butter or margarine 2 cups skim milk Salt, pepper and marjoram

1. Wash water cress, remove stems and chop up leaves very fine. 2. Bring chicken stock to a boil, add chopped water cress, then simmer for 10 minutes. 3. In another saucepan melt the butter or margarine and blend in flour. When smooth, slowly add the milk, then bring to a boil, stirring continuously. Let simmer 5 minutes. 4. Combine the mixtures, season with salt and pepper, and a pinch of marjoram. Serve at once.

CALORIES IN DESSERTS (Approximate)
AVOID ALL HIGH CALORIE DESSERTS

APPLE PIE (1 small piece)  Made with Sugar — 375 Made with Dietetic Sweetener — 175	**BAKED APPLE (1 apple)**  Made with Sugar — 140 Made with Dietetic Sweetener — 80
COOKIES (1 cookie)  Regular Cookies — 60 to 100 Dietetic Cookies — as low as 10	**CUSTARDS (1 serving)**  Regular Custards — 200 Made with Dietetic Sweetener — 70
CHOCOLATE LAYER CAKE (1 piece) 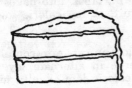 Made with Sugar — 310 Made with Dietetic Sweetener — 160	**GELATIN DESSERTS (1 serving)** Jell-O — 83 D-Zerta — 12 Glow — 7-1/2
PUDDINGS (1 serving) Average Chocolate Pudding — 200 Special Low Calorie Pudding — 45	**ICE CREAM (1/2 cup serving)**  Regular Ice Cream — 240 Made with Dietetic Mix — 80

171

LOW-CALORIE GELATIN DESSERTS

There are a number of low-calorie gelatin desserts which are sweetened with saccharin or other sugar-substitute sweetening agents.

Two of the best of these low-calorie gelatin desserts are called "D-Zerta," made by General Foods Corporation, New York City, and "Glow," made by Charles Killgore Company, Yonkers, New York.

Both bear the acceptance seal of the American Medical Association's Council on Foods and Nutrition. D-Zerta contains 12 calories, Glow contains 7½ calories; both may be eaten plain almost without counting the calories, so you can enjoy nearly all you want. Both Glow and D-Zerta are sold in diet food stores, department store food departments and in many leading drug stores.

Here are 6 different simple ways to serve D-Zerta or Glow. Use any of the 6 flavors—Strawberry, Raspberry, Cherry, Orange, Lemon or Lime.

SOLID: Dissolve in ½ cup hot water, as directed on package. Turn into mold and chill until firm. If necessary to hasten setting, place mold in ice water. Serve plain or garnish with touch of Dietician Brand low-calorie jam or jelly substitutes.

FLAKES: Mold in shallow layer. When firm, break into flakes with a fork. Serve plain, or garnish with fruit, or low-calorie mayonnaise substitute.

RICED: Mold 2 flavors of contrasting colors in separate containers. When firm, put each through ricer. Serve in alternate layers in parfait glasses. Serve plain or with low-calorie jam or jelly substitute between layers. Top with fruit.

CUBES: Mold gelatin in ½-inch layer. When firm, cut in cubes, using warm knife. Serve plain or combined with fruits. Garnish with mayonnaise substitute or top with one of the several good low-calorie strawberry or raspberry concentrates.

WHIP: Chill dissolved gelatin until cold and sirupy. Place bowl in cracked ice or ice and water and beat until fluffy and thick like whipped cream. Turn into individual molds or sherbet glasses. Chill until firm.

CRESTED WHIP: Dissolve 1 envelope D-Zerta or Glow as directed. Pour 2 tablespoons of the mixture into 2 individual molds and chill until firm. Whip the remainder of the mixture as directed above and place this over the firm layers in the molds. Chill and garnish with fruit.

ORANGE SLICES

Makes 1 serving (50 calories).

Raoul Dufy, the famous painter, insisted that our first dinner in Madrid must be at the Jockey Club, and it more than lived up to his glowing description. But dinner in Spain starts at 9 P.M.—even 10 P.M. is not late—so that on this occasion it was almost midnight before the dessert order was taken and we weakly pointed to the orange slices at the next table, held up two fingers, and to show we knew at least a word of Spanish, said "Dos!"

The "maitre dee" himself placed a large orange on a long-handled fork, held it high in the air, and with an impressive slim knife skinned down the orange to the very edge of the fruit, with the long winding peel suspended in air until the end, when it dropped, from sheer exhaustion no doubt.

The peeled orange, held by the long fork, was then thinly sliced, and sugared. And the taste was like nectar and ambrosia combined. The secret no doubt lies in finding big fully-ripened oranges, no tiny job today in Spain, where only mean little fruit is available for home consumption, and the good fruit is exported.

So find yourself a good juicy orange, take a long-handled fork and knife—and have fun. Except use a no-calorie liquid sweetener instead of sugar.

Orange slices contain not one more calorie than the juice of the same orange, yet are more filling, more satisfying. True, they take a little longer to prepare, a little longer to eat . . . but your health is at stake, and you've promised to help make this diet a success!

1 medium orange, chilled   ¼ teaspoon no-calorie sweet-
                               ener

1. Peel orange carefully. Remove any white inner skin which remains on fruit. 2. Slice very thinly. Sprinkle with ¼ teaspoon sweetener. Chill before serving.

STRAWBERRY BAVARIAN

Makes 4 servings (172 calories). Calories in 1 serving: 43.

2 envelopes strawberry flavor   milk (chilled for several
   low-calorie gelatin   hours)
⅜ cup well-chilled evaporated   ½ cup crushed fresh straw-
                                    berries (not frozen)

1. Dissolve gelatin in ½ cup boiling water. Chill until sirupy. 2. Add crushed strawberries. 3. Whip the evaporated milk until almost stiff and fold in the gelatin mixture. 4. Pour into dessert glasses and chill until firm.

VANILLA RENNET CUSTARD DESSERTS

Makes 5 servings (176 calories). Calories in 1 serving: 35.

1 Junket rennet tablet
2 cups skim milk
1½ teaspoons vanilla

1 teaspoon Sacrose liquid sweetener or 6 Sucaryl tablets (⅛ gram size)

1. Dissolve rennet tablet by crushing it in 1 tablespoon cold water. **2.** Add the sweetener and vanilla to the milk. Warm very slowly until lukewarm, stirring constantly. Test temperature on inside of your wrist, and when liquid is comfortably warm (110°F.), not hot, remove from heat immediately. Stir in the dissolved rennet tablet quickly, for a few seconds only. **3.** Have 5 dessert glasses ready and pour in mixture at once, while still liquid. Do not disturb for about 10 minutes, while milk sets. Then chill.

Variations: (all having about the same calorie count—44 in a serving)

ALMOND RENNET DESSERT: Follow basic recipe but omit vanilla and add 1¼ teaspoons almond flavoring.

LEMON RENNET DESSERT: Follow basic recipe but omit vanilla and add 1 teaspoon lemon extract and a few drops yellow food coloring.

ORANGE RENNET DESSERT: Follow basic recipe but omit vanilla and add 1 teaspoon orange extract and a few drops orange food coloring.

PEPPERMINT RENNET DESSERT: Follow basic recipe but omit vanilla and add 2 drops oil of peppermint and a few drops red food coloring.

CRISPY COOKIES

Makes 2 dozen cookies (358 calories). Calories with 1 tablespoon sugar: 406. Calories with 2 tablespoons sugar: 454. Calories in 1 cookie without sugar: 15. Calories in 1 cookie using 1 tablespoon sugar: 17. Calories in 1 cookie using 2 tablespoons sugar: 19.

2 egg whites
1 teaspoon Sacrose no-calorie sweetener
¼ teaspoon almond extract

1 or 2 tablespoons sugar, optional
2 cups Kellogg's Corn Soya cereal

1. Place egg whites, Sacrose and almond extract in a mixing bowl. **2.** Beat until egg whites are stiff, gradually adding the sugar, if used. **3.** Fold in Corn Soya shreds. Drop mixture, by teaspoonful, 1 inch apart on lightly greased cookie sheet. **4.** Bake in moderately hot oven (375°F.) until lightly browned and crisp, about 10 minutes.

LEMON JELLY

Makes 4 servings (30 calories). Calories in 1 serving: 7½.

4 envelopes lemon flavor low-   Rind of ½ lemon
calorie gelatin

1. Place 2 cups water in a saucepan with the lemon rind. Bring to a boil and remove rind. 2. Dissolve gelatin in the boiling water. Mix thoroughly. Do not cook. 3. Allow to cool and pour into serving dish or mold. Chill in refrigerator until set.

NEAPOLITAN GELATIN

Makes 3 servings (36 calories). Calories in 1 serving: 12.

1 envelope each of orange,   low-calorie gelatin
lime and raspberry flavors,

1. Dissolve the 3 envelopes of gelatin separately, each in ½ cup boiling water. Chill until all are sirupy. 2. Pour raspberry into square glass ice-box dish, then layer of lime and on top, layer of orange. 3. Chill till firm. Slice with warm knife and serve.

MOCHA CREAM

Makes 2 servings (32 calories). Calories in 1 serving: 16.

1 teaspoon plain unflavored   1 tablespoon Choc-low low-
gelatin   calorie substitute for choco-
¾ cup hot coffee   late sirup

1. Soak the gelatin in 1 tablespoon cold water. 2. Stir Choc-low sirup into the hot coffee until blended. 3. Add gelatin and stir until dissolved. 4. Chill in refrigerator until thick and sirupy, but not set. 5. Remove from refrigerator and whip with rotary beater or electric mixer until very light and frothy. 6. Pour into ½-pint mold or small bowl and return to refrigerator until firm. 7. Unmold and serve at once.

RHUBARB STRAWBERRY GELATIN

Makes 1 serving (17 calories).

1 envelope strawberry flavor   Scant ¼ cup fresh rhubarb,
D-Zerta low-calorie gelatin   diced
dessert

1. Add rhubarb to ½ cup hot water and simmer until tender. 2. Measure and add hot water to make ⅝ cup. Add gelatin and stir until dissolved. 3. Turn into individual mold or parfait glass. Chill until firm.

DIET "WHIPPED CREAM" (using evaporated milk)

Makes 2¼ cups (224 calories). Calories in ¼ cup: 25; in 1 tablespoon: 6.

1 small can evaporated milk, 5 oz.	2 teaspoons Sacrose saccharin liquid sweetener (or
1 tablespoon lemon juice	Sucaryl)

1. Pour evaporated milk into freezing tray of refrigerator and freeze until ice crystals begin to form around edge. **2.** Pour chilled milk into a cold bowl and whip with a cold beater until stiff. **3.** Add lemon juice and Sacrose and continue beating until well mixed. **4.** Serve as topping for stewed fruits, or blend with Sacrose-sweetened puréed fruits for fruit whips, frozen desserts, or "Glow" low-calorie gelatin desserts.

DIET "WHIPPED CREAM" (using skim milk powder)

Makes 2¼ cups whipped topping (220 calories). Calories in ¼ cup: 25; in 1 tablespoon: 6.

1 tablespoon lemon juice	½ cup non-fat dry milk solids
2 teaspoons saccharin liquid sweetener or Sucaryl	(skim milk powder)

1. Place ½ cup cold water in bowl. Add lemon juice, Sacrose and milk powder. **2.** Beat with rotary beater or electric mixer until as thick as marshmallow cream. **3.** This topping will stay light and fluffy for about 30 minutes.

Variation: SPICY FLUFFY TOPPING
Calories in 1 tablespoon: 7.
Add to the above recipe before beating, ¼ teaspoon cinnamon and ⅛ teaspoon nutmeg.

Variation: WHIPPED COFFEE TOPPING
Calories in 1 tablespoon: 8.
Add 1 teaspoon instant coffee before beating.

Variation: WHIPPED ORANGE TOPPING
Calories in 1 tablespoon: 8.
Add 1 tablespoon grated orange rind after beating. Blend in.

PINEAPPLE CHEESE DESSERT

Makes 4 servings (160 calories). Calories in 1 serving: 40.

½ cup pineapple tidbits, fresh or unsweetened canned	4 tablespoons cottage cheese 2 tablespoons orange juice

1. Blend all the ingredients, set in 4 serving glasses, chill and serve.

STRAWBERRY SPONGE

Makes 2 servings (36 calories). Calories in 1 serving: 18.

2 envelopes strawberry flavor low-calorie gelatin dessert

½ stiffly beaten egg white

Dietician Brand apricot jam substitute

Nutmeg, to taste

1. Dissolve gelatin in 1 cup boiling water. **2.** When mixture begins to thicken, beat until frothy and fold in egg white. **3.** Pour into sherbet glasses, garnish with jam substitute and sprinkle with nutmeg.

BERRY WHIP

Makes 2 servings (about 35 calories). Calories in 1 serving: about 18.

1 envelope strawberry or raspberry flavor Glow or D-Zerta low-calorie gelatin

Scant ½ cup fresh or water-packed canned sliced strawberries or ⅜ cup raspberries

1. Dissolve gelatin in ½ cup boiling water. Chill until sirupy. **2.** Place bowl in ice and water or cracked ice and beat for about 4 minutes until thick and fluffy. **3.** Fold in berries. **4.** Turn into sherbet or parfait glasses or individual molds and chill until firm.

Variation: PEACH WHIP
Calories in 1 serving: 15.
Substitute orange flavor low-calorie gelatin and 5 tablespoons, unsweetened peaches, finely cut, in above recipe.

Variation: CHERRY WHIP
Calories in 1 serving: 21.
Substitute cherry flavor low-calorie gelatin and 14 pitted, unsweetened, red cherries in above recipe.

Variation: APRICOT WHIP
Calories in 1 serving: 18.
Substitute lime or strawberry flavor low-calorie gelatin and 2 small unsweetened fresh or canned apricots, finely cut, in above recipe.

LEMON–APRICOT FLUFF

Makes 2 servings (38 calories). Calories in 1 serving: 19.

2 envelopes lemon flavor low-calorie gelatin dessert (Glow or D-Zerta)

2 tablespoons Dietician Brand apricot jam substitute

¼ grated lemon rind

Mint leaves

1. Dissolve gelatin in 1 cup boiling water. Do not cook. Allow to cool and chill until slightly thick. 2. Beat light and fluffy. Add jam substitute and grated lemon rind. Mix well. 3. Pour into sherbet glasses. Add mint leaf.

FRUIT JELLY

Makes 3 servings (70 to 90 calories). Calories in 1 serving: 23 to 30.

3½ envelopes lemon or lime flavor low-calorie gelatin	Cut-up sections of orange or grapefruit, or of other low-calorie fruit

1. Add gelatin to 1¾ cups boiling water and stir until dissolved. 2. When gelatin is nearly set, stir in fruit. Place in mold and chill in refrigerator.

COFFEE GELATIN DESSERT

Makes 6 servings (150 calories). Calories in 1 serving: 25.

1 tablespoon unflavored gelatin (1 envelope Knox's)	1 teaspoon vanilla
1 cup skim milk	½ teaspoon salt
1 cup cold strong coffee	1 teaspoon Sacrose or other no-calorie liquid sweetener
2 egg whites, stiffly beaten	

1. Soak the gelatin in the cold milk for 5 minutes, in the top of a double boiler. Then stir over hot water until the gelatin is dissolved. 2. Add the Sacrose and salt, and stir until dissolved, then add the coffee. 3. Chill in refrigerator until the mixture becomes about as thick as raw egg white, then add the vanilla and beat until foamy. 4. Fold the mixture into the 2 stiffly beaten egg whites. Pour into a mold or serving dish, and chill until set.

BUTTERSCOTCH CHARLOTTE GLACÉ

Makes 2 servings (52 calories). Calories in 1 serving: 26.

1 envelope Dietician Brand butterscotch flavor pudding	2 Sweetlow calorie reduced sandwich wafers (or 2 halves of Nabisco sugar wafers)
½ teaspoon vanilla	
Pinch of ginger or nutmeg	

1. Prepare the pudding according to directions on the package. 2. When slightly cool, season with vanilla and ginger or nutmeg, to taste. Blend well. 3. Fill in individual molds or glasses and put in freezing compartment of the refrigerator. Stand Sweetlow Wafer in side of each serving dish.

SPICED BUTTERSCOTCH PUDDING

Makes 2 servings (52 calories). Calories in 1 serving: 26.

1 envelope Dietician Brand
    butterscotch pudding
½ tablespoon strong coffee
Rind of ¼ lemon, grated

⅛ teaspoon cinnamon
⅛ teaspoon cloves
⅛ teaspoon allspice

1. Prepare pudding according to directions on package. 2. When slightly cool, blend well with coffee and spices. 3. Pour into 2 dessert glasses and chill until set. Serve topped with grated lemon rind.

GINGER PEAR DESSERT

Makes 1 serving (27 calories).

1 envelope D-Zerta or Glow
    low-calorie gelatin dessert,
    any flavor
⅛ teaspoon ginger
⅛ teaspoon salt

2 tablespoons fresh or canned
    unsweetened pears, diced
1 tablespoon Choc-low low-
    calorie sirup

1. Dissolve gelatin, ginger and salt in ½ cup hot water. 2. Chill and, when slightly thickened, fold in pears. 3. Turn in individual mold and chill until firm. 4. Unmold, and serve with tablespoon Choc-low sirup.

BANANA GELATIN

Makes 4 servings (120 calories). Calories in 1 serving: 30.

4 packages low-calorie gela-
    tin, any flavor

1 ripe banana

1. Dissolve gelatin in 2 cups boiling water. Chill until slightly thickened. 2. Partly fill 4 dessert glasses with gelatin and add slices of banana. 3. Fill mold with remaining gelatin. Chill until firm. Garnish each dish with banana slice, berry, or other fruit slice.

FROZEN ORANGE DESSERT

Makes 2 servings (60 calories). Calories in 1 serving: 30.

2 envelopes orange flavor low-
    calorie dessert (Glow or
    D-Zerta)

Grated rind of ¼ orange

1. Dissolve gelatin in 1 cup boiling water. 2. Mix well with grated orange rind. 3. Cool mixture and pour into molds. Chill.

SELF-LAYERING FRUIT DESSERT

Makes 1 serving (30 to 40 calories).

1 envelope orange flavor D-Zerta low-calorie gelatin dessert
One of these 4 combinations of fruit:
1 tablespoon cooked pineapple, diced, and 1½ tablespoons fresh strawberries, sliced

or

2 to 3 slices cooked peaches, diced, and 1 rounded table-spoon blueberries

or

1 rounded tablespoon cooked pears, diced, and 5 or 6 blackberries

or

½ cooked apricot, finely cut, and 2 teaspoons raspberries

1. Dissolve gelatin in ½ cup hot water. Pour into parfait or sherbet glasses or individual molds. 2. Add fruits, using one of the above combinations. The heavy fruits will sink to the bottom and the light fruits will float. 3. Chill until firm.

Variation: LEMON FLAVOR FRUIT DESSERT
Substitute in the above recipe lemon flavor low-calorie gelatin and one of these two fruit combinations:

3 to 4 slices cooked peaches, diced, and 5 or 6 blackberries

or

1 tablespoon cooked raspberries, and 4 medium melon balls

SACROSE SWEETENED CANNED FRUITS

Makes 2½ cups (about 175 calories). Calories in ½ cup: 35.

1 No. 2 can water-pack fruit   1 to 2 teaspoons Sacrose liquid saccharin

1. Pour fruit into jar with tight-fitting cover. Lightly mix in the Sacrose. 2. Allow to stand for a few hours, preferably overnight, in the refrigerator.

One teaspoon of Sacrose will sweeten the fruit to the equivalent of fruit packed in a light sirup.

Two teaspoons of Sacrose will sweeten the fruit to the equivalent of fruit packed in heavy sirup.

High quality water-packed fruit meant for table use may be purchased in No. 2 cans in the following varieties: apricots, cherries, peaches, pears and fruit salad.

FRUIT BOWL

Makes 6 servings (300 calories). Calories in 1 serving: 50.

2 medium fresh peaches
1½ cups strawberries
½ cup huckleberries or blueberries

1 slice pineapple, ¾ inch
  thick
½ teaspoon lemon juice
Mint leaves

1. Peel and slice peaches, wash berries, hull strawberries, crush pineapple. **2.** Arrange fruit in interesting pattern in bowl, sprinkle with lemon juice, and chill for 1 hour or more. **3.** Garnish with mint leaves and serve at once.

STEWED APRICOTS

Makes 4 servings (200 calories). Calories in 1 serving: 50.

20 halves dried apricots
Lemon juice

Powdered ginger

1. Wash apricots thoroughly and soak for about 2 hours in just enough hot water to cover fruit. **2.** Simmer, covered, in soaking water until tender. Add lemon juice and ginger to taste.

APPLE MOUSSE

Makes 6 servings (300 calories). Calories in 1 serving: 50.

2 cups hot applesauce, unsweetened
1 egg white, stiffly beaten

2 tablespoons currant jelly
Cinnamon or nutmeg

1. Pour applesauce over jelly; stir until jelly is dissolved. Cool. **2.** Fold in egg white. Pour into 6 sherbet glasses, sprinkle with cinnamon or nutmeg, and chill for 1 hour before serving.

SNOW PUDDING

Makes 6 servings (270 calories). Calories in 1 serving: 45.

4 envelopes lemon flavor low-
  calorie gelatin

Grated rind of ½ lemon
2 egg whites, stiffly beaten

1. Prepare recipe for Lemon Jelly (see p. 175) but chill only until gelatin is as thick as raw egg white. **2.** Beat until foamy. Add grated lemon rind. **3.** Fold this foamy mixture into the stiffly beaten egg whites and continue beating until it holds its shape. **4.** Pour into serving dish and chill in refrigerator until firm. Unmold and serve.

APPLESAUCE GELATIN DESSERT

Makes 4 servings (208 calories). Calories in 1 serving: 52.

3½ envelopes lemon flavor   ½ teaspoon vanilla
low-calorie gelatin   4 sprigs of mint
3 small apples

1. Make applesauce with apples by cooking them in 1 cup water. When they are tender, rub through a sieve, then add vanilla. If apples are tart, add a few drops of non-calorie sweetener, and mix in thoroughly. 2. Add ¾ cup water to gelatin and stir until dissolved. Add to applesauce. 3. Place in refrigerator and when it begins to stiffen, beat until light. Heap in serving glasses.

CHILLED GRAPEFRUIT

Makes 4 servings (208 calories). Calories in 1 serving: 52.

2 medium grapefruits   1 lime

1. Halve grapefruits and free the sections. 2. Squeeze lime juice over the fruit and chill for 1 hour or more.

STEWED FRUITS

INGREDIENTS			NUMBER OF SERVINGS	TOTAL CALORIES	CALORIES IN ONE SERVING
FRUIT	WATER	SACROSE			
Apples 2 lbs.	½ cup	1 t.	4	232	58
Plums 1 lb.	½ cup	1 t.	3	195	65
Peaches 1 lb.	½ cup	1 t.	3	183	61
Dried Apricots 6 oz.	1½ cups	1½ t.	4	445	111*
Cranberries 1 cup	½ cup	1 T.	3	54	18

t = teaspoon   T = tablespoon

While Sacrose was used in testing, other non-caloric liquid sweeteners are equally satisfactory.

*Since dried apricots are comparatively high in calories, a partial portion may be mixed with other fruits.

STEWED FRUIT SPECIAL DIRECTIONS

APPLES

Wash apples. Core and cut in eighths. Place in saucepan. Add water. Cover and bring to boil. Simmer until apples are tender, about 15 minutes. Press through sieve or food mill. Add Sacrose and about ⅛ teaspoon nutmeg or cinnamon, mixing thoroughly. Makes 2¼ cups applesauce, or 4 servings.

PLUMS

Wash plums. Place in saucepan and add water. Cover and bring to boil. Simmer until plums are just tender. Remove from heat. Add sweetener and mix gently. Let stand at least 10 minutes. Serve warm or cold. Makes 3 servings.

PEACHES

Peel peaches. Halve peaches and remove pits. Place peaches in saucepan. Add water. Cover and bring to boil. Simmer until peaches are tender, about 10 minutes. Remove from heat. Add Sacrose and about 1/16 teaspoon cloves. Mix gently. Let stand at least 10 minutes. Serve warm or cold. Makes 3 servings.

DRIED APRICOTS

Place apricots in saucepan. Add water. Cover and bring to boil. Let simmer until apricots are soft and plump, about 25 minutes. Remove from heat. Add Sacrose and mix gently. Let stand at least 10 minutes. Serve warm or cold. Makes 4 servings.

CRANBERRY SAUCE

Pick over cranberries, removing any stems or soft berries. Place in saucepan. Add water. Bring to boil and let cook partially covered over moderate heat until all berries burst, about 10 minutes. Remove from heat. Add Sacrose and mix gently. If desired, put berries through sieve or food mill before adding the Sacrose. Cool before serving. Makes about ¾ cup, 3 servings.

PINEAPPLE WHIP

Makes 6 servings (330 calories). Calories in 1 serving: 55.

1¾ cups unsweetened grape-fruit juice	1 tablespoon unflavored gelatin (1 envelope Knox's)
¾ cup fresh or canned unsweetened pineapple tidbits	1 tablespoon shredded coconut ⅛ teaspoon salt

1. Heat 1¼ cups of the grapefruit juice. 2. Soften gelatin in a bowl, in remaining ½ cup cold grapefruit juice. 3. Add the hot juice; stir until gelatin is dissolved. 4. Add salt and pineapple and mix well. 5. Chill until slightly thickened, then beat mixture until light and fluffy. 6. Pour into 6 glasses and chill for 2 hours, or until firm. Decorate with shredded coconut before serving.

APPLESAUCE DESSERT

Makes 1 serving (32 calories).

1 envelope lemon or lime D-Zerta or Glow low-calorie gelatin

¼ cup (generous) unsweetened applesauce

1. Dissolve gelatin in ½ cup hot water. Chill until cold and sirupy. 2. Place bowl into pan of cracked ice or ice water and beat until fluffy and thick like whipped cream. 3. Fold in applesauce. Pile in sherbet glass.

STEWED PRUNES

Makes 6 servings (300 calories). Calories in 1 serving: 50.

12 medium to large prunes Lemon juice

Several slivers orange rind

1. Cover prunes with boiling water until plump, about 1 hour. 2. Simmer, covered, with orange rind, until tender. 3. Add lemon juice, as desired.

MELON BALLS WITH STRAWBERRIES

Makes 4 servings (220 calories). Calories in 1 serving: 55.

2 cups melon balls 2 tablespoons fresh orange juice

1⅓ cups fresh strawberries Mint leaves

1. Blend ingredients. If desired, sweeten slightly with Sacrose liquid sweetener. 2. Chill for 1 hour and serve in individual glasses. Garnish with springs of mint.

LEMON OR ORANGE WHIP

Makes 1 serving (40 calories).

1 envelope low-calorie gelatin dessert, lemon or orange flavor

2 tablespoons cottage cheese ¼ teaspoon powdered cinnamon or nutmeg

1. Dissolve gelatin in ½ cup boiling water; chill until cold and sirupy. 2. Whip with rotary egg beater until fluffy. 3. Blend 2 tablespoons of cottage cheese with powdered cinnamon or nutmeg to taste and mix with gelatin. Chill.

BUTTERMILK SHERBET

Makes 6 servings (240 calories). Calories in 1 serving: 40.

1 tablespoon plain gelatin   6 tablespoons cottage cheese
  (1 envelope Knox's)   1 teaspoon vanilla flavoring
1 cup buttermilk

1. Soften gelatin in bowl, in ¼ cup cold water, for 5 minutes. **2.** Add ¾ cup hot water and stir until gelatin is dissolved. **3.** Place bowl in pan of ice water and stir until mixture begins to thicken. **4.** Thoroughly blend buttermilk, cheese and flavoring. **5.** Pour in 6 individual molds, chill until firm, about 2 hours. Unmold and serve at once.

FRUIT WHIP

Makes 1 serving (47 calories).

1 envelope lemon flavor low-   ¼ teaspoon cinnamon or nut-
  calorie gelatin   meg
2 tablespoons cottage cheese

1. Dissolve gelatin in ½ cup boiling water. Chill until sirupy. **2.** Whip with rotary egg beater until fluffy. **3.** Blend 2 tablespoons cottage cheese with cinnamon or nutmeg and mix into gelatin. Chill.

SPONGE CAKE

Makes 9-inch cake—about 20 servings (1140 calories). Calories in 1 serving: 57.

5 egg whites   1 tablespoon Sacrose no-cal-
5 egg yolks   orie sweetener
1 cup sifted cake flour   ¼ teaspoon cream of tartar
½ cup sugar   ¼ teaspoon salt
1 tablespoon lemon juice

1. Beat egg whites, salt and cream of tartar together until frothy, with rotary beater. Continue beating until whites stand up in peaks, gradually adding sugar. **2.** Place 2 tablespoons cold water, Sacrose, lemon juice and egg yolks in another mixing bowl and beat until frothy. Then beat in flour until smooth. **3.** Fold yolk mixture gently into beaten egg whites until no streaks remain. Pour into ungreased 9-inch tube pan. **4.** Bake in moderate oven (350°F.) until cake springs back into shape after being pressed lightly with fingers, about 45 minutes. **5.** Invert cake on drying rack immediately and allow to cool before removing from pan.

DUTCH CIDER DESSERT

Makes 4 servings (228 calories). Calories in 1 serving: 57.

3½ envelopes lemon flavor
dessert low-calorie gelatin
1 well-beaten egg

1 cup sweet cider
4 sprigs of mint
4 pieces of cherry

1. Boil 1¾ cups water. Add gelatin and stir until dissolved. Stir into beaten egg slowly. **2.** Cook mixture in double boiler, stirring constantly until it thickens. **3.** Remove from stove, stir in cider and cool. When it begins to thicken, place in a pan of chopped ice and beat until mixture holds its shape. **4.** Heap in sherbet glasses and garnish with a sprig of mint or with small pieces of cherry.

BISCUIT TORTONI

Makes 4 servings (228 calories). Calories in 1 serving: 57.

2 tablespoons lemon juice
½ cup non-fat dry milk solids
(skim milk powder)
¼ teaspoon almond extract

2 teaspoons liquid saccharin
sweetener
2 vanilla wafers

1. Place ½ cup cold water and lemon juice in a mixing bowl. Add milk powder and beat with rotary beater until stiff. **2.** Add Sacrose and almond extract. Beat in until thoroughly mixed. **3.** Pour mixture into freezing tray or four 5-ounce custard cups. Sprinkle lightly with finely crushed vanilla wafers. **4.** Freeze as quickly as possible with refrigerator turned to coldest setting. Serve when just frozen.

PEACH SHERBET

Makes 6 servings (350 calories). Calories in 1 serving: 58.

4 medium fresh peaches,
peeled
1½ cups buttermilk

¼ cup lemon juice
Grated rind of 1 lemon
Few grains salt

1. Remove peach pits and mash peeled peaches with fork until light and fluffy. At same time work in lemon juice and grated rind. **2.** Add buttermilk and salt. **3.** Pour into an ice-cube tray and set in freezing compartment of refrigerator. **4.** When mixture is frozen almost solid, whip until very light. Return to ice-cube tray and freeze until set. **5.** Unmold and serve at once.

GINGER BAKED PEAR

Makes 2 servings (140 calories with orange juice; 126 with water). Calories in 1 serving: with orange juice—70; with water—63.

2 ripe pears

3 tablespoons orange juice or water

⅛ teaspoon ginger

2 teaspoons Sacrose liquid saccharin sweetener

1. Wash and halve pears. Remove cores. 2. Stand two pear halves in each custard cup or individual baking dish. 3. Combine the remaining ingredients and pour over the two pears. 4. Bake in moderately hot oven (375°F.) until tender and juicy, about 30 minutes. Serve warm or cold.

FRUIT COCKTAIL WITH YOGURT OR SOUR CREAM

Makes 4 servings (about 264 calories). Calories in 1 serving: about 66.

⅛ cup fresh or frozen strawberries

⅛ cup fresh pineapple

⅛ cup sliced bananas

½ cup Dannon Yogurt or sour cream (¼ pint)

Dietician Sugarless Sweetener

1. Into 4 serving glasses distribute the strawberries and cover with 2 teaspoons yogurt or sour cream in each glass. 2. Next, make a layer of pineapple, and then another layer of yogurt or sour cream. 3. Add the bananas, and a final layer of yogurt. Top off with a large strawberry rolled in Dietician Sugarless Sweetener.

PINEAPPLE BUTTERMILK FROST

Makes 6 servings (400 calories). Calories in 1 serving: 67.

1 cup drained canned crushed pineapple

2 cups buttermilk

1 egg white, stiffly beaten

1 teaspoon non-caloric liquid sweetener

1. Combine pineapple, buttermilk and sweetener and pour into freezing tray of refrigerator. Turn refrigerator to coldest point and put tray into freezing compartment. 2. When firm (about 1 hour) turn into chilled bowl. mash with fork and add beaten egg white. Beat until fluffy but not melted. 3. Return to freezer, covering with waxed paper. Freeze until firm (about 2 hours).

SPANISH PUDDING

Makes 1 serving (68 calories).

1 envelope low-calorie gelatin   ½ cup hot skim milk
(any flavor)   1 egg white, stiffly beaten

1. Dissolve gelatin in hot milk. Cool until it begins to thicken, dropping from the mixing spoon in sheets. 2. Fold in the stiffly beaten egg white. 3. Pour into rather large individual mold and chill until set.

COFFEE SPONGE

Makes 5 servings (344 calories). Calories in 1 serving: 69.

1 tablespoon instant coffee   1 tablespoon unflavored gela-
1 cup skim milk, scalded   tin (1 envelope Knox's)
2 egg whites, stiffly beaten   ¼ cup sugar

1. Soften gelatin in ¼ cup cold water for 5 minutes. 2. Dissolve coffee and sugar in milk. Pour over gelatin, stirring until dissolved. Chill until slightly thickened. 3. Fold in beaten egg whites. Pour into individual molds and chill until firm.

APRICOT-APPLE COMPOTE

Makes 6 servings (420 calories). Calories in 1 serving: 70.

10 dried apricot halves, soaked   ⅛ teaspoonful grated lemon
4 medium apples   rind
Lemon juice, to taste   Cinnamon to taste

1. Pare, quarter and core apples. Cut into eighths. 2. Place apples in saucepan, add apricots and few tablespoons of water in which apricots have soaked. 3. Cover and simmer until apples are tender, about 20 minutes. 4. While hot, add cinnamon, lemon juice and grated rind. Serve hot or cold.

WINED GRAPEFRUIT

Makes 1 serving (83 calories). If Dietician Sugarless Sweetener is used instead of brown sugar, calories are reduced to 63. Or, a teaspoonful of the sugarless sweetener can be mixed with the brown sugar if the Wined Grapefruit is not sweet enough. In this case the calorie count remains at 83.

½ grapefruit   1 slightly rounded teaspoon
1 tablespoon sherry   brown sugar

1. Core the grapefruit and fill center with sugar and sherry. 2. Heat in moderate oven (350°F.) until sugar is melted.

PINEAPPLE À LA BIRD & BOTTLE

We call this a Bird & Bottle recipe because we first encountered this delectable dish at the famous Bird & Bottle Restaurant, in Garrison, New York. Picture yourself sitting beside a stream, under the stars, on a lovely night in July. After a heavenly meal, this colorful, yet utterly simple, pineapple dish is brought before you. We have since served it many times, always with success. Fortunately, it fits into many restricted diets.

Makes 4 servings (372 calories). Calories in 1 serving: 93.

1 whole, fresh pineapple   4 tablespoons Kirsch

1. Leave the pineapple whole, do not peel or cut off top. Lay whole pineapple on its side, cut in half lengthwise, leaves and all. Then cut halves again lengthwise, making quarters, and still leaving on the leaves. 2. Take each of the quarters, and with a sharp paring knife cut out the centers but leave a ½-inch strip along the top of the fruit, like a basket handle. 3. Slide out the center section, cut across in wedges ½-inch thick. Do this with each of the four sections. 4. Soak the groups of wedges in the Kirsch in a flat dish for about an hour, turning pieces on all sides. Then replace the pineapple wedges in each shell with the pieces sticking out alternately, a little on each side, so that they are easy to get at with a fork.

BAKED BANANAS

Makes 4 servings (400 calories). Calories in 1 serving: 100.

4 firm medium bananas   Carbonated water
½ lemon

1. Peel and halve bananas lengthwise. Put flat side down in shallow baking dish. 2. Squeeze few drops lemon juice over each banana and pour 4 tablespoons carbonated water over all. 3. Bake in slow oven (300°F.). Serve at once.

ORANGE AND BANANA AMBROSIA

Makes 6 servings (600 calories). Calories in 1 serving: 100.

2 medium-size oranges   2 tablespoons sugar
2 ripe bananas   ½ cup shredded coconut

1. Peel oranges and cut crosswise into thin slices, removing seeds and fibrous portions. 2. Peel and slice bananas. 3. Arrange a layer of orange slices on a serving dish, and sprinkle with sugar. Then make a layer of banana slices. 4. Make additional alternate layers of oranges and bananas until the fruit is used up. 5. Top with coconut, chill for 1 hour and serve.

JELLIED ORANGE JUICE

Makes 4 servings (146 calories). Calories in 1 serving: 37.

1 tablespoon unflavored gelatin (1 envelope Knox's)
1 cup orange juice
1 tablespoon lemon juice

½ teaspoon saccharin liquid
sweetener
¼ teaspoon salt

1. Soften gelatin in ¼ cup cold water. Add ½ cup boiling water
and stir until dissolved. Add sweetener and salt; stir until dissolved. Increase sweetening if desired. 2. Add orange and lemon
juices. 3. Chill in refrigerator until mixture is as thick as raw egg
white. Then stir, and if desired, set in a few very small sections
of orange. 4. Pour into mold or serving dish and chill until set.

CHOCOLATE PUDDING

Makes 4 servings (328 calories). Calories in 1 serving: 82.

3 tablespoons cornstarch
3 tablespoons cocoa
¼ teaspoon salt
2 cups fresh skim milk (or reliquefied skim milk powder)

1 teaspoon vanilla
Dash of cinnamon
1½ teaspoons Sacrose saccharin liquid sweetener

1. Mix cornstarch, cocoa and salt with ¼ cup of milk until smooth.
Meanwhile scald the remaining milk in double boiler. 2. Pour a
little of the scalded milk into the cornstarch mixture and blend
smooth. 3. Stir this slowly into remaining scalded milk, then cook,
stirring constantly, until the pudding is thick and smooth. 4. Remove the spoon, cover the double boiler, and cook 20 minutes,
stirring occasionally. 5. Cool slightly, then add Sacrose, cinnamon
and vanilla, stirring in well. Pour pudding into four 5-ounce custard cups and chill before serving.

BROILED GRAPEFRUIT

Makes 4 servings (300 calories). Calories in 1 serving: 75.

2 medium grapefruits
Cinnamon and mace

Sprigs of mint or very tiny
pieces of maraschino cherry

1. Halve grapefruits. Core, loosen sections, remove seeds. Preheat
broiler. 2. Place fruit in shallow pan, sprinkle with cinnamon and
mace. 3. Broil on rack about 3 inches below heat. Broil 15 minutes,
or until skin starts to brown and fruit is hot. 4. Garnish with mint
or pieces of cherry.

BANANA ORANGE HALF-AND-HALF

No Statue of Liberty hailed my father's tiny mother when she came to the New World in 1880. A fire at sea, a transfer to another boat, a storm—and then at long last, arrival in Philadelphia, where she was promptly greeted by a sight which scared her so, her one mad desire was to rush back home. Silly as it seems today, the cause of my grandmother's fright was just a tall colored man sitting happily on the dock eating a banana. She had never before seen a Negro, never before seen a banana, and to this mite of a woman with her immigrant brood, America appeared as a place too different ever to be home. Grandma eventually conquered the banana, and served it for breakfast, dinner and supper.

Bananas are a good filling start for the diet day . . . but you will probably have to restrict yourself to the smaller or medium-size bananas. A small banana contains about 70 calories, a medium banana 90—but a large banana contains over 115 calories, and that usually eats too deeply into your calorie allowance. Bananas are filling, contain a good amount of Vitamin A and a fair quantity of other vitamins.

Makes 2 servings (168 calories). Calories in 1 serving: 84.

1 medium orange
½ teaspoon sugarless sweetener, powdered or liquid

1 medium banana
Few shreds coconut, or very tiny pieces maraschino cherry

1. Flute the peeled banana, by running the prongs of a fork down lengthwise. Then slice the banana crosswise. 2. Carefully peel the orange, down to the fruit, and slice thinly. Lay out the slices on 2 serving plates and sprinkle with Sacrose, Sucaryl or other sugarless sweetener. 3. Place one slice of banana over each slice of orange, add more sweetener if desired, and then top off each banana with a piece or two of shredded coconut or just enough maraschino cherry to add a touch of color.

OLD-FASHIONED RICE PUDDING

Makes 6 servings (521 calories). Calories in 1 serving: 87.

¼ cup rice
1 quart skim milk
1 teaspoon vanilla extract
¼ teaspoon nutmeg

¼ teaspoon salt
1 teaspoon no-calorie sweetener

1. Scald the milk, add sweetener and salt. Stir until thoroughly dissolved. 2. Add rice, vanilla and nutmeg. 3. Pour into 1½-quart casserole and bake in very slow oven (250°F.) about 2 hours. Stir several times during the first hour. Chill before serving.

WAFFLES

Makes 4 waffles (476 calories). Calories in 1 waffle: 119.

1 tablespoon butter or margarine	1 cup Diet-mix self-rising gluten flour

1. Stir until smooth 1 cup Diet-mix in 1 cup water. You can use 1 cup skim milk instead of water, but add 87 calories for the 4 waffles—22 calories for 1 waffle. **2.** Heat waffle iron, grease lightly. Pour batter and bake 5 to 7 minutes until waffle is brown.

GRIDDLE CAKES

Makes 10 to 12 griddle cakes (460 calories, using water). Calories in 1 serving (3 griddle cakes): about 120. If milk is used, add 10 calories for each tablespoon of milk.

1 egg, beaten	Milk or water as described
¾ cup Diet-mix gluten flour	below

1. Put beaten egg into measuring cup and add enough milk (or water—or a mixture of both) to fill ¾ cup. **2.** Stir into this ¾ measured cup Diet-mix gluten flour. **3.** Beat until smooth, then drop by spoonfuls on greased griddle. Turn over when first side is brown.

FRESH FRUIT CUP

Makes 6 servings (444 calories). Calories in 1 serving: 74.

1 medium orange	Dash of vanilla or almond flavoring
1 medium grapefruit	
1 medium banana	Note—The fruit above can be varied, depending on fresh fruits available. The calories have been calculated on the above mixture, but slight variations will not seriously change the calorie count.
1 medium apple (preferably "Delicious")	
1 medium fresh apricot	
6 grapes, 2 strawberries, 6 raspberries, 3 cherries	
Juice of 1 lemon	

1. Halve grapefruit and orange, remove the sections and cut in half again. **2.** Peel and slice banana, core and dice apple. Sprinkle with lemon juice. **3.** Peel and dice apricot, peel and pit grapes, pit cherries, hull and cut up strawberries. (Do not use raspberries yet.) Mix and sprinkle on the flavoring lightly. **4.** Mix all the ingredients together and chill, covered, for at least 30 minutes. **5.** Serve in glasses, with raspberry set in center.

CHOCOLATE JUNKET

Makes 5 servings (404 calories). Calories in 1 serving: 81.

1 box chocolate flavor Junket   2 cups (1 pint) skim milk
rennet powder

1. Set out 5 dessert glasses. **2.** Warm milk in saucepan, stirring constantly. Test a drop on inside of wrist frequently. When comfortably warm (110°F.) remove at once from heat. If milk gets too hot, let cool to proper warmth, as heat destroys the rennet enzyme. **3.** Quickly stir contents of Junket powder into warm milk until it dissolves—not more than one minute. Pour at once, while still liquid, into dessert glasses. Do not move until set—about 10 minutes. Then chill in refrigerator.

Variations: Junket powder also comes in these flavors: Raspberry, Vanilla, Maple, Lemon, Orange. All these flavors run a little lower in calories than the Chocolate flavor—they contain approximately 360 calories in 5 servings or 72 calories in 1 serving.

APPLESAUCE PLEASURE

Makes 4 servings (315 calories). Calories in 1 serving: 79.

2 cups unsweetened apple-   1 cup creamed cottage cheese
sauce, chilled   Pinch of cinnamon
                                Berry or orange slice

1. Into each of 4 dessert glasses place ½ cup applesauce. **2.** Cover with ¼ cup cottage cheese and sprinkle with cinnamon. (If desired, mix.) **3.** Garnish with fresh berry or orange slice and serve at once.

PUFFED WHEAT MERINGUE SHELLS

Makes 6 servings (600 calories). Calories in 1 serving: 100.

2 egg whites   ½ teaspoon vinegar
1 cup Quaker Puffed Wheat   1 teaspoon vanilla
¼ teaspoon salt   ⅔ cup sugar

1. Add salt, vinegar and vanilla to egg whites (room temperature); beat until egg white is frothy. Add sugar, 1 tablespoon at a time, beating well after each addition. Continue beating until mixture is stiff and glossy. Fold in puffed wheat. **2.** Drop meringue in 6 portions on a cookie sheet covered with greased heavy unglazed paper. Hollow out centers with a spoon. **3.** Bake in slow oven (300°F.) for 30 to 35 minutes. Remove immediately from paper with a spatula. Cool on wire rack.

EASY SPONGE CAKE

Makes one 10-inch cake (1392 calories). Calories in 1 serving (1/12 cake): 116.

5 eggs, separated	1 teaspoon cream of tartar
1 cup cake flour, sifted 3 times	1 teaspoon vanilla extract
	1 teaspoon lemon extract
1 cup superfine sugar	½ teaspoon salt

1. Beat egg whites until foamy at medium electric mixer speed. 2. Add cream of tartar and salt. Beat until stiff. 3. Beat, in another bowl, at medium speed, egg yolks, sugar and 5 tablespoons cold water, until light yellow and fluffy. 4. Add cake flour, and vanilla and lemon extracts, to yolk mixture. Blend well, at low speed. 5. Fold in egg whites and blend. 6. Pour into ungreased 10-inch x 4-inch tube pan. Bake 70 minutes in slow oven (300°F.). Turn upside down to cool.

DEEP DISH APPLE PIE

Makes 3 servings (530 calories). Calories in 1 serving: 177.

2½ cups diced peeled apples	1 teaspoon Cream of Rice or tapioca
⅓ cup cake flour	
2 teaspoons Sacrose or other liquid saccharin sweetener	⅛ teaspoon nutmeg
	⅛ teaspoon cinnamon
4 teaspoons melted fat	Dash of salt

1. Place apples in mixing bowl. Sprinkle in the rice or tapioca, Sacrose, nutmeg and cinnamon. 2. Mix lightly together. Divide apple mixture evenly among three shallow 3-inch casseroles or three 5-ounce custard cups. 3. Place flour and salt in a mixing bowl. Combine and add the melted fat and 1 tablespoon cold water. Mix thoroughly with fork. 4. Divide pastry into three portions. Roll out each portion on lightly floured board to size of top of casseroles or custard cups. Slash pastry circles to allow steam to escape. 5. Top each pie with pastry circle. Bake in hot oven (400°F.) until pastry is lightly browned and apples are just tender, about 30 minutes. Cool to room temperature and serve.

GRAPE EGG WHITE

Makes 1 serving (43 calories).

2 tablespoons grape juice	1 egg white

1. Place grape juice in bottom of wine glass. 2. Beat egg white and add to grape juice with a little crushed ice.

COFFEE CAKE

Makes 9 servings (calories in cake alone, 802; calories in topping alone, 308; total calories: 1110). Calories in 1 serving: 123.

1 package active dry yeast	2 teaspoons Sacrose or other
⅓ cup milk, scalded	liquid saccharin sweetener
1 tablespoon sugar	½ teaspoon salt
1 egg, beaten	1½ cups enriched flour

1. Soften yeast in ¼ cup lukewarm water. Cool scalded milk to lukewarm. 2. Add to the milk: softened yeast, sugar, Sacrose, salt, egg and half of flour. Beat well. 3. Add remaining flour to make a thick batter. Cover and let rise until double, about one hour. 4. Spread dough in greased square baking pan, 8 x 8 x 2 inches. Sprinkle with crumble topping. Let rise until double again. 5. Bake in hot oven (400°F.) until done, about 30 minutes.

CRUMBLE TOPPING

1 tablespoon soft butter	⅛ teaspoon cinnamon
1 teaspoon Sacrose	¼ cup fine dry bread crumbs

1. Blend together in small bowl the butter, Sacrose and cinnamon. Sprinkle in the bread crumbs. 2. Stir until well blended. Use as topping for Coffee Cake.

BROILED FRUIT CUP

Makes 4 servings (332 calories). Calories in 1 serving: 83.

2 medium oranges	4-ounce bunch of grapes
1 large apple, diced	

1. Halve the oranges and remove sections. Clean out orange skins. 2. Halve and pit the grapes. 3. Mix diced apple, orange sections and grapes. Sweeten with Sacrose if desired. 4. Fill into orange skins and place in shallow pan on broiler rack. 5. Broil under medium heat about 3 inches away from broiler, until heated through and the tops begin to brown. Serve at once.

PINEAPPLE AMBROSIA

Makes 1 serving (77 calories).

6 tablespoons (⅜ cup) pineapple tidbits (canned, unsweetened)	1 tablespoon sherry wine
	1 teaspoon shredded coconut

1. Chill pineapple cuts. Drain off liquid. 2. Mix in the sherry, and let soak. 3. Place in serving dish and sprinkle with coconut.

PUMPKIN TART

Makes 3 tarts (220 calories). Calories in 1 tart: 73.

3 tablespoons non-fat dry milk solids (skim milk powder)
1 tablespoon liquid saccharin sweetener
¾ cup canned or cooked pumpkin

1 egg, beaten
¼ teaspoon salt
⅛ teaspoon ginger
⅛ teaspoon nutmeg
1 teaspoon grated orange rind
2 vanilla Sweetlow wafers, optional

1. Place ¾ cup water and milk powder in bowl. Beat until smooth with rotary beater. 2. Add, and beat in, the remaining ingredients. 3. Pour into three lightly-oiled 5-ounce custard cups. 4. Bake in moderate oven (350°F.) for 30 minutes. 5. Remove from oven. If you sprinkle with finely crumbled vanilla wafers, each tart will have 85 calories. Serve hot or cold.

BROILED BANANAS

Makes 4 servings (440 calories). Calories in 1 serving: 110.

4 firm bananas
1 tablespoon melted butter

Pinch of salt

1. Peel bananas and place on broiler rack. 2. Brush with butter and sprinkle lightly with salt. 3. Broil 3 to 4 inches from heat about 5 minutes on each side or until brown and tender.

Variation: BROILED BANANAS WITH APPLESAUCE

Calories in 1 serving: 145.

Cover each banana with ¼ cup unsweetened applesauce.

BAKED APPLE

Makes 2 servings (160 calories). Calories in 1 serving: 80.

2 baking apples, about 6 ounces each
⅛ teaspoon cinnamon

2 teaspoons liquid saccharin sweetener

1. Wash and core apples. Peel off skin to about a third of the way down from the top. 2. Place each apple in an individual casserole, or shallow custard cup. 3. Combine sweetener and cinnamon with ¼ cup water, and pour over the apples. 4. Bake in moderately hot oven (375°F.) until the apples are tender and juicy, about 45 minutes. Serve warm or cold.

SWEDISH OMELET DESSERT

A prized recipe of Alfred Lunt's and Lynn Fontanne's, famous stage stars.

Makes 6 servings (738 calories). Calories in 1 serving: 123.

4 eggs	1 teaspoon sugar or few drops
1½ cups scalded milk (cooled)	Sacrose
2 teaspoons butter	1 cup crushed fresh fruit

1. Beat the eggs. Add milk and sugar. **2.** Heat a casserole and grease with butter. Pour in mixture. **3.** Bake 15 to 20 minutes in hot oven (400°F.). Serve with crushed fruit.

BAKED CUSTARD

Makes 4 servings (284 calories). Calories in 1 serving: 71.

1½ cups fresh skim milk (or re-liquefied skim milk powder)	½ teaspoon Sacrose or other non-caloric liquid sweetener
2 medium eggs	Dash of salt
¼ teaspoon vanilla	Dash of nutmeg

1. Scald milk. Beat eggs, Sacrose, salt and vanilla together until well mixed. Add the scalded milk gradually, while stirring constantly. **2.** Pour custard into four 5-ounce custard cups. Sprinkle with nutmeg. **3.** Place in shallow pan. Add hot water to level of custard mixture in cups. **4.** Bake in moderately slow oven (325°F.) for 45 minutes, or until the tip of a sharp knife comes out clean when inserted in center of custard. **5.** Chill and serve. Top with Sacrose sweetened fruit purée or diet "Whipped Cream," if diet allowance permits.

ZABAGLIONE

Makes 4 servings (516 calories). Calories in 1 serving: 129.

6 egg yolks	3 tablespoons sherry flavoring
3 tablespoons sugar	Few grains salt

1. Beat egg yolks slightly. Add sugar, salt, sherry flavoring and 2 tablespoons water. **2.** Place over hot water in double boiler, but do not let water boil. **3.** Beat with rotary beater about 3 minutes, or until thick. Serve at once.

THE LOW SODIUM DIET

(Sometimes called the "Salt Free" diet)

More and more people are being put on low sodium diets by their physicians, who have found this regimen valuable in the treatment of many types of heart and kidney disorders, high blood pressure, and other conditions. Each person embarking on such a diet should have a clear understanding of what it is, to insure the best results.

Sodium is one of the mineral elements which is found in practically all foods in varying amounts. It is an essential part of the fluids of the body. Normally, the amount of sodium in your body remains about the same. If you eat more salt or other sodium foods than the body needs, it easily gets rid of the surplus. For example, you know that salty foods make you thirsty, so you drink a lot of water. This is nature's way of washing out the excess sodium.

The job of the low sodium diet is to reduce the amount of sodium in your body. This means you must become a sodium-watcher, in the same manner that the person on a reducing diet must become a calorie-watcher. Sodium is measured in milligrams, and each milligram is a very small amount, but these little milligrams can mount up if you are not careful. Your doctor will tell you the number of milligrams of sodium you can have each day; maybe as little as 200, perhaps considerably more. Whatever the amount, you must plan a menu whose total sodium content does not exceed it.

This section presents a number of pictorial charts and many recipes to help you plan these menus, and to make your diet more enjoyable. Before turning to them, here are five points to remember:

1. *Change your seasonings.* Push the salt cellar away . . . table salt is almost entirely sodium chloride, which consists of nearly one third pure sodium, a tremendously high percentage. Use no

table salt or vegetized salts in cooking or at the table. Salt substitutes sold in drug stores or at diet-food counters may be used if specifically recommended by your physician. Rely mainly on seasoning with the many herbs and spices available, all of which, except dried celery and dried parsley, are low in their sodium content. Remember that while onion, garlic and celery salts are taboo, onions and garlic may be used liberally to season foods.

2. *Get the most nourishment and enjoyment for your sodium allowance.* There are plenty of tasty, low sodium foods, including many vegetables, cereals, fruits, fresh-water fish, and an increasing number of specially prepared low sodium foods. Unsalted butter is usually available; if not, it's fun to churn your own. Canned foods labeled "no salt added" can be had wherever special diet foods are sold, but make sure that the total sodium content of the ingredients is low. Read the label . . . it should tell you the approximate sodium content in the package. For example, a vegetable soup free of salt and sodium glutamate might be excellent for your diet, while a salt-free beef soup might contain considerable sodium extracted from the meat. A bread might be advertised as "salt-free," and yet be high in sodium because of the baking soda and other ingredients added. If you cannot obtain a true low sodium bread in your neighborhood bake your own, or use a low sodium hot-roll-mix sold in diet-food stores. Low sodium milk—Lonalac—has many uses in your kitchen for reducing the sodium content of recipes.

3. *Ask about the water you use.* The sodium content of water varies in different parts of the country . . . in certain places it may be unsafe for use in a sodium-restricted diet. If you use city or town water, the sodium content will be known by the local Department of Water Supply or other supplier. If you have a local well or spring, some information as to the sodium concentration of the water in the vicinity will probably be available from the local or State Health Department. Where the sodium content is known to be high, it may be necessary for you to use a special source for your drinking and cooking water. In hard water areas, watch out for certain water softeners, which add sodium to the water. When you travel, it may be advisable to avoid places where the salt-content of the water is very high, or use special bottled water. In sections where the local water supply is deficient in iodine, your physician may prescribe iodine

to replace what you have been previously getting by using iodized salt.

4. *Do not use any medicines whatsoever unless prescribed by your physician.* Many indigestion remedies, laxatives, tonics, sleeping pills and other drugs contain sodium, and can undo the beneficial effects of a well-maintained diet.

5. *Acquire a working group of low sodium recipes.* Many of your favorite protein sources, such as meats and cheeses, have a high or medium sodium content, and it is in limiting these without stinting yourself that the greatest ingenuity will be required. Our recipes give you tempting dishes with a minimum of the higher sodium ingredients. They tell you how to prepare your own low sodium salad dressings, condiments, conserves, which you should always have ready in your refrigerator to use in dressing up your foods. These pages also supply you with recipes for tasty desserts to make your meals more interesting.

Note—No restricted diet of any kind should be undertaken unless supervised by a physician. This is particularly true of the low sodium diet . . . patients must check with the doctor regularly. In kidney disorders, use no salt substitute unless the physician consents.

ANN PILLSBURY'S LOW SODIUM BREAD

Makes 2 loaves of about 20 slices to a loaf. Each slice contains about 3 milligrams sodium; 69 calories.

1 cup (½ pint) milk
2 tablespoons sugar
1½ tablespoons vegetable shortening

1 compressed yeast cake
5½ to 6 cups enriched flour, sifted

1. Scald the milk and combine with sugar and shortening. Cool to lukewarm. **2.** Soften yeast cake in 1 cup of lukewarm water and add this to the milk mixture. Then blend in the flour. **3.** Knead the dough on a floured board. Fold toward you, pushing away with a rocking motion, using the heels of your palms. Turn the dough slightly and repeat the folding-pushing process, with a rhythmic motion. If dough sticks, add a little flour to the board. Knead for 10 minutes to obtain a fine grain. **4.** Place dough in a greased bowl and cover it. Let rise in a warm place (80° to 85°F.) about 1½ hours, or until dough will retain the impression of a finger. Punch out the gas by plunging your fist in the center of the dough. Fold over the edges; turn upside down and cover. **5.** Let rise in a warm place about ½ hour. **6.** Flatten dough on a floured board and divide into two pieces. Mold into balls; allow to stand, closely covered, for 15 minutes and shape into loaves. Place in greased bread pans (9 x 4 x 3-inch pans) and cover. 7. Allow to stand in a warm place about 1¼ hours, until dough fills the pan and the center is well above the top. Bake in a moderately hot oven (375°F.) for about 45 minutes. Do not store the loaves until they are cold.

UNSALTED BUTTER

Where to buy it; how to make it

In Europe, sweet butter is the favorite; the finest chefs make their choicest dishes with it, and it is the standard for table use. But in America we have come to use salt butter, and for those on low sodium diets, it is sometimes a problem to obtain unsalted butter. In the large cities, sweet butter can be bought in many independent grocery stores, and at some chain stores. Grocers and delicatessens catering to Jewish trade usually carry sweet butter, since many people of this faith prefer it.

Frank E. Pilley, a well-known butter man and distributor of Hanford's sweet butter in many Eastern and Midwestern cities, suggests that in rural sections anyone who needs unsalted butter should ask the local creamery to make it up specially. As unsalted butter keeps even better in the freezer than salted butter, persons who own freezers can safely purchase several pounds at a time.

H. F. Judkins of the National Dairy Products Company suggests that where unsalted butter cannot be bought locally, the low sodium dieter can make sweet butter just by whipping sweet cream until it solidifies; then pack it into a bowl or container and chill it. National Dairy and Beatrice Foods Co. have many affiliated companies which distribute sweet butter, principally in larger cities.

Churns—The Dazey Corporation of St. Louis, Mo., makes a number of splendid churns for home use. They have a one-gallon churn which sells for less than $5, and makes about two pounds of butter. It is quick, easy, and the butter has that good homemade flavor. There is also a two-gallon hand churn, and four sizes of Dazey electric churns. While these churns are usually sold only in hardware stores in rural communities, most of the leading hardware and general stores can obtain one for you promptly, if the churns are not carried in stock.

Margarine—Unsalted margarine is not usually obtainable, but diet food stores often sell a soy spread without added salt.

LOW SODIUM FOODS

BEVERAGES

Coffee, tea, Postum, ginger Ale, Coca Cola.

BREADS

Salt-free bread and rolls. Salt-free crackers and cookies. Unsalted matzohs.

CEREALS

Puffed Wheat, Shredded Wheat. Any cooked cereal made without salt.

DESSERTS

All types of fruit except dried fruit. Fruit juices. Any home-made dessert prepared without salt, baking powder or baking soda.

FATS

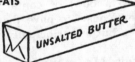

Unsalted ("sweet") butter. Salt-free margarine. Vegetable Shortening

FISH

Any fresh water fish prepared without salt.

LOW SODIUM FOODS

SALADS

All salads, with home-made salt-free dressings, or with prepared, salt-free dietetic dressings such as Frenchette.

SEASONiNGS

Vinegar, lemon juice, pepper, and all herbs and spices except parsley flakes and celery flakes.

SOUPS

Home-made broths prepared without salt (not made from bouillon cubes). Creamed soups made from low sodium milk such as Lonalac.

VEGETABLES

Fresh vegetables prepared without salt, except celery, chard, kale, dried peas.

MISCELLANEOUS FOODS

Cranberry sauce, cocoa, unsalted nuts. Grains such as barley, rice, wheat germ and wheat flour (but not self-rising flour.)

COMPARATIVELY HIGH SODIUM FOODS

EGGS

One egg has 44 mg. sodium.
One egg yolk has 6 mg. sodium.
One egg white has 38 mg. sodium.

MEAT

Beef, veal or pork.
Chicken or turkey.
Liver, kidneys, sweetbreads or brains.

MILK

One cup of whole or skim milk has 125 mg. sodium.
(One cup of Lonalac low sodium milk has 32 mg. sodium.)

MOST CANNED or FROZEN VEGETABLES

SALT WATER FISH

Cod, halibut, salmon, tuna, etc.

HIGH SODIUM FOODS	**TABLE SALT** 
VEGETABLE SALTS   Onion Salt / Garlic Salt	**BAKING POWDER and BAKING SODA** 
SALTED CRACKERS, etc.  Salted nuts, potato chips, pretzels, salted popcorn.	**ORDINARY BREAD or ROLLS**  Bread made with salt, baking powder, baking soda or self-rising flour.
PREPARED SEASONINGS   Catsup, chili sauce, mustard, Worcestershire sauce.	**SAUSAGE MEATS** 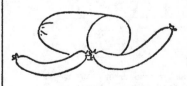 Bologna, sausages, frankfurters.

HIGH SODIUM FOODS

SALTED MEATS

Ham, bacon, salt pork, dried beef, corned beef.

SALTED FISH

Anchovies, caviar, smoked salmon, dried cod, pickled herring.

CHEESE

All types of cheese. Processed cheeses such as Velveeta have more sodium.

DRY CEREALS

Cornflakes, Bran Flakes, All-Bran, Grape-nuts, etc.

SOUPS or GRAVIES

Soups or gravies prepared from bouillon cubes or meat extract. Also most canned soups.

DESSERTS

Desserts made from rennet tablets (Junket). Baked goods made with salt or baking powder.

MISCELLANEOUS FOODS

Olives, sauerkraut, peanut butter, pickles.

LOW SODIUM WHITE BREAD NO. 2

Makes 2 loaves of about 20 slices each. Each slice contains 1 milligram sodium; 69 calories.

5 cups sifted flour, plus flour for dusting board
½ cup low sodium milk powder
1 yeast cake (1 ounce)
2 tablespoons sugar

¼ cup unsalted butter, Crisco or Spry. Extra butter or vegetable oil to brush on loaves
Grated rind of ¼ lemon

1. Melt butter or shortening in saucepan with 2 cups water and pour this mixture into a large bowl. Add the sugar and lemon rind. 2. When mixture is lukewarm, crumble in the yeast cake and stir until perfectly smooth. 3. Mix the low sodium milk powder with 2 cups of the flour. Sift twice and then stir well into the mixture. Stir in the other 3 cups of flour. 4. Knead dough on well-floured board, until smooth. Return dough to bowl and brush with melted butter or vegetable oil. Cover and let rise until twice the size. 5. Cut the dough through to break the air bubbles, turn out on board again, and knead into loaf shape. Place in 2 well-greased pans, filling only half full. When dough again rises to double its bulk, bake in moderate oven (350°F.), for 45 to 50 minutes, or until bread is brown and shrinks from pan.

QUICK, EASY HOT ROLLS

Makes 10 rolls. Each roll contains about 5 milligrams sodium; 160 calories.

1 jar Killgore's Hot Roll Mix (this contains packet of yeast)

1. Remove envelope of yeast from inside of package. 2. Measure 4 ounces (½ cup) very warm water into a mixing bowl, making sure this is 115° to 125°F. (much warmer than lukewarm). Sprinkle yeast over water and stir until dissolved. Add entire package of Roll Mix immediately. Mix well. Grease top lightly and cover. 3. Permit it to rise in a warm place, 85° to 90°F., until double in bulk, from ½ hour to 1 hour. Prewarmed oven with the door left open is satisfactory. CAUTION! Do not make this overly warm since excessive heat destroys the action of the yeast. 4. Take out leavened dough and knead about 30 strokes. Shape this into small rolls by rolling in the hand. Make sure hands are greased so dough doesn't stick. To make clover leaf rolls, use three small balls for each roll. 5. Place each roll in a greased pan. Dough should fill half the pan. Permit this to rise in a warm place, until it is double in bulk again. Bake in a hot oven (400°F.) approximately 15 minutes.

Variations: Nuts, fruits or spices may be added to this mix, or rolls may be coated with sirup as they are baked.

SCOTCH SHORTBREAD

Makes 8 servings. Each serving contains 2 milligrams sodium; 338 calories.

1 cup unsalted butter
½ cup sugar

2 cups sifted flour

1. Cream the butter and sugar. Add flour gradually. Knead by hand on floured board until dough can be rolled out. It is important to knead for a long time. Best results are obtained in a cool room. **2.** Chill shortbread and roll to ¼-inch thickness. Make into large circle, pinch like pie crust and cut into four sections. **3.** Bake until a delicate brown in moderately slow oven (325°F.) for about 20 minutes.

PECAN BUTTERSCOTCH BUNS

Makes 16 buns. Each bun contains 13 milligrams sodium; 170 calories.

1 package dry yeast or 1 cake compressed yeast
⅓ cup milk
½ teaspoon lemon juice
2 tablespoons sugar
2 tablespoons vegetable shortening
1 egg, well beaten
¼ teaspoon grated lemon rind

2 cups all-purpose flour
⅔ cup brown sugar
1 teaspoon cinnamon
3 tablespoons melted butter or margarine
½ cup seedless raisins
¼ cup dark corn sirup
¼ cup broken pecan meats

1. Scald milk in saucepan. Remove from stove and add lemon juice, sugar and shortening. Blend well and set aside until lukewarm. **2.** Sprinkle yeast or crumble yeast cake into mixing bowl, let stand a little, then stir until dissolved. **3.** Stir in milk mixture. Add egg and lemon rind. Sift flour and measure. Add 1 cup to mixture and beat smooth. Stir in remainder. **4.** Turn out on floured board; knead until dough springs back when pressed lightly. Wash and grease a bowl and place dough in bowl. Turn over dough to grease entire surface. Cover with towel and let rise in warm place (80°F.) until it doubles, or about 1 hour. **5.** Mix brown sugar and cinnamon. Use half the butter to grease 9-inch square pan; spread half of sirup on bottom. Sprinkle on half of sugar mixture, all of pecan pieces. **6.** Roll raised dough on lightly floured board, into a rectangle about 8 inches by 16 inches. Spread with remaining butter, then spread on sirup; sprinkle on remaining sugar, then the raisins. **7.** Roll up like long strudel or jelly roll. Slice into 16 one-inch pieces, using long sharp knife. Pat slices into rounds if they get out of shape. Place slices cut side down in the pan. Cover with towel and let rise in warm place (80°F.)

for about 1 hour, or until buns are light and double in bulk. **8.** Bake in moderately slow oven (325°F.) for 35 to 40 minutes. Stand on rack about a minute, then turn upside down on shallow pan or tray. Separate with fork and serve warm.

NORWEGIAN CHRISTMAS BREAD

One ½-inch slice contains about 15 milligrams sodium (citron not calculated); 300 calories.

1 pint milk	½ box raisins
1 cake yeast	½ cup citron
½ pound unsalted butter	1 teaspoon cardamom
1 cup sugar	2 pounds flour (approximately)

1. Mix the yeast in 1 cup of milk and a little flour. Let stand in a warm place until it rises (about an hour). **2.** Mix the butter (half of it melted, the other solid), sugar, raisins (which have been rinsed), citron, cardamom (which has been powdered) and the rest of the milk and about 1½ pounds of flour. Add the yeast. **3.** Let stand in a warm place again until it rises. Knead with more flour and put in greased forms. **4.** Let stand to rise again. When it has risen, place in moderate oven (350° to 400°F.). **5.** Do not bake too long, about 40 minutes.

WELSH LEEK SOUP

Makes 6 servings. Each serving contains 3 milligrams sodium; 142 calories.

4 large leeks	2 tablespoons unsalted butter
4 medium potatoes	or salad oil
1 medium onion, finely	2 egg yolks
chopped	Pinch of oregano or basil
2 tablespoons flour	

1. Wash and trim leeks; cut in half lengthwise, then crosswise in small pieces. **2.** Peel and slice potatoes. Simmer in 6 cups water, until tender. **3.** Melt butter or oil in a skillet and cook the chopped onion and leeks until not quite brown. **4.** Stir in the flour and cook a few minutes longer until flour is blended. Moisten with a little of the potato water and stir to a smooth paste. **5.** Put leek-and-onion mixture into saucepan with the potatoes and continue to simmer until potatoes are very soft. Turn into a sieve and force the vegetables through. **6.** Return the puréed soup to the saucepan and reheat. Add pinch of oregano or basil. Beat the egg yolks and place in a soup tureen. Pour the hot soup over the eggs, and stir. Serve at once.

TOMATO AND BARLEY SOUP

Makes 4 servings. Each serving contains 24 milligrams sodium; 185 calories.

½ cup fine barley
2 cups stewed or canned
unsalted tomatoes
1 onion

2 tablespoons unsalted butter, or salad oil
2 tablespoons flour
Salt substitute

1. Rinse barley in cold water. Put in pot with tomatoes, onion and 4 cups water. 2. Cook over medium flame 45 minutes, or until barley is tender. Put through sieve. 3. Heat the butter or oil, mix with flour, and stir in a little of the soup. Cook 3 minutes and add to soup. Simmer for few minutes. Add salt substitute.

SCANDINAVIAN CREAM SOUP

Makes 8 servings. Each serving contains 35 milligrams sodium; 310 calories.

½ pound sago or pearl tapioca
1 pint cream
3 egg yolks
¾ cup white wine
2 tablespoons cognac
⅓ cup raisins

1 tablespoon grated lemon peel
4 almonds
Sugar, to taste (calories calculated for ¼ cup sugar)

1. Cook sago or pearl tapioca for 3 hours in 6 quarts of water, covered, over low flame. 2. Add raisins, grated lemon peel, almonds, wine and cognac. 3. Beat yolks and cream separately. Add to soup just before serving. Sugar to taste.

DRIED FRUIT SOUP (HOT OR COLD)

A cold soup, somewhat like this, is called Hedelmakeitto, in case you are interested.

Makes 6 servings. Each serving contains 5 milligrams sodium; 160 calories.

6 prunes
3 dried apricot halves
3 dried pear halves
½ cup seedless raisins
½ cup sugar

1 piece cinnamon (2-inch stick)
1½ tablespoons Minute Tapioca or cornstarch

1. Wash fruit in hot water. Pour over 1 quart boiling water and let stand until fruit is plump. 2. Add all other ingredients, cover, and cook slowly for about 1 hour, until fruit is tender and tapioca clear. (If cornstarch is used instead of tapioca, mix it with the sugar first, before adding to the fruit water.) Serve hot or cold.

CHERRY SOUP

Makes 4 servings. Each serving contains 2 milligrams sodium; 155 calories.

1 No. 2 can pitted cherries	Pinch of cinnamon
¼ cup rice	Raspberry juice
1 tablespoon potato flour	Sugar, to taste (calories calcu-
3 drops lemon juice	lated for ¼ cup sugar)

1. Cook rice in a quart of boiling water. **2.** When almost tender add all other ingredients except potato flour. **3.** Mix 1 tablespoon of potato flour in 2 tablespoons cold water, and stir this into soup.

COLD FRESH FRUIT SOUP

Makes 6 servings. Each serving contains 3 milligrams sodium; 105 calories.

2 cups fresh fruit—cherries, strawberries, raspberries or plums	1 piece cinnamon (2-inch stick)
½ cup sugar	1 tablespoon Minute Tapioca or cornstarch
Grated rind of 1 lemon	¼ cup white wine

1. Cook all ingredients, except wine, in 1 quart of water. Cook until fruit is soft and tapioca clear. (If cornstarch is used, mix with sugar first, before adding to water.) **2.** Put through a fine sieve. Cool and add wine. Serve very cold.

STUFFED MEAT LOAF WITH TOMATOES

Makes 6 servings. Each serving contains about 73 milligrams sodium; 480 calories.

1 green pepper, ½ finely diced and ½ sliced	1 minced onion
2 tablespoons vegetable short-ening or oil	2 cups soft crumbs of low-sodium bread
1 tablespoon tarragon vinegar	1 can unsalted tomatoes
	1½ pounds ground meat
	Pepper

1. Cook diced green pepper and onion in fat until they begin to brown. **2.** Mix with bread crumbs and add enough liquid from a can of tomatoes to make a moist stuffing. **3.** Season ground meat with tarragon vinegar and pepper and divide in half. **4.** Place one half in baking dish to form layer and top with stuffing. Cover with remaining meat. **5.** Decorate top with sliced green pepper. Pour remaining tomatoes over meat. Bake in a moderate oven (350°F.) 1 hour.

MEAT PATTIES

Makes about 18 patties. Each patty contains about 29 milligrams sodium; 90 calories.

1⅔ cups cooked rice
2 tablespoons chopped onion
1 pound ground lean beef

1 cup evaporated milk
1 egg
1 teaspoon salt substitute

1. Combine all ingredients, with ⅔ cup water, and mold into patties. 2. Place in greased pan, add 3 tablespoons boiling water and bake in a hot oven (400°F.).

VEAL VIENNA

Makes 4 servings. Each serving contains 68 milligrams sodium; 305 calories.

3 medium onions
2 tablespoons vegetable
shortening
1 veal cutlet, 1½ inches thick
½ cup flour
⅛ teaspoon pepper
¼ tablespoon paprika

1 cup (1 container) yogurt
1 tablespoon fresh grated
horseradish
¼ teaspoon nutmeg
¼ teaspoon rosemary
1 teaspoon sugar

1. Slice onions; brown in hot fat. Remove from frying pan. 2. Dredge cutlet with flour, pepper and paprika mixed; brown well on both sides in remaining fat. Return onions to pan. 3. Combine yogurt, horseradish, nutmeg, rosemary and sugar; pour into pan; cover. 4. Simmer about 1 hour, or until meat is tender.

VEAL SCALLOPINI NO. 1

Makes 4 servings. Each serving contains 61 milligrams sodium; 350 calories.

1 pound veal cutlet, very thinly
sliced, and pounded
2 tablespoons olive oil or cooking oil
1 clove garlic, crushed
½ cup white wine

2 teaspoons lemon juice
Flour
Pinch of marjoram
Pinch of thyme
Dash of pepper

1. Cut meat in pieces about 3 inches long. Roll in peppered flour. 2. Place oil and crushed garlic in skillet, heat, and add seasonings. Brown the meat in this. 3. Add the wine, lemon juice and ½ cup water. Cover and simmer about 30 minutes, or until meat is tender.

VEAL SCALLOPINI NO. 2

Makes 1 serving. Contains 110 milligrams sodium; 294 calories.

1 large veal chop (8 ounces)
1 teaspoon vegetable shortening
½ tablespoon flour
1 tablespoon sherry
¼ clove garlic, cut in slivers

1. Dip chop in flour. Heat fat, brown chop quickly on both sides. **2.** Pour sherry and ¼ cup water over meat. Place slivered garlic on top. **3.** Cover and simmer 25 to 30 minutes, or until tender, replenishing water if necessary. **4.** When serving, spoon liquid from pan over the chop.

BEEF PIE

Makes 8 servings. Each serving contains about 90 milligrams sodium; 504 calories.

3 pounds beef, economical cut
6 small onions, finely chopped
2 tablespoons suet, or vegetable shortening
2 small fresh carrots, diced
¼ pound raw mushrooms,
sliced
1 teaspoon black pepper
¼ teaspoon dried tarragon
¼ teaspoon ground ginger
¼ teaspoon ground cinnamon
¾ cup red wine
Pastry for 1-crust pie, made
without salt
Melted butter, unsalted, to
brush on pie crust

1. Dry and cube meat; sauté in suet or shortening until light brown, then cook slowly with 1 cup water for 1 hour. **2.** Add onions, carrots, mushrooms, seasonings. Cook slowly for ½ hour more. Then pour into baking dish and add the wine. **3.** Set pastry top on pie, crimp edge and prick with fork tine to let out steam. **4.** Brush top with butter. Bake in hot oven (425°F.) for 20 to 30 minutes.

PORK WITH HORSERADISH

Makes 4 servings. Each serving contains 70 milligrams sodium; 440 calories.

1 pound lean tender pork
½ cup vinegar
2 tablespoons ground horseradish (homemade)
4 onions
1 bay leaf
Unsalted butter
Pepper

1. Slice onions and brown lightly in butter. Cut pork into 2- to 3-inch lengths and add to onions. **2.** Cover with ½ cup boiling water and the ½ cup vinegar. Crush bay leaf and add. **3.** Sprinkle on pepper and simmer very gently until meat is tender—about 1 hour. **4.** When done, place on hot platter and sprinkle with the grated horseradish.

ROAST BEEF IN WINE

Makes 6 servings. Each serving contains 120 milligrams sodium; 700 calories.

3 pounds top sirloin of beef, or bottom round	1 bay leaf
1 pint red wine	3 thin slices lemon
1 finely chopped clove garlic	4 thin slices onion
⅛ teaspoon thyme	Beef drippings or vegetable shortening

1. Mix wine, seasonings, lemon and onion slices. Pour over the roast and let stand in cool place for at least 5 hours. 2. Remove from marinade; save sauce. Place beef in roasting pan and dot top well with beef drippings or Crisco. 3. Place, uncovered, in moderate oven (350°F.) until meat begins to brown. Then add marinating sauce, with ½ cup boiling water. 4. Cover pan and cook 3 or 4 hours longer, basting occasionally, until meat is tender.

VEAL STEAK PROVENÇALE

Makes 2 servings. Each serving contains 63 milligrams sodium; 520 calories.

2 veal steaks, 6 ounces each	2 tomatoes, peeled and chopped
¼ cup olive oil	6 tablespoons dry white wine
4 large raw mushrooms, sliced	Flour
1 clove garlic, crushed	

1. Roll meat in flour and fry in olive oil until brown on both sides. 2. Remove meat from pan and use pan to fry mushrooms in the olive oil, for 2 minutes. 3. Add crushed garlic, fry 1 minute more, then pour in wine. Let this simmer until wine is absorbed, then stir in the tomatoes. 4. Add the meat and simmer for 10 minutes.

CHICKEN LIVERS AND GIZZARDS

Makes 6 appetizer servings. Each serving contains about 42 milligrams sodium; 150 calories.

5 chicken livers	2 tablespoons unsalted butter, or vegetable shortening
3 chicken gizzards	½ teaspoon minced parsley
1 small onion, finely chopped	4 lettuce leaves
2 hard-boiled eggs	

1. Simmer gizzards and livers in boiling water for about 10 minutes, or until tender. 2. Sauté chopped onion with the livers. 3. Chop gizzards, eggs, livers and onion together. Add parsley. 4. Force through a sieve, shape into a mound and serve cold, on lettuce.

ROAST LEG OF LAMB

3½ ounces serving contains 78 milligrams sodium; 210 calories.

Leg of lamb
2 cloves garlic

Rosemary

1. It is not necessary to remove the thin paper-like covering called the "fell," although it makes carving easier if this is stripped off. **2.** Place the lamb, skin-side down, on a low rack in a shallow open pan. Insert a peeled clove of garlic at each end, and sprinkle the roast with rosemary. Insert a meat thermometer into center of the leg. **3.** Roast in moderately slow oven (325°F.) until the thermometer indicates the degree of doneness desired—medium (170°F.), or well done (182°F.). Remove to hot platter or smaller pan to keep lamb hot.

PORK CHOPS WITH ORANGE SLICES

Makes 1 serving. Contains 100 milligrams sodium; 650 calories.

2 four-ounce pork chops
2 orange slices

Unsalted butter
Paprika

1. Broil chops, and when nearly done, place orange slice on top of each chop. **2.** Brush with melted butter, and continue broiling until orange is browned. Sprinkle with paprika.

EAST INDIA CURRY OF CHICKEN

Makes 6 servings. Each serving contains about 286 milligrams sodium; 400 calories.

4 pounds frying chicken, cut up
¼ cup olive oil or salad oil
2 medium onions, chopped
1 clove garlic, finely chopped
2 bay leaves
1 teaspoon paprika

2 teaspoons curry powder
Few peppercorns
Flour for thickening
1½ cups cooked rice
Toasted coconut or onions French-fried in vegetable oil

1. Pour oil in heavy saucepan, add onions, and cook slowly until golden brown. **2.** Add pieces of chicken, and all other spices except curry powder. Cook for 10 minutes. **3.** Add enough boiling water to cover chicken, and simmer until meat is tender. Add curry powder and simmer for 5 minutes more. Thicken with flour and water. **4.** Remove chicken and arrange on a warm platter with a ring of boiled rice around it. Cover both rice and chicken with the curry sauce. Garnish with toasted coconut or French-fried onions.

LOIN OF PORK

Makes 8 servings. Each serving contains 135 milligrams sodium; 750 calories.

5-pound pork loin
2 cups white wine
2 tablespoons lard
2 tablespoons sugar sirup

2 tablespoons sugar
Juice of 1 orange
Flour
Pepper, parsley sprigs

1. Rub meat with pepper. Heat the lard and brown the meat. **2.** Add wine, sugar sirup, and enough boiling water to cover. **3.** Cover and cook slowly until tender. Turn several times at 5-minute intervals, then at 10-minute intervals. Remove and sprinkle the sugar over meat. **4.** Place meat under broiler until brown crust forms. **5.** Stir orange juice into meat gravy and thicken with flour. Pour over the meat and garnish with sprigs of parsley.

FRIED SALMON

Makes 4 servings. Each serving contains about 72 milligrams sodium; 375 calories.

4 slices fresh salmon, ½ inch
thick
¼ cup salad oil
¼ cup lemon juice

1 egg, beaten
¼ cup matzo meal or unsalted matzos
Parsley, lemon slices

1. Mix together oil and lemon juice. Pour over fish and let stand for a few hours. **2.** Remove fish, drain, and dip into egg-and-cracker meal mixture. Fry to a golden brown. **3.** Garnish with parsley and lemon slices.

FISH PURÉE

Makes 4 servings. Each serving contains about 140 milligrams sodium; 370 calories.

2 pounds freshwater fish in
season
1½ teaspoons lemon juice
1 small carrot
1 stalk celery

1 small onion
1 small parsnip
1 leek
1½ bay leaves
5 peppercorns

1. Boil water, add carrot, celery, onion, parsnip, leek, bay leaves and peppercorns. Simmer 15 minutes. **2.** Add half the fish and cook until it begins to fall apart. Force through a sieve and return to pot. Bring to a boil. **3.** Slice the rest of fish and add to stock. Cook for 15 minutes. **4.** Before serving, add lemon juice.

SPICE SUGGESTIONS FOR LOW SODIUM DIETERS

Turmeric is a spice that adds something nice to creamed eggs, fish, seafood. As with most spices, a little goes a long way.

Add a dash of allspice to tomato sauce.

A touch of cayenne, plus ¼ teaspoon of paprika, added to 2 or 3 tablespoons of sweet butter makes an excellent sauce for vegetables.

For a tastier meat stew, add a small onion, studded wtih 2 or 3 whole cloves.

Rub chicken inside and out with a mixture of ginger and salad oil, before roasting.

Add a teaspoon of curry powder to a can of salt-free tomato soup.

A teaspoon of ground mace added to a pint of whipped cream increases its delicacy, and cuts oiliness.

A pinch of nutmeg adds flavor to the crust for meat pie.

For a real sophisticated touch, add mixed pickling spice to boiling beets and cabbage. About a tablespoon to 4 or 6 servings.

A new and delicious snack is made of French fried slices of raw pumpkin, dusted lightly with pumpkin pie spice.

To add golden color and rich flavor to rice, do as the Spanish do, and boil a pinch of saffron in the water for a moment before adding the rice.

Chili powder is a good seasoning for hamburgers and other ground meat dishes.

SEEDS WHICH SHARPEN FLAVOR

Caraway seeds (kümmel), so good on cabbage, also add flavor to canned asparagus. Sprinkle with caraway before heating.

Ground cardamom seeds make iced melon taste more delicious. Try this the next time you serve honeydew, cantaloupe or Persian melon for dessert or breakfast.

For a flavor that is different, add about ½ teaspoon of celery seed to a head of braised lettuce.

Coriander seed, ground of course, should be rubbed on fresh pork before roasting.

Sprinkle dill seeds on potato salad, or on cooked macaroni.

Add a dash of fennel seed to apple pie for an unusually good flavor.

Add poppy seed to noodles blended with sweet butter, and mix thoroughly.

HERB IDEAS FOR THE SALTLESS DIET

Chervil perks up broiled fish. Sprinkle it, finely chopped, over the fish before removing from the broiler.

Sprinkle chopped basil leaves over lamb chops before cooking.

SPICES, HERBS, AND OTHER LOW SODIUM SEASONINGS

MEAT and FISH SAUCES

Cayenne, Mace, Marjoram, Mustard, Pepper, Tarragon.

POULTRY and POULTRY STUFFING

Coriander, Marjoram, Pepper, Rosemary, Sage, Savory, Thyme, Turmeric.

STEWS and GRAVIES

Allspice, Bay leaf, Chili, Marjoram, Mustard, Oregano, Pepper, Rosemary, Thyme.

PASTA SAUCES

For Spaghetti, Macaroni and Pizza—Basil, Bay leaf, Oregano, Pepper.

VEGETABLES

Basil, Marjoram, Pepper, Savory.

SPICES, HERBS, AND OTHER LOW SODIUM SEASONINGS

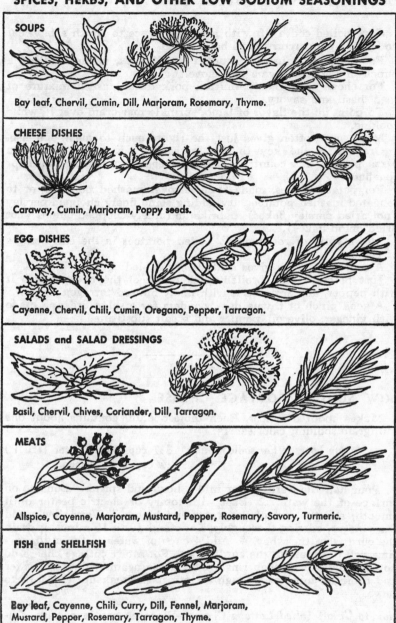

SOUPS

Bay leaf, Chervil, Cumin, Dill, Marjoram, Rosemary, Thyme.

CHEESE DISHES

Caraway, Cumin, Marjoram, Poppy seeds.

EGG DISHES

Cayenne, Chervil, Chili, Cumin, Oregano, Pepper, Tarragon.

SALADS and SALAD DRESSINGS

Basil, Chervil, Chives, Coriander, Dill, Tarragon.

MEATS

Allspice, Cayenne, Marjoram, Mustard, Pepper, Rosemary, Savory, Turmeric.

FISH and SHELLFISH

Bay leaf, Cayenne, Chili, Curry, Dill, Fennel, Marjoram,
Mustard, Pepper, Rosemary, Tarragon, Thyme.

219

Give boiled cod a lift with a tomato sauce to which a bay leaf and whole peppercorns have been added.

For lamb stew, use a "bouquet garni" sack, or tie together a bunch of parsley, thyme and clove.

For chops and other permitted pork dishes, use a mixture of sage, basil and savory.

To point up the flavor of lamb, sprinkle marjoram over it, while cooking.

Mint sauce often gives just the right touch to meat and fish.

Orégano is the key to the increasing popularity of Italian pizza pies in this country. Sprinkle orégano into meat sauce for spaghetti.

For potato patties, made from leftover mashed potatoes, or to reheated mashed potatoes, try adding some finely chopped parsley (not dried parsley flakes), paprika and finely chopped onions (not dried onion flakes).

Add a sprig of rosemary to boiled potatoes in the early stages of cooking.

A pinch of savory gives a lift to scrambled eggs.

Just before taking broiled chicken out of the oven, season it with pepper, and sprinkle it with finely minced tarragon.

A good pinch of thyme does wonders for a salad dressing made with vinegar, olive oil, pepper and a salt substitute.

LOW SODIUM COTTAGE CHEESE

Makes about 6 ounces. Each tablespoonful contains about one milligram sodium; calories: 14.

1 cup Lonalac low sodium milk powder   3½ cups warm water (120°F.)   ¼ cup white vinegar

1. Pour half the warm water into a bowl and sprinkle Lonalac on surface of the water. 2. Beat with rotary or electric beater until smooth; add the rest of the water and blend. 3. Very slowly add the vinegar, stirring thoroughly. Let stand 10 to 15 minutes; drain the curd from the whey. 4. Add 4 cups of water to the curd, stirring well to break up the curd. Drain. For a tart cottage cheese do not stir too much when rinsing. 5. Rinse again with fresh water and drain 30 minutes through a cloth bag. Break up with fork to serve.

How to Unsalt Salted Cottage Cheese—Place cheese in a sieve. Immerse it in a pot of cold water. Shake a bit. Change water 3 times, allowing 1 minute immersion each time. Grated onion and some dill make a good flavoring.

FLOUNDER GRECHESKI

Makes 6 servings. Each serving contains about 168 milligrams sodium; 160 calories.

3 pounds flounder (or had-dock) fillets

3 tablespoons vegetable short-ening

2 medium onions, finely chopped

2 scallions, sliced, including tops

4 cloves garlic

3 ripe tomatoes, peeled and coarsely chopped

¾ pound spinach, chopped

½ pound sorrel (sour grass), chopped

1 tablespoon minced parsley

3 cups hot water

Pepper

Lemon slices

1. Brown the chopped onions and garlic in shortening. Add chopped tomatoes, spinach, sorrel and sliced scallions. Sauté until vegetables are tender. 2. Add parsley. Stir in hot water. Add pepper, cover, and bring to slow boil. 3. Place fish on top of vegetables, cover, and poach for not more than 10 minutes. 4. Remove fish to hot platter and keep hot. Drain off and retain about three-quarters of the vegetable stock. Boil down the rest of the stock to half its quantity. 5. Pour vegetables and stock over fish. Garnish with lemon slices. Serve at once.

SCRAMBLED EGG MOUNTAINS

The heaped-high egg specialty of The Californian Restaurant, in New York City, adapted to this diet.

Makes 1 serving. Contains 90 milligrams sodium; 350 calories.

2 tablespoons vegetable short-ening

2 eggs

Pepper and herbs or salt sub-stitute

1. Use eggs only—no cream, milk or water. Beat eggs several hours in advance (or, better yet, the night before) and keep in refrigerator until cooking time. 2. Briefly beat up eggs again and season with pepper and herbs. Have ready a large fork from a carving set. 3. Heat shortening in heavy frying pan, pour in eggs, and just as eggs begin to set, slip one tine of the carving fork underneath the egg, across the pan. 4. Rotate the fork slowly to roll the egg up on fork as it cooks, and to let the uncooked part move to the edge of the pan. 5. When most of the egg is cooked, raise the fork, pulling the center of the egg up into a high mountain, and letting the rest of the uncooked egg roll against the side of the pan. Then slip it off onto a warm serving platter. Directions must be followed accurately to have success with this recipe.

NORWEGIAN FISKEPUDDING

Makes 6 servings. Each serving contains 121 milligrams sodium; 166 calories.

2 pounds fresh haddock
½ cup light cream
3 eggs
1 tablespoon unsalted butter

1 tablespoon white flour
2 tablespoons potato flour
½ teaspoon nutmeg

1. Skin, clean and bone fish. Grind at least 4 times, twice with fine cutter. 2. Blend white flour, potato flour, butter and eggs into fish. Add nutmeg. Add the cream gradually, until butter has a good dough consistency. 3. Grease a deep baking dish well and fill ¾ full with dough. Set dish into a shallow pan of water. 4. Bake about one hour in medium oven (350°F.), testing with toothpick as for cake. If top of Fiskepudding browns too quickly, cover with greased paper. 5. Cool for a few minutes before turning out onto hot platter. Serve with white sauce, tomato sauce, shrimp sauce, or simply a lemon wedge.

SCRAMBLED EGGS AND MUSHROOMS

Makes 1 serving. Contains 58 milligrams sodium; 130 calories.

½ cup raw mushrooms, sliced
1 egg
4 teaspoons milk

1 teaspoon olive oil
Pepper
Paprika

1. Fry mushrooms in olive oil for 5 minutes. 2. Place in double boiler top and add egg, milk and pepper. Cook slowly, stirring until creamy. Sprinkle with paprika.

ASPARAGUS OMELET

Makes 1 serving. Contains 48 milligrams sodium; 111 calories.

1 medium egg
½ No. 2 can or 1 Picnic can Diet Delight brand dietetic asparagus

½ teaspoon vegetable shortening
Dash of pepper

1. Beat egg yolk and mix in pepper. Beat egg white stiff and fold in. 2. Grease heated frying pan with vegetable shortening, add omelet mixture and cook over low heat until bottom is browned. 3. Place in moderate oven (350°F.) a few minutes to dry out top. 4. Meanwhile heat the asparagus. Cut omelet part way through center, put drained asparagus on one half, fold over and serve.

CHINESE BOILED RICE

The Chinese, fortunately, do not use salt in preparing plain rice. The trick in preparing rice, says the good Chinese cook, is to have all the moisture completely absorbed into each grain and not left between the grains. "Properly cooked rice," says Buwei Yang Chao, "should be dry and uniform in texture." Here is how to do it:

Makes 4 servings. Each serving contains 4 milligrams sodium; 173 calories.

1 cup rice

1. Wash rice; drain. Bring long-grained rice to a boil in 2 cups of water if a rather soft rice is desired; 1½ cups if you prefer it less soft. If rice is the oval-grained variety, increase the water by ½ cup. **2.** Boil over high flame, but stir occasionally to prevent sticking. After 5 minutes of boiling, or as soon as the free water is boiled off, reduce the flame as low as possible. **3.** Cover and simmer for 20 minutes or until rice is soft and dry, and has lost its shiny, wet appearance. Oval-grained rice should simmer for 30 minutes, and half-way through should be turned over to insure more uniform cooking. Be sure to re-cover pot after turning rice.

DRY STEAMED RICE—CHINESE CHANGSHA STYLE

Makes 4 servings. Each serving contains 4 milligrams sodium; 173 calories.

1 cup rice

1. Wash rice; drain. If rice is long-grained Louisiana or Mississippi variety, bring to a boil in 2 to 3 cups cold water; if oval-grained rice, use 3 to 4 cups water. Boil for 3 minutes. **2.** Drain off the liquid and place rice in a steaming tier or colander, and steam for 30 minutes if rice is long-grained, or 45 minutes if rice is oval-grained.

DRY STEAMED RICE—CANTONESE STYLE

Possibly you may not feel it worthwhile spending an hour to an hour and a half steaming rice. But the Chinese, who are probably the largest consumers of rice, willingly devote themselves to the process, so give it a trial.

Follow same directions as for Changsha style rice, except boil for 5 minutes instead of 3, and steam the rice in 4 individual bowls. Long-grained rice made this way should be steamed for 1 hour, oval-grained rice for 1½ hours.

CHICKEN SALAD

Makes 4 servings. Each serving contains 95 milligrams sodium; 165 calories.

1 cup leftover roast chicken	1 tablespoon unsalted butter
2 stalks celery	½ teaspoon dry mustard
Lettuce leaves	½ tablespoon sugar
2 eggs, hard-boiled	¼ teaspoon white pepper
2 eggs, raw	Lemon juice
¼ cup vinegar	

1. Cut chicken, celery, lettuce and hard-boiled eggs into strips. Mix. 2. Heat vinegar and butter together in double boiler. 3. Beat raw eggs in a bowl and add mustard, sugar, white pepper and a little lemon juice. Add to vinegar and butter mixture and stir until thickened. 4. Cool and pour over chicken and vegetables lightly.

MASHED POTATO SALAD

Makes 6 servings. Each serving contains 5 milligrams sodium; 150 calories.

6 hot potatoes, mashed	Pepper
2 egg yolks	Vinegar
1 tablespoon unsalted butter	Sugar (each tablespoon sugar
2 tablespoons cream	has 48 calories)
1 teaspoon chives, chopped	Lemon slices
Parsley, chopped	

1. Cream the butter and add egg yolks, cream, parsley, chives, pepper and small equal amounts of sugar and vinegar, to taste. 2. Add mashed potatoes and mix well. Serve trimmed with parsley or lemon slices.

SPRING SALAD

Makes 1 serving. Contains 13 milligrams sodium; 44 calories.

3 tablespoons diced cucumber or cabbage	⅔ cup Diet Delight brand dietetic tomato juice
3 sliced radishes	¼ teaspoon grated onion
1 envelope lemon flavor Glow low-calorie gelatin	1 lettuce leaf

1. Soften gelatin in 1 tablespoon tomato juice. Heat remainder of tomato juice and dissolve softened gelatin in it. 2. Blend in onion. Chill until sirupy. 3. Fold in cucumber and radishes. Chill until firm. Serve on lettuce.

PARTY SALAD

Makes 6 servings. Each serving contains 21 milligrams sodium; 340 calories.

4 cups cranberries
1½ cups sugar
1 cup diced celery
¾ cup chopped walnuts

1½ tablespoons gelatin (1½ envelopes Knox's unflavored gelatin)
1 tablespoon lemon juice

1. Boil sugar and 1 cup water for 5 minutes. Add cranberries and cook slowly, without stirring, 5 minutes, or until all the skins pop open. 2. Soften gelatin in ¼ cup cold water; dissolve in hot sauce. Add lemon juice. 3. Cool sauce. When it begins to thicken, fold in nuts and celery. Transfer to mold and chill until firm.

BANANA SPLIT LUNCHEON SALAD

Makes 4 servings. Each serving contains 219 milligrams sodium; 200 calories.

4 ripe medium bananas
4 teaspoons lemon juice
1⅓ cups cottage cheese
2 small oranges
4 lettuce leaves or other salad greens

4 maraschino cherries
Few blueberries, strawberries, grapes or cubes of red apple with skin left on, for garnishing

1. Peel bananas and cut in half lengthwise. Sprinkle with lemon juice. 2. Place banana halves on salad greens, cut side down. Pile ⅓ cup cottage cheese over the center of each banana and put a cherry on top. 3. Peel oranges and arrange sections, or very thin slices, around cheese. Garnish.

POTATO PANCAKES

Each potato pancake contains negligible amount of sodium, but is high in calories.

Fresh or leftover mashed potatoes

Small lump unsalted butter
Flour

1. Mash boiled potatoes thoroughly while still warm (or use leftover mashed potatoes). Add butter, and mix well. Place in refrigerator to chill. 2. Work in just enough flour to keep mixture together when rolled out. 3. Take small portion at a time and roll out into round cakes the size of small skillet. 4. Fry in ungreased skillet over slow fire.

VEGETABLES WITH HERBS

Pickled beets: Heat a sprig of dill with vinegar and pour over cooked beets.

Turnips and carrots: Cook a good-sized sprig of rosemary with equal parts of diced turnips and carrots. Remove rosemary, and mash vegetables if desired. Season with pepper and unsalted butter.

Fresh spinach: Add about ¼ teaspoon minced fresh sweet marjoram to butter when melting, and pour over 1 pound spinach, cooked.

Braised radishes: Clean 2 bunches of radishes but do not peel; slice and cook in small amount water 10 minutes. Drain. Melt 2 tablespoons unsalted butter, add ¼ teaspoon finely chopped fresh thyme and radishes; cook slowly 5 minutes and add ⅓ cup light cream. Heat thoroughly but do not boil. Makes 6 servings.

Fresh tomatoes: "Thyme and fresh tomatoes go together like hand and glove," says that splendid booklet, "The A.B.C. of Spice Cookery." Sprinkle thyme over sliced tomatoes in a bed of lettuce, use vinegar and olive oil dressing with pepper and a salt substitute.

Canned dietetic unsalted tomatoes: Season with pepper, and sugar if desired, and unsalted butter and heat with 1 sprig sweet basil. Remove sweet basil.

Fresh carrots: Add a pinch of dried thyme, or good-sized sprig fresh thyme.

Fresh green peas: Cook with a sprig of mint or summer savory.

STEAMED CARROT PUDDING

Makes 3 servings. Each serving contains 87 milligrams sodium; 90 calories.

1 cup grated or finely shredded carrots	1 egg
2 teaspoons grated lemon rind	1 tablespoon lemon juice
1 cup corn flakes	1 teaspoon Sacrose no-calorie sweetener

1. Place carrots, lemon rind and corn flakes in mixing bowl. 2. Beat the egg, lemon juice and Sacrose together until thoroughly mixed. Add to carrot and mix well. 3. Place pudding mixture in three lightly oiled 6-ounce custard cups. Cover tightly with waxed paper or aluminum foil. 4. Place on rack in kettle. Add boiling water to depth of one inch in kettle. 5. Cover tightly and steam for one hour. Serve pudding hot with a Sacrose-sweetened fruit purée or diet "Whipped Cream," if diet permits.

CORN ON COB

A reader of *The New York Times* writes its food editor that her ideas on the secrets of good corn are excellent "except the horror of cooking in salted water. Salt never, sugar always."

Each medium ear plus 1 teaspoon unsalted butter contains 1 milligram sodium; 120 calories.

Uniform medium ears of corn, fresh not canned	Sugar—about a teaspoon for 8 ears
Unsalted butter or margarine	Pepper

1. Husk corn and remove silk. 2. Cover corn with boiling sugared water. 3. Cover pot and boil 5 to 7 minutes. Drain. 4. Butter corn and season with pepper.

EGGPLANT AU GRATIN

Makes 4 servings. Each serving contains 54 milligrams sodium; 68 calories.

1 medium eggplant	½ tablespoon unsalted butter or margarine for greasing baking dish
¼ cup grated cheddar cheese	
¼ cup dry bread crumbs from low-sodium bread	Lemon juice

1. Peel eggplant, cut into ¾-inch slices and sprinkle with lemon juice. 2. Grease baking dish lightly and place several eggplant slices at bottom of dish. Sprinkle with cheese and then with bread crumbs. 3. Make layers of eggplant, cheese and bread crumbs, topping with cheese. 4. Bake for about 30 minutes, or until tender, in moderately hot oven (375°F.).

CANDIED YAMS

Makes 3 servings. Each serving contains about 6 milligrams sodium (without skins); 650 calories.

3 medium yams, orange-colored	1½ cups sugar
	1 medium orange
1 tablespoon unsalted butter, or vegetable oil	1 medium lemon

1. Boil yams in skins until done. Then peel and cut through lengthwise. Arrange in buttered baking dish. 2. Cut up orange and lemon finely, including peels. Boil sugar in 1½ cups water, with the orange and lemon, until sugar is melted, then boil 2 minutes longer. Strain this mixture over the yams. 3. Bake in hot oven (400°F.) until yams and sirup are golden brown.

STRING BEANS WITH MUSHROOMS

Makes 4 servings. Each serving contains 4 milligrams sodium; 88 calories.

1 pound fresh young string beans	2 tablespoons unsalted butter
⅓ pound raw mushrooms	Thyme or marjoram, to taste

1. Split beans lengthwise (French style) or cut into 1-inch pieces. Cook in small amount of boiling water, to which pinch of thyme or marjoram has been added. Cook until tender. 2. While beans are cooking, sauté sliced mushrooms in butter until slightly browned. Keep stirring to prevent burning. 3. Add mushrooms to thoroughly drained beans. Serve at once.

BROILED MUSHROOM CAPS

Makes 3 servings. Each serving contains 6 milligrams sodium; 100 calories.

12 large raw mushroom caps	¼ clove garlic, minced
2 tablespoons fine crumbs of low-sodium bread	2 tablespoons vegetable oil
	Pepper
1 tablespoon chopped parsley	Herbs or salt substitute

1. Mix together the crumbs, parsley and garlic. 2. Brush mushroom caps with oil and roll in crumbs. Sprinkle with herbs and pepper. 3. Broil under moderate heat about 5 minutes on each side. Sprinkle with more oil, if necessary.

EGGPLANT STEW

Makes 4 servings. Each serving contains 107 milligrams sodium; 48 calories. Use as a main luncheon dish.

1 medium eggplant	1 bay leaf
1½ canned pimientos, chopped	Paprika
½ pound raw mushrooms, sliced	1 teaspoon tarragon vinegar
	1 hard-boiled egg, chopped
¾ cup tomato juice	Lemon juice

1. Wash but do not peel eggplant. Cut into 1-inch cubes. Sprinkle at once with lemon juice to prevent discoloration. 2. Heat tomato juice in saucepan, add diced eggplant, sliced mushrooms, chopped pimientos and bay leaf. 3. Cover tightly, simmer until tender and remove bay leaf. Season with tarragon vinegar and paprika. 4. Sprinkle with chopped egg before serving.

TOMATO CATSUP

Some call it ketchup or catchup, but catsup seems to be winning out as the standard. All three names come from the same source —an East Indian pickle—and apply to the same sauce.

Every committee in charge of the hamburger booth or the steamed clam booth at the local church supper or American Legion carnival, has its own pet homemade catsup recipe. We merely submit one more favorite, successfully prepared without salt. Vary it, as you like.

Makes about 3 quarts. Each teaspoon contains about 1 milligram sodium; 5 calories.

1 peck ripe tomatoes (8 quarts)
6 onions, sliced
½ clove garlic
2 long red peppers, seeded
2 small bay leaves
1 cup brown sugar
2 cups cider vinegar

Spice bag containing:
1 tablespoon whole allspice
2-inch stick cinnamon
1 tablespoon whole cloves
1 tablespoon black peppercorns
1 tablespoon whole mace
1 tablespoon cassia-buds (or mustard seed)
1 clove garlic

1. Wash tomatoes, cut into pieces. Boil until soft, with sliced onions, garlic, red peppers and bay leaves. 2. Press through colander and fine sieve, and add brown sugar. Add the spice bag. 3. Cook rapidly, stirring frequently to prevent scorching, until thick or reduced in half, about 1½ hours of boiling. 4. Remove the spice bag, add the vinegar (and ¼ tablespoon cayenne pepper if your taste wishes it). 5. Boil for 10 minutes longer and bottle immediately, in small sterilized bottles or jars. Seal bottles with sealing wax. When cold, store in a cool dry place.

CRANBERRY CATSUP

Makes 2 quarts. Each teaspoon contains about 1 milligram sodium; 13 calories.

4 pounds cranberries
2 cups vinegar
5 cups brown sugar

2 teaspoons cinnamon
1 teaspoon cloves
1 teaspoon allspice

1. Cook cranberries with vinegar and 2 cups water, until all the skins pop open. 2. Put through a fine sieve. 3. Combine strained cranberries with all other ingredients, and cook together 5 minutes. 4. Seal in hot sterilized jars. Serve with meats, hot or cold, and fish.

LEMON CATSUP

Makes about 2 quarts. Each tablespoon contains about 1 milligram sodium; 18 calories.

Juice of 12 large lemons
Grated rind of 12 large lemons
4 tablespoons mustard seed
2 tablespoons sugar
2 tablespoons freshly grated horseradish
1 tablespoon white pepper
1 tablespoon turmeric
1 shallot or scallion
1 teaspoon mace
1 teaspoon cloves
Few grains cayenne pepper

1. Mix together all ingredients, and let stand in a cool place 3 hours. 2. Bring to a boil, and cook for 30 minutes. 3. Pour into a crock, cover tightly with weight on top, and let stand for 2 weeks. Stir well every day. 4. Strain, fill into sterilized bottles, and seal.

GRAPE CATSUP

A catsup to serve with hot or cold fish.

Makes about 4 quarts. Each tablespoon contains 1 milligram sodium; 30 calories.

10 pounds grapes (not seedless)
6 pounds sugar
1 quart vinegar
2 tablespoons allspice
2 tablespoons ground cinnamon
2 tablespoons ground clove
1 tablespoon ground pepper

1. Pick over, wash and crush grapes in large saucepan. 2. Simmer, without water, until fruit is soft and juice flows. 3. Press through sieve or cheesecloth; discard seeds and skins. 4. Return pulp to pan, add all other ingredients, and simmer very slowly until catsup is as thick as desired. Fill into sterilized jars, and seal.

INDIA RELISH

Makes about 2 quarts. Each tablespoon contains 1 milligram sodium; 15 calories.

6 green tomatoes
6 tart apples
1 large onion
1 pimiento
2½ cups vinegar
2½ cups sugar
1½ teaspoons ginger
½ teaspoon red pepper
½ teaspoon turmeric

1. Peel and core apples. Put through food chopper, with tomatoes, pimiento and onion. 2. Boil vinegar, sugar and seasonings, then add the chopped ingredients. 3. Cook for 30 minutes, fill into sterilized jars, and seal.

LOW SODIUM FRENCH DRESSING

There is now a ready-made low sodium dressing available at diet food counters. It is called Frenchette Dressing, salt-free style; very good, and contains only 3 calories in a teaspoonful. Here is a recipe for a higher calorie low sodium dressing.

Makes about ¾ cup. Each tablespoon contains negligible sodium; 82 calories.

½ cup salad oil or olive oil	Dash of paprika
3 tablespoons lemon juice	Few grains pepper
½ clove garlic	

1. Cut garlic in several places, rub the bowl with it, then leave garlic in the bowl. **2.** Add other ingredients, mix vigorously with a fork, and let stand for half hour. **3.** Remove garlic and beat dressing with hand beater until well mixed. Place in refrigerator until ready to serve.

WATERMELON PICKLES

This recipe comes from the United States Department of Agriculture, which wants you to get the most out of your watermelons. Long after the luscious red part of the watermelon has been eaten, the rind can remind you of its goodness.

Makes about 6 pints. Each tablespoon contains less than 1 milligram sodium; 10 calories.

4 pounds watermelon rind	2 tablespoons whole cloves
Limewater, made with 2 quarts cold water and 1 tablespoon of lime (calcium oxide purchased from drug store)	10 2-inch pieces stick cinnamon
	1 quart vinegar
	4 pounds sugar
2 tablespoons whole allspice	

1. Select thick rind from a firm, not overripe, melon. Trim off the green skin and pink flesh. Weigh 4 pounds of the remaining portion, cut up into 1-inch cubes. **2.** Soak for an hour in limewater. Drain; cover with fresh water and cook for 1½ hours, or until tender. Add more water as needed. Drain. **3.** Put spices loosely in a clean, thin white cloth; tie top tightly. Bring to a boil the spices, vinegar, 1 quart of water and sugar. Add watermelon rind and boil gently for 2 hours. Remove spice bag.* **4.** Pack rind in clean, hot jars which have just been boiled 15 to 20 minutes. Fill jars to top with hot sirup. Seal tightly.

*Note: If preferred, let the watermelon stand overnight covered with the sirup. In the morning, remove spice bag. Boil 1 minute. Then pack into jars, cover with sirup and seal tightly.

HORSERADISH SAUCE

For cold boiled fish.

Makes 4 servings. Each serving contains 23 milligrams sodium; 95 calories.

¾ cup sour cream
2 teaspoons fresh grated horseradish

Sugar, to taste
Lemon juice, to taste

1. Whip sour cream and blend in horseradish. 2. Add a little sugar and lemon juice, to taste. Chill.

BUTTER AND EGG SAUCE

Makes 4 servings. Each serving contains 27 milligrams sodium; 278 calories.

½ cup unsalted butter   2 eggs, hard-boiled

1. Chop eggs fine. Bring butter to a boil and remove scum. 2. Add finely chopped eggs. Serve on boiled fish.

CRANBERRY–ORANGE RELISH

Makes about 1 quart. Each tablespoon contains less than 1 milligram sodium; 25 calories.

4 cups cranberries   2 cups sugar
1 large orange

1. Cut orange, unpeeled, into eighths; remove seeds. 2. Wash and pick over cranberries. Run both cranberries and orange through a food chopper. 3. Mix, add the sugar, and stir until thoroughly mixed. 4. Let stand for several hours, then fill into sterilized glasses, and seal.

LOG CABIN CRANBERRY RELISH

Makes 3 cups. Each tablespoon contains 7 milligrams sodium; 34 calories.

½ medium-sized lemon   1½ cups Log Cabin Syrup
4 cups raw cranberries

1. Remove seeds from lemon. Put lemon and cranberries through medium grinder. 2. Add Log Cabin Syrup and mix well. 3. Chill in refrigerator several hours or longer, to blend flavors. Serve with meat or fowl. Relish will keep several days in refrigerator.

SOUR CREAM SAUCE

Makes about 1 cup. Each tablespoon contains about 7 milligrams sodium; 43 calories.

¾ cup sour cream (or sweet cream with additional vinegar)

2 egg yolks, lightly beaten
1 teaspoon tarragon vinegar

1. Combine the lightly beaten egg yolks with the cream and vinegar and cook in double boiler over hot water—not boiling water—until thickened.

COOKED SALAD DRESSING

Makes ¾ cup—about 8 servings. Each serving contains 32 milligrams sodium; 62 calories.

¼ cup non-fat dry milk solids (skim milk powder)
2 tablespoons flour
1 teaspoon dry mustard
1 egg, beaten

2 tablespoons vegetable oil
¼ cup lemon juice
1 teaspoon saccharin liquid or other no-calorie sweetener

1. Place milk powder, flour, mustard and 1 cup water in glass jar with tight-fitting cover. 2. Shake until well blended. Pour into saucepan and cook over moderate heat, stirring constantly, until mixture thickens. 3. Blend together and add the egg, oil and lemon juice. Stir cooked mixture into beaten egg mixture gradually. 4. Return to saucepan and cook over very low heat 5 minutes longer, stirring constantly. 5. Remove from stove and stir in sweetener. Cool. Store in refrigerator.

RED CURRANT PRESERVE

Makes 2 quarts. Each tablespoon contains 1 milligram sodium; 60 calories.

2 quarts red currants (do not wash until ready to use)
2 large oranges

2 quarts sugar (8 cups)
2 cups seedless raisins

1. Wash and stem the currants. Peel the oranges and finely shred the peel. 2. In a large kettle make alternate layers of currants, orange pulp and peel, and sugar. 3. Let stand overnight and in the morning bring slowly to a boil, stirring gently. Then simmer for 25 minutes. 4. Add the raisins and continue cooking until thickened. Turn into hot sterilized jars, and seal.

CUMBERLAND SAUCE

Makes about ¾ cup. Each tablespoon contains 1 milligram sodium; 20 calories.

3 tablespoons red currant jelly
3 tablespoons thinly peeled orange rind
2 tablespoons port wine
2 tablespoons orange juice

1 tablespoon lemon juice
1 teaspoon dry mustard
1 teaspoon paprika
½ teaspoon ground ginger

1. Finely shred and scald the orange peel. Cover with cold water, bring to a boil, and drain. 2. Melt the jelly over a low flame. 3. When melted jelly has cooled, add all other ingredients. Serve at room temperature.

FOAMY YELLOW SAUCE

Makes about 2 cups. Each tablespoon contains 2 milligrams sodium; 31 calories.

½ cup unsalted butter
1 cup confectioners' sugar

1 egg, separated
¼ cup orange juice

1. Cream the butter until it is soft and smooth. 2. Add the sugar gradually, continuing to cream the butter. 3. Beat the egg yolk until light and add this and the orange juice to the butter and sugar. 4. Beat the egg white until stiff but not dry and fold it into the sauce. Serve at once.

VANILLA SAUCE

This is a good tested recipe, but if you want a ready-prepared low sodium Vanilla Sauce, get a box of Dietician Vanilla Pudding, and follow the easy directions for making an excellent sauce. It's sugar-free and low in calories too—only 39 calories per portion, including the 3 ounces of milk with which it is made.

Make about 2¼ cups. Each tablespoon contains negligible sodium; 24 calories.

½ cup sugar
¼ cup unsalted butter
2 teaspoons lemon juice

2 tablespoons cornstarch
2 teaspoons vanilla extract

1. Combine sugar and cornstarch in a saucepan. 2. Add 2 cups boiling water slowly. Stir constantly. 3. Simmer until pudding thickens—about 5 minutes—stirring constantly. 4. Remove from stove and stir in butter, vanilla, and lemon juice.

HARD SAUCE

Each tablespoonful contains less than 1 milligram sodium; 57 calories.

1 cup confectioners' sugar or
¾ cup granulated sugar
⅓ cup unsalted butter

⅔ teaspoon vanilla extract or
other flavoring

1. Let butter stand until soft, but not melted. Cream thoroughly and beat in sugar gradually, until mixture is smooth and fluffy. If an electric mixer is used, scrape down the sides of the bowl once or twice during beating. 2. Add the flavoring drop by drop, to prevent it from separating. Chill sauce in refrigerator before serving.

Variations: LEMON HARD SAUCE: Add ⅓ teaspoon lemon extract, or 1 teaspoon lemon juice and 1 tablespoon grated rind.

STRAWBERRY HARD SAUCE: Wash, hull and drain ⅔ cup strawberries. Beat into mixture one at a time.

BRANDY SAUCE: Flavor with 1 teaspoon brandy.

APPLE BUTTER

Makes about 3 pints. Each tablespoonful contains less than 1 milligram sodium; 21 calories.

2 quarts apples
1 quart cider or cider vinegar
1½ cups sugar

¾ teaspoon cinnamon
½ teaspoon allspice
½ teaspoon ground cloves

1. Wash apples and cut into small pieces. 2. Cover with cider and cook slowly until soft. Press through sieve to remove seeds and skins. Add sugar and spices. 3. Cook in large kettle until thick and apple butter mounds up when dropped from a spoon. Pour into hot sterilized jars, and seal.

SPICED CRANBERRIES

Makes 1 quart. Each tablespoon contains less than 1 milligram sodium; 34 calories.

4 cups cranberries
2½ cups sugar
2 sticks cinnamon (2-inch lengths)

2 tablespoons lemon juice
Grated rind of 1 lemon
1 teaspoon whole cloves

1. Combine sugar, spices, lemon juice, rind and ½ cup water. Boil 5 minutes. 2. Add cranberries and cook slowly, without stirring, until all the skins pop open. 3. Seal in sterilized jars or chill for immediate use.

STREUSEL COFFEE CAKE

Makes 16 servings. Each serving contains 7 milligrams sodium; 166 calories.

3 cups sifted flour	½ cup sugar
2 egg yolks	6 tablespoons melted butter,
1 yeast cake	unsalted
¾ cup hot milk	Nutmeg

1. Place scalded milk and sugar in a large bowl. When the mixture is lukewarm, crumble yeast over the surface of the liquid. **2.** Add 1½ cups of the sifted flour and beat vigorously. Cover and let rise until the sponge is double in bulk, about ¾ hour. Add egg yolks and melted shortening, and enough flour to form a soft dough. **3.** Turn out on a floured board and knead lightly for half a minute. Brush surface with melted shortening and cover with a towel; allow to double in bulk again. **4.** Knead for 1 minute, or until there are no large air bubbles in the dough. Roll ½ inch thick and then place in a buttered 8-inch square cake pan. Cover and allow to rise for half hour. Sprinkle top lightly with nutmeg and streusel, which is made as follows:

¼ cup unsalted butter	½ cup flour
¼ cup sugar	2 teaspoons cinnamon

5. Cream the butter until light. Mix sugar with flour and cinnamon. Cream this mixture into the butter. Bake cake in hot oven (400°F.) 10 minutes. Reduce heat to 350°F. and bake 20 to 25 minutes longer.

APPLESAUCE PIE

Makes 6 servings. Each serving contains less than 10 milligrams sodium; 380 calories.

6 or 8 sour, juicy apples	Cider
½ cup seedless raisins	Flour
½ cup sugar	Uncooked 9-inch pie shell and
½ teaspoon cinnamon	pastry strips, made without
¼ teaspoon ground cloves	salt, or with salt substitute
Dash of nutmeg	

1. Prepare apples as for applesauce. Place in saucepan with raisins and add cider to cover. **2.** Cook slowly until apples are soft. Remove from stove, stir in a little flour if sauce seems too thin. **3.** Add sugar and spices. When cool, pour into raw pie shell. **4.** Put strips of pastry on top and bake in very hot oven (450°F.) 10 minutes, then reduce heat to 350°F. and continue baking another 30 minutes, or until brown.

SPONGE CAKE

Gunvor Storlien, our good friend from Norway, follows this recipe, but she uses plain white flour instead of cake flour—says she saw the plain flour in the canister and thought it looked so much lovelier than the flour she had in Norway, she was delighted to use it without question—in fact, she never knew a cake flour existed. And as for sifting, she never bothers. But Gunvor has a white thumb and everything she makes comes out right, so follow the recipe, use cake flour—and sift it.

Makes 12 servings. Each serving contains 19 milligrams sodium; 137 calories.

1 cup sifted cake flour (not self-rising flour)	1½ tablespoons lemon juice
	Grated rind of ½ lemon
1 cup sugar	1 teaspoon vanilla
5 eggs, separated	

1. Sift flour at least 4 times. 2. Beat egg yolks, add vanilla, lemon juice and rind and beat until very thick. 3. Beat egg whites until stiff but not dry; then fold in sugar very gradually. Fold in the stiffly beaten egg yolks. 4. Sift about ¼ of the flour at a time over the mixture, and fold in. 5. Use a 9-inch ungreased tube pan and bake in moderately slow oven (325°F.) for 1 hour. Turn pan upside down until cake is cold.

DEEP DISH APPLE PIE

Makes 3 servings. Each serving contains less than 5 milligrams sodium; 177 calories.

2½ cups diced peeled apples	1 teaspoon Cream of Rice or tapioca
⅓ cup cake flour (not self-rising flour)	4 teaspoons melted shortening
2 teaspoons Sacrose or other liquid saccharin sweetener	⅛ teaspoon nutmeg
	1/16 teaspoon cinnamon

1. Place apples in mixing bowl. Sprinkle in the rice or tapioca, Sacrose, nutmeg and cinnamon. 2. Mix lightly together. Divide apple mixture evenly among three shallow 3-inch casseroles or three 5-ounce custard cups. 3. Place flour in a mixing bowl. Combine and add the melted shortening and 1 tablespoon cold water. Mix thoroughly with fork. 4. Divide pastry into three portions. Roll out each portion on lightly floured board to size of top of casseroles or custard cups. Slash pastry circles to allow steam to escape. 5. Top each pie with pastry circle. Bake in hot oven (400°F.) until pastry is lightly browned and apples are just tender, about 30 minutes. Cool to room temperature and serve.

SHREDDED WHEAT

Neither the Nabisco nor the Kellogg brand of Shredded Wheat has salt added. One biscuit contains less than 1 milligram sodium; has 102 calories.

Rated among the most popular cereal foods, Shredded Wheat can be served with sugar and cream, or with:

bananas	strawberries	raspberries
blueberries	blackberries	peaches
applesauce	stewed prunes	stewed apricots
stewed pears	stewed cherries	stewed rhubarb
sliced pineapple	stewed plums	stewed raisins

Here are several additional variations:

BROILED WITH BUTTER, SERVED WITH JAM: Crumble Shredded Wheat, mix with melted sweet butter, brown lightly under broiler. Serve with dab of jam or jelly, and cream.

WITH CINNAMON AND SUGAR: Add 1 teaspoon cinnamon and ½ teaspoon sugar to 1 cup top milk. Heat and serve on Shredded Wheat biscuit.

WITH EGG, CINNAMON AND NUTMEG: Beat 1 egg, add 1 cup milk, ½ teaspoon cinnamon, ⅛ teaspoon nutmeg. Mix well and pour over Shredded Wheat biscuit.

SHREDDED WHEAT PUDDING

Makes 4 servings. Each serving contains 89 milligrams sodium; 383 calories.

2 Shredded Wheat biscuits	1 tablespoon unsalted butter
2 eggs, slightly beaten	1 teaspoon cinnamon
2 cups low-sodium milk	¼ teaspoon nutmeg or mace
¾ cup molasses	

1. Break Shredded Wheat into a baking dish. 2. Mix all other ingredients, except the butter, in a bowl, and pour over Shredded Wheat. Dot with the butter. 3. Bake in moderate oven (350°F.) for 45 minutes. Serve with hard sauce or whipped cream if diet permits.

SHREDDED WHEAT PIE SHELL

Makes 1 pie shell; 12 servings. Each serving contains less than 1 milligram sodium; 100 calories.

6 Shredded Wheat biscuits, finely rolled	¼ teaspoon salt substitute
¼ cup sugar	¼ cup softened sweet butter

THE LOW SODIUM DIET

1. Mix thoroughly Shredded Wheat crumbs, sugar, butter and salt substitute. **2.** Add 1½ teaspoons water; mix well. Press mixture firmly against sides and bottom of lightly greased 9-inch pie pan. **3.** Bake in a hot oven (400°F.) 10 minutes. Cool; fill with a favorite filling.

SHREDDED WHEAT BASKETS FOR SERVING FRESH FRUIT, DRIED FRUIT WHIPS, CUSTARD, ETC.

Makes 12 baskets. Each basket contains 12 milligrams sodium; 195 calories.

1½ cups brown sugar	½ cup milk
6 Shredded Wheat biscuits, crumbled	¼ cup unsalted butter
	2 teaspoons corn sirup

1. Combine sugar, sirup, milk and butter. **2.** Cook, stirring occasionally, to soft ball stage (238° to 240°F.). **3.** Pour hot sirup over crumbled Shredded Wheat, in buttered mixing bowl. Mix well. **4.** Pack in well-greased muffin pans, shaping to form cups. Chill until firm. To serve, unmold and fill center with sliced peaches, berries, etc.

RÖDGRÖT

A favorite Swedish recipe of Alfred Lunt, famous stage star.

Makes 4 servings. Each serving contains about 3 milligrams sodium; about 220 calories.

2 cans red raspberries	Potato flour
1 glass currant jelly	

1. Strain berries through a fine sieve into an enamel pot. Add jelly. **2.** Cook until jelly is completely dissolved. **3.** Thicken with a mixture of water and potato flour, being careful not to thicken too much.

STEWED FRUIT PUDDING

Makes 4 servings. Each serving contains 7 milligrams sodium for prunes, 12 for apricots; 294 calories.

1 pound prunes or dried apricots	1 tablespoon lemon juice
½ cup sugar	1 tablespoon potato flour

1. Soak prunes overnight in water. In the morning add sugar and cook on low flame until prunes are tender. **2.** Remove prunes from liquid and add lemon juice to the liquid. Thicken with potato flour dissolved in 2 tablespoons cold water. **3.** Bring liquid to a boil and pour over prunes. Serve chilled.

BATTER FOR PANCAKES, WAFFLES, FRENCH TOAST

1 egg
1½ teaspoons sugar
¾ cup milk
1 cup flour

3 egg whites
3 tablespoons vegetable shortening

FOR PANCAKES:

Makes 8 4-inch pancakes. One 4-inch pancake contains 35 milligrams sodium; 136 calories.

1. Combine egg, sugar and milk. Add the flour and mix until smooth. 2. Beat egg whites very stiff and fold into batter. 3. Fry on hot greased griddle.

FOR WAFFLES:

Makes 4 waffles. One waffle contains 70 milligrams sodium; 270 calories.

1. Use batter in waffle iron.

FRENCH TOAST:

One piece of French toast (not counting the sirup) contains about 22 milligrams sodium; 110 calories.

1. Use slices of dry or stale salt-free bread. Dip in batter and fry in butter. Serve with sirup.

APPLE TART

Makes 3 servings. Each serving contains 27 milligrams sodium; 108 calories.

1½ cups unsweetened applesauce
1 egg, beaten
⅛ teaspoon nutmeg
1½ teaspoons liquid saccharin or other non-food sweetener

⅛ teaspoon cinnamon
1 teaspoon melted sweet butter or vegetable oil
3 tablespoons fine dry low-sodium bread crumbs

1. Heat applesauce. Beat egg in bowl and gradually beat in hot applesauce. 2. Add nutmeg, cinnamon and 1 teaspoon of the sweetener, mixing well. 3. Place apple mixture in three lightly oiled 5-ounce custard cups. Blend together melted butter and ½ teaspoon sweetener. 4. Combine with bread crumbs and sprinkle over apple mixture. 5. Bake in moderately hot oven (375°F.) until crumbs are lightly browned, about 30 minutes.

TONI'S TARTS

This recipe is worth the price of the book. Normally, salted butter is used and the salt in the butter adds to the flavor. But unsalted butter does not greatly lessen the dreaminess of these tarts. Try them once without a salt substitute, then if you feel a need for it, use a teaspoon of one of the salt substitutes.

Makes 6 tarts. Each tart contains 36 milligrams sodium; 315 calories.

⅓ cup cream cheese
⅔ cup sweet butter
1 cup flour

2 tablespoons ice water
6 teaspoons apricot jam
Small amount egg yolk or milk

1. Press cream cheese through coarse sieve, then knead together all ingredients. **2.** Refrigerate at least 1 hour (overnight is better). **3.** Roll out thin (⅛ inch) and make squares 3 inches x 3 inches. **4.** Place a teaspoon of apricot jam in the center of each square and fold the dough over in triangle like a diaper. Press all edges together. **5.** Paint top with egg yolk or milk. Bake 10 to 15 minutes in hot oven (400°F.).

RICE DUMPLINGS

Makes about 30 dumplings. Each dumpling contains about 5 milligrams sodium; 20 calories.

¾ cup milk
1 teaspoon unsalted butter
1 egg

¾ tablespoon sugar
Vanilla or lemon flavoring
Rice flour

1. Add butter to milk and bring to a boil. **2.** Sprinkle in rice flour, stirring constantly, until mixture is firm. Let boil, while kneading with spoon. **3.** Beat egg with sugar and a drop of vanilla or lemon flavoring. Add rice flour mix, after mixture has been taken off stove and allowed to cool. **4.** Form small dumplings with teaspoon and let simmer in soup or other stock for five minutes. Turn on other side for a few minutes, remove to warm dish until all are done.

APPLE BETTY

Makes 6 to 8 servings. Each serving contains 10 milligrams sodium; 212 calories.

6 cups sliced apples
1½ cups soft bread crumbs
  made of low-sodium bread
½ cup white sugar
¼ cup melted butter, unsalted

¼ cup brown sugar, firmly
  packed
¾ teaspoon ground cinnamon
½ teaspoon ground nutmeg

1. Place 2 cups sliced apples in greased baking dish. 2. Mix bread crumbs, sugars, cinnamon, nutmeg and melted butter. Sprinkle apples with ⅓ of this crumb mixture. 3. Repeat the process, making 2 more layers the same way. 4. Dribble ⅓ cup hot water over top of crumbs and bake in moderate oven (350°F.) 45 to 50 minutes. Serve with hard sauce—see recipe.

APRICOT RICE

Makes 6 servings. Each serving contains 4 milligrams sodium; 175 calories.

1 can (No. 2½) apricot halves, drained	⅔ cup Minute Rice
	¼ teaspoon grated lemon rind
1¾ cups water mixed with sirup from can of apricots	1 teaspoon lemon juice
	1 tablespoon unsalted butter

1. Combine Minute Rice, water and apricot sirup, apricot halves, and lemon rind and juice. Bring quickly to a boil, cover, and simmer 5 minutes. 2. Remove from heat and let stand 10 minutes. 3. Add butter and cool to room temperature. Then chill slightly before serving. Serve plain or with whipped cream.

GRAPEFRUIT TAPIOCA

Makes 10 servings. Each serving contains 6 milligrams sodium; 80 calories.

½ cup sugar	1 cup grapefruit juice
6 tablespoons quick-cooking tapioca	1 tablespoon lemon juice
	1 egg white, stiffly beaten
1 egg yolk, beaten	

1. Cook 1½ cups boiling water, sugar and tapioca, in double boiler over rapidly boiling water until clear. Stir occasionally. 2. Remove from fire and stir in egg yolk. 3. Add grapefruit juice and lemon juice. 4. Fold in egg white. 5. Chill. Decorate each serving with 2 or 3 grapefruit segments.

ORANGE FRUIT COMPOTE

Makes 6 servings. Each serving contains less than 1 milligram sodium; 120 calories.

1½ cups reconstituted (water added) frozen orange juice	3 cups diced fresh fruits in season, such as grapes,
1 tablespoon sugar	peaches, banana, cantaloupe

1. Combine orange juice and sugar. Add fruit. Chill.

VANILLA ICE CREAM

Makes 4 to 6 servings. Total recipe contains 45 milligrams sodium; 1405 calories. Each serving contains 10 to 7 milligrams sodium; 350 to 234 calories.

1 teaspoon plain gelatin
1 cup (4¼ ounces) low-sodium milk powder
½ cup granulated sugar
2 tablespoons corn oil
2 egg yolks
1½ teaspoons vanilla extract

1. Soften gelatin in 2 tablespoons cold water. Then dissolve over boiling water. 2. Measure 1½ cups warm water into the large bowl of an electric mixer. Sprinkle milk powder over the surface of the water. Beat with electric mixer until smooth. Add sugar, corn oil, egg yolks and vanilla, and mix well. Then beat in dissolved gelatin. 3. Pour into freezer tray. Have control on coldest setting. When frozen but not hard, turn into mixer bowl and beat until smooth but not melted. Return to freezer tray, and freeze until firm. Then move control to medium setting until served.

CHOCOLATE ICE CREAM

Makes 4 to 6 servings. Total recipe contains 45 milligrams sodium; 1740 calories. Each serving contains 10 to 7 milligrams sodium; 435 to 290 calories.

1 teaspoon plain gelatin
1 cup (4¼ ounces) low-sodium milk powder
1-ounce square unsweetened chocolate (melted)
¾ cup granulated sugar
2 tablespoons corn oil
2 egg yolks
1 teaspoon vanilla extract

1. Follow directions for Vanilla Ice Cream with the exception that the melted chocolate must be beaten into the mixed warm water and milk before adding the rest of the ingredients.

BANANA ICE CREAM

Makes 4 to 6 servings. Total recipe contains 40 milligrams sodium; 1536 calories. Each serving contains 10 to 7 milligrams sodium; 384 to 256 calories.

1 teaspoon plain gelatin
1 cup (4¼ ounces) low-sodium milk powder
½ cup granulated sugar
2 tablespoons corn oil
1 egg yolk
1 teaspoon vanilla extract
2 medium or 1½ large bananas
2 teaspoons lemon juice

1. Follow directions for Vanilla Ice Cream, except add only 1 cup warm water in Step 2 (instead of 1½ cups). 2. After the ice

cream has been frozen the first time, slice bananas into a large mixing bowl. Add lemon juice. Mash by mixing with electric mixer. Add the ice cream, beat until smooth, and return to freezer as in directions for Vanilla Ice Cream.

FRESH STRAWBERRY ICE CREAM

Makes 4 to 6 servings. Total recipe contains 40 milligrams sodium; 1524 calories. Each serving contains 10 to 7 milligrams sodium; 381 to 254 calories.

1½ cups fresh ripe strawberries (cleaned and cut in small pieces)
2 teaspoons lemon juice
2 tablespoons granulated sugar
1 teaspoon plain gelatin
1 cup (4¼ ounces) low-sodium milk powder
½ cup granulated sugar
2 tablespoons corn oil
1 egg yolk
1 teaspoon vanilla extract

1. Purée one cup of the strawberries. Add the lemon juice and the 2 tablespoons of sugar to the purée. Chill the purée and the rest of the strawberries separately in the refrigerator. 2. Then prepare the ice cream according to the directions for Vanilla Ice Cream except use only 1 cup warm water in Step 2. 3. After the base has been frozen the first time, add the puréed strawberries. Mix with electric mixer until smooth. Stir in the rest of the strawberries, and return to freezer as in the directions for Vanilla Ice Cream.

CANNED PEACH ICE CREAM

Makes 4 to 6 servings. Total recipe contains 47 milligrams sodium; 1512 calories. Each serving contains 10 to 8 milligrams sodium; 378 to 252 calories.

1½ cups canned peaches (diced and drained)
¼ cup liquid from canned peaches
2 teaspoons lemon juice
1 teaspoon plain gelatin
1 cup (4¼ ounces) low-sodium milk powder
½ cup granulated sugar
2 tablespoons corn oil
1 egg yolk
1 teaspoon vanilla extract

1. Purée 1 cup of the peaches. Add the lemon juice and peach liquid to the purée. Chill the purée and the rest of the diced peaches separately in the refrigerator. 2. Then prepare the ice cream according to the directions for Vanilla Ice Cream except add only 1 cup warm water in Step 2. 3. After the base has been frozen the first time, add the puréed peaches. Mix with electric mixer until smooth. Stir in the diced peaches, and return to freezer.
Note: For *fresh* peach ice cream, follow the recipe for fresh strawberry ice cream substituting fresh ripe peaches for the strawberries. (Total recipe contains 40 milligrams sodium.)

NESCAFÉ ICE CREAM

Makes 6 servings. Each serving contains 17 milligrams sodium; 227 calories.

2 teaspoons Nescafé
¾ cup sugar

1 teaspoon cornstarch
½ pint heavy cream, whipped

1. Mix Nescafé, sugar and cornstarch; add ¾ cup hot water; cook 20 minutes in top of double boiler, stirring frequently; cool. **2.** Fold in whipped cream. Freeze in tray in freezing compartment of refrigerator until firm, stirring after ½ hour and again at end of 1 hour.

CHOCOLATE SUNDAE SIRUP

Total recipe contains 15 milligrams sodium; 1700 calories. Two tablespoons contain 1 milligram sodium; 110 calories.

½ cup low-sodium milk
    powder
1½ cups granulated sugar
6 peaked tablespoons breakfast

cocoa (plain) or two 1-ounce squares unsweetened chocolate

1. Mix milk powder, sugar and cocoa. (If chocolate is used, do not mix in, but add during beating.) Sift together twice. **2.** Measure 1 cup water into a bowl. Pour milk mixture on top of the water. Mix with an egg beater or electric beater until smooth. **3.** Heat mixture to a boil (add cut-up chocolate, if chocolate is used). Simmer for 5 minutes. Stir constantly. **4.** Refrigerate until used.

OATMEAL FLOUR COOKIES, NOT TOO SWEET

Makes 36 cookies. Each cookie contains about 1 milligram sodium; about 36 calories.

1½ cups sifted oatmeal flour
⅓ cup unsalted butter
1 tablespoon grated orange
    rind

¼ cup yellow sugar
1 teaspoon vanilla extract or
1 tablespoon orange juice

1. Cream the butter, with the sugar, until light and fluffy. Add the orange rind. Add the vanilla extract or orange juice. **2.** Be sure the flour is well-sifted and smooth. Add to the mixture and mix thoroughly. **3.** Roll into little balls, between the palms of the hands. The recipe should make 36 balls. **4.** Put balls on a greased and floured cookie sheet, and press with a fork, to flatten them. Press one way. **5.** Bake 15 minutes at 300° to 325°F.

VANILLA COOKIES

Makes about 30 cookies. Each cookie contains 2 milligrams sodium; 50 calories.

¾ cup flour
½ cup unsalted butter
⅓ cup sugar

1 egg
3 tablespoons chopped almonds
1 teaspoon vanilla

1. Cream the butter and add the sugar a little at a time, beating well. **2.** Beat the egg separately, then beat it into the creamed butter. Add the flour a little at a time. Add the vanilla. **3.** Drop the mix from end of a teaspoon to an ungreased cookie sheet. With knife dipped in cold water, press each cookie until very thin. **4.** Sprinkle with chopped almonds. Bake in moderately hot oven (375°F.) for about 10 minutes.

CHOCOLATE PUDDING

Makes 4 servings. Each serving contains 69 milligrams sodium; 82 calories.

3 tablespoons cornstarch
3 tablespoons cocoa
2 cups fresh skim milk (or reliquefied skim milk powder)

1 teaspoon vanilla
Dash of cinnamon
1½ teaspoons liquid saccharin
sweetener

1. Mix cornstarch and cocoa with ¼ cup of milk until smooth. Meanwhile scald the remaining milk in double boiler. **2.** Pour a little of the scalded milk into the cornstarch mixture and blend smooth. **3.** Stir this slowly into remaining scalded milk, then cook, stirring constantly, until the pudding is thick and smooth. **4.** Remove the spoon, cover the double boiler, and cook 20 minutes, stirring occasionally. **5.** Cool slightly, then add sweetener, cinnamon and vanilla, stirring in well. Pour pudding into four 5-ounce custard cups and chill before serving.

BAKED PEARS

Makes 6 servings. Each serving contains 8 milligrams sodium; 145 calories.

6 baking pears
1½ teaspoons vanilla or ¼
teaspoon cinnamon

¼ cup sugar
Unsalted butter or vegetable
shortening for pan greasing

1. Stand pears in a greased glass baking dish. **2.** Place sugar, vanilla or cinnamon and 2 cups water in a saucepan and bring to a quick boil. Pour over pears. **3.** Preheat oven to 300°F. and set dish in. Cook at same slow heat for about 2½ hours or until pears are tender.

CINNAMON TOAST

Makes 5 servings. Each serving contains 8 milligrams sodium*; 170 calories.

5 slices low-sodium bread
2 tablespoons unsalted butter

4 tablespoons sugar
1 tablespoon cinnamon

1. Cream the butter, sugar and cinnamon to a consistency that will spread easily. 2. Toast bread in broiler, on one side only. 3. Spread untoasted side with the mixture, and put in hot broiler until sugar bubbles.

*This figure calculated from the average sodium content of several commercial brands of low-sodium bread.

ORANGE RICE CUSTARD

Makes 1 serving. Contains 35 milligrams sodium; 300 calories.

1 tablespoon washed rice
3 tablespoons light cream
2 tablespoons heavy cream
2 teaspoons sugar

4 teaspoons orange juice
2 sections of orange
¼ teaspoon grated orange rind
Mint leaf

1. Place rice, light cream and 4 teaspoons water in double boiler top. Cover and steam until rice is tender. 2. Take off stove and add sugar, orange juice and orange rind. 3. Whip the heavy cream and fold into the mixture. Pour into custard cups and set in refrigerator to chill. 4. Unmold and trim with bits of orange and mint leaf.

JELLIED ORANGE FRUIT CUP

Makes 8 servings. Each serving contains 1 milligram sodium; 94 calories.

1 tablespoon unflavored gela-
    tin (1 envelope Knox's)
½ cup orange juice, heated
¾ cup orange juice, unheated
2 tablespoons lemon juice

½ cup sugar
1 cup Sunkist orange pieces
½ cup sliced bananas
½ cup raspberries, or other
    fresh fruit

1. Soften gelatin in ½ cup cold water 5 minutes. Add the hot orange juice. Stir to dissolve gelatin. 2. Add cold orange juice, lemon juice, sugar. Stir. 3. When slightly thickened add orange pieces, banana slices and raspberries. Pour into shallow pan. 4. Chill. When set, serve in dessert glasses. Garnish with additional orange sections and berries.

LEMON FLUFF

Makes 4 servings. Each serving contains 46 milligrams sodium; 184 calories.

4 eggs, whites and yolks separated
½ cup sugar
Juice of ½ lemon

Grated rind of ½ lemon
1 tablespoon unflavored gelatin (1 envelope Knox's)

1. Whip yolks alone. Add sugar and whip again. Add grated lemon rind. 2. Whip the whites stiff. 3. Dissolve gelatin in a little water, mix with lemon juice and add to egg yolks. 4. Delicately fold in whites and pour mixture into a mold. Chill until firm.

SUNBEAM TAPIOCA

Makes 6 servings. Each serving contains 2 milligrams sodium; 188 calories.

¼ cup Minute Tapioca
¾ cup sugar
½ cup pineapple juice
½ cup orange juice
1½ tablespoons lemon juice

1 orange, sectioned and free
from membrane
1 cup drained diced or crushed
canned pineapple

1. Combine Minute Tapioca, sugar, pineapple juice and 1 cup water in saucepan. 2. Place over medium heat and cook until mixture comes to a full boil, stirring constantly. Remove from heat. 3. Add remaining fruit juices. Cool, stirring occasionally. Add fruit. Chill. Serve in sherbet glasses.

TROPICAL RHUBARB

Makes 4 servings. Each serving contains about 4 milligrams sodium; 280 calories.

½ cup sugar
1 box (1 pound) frozen rhubarb

1 orange, peeled and sliced
¼ teaspoon grated orange rind

1. Place sugar and ½ cup water in saucepan and bring to a boil. Add rhubarb. Bring again to a boil, separating pieces with a fork; then boil gently 4 minutes. 2. Add orange slices and continue boiling 1 minute longer. Add orange rind.

ORANGE AND BANANA AMBROSIA

Makes 6 servings. Each serving contains 2 milligrams sodium; 100 calories.

2 medium-size oranges
2 ripe bananas

2 tablespoons sugar
½ cup shredded coconut

1. Peel oranges and cut crosswise into thin slices, removing seeds and fibrous portions. 2. Peel and slice bananas. 3. Arrange a layer of orange slices on a serving dish, and sprinkle with sugar. Then make a layer of banana slices. 4. Make additional alternate layers of oranges and bananas until the fruit is used up. 5. Top with coconut, chill for 1 hour and serve.

COFFEE FONDANT BONBONS

Makes 1 pound fondant—32 bonbons. Each piece contains less than 1 milligram sodium; 50 calories.

1 tablespoon Nescafé	2 cups sugar
1 teaspoon vanilla	2 tablespoons light corn sirup

1. Dissolve Nescafé in 1¼ cups hot water; combine with sugar and corn sirup in deep saucepan. 2. Cook, stirring constantly, until sugar is dissolved. Remove spoon and cook without stirring until mixture begins to boil. 3. Cover saucepan; cook 3 minutes to wash down sugar crystals. Remove cover; cook to 240°F. (from time to time wash away sugar crystals with fork covered with cheesecloth and dipped in cold water). 4. Remove from heat; pour at once on cold, wet platter; cool to 110°F. (lukewarm). Add vanilla and beat with spatula until creamy; knead with hands until smooth. Place in covered glass jar and let "ripen" 2 to 3 days before using. 5. After fondant has ripened, shape it as desired and decorate with colored sprills, silver dragees, nutmeats, semi-sweet chocolate morsels, coconut, etc.

PINEAPPLE AND STRAWBERRY JAM

Makes about 8 six-ounce glasses. Each glass contains 2 milligrams sodium; 410 calories. 1 tablespoon contains negligible sodium; 34 calories.

1 (12-ounce) box frozen sliced strawberries	2⅓ cups (1 No. 2 can) crushed pineapple
3½ cups (1½ pounds) sugar	1 box Sure-Jell fruit pectin

1. Thaw strawberries as directed on package. Measure sugar and set aside. Combine strawberries, crushed pineapple, ⅓ cup water, and Sure-Jell in a very large saucepan; mix well. 2. Place over high heat and stir until mixture comes to a hard boil. At once stir in sugar. 3. Bring to a *full rolling boil* and *boil hard 1 minute*, stirring constantly. 4. Remove from heat and skim off foam with metal spoon. Then stir and skim by turns for 5 minutes to cool slightly, to prevent floating fruit. Ladle quickly into glasses. 5. Cover jam at once with ⅛ inch hot paraffin.

DIET "WHIPPED CREAM" SUBSTITUTE

Makes 2¼ cups whipped topping. Each tablespoon contains 12 milligrams sodium; 7 calories.

1 tablespoon lemon juice	½ cup non-fat dry milk solids
2 teaspoons Sacrose or other liquid saccharin	(skim milk powder)

1. Place ½ cup cold water in bowl. Add lemon juice, Sacrose and milk powder. 2. Beat with rotary beater or electric mixer until as thick as marshmallow cream. 3. This topping will stay light and fluffy for about 30 minutes.

SPICY FLUFFY TOPPING: Add to the above recipe before beating, ¼ teaspoon cinnamon and ⅛ teaspoon nutmeg.

WHIPPED COFFEE TOPPING: Add 1 teaspoon instant coffee before beating. *Calories in 1 tablespoon: 8.*

HOT FRUIT COMPOTE

Makes 12 servings. Each serving contains 10 milligrams sodium; 145 calories.

1 pound can purple plums	3 pears
1 No. 2½ can (3½ cups) whole apricots	½ cup sugar
	¼ cup lemon juice
3 apples	Peel of 1 small orange

1. Peel, core and quarter the apples. Peel, core and halve the pears. Cut the orange peel into slivers. 2. Place the apples, pears and orange peel in a saucepan, with 3 cups water. Add the sirup of the apricots, the sugar and lemon juice. 3. Simmer for 30 to 40 minutes, until apples and pears are tender. 4. Drain the plums, and add plums and apricots to the compote. Heat through, and serve hot.

ROAST DUCK STUFFING

Makes 6 servings. Each serving contains 48 milligrams sodium; 370 calories.

1½ loaves salt-free bread, cubed	⅛ pound unsalted butter
	1 egg
1 large stalk celery, chopped	Marjoram
2 large onions, chopped	

1. Fry the bread, onions and celery together in the butter. 2. Stir in the egg. Season to taste with marjoram.

THE HIGH RESIDUE OR "REGULARITY" DIET

(Anti-constipation)

There are several different factors which may cause constipation, and these require different types of treatment. Some of these treatments are the opposite of others, and a special diet which helps one person may be the worst one possible for another. Your doctor, the only one who can determine this, may have told you that you are suffering from the atonic type of constipation, in which the muscles in the bowel walls have lost their tone and become flabby. This is one of the commonest varieties, and is treated with the aid of a high residue diet.

Normally, the food wastes keep moving along the intestinal tract by means of peristalsis, an intermittent contraction of the intestinal muscles. If this caterpillar-like motion is weak or irregular, the muscles become flabby and atonic constipation results. This is frequently the consequence of eating foods which do not produce enough bulk to keep the muscles well exercised. A corrective diet which supplies sufficient bulk stimulates the intestinal muscles, and with renewed use, they regain their tone.

DRESSING UP THE VEGETABLES—The principal and most satisfactory form of intestinal bulk comes from cellulose. Cellulose is the fiber framework of vegetables, fruits and grains, which resists the action of the digestive ferments, and passes through the gastrointestinal tract practically unchanged. If you have habitually shunned the high fiber vegetables, possibly since childhood, you must realize that this is most likely a cause of your present constipated condition and you should seek recipes which make these vegetables inviting. In this section there are many such recipes, which present the bulk-producing vegetables in a manner that will help you enjoy them, and even ask for more.

FRUIT HELPS IN TWO WAYS—Most of the fruits provide a great deal of bulk-producing cellulose, and in addition they contain certain natural chemicals which healthfully stimulate the

251

activity of the intestinal muscles. So another group of recipes in this section presents attractive ways of preparing fruits, particularly those high in crude fiber.

WHOLE GRAINS—High in cellulose are the whole grains, the flour or meal into which all of the grain kernel has been ground. Many good recipes are available for using whole grains of wheat, corn, rye or oats; some such recipes are included in this section. A word about bran: some medical authorities believe that the combined effect of bran's crude fiber and vitamin B is good, while others feel that bran may be too irritating. Ask your doctor specifically whether you should eat 100% bran cereals. We have included some recipes containing bran in such small amounts as hardly to be troublesome to anyone.

LIQUIDS MAKE THE CELLULOSE WORK—Cellulose by itself is not bulky—it only becomes so when it absorbs liquid. A sea-sponge is almost pure cellulose, which swells up when soaked in water. In your anti-constipation diet, you must drink enough liquids to act with the cellulose obtained from the vegetables, fruits and grains. This helps prevent the intestinal contents from packing down into hard masses which offer no stimulus to the muscles. Plain drinking water is highly recommended for the high residue diet, but since water may become monotonous, we have given you a number of recipes to help vary the liquid portion of your diet, so that drinking the necessary amount of fluids will become a pleasure.

There is usually no harm in drinking liquids with your meals, but be moderate . . . don't shock your stomach with drinks too cold, and don't use water, coffee or other liquids to wash down morsels of unchewed food. If liquids disturb your sleep during the night, limit them after 6 P.M. Alcoholic beverages are not a water substitute—in fact alcohol actually draws water from the tissues.

Contrary to general belief, milk possesses no constipating properties . . . but milk is a concentrated food which leaves little residue and can contribute to constipation if you don't eat enough bulky foods. On a high cellulose diet, the average person can enjoy all the benefits of milk and milk-drinks, without fear of their being binding.

FOODS FOR THE HIGH RESIDUE (Anti-Constipation) DIET

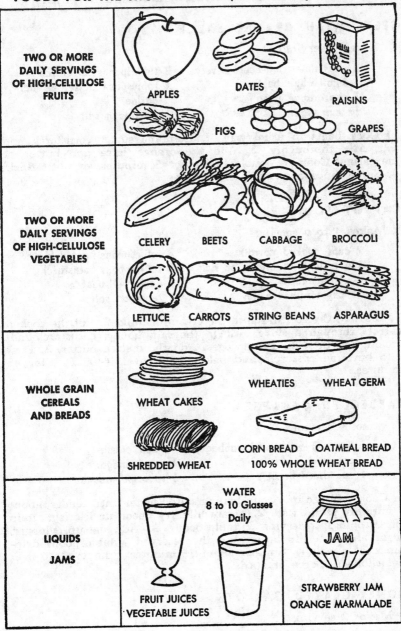

TWO OR MORE DAILY SERVINGS OF HIGH-CELLULOSE FRUITS	APPLES DATES RAISINS FIGS GRAPES
TWO OR MORE DAILY SERVINGS OF HIGH-CELLULOSE VEGETABLES	CELERY BEETS CABBAGE BROCCOLI LETTUCE CARROTS STRING BEANS ASPARAGUS
WHOLE GRAIN CEREALS AND BREADS	WHEAT CAKES WHEATIES WHEAT GERM SHREDDED WHEAT CORN BREAD OATMEAL BREAD 100% WHOLE WHEAT BREAD
LIQUIDS **JAMS**	WATER 8 to 10 Glasses Daily FRUIT JUICES VEGETABLE JUICES JAM STRAWBERRY JAM ORANGE MARMALADE

253

BEETS WITH ORANGE SAUCE

Makes 4 servings.

2 cups shoestring beets or very small whole beets
1 cup orange juice
⅓ cup sugar

2 tablespoons cornstarch
1 tablespoon butter or margarine
⅛ teaspoon salt

1. Cook beets in usual way. 2. Combine sugar, cornstarch and salt. Mix thoroughly. 3. Add the orange juice and butter or margarine. Cook in double boiler for 5 minutes, or until thick. 4. Serve sauce over warm or cold beets.

CARROT SOUFFLÉ

Makes 4 to 6 servings.

2 cups cooked carrots
1¼ cups light cream or rich whole milk
¼ cup strained honey

4 tablespoons melted butter
3 tablespoons cornstarch
3 eggs, well beaten
1 teaspoon salt

1. Dissolve the cornstarch in the cream or milk. 2. Put the cooked carrots through a sieve. Stir in the salt, honey, cornstarch-and-cream, and then the beaten eggs. Add the melted butter. 3. Pour into buttered casserole and bake in hot oven (400°F.), for 45 minutes.

BARBECUED CABBAGE

Makes 4 servings.

1 head (1½ pounds) cabbage, cut in quarters
1 cup diced bacon

½ cup catsup
¼ cup vinegar
1 tablespoon sugar

1. Cook cabbage in ½ cup boiling salted water until tender, about 5 minutes. Drain well. 2. Meanwhile, fry bacon until crisp. Drain off drippings, reserving 2 tablespoons. 3. Add catsup, vinegar, sugar and water to bacon and the reserved 2 tablespoons drippings. Mix well. 4. Simmer about 15 minutes. Pour mixture over hot cabbage. Serve at once.

HONEY-GLAZED CARROTS

Makes 2 servings.

8 small carrots
⅓ cup strained honey

2½ tablespoons butter or margarine

1. Scrub carrots and boil whole, with very small amount of water, which should cook off in boiling. Boil until carrots are tender, but firm. **2.** To dry carrots add butter or margarine, and honey. Simmer slowly, until carrots are glazed and brown. Turn once or twice during cooking.

GUACAMOLE

The Tacuba Restaurant in Mexico City is not fancy, but it is a happy place in which to eat. Families fill its tables with laughter and good talk, while substantial, crisply dressed waitresses move about cheerfully, against a background of clean, colorful tiles. It was here that Suzie obtained the guacamole recipe which has been so successful at parties and buffet suppers. Despite its chili powder or tabasco sauce, the dish is smooth and not overly spicy.

Makes 2 to 3 servings.

1 good ripe avocado	½ teaspoon oil
1 small onion, finely chopped	1 teaspoon cider vinegar
½ small can pimientos, finely sliced	Salt
	Chili powder or tabasco sauce

1. Peel, quarter and pit avocado. Purée avocado through coarse sieve. **2.** Add the finely chopped onion and sliced pimiento. Add oil, vinegar and salt. Add generous dashes of tabasco (or chili powder) and mix thoroughly. **3.** Place in serving bowl and either serve at once or place in refrigerator to preserve the lovely green color of the avocado. **4.** Serve on Melba toast as an hors d'oeuvre or on a lettuce leaf as a salad course with meat.

GREEN PEPPERS ITALIENNE

Makes 4 servings.

4 large green peppers	2 teaspoons sugar
2 cups canned tomatoes	2 cloves garlic, finely chopped
4 tablespoons olive oil	½ teaspoon basil
1 medium onion, sliced	⅛ teaspoon pepper
2 teaspoons salt	

1. Cut thin slice off stem end of peppers; remove seeds and membranes. Cut peppers into strips 1½ inches wide; cut strips in half. **2.** Heat 3 tablespoons of the oil in a large skillet, and sauté peppers 10 minutes, or until slightly browned. Then add ¼ cup boiling water and 1 teaspoon salt. **3.** Cover, and simmer for 20 minutes, or until tender. **4.** Sauté sliced onion and chopped garlic in a saucepan, using remaining tablespoon oil. When onion and garlic are golden brown, add peppers and all other ingredients. **5.** Simmer, uncovered, for 30 minutes, or until thickened. Place drained peppers in serving dish and pour on sauce.

BAKED CARROTS WITH WINE

Makes 4 servings.

4 cups shredded raw carrots
½ cup sauterne or other white table wine
½ teaspoon salt

1 teaspoon sugar
2 tablespoons butter or margarine
Dash of pepper

1. Place carrots in a greased casserole; add wine, salt, pepper, and sugar, and stir well. Dot with butter. **2.** Cover and bake in moderate oven (350°F.) for 30 minutes. Serve right from casserole.

SAUTÉED CORN AND SWEET PEPPER

Makes 4 servings.

1 medium-large sweet green pepper, chopped fine
1 can corn kernels (12 ounces)

2 tablespoons shortening
¾ teaspoon salt

1. Cook chopped pepper in shortening until almost done, then add corn and salt. **2.** Cook for another 5 minutes, or until tender and lightly browned. Serve quickly.

CUCUMBERS AND ONIONS WITH PENNSYLVANIA DUTCH DRESSING

Makes 4 servings.

2 medium cucumbers
3 small white onions
1 cup sour cream
2 tablespoons white vinegar

2 tablespoons sugar
½ teaspoon dry mustard
¼ teaspoon salt
Few grains celery salt

1. Thinly slice the cucumbers. Slice onions particularly thin. Toss all into ice water, to crisp. Drain. **2.** Whip together all other ingredients except vinegar; when they are thoroughly blended, add the vinegar. Pour this dressing over the drained cucumber and onion slices.

CREAMED GREEN PEPPERS

Makes 6 servings.

6 medium peppers
2 cups milk
2 tablespoons butter, margarine or oil

2 tablespoons flour
1 teaspoon salt
¼ teaspoon pepper

1. Place peppers right on burners, over medium heat. Turn, often, until entire surfaces are charred. **2.** Under running water, scrape off the blackened skin with a sharp knife. Cut peppers open, re-move seeds and membranes. **3.** Cut peppers into slivers with scissors, and combine with butter in a saucepan. Add the flour when butter is melted; stir to smoothness. Stir in milk, salt, pepper. **4.** Simmer about 15 minutes, or until sauce has thickened and peppers are tender. Stir often. Thin with milk if necessary.

OKRA WITH HOLLANDAISE SAUCE

Makes 2 servings.

2 dozen fresh young okra pods   Salt
Hollandaise sauce

1. Wash okra. Do not cut off the stem end. **2.** Drop whole pods in rapidly boiling, lightly salted water. Boil exactly 7 minutes from time water resumes boiling. **3.** Drain and serve on individual plate, like oysters-on-half-shell, with small bowl of Hollandaise sauce in center and okra arranged in fan shape around it. Eat okra by lifting stem end with fingers and dipping into Hollandaise.

BRAISED RADISHES

Makes 6 servings.

3 bunches radishes   3 tablespoons butter
¼ cup cream   ½ teaspoon salt

1. Wash radishes; remove roots and leaves. Slice. **2.** Place in saucepan; cover with water. Boil, uncovered, for 10 minutes; drain. **3.** Cook in butter for 5 minutes, add the salt and cream. Cover and simmer 5 minutes more.

STEAMED AND GLAZED PARSNIPS

Here is an excellent winter vegetable which deserves greater popularity. When steamed, parsnips have a rich, nutty flavor, enriched by glazing.

Makes 4 servings.

1 pound parsnips   Salt
¼ cup melted butter   Paprika
¼ cup brown sugar

1. Wash parsnips, but do not peel. Place in covered saucepan with about ½ cup water, and steam until tender. **2.** Now peel and slit lengthwise. If cores are large, scoop out with point of a knife. **3.** Cut parsnips in quarters, lengthwise, and dip in melted butter. **4.** Sprinkle with salt, paprika and sugar; place in heavy skillet over a low fire until parsnips are well glazed. Baste occasionally with melted butter.

SNAP BEANS AMANDINE

Makes 4 servings.

1 pound young whole string
beans, wax or butter beans
1 cup bouillon

¼ cup shredded almonds
2 tablespoons butter

1. Heat bouillon and add whole beans. Cook until done; drain.
2. Brown the butter lightly and add almonds. Then add to the
beans. **3.** Mix lightly and serve piping hot, like asparagus, on
lightly buttered toast squares.

SNAP BEANS AND MUSHROOMS IN SOUR CREAM

Makes 4 servings.

2 cups cooked string beans or
other snap beans
1 cup mushrooms
⅓ cup sour cream
¼ teaspoon salt

2 tablespoons butter or margarine
2 teaspoons chopped parsley
or basil

1. Sauté mushrooms in the butter or margarine. **2.** Add the cooked
beans, sour cream and salt. **3.** Heat and serve with chopped
parsley or basil.

BAKED SUCCOTASH

Makes 3 servings.

¾ cup cooked green peas
½ cup cooked corn kernels
½ cup baby lima beans
¼ cup light cream

⅛ cup finely chopped canned
pimiento
½ teaspoon salt
½ teaspoon sugar

1. Mix together all ingredients and place in a covered baking
dish or casserole. **2.** Heat in moderate oven (350°F.) for 30
minutes.

BAKED TURNIPS

Makes 6 servings.

2 pounds turnips
¼ cup butter or margarine
1½ teaspoons salt

1½ teaspoons granulated or
brown sugar

1. Peel and cube turnips. **2.** Place in baking dish with butter,
sugar and salt. Cover tightly. **3.** Bake in moderate over (350°F.)
about 1 hour, or until tender.

SPINACH AND CELERY PIQUANT

Makes 6 servings.

1 box (14 ounces) frozen spinach or chopped spinach
1 cup sliced celery
½ teaspoon salt
2 tablespoons butter

2 tablespoons prepared horseradish
½ teaspoon salt
⅛ teaspoon pepper
¼ cup cream

1. Cut frozen block of spinach into 1½-inch cubes. Add celery and ½ teaspoon salt to 1½ cups boiling water in saucepan. 2. Cook until celery is almost tender. Then add spinach, bring again to a boil, and cook gently 4 to 6 minutes, or until spinach is just tender. 3. Drain well. Add remaining ingredients and mix well. 4. Heat thoroughly. Serve on hot platter with slices of hot boiled tongue, luncheon meat, or sliced chicken.

ZUCCHINI WITH BUTTER SAUCE

Makes 1 serving.

Small, tender zucchini (Italian
squash)

Melted butter
Salt and pepper

1. Scrape zucchini lightly, removing only the darkest green. 2. Lay whole in a covered pot with a very small amount of water—enough to barely cover the bottom of the pot. Steam until just tender, or about 25 minutes, checking from time to time to make sure zucchini doesn't burn. 3. Turn out carefully into serving dish and pour on melted butter. Season with salt and pepper.

CAROTENE SALAD

Makes 6 servings.

1½ cups Sunkist orange pieces
1½ cups finely cut carrot
½ cup raisins

½ cup chopped peanuts
French dressing, lettuce leaves
or shredded cabbage

1. Toss together lightly with 2 forks the orange pieces, carrot and raisins. 2. Add French or other salad dressing to moisten. 3. Serve on lettuce or shredded cabbage and garnish with peanuts.

COOKED CRANBERRY APPLE RELISH

Makes about 1 pint.

1 cup sugar
¼ teaspoon cinnamon
Grated rind of 1 orange
Grated rind of 1 lemon

½ pound (one pint) cranberries
1 large cooking apple, peeled
and sliced

1. Mix sugar, ½ cup water, cinnamon and fruit rind. Heat, stirring until sugar is dissolved and mixture is boiling. 2. Add cranberries and apples and simmer without stirring until skins of cranberries pop open and apple is tender. 3. Cool and serve with poultry, pork or game.

CHOPPED CRANBERRY APPLE RELISH

Makes 1½ quarts.

4 cups cranberries	1 lemon
2 apples	2½ cups sugar
2 oranges	

1. Peel and core apples. Put through food chopper, with the cranberries. 2. Quarter the oranges and lemon, unpeeled; remove seeds. Put through chopper, add sugar, and blend well. 3. Chill in refrigerator several hours before serving. This sauce will keep in refrigerator for several weeks.

WINTER VEGETABLE SALAD

Makes 6 servings.

1 package lemon Jell-O	½ cup finely shredded cabbage
1 tablespoon vinegar	2 tablespoons thinly sliced pimiento
¾ teaspoon salt	
1 cup cooked peas	
½ cup diced celery	

1. Dissolve Jell-O in 1 cup *hot* water. 2. Add 1 cup cold water, vinegar and salt. Chill until slightly thickened, then fold in vegetables. 3. Turn into individual molds. Chill until firm. Unmold on crisp lettuce. Serve with mayonnaise.

FROZEN DATE AND CHEESE SALAD

Makes 6 to 8 servings.

1 package cream cheese (3 ounces)	½ cup sliced dates
3 tablespoons milk	½ cup blanched chopped almonds
½ cup mayonnaise	2 teaspoons lemon juice
¼ cup heavy cream, whipped	Lettuce leaves

1. Blend cream cheese with milk, stir in mayonnaise. Fold in cream, dates, almonds and lemon juice. 2. Turn into freezing tray of refrigerator, freeze 2 to 4 hours or until firm. 3. Unmold, slice and serve on crisp lettuce with a cream dressing.

WALDORF SALAD

Makes 4 servings.

1½ cups cubed apple (if red apple, leave on peel)
¾ cup finely diced celery
⅓ cup chopped walnuts or pecans

½ cup boiled dressing or mayonnaise
Juice of ½ lemon
4 lettuce leaves or salad greens

1. Sprinkle cubed apples with lemon juice. **2.** Mix all the ingredients together and serve on greens.

DATE-ORANGE SALAD

Makes 4 servings.

½ package dates
4 oranges
4 lettuce leaves

4 tablespoons cottage cheese
4 maraschino cherries

1. Cut dates in half. **2.** Pare 4 oranges as you would an apple, cutting a continuous circular peel to remove the outside membrane surrounding the sections. Cut out each segment separately. **3.** Arrange the date halves and orange segments alternately on a lettuce leaf. Top with a tablespoonful of cottage cheese and a maraschino cherry. Serve with Fruit Frenchette Dressing.

TUNA-APPLE MOLDED SALAD

Makes 8 servings.

2 packages lemon flavor gelatin
1 tin fancy tuna (7½ ounce can)
1 cup shredded apple

¼ cup shredded carrot
2 tablespoons chopped celery
Lettuce leaves, radishes and parsley

1. Dissolve gelatin in 1 cup hot water; add 2 cups cold water; cool. **2.** Add well-drained tuna, apple, carrot, celery. **3.** Chill several hours. Unmold on lettuce leaves; garnish with radish rosettes and parsley.

ORANGE FRUIT SOUP

Makes 5 or 6 servings.

2 tablespoons Minute Tapioca
1 tablespoon sugar
½ cup concentrated frozen orange juice

2½ cups diced fresh fruit (bananas, grapes, cantaloupes, peaches, etc.)
Dash of salt

1. Place tapioca and 1½ cups water in saucepan. Bring to a boil, stirring constantly. 2. Remove from stove. Add sugar, salt, and concentrated orange juice; blend. 3. Cool, stirring once after 15 to 20 minutes. Cover and chill. Before serving, add fruit.

COLD FRESH FRUIT SOUP

Makes 4 servings.

2 cups fruit—cherries, strawberries, raspberries or plums
Grated rind of 1 lemon
1 piece cinnamon (2-inch
stick)

½ cup sugar
1 tablespoon Minute Tapioca
or cornstarch
Dash of salt
¼ cup white wine

1. Cook all ingredients except wine in 1 quart of water. Cook until fruit is soft and tapioca clear. (If cornstarch is used, mix with sugar first, before adding to water.) 2. Put through a fine sieve. Cool and add wine. Serve very cold.

DRIED FRUIT SOUP (HOT or COLD)

Makes 6 servings.

6 prunes
3 dried apricot halves
3 dried pear halves
½ cup seedless raisins
½ cup sugar or honey

½ teaspoon salt
1 piece cinnamon (2-inch
stick)
1½ tablespoons Minute Tapioca or cornstarch

1. Wash fruit in hot water. Pour over 1 quart boiling water and let stand until fruit is plump. 2. Add all other ingredients, cover, and cook slowly for about 1 hour, until fruit is tender and tapioca clear. (If cornstarch is used instead of tapioca, mix it with the sugar first, before adding to the fruit water.) Serve hot or cold.

ONION SOUP

Makes 6 servings.

4 large onions, sliced thin
4 tablespoons fat
6 Souplets vegetable bouillon
tablets

6 thick slices French bread,
oven toasted
Grated Parmesan cheese
Salt and pepper

1. Cook onions in fat until brown. 2. Dissolve Souplets tablets in 6 cups boiling water and pour over onions. Simmer covered 45 minutes. 3. Season to taste. Place 1 slice of toast in each serving dish; fill dishes with soup; sprinkle with cheese. 4. Soup may be placed under broiler for a few seconds, if desired.

SCANDINAVIAN OAT SOUP

Makes 8 servings.

¾ cup rolled oats
18 pitted prunes or ¾ cup
    raisins

10 almonds
3½ cups milk
Sugar and salt

1. Simmer oats in 2½ pints water about 1 hour, or until soft. Put through strainer. **2.** Wash prunes or raisins, cover with cold water and simmer until tender. **3.** Scald the almonds, remove skins, and cut into strips. **4.** Bring milk to a boil and add to pot containing oats. Add prunes or raisins, together with their cooking water. Add slivers of almond. Season with salt, and add sugar to taste. **5.** Heat thoroughly and serve hot.

CARROT AND FIG CONSERVE

Makes about 10 pints.

1½ pounds large firm carrots
1 large beet
3 pounds sugar
1 pound dried figs
1½ cups seedless raisins

⅝ cup wine vinegar
2 large oranges
1 large grapefruit
1 large lemon

1. Scrape carrots thinly and chop fine. Peel and chop beet fine. **2.** Squeeze the citrus-fruit juices, and combine. Finely chop the rinds of the oranges, grapefruit, lemon. Finely chop the figs and raisins. **3.** Combine chopped carrots, chopped beet, chopped rinds, raisins, figs, with fruit juices, vinegar and sugar, in large kettle. **4.** Add 2 cups water, stir thoroughly to blend ingredients, and let stand for 3 hours. **5.** Stir again and cook gently, stirring constantly until the mixture boils. Cook 40 minutes, then turn into small sterilized jars, and seal.

RED CURRANT PRESERVE

Makes 2 quarts.

2 quarts red currants (do not
    wash until ready to use)
2 large oranges

2 quarts sugar
2 cups seedless raisins

1. Wash and stem the currants. Peel the oranges and finely shred the peel. **2.** In a large kettle make alternate layers of currants, orange pulp and peel, and sugar. **3.** Let stand overnight and in the morning bring slowly to a boil, stirring gently. Then simmer for 25 minutes. **4.** Add the raisins and continue cooking until thickened. Turn into hot sterilized jars, and seal.

LEMON CELERY VICTOR

1 bunch celery, tender portions, or 3 celery hearts	1 teaspoon salt
1 pint beef broth or consommé	1 tablespoon sugar
1 teaspoon celery seed	1 large or 2 small Sunkist lemons, cut in thin slices
6 peppercorns	¼ cup minced pimiento
4 tiny, dry red peppers	

1. Cut celery or celery hearts into desired lengths (1 to 4 inches). **2.** Parboil in salted water 10 minutes. Drain. Cook 10 to 15 minutes longer in broth made by combining other ingredients. **3.** Marinate until cold. Drain off liquid, retaining spices and lemon slices. **4.** Serve as an appetizer or a meat accompaniment.

LEMON FRUIT COCKTAIL SAUCE

Makes 6 servings.

½ cup sugar	3 cups any diced fruit mixture or melon balls
¼ cup any red jelly	
¼ cup lemon juice	

1. Boil sugar and jelly with 1 cup water, for 5 minutes. Chill. **2.** Add lemon juice. **3.** Pour over fruit and serve in cocktail glasses.
Variation: SPICED LEMON COCKTAIL SAUCE
For jelly, substitute ⅛ teaspoon each of cinnamon and nutmeg.

GRAPEFRUIT HORS D'OEUVRES

In center of tray or large plate, place a Sunkist grapefruit, stuck with toothpicks or gaily colored cocktail picks. Around this arrange the following appetizers made by combining grapefruit segments with:

Coconut, Nuts, Grated Cheese, or Mint: Roll segments in toasted coconut, chopped nuts, grated cheese, or chopped mint.

Anchovies: Top segments with rolled anchovies.

Prunes: Stuff cooked and pitted prunes with segments. Skewer together with picks.

Celery: Stuff finger-lengths of celery with cream cheese, moistened with grapefruit juice. Top with half-segments of grapefruit.

Shrimps: Curl shrimps over segments.

Olives, Cherries, or Cheese Balls: With a pick, skewer segments around whole stuffed olives, maraschino or mint cherries, or balls of cream cheese.

BAKED APPLES STUFFED WITH DATES

Makes 6 servings.

6 large apples, cored   ¾ cup brown sugar
12 sliced dates

1. Fill centers of cored apples with sliced dates. Slit the skin of the apples to prevent bursting in the oven. **2.** Place in baking pan. Dissolve sugar in 1½ cups boiling water and pour over the apples. **3.** Bake in hot oven (400°F.) until tender, basting occasionally. Serve warm or cold with cream.

FRESH FIGS

Kadota figs—green   Mission figs—almost black
Calimyrna figs—almost white   Celeste figs—light green
outside, brown inside

Buy and eat fresh figs only when fully ripe—fairly soft to the touch—but not bruised or injured. Overripe figs ferment quickly. To serve, wash and pare off outer skin. Serve whole, cut in halves, or sliced, with cream. Or split figs and serve on lettuce with topping of cottage cheese and chopped nuts.

STEWED DRIED FIGS

Short soaking and quick cooking is the modern way of preparing dried figs. Rinse and drain, cover with water, and let simmer for about 20 to 30 minutes. After about 15 minutes of cooking, add 1 tablespoon sugar for each cup of figs. Grated lemon or orange rind, whole cloves, cinnamon or candied ginger may also be added to the cooking water to improve the flavor of the figs.

Variation: Another stewed figs recipe is:

1 pound dried figs   1 piece lemon rind
2½ tablespoons lemon juice   Sugar equal to ½ of juice (see
1 large piece ginger root (if   directions)
available)   1 tablespoon sherry wine

1. Wash figs and remove stems. **2.** Add cold water to cover well. Add 1½ tablespoons of the lemon juice, lemon rind and ginger root. **3.** Stew figs, covered, until soft. Drain off juice and measure. Add half as much sugar as there is juice, then simmer the sirup until thick. Add remaining tablespoon lemon juice. **4.** Replace figs in the sirup and cook for one minute more. Cool and add the sherry. Chill and serve with cream.

STEAMED FIGS WITH CHEESE AND NUTS

Makes 6 servings.

2 dozen dried figs   ¼ cup walnut meats
1 pound cottage cheese   Salt

1. Steam the figs until tender and trim the stems. **2.** Chop the walnuts, combine with the cheese, and season to taste. **3.** Halve the figs and stuff with the cheese filling.

LIQUEURED FIGS AND SOUR CREAM

Makes 2 or 3 servings.

1 large can Kadota figs   1 tablespoon crème de cacao
½ cup sour cream   ½ teaspoon sugar

1. Drain figs well. Chill. **2.** Add crème de cacao to sour cream. Add sugar. **3.** Place chilled figs in serving dish and cover with sour cream mixture.

FIG TAPIOCA

Makes 6 servings.

2 cups diced cooked figs   ½ teaspoon grated lemon rind
½ cup quick-cooking tapioca   ½ teaspoon vanilla
½ cup granulated sugar   ¼ teaspoon salt
2 tablespoons lemon juice

1. Put the top part of a double boiler directly on the stove and boil 3 cups of water. At the same time, half fill the bottom part of the double boiler with water, and set on stove to boil. **2.** Combine the tapioca, sugar and salt. Shake this gently into the water and again bring to the boiling point, stirring constantly. **3.** Set the top of the boiler over the bottom, which by now should contain boiling water, and cook 5 minutes longer. **4.** Add the figs, lemon juice, grated lemon rind and vanilla. **5.** When partly cooled, turn the mixture (which by then should be quite thick) into a serving dish and set in refrigerator to chill. Serve with whipped or plain cream.

FIG DUMPLINGS

Use one fresh, ripe fig for each dumpling. Enclose each in a square of biscuit dough and steam for about 25 minutes. Serve with a favorite sauce—hard sauce, foamy yellow sauce or other sauce.

FRESH FIGS MELBA

Makes 6 servings.

1 cup fresh raspberries
¼ cup sugar

12 large fresh peeled Mission figs
6 servings vanilla ice cream

1. Make sauce by crushing and straining the raspberries, adding the sugar and cooking to a heavy sirup. This is enough for 6 servings. **2.** Gently press 2 figs into each serving of vanilla ice cream and top with the raspberry sauce.

FRESH FIG MARMALADE

Fresh figs

Sugar to equal cooked figs

1. Wash a quantity of figs, place in a little water and bring to a boil. **2.** Measure cooked figs and add 1 cup of sugar for each cup of figs. Cook for one hour, stirring constantly to prevent burning. **3.** Turn into sterilized jars, and seal.

STUFFED FIGS

½ pound figs
2 tablespoons sugar
1 teaspoon lemon juice

Chopped salted almonds
½ cup sherry or other wine
(or water)

1. Wash figs and stuff with chopped almonds. **2.** Put sugar, lemon juice and wine (or water) in saucepan. Heat, and add figs. **3.** Cover pan and cook until figs are tender. Turn and baste frequently, so figs absorb full flavor.

FIG GINGER PUDDING

Makes 6 servings.

1 cup dried figs
1 cup light molasses
½ cup melted shortening
2 cups sifted flour

1 tablespoon ginger
1 egg
1 teaspoon baking soda
¼ teaspoon salt

1. Rinse figs, remove stems, and chop coarsely. Beat the egg. **2.** Combine figs with egg, molasses and melted shortening. **3.** Sift together the dry ingredients and add half of this to the fig mixture, then add ½ cup water, the rest of the fig mixture, and another ½ cup of water. Stir while you do this, and beat the mix to blend thoroughly. **4.** Turn into one large or 6 small greased molds. Cover with greased paper or the cover of the molds, and steam the pudding for 1½ hours if it is in 1 large mold. If in small molds, steam for about 45 minutes. **5.** Serve with vanilla custard sauce.

FIG CHARLOTTE

Makes 6 servings.

1 envelope (1 tablespoon) unflavored gelatin
1 cup canned figs
1 cup canned fig juice
½ cup heavy cream, whipped

⅓ cup sugar
1 tablespoon lemon juice
⅛ teaspoon almond extract
⅛ teaspoon salt

1. Soften the gelatin in ¼ cup cold water. Slice half the figs; dice the other half and set them aside. 2. Combine the fig juice, sugar and salt in a saucepan. Bring to a boil and cook for 3 minutes, or until the sugar dissolves completely. Then pour in the softened gelatin and stir until this is dissolved. Cool a little and add the lemon juice and almond extract. Chill until mixture thickens, but does not set. 3. Wet a mold and arrange the sliced figs in the bottom of the mold. 4. Fold the whipped cream into the thickened gelatin and cover the sliced figs in the mold with a layer of this mixture. 5. Now quickly fold the diced figs into the remaining whipped cream mixture, and add this to the mold. Chill. When unmolded, garnish with whipped cream, if desired.

FIG FRITTERS

Makes 6 servings.

¾ cup steamed cold dried figs
1 whole egg plus 1 egg yolk
⅔ cup milk, to which few
drops vanilla or almond extract have been added

1½ cups sifted flour
2 teaspoons baking powder
¼ teaspoon salt
Deep fat

1. Sift flour, baking powder and salt. 2. Mix to a batter with the egg, egg yolk and enough milk to make a light drop batter. 3. Chop the figs coarsely and stir them into the batter. Drop the mixture from tip of tablespoon into deep hot fat (375°F.) and fry to a golden brown, turning to brown all sides. 4. Drain on soft crumbled paper and serve as hot as possible with hard sauce or lemon sauce.

CREAMED PRUNES AND DATES

1 cream cheese (3 ounces)
2 tablespoons milk

Pitted prunes and dates

1. Soften cream cheese with milk. 2. Force the softened cream cheese through a pastry tube into the pitted fruit.

INTERESTING MIXTURES FOR STUFFING DATES
(Enough to stuff 1 package of Dromedary dates)

ORANGE PEANUT:
To ⅓ cup peanut butter, slowly add 5 tablespoons orange juice and ½ teaspoon grated orange rind. Sprinkle stuffed dates with chopped salted peanuts.

APRICOT COCONUT:
Wash ½ cup dried apricots. Put through food chopper alternately with ¼ cup nutmeats and ⅓ cup shredded coconut. Add 1 tablespoon orange juice. Mix until well blended. Stuff dates and roll in sifted confectioner's sugar.

MARSHMALLOW COCONUT:
Cut ¼ pound marshmallows into quarters with wet scissors. Place a piece of marshmallow, cut side up, in each date. Dip the sticky surface of the marshmallow into shredded coconut.
Other suggestions: Stuff dates with walnut or pecan halves; stuff dates with softened cream cheese; stuff with shredded coconut.

MAGIC DATE AND NUT ROLL

2 cups (½ pound) vanilla wafer crumbs	½ cup Eagle Brand sweetened condensed milk
1 cup chopped dates	2 teaspoons lemon juice
½ cup chopped nutmeats	

1. Combine wafer crumbs, dates, and nutmeats. 2. Blend condensed milk and lemon juice. 3. Add to crumb mixture and knead well. Form into roll and cover with waxed paper. Chill in icebox 12 hours, or longer. 4. Cut in slices. Serve with whipped cream or hard sauce.

BRAN-DATE BALLS

Makes 3 dozen candies.

2 cups Post's 40% bran flakes	1 tablespoon butter
¾ cup dates, pitted	2 teaspoons lemon juice
½ cup pecan meats	Confectioners' sugar
2 tablespoons honey	

1. Put bran flakes, dates and nutmeats through meat grinder. 2. Add honey, butter and lemon juice. Knead mixture until well blended. 3. Shape into 1-inch balls or fingers and roll in confectioners' sugar.

LOUISIANA DATE STRIPS

Makes 36 to 48 date strips.

1 package pie-crust mix
Small amount melted butter
6 tablespoons brown sugar
6 tablespoons shredded coconut

⅔ cup finely chopped dates
¼ teaspoon salt
Dried fruits and peels, toasted coconut, chopped nuts or sifted confectioners' sugar

1. Prepare pie-crust mix according to directions on the package. Roll out to ½-inch thickness and brush with butter. **2.** Combine sugar, shredded coconut, dates and salt. Spread this over one-half of the pastry. **3.** Fold over the other half and cut into strips about 1½ by 3 inches. **4.** Bake 15 minutes in hot oven (400°F.). Decorate baked date strips with dried fruits and peels, coconut, chopped nuts or sifted confectioners' sugar. Date strips may be frosted with confectioners' sugar and water frosting before decorating.

DATE AND WALNUT DELIGHT

Makes 4 servings.

24 graham crackers, finely rolled (2 cups crumbs)
½ pound marshmallows, quartered

1 cup chopped walnut meats
7¼-ounce package pitted dates, finely cut
½ cup heavy cream

1. Reserve 3 tablespoons graham cracker crumbs. Blend remainder with other ingredients. **2.** Shape in a roll. Coat with reserved crumbs, roll in waxed paper. **3.** Chill 4 hours. Serve in slices with whipped cream.

DATE REFRIGERATOR DESSERT

Makes 6 servings.

1 cup dates cut in pieces
1 cup marshmallow pieces
2 tablespoons milk
Few grains salt

½ teaspoon vanilla
16 graham crackers (¼ pound)
¼ cup chopped nutmeats
½ cup heavy cream, whipped

1. Cut the dates and marshmallows into small pieces with wet scissors. **2.** Add milk, salt, vanilla, and nutmeats. Mix well. Crush the graham crackers with a rolling pin. Add all the crumbs excepting 2 tablespoonfuls to the date mixture. **3.** Fold in the whipped cream. Form into a roll. Sprinkle the sides with the 2 tablespoons of graham cracker crumbs. **4.** Store in refrigerator for 24 hours. Slice and serve with sweetened whipped cream or ice cream.

DATES IN BLANKETS

Makes 32 pastries.

Dates, split lengthwise
Whole nut meats
Pastry

Small amount of cream
Chopped nuts

Stuff dates with nuts. Roll pie-crust dough thin (use a package mix). Cut pieces 3 inches x 1¼ inches. Wrap pastry pieces around stuffed dates. Brush with cream. Bake 10 to 12 minutes in very hot oven (450°F.). Frost if you like. Roll in chopped nuts.

DATE PEANUT BUTTER COOKIES

Makes 24 cookies.

1 cup (½ package) dates,
  finely chopped
¾ cup all-purpose flour
½ teaspoon soda
¼ teaspoon baking powder

¼ teaspoon salt
¼ cup shortening
¼ cup peanut butter
½ cup brown sugar
1 egg, well beaten

1. Mix and sift flour, soda, baking powder and salt. Cream shortening and peanut butter together. (*Note:* ½ cup of butter or margarine may be substituted for the shortening and peanut butter.) **2.** Stir in sugar, and egg. Blend in flour mixture and dates. Chill in refrigerator for at least one hour. **3.** Form into small balls. Place on greased cookie sheet and flatten with a fork. **4.** Bake in moderately hot oven (375°F.) 8 to 10 minutes.

DATE BARS

Makes 32 bars.

1 package dates
½ cup sugar

¼ cup chopped walnut meats

CRUMB MIXTURE:

1½ cups sifted flour
1 teaspoon soda
¼ teaspoon salt

1½ cups quick oatmeal
¾ cup brown sugar
¾ cup shortening

1. Cut dates in quarters, add sugar and 1 cup water. Cook over low flame until thick. Stir in nutmeats. Cool. **2.** Sift flour, soda and salt into large bowl. Add oatmeal and brown sugar. Mix together thoroughly. **3.** Cut in shortening with pastry blender or two knives until mixture is crumbly. **4.** Grease 8 x 8 x 2-inch square pan; pat half the crumbs into the bottom. Spread date mixture evenly over the top. Pat on the remaining crumbs. **5.** Bake in hot oven (400°F.) 25 to 30 minutes. When cool, cut into 1 x 2-inch bars.

HONEY DATE BARS

Makes 16 small squares.

1 cup dates chopped
½ cup all-purpose flour
½ teaspoon baking powder
¼ teaspoon salt
¼ cup shortening

½ cup honey
1 egg or two yolks, unbeaten
½ cup chopped nuts
½ teaspoon vanilla
Confectioners' sugar

1. Mix and sift flour, baking powder and salt. 2. Cream shortening and honey together. Beat in egg. Stir in flour mixture. 3. Fold in dates, nuts and vanilla. Spread in greased 8 x 8 x 2-inch square pan. 4. Bake in moderate oven (350°F.) 30 to 35 minutes, or until golden brown. Cool. 5. Cut into squares. Roll in confectioners' sugar.

DATE TORTE

Makes 6 servings.

½ cup flour
⅛ teaspoon salt
1 teaspoon baking powder
2 eggs

½ cup sugar
½ teaspoon vanilla
1 cup chopped nutmeats
1 package dates, sliced

1. Sift flour, salt and baking powder. 2. Beat eggs until stiff; beat in sugar gradually. Add vanilla, nuts and dates. 3. Stir in sifted dry ingredients. Pour into a shallow pan, lined with greased waxed paper. 4. Bake in moderately slow oven (325°F.) 1 hour. Cool. Cut into squares. 5. Serve with whipped cream or ice cream.

HONEY FRUIT BARS

Makes 35 bars (10½ x 15-inch pan).

¼ cup shortening
½ cup sugar
½ cup honey
1 egg
1½ cups Kellogg's Pep
1½ cups sifted flour

1½ teaspoons baking powder
¼ teaspoon soda
¼ teaspoon salt
½ cup milk
1 cup seedless raisins

1. Blend shortening, sugar and honey thoroughly. Add egg and beat well. 2. Crush Pep into fine crumbs and mix with sifted dry ingredients. Add to shortening mixture alternately with milk. 3. Stir in raisins. Spread batter about ½ inch thick in greased shallow pan. 4. Bake in moderate oven (350°F.) 15 to 20 minutes. Cool and cut into bars.

WASHINGTON APPLE FOAM

Makes 4 servings.

1 pint apple juice	1 teaspoon lemon juice
1 egg white	Cinnamon
1 tablespoon sugar	Sugar

1. Chill apple juice. Beat egg white stiff; add sugar, beating constantly. 2. Add apple and lemon juices. Pour into glasses. 3. Mix a little cinnamon and sugar; sprinkle on fruit juice mixture.

CRUSTED PEARS

Makes 6 servings.

3 fresh pears*	1 tablespoon butter or margarine
1 tablespoon lemon juice	
¼ cup honey	⅛ teaspoon nutmeg
1½ cups Rice Krispies	

1. Pare fruit and cut in half lengthwise; remove cores. Dip halves in mixture of lemon juice and honey. 2. Roll in finely crushed Rice Krispies. Place cut side up in greased baking dish. Dot with butter and sprinkle with nutmeg. 3. Bake in hot oven (400°F.) about 55 minutes or until tender. 4. Serve pears either hot or cold with Custard Sauce or cream.

*If cooked or canned pears are used, drain carefully, use same method except decrease baking time to 15 to 20 minutes.

CUSTARD SAUCE

1 egg	1 cup scalded milk
2 tablespoons honey	¼ teaspoon vanilla
Pinch of salt	

1. Beat egg slightly; add honey and salt. Gradually stir in scalded milk. 2. Cook over hot water, stirring constantly until mixture coats a metal spoon. Remove from heat; add vanilla. Cool.

HONEYDEW MELON WITH LIME

Makes 6 servings.

1 large ripe honeydew melon	Grated nutmeg
3 limes	

1. Chill honeydew for several hours and cut into 6 even slices. 2. Just before serving squeeze juice of half a lime over each slice and sprinkle with grated nutmeg.

FROZEN PINEAPPLE-MINT

Makes 4 servings.

½ cup sugar
½ teaspoon mint extract
½ cup lemon juice

½ cup crushed pineapple
1 cup ginger ale
Green food coloring

1. Put ½ cup water in saucepan, add sugar, mint extract and green coloring, and simmer for 10 minutes. 2. Add lemon juice, crushed pineapple and ginger ale, and pour into refrigerator tray. Set into freezing compartment. 3. When frozen, turn into sherbet or parfait glasses.

CRANBERRY–MIXED FRUIT JAM

Makes about 1 quart.

4 cups cranberries
1 cup mixed dried fruit
1 tart apple, peeled and cored

1 lemon, quartered and seeded
2 cups sugar
½ teaspoon mace

1. Grind cranberries, dried fruit, apple and lemon in a food chopper with coarse blade. 2. Combine mixture with sugar, mace and 1½ cups water and cook slowly until mixture is thick—about 20 to 30 minutes. Stir occasionally to avoid sticking. Pack in hot sterilized jars; seal with paraffin.

PEACH JAM

Well-ripened peaches

Sugar to equal cooked peach pulp

1. Cut peaches into small pieces. 2. Put into large kettle. Cook slowly, without water, for 20 minutes, or until peaches are slightly softened. 3. Measure peach pulp and add one cup sugar for each cup peaches. 4. Cook until desired consistency is reached. Pour into sterilized jars and seal.

LEMON MARMALADE

Makes eight 6-ounce glasses.

6 unpeeled Sunkist lemons,
sliced very thin and cut
crosswise into small pieces

1. Measure fruit. Add 3 times as much water. Boil about 20 minutes or until tender. 2. Replace liquid boiled away with water. Allow ¾ cup sugar to each cup fruit juice. 3. Cook in 2-cup lots to the jelly test—thick, reluctant drops from the spoon (about 10 minutes). 4. Pour into sterilized jelly glasses. Cover with paraffin.

MARMALADE RICE

Makes 4 or 5 servings.

1⅓ cups (5-ounce package)   3 tablespoons orange marma-
Minute Rice   lade
½ teaspoon salt

1. Combine rice, 1½ cups water, and salt in saucepan. Mix just
until all rice is moistened. 2. Bring quickly to a boil over high
heat, uncovered, fluffing rice gently once or twice with a fork. (Do
not stir.) 3. Cover and remove from heat. Let stand 10 minutes.
Add marmalade and mix lightly with a fork.

SIRUPED APPLE SLICES

Makes about 2 cups.

¾ cup Log Cabin Syrup   3 tart apples
Dash of salt

1. Pare and core apples, cut in eighths. 2. Combine sirup and
salt in saucepan. Add apples and cook, covered, 5 minutes. 3. Remove cover and continue cooking until apples are soft and transparent and sirup is absorbed, turning apples frequently. 4. Serve
hot or cold as a meat accompaniment.

RAISIN OATMEAL

Makes 4 to 6 servings.

1½ cups Quaker or Mother's   ¾ teaspoon salt
Oats (quick or old-fashioned,   ½ cup raisins
uncooked)

1. Bring 3½ cups water to a boil. Add salt and raisins. 2. Stir in
rolled oats. Cook 2½ to 5 minutes or longer, stirring occasionally.
3. Turn off heat and let stand for 5 minutes.

Variation: 1. Use 2 cups milk and 1½ cups water. 2. Add ½ teaspoon cinnamon and ⅛ teaspoon nutmeg to water in Step 1 of
above recipe.

Oatmeal Variations:

CHOCOLATE CHIP CEREAL: Fold ½ cup semi-sweet chocolate chips into 4 servings cooked cereal.

EGG NOG TOPPING: Combine 1 beaten egg, 2 teaspoons
sugar, 1 cup top milk and ¼ teaspoon vanilla. Serve over hot
cereal.

FRUIT CEREAL: Add ½ cup chopped dates, cooked dried
apricots, figs, or prunes to four servings of cooked cereal.

DATE OATMEAL MUFFINS

Makes 8 to 16 muffins.

1 cup quick or old-fashioned oats uncooked
1 cup buttermilk
1 cup sifted flour
¼ cup sugar
½ teaspoon soda

2 teaspoons baking powder
½ teaspoon salt
½ cup chopped dates
1 beaten egg
3 tablespoons melted fat

1. Pour buttermilk over oats and let stand a few minutes. **2.** Sift together dry ingredients; add to oats mixture with chopped dates. **3.** Fold in beaten egg and melted fat. Fill greased muffin pans ⅔ full and bake in hot oven (425°F.) 15 to 25 minutes, depending on size of muffins.

HONEY CURRANT BUNS

Makes 12 buns 2½ inches in diameter.

½ cup currants
¾ cup milk
¼ cup honey
2 cups sifted flour

4 teaspoons baking powder
1 teaspoon salt
¼ cup shortening
½ cup Kellogg's All-Bran

1. Combine currants, milk, bran and honey; let stand 10 minutes. **2.** Sift together flour, baking powder and salt. Cut in shortening until mixture resembles coarse cornmeal. **3.** Add bran mixture, stirring to form a soft dough. Turn onto lightly floured board and shape into roll. **4.** Divide into 12 equal pieces, shape into balls and flatten to about ½-inch thickness. **5.** Place on greased pan, brush with honey and bake in hot oven (425°F.) about 20 minutes. Serve while warm.

HONEY FRUIT BRAN BREAD

Makes 1 loaf.

1 egg, well beaten
⅔ cup honey
1½ cups Kellogg's All-Bran
1 cup buttermilk
2 cups sifted flour
2 teaspoons baking powder

½ teaspoon soda
1 teaspoon salt
½ cup chopped figs
½ cup chopped dates
½ cup raisins
½ cup chopped nutmeats

1. Combine egg, honey, bran and buttermilk. **2.** Sift together flour, baking powder, soda and salt; add to bran mixture with fruits and nutmeats. Stir only until flour disappears. **3.** Spread in greased loaf pan—4¼ x 9½ inches—with waxed paper in bottom and bake in moderate oven (350°F.) about 45 minutes.

TWO-FRUIT MUFFINS

Makes 8 muffins.

1½ cups sifted flour
½ teaspoon salt
½ teaspoon soda
1 teaspoon baking powder
½ cup sliced dates
½ cup sour cream

1 cup mashed banana (3 bananas)
1 egg, slightly beaten
2 tablespoons melted shortening

1. Sift flour, salt, soda and baking powder over dates. To mashed banana add sour cream, egg and melted shortening. Beat well. 2. Add dry ingredients to dates, stir until just blended (batter will be lumpy). 3. Fill greased muffin tins ⅔ full. Bake in hot oven (400°F.) 20 to 30 minutes.

PETTIJOHNS MUFFINS

Makes 12 muffins.

1¼ cups sifted enriched flour
¼ cup sugar
3 teaspoons baking powder
1 cup Pettijohns Rolled Wheat, uncooked

½ teaspoon salt
1 beaten egg
1 cup milk
¼ cup melted shortening

1. Sift together flour, sugar, baking powder and salt; mix with Pettijohns. 2. Add egg and milk to dry ingredients, stirring lightly. Fold in cooled shortening. 3. Fill greased muffin pans ⅔ full. 4. Bake in hot oven (425°F.) 15 to 25 minutes.

Variation: CINNAMON TOPPING
Combine ⅓ cup brown sugar, 2 teaspoons cinnamon and 1 tablespoon melted butter. Sprinkle over muffins before baking.

Variation: DATES
Add ½ cup chopped dates to batter in Step 2.

Variation: RAISINS
Add ½ cup raisins to batter in Step 2.

WHEAT GERM MUFFINS

Makes about 8 muffins.

1 cup wheat germ
1 cup flour
4 tablespoons brown sugar
1 egg, well beaten
1 cup milk

2 tablespoons melted butter or shortening
4 teaspoons baking powder
¾ teaspoon salt

1. Mix milk and egg in bowl. Add wheat germ and let mixture stand a few seconds until wheat germ absorbs some moisture. 2. Sift in flour, salt, baking powder, brown sugar. Mix well. 3. Add melted butter. Stir. Half fill greased muffin tins and bake 20 to 25 minutes in hot oven (400°F.) as near center of oven as possible.

BRAN FRUIT SQUARES

Makes about 5 dozen pieces.

3 cups 40% bran flakes
1½ cups chopped raisins
¾ cup chopped dried figs
¾ cup chopped dates
1 cup chopped walnut meats

¾ cup sweetened condensed milk
1 tablespoon honey
1 tablespoon lemon juice

1. Combine bran flakes with remaining ingredients and mix until blended. 2. Press into 9 x 9 x 2-inch pan and cut in small squares, or roll in balls or in finger shapes. 3. Place shaped candy on platter and dry several hours. Wrap in waxed paper.

FILLED BRAN SQUARES

Makes 2 dozen cookies—2 inches square.

FILLING:

1 cup chopped dates or figs
½ cup brown sugar
2 tablespoons water

2 tablespoons orange juice
½ teaspoon grated orange rind

1. Combine ingredients and cook over moderate heat until thickened. Cool.

DOUGH:

½ cup shortening
¾ cup brown sugar
1 egg
1 cup Kellogg's All-Bran
2 cups sifted flour

1 teaspoon baking powder
½ teaspoon soda
½ teaspoon salt
¾ cup sour milk or buttermilk

1. Blend shortening and sugar thoroughly; add egg and beat well. Stir in bran. 2. Sift flour with baking powder, soda and salt; add to first mixture alternately with milk. 3. Spread ½ the dough in a greased shallow pan, about 8 x 14 inches. Drop filling by teaspoonfuls on top of dough and spread evenly. Cover filling with remaining dough, spreading carefully. 4. Bake in hot oven (400°F.) about 25 minutes.

FRUIT-FILLED COFFEE CAKE

3 cups sifted flour
4 teaspoons Calumet baking powder
1 teaspoon salt
½ cup sugar

½ cup shortening
1 egg, slightly beaten
¾ cup milk
Fruit Filling

1. Sift flour once, measure, add baking powder, salt, and sugar, and sift again. Cut in the shortening. 2. Combine egg and milk. Add to flour mixture and stir until soft dough is formed. Turn out on lightly floured board and knead 30 seconds to shape. Place dough on inverted baking sheet and pat or roll into 15 x 10-inch rectangle. 3. Place fruit filling down center of dough in 2-inch strip. Cut dough in 1-inch strips from filling to outside edge. Lace strips over filling by lifting 1 strip from each side and crossing in center. 4. Bake in moderately hot oven (375°F.) 45 minutes, or until done. Remove from oven. 5. While hot, brush lightly with thin icing made by mixing 4 tablespoons confectioner's sugar with 1½ teaspoons hot water. Serve warm.

FRUIT FILLING

⅓ cup chopped, cooked prunes
⅔ cup chopped apples
⅓ cup brown sugar (firmly packed)

2 teaspoons vinegar
⅛ teaspoon salt
⅛ teaspoon cinnamon

1. Combine all ingredients, add ⅓ cup water and boil gently 5 minutes, stirring often. Cool before using.

SHREDDED WHEAT COOKIES

Makes about 5 dozen cookies.

½ cup shortening
½ cup honey
½ cup sugar
1 egg
1½ cups sifted flour
½ teaspoon baking soda
1 teaspoon salt

1 teaspoon cinnamon
¼ cup milk
½ cup raisins
½ cup nutmeats, chopped
4 Shredded Wheat biscuits, crumbled

1. Cream shortening and sugar; add honey. Add egg, beating well. 2. Sift flour, soda, salt, cinnamon. Add alternately with milk to first mixture. Stir in remaining ingredients. 3. Let stand 5 minutes. Drop by teaspoonfuls on greased cookie sheet. 4. Bake in moderately hot oven (375°F.) about 12 minutes.

ALL-BRAN MUFFINS OR PAN BREAD

Makes 9 medium muffins, 2½ inches in diameter, or nine 2½-inch squares.

2 tablespoons shortening	2½ teaspoons baking powder
1 cup Kellogg's All-Bran	½ teaspoon salt
¾ cup milk	¼ cup sugar or molasses
1 cup sifted flour	1 egg

1. Combine All-Bran and milk in mixing bowl. 2. Sift together flour, baking powder and salt; add to soaked bran with sugar or molasses, egg and shortening. Stir only until combined. 3. Fill greased muffin pans ⅔ full, or pour into greased pan (8 x 8 x 2 inches). Bake in preheated hot oven (400°F.) 25 to 30 minutes.

ALL-BRAN MUFFIN VARIATIONS:

SOUR MILK OR BUTTERMILK: Use in place of sweet milk; reduce baking powder to 1 teaspoon and add ½ teaspoon soda.

RAISIN OR DATE: Add ½ cup raisins or chopped dates to dry ingredients.

BACON: Add ¼ cup crisp, diced bacon to dry ingredients.

ORANGE: Add 2 tablespoons grated orange rind to dry ingredients.

SPICY APPLE: Roll thin apple slices in cinnamon and sugar and place on top of muffins just before baking.

SPICED: Use the molasses in place of sugar and add ½ teaspoon ginger and 1 teaspoon cinnamon to dry ingredients.

CARROT MUFFINS

Makes 2 dozen muffins.

⅓ cup raw carrots, grated	2½ teaspoons baking powder
¼ cup stewed prunes, chopped	½ teaspoon salt
¼ cup almonds, chopped	½ teaspoon nutmeg
1 cup milk	¼ teaspoon ground cloves
1 egg	2¼ tablespoons sugar
2 cups flour	2 tablespoons butter

1. Combine and sift flour, baking powder, salt, nutmeg and cloves. 2. Cream the butter while working in the sugar. Beat in egg until fluffy. Add flour mixture and milk, a little of each alternately, and stir just enough to blend. 3. Gently stir in the grated carrots, chopped prunes and almonds. Bake in well-greased muffin pan in hot oven (400°F. to 425°F.) for 20 to 25 minutes. Turn out at once and serve.

100% WHOLE WHEAT COFFEE CAKE

Makes 9 to 12 servings.

CAKE:

2 cups sifted Wheatsworth whole wheat flour
1 tablespoon baking powder
1/3 cup sugar
1/2 teaspoon salt
1/4 cup shortening
2/3 cup milk (about)

TOPPING:

1/2 cup brown sugar, firmly packed
1/4 cup Wheatsworth flour
1/4 cup melted butter or margarine
1 tablespoon cinnamon

1. Sift together flour, baking powder, sugar, and salt. **2.** Cut in shortening until fine as meal. Add about 2/3 cup milk, mixing to form soft dough. **3.** Pat out to 1/2-inch thickness in greased 9-inch square pan. **4.** Make topping: Mix together brown sugar, melted butter or margarine, flour, and cinnamon. Spread on top of dough. **5.** Bake in hot oven (425°F.) 25 to 30 minutes. Serve warm.

APRICOT RAISIN BRAN PUDDING

Makes 6 servings.

1 cup sifted flour
3/4 teaspoon Calumet baking powder
1/4 teaspoon soda
1/4 teaspoon salt
1 1/4 cups raisin bran
1 egg, well beaten
1/2 cup dark corn sirup
1/4 cup apricot juice
1 teaspoon grated orange rind
1 teaspoon vanilla
4 tablespoons melted shortening
2 tablespoons butter
16 to 18 canned apricot halves, well drained

1. Sift flour once, measure, add baking powder, soda and salt, and sift together three times. **2.** Add bran and mix well. Combine egg, 1/2 cup corn sirup, apricot juice, orange rind, vanilla and shortening. **3.** Add to flour mixture, stirring only enough to dampen all flour. **4.** Melt butter in 8 x 8 x 2-inch pan. On this arrange apricots. Turn batter out on contents of pan. **5.** Bake in moderate oven (350°F.) 50 minutes, or until done. Loosen pudding from sides of pan with knife or spatula. **6.** Turn upside down on dish with apricots on top. Serve warm with whipped cream or fruit sauce.

Note: The following fruits may be substituted for canned apricot halves in the above recipe: 30 slightly sweetened stewed dried apricots, 24 slightly sweetened stewed prunes, pitted, 1 1/4 cups sliced peaches, or 4 slices pineapple, cut in quarters.

BOSTON BROWN BREAD

Makes 2 loaves.

1½ cups whole wheat flour	1½ teaspoons cinnamon
1½ cups yellow corn meal	1½ teaspoons ginger
1½ cups enriched white flour	2 eggs, slightly beaten
1½ teaspoons baking soda	1½ cups molasses
1 cup raisins	1¼ cups sour milk

1. Mix eggs, molasses and sour milk in one bowl, mix dry ingredients in another bowl and add to liquid mixture. Stir well. **2.** Into 2 well-greased, tall tins, spoon equal parts of the brown bread mix. **3.** Cover tightly with lids or waxed paper tied on firmly. Put tins in a kettle of boiling water and steam for 3 hours.

OLD-FASHIONED SOFT MOLASSES COOKIES

Makes 2½ dozen cookies.

⅓ cup shortening	3 cups sifted flour
⅓ cup brown sugar	1 tablespoon soda
1 cup molasses	¼ teaspoon salt
1 cup Kellogg's All-Bran	Nuts and raisins, if desired

1. Beat shortening until creamy. Add sugar gradually, mixing until thoroughly blended. **2.** Stir in molasses, bran, nuts and raisins. **3.** Add sifted dry ingredients alternately with ½ cup water, stirring to make a soft dough. **4.** Drop by tablespoonfuls onto greased cookie sheets; flatten if desired. **5.** Bake in moderately hot oven (375°F.) about 15 minutes.

WHEAT GERM HONEY COOKIES

Makes about 24 cookies.

¾ cup honey	¼ cup butter or margarine
1 cup wheat germ	½ teaspoon soda
2¼ cups wheat flour	½ teaspoon cloves
1 cup raisins	½ teaspoon cinnamon
1 egg, beaten	½ teaspoon salt

1. Heat the honey and mix in butter. Cool. Add egg. **2.** Stir in the dry ingredients and raisins and beat well. **3.** Drop by teaspoonfuls onto a greased baking sheet. Bake in moderate oven (350°F.) for the first few minutes, then lower heat to about 300° to 325°F. and bake for about 8 minutes more.

OATMEAL PANCAKES

Makes 12 to 14 pancakes.

2 cups milk
1½ cups quick oats, uncooked
1 cup sifted enriched flour
2½ teaspoons baking powder

1 teaspoon salt
2 tablespoons sugar
2 beaten eggs
⅓ cup melted shortening

1. Pour milk over oats and let stand 5 minutes. 2. Sift together flour, baking powder, salt and sugar. 3. Add beaten eggs to oats mixture. Add sifted dry ingredients. 4. Fold in melted shortening. 5. Bake on hot lightly-greased griddle until golden brown, turning only once.

APPLE BRAN BREAD

1 teaspoon soda
½ cup molasses
1½ cups sour milk

1½ cups flour
1½ cups bran
1 cup Musselman's applesauce

1. Dissolve soda in molasses, add milk, flour, bran and applesauce. 2. Bake 45 minutes in moderate oven (350°F.) in greased loaf pan.

PETER'S PLUM CAKE

2 pounds fresh blue plums
1½ cups flour
½ cup butter

¼ cup sugar for pastry
Cinnamon and sugar for top

1. With hands or pastry blender mix together flour, butter and about ¼ cup of hot water until a solid mass of dough. 2. Press dough into 9-inch pan, sides and bottom. 3. Cut plums almost in half to remove pits, place on ends very close together on the crust, starting on the outside and ending in the center. 4. Sprinkle with sugar and cinnamon and dot with butter. 5. Bake for 5 minutes in a hot oven (400° to 450°F.), then reduce heat to moderate (350°F.) and bake 20 minutes longer.

PRUNE–APRICOT UPSIDE DOWN CAKE

Makes 4 to 6 servings.

½ cup Karo sirup (blue label)
2 tablespoons melted butter or margarine
¼ cup brown sugar, firmly packed

1 package cake mix
20 stewed, drained apricot halves
20 stewed, drained prune halves

1. Combine first three ingredients in a 9 x 9 x 2½-inch pan.

2. Arrange fruit on top of sirup mixture. Use prepared cake mix according to package directions. **3.** Pour over sirup-fruit mixture. **4.** Bake in moderately hot oven (375°F.) 45 to 50 minutes. **5.** Let cool in pan about 2 minutes; then invert on serving plate. Serve warm, plain or with whipped cream.

SHREDDED WHEAT APPLE CRISP

Makes 4 to 6 servings.

5 cups sliced unpeeled apples, ¼-inch slices
¼ cup honey
2 teaspoons lemon juice
3 Shredded Wheat biscuits, finely rolled
3 tablespoons flour
4 tablespoons sugar
½ teaspoon cinnamon
2 tablespoons butter or margarine
Dash of salt
Light cream

1. Place apple slices in greased casserole. Pour over them honey and lemon juice. **2.** Mix together crushed Shredded Wheat, flour, sugar, cinnamon, butter and salt. Sprinkle over apples. **3.** Bake in hot oven (400°F.) 40 minutes. Serve warm with cream.

GRAHAM CRACKER FRUIT CAKE

Makes 8 to 10 servings.

¾ cup shortening
1 cup sugar
3 eggs, separated
1½ cups finely chopped seeded raisins
½ cup finely chopped maraschino cherries
¼ cup finely cut citron
½ cup finely chopped walnut meats
1 teaspoon grated orange rind
1 tablespoon orange juice
28 graham crackers, finely rolled (2⅓ cups crumbs)
¼ teaspoon salt
1½ teaspoons baking powder
¼ teaspoon cinnamon
⅛ teaspoon cloves
⅛ teaspoon nutmeg
½ cup milk
1 teaspoon vanilla

1. Cream together shortening and sugar, beating until light and fluffy. Slightly beat egg yolks; add to creamed mixture. **2.** Combine raisins, cherries, citron, walnut meats and orange rind; add to creamed mixture, together with orange juice. **3.** Combine graham cracker crumbs with salt, baking powder, cinnamon, cloves and nutmeg. Add these dry ingredients, alternately with milk, to first mixture, stirring until well mixed. **4.** Beat egg whites stiff, but not dry; add vanilla. Fold into batter. Pour into greased 10-inch tube pan. **5.** Bake in moderately slow oven (325°F.) about 1 hour and 15 minutes. Cool thoroughly; remove from pan.

DARK SPICED FRUIT CAKE

Makes about 3 pounds fruit cake.

1½ cups sifted flour
½ teaspoon Calumet baking powder
½ teaspoon salt
1 teaspoon cinnamon
½ teaspoon mace
¼ teaspoon nutmeg
¼ teaspoon allspice
⅛ teaspoon cloves
¼ cup raisins
¼ cup coarsely cut candied pineapple
¼ cup coarsely cut candied cherries
¼ cup currants
¼ cup finely cut candied orange peel
¼ cup finely cut candied lemon peel
⅓ cup finely cut citron
¼ cup coarsely chopped nut-meats
½ cup shortening (part butter)
1 cup brown sugar, firmly packed
3 eggs, unbeaten
¼ cup jelly
¼ cup fruit juice

1. Sift flour once before measuring. Measure 1 cup of the flour and sift together with baking powder, salt and spices. 2. Combine fruit, nutmeats, and remaining ½ cup of the flour; blend well. 3. Cream shortening, add sugar gradually, and cream together until light and fluffy. Add eggs, one at a time, beating well after each. Break jelly with a fork, add to egg mixture, and mix thoroughly. 4. Stir in fruit mixture. Add flour, alternately with fruit juice, blending well after each addition. 5. Turn into 8 x 4 x 3-inch loaf pan which has been greased, then lined on bottom and sides with brown paper. Bake in very slow oven (275°F.) 2½ hours, or until done. (If cake browns too quickly, cover with heavy brown paper.)

To store: Cool cake thoroughly. Wrap in cheesecloth which has been dampened with brandy or fruit juice. Then wrap in aluminum foil or cellophane to make airtight. Redampen cheesecloth about every two weeks.

NORWEGIAN PRUNE PUDDING

Makes 4 to 6 servings.

2 cups cooked pitted prunes, with juice
2 tablespoons cornstarch
1 tablespoon lemon juice
1 teaspoon cinnamon or nut-meg

1. Cut up prunes and bring prunes, lemon juice and cinnamon to a boil. 2. Blend cornstarch and ¼ cup cold water until smooth. Stir into prune mixture until thick. 3. Simmer 5 minutes. Chill and serve with custard sauce.

GRAHAM PRUNE WHIP

Makes 4 servings.

½ cup unsweetened, cooked prunes
¼ cup and ⅓ cup sugar
¼ teaspoon powdered cloves
1 teaspoon vanilla

½ cup heavy cream
12 graham crackers, finely rolled (1 cup crumbs)
2 egg whites

1. Pit and cut prunes. Blend thoroughly together the prunes, ¼ cup sugar, cloves and vanilla. 2. Whip cream. Beat prune mixture into whipped cream. Fold in graham cracker crumbs. 3. Chill thoroughly. Beat egg whites stiff, but not dry; gradually add remaining sugar, beating constantly. 4. Fold into chilled mixture. Serve very cold.

ICE-BOX PUDDING

Makes 6 servings.

½ cup wheat germ
6 macaroons, crushed
½ cup butter
½ cup sugar
⅓ cup crushed fruit

2 eggs
16 ladyfinger cookies
⅓ cup chopped nuts
Whipped cream

1. Cream butter and sugar and add 1 egg. Beat well. Add second egg and beat again. 2. Stir in crushed fruit and nuts. 3. Split some of the ladyfingers and arrange, flat side down, on the bottom of cake pan. 4. Mix together the crushed macaroons and wheat germ. Pour over ladyfingers. 5. Add fruit and egg mixture, top with more ladyfinger halves and chill. Serve with whipped cream on top.

COCONUT–APRICOT CANDY

Makes about 2 dozen balls.

¾ cup dried apricots
¾ cup Baker's coconut
½ teaspoon grated lemon rind

½ teaspoon grated orange rind
1 tablespoon orange juice

1. Wash apricots, cover with boiling water, and let stand 5 minutes; then drain. Put apricots and coconut through food chopper. 2. Add orange and lemon rind and orange juice and knead mixture until blended. If candy is dry, add enough additional orange juice to moisten. 3. If too moist, work in a small amount of confectioners' sugar. Shape in 1-inch balls. Roll in granulated sugar, additional coconut, or finely chopped nuts.

FIG NEWTON PARFAIT

Makes 4 servings.

1 package Fig Newtons
½ cup milk
½ cup drained crushed pineapple

¼ teaspoon salt
1 teaspoon lemon juice
1 cup heavy cream
½ teaspoon vanilla

1. Mix Fig Newtons and milk with fork until smooth. **2.** Add pine-apple, salt and lemon juice. Whip cream stiff; add vanilla; fold carefully into Fig Newton mixture. **3.** Freeze several hours in coldest unit of refrigerator.

Variation: For an orange variation use ½ cup orange juice in place of milk, omit pineapple and add ¼ teaspoon orange rind.

FRUIT PARFAITS

Makes 6 servings.

1 cup heavy cream
1 teaspoon vanilla
1 egg white
2 tablespoons sugar

18 Lorna Doone shortbread
cookies, coarsely crumbled
(1½ cups crumbs)
1 cup crushed strawberries

1. Whip cream stiff; add vanilla. Beat egg white stiff, but not dry; gradually add sugar; fold into cream. **2.** Alternate layers of Lorna Doone crumbs, strawberries and cream mixture. Garnish with strawberries.

Variations:

CHERRY PINEAPPLE PARFAIT
   Follow above recipe using crushed pineapple for the fruit and 38 Nabisco chocolate snaps for the crumbs. Garnish with mara-schino cherries.

GINGER AMBROSIA PARFAIT
   Follow above recipe using 2 sliced bananas marinated in orange juice for the fruit and 21 ginger snaps for the crumbs. Alternate crumbs, coconut, bananas and cream mixture.

PLOMBIERE SAUCE (for Ice Cream)

Makes ¾ cup.

½ cup orange marmalade   ¼ cup toasted coconut

1. Combine the marmalade with 2 tablespoons water. Add the coconut.

FIG ICE CREAM

Makes 4 servings.

1 package ice cream mix   ¼ cup milk or cream
½ package Fig Newtons

1. Prepare refrigerator vanilla ice cream according to your own favorite recipe or use packaged ice cream mix. **2.** Place mixture in tray of refrigerator freezing unit until ready to beat a second time, as stated on mix package or directions. **3.** Soften ½ package Fig Newtons in ¼ cup milk or cream, using fork to blend into a smooth mixture. **4.** After beating ice cream, gently stir in Fig Newton mixture; return to freezing unit and freeze until firm.

FIG MOLD WITH WHITE WINE

Makes 4 servings.

1 pound dried figs   1 tablespoon unflavored gelatin
¾ cup sugar   (1 envelope Knox's)
1 cup white wine   Strips of lemon rind

1. Chop the figs and put in a saucepan with the sugar, wine, 1 cup water and lemon rind. **2.** Simmer gently until figs puff out and are tender. **3.** Dissolve gelatin in a little warm water. Add to the mixture and pour into a mold and chill until set.

PINEAPPLE MINT SHERBET

Makes about 3 quarts.

3 cups sugar   1 cup crushed pineapple
1 cup fresh mint leaves   3 ripe bananas, mashed
Juice of 2 lemons   2 egg whites
Juice of 3 oranges   Vegetable coloring

1. Cook sugar and 3 cups water in a saucepan until all the sugar has dissolved and the sirup boils. **2.** Wash and crush the mint leaves slightly (with fingers or back of spoon) to release some of the juices. Add mint to the sugar-and-water sirup and let the mixture steep for about 1 hour. **3.** Strain out all the leaves, add the lemon juice, orange juice, crushed pineapple, mashed bananas, and a little green vegetable coloring to the sirup. **4.** Beat the egg whites until they stand in soft points, then mix into the fruit mixture very gently, but thoroughly. Pour sherbet into a hand freezer (or freeze in refrigerator trays), add 4 parts of crushed ice to 1 part of salt to the ice container, and start cranking. When the handle begins to move stiffly, sherbet is finished.

SPRING FRUIT TAPIOCA

Makes 8 servings.

¼ cup Minute Tapioca
1½ cups sugar
2½ cups rhubarb, cut in ½-
     inch pieces

½ teaspoon salt
1 cup shredded fresh pine-
     apple

1. Combine tapioca, sugar, salt, rhubarb, and 2½ cups water in saucepan. **2.** Place over medium heat and cook until mixture comes to a full boil, stirring constantly. **3.** Remove from stove. Cool, stirring occasionally. Add pineapple. Chill.

STRAWBERRY TAPIOCA

Makes 6 servings.

2 cups fresh strawberries,
     sliced
¾ cup sugar
2 cups berry juice and water

¼ cup Minute Tapioca
¼ teaspoon salt
2 tablespoons lemon juice

1. Sweeten strawberries with ¼ cup of the sugar and let stand 30 minutes. **2.** Drain; add enough water to juice to make 2 cups. Combine berry juice and water, tapioca, remaining sugar, and salt in saucepan and mix well. **3.** Place over medium heat and cook until mixture comes to a full boil, stirring constantly. Remove from stove. **4.** Cool, stirring occasionally. Add berries and lemon juice. Chill.

LEMON COCKTAIL PUNCH

Makes 1 serving.

1 tablespoon lemon juice
Ginger ale

Lemon sherbet
Sprig of mint

1. Put lemon juice in cocktail glass. **2.** Fill ⅔ full with chilled ginger ale. Add a spoonful of lemon sherbet. **3.** Garnish with a sprig of mint. This is a most delicious and refreshing appetizer.

PIED PIPER FRUIT CUP

Serve over any fruit cocktail mixture a combination of finely cut dates, dried prunes, raisins, candied or maraschino cherries, and a generous portion of lemon juice.

MELON À LA HOLLYWOOD

Serve 1 or more Sunkist lemon quarters with chilled cantaloupe, honeydew, casaba, or Persian melon.

RASPBERRY SIRUP DRINKS

Dr. Berthold Loeb, a lovely gentleman who is the picture of all old German doctors with Dignity and a big sweeping mustache, feels that the American people should get to know raspberry sirup better. In Europe it has been highly popular, and justifiably so. Mrs. Bauer's raspberry sirup is the preferred brand, although other good ones are now available. A little sirup makes a good drink just with carbonated water or cold water. Or, mix it with juices, in these proportions:

1 part raspberry sirup
1 part orange juice
2 parts grapefruit juice

or

1½ parts orange juice
½ part raspberry sirup
2 parts grapefruit juice

or

2 parts apple juice
½ part raspberry sirup
½ part orange juice
1 part grapefruit juice

HOT SPICED APPLE PUNCH

Makes about 2 quarts.

1 quart apple juice or cider
1 pint pineapple juice
3 tablespoons diced, candied ginger

1 cup strong tea
1 peeled orange cut into eighths
Thin, yellow rind of 1 orange

1. Place tea, ginger, orange, and rind in container of electric blender, in order named. 2. Put on cover and run blender until contents are thoroughly blended. 3. Pour into saucepan, add other ingredients and heat. 4. Serve hot in mugs.

GRAPE PUNCH

Makes 3 pints.

1 pint grape juice
1 cup strong cold tea
4 slices canned pineapple

1 cup pineapple juice
½ cup port wine
1 tablespoon lemon juice

1. Place tea, lemon juice, and sliced pineapple in container of electric blender. 2. Put on cover and run blender until contents are thoroughly blended. 3. Pour grape juice, pineapple juice, and port wine into pitcher partly filled with ice. Add blended ingredients. 4. Stir and serve.

FRUIT SALAD NECTAR

Makes about 1 pint.

1 cup unsweetened pineapple
juice
1 cup canned fruit salad

1 cup finely cracked ice (not
ice cubes)

1. Place juice in container of Waring Blendor. 2. Add other ingredients and put on cover. 3. Turn on blender and run until thoroughly blended, about 2 minutes.

OTHER FRUIT NECTARS:

Honeydew Nectar

1 cup orange juice
1 tablespoon lemon juice

1 cup diced honeydew melon

Pear Nectar

1 cup unsweetened pineapple
juice
1 cup finely cracked ice

1 cup canned pears
2 tablespoons sherry

Prune Nectar

1 cup apple juice or cider
½ cup soaked, pitted, dried
prunes

1½ cups finely cracked ice
Dash of cinnamon or Angostura
bitters

Strawberry Nectar

1 cup orange juice
1 cup finely cracked ice
1 cup fresh strawberries

2 tablespoons sugar or ½ cup
quick-frozen strawberries

1. Follow same directions as for Fruit Salad Nectar. Run blender 15 seconds to 3 minutes, as required.

APRICOT MILK SHAKE

Makes 2 small servings. Each serving contains 83 milligrams sodium; 73 calories.

¼ cup drained stewed dried
apricots, unsweetened
1 cup cold water
3 tablespoons non-fat dry milk
solids (skim milk powder)

1 teaspoon Sacrose no-calorie
sweetener
1 teaspoon lemon juice

1. Place all ingredients in deep bowl. 2. Beat until smooth with rotary egg beater. 3. Pour over ice cubes in tall glass and serve immediately.

RHUBARB JUICE

2 pounds rhubarb   Sugar as required

1. Split rhubarb stalks and cut in small pieces. Let boil in 1 quart water until rhubarb becomes very mushy. 2. Place into flannel bag and let drip. 3. To each quart of juice, add a pound of sugar. 4. Let boil fifteen minutes, skim, fill into hot, clean bottles, cork and seal.

PINEAPPLE TEA PUNCH

¾ cup cold tea   1 tablespoon lemon juice
2 tablespoons pineapple juice   Sugar to taste

1. Combine all ingredients and pour over ice cubes in tall glass.
2. Let stand two or three minutes, then serve.

APRICOT OR STRAWBERRY DRINK

Makes 1¼ cups.

¼ cup chilled, unsweetened,   ¼ teaspoon lemon juice
  stewed purée of dried apri-   1 cup milk
  cots or ⅓ cup uncooked, unsweetened strawberry purée

1. Combine lemon juice and apricot or strawberry purée. 2. Gradually stir in milk, blending well. Serve at once.

SPICED CIDER

Makes 8 servings.

2 quarts cider   4 whole allspice
½ cup light brown sugar   1 stick cinnamon
4 whole cloves   3 or 4 apples

1. Simmer cider, sugar and spices 15 minutes. Let stand several hours. 2. Bake the apples whole. 3. Strain the cider and reheat. Place in a large bowl, with the baked apples bobbing in it. Serve hot.

THE BLAND DIET

Frequently prescribed in the treatment of peptic ulcers and other gastrointestinal disorders

In the course of digestion, the food you eat is conveyed through about 30 feet of gastrointestinal tract. During the process this food is subjected to a complex series of chemical changes which enable your body to use the various nutrients in it.

Certain components of the normal diet, such as indigestible fruit and vegetable fibers, coarse particles, seasonings and spices are useful and even desirable for people with healthy gastrointestinal tracts. But when something goes wrong, these substances may have to be reduced or eliminated from the diet.

Because of its length and complexity, the digestive tract is often upset at any one of a number of places. These disturbances can be relatively mild, like indigestion or simple diarrhea, and respond quickly to treatment; or they may be as severe as peptic ulcer or colitis, and require months or years of continual therapy. But, mild or severe, the physician usually corrects the diet to cut out all but the blandest and least irritating food substances during the course of treatment. A diet of this type is called a bland diet and consists of soft, smooth, gentle foods. If the disturbance is in the colon, your doctor may recommend a bland and low residue diet that will be so thoroughly absorbed by the body that it leaves the lowest possible residue of waste matter for the colon to handle.

The object is to give a rest to the irritated or disturbed area —to relieve it of added work and mechanical irritation. Mechanical irritation is reduced by avoiding coarse cereals, raw fruits, raw vegetables and tough meat. In this way, cellulose fibers and other indigestible carbohydrates and connective tissues are reduced to a minimum.

The reduction of gastric acidity is usually accomplished through protein foods, together with the physician's alkaline medication. Proteins are rather effective antacids.

293

Foods that stimulate the gastric secretion are usually forbidden. These include coffee, tea, cola drinks, spices, condiments, meat extracts, cabbage and other highly flavored vegetables, and extremely hot or cold foods. Be sure to get your own doctor's list as to which foods to include in your diet, since he knows your individual requirements best. He may permit certain foods like weak tea with milk or mild beef tea, which he would exclude from another patient's diet.

It is entirely possible to prepare a bland diet so that it will contain an adequate amount of essential nutrients. However, strict bland diets are likely to be deficient in some of the nutrients; for this reason, doctors usually make every attempt to have their patients return to a less restricted diet as soon as possible.

The recipes in this section are designed to help you get the smooth, soft, bland foods which your doctor orders, and at the same time help you obtain the greatest possible variety and brightness in your meals, to avoid the monotony and dullness which are the principal bugaboos of the bland diet.

For the low residue diet, the bland diet is usually modified by the elimination of all whole grain breads and cereals, and by the exclusive use of ground meats and strained fruits and vegetables. Ask your physician to check the recipes he approves in your case.

Dr. Dorothea Turner, Editor of the Journal of the American Dietetic Association, tells how to cook the strongly flavored or "gas forming" vegetables (onions, leeks, radishes, dried beans, and vegetables of the cabbage family) so that many bland diet patients can eat them without particular discomfort. These vegetables contain sulphur in the form of sinigrin. To prevent the decomposition of this sinigrin and other substances which cause discomfort, heat these vegetables quickly. Keep the kettle uncovered to prevent the water from becoming acid. Make the cooking period as short as possible, and drain and serve the vegetable immediately when it is done.* This method has been tested and found to be effective, so that only the vegetables which the individual patient cannot tolerate need usually be barred from the diet, instead of eliminating all strongly flavored vegetables.

*Handbook of Diet Therapy.

FOODS <u>USUALLY</u> ALLOWED on the BLAND DIET

(Be sure to have this list checked by your doctor, before starting on diet.)

BEVERAGES

Milk (fresh, evaporated
   or dried)...Cocoa made
   with milk...Postum
Sanka Coffee...Weak tea
Light coffee (half milk)
   not more than once
   daily

BREADS

Enriched white bread
Fine whole wheat
Rye without seeds
White crackers...Toast
Plain white rolls
Zwieback
Milk toast

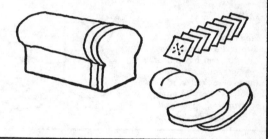

CEREALS

Corn flakes...Puffed rice,
   and similar prepared
   cereals
Cooked fine cereals:
   Enriched farina,
   Cream of Wheat, corn
   meal, rice, hominy grits
   ...Strained coarse
   cereals: oatmeal, Pettijohns, whole wheat

DESSERTS

Custard, cornstarch
   pudding, Junket,
   tapioca, rice pudding,
   bread pudding...
   Ice cream
Plain cakes and cookies...
   Pie made with Zwieback
   crust
Gelatin desserts...
   frozen desserts

No raw fruits; No nuts

FOODS USUALLY ALLOWED on the BLAND DIET

(Be sure to have this list checked by your doctor, before starting on diet.)

FATS, EGGS and CHEESE

Butter and margarine
Eggs, soft-boiled,
  poached or coddled
Mild soft cheese—
  cream, cottage
Moderate amount of grated
  American cheese in sauce
  or cooking

FRUITS

Ripe banana...Avocado
Strained cooked apples,
  pears, peaches, prunes,
  plums, apricots, cherries
Puree of cooked dried fruits
Strained juices of orange,
  grapefruit, pineapple,
  apple, prune, tomato

**MEAT and FISH (Without
  bones, gristle or
  excessive fat. Ground,
  unless very tender)**

Beef...Veal...Lamb
Poultry
Liver...Sweetbreads
All fresh fish
Canned tuna and salmon

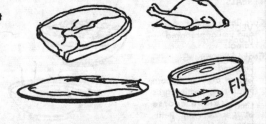

POTATO, etc.

White or sweet
  potatoes—
  any way but fried
  —no skins
Rice
Noodles, spaghetti,
  macaroni, pastina,
  semolina

FOODS <u>USUALLY</u> ALLOWED on the BLAND DIET

(Be sure to have this list checked by your doctor, before starting on diet.)

SALADS and DRESSINGS

Salads of permitted
   vegetables (cooked,
   strained)
Salads of permitted fruits
No greens
Home-made, cream-type
   salad dressings, made
   with salt, but without
   condiments

SOUPS

Cream soups made
   without stock—
   made with permitted
   vegetables
Clear broth not prepared
   from stock
Bland chowders

VEGETABLES
(Cooked and Strained)

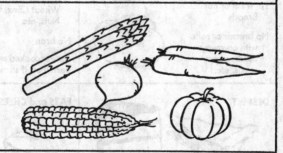

Asparagus...Beets
Carrots...Celery
Chard and Spinach
Corn...Lentils
Lima and String Beans
Peas—fresh or dried
Pumpkin and Squash

MISCELLANEOUS

Moderate amounts of:
   Jellies (clear)
   Marmalade...Syrup
   Honey...Molasses
   Plain candy
Sugar
Salt to make food palatable
Salt substitutes

FOODS
NOT USUALLY ALLOWED
on the BLAND DIET

Ask Your Physician

No carbonated drinks

No cola drinks

Coffee or tea only
in amounts
allowed

BREADS

No whole grain crackers

No coarse dark breads

No fresh or hot
breads

No breads or rolls
with caraway
seeds, poppy
seeds, etc.

CEREALS

No coarse dark
cereals such as
Shredded Wheat,
Wheat Chex, Grape
Nuts, etc.

No bran

Coarse cooked cereals only
permitted if strained

DESSERT

No rich pastries

No desserts containing
nuts or whole fruits

FATS and CHEESE

No fried foods

No nuts

No excess meat fats

No strongly flavored types
of cheese

No cooked cheese dishes
(Welsh rarebit)

FOODS
NOT USUALLY ALLOWED
on the BLAND DIET

Ask Your Physician

FRUITS

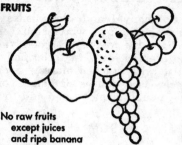

No raw fruits
except juices
and ripe banana

No skins or seeds

Eat only fruits on
allowed list

MEAT and FISH

No salted, smoked
or pickled meat
or fish

No bologna, frank-
furters, Spam,
Treet or other prepared
meat products. No Pork

No gristle, bones or
excess fat

SOUPS

No soup prepared
with meat stock

No chicken broth,
if prepared
with meat stock

VEGETABLES

No raw and coarse
vegetables

No strongly flavored
vegetables if they
disagree (cabbage,
cauliflower, broccoli,
Brussels sprouts, green
peppers, onion, turnip)

MISCELLANEOUS

No popcorn

No rich gravies
or sauces

No seasonings, spices,
vinegar, olives, pickles,
pepper, garlic, mustard,
catsup, chili sauce, horseradish, Worcestershire
sauce, etc.

299

BEEF, CHICKEN, AND VEAL STOCKS

So many bland diet dishes are based upon beef consommé, chicken broth or white stock, it behooves the cook to take time and trouble to prepare good, rich, homemade stocks, tempered to the dieter's taste, and clarified to suit his need. Fresh, uncooked meat, with cracked marrow bones or chicken feet, makes the best stock. Two ounces of bones contain as much thickening gelatin as a pound of meat, and add to the strength of the soup.

BEEF CONSOMMÉ

For good rich beef stock or "consommé," follow this rule:

Use 1 to 1½ pounds lean beef to each quart of water
Use ½ pound of cracked bone (or chicken feet) for each pound of meat
Use 2 cups of mixed, chopped, sliced or diced vegetables from the permitted list, for each quart of liquid after the meat and bones have cooked. For example: sliced onions, diced celery, quartered carrots, cut-up parsley and leek, diced parsnip, etc.

1. Cut the meat into 1-inch cubes and put into a pot with the bones, water and 2 teaspoons salt. Let stand 1 hour. **2.** Bring slowly to a boil, let simmer a few minutes, and very carefully skim off scum. **3.** Simmer, covered, for 3½ hours. Skim again and add the vegetables. A little thyme, bay leaf, or marjoram may also be added if desired. Simmer, covered, for 1 hour longer. **4.** Strain through a fine sieve. Set to cool in a crockery bowl, then chill quickly in refrigerator. Faithfully remove the fat and reheat soup. Add salt or several broken-up Souplets tablets if seasoning is required. **5.** Strain through fine strainer, lined with double thickness of cheesecloth, or use a flannel bag.

CHICKEN BROTH AND WHITE STOCK

Chicken broth is made in exactly the same way as beef consommé, with chicken substituted for the beef, pound for pound.

Veal stock, or "white stock," is made with veal and poultry trimmings substituted for beef, pound for pound.

JELLIED CHICKEN BROTH

Makes 4 servings.

2 tablespoons unflavored gelatin (2 envelopes Knox's)
1 quart chicken broth
Salt

1. Soak gelatin in ½ cup cold water 5 minutes. Add hot chicken broth. Add a little salt. **2.** Pour into mold rinsed in cold water. Chill. **3.** Unmold, beat slightly and serve in cold bouillon cups.

CONSOMMÉ ROYALE

Into each plate of consommé, put 8 or 10 cubes of egg custard, which are made this way:

3 egg yolks	Few grains salt
⅓ cup consommé	Few grains nutmeg

1. Beat egg yolks slightly, add ⅓ cup consommé, salt and nutmeg. 2. Pour into small buttered cup, place in pan of hot water and bake until firm. Remove from cup and slice into ¼-inch cubes.

CONSOMMÉ ALFREDO

Into each plate of consommé, put:

1 poached egg	Grated Parmesan cheese sprinkled on top

BEET SOUP

Makes 4 servings.

2 bunches young beets	2 tablespoons butter
½ cup chopped celery	1 tablespoon flour
1 cup milk	1 teaspoon salt
½ cup cream	

1. Scrub beets thoroughly and grate into a saucepan. Add celery, salt and 2 cups cold water. 2. Boil gently 10 to 15 minutes. 3. Press through sieve and add milk and cream. 4. Reheat gently. Cream the butter and flour, and add to soup, to thicken. Serve hot.

ATTRACTIVE AVOCADO SOUP

Makes 4 servings.

1 small or ½ large avocado	2 tablespoons butter
2 cups milk (or milk and cream)	2 tablespoons flour
2 cups chicken stock or canned chicken soup, strained	1 onion, finely chopped
	Few celery leaves, chopped

1. Cook minced onion and celery leaves in butter about 5 minutes on low flame, until onion is soft and light yellow. 2. Stir in flour and blend thoroughly. Then add chicken stock or canned chicken soup and milk (or half milk and cream). 3. Bring to a boil, stirring constantly; then simmer 5 minutes. Keep soup hot in double boiler top, until 10 minutes before it is ready to be served. 4. Run the avocado through a coarse strainer and add mashed pulp to the soup. 5. Stir well, heat to a boil, salt and serve.

CREAM OF CHICKEN SOUP

Makes 4 servings.

3 cups chicken broth
2 tablespoons butter
2 tablespoons flour

1 cup half milk–half cream
½ teaspoon salt
¼ teaspoon celery salt

1. Melt butter in double boiler top and blend in the flour. Add milk-cream, salt and celery salt. Stir constantly. 2. Cook until sauce thickens, add chicken broth. Stir. 3. Cook about 10 minutes, or until soup is hot. Stir every few minutes.

CREAM OF CARROT SOUP

Makes 4 servings.

2 cups milk
1 small onion, sliced
2 tablespoons butter
2 tablespoons flour
1 teaspoon salt

1½ cups carrot juice (or one 12-ounce can Eveready carrot juice)
Celery salt, if desired

1. Scald milk with onion added. Melt butter, stir in flour, milk, and seasoning. 2. Bring to the boiling point, add carrot juice. Heat thoroughly. 3. Serve topped with corn flakes, or a dash of whipped cream.

CREAM OF PEA PODS SOUP

Makes 6 servings.

2 quarts young tender pea pods, with peas removed
1 quart milk
1 cup shredded lettuce
1 small onion, minced
1 bay leaf
4 sprigs parsley

2 egg yolks
1 tablespoon butter
1 tablespoon flour
Dash of nutmeg
Salt
Croutons

1. Wash and pick over pea pods. Drop into pot with 1 quart boiling water. Add lettuce and onion. 2. Boil until pods are very tender. Rub through sieve into clean saucepan. 3. Scald milk with bay leaf and parsley. Strain, and remove bay leaf and parsley. Add milk to pea purée, and bring to boil. Season with salt, add dash of nutmeg. Remove from stove. 4. Knead butter with flour; beat egg yolks well. Alternately add some of each of these to the soup, until all of beaten egg yolk and flour-butter mix are added. Beat thoroughly during this process. 5. Reheat, but do not boil. Serve with croutons.

SCOTCH LAMB BROTH

Makes 4 to 6 servings.

2 pounds breast of lamb, cut in 1½-inch pieces
½ cup split peas
¼ cup barley
4 carrots, diced

2 medium onions, sliced
2 stalks celery, finely sliced
1 tablespoon chopped parsley
1 teaspoon salt

1. Soak split peas and barley in cold water overnight. 2. Put meat in heavy soup pot, cover with 1½ quarts cold water, bring to a boil, and simmer very slowly for about 1¼ hours. 3. Spoon off scum, strain, cool, and remove all fat. Pick meat from bones, removing all skin and gristle, and return meat to the pot, with the broth. 4. Drain split peas and barley and add to broth. Add vegetables and salt. Let simmer 1½ hours longer, or until vegetables are tender. Serve with meat in soup, or serve meat separately.

BEEF JUICE TEA

Makes ½ to ⅓ cupful.

1 pound lean round steak   Pinch of salt

1. Cut meat into very small cubes, or run through grinder. 2. Place in a quart mason jar, add 1 cup cold water and pinch of salt. Cover jar lightly. 3. Place jar in saucepan of cold water, with the water as high as possible without upsetting jar. Bring to a slow boil and boil gently 1 hour. 4. Remove jar and place on cake-cooling rack, to cool quickly. Strain the juice, remove all fat, and store in covered container in cold part of refrigerator. 5. When ready to serve, reheat over hot water kept below boiling point.

CREAM OF MUSHROOM SOUP

Makes 4 servings.

½ pound mushrooms
1 quart rich milk
2 tablespoons butter
2 tablespoons flour

2 egg yolks
2 Souplets vegetable broth tablets
Salt

1. Wash, peel and chop mushrooms fine. Cook in double boiler top, with the butter, until mushrooms are soft. Blend in the flour. 2. Reserve 1½ ounces (3 tablespoons) milk and add the rest of the quart to the mushrooms. 3. Place pot directly on the flame, bring to boil, and simmer 15 minutes. Rub through sieve, and put back on stove. 4. Beat egg yolks with remaining milk. Bring soup to a boil and add beaten yolks. 5. Break up Souplets, and add to pot (or soften first with a little of the soup). Cook soup 1 minute, stirring continuously. Taste, and add salt if needed.

COMBINATION CREAM SOUPS

Makes 3 to 4 servings.

2 containers Heinz Strained Food*
1 tablespoon butter

2 cups milk
Salt to taste

Combine all ingredients. Heat just to simmering, stirring constantly. *Any of the following combinations of Heinz or other strained foods may be used:

Strained Beef Broth with Beef and Barley—and Strained Carrots
Strained Beef Broth with Beef and Barley—and Strained Vegetable Soup
Strained Carrots—and Strained Green Beans
Strained Carrots—and Strained Peas
Strained Carrots—and Strained Vegetables and Lamb
Strained Green Beans—and Strained Vegetable Soup
Strained Spinach—and Strained Vegetable Soup
Strained Tomato Soup—and Strained Vegetable Soup
Strained Vegetables and Lamb—and Strained Vegetable Soup
Strained Vegetables and Bacon—and Strained Vegetable Soup

PURÉED TOMATO AND BARLEY SOUP

Makes 4 to 6 servings.

½ cup fine barley
2 cups canned or stewed tomatoes
1 onion, peeled and chopped
2 tablespoons butter

2 tablespoons flour
½ teaspoon salt
Milk or light cream, or combination

1. Rinse barley in cold water. Put in pot with tomatoes, onion, salt and 4 cups water. Cook over medium flame 45 minutes, or until barley is tender. 2. Put through strainer. 3. Heat butter, mix with flour, stirring in a little of the soup. Cook 3 minutes and add to soup. Add milk or cream as desired. Simmer for few minutes.

PURÉED POTATO SOUP

Makes 4 servings.

3 medium potatoes peeled and diced
1 onion, peeled and chopped
1 small carrot, diced

1 cup milk
2 tablespoons butter
Salt

1. Cook potatoes, carrot and onion 20 minutes in 2 cups cold water. 2. Press through sieve, add milk, salt to taste. Heat and add butter. Serve with croutons or toast.

BREAD-THICKENED VEGETABLE SOUP (PANADE)

Makes about 8 cups.

6 cups diced bread
2 cups finely chopped celery, leeks or onions
2 tablespoons butter
2 cups rich milk

1 large egg
1 teaspoon salt
Chopped parsley
Nutmeg, freshly grated

1. Slowly cook vegetables, covered, in butter, until soft but not brown. Leafy vegetables should come down more than half. **2.** Add salt, bread and 4 cups hot water. Stir well. Bring mixture to a boil, lower heat and simmer ½ hour. Beat well until smooth, using wire whisk. **3.** Combine milk and egg and stir slowly into the hot soup. Heat through, but do not boil. **4.** Serve with chopped parsley and freshly grated nutmeg.

CREAMED VEGETABLE SOUP

Makes 2 servings.

3 tablespoons butter
2 tablespoons flour
1 cup cooked vegetable, strained—asparagus, celery, corn, spinach, lettuce, carrots, etc.

1 onion, finely chopped
1½ cups milk or milk-and-cream
Buttered or dry croutons, oysterettes or other crackers
½ teaspoon salt

1. Melt 2 tablespoons butter with the flour, in saucepan, over medium flame. Rub with spoon until smooth, but not brown. **2.** Heat onion with remaining butter, in double boiler top and add to flour mix. Stir in milk slowly, and cook 1 minute. **3.** Add salt and cooked strained vegetable, bring to slow boil, stirring continuously while cooking. Serve with croutons or crackers.

COLD LETTUCE SOUP

Makes 4 to 6 servings.

1 large head lettuce
1 small onion, chopped
3 tablespoons butter
2 cups cooked peas

1 quart (4 cups) chicken broth
¾ cup heavy cream
Salt

1. Wash lettuce leaves carefully, drain, and shred finely. Put in double boiler top with onion and butter. **2.** Cover and cook over boiling water until lettuce is tender. Turn into saucepan, add broth and peas, and simmer, directly over the flame, ½ hour. **3.** Press through sieve, cool, and chill in refrigerator. **4.** When ready to serve, whip cream and fold into soup; add salt. Serve in chilled cups.

LENTIL SOUP

Makes 6 servings.

1½ to 2 pounds soup meat	1 carrot
1½ cups lentils	1 onion, peeled and chopped
1 medium potato	Salt
2 stalks celery	

1. Put 2 quarts cold water in soup pot, add meat and bring to a quick boil. Skim carefully. **2.** Cut up celery and carrot, and put into pot. Add lentils, potato, onion and salt. **3.** Simmer 1½ hours or until meat is tender. Cool, remove fat carefully, reheat, and serve.

Variation: LENTIL AND BARLEY SOUP
Add ½ cup barley when vegetables are added.

CREAMED LEGUME PURÉE

Makes 4 servings.

1 cup dried lima beans, whole peas, split peas, or lentils	2 teaspoons salt
2 bay leaves	Milk or light cream, or combination
1 onion, peeled and chopped	Butter

1. Soak legumes in cold water overnight if possible, or for at least 2 hours. **2.** Drain legumes, place in pot, add onion, bay leaves, salt and 6 cups water. **3.** Cook, covered, 1½ hours, over medium heat. **4.** Press through strainer. Use some of pot liquid to help force legumes through strainer. **5.** Add milk or cream to desired strength. Add 1 teaspoon butter to each serving.

OLD FASHIONED VEGETABLE-NOODLE SOUP

Makes almost 4 quarts.

2 pounds beef brisket	4 carrots
1 beef bone, 2 pounds	1 onion, peeled and chopped
1 veal bone, 2 pounds	1 stalk celery, including leaves
1 No. 2 can tomatoes	1 bunch parsley
½ pound string beans or wax beans	2 teaspoons salt
	1½ cups fine noodles, broken

1. Place 1 gallon cold water in soup pot; add beef, bones, onion, tomatoes and salt. Cover pot tightly and simmer 3½ hours. **2.** Cut up remaining vegetables and add to pot. Simmer ½ hour longer. **3.** Remove meat and carefully strain the soup through cheesecloth. Chill, and remove all fat. **4.** Reheat, and add broken noodles. Simmer 10 to 15 minutes, or until tender.

SPLIT PEA SOUP

Adapted from recipe of George Rector, famous restaurateur and author.

Makes 6 servings.

2 cups split peas
1 small onion, finely chopped
½ small bay leaf

2 cups milk
4 tablespoons butter
1 teaspoon salt

1. Wash peas and soak in water overnight, with onion and bay leaf. **2.** Cook gently in 2 quarts cold water, for 2 to 3 hours or until peas are soft enough to sieve. **3.** Rub through coarse sieve, then add milk, butter and salt. Re-heat and serve.

CREAM OF CLAM SOUP

Makes 4 servings.

1 pint (2 cups) chopped clams
2 cups milk
1 tablespoon flour
1 tablespoon butter

1 teaspoon scraped onion
¼ teaspoon celery salt
Pinch of salt

1. Melt butter in large saucepan. Add onion and cook slowly 5 minutes. **2.** Add flour and press smooth with bowl of a spoon. Add milk slowly. Stir constantly and cook a few minutes, until milk boils up once. **3.** Add minced clams, celery salt and salt. Reheat to just under a boil.

OYSTER SOUP

Makes 4 servings.

2 dozen oysters with their juice
2 egg yolks
2 tablespoons butter
2 tablespoons flour
2 tablespoons finely chopped parsley

2 shallots, chopped
1 teaspoon celery powder, or celery salt
1 bay leaf or ¼ teaspoon thyme
½ teaspoon salt

1. Strain oyster liquor through cheesecloth. Remove and discard round muscle from oysters. Cut oysters in halves or thirds. **2.** Melt butter in double boiler top and blend in the flour. Add oyster liquor, 2 cups cold water, shallots, parsley, celery powder, bay leaf or thyme. **3.** Stir until smooth, bring to a boil, then lower flame and let simmer 5 minutes. Add the oysters and simmer 5 minutes longer. **4.** In a mixing bowl, beat the egg yolks with the salt, and pour in oysters and liquid. Continue beating eggs while soup is being poured in. Remove bay leaf. Serve at once.

CREAM OF CRAB SOUP

Makes 4 servings.

1 pound crabmeat
1 quart milk
½ cup heavy cream
3 tablespoons butter
3 tablespoons flour

1 or 2 gratings of onion
½ teaspoon celery salt
½ teaspoon salt
¼ teaspoon onion salt (optional)

1. Melt butter in double boiler top and blend in the flour. Add milk and seasonings. 2. Cook until mixture thickens, stirring constantly. 3. Add crabmeat and cook until hot. 4. Whip the cream and add to soup after it is served into plates.

FISH STEW

Makes 6 servings.

1 pound whitefish
1 pound pike
6 potatoes, cut in ¾-inch cubes
3 large onions, sliced

2 carrots, quartered
1 bay leaf
2 teaspoons salt
½ lemon

1. Wash and slice fish. Sprinkle with lemon juice and place in refrigerator for several hours. 2. Wash fish gently and cook in 8 cups water. 3. Add all other ingredients and simmer one hour. Remove bay leaf. Serve very hot.

LIVER BALLS FOR SOUPS

Makes 6 to 12 servings.

¼ pound liver—calf's liver for beef soup, chicken liver for chicken soup, lamb's liver for mutton broth
½ cup sifted bread crumbs
2 tablespoons melted butter
1 egg, separated

1 teaspoon celery powder
1 teaspoon finely chopped parsley
2 tablespoons onion juice
½ teaspoon salt
1 grating of nutmeg
Milk

1. Shred liver with fork. Discard skin and veins. Mix with bread crumbs, butter and seasonings. 2. Beat egg yolk and add. Beat egg white stiff and add. If more moisture is needed, add milk by the teaspoon; if too soft, sprinkle in a little flour. If in doubt as to consistency, drop a ball of the mixture into boiling water before adding milk or flour. 3. Form into balls a little larger than marbles. 4. Drop into gently boiling soup and cook 5 to 7 minutes.

ROAST BEEF

Standing rib roast   Salt
¾ to 1 cup beef consommé

1. Take meat out of refrigerator 30 minutes to an hour before using. Then wipe with damp towel and rub with salt. 2. Place beef on its ribs in dry roasting pan, with fat side up. 3. Preheat oven to slow (300°F.), and cook 20 minutes per pound for a rare roast; 25 minutes per pound for a medium roast; 30 minutes per pound for a well-done roast. During this time, baste every 15 minutes with meat's own pan juices, mixed with beef consommé. 5. When roast is cooked, pour pan gravy into a small bowl set in ice water. Skim off fat, return gravy to roasting pan, and reheat.

HAMBURGERS WITH CELERY

Makes 4 servings.

1 pound finely chopped beef   1 cup grated or very finely
  round   chopped celery
1 egg   3 tablespoons butter
¼ cup milk   ⅓ cup bread crumbs
1 medium onion, finely chopped   1 teaspoon salt

1. Beat egg and add salt and milk. Stir together, then add onion, grated celery, bread crumbs, meat. 2. Mix together lightly, and shape into 4 flat patties. 3. Place patties in a pan greased with part of the butter, and put the rest of the butter on top of the hamburgers. 4. Broil under medium broiler 5 minutes. Turn over, baste with the melted butter and broil about 4 minutes more.

BROILED LAMB KIDNEYS

Makes 1 serving.

3 kidneys   Buttered toast

1. Remove skin which covers kidneys. Split in half lengthwise and remove tubes and center fat part. 2. Soak in lightly salted water for about a half hour. 3. Broil about 5 minutes, then turn kidneys and broil 5 minutes on other side. Serve on buttered toast.

LAMB STEAK

½- to ¾-inch-thick steaks   Salt
  from leg of young lamb (cut
  same as a veal steak)

1. Salt both sides. Broil in hot broiler 3 minutes on each side. One steak makes a serving.

OVEN-BROILED BACON

No other style bacon is permitted on this diet.

Place bacon slices on broiler rack, in a dripping pan. Broil in very hot oven (425°F.). Turn once, to insure crisp broiling throughout. Drain well on absorbent paper.

BEEF AND LIVER SOUFFLÉ

Makes 2 servings.

2 tablespoons butter or margarine	1 container Heinz strained beef and liver soup.
3 tablespoons flour	½ cup grated process American cheese
¼ cup milk	
Dash of salt	2 egg whites

1. Preheat oven to moderately slow (325°F.). Melt butter. Add flour and blend thoroughly. Add milk gradually, then salt and strained soup. 2. Cook, stirring constantly, until mixture comes to a boil. Add cheese. Heat, stirring constantly, until cheese is melted. 3. Cool slightly. Beat egg yolks slightly, and add to soup mixture. 4. Pour into ungreased, individual baking dishes. Set in a pan of warm water. Bake 45 minutes.

PASHTET OF BEEF

Makes 6 to 8 servings.

2 pounds round steak, cut thin	Milk
6 hard rolls	Butter
4 large potatoes	Bread crumbs
2 onions, finely sliced	Salt
3 eggs	

1. Cut steak into thin strips about 2 inches by ½ inch. Pound with potato masher. 2. Boil potatoes in their skins. Drain, cool, peel and slice. Soak rolls in milk for ½ hour, then mash with fork. 3. Butter baking dish and sprinkle bottom with bread crumbs. Arrange layer of onions, then layer of meat. Season lightly with salt (also herbs as desired—marjoram or oregano, etc.). 4. Add another layer of onions and layer of sliced potatoes; dot with butter, then add layer of meat; add light seasonings. Repeat until ingredients are used up. 5. Beat eggs, add rolls-and-milk mixture, seasoned gently with salt. Turn into baking dish. Sprinkle with bread crumbs. 6. Bake in moderate oven (350°F.) about 35 minutes, or until brown.

BAKED FISH

Use non-oily fish—bass, whitefish, red snapper, haddock, etc. Have fish cleaned but not split. Allow ½ to ¾ pounds per person.

3 tablespoons butter	¾ cup fish or chicken stock
1 bay leaf	2 egg yolks
3 thin slices onion	Salt
1 tablespoon chopped parsley	

1. Rub softened butter and salt on fish surface. Cut diagonal gashes through the skin about 1½ to 2 inches apart on both sides of the fish. Force butter into the cuts. **2.** Line a baking pan with aluminum foil or waxed paper. Butter this lining thoroughly and put in fish. **3.** Add butter, bay leaf, thin slices of onion, chopped parsley and fish or chicken stock. **4.** Bake in moderate oven (350°F.) for 12 to 14 minutes per pound of fish. Baste every 10 minutes or so with pan liquid. **5.** Make sauce by straining pan liquid, and beating in the 2 egg yolks, one after another. If there is too much liquid, boil down first, before adding egg yolks.

BROILED FISH

Use non-oily fish—brook trout, flounder, cod, halibut, etc. Small fish broiled whole, larger fish split open lengthwise, and steaks of large fish:

1. Sprinkle with salt and rub fish surface lightly with softened or melted butter. **2.** Broil small whole fish about 2 inches from flame, 3 or 4 minutes on each side. Broil split fish 3 inches from flame, skin side down, 10 to 12 minutes without turning. Broil steaks 3 inches from flame, 4 to 5 minutes on each side.

COURT BOUILLON FOR BOILING FISH

1 medium onion, peeled and sliced	2 bay leaves
	Sprig of thyme
2 carrots, scraped and sliced	1 tablespoon lemon juice
½ bunch parsley	2 teaspoons salt

1. Tie the parsley, bay leaves and thyme together. **2.** Put all the ingredients in a pot, with 3 quarts of cold water, and simmer ¼ hour before adding it to the fish (or before adding the fish to it). If *sliced* fish is to be used, bring the bouillon to a quick boil first.

BOILED FISH

Use cod, sea trout, haddock, halibut, flounder, red snapper and similar fish. Know the weight of the fish. Never use too-thin slices.

1. Mop fish in clean cheesecloth and put it in large pot, with enough hot Court Bouillon to cover. **2.** Bring to simmering and cook 10 minutes for the first pound, and 8 minutes for each additional pound (for example: a 3-pound fish cooks in the bouillon 26 minutes). Remove fish as soon as done.

FISH STOCK

Bones and skin of non-fatty fish
1 onion, sliced
1 carrot, sliced

3 sprigs of parsley
1 teaspoon lemon juice
Salt

1. Break up bones and place, with fish skin, in pot. Add just enough cold water to cover. Add other ingredients. **2.** Bring to a boil, reduce flame, and simmer 25 minutes. **3.** Strain through double thickness of cheesecloth.

FISH SOUFFLÉ

Makes 6 servings.

1 pound boiled fish
2 cups top milk or cream
¼ pound butter
¾ cup flour

3 eggs
1 teaspoon salt
Cracker meal

1. Separate boiled fish into flakes. Beat eggs well. **2.** Melt butter, add flour and gradually the top milk, salt, and the well-beaten eggs. **3.** Pour into a greased baking dish, sprinkle with cracker meal and bake in a moderate oven (350°F.) for about 45 minutes. Serve with melted butter.

CHICKEN POT PIE

Makes 6 to 8 servings.

1 chicken (4-pound hen)
4 medium potatoes, sliced
2 tablespoons finely chopped parsley

1½ teaspoons salt
2 cups flour
2 eggs

1. Cut up chicken into serving pieces, as for fricassee. Cover with water and cook until tender; add 1 teaspoon salt. **2.** Add the potato slices when chicken is almost soft. **3.** Make a stiff dough as follows: Form a well in the flour and drop in eggs and ½ teaspoon salt. Work together; add water or milk if too dry. Roll out thin—⅛ inch—and cut into 1-inch squares. **4.** Drop dough squares into the pot of boiling chicken which should have a good covering of broth by now. Add chopped parsley.

MACARONI WITH CHEESE

Makes 6 servings.

1 package macaroni (8-ounce)   1 teaspoon salt
4 tablespoons butter   ¼ pound cheese, cut in small
4 tablespoons flour   pieces
2 cups milk

1. Cook the macaroni as directed on the package. Melt the butter, add the flour, season, and blend. **2.** Add the milk slowly and cook at low temperature until thick and smooth. **3.** Add the cheese and stir until the cheese has melted. Place the macaroni in a greased 2-quart baking dish. Pour cheese sauce over it. **4.** Bake in moderately hot oven (375°F.) for 25 to 30 minutes.

Variations: Boiled spaghetti, broad noodles, or 3 cups cooked rice may be used in place of macaroni.

Add chopped cooked ham, chicken or liver to the sauce before pouring over the macaroni.

GNOCCHI

Makes 6 servings.

¾ cup quick-cooking farina   1 teaspoon salt
4 tablespoons butter   ½ cup light cream
1 egg, slightly beaten   ⅓ cup grated cheese

1. Add salt to 3 cups water and bring to a boil. Sprinkle farina gradually into the boiling water, stirring constantly. **2.** Cook over medium flame for 5 minutes. **3.** Take off stove, add butter, and slightly beaten egg. Stir until blended. **4.** Pour into buttered dish (about 8 inches square). Chill in refrigerator. **5.** Cut into 1½-inch squares and place in buttered shallow baking dish. Pour light cream over the squares, sprinkle with cheese and dot with butter. **6.** Bake in moderately hot oven (375°F.) for 30 minutes, or until golden brown.

BAKED VEGETABLE CUSTARD

Makes 2 servings.

1 egg   ½ cup milk, scalded
1 container strained vegetable   Salt to taste

1. Heat oven to 350°F. (moderate). Beat egg well with fork. **2.** Add strained food and beat until blended. Add milk and salt. **3.** Pour into custard cups; place in a pan of warm water up to the level of the custard. **4.** Bake in a moderate oven (350°F.) 50 minutes or until a silver knife, when inserted, comes out clean. Serve at once.

VEGETABLE RAREBIT

Makes 3 servings.

1 tablespoon butter or margarine
1 tablespoon flour
½ cup grated process American cheese*
½ cup milk

1 container Clapp, Gerber or other good brand of any strained vegetable
Salt to taste
3 slices toast

1. Melt butter. Add flour. Blend thoroughly. **2.** Add milk and cheese. Cook, stirring constantly, until thickened. **3.** Add vegetable and salt. Serve hot over triangles of toast.

VEGETABLE SOUFFLÉ

Makes 2 to 3 servings.

2 tablespoons butter or margarine
2 tablespoons flour
½ container strained vegetable

¼ cup milk
¼ teaspoon salt
1 egg, separated
Cheese*

1. Preheat oven to moderately slow (325°F.). Melt butter; add flour and blend. **2.** Slowly add milk, then strained or junior food and salt. Cook until bubbling, stirring constantly. Add slowly to slightly beaten egg yolk, stirring constantly. **3.** Beat egg white until stiff but not dry. Fold into vegetable mixture. Pour into ungreased individual baking dishes, filling ¾ full. **4.** Place in a pan of warm water. Bake 35 to 40 minutes. Serve immediately.

* If cheese is desired, 2 tablespoons grated process American cheese may be added before egg white is folded in.

BREAD OMELET

Makes 4 to 6 servings.

3 eggs, separated
1½ cups milk
1 cup dry bread crumbs
2 tablespoons butter

1 tablespoon cornstarch
½ teaspoon salt
½ teaspoon baking powder

1. Soak bread crumbs in the milk for 10 minutes. **2.** Beat egg yolks and add to bread crumbs. Add salt, baking powder, and cornstarch. **3.** Beat egg whites to stiffness and fold into mixture. **4.** Melt butter in heavy pan, add egg mixture, reduce flame slightly, and cook like a regular omelet. Fold in half and serve on hot platter.

PLAIN SOUFFLÉ

Makes 4 servings.

4 eggs, separated
2 tablespoons butter
2 tablespoons flour

1 cup milk
1 cup cream
½ teaspoon salt

1. Scald the milk and cream together. 2. Cream the butter, blend in the flour well, and pour on the scalded milk-cream. Stir constantly. Cook 5 minutes in double boiler top. 3. Beat egg yolks until thick and pale; add to creamy mixture, stirring constantly. 4. Remove from stove, add salt. Beat egg whites stiffly, and when the egg yolk mixture is cool, fold in the whites. 5. Turn into buttered baking dish and place dish in pan of warm water. Bake in slow oven (300°F.) about 50 minutes or until delicately browned on top, and soufflé is barely firm. Serve immediately, right from baking dish.

CARROT SOUFFLÉ

Makes 6 servings.

2 cups cooked carrots
1¼ cups light cream or rich milk
3 tablespoons cornstarch

3 eggs
¼ cup strained honey
4 tablespoons melted butter
1 teaspoon salt

1. Put carrots through a sieve. 2. Dissolve cornstarch in the milk. Stir this into the carrot purée and also blend in the salt and honey. 3. Beat eggs well and add to the mixture; then add melted butter. 4. Turn into greased casserole. Bake in hot oven (400°F.) for 45 minutes.

EGG IN SPINACH NEST

Makes 2 servings.

2 eggs
¼ teaspoon salt
½ container Heinz strained spinach
2 tablespoons butter

2 tablespoons grated process American cheese
2 toast rounds—2-inch diameters

1. Preheat oven to moderate (350°F.). Separate eggs. Add salt to egg whites. Beat until stiff, but not dry. 2. Fold strained food into egg white. On a cookie sheet or in large custard cups (5½ x 2 inches) mound the spinach mixture into two portions. 3. Place a toast round in the center of each spinach mold; slip egg yolk onto it. 4. Dot surface with butter and sprinkle with cheese. Bake in moderate oven (350°F.) 12 minutes.

SHIRRED EGGS

Makes 1 serving.

1 egg	Salt
1 tablespoon cream	

1. Pour cream into individual baking dish. **2.** Break an egg into the dish. Sprinkle with salt. **3.** Bake in moderate oven (350°F.) from 15 to 20 minutes until the egg is set.

Variations: Place a thin slice of ham in each dish. Add an egg. Cover with thin white sauce. Sprinkle with grated cheese. Bake as for shirred eggs.

Place rounds of thin toast in each dish. Add an egg. Place a few cooked string beans or small spears of cooked asparagus around the egg. Cover with thin white sauce and bake as for shirred eggs.

SCALLOPED EGGS WITH MUSHROOMS

Makes 6 servings.

6 eggs	2 scant tablespoons flour
½ pound mushrooms, sliced	1 tablespoon chopped parsley
1¾ cups chicken broth	2 tablespoons chopped celery
¼ cup cream	Grated cheese
3 tablespoons melted butter	Salt

1. Place 2 tablespoons of the melted butter in double boiler top, mix in sliced mushrooms. Blend in flour, and cook slowly for about 3 minutes. **2.** Add cream, broth, parsley and celery, and salt to taste. Simmer for 6 minutes. **3.** Turn into a shallow baking dish. Drop in eggs one at a time; keep separate from each other. Sprinkle lightly with salt and cheese. Moisten with remaining melted butter. **4.** Bake in moderate oven (350°F.) until whites set and cheese is lightly colored.

BAKED OMELET

Makes 2 to 3 servings.

4 eggs, separated	½ teaspoon salt
2 teaspoons butter	

1. Add salt and 3 tablespoons hot water to egg yolks, and beat until thick and pale. **2.** Beat egg whites stiff, and fold into yolks. **3.** Heat butter in heavy frying pan, in the oven. When butter bubbles, turn in eggs, spreading evenly. **4.** Cook in moderate oven (350°F.), until omelet is firm. Loosen with spatula and slide onto hot serving platter.

FRENCH OMELET

Makes 1 serving.

2 eggs
2 tablespoons cream

2 tablespoons butter
¼ teaspoon salt

1. Select a frying pan and saucepan combination that permits the frying pan to sit inside the saucepan which is to be half full of briskly boiling water, with the water coming around the sides of the frying pan. **2.** Combine eggs, cream and salt in mixing bowl. Beat gently with fork. Melt butter in perfectly clean frying pan and make sure entire bottom of pan is greased. **3.** Turn eggs into pan, let cook until bottom sets, about 1 minute. As bottom of omelet gets done, lift edges with spatula, to allow liquid part to run under the cooked part. **4.** When omelet is done, fold over on itself with spatula, and slide onto a hot platter. If the oven is going, slip omelet under the broiler, to brown the top, before placing on platter.

SPINACH AND RICE CASSEROLE

Makes 3 servings.

1 egg
2 containers strained spinach
2 tablespoons butter, melted

Salt to taste
1 cup cooked rice
½ cup milk

1. Preheat oven to moderately slow (325°F.). Combine all ingredients and mix well. **2.** Pour into buttered baking dish and place in a pan of warm water. Bake in moderately slow oven (325°F.) 55 minutes.

HUNGARIAN CHEESE DUMPLINGS

Makes 6 servings.

1 pound dry pot cheese or uncreamed cottage cheese
2 eggs
1 tablespoon butter
3 tablespoons semolina or Cream of Wheat

3 tablespoons bread crumbs
Pinch of salt
Flour
Bread crumbs roasted in melted butter, or sugar

1. Press cheese through sieve. Thoroughly mix cheese, eggs, butter, semolina and bread crumbs, with enough flour to give a dough not too stiff. Add a pinch of salt if cheese is unsalted. **2.** Shape dumplings the size of an egg. Drop into boiling water. After dumplings rise to surface, boil for another 5 minutes. **3.** Drain and serve with bread crumbs roasted in melted butter or just sprinkle with sugar.

YORKSHIRE PUDDING

Makes 8 servings.

1 cup flour	3 eggs
1 cup milk	½ teaspoon salt

1. Sift flour and salt together. Beat eggs well and add flour-salt mixture. Add milk and beat 2 minutes, or until smooth. **2.** Place about 4 tablespoons of hot roast beef drippings in a pan; then pour in the batter. **3.** Preheat oven to 425°F., put in batter and bake 15 minutes. Reduce heat to 375°F. and bake 15 minutes longer. If same oven is used as for the roast beef, use a 400°F. oven throughout, and bake pudding 30 minutes. In this case, reduce the oven time for the roast beef, so as not to overcook the beef. Use meat thermometer to test doneness. **4.** Cut pudding in squares and serve with roast.

NOODLE PIE

½ pound noodles	4 tablespoons butter
1¼ cups milk	Salt
3 eggs, separated	

1. Break up noodles into small pieces and cook in milk until tender. Cool, but do not drain. **2.** Cream the butter and beat in egg yolks one at a time, beating constantly. **3.** Separate noodles from the milk and add noodles to the butter-and-eggs. Beat egg whites until stiff but not dry; fold into mixture. Add salt to taste. **4.** Thickly butter a large frying pan, and turn in mixture. Spread out evenly. **5.** Bake in moderate oven (350°F.) about 45 minutes, until light brown. Cool a little and loosen rim. Turn out on warm platter and serve in pie-shaped wedges, with meat or fish dishes, or cut into smaller pieces to serve in chicken broth or other soups.

WHIPPED SWEET POTATOES IN ORANGE SHELLS

Makes 8 servings.

8 oranges	2 teaspoons salt
4 cups boiled or baked sweet potatoes	2 tablespoons melted butter
	8 marshmallows

1. Cut off tops of oranges and remove pulp and juice with a sharp knife and spoon. **2.** Whip sweet potatoes with salt, butter and orange juice to moisten to desired consistency. Use the juice that comes out when preparing the shells. **3.** Fill orange shells and top each with a marshmallow. Brown in moderate oven (350°F.) until heated through.

BAKED MASHED POTATOES AND CARROTS

Makes 8 servings.

4 cups mashed potatoes
1 cup mashed carrots
¼ cup cream

1 egg
½ teaspoon salt
Butter

1. Mix all ingredients together, thoroughly. 2. Place in buttered baking dish and bake in moderately hot oven (375°F.) for 25 minutes.

DUTCH POTATO FILLING

2 cups hot mashed potatoes
1 tablespoon minced parsley
1 egg
2 tablespoons butter
1 onion, finely chopped

4 cups cubed toast (use stale bread for toasting)
½ cup diced celery
1 teaspoon salt

1. Brown the onion in the butter, in top of double boiler. 2. Beat the egg well, and mix with the potatoes. 3. Mix in all the other ingredients. 4. Use for stuffing fowl or meat.

NEW POTATOES IN SOUR CREAM

Makes 4 to 6 servings.

2 pounds new potatoes (small potatoes of uniform size)
1 cup sour cream

3 tablespoons butter
2 teaspoons flour
Salt

1. Scrape skin off potatoes and rub with salt. Wash in cold water, drain, and put into heavy saucepan. Add a good sprinkling of salt. 2. Cook, covered, over low heat for 10 minutes. Shake constantly. 3. Drain off any liquid. Cream the butter, blend in the flour, and add to the potatoes. Stir in the sour cream. 4. Mix well, and cook, covered, over low flame, until potatoes are done. 5. Serve at once. Add more sour cream if desired.

ORANGE BEETS

Makes 6 servings.

2½ cups sliced raw beets
1 cup orange juice

1 tablespoon butter
1 teaspoon salt

1. Peel raw beets and slice thin into buttered casserole. Pour on remaining ingredients. 2. Cover and bake in moderate oven (350°F.) about 1 hour.

CREAMED GREENS, FRENCH STYLE

Makes 4 servings.

1½ pounds spinach or other tender leafy greens
¾ cup chicken stock
¼ cup light cream
1 tablespoon finely chopped onion

2 tablespoons butter
2 tablespoons flour
Pinch of thyme
Pinch of nutmeg
1 teaspoon salt

1. Remove roots and any tough stems from greens and wash thoroughly. **2.** Cook, covered, in water that clings to the leaves, about 5 minutes, or until tender, adding ½ teaspoon salt after greens are half done. **3.** Drain well and chop or force through a food mill or coarse sieve. **4.** Heat butter, add onion and cook, stirring, till lightly browned. Blend in flour. Add stock, cream, remaining salt, thyme and nutmeg, and cook till thickened. **5.** Add chopped greens to the sauce and boil, stirring until well blended.

CHEESE BALLS WITH JELLY

Makes 10 servings.

1 pound farmer cheese or pot cheese
¼ pound butter
3 eggs

½ cup farina
Sugar
Melted butter
Quince or other tasty jelly

1. Mix cheese, butter, eggs and farina with a fork. When thoroughly mixed, form a ball, and let stand 1 hour. **2.** Take mixture out of bowl with spoon, and with wet hands form balls the size of a peach. **3.** Place in salted water. Let cook very slowly ¾ hour, uncovered. **4.** When cheese balls rise, cut in 4 pieces, sprinkle with sugar, pour on hot melted butter, and serve with jelly.

BEET AND COTTAGE CHEESE SALAD

Makes 2 servings.

1½ teaspoons unflavored gelatin (½ envelope Knox's)
2 teaspoons Heinz cider vinegar or lemon juice

1 container Beech-Nut, Libby or other good brand of strained beets
Salt to taste
¼ cup cottage cheese

1. Soften gelatin in ¼ cup cold water 5 minutes. **2.** Add ½ cup boiling water and stir until dissolved. Cool. **3.** Add vinegar, strained beets, and salt. Pour into molds. Chill. **4.** Unmold when firm. Top with cottage cheese.

BASIC WHITE SAUCE

1 cup milk	2 tablespoons flour
2 tablespoons butter	¼ teaspoon salt

1. Melt butter in small flat-bottom saucepan or double boiler top. Add flour and salt, and stir until well blended. Use wire whisk, to obtain smoothness. **2.** Pour on milk gradually; stir constantly. **3.** Bring to a boil; boil 2 minutes. **4.** Cook in double boiler top for 15 minutes. Stir well. If sauce becomes too thick, thin with a little more milk. Taste, and add more salt if needed.

Variations: THIN WHITE SAUCE: Use 1 tablespoon butter and 1 tablespoon flour, instead of 2.

THICK WHITE SAUCE: Use 4 tablespoons butter and 4 tablespoons flour.

CREAM SAUCE: Use cream instead of milk. If too thick, thin out with milk.

WHITE SAUCE WITH EGG: Stir in 1 slightly beaten egg yolk, just before serving.

MOCK HOLLANDAISE: Just before serving, stir in 2 egg yolks, 6 tablespoons butter (1 tablespoon at a time), and 1 tablespoon lemon juice.

CELERY SAUCE: Cook 1½ cups thinly-sliced celery until soft. Rub through sieve and add to white sauce. Use all milk, or half chicken stock or celery water, in making sauce.

MUSHROOM CREAM SAUCE

½ pound small mushrooms	1 cup cream
2 tablespoons butter, preferably *sweet*	2 tablespoons cream sauce
	Salt

1. Clean mushrooms and stew lightly in saucepan, with the butter. **2.** Add cream and cook 7 or 8 minutes. **3.** Thicken with cream sauce and season with salt.

HOLLANDAISE SAUCE

3 fresh egg yolks	Salt
¼ pound best butter, preferably *sweet* butter	Lemon juice, if desired

1. Place egg yolks in a small bowl; add 1 tablespoon water. **2.** Place bowl over hot water—not boiling. Whisk with a wire whisk until creamy. **3.** Add the butter bit by bit, whisking gently but constantly. **4.** Add salt to taste (add a squeeze of lemon juice if desired) and strain through cheesecloth.

EGGNOG SAUCE

Makes about 2 cups eggnog sauce.

2 tablespoons sugar	⅛ teaspoon nutmeg
1 tablespoon flour	¼ teaspoon rum extract
Dash of salt	1 egg white
1 egg yolk	1 tablespoon sugar
1¼ cups milk	

1. Combine 2 tablespoons sugar, flour, and salt in double boiler top. Add egg yolk and beat well. Then add milk slowly, stirring constantly. 2. Cook over rapidly boiling water 5 minutes, stirring occasionally. Remove from stove. Cool. Add the nutmeg and rum extract. 3. Beat egg white until foamy. Add 1 tablespoon sugar gradually, beating constantly until mixture will stand in soft peaks. Fold in custard mixture.

CUSTARD SAUCE

Makes 2¼ cups.

1 tablespoon cornstarch	2 egg yolks
¼ cup sugar	2 cups milk
¼ teaspoon salt	1 teaspoon vanilla

1. Mix cornstarch, sugar and salt in top of double boiler. 2. Add egg yolks and mix well. Gradually stir in milk. 3. Place over boiling water and cook, stirring constantly, until mixture is slightly thickened (about 5 minutes). 4. Remove from heat, cool; add vanilla. Chill thoroughly before serving.

CHEESE SALAD DRESSING

Makes ½ cup.

¼ cup cream cheese	2 teaspoons lemon juice
¼ cup Heinz strained carrots	½ teaspoon salt
2 teaspoons olive oil	

1. Combine all ingredients and mix until smooth. Serve on salads, if diet permits.

MAGIC LEMON MAYONNAISE

Makes 1¼ cups.

1 egg yolk	¼ cup lemon juice
⅔ cup sweetened condensed milk	¼ cup melted butter
	½ teaspoon salt

1. Beat or shake until mixture thickens. Add ¼ cup more of lemon juice for a tarter flavor.

BAKED CUSTARD

Makes 4 cups of custard.

2 eggs
2 cups milk
2 tablespoons sugar

⅛ teaspoon salt
Nutmeg

1. Beat eggs slightly, add sugar, salt, and milk. Pour in custard cups and sprinkle with nutmeg. 2. Place the cups in a pan of hot water and bake in a moderate oven (350°F.) until the custards are firm and the mixture does not adhere to a knife when inserted.

FLAN (Caramel Custard)

Makes 8 servings.

1 quart light cream or half milk–half cream
12 egg yolks
5 tablespoons sugar

1 cup sugar for caramelized sirup
Juice of 1 lime

1. Scald cream in double boiler top. Beat egg yolks and sugar together. Pour cream over egg mixture, very slowly, stirring constantly. Add lime juice. 2. Caramelize the cup of sugar and thickly coat the sides and bottom of a 2-quart baking dish. 3. Pour in the cream mixture and set the baking dish in a pan of hot water. 4. Bake in moderate oven (350°F.) about 1 hour, or until a silver knife inserted in center comes out clean. Cool and chill. Serve very cold.

CAKE 'N FRUIT CUSTARD

Makes 2 to 3 servings.

⅛ teaspoon salt
1 egg white
2 tablespoons sugar
1 egg yolk
1 container Libby, Beech-Nut or other good strained apricots and applesauce

½ teaspoon lemon juice
1 tablespoon melted butter
2 tablespoons sugar
2 tablespoons flour
½ cup milk

1. Preheat oven to moderate (350°F.). Add salt to egg white, beat until moist peaks form when beater is raised. Gradually add 2 tablespoons sugar, beating until stiff. 2. Beat egg yolk with apricots and applesauce, lemon juice and melted butter. Stir 2 tablespoons sugar mixed with flour; add milk. Fold in beaten egg white. 3. Pour into individual greased custard cups, filling to within ½ inch from top. Set in pan containing ½-inch hot water. 4. Bake in moderate oven (350°F.) 55 to 60 minutes, or until firm on top and browned. Serve chilled or slightly warm.

MILK RICE, HOT OR COLD

Makes 8 servings.

½ cup rice
3½ cups milk
½ cup sugar

2 tablespoons butter
½ teaspoon salt
Cinnamon, powdered sugar

1. Bring milk to a boil in double boiler top, or in saucepan. Add rice and cook slowly for 15 minutes, stirring occasionally. **2.** Add salt and continue cooking until rice is soft but not mushy. **3.** Remove from stove, and blend in butter and sugar thoroughly. **4.** Serve hot with sprinkling of cinnamon and sugar, or serve chilled or lukewarm, pile rice on Pyrex dish, add a good sprinkling of powdered sugar and slip under broiler for few minutes to brown top.

MOLDED PUDDING

Makes 8 servings.

2 cups light cream
1 cup chilled heavy cream
½ cup vanilla sugar (sugar in which a vanilla bean has been kept)

1 tablespoon gelatin (1 envelope Knox's)
4 tablespoons flour
2 teaspoons lemon or almond extract

1. Combine light cream, flour and half the vanilla sugar in double boiler top. Cook until mixture thickens, stirring constantly. **2.** Remove from stove and pour into a bowl. Beat until cool. **3.** Dissolve gelatin in ½ cup boiling water, add to light cream mixture, and beat. **4.** Whip the heavy cream and gradually add remaining ¼ cup vanilla sugar. When mixture is stiff, fold into cooked mixture and add lemon or almond. **5.** Beat again and turn into mold. Chill to set. Unmold; serve with fruit sauce or stewed fruits.

CEREAL PUDDING

Makes 3 servings.

1 cup Heinz precooked cereal food or precooked oatmeal
¼ cup light brown sugar, firmly packed
Dash of salt

2 cups milk, scalded
1 teaspoon vanilla
2 tablespoons butter
Graham cracker crumbs
Cube of red gelatin or jelly

1. Combine first 3 ingredients and mix well. Gradually add milk. **2.** Cook until sugar is dissolved, stirring frequently. Add vanilla and butter. Pour into dessert dishes. **3.** Top with graham cracker crumbs and garnish with gelatin or jelly cube. Chill.

SNOW TORTE

1 cup sifted cake flour
3 cups sifted confectioners' sugar
¾ cup melted butter, lukewarm
¾ cup sifted cornstarch
12 egg whites
2 teaspoons vanilla
Dry bread crumbs

1. Beat egg whites until stiff but not dry. Add vanilla. **2.** Sift dry ingredients together and add to egg whites. Stir in lukewarm butter. Blend ingredients thoroughly. **3.** Grease a spring mold and dust with dry bread crumbs. Turn in mixture. **4.** Bake in moderate oven (350°F.) for 1 hour. When cake cools, decorate with lemon frosting.

SPANISH CREAM PARFAIT

Makes 6 servings.

1 tablespoon unflavored gelatin (1 envelope Knox's)
2 cups milk
2 eggs, separated
3 tablespoons sugar
⅛ teaspoon salt
½ teaspoon vanilla
2 containers Heinz strained apricots and applesauce
2 tablespoons lemon juice
1 tablespoon sugar

1. Soften gelatin in ⅓ cup of the milk 5 minutes. Scald remainder of milk, then add gelatin, stirring until dissolved. **2.** Combine slightly beaten egg yolks with sugar, salt and vanilla, then add slowly to gelatin mixture. **3.** Chill until mixture congeals. Beat with a rotary beater until soft. Beat egg whites until stiff, but not dry, and fold into custard mixture. **4.** Combine strained apricots and applesauce, lemon juice and sugar, blending thoroughly. **5.** Place custard mixture and apricots and applesauce alternately into tall glasses. Chill.

VIENNA POPOVERS

Makes 24 small or 16 large popovers.

2 cups flour
5 eggs
1½ cups milk
2 tablespoons melted butter
Sugar and stewed fruits

1. Thoroughly blend flour and milk, until very smooth. **2.** Beat eggs until foamy, then stir into flour mixture. Add melted butter, beat well, and let stand 30 to 40 minutes. **3.** Turn into well-greased muffin tins, about ¾ full. **4.** Bake in moderate oven (325° to 350°F.) for 45 minutes. Serve hot, sprinkled with sugar. May also be served with stewed fruits.

FARINA PUDDING

Makes 8 servings.

¼ cup farina
2 cups milk
3 eggs, separated
3 tablespoons sugar

2 tablespoons butter
1 lemon peel
1½ cups stewed fruits

1. Combine farina, milk, butter, sugar and lemon peel in double boiler top. Cook 15 to 20 minutes, or until mushy. **2.** Cool to lukewarm, then remove lemon peel. **3.** Beat egg yolks and add to the farina. Add more sugar if needed. Beat egg whites to stiffness, but not dry, and fold into farina. **4.** Line a greased Pyrex dish with stewed fruits. Pour on the farina mush. Bake in moderately slow oven (325°F.) for 45 minutes. Serve from the baking dish.

BLANC MANGE

Makes 6 to 8 servings.

½ cup sugar
5 tablespoons cornstarch
¼ teaspoon salt

4 cups milk
1½ teaspoons vanilla

1. Mix sugar, cornstarch and salt in top of double boiler. Gradually add milk, mixing until smooth. **2.** Place over boiling water and cook, stirring constantly, until mixture thickens. **3.** Cover and continue cooking 10 minutes longer, stirring occasionally. Remove from heat. Add vanilla; cool. **4.** Pour into serving dish and chill.

Variations: MOLDED BLANC MANGE: Use 6 tablespoons cornstarch.

CUSTARD BLANC MANGE: Follow above recipe. When cooked, remove from heat. Pour gradually over 2 well-beaten eggs, stirring constantly. Return to double boiler and cook 2 minutes longer, stirring constantly.

PEACH TORTE

1½ cups zwieback
2 cups canned sliced peaches
2 eggs
⅓ cup sour cream

⅔ cup sugar
2 teaspoons vanilla or almond extract
⅛ teaspoon cinnamon

1. Roll zwieback into fine crumbs and put ⅔ of these crumbs in a well-buttered loose-bottom layer cake pan. **2.** Smooth crumbs flat, and cover with the canned, sliced peaches. **3.** Mix the beaten eggs, sour cream, sugar, vanilla, and cinnamon and pour over peaches. **4.** Sprinkle with remaining crumbs and bake in moderately hot oven (375°F.) about 20 minutes, or until peaches are cooked.

ORANGE BAVARIAN

Makes 8 servings.

1 tablespoon unflavored gelatin (1 envelope Knox's)
1½ cups orange juice
½ cup sugar

⅔ cup evaporated milk or whipping cream, thoroughly chilled
1 tablespoon lemon juice

1. Soften gelatin in ¼ cup of the orange juice and liquefy over hot water. 2. Combine remaining 1¼ cups orange juice with sugar. Add gelatin and set in cold place, stirring occasionally to dissolve sugar. 3. When mixture is set to a soft jelly, whip milk or cream stiff. 4. Fold in lemon juice, then orange-gelatin mixture. Pour into a mold to set.

CRÈME BRULÉE

Makes 6 to 8 servings.

8 egg yolks
4 cups cream (2 pints)
2 tablespoons sugar

1 teaspoon vanilla
Light brown sugar

1. Place cream in saucepan and heat, but do not boil. Beat egg yolks well, and stir into hot cream. Add sugar and vanilla. 2. Mix well and pour into shallow baking dish. 3. Set in pan of hot water and bake in slow oven (300°F.) for 15 to 25 minutes, or until custard is set. Test with silver knife, which should come out clean, or tip dish to make sure the custard center does not move under the crust. 4. As soon as cool, set in refrigerator, and when thoroughly cold, spread on ⅜-inch layer of light brown sugar, and smooth down. 5. Slide dish under a very hot broiler, leaving door open if possible, as this phase of the recipe needs very careful watching. If custard starts to smoke, instantly remove from oven, let cool a little, turn dish around, and return to the oven. A smooth glaze of caramel, without any burning, is desirable. 6. Place in refrigerator until very cold.

APPLE FLUFF

Makes 6 to 8 servings.

1 package orange, lime, or lemon flavor Jell-O
1 cup applesauce

1. Dissolve Jell-O in 1 cup *hot* water. Add ¾ cup cold water. Chill until slightly thickened. 2. Place in bowl of ice and water and whip with rotary egg beater until fluffy and thick like whipped cream. 3. Fold in applesauce. Turn into individual molds, or turn into shallow pan to a depth of 1 inch. 4. Chill until firm. Unmold or cut in squares. Serve plain or with custard sauce.

ZWIEBACK PIE CRUST

½ cup butter   2 cups grated zwieback

1. Cream the butter until soft, then knead thoroughly into zwieback crumbs. 2. Spread mixture evenly over bottom and sides of 9-inch pie plate, and press firmly into place. 3. For pies and other dishes requiring baking with the crust, follow those recipes. Remove from tin only when cool. 4. For use with cooked fillings, bake zwieback pie crust in moderately slow oven (325°F.) for 12 to 15 minutes, and cool at room temperature before adding fillings.

Do not store this crust when baked. Eat fresh only.

APPLE BUTTER PIE

1 zwieback pie crust	1½ tablespoons cornstarch
½ cup apple butter	1 teaspoon cinnamon
2 eggs	2 cups milk
½ cup sugar	

1. Add sugar, eggs, cornstarch and cinnamon to apple butter and mix well. 2. Add milk gradually to mixture and blend together. Pour into an unbaked zwieback pie shell. Bake 35 minutes in moderate oven (350°F.).

QUICK MORAVIAN SUGAR CAKE

Makes about 36 squares.

2 packages yeast	1 cup milk, scalded
1 pound light brown sugar	2 eggs, slightly beaten
½ cup sugar	5 cups sifted flour (approximate)
1½ teaspoons salt	
1 cup butter	Cinnamon and nutmeg

1. Soften yeast in ⅔ cup warm water. Add sugar, salt and 3 tablespoons butter to the scalded milk. Cool milk to lukewarm, stirring until sugar is dissolved. Add yeast and slightly beaten eggs. 2. Add to flour and stir until blended. Dough must be soft. Turn out on a floured board and knead till smooth. 3. Place in a greased bowl; grease surface and let rise in a warm place (80° to 85°F.) until double in bulk, or about 1¼ hours. 4. Press portions of the dough into three greased pans (7 x 11 inches) for thick cakes or into two pans (11 x 15 inches) for thinner cakes. Grease surfaces and let rise till double, or about 30 minutes. 5. "Pinch" dough all over with thumb and finger to make wells in it. Sprinkle lightly with cinnamon and nutmeg and very generously with light brown sugar. Dot with bits of remaining butter. 6. Bake in a hot oven (400°F.) about 20 minutes, or until brown and the topping is bubbly. Serve warm or reheat. It is traditional to sprinkle the cake with confectioners' sugar before serving.

BAKED ALASKA

For sheer luxuriousness, our favorite of favorite restaurants is the Ambassadeurs, in Mexico City. On one occasion, a large Mexican family at a table adjoining was being served a Baked Alaska, and as our eyes lit up, the waiter asked if we would like to have some. Taking for granted we were to share in the same Alaska being served our neighbors, we enthusiastically accepted the invitation. But woe! We soon realized that a special Baked Alaska had been made for just the two of us—and one almost as large as had been served to ten! In the end, all collapsed . . . we, and the remains of the Baked Alaska . . . but how wonderful while it lasted!

Makes 6 to 8 servings.

1½ quarts ice cream—vanilla, chocolate or coffee flavor— molded like a brick or a melon
6 egg whites
6 tablespoons powdered sugar
½ teaspoon vanilla

½-inch layer of sponge cake, same shape as ice cream, but 1 inch larger all around. Use 2 pieces of cake if necessary
Pinch of salt

1. Cover meat plank or bread board with a sheet of heavy paper or flat aluminum foil. Place cake in center. **2.** Light oven and set at very hot—(450°F.). **3.** Add pinch of salt to egg whites and beat to stiffness, in a chilled bowl. After eggs are stiff, add powdered sugar and vanilla gradually, while continuing beating. **4.** Now work fast. Unmold ice cream onto cake and very quickly, but thoroughly, spread meringue all over ice cream and cake, with a spatula. **5.** Slide Alaska into the hot oven, to brown the meringue. This happens quickly, so peek in frequently, but do not open oven door wide as a sudden chill can ruin the meringue. When nicely browned, slide off paper or foil, onto serving platter.

FROZEN FRUIT CUSTARD

Makes 4 servings.

1 egg
¼ cup sugar
¼ teaspoon salt
½ cup hot milk
2 teaspoons lemon juice

2 containers Gerber, Clapp or other good brand of strained fruits or 1 container strained prunes
1 cup thin cream
½ teaspoon vanilla

1. In double boiler top, beat egg well with fork. **2.** Add sugar, salt and hot milk, stirring constantly. Cook over boiling water until thickened. **3.** Cool. Add remaining ingredients. Mix well. **4.** Pour into refrigerator tray and stir occasionally while freezing until firm.

ANGEL FOOD CAKE

1 cup sifted Swans Down cake flour	1¼ teaspoons cream of tartar
	¼ teaspoon salt
1½ cups sifted sugar	1 teaspoon vanilla
1¼ cups (10 to 12) egg whites (at room temperature)	¼ teaspoon almond extract

1. Sift flour once, measure, add ½ cup sugar, and sift together 4 times. Beat egg whites and salt with flat wire whisk or rotary egg beater until foamy.* **2.** Sprinkle in cream of tartar and continue beating until egg whites are stiff enough to hold up in soft peaks but are still moist and glossy. **3.** Sprinkle rest of sugar over egg whites, 4 tablespoons at a time, and beat after each addition to blend (25 strokes). Beat in flavoring (10 strokes). **4.** Sift about ¼ of flour over mixture and fold in lightly (15 fold-over strokes), turning the bowl gradually. Fold in flour by fourths in this way, folding well after last addition (10 extra strokes). **5.** Turn into ungreased round 10-inch tube pan. Bake in moderately hot oven (375°F.) 30 to 35 minutes. Remove from oven, invert pan, and let stand 1 hour, or until cool.

* TO USE ELECTRIC MIXER, beat egg whites and salt in large mixing bowl at medium to high speed until foamy. Add cream of tartar; beat until stiff enough to hold up in definite peaks, but not dry. Continue beating at high speed, adding sugar rapidly, 1 tablespoon at a time. Beat only until sugar is just blended. Add flavoring. Remove bowl from mixer. Fold in flour mixture by hand, as above.

Variations: FROSTED ANGEL FOOD:

Spread angel food with Butterfly Frosting or Chocolate Glaze.

ANGEL FOOD DREAM CAKE:

Makes 14 to 16 servings.

Cut Angel Food (large) to make 3 layers. Whip 1½ cups heavy cream with 1 cup dark brown sugar and ¾ teaspoon vanilla. Spread this amber whipped cream between layers and over cake. Chill in refrigerator 2 hours before serving. Cut in wedges.

FRUITED CREAM

Makes 2 servings.

1 container Heinz or other strained fruit, chilled	1 teaspoon lemon juice
	⅓ cup whipping cream, whipped
1 teaspoon confectioners' sugar	

1. Combine strained fruit, sugar and lemon juice. Fold in whipped cream.

HOT MILK SPONGE CAKE

⅔ cup sifted Swans Down cake flour

¾ teaspoon baking powder

⅛ teaspoon salt

2 eggs (at room temperature)

⅔ cup sugar

1½ teaspoons lemon juice

¼ cup hot milk

1. Sift flour once, measure, add baking powder and salt, and sift together three times. **2.** Beat eggs in deep bowl with rotary egg beater until very thick and light (about 5 minutes). **3.** Add sugar gradually, beating constantly. Add lemon juice. Then fold in flour, a small amount at a time. Add hot milk and stir in quickly and thoroughly until completely blended. **4.** Turn batter at once into ungreased 8 x 8 x 2-inch pan. Bake in moderately hot oven (375°F.) 20 minutes, or until done. Remove from oven and invert pan until cold.

BUTTERFLY FROSTING

2 tablespoons butter

2½ cups sifted confectioner's sugar

1 egg white, unbeaten

1 tablespoon cream (about)

¾ teaspoon vanilla

⅛ teaspoon salt

Coloring

1. Cream butter; add part of the sugar gradually, blending after each addition. Add remaining sugar, alternately with egg white, then with cream, until of right consistency to spread. **2.** Beat after each addition until smooth. Add vanilla and salt. Tint delicately with coloring. **3.** For assorted frostings, divide untinted frosting into 4 small bowls. Use 1 plain or flavor with ½ square melted Baker's unsweetened chocolate. Tint the remaining frostings to give delicate, yet decided, shades of yellow, green, and pink. **4.** While using assorted frostings, keep bowls covered to avoid crusting. If necessary, 1 or 2 drops cream or milk may be added to keep frostings of right consistency to spread.

FROZEN CHOCOLATE-MINT MARSHMALLOW CREAM

Makes 6 to 8 servings.

2 cups milk

1 cup cream, whipped

2 squares unsweetened chocolate

32 marshmallows

2 or 3 drops peppermint extract

1. Scald 1 cup milk. Shave chocolate into milk and stir until melted. **2.** Remove from stove and add marshmallows. Stir lightly until nearly melted. **3.** Add remaining cup of cold milk and extract. Fold mixture until smooth. **4.** Pour into refrigerator tray to chill while whipping cream. **5.** Fold in whipped cream and return to refrigerator. Stir once during freezing.

CHOCOLATE CREAM FILLING

Makes 2 cups filling.

4 to 6 tablespoons sugar	¾ cup milk
2 tablespoons flour	1 tablespoon butter
Dash of salt	1 teaspoon vanilla
1 square Baker's unsweetened chocolate	½ cup cream, whipped

1. Combine sugar, flour, and salt in top of double boiler; add milk gradually, stirring until well blended. Add chocolate and cook over boiling water until thickened, stirring constantly. 2. Continue cooking 5 minutes, stirring occasionally. Add butter and vanilla. Chill thoroughly. Fold in whipped cream.

SEA FOAM CAKE FROSTING

Makes enough frosting for two 9-inch layers.

1½ cups firmly packed dark brown sugar	2 egg whites
	1 teaspoon vanilla extract

1. Mix egg whites, unbeaten, with sugar and ⅓ cup water, in saucepan or double boiler top. Stir with spoon until smooth and well mixed. 2. Beat over briskly boiling water until frosting looks fluffy and holds a soft gentle shape. This should take 7 minutes with egg beater or 3 to 4 minutes with electric mixer. 3. Lift pot away from boiling water and add vanilla. Continue beating until frosting stands in peaks.

BOILED FROSTING

Makes enough frosting to cover tops and sides of two 8-inch layers, two 9-inch layers, or top and sides of 13 x 9 x 2-inch cake, or tops of 20 large cupcakes.

1½ cups sugar	2 egg whites
Dash of salt	1 teaspoon vanilla
½ teaspoon light corn sirup	

1. Combine sugar, salt, corn sirup, and ⅔ cup boiling water. Bring quickly to a boil, stirring only until sugar is dissolved. 2. Boil rapidly, without stirring, until small amount of sirup forms a soft ball in cold water, or spins a long thread when dropped from the tip of the spoon (240°F.). 3. Beat egg whites with flat wire whisk or rotary egg beater until stiff enough to hold up in moist peaks. Pour sirup in fine stream over egg whites, beating constantly. Add vanilla. 4. Continue beating 10 to 15 minutes, or until frosting is cool and of right consistency to spread. (If too stiff for rotary egg beater, use a wooden spoon.)

CHOCOLATE SAUCE

Makes 2½ cups sauce.

2 squares Baker's unsweetened chocolate
2 cups milk
⅔ cup sugar

2½ tablespoons flour
⅛ teaspoon salt
2 tablespoons butter
1 teaspoon vanilla

1. Heat chocolate and milk in double boiler. When chocolate is melted, beat with rotary egg beater until blended. **2.** Combine sugar, flour, and salt; add gradually to chocolate mixture. Cook until thickened, stirring constantly. Cook 5 minutes longer, stirring occasionally. Add butter and vanilla. Serve on cottage pudding or other dessert.

MINIKIN JELLY ROLLS

Makes 6 servings.

½ cup sifted Swans Down cake flour
½ teaspoon Calumet baking powder
Dash of salt

2 eggs (at room temperature)
½ cup sugar
½ teaspoon vanilla
¾ to 1 cup tart red jelly
Powdered sugar

1. Sift flour once and measure. Combine baking powder, salt, and eggs in bowl. Beat with rotary egg beater, adding sugar gradually until mixture becomes thick and light-colored. **2.** Gradually fold in flour, then the vanilla. Turn into 15 x 10-inch pan which has been lined with paper, then greased. **3.** Bake in hot oven (400°F.) 10 minutes. Turn cake out on cloth or towel, dusted with powdered sugar. **4.** Quickly remove paper and cut off crisp edges of cake. Cut lengthwise, then crosswise twice, to make 6 pieces of equal size. **5.** Spread each with jelly, and roll into individual jelly rolls. Cool on cake rack. **6.** Rolls may be decorated, if desired. Use sweetened whipped cream and force it through pastry tube to make borders at ends of each roll and rosettes on top.

Variations: JELLY ROLL TEA SLICES: Cut Minikin Jelly Rolls in ½-inch slices. Makes 4½ dozen slices to serve with tea or fruit punch.

BRAMBLE CAKES: Bake sponge sheet for Minikin Jelly Rolls and cool on rack without rolling. Cut sheet in half. Put together as layers, spreading blackberry jam or jelly between. Cut in 18 pieces. Spread Seven Minute Frosting (½ recipe) over tops and sides of each cake. Or use Chocolate Cream Filling instead of jelly and frosting.

BAKED BANANAS

Makes 4 servings.

4 ripe bananas	Salt
1½ tablespoons melted butter	Boiled lime juice, if desired

1. Use ripe all-yellow or slightly green-tipped bananas. Peel, and place in a well-greased baking dish. **2.** Brush well with butter and sprinkle lightly with salt. Add just a little boiled lime juice, if desired. **3.** Bake in moderately hot oven (375°F.) for 15 to 18 minutes, or until bananas are tender—easily pierced with a fork. **4.** When browning is desired, place the baked banana under broiler heat for 1 to 2 minutes. **5.** Serve hot as a vegetable, or as a dessert with cream, sirup or a hot fruit sauce.

Variations: BAKED BANANAS WITH SOUR CREAM: To serve as a vegetable, top each hot banana with ¼ cup sour cream.

BANANAS BAKED WITH CRANBERRIES: Pour ¾ cup hot cranberry sauce over bananas. Bake as above. Serve hot with beef, chicken or turkey.

BANANAS BAKED WITH BROWN SUGAR: Sprinkle bananas lightly with brown sugar. Bake as above. Serve hot as a sweet entrée with beef, lamb or chicken, or as a hot dessert.

BANANAS BAKED WITH APPLESAUCE OR APPLE BUTTER: Spread bananas evenly from tip to tip with applesauce or apple butter. Use ¼ cup for each banana. Bake as above. Serve as a hot dessert.

BANANAS BAKED WTH ORANGE SAUCE: Pour over the bananas ¾ cup hot orange sauce made without orange peel. Bake as above. Serve hot as a sweet entrée, or as a hot dessert.

BROILED BANANAS

Makes 4 servings.

4 firm ripe bananas (all yellow or slightly green-tipped)	Melted butter Salt

1. Peel bananas and place on broiler rack or into pan containing rack. Brush bananas well with butter; sprinkle lightly with salt. **2.** Broil 3 to 4 inches from heat, about 5 minutes on each side, or until bananas are browned and tender—easily pierced with fork. Serve hot as a vegetable.

Variations: BROILED BANANAS WITH CREAM: To serve as a hot dessert, top each banana with plain, whipped or sour cream, sprinkle with sugar, nutmeg or cinnamon, if desired.

To serve as a vegetable, top each banana with ¼ cup sour cream.

RENNET MILK DRINKS

RENNETIZED MILK DRINK: To each cup of cold milk (not canned), add 1 rounded tablespoon Junket rennet powder (any flavor*). Beat with rotary beater or shake in a milk shaker until dissolved. To make even more readily digestible, let stand 15 minutes before serving.

CREAMY RENNETIZED MILK DRINK: Warm 1½ cups milk (not canned) slowly, stirring constantly. Test a drop on inside of wrist frequently. When comfortably warm (110°F.), not hot, remove at once from heat. Stir ¼ cup Junket rennet powder (any flavor—for chocolate use ⅓ cup) into milk quickly until dissolved—not over one minute. Do not move until set—about 10 minutes. Then chill. Just before serving, add 1½ cups cold milk (not canned) and beat well with rotary beater. Makes 3 servings.

BANANA RENNETIZED MILK DRINK: Beat ½ cup sliced bananas with rotary beater until smooth. Strain, if desired. Add 1 cup cold milk (not canned) and 2 tablespoons vanilla rennet powder to the banana purée and beat with rotary beater or shake in a milk shaker until dissolved.

CHOCOLATE HONEY RENNETIZED MILK DRINK: Add 2 tablespoons chocolate rennet powder and ½ tablespoon honey to 1 cup cold milk (not canned). Beat with rotary beater or shake in a milk shaker until dissolved.

EXTRA-RICH RENNETIZED MILK DRINK: Add ¼ cup rennet powder (any flavor—for chocolate use ⅓ cup) to 1 cup light cream and 1 cup cold milk (not canned). Beat with rotary beater or shake in a milk shaker until dissolved. To make even more readily digestible, let stand 15 minutes before serving. Makes 2 servings.

FLAVORED EGG NOG: Add 1 rounded tablespoon rennet powder (any flavor*) to 1 cup cold milk (not canned). Beat with rotary beater or shake in a milk shaker until dissolved. Beat 1 egg until frothy. Stir into milk and serve.

*Chocolate requires 2 tablespoons for each cup of milk.

MAPLE CREAM CHEESE FUDGE

1 package Philadelphia cream cheese (3 ounces)	2½ cups sifted confectioner's sugar
10 drops maple flavoring	Dash of salt

1. Place cream cheese in a bowl. Cream it until soft and smooth. Add 1 teaspoon cream if a soft fudge is desired. 2. Slowly blend in sugar. Add maple flavoring and salt. Mix well until thoroughly blended. 3. Press into well-buttered shallow pan. Place in refrigerator until firm, about 15 minutes. Cut into squares.

THE LOW FAT - LOW CHOLESTEROL DIET

Frequently prescribed as part of the treatment of athero-
sclerosis and certain gall bladder and liver disorders

WHEN YOUR DOCTOR decides to put you on a low fat diet, it is usually because your gall bladder or liver may not be functioning normally; fats will overburden these organs and can cause distress, even serious trouble. Therefore the recipes in this section seek to give you interesting dishes with less fat.

The low cholesterol diet strives for something more than a *reduction* in fat...it aims for a change in the *kind* of fat your body receives.

When the doctor decides you should be on a low cholesterol diet, it is because he is concerned about your heart...and there appears to be a relationship between heart attacks and the ingestion of fats that are high in cholesterol. He therefore prescribes a diet that is low in cholesterol as one precaution against coronary thrombosis, which is a medical term for a closure or roadblock in your blood vessels. When this happens, the blood cannot get through to your heart—and the result is a heart attack, a stroke, and even sudden death.

Bear in mind, a low fat diet is not a no fat diet. Fat has a number of functions in human nutrition, one of which is to supply certain body chemicals that are necessary to good health. We cannot ban them entirely. Nor can we completely bar cholesterol; it too has a useful function in the body. But we must modify the diet so that the proportion of overly high cholesterol-bearing fats is reduced, and the low cholesterol fats are given more emphasis.

WHAT IS CHOLESTEROL?

Cholesterol is a tasteless substance found in butter, lard and other animal fats and oils, in egg yolks, and in all milk products, including cheese. It is also found in vegetable oils that have been "hydrogenated," or hardened. This includes all margarines, Crisco, Spry and all similar shortenings.

When cholesterol piles up on the inside of blood vessels, it closes down the opening so the blood requires extra pressure to push through to the heart. Just picture your kitchen sink's drainpipe clogged up with lamb fat, bacon fat and other substances so no water can go through. In that case you can call a plumber; but when your arteries or veins get clogged up, even the physician can't always bring you help. That's why your doctor says to cut down on cholesterol-making fats before the blood "pipes" become encrusted with cholesterol and before the encrustation is so bad it forms a blood clot or causes a heart attack.

MEN MORE FREQUENT VICTIMS THAN WOMEN

Because of the growing importance of the low cholesterol diet in the treatment of atherosclerosis (hardening of the arteries), we have given you a variety of recipes that we hope will make your diet more endurable. And since it is a fact that more men than women suffer from heart conditions, many recipes lean to the foods men usually prefer. Up to the period of menopause, women are, by some wondrous body secretion or ovarian activity perhaps, protected against coronary diseases; after menopause they rival men as possible victims.

While middle-aged men are the ones most carefully watched by their doctors for signs of hardening of the arteries, all of us these days may be overindulging in fatty foods. An average of 40% to 45% of the total food intake of the American diet comes from fat. We have developed into a nation of fryers—we eat French fries by the ton—and are eating 15% more each year over the last. One group of hamburger restaurants sells so many French fries that it uses 10% of the entire potato crop of America. Besides French fries, we gobble up potato chips, doughnuts, Chinese egg rolls, all fried in deep fat, plus fried chicken, fried eggs, fried fish, fried sausages, and a multitude of other fried foods. We love our double-dips of ice cream and our pieces of cake, which are loaded with fat, and we sit through movies consuming bucketfuls of buttered popcorn. Our consumption of meat—particularly hamburgers, hot dogs, Sloppy Joes, Heroes and chili—has gone sky-high, and here too one of the main ingredients is fat, the kind of fat that tends to raise the cholesterol level of the blood. Another hidden source of fat is the so-called "convenience foods"—the mixes and other ready-to-use products which contain shortenings and other ingredients that violate this diet.

THE DESIRABLE FATS

Fortunately for the person on a low cholesterol diet, there is a certain kind of fat which does NOT increase the cholesterol level of the blood; in fact, it actually tends to LOWER it. These fats are called "polyunsaturates" and are found in such liquid vegetable oils as corn oil, soybean oil, cottonseed oil and safflower oil. These same desirable fats are also in fish, poultry, in whole grain foods, in certain nuts—walnuts, pecans, almonds, peanuts (which means peanut butter too).

The recipes in this section aim to supplant undesirable (saturated) fats with desirable (polyunsaturated) fats, or to avoid fats entirely. For many people, desserts are the most difficult to do without, and while fruits are the safest form of dessert for low cholesterolites, you will also find a number of acceptable dessert recipes. The taboo is very clear on store-bought ice cream, cakes, pies, Danish pastry, cookies, etc.—they are high in calories, and from half to three quarters of those calories are in cholesterol-forming fat.

For all we have said about cholesterol-laden fats, there are these three words of advice: Don't go overboard. If a little butter or egg yolk or bacon fat gets into your diet, don't let it send you to a psychiatrist. The idea is to get more fat balance in your diet, not necessarily to eliminate all saturated fats entirely. In fact, in following *any* restricted diet, it is a pretty good rule to know and understand your basic goal and to hew as close to it as you can without going crazy over it...unless your condition is VERY bad and your doctor advises utmost strictness.

"YES" FOODS ON THIS DIET

These are the permitted foods on the low fat–low cholesterol diet. As you scan this list, you will see that, while there are numerous omissions, such as mayonnaise, gravies, chocolate, pies, and pastries, there are plenty of things you can eat. As with all other special diets, you must reeducate and retrain your tastes and your eating habits. But since the very important matter of your health is at stake, it does make the effort worthwhile.

FISH—All fish is permitted—fresh, frozen, dried, smoked. Also any canned fish packed in vegetable oil; if packed in olive oil, drain well. Shellfish is permitted only occasionally and in moderation (lobster, crab, shrimp, oysters).

MEAT—Lean meats only. Trim off all visible fat.
   Veal—the leaner cuts, scaloppine, well-trimmed loin chops, leg, rump or shoulder, eye roast.
   Lamb—leg.
   Beef—eye, top or bottom round, lean ground round.

Pork—well-trimmed ham steak, lean loin of pork, Canadian bacon. [Eat organ meats (liver, heart, kidneys, tongue) only occasionally, or avoid altogether.]

POULTRY—Especially desirable on this diet.
Chicken—gives preference to young chicken and to the white meat.
Turkey—same as chicken, young and the white meat.

DAIRY PRODUCTS—Milk—skim milk only, fresh or the dry powder reliquefied.
Eggs—the whites only are freely permitted; the yolks are high in cholesterol and should be eaten sparingly.
Cheese—uncreamed cottage cheese, farmer cheese, or pot cheese; cottage cheese "creamed" with skim milk; Sap Sago or "green" cheese; hoop cheese.
Margarine—Diet Chiffon or other diet margarines.

SOUPS—any fat-free soup, including clear consomme, bouillon, madrilene, fruit soups and well-skimmed vegetable or chicken soup; home-made imitation cream soups (prepared with skim milk).

VEGETABLES—all vegetables cooked without animal fats fit into this diet.

SALADS—all greens, tomatoes, cucumber, celery, etc., are fine; serve with lemon juice, or diet salad dressings such as Frenchette or Mayonette. Aspics are good.

CEREALS—all breakfast cereals are permitted, with skim milk and any sweetener; rice, spaghetti, macaroni, barley.

FRUITS—all fruits, fresh, frozen or canned.

BREADS—all breads and rolls made without shortening—whole wheat bread, rye bread, French or Italian bread.

CAKES—any home-made cakes or pastries made without animal fats or hard shortenings (hydrogenated)—angel cake and meringues, pancakes, waffles (use syrup, honey, jam, cinnamon-and-sugar, etc., but diet margarine instead of butter).

DESSERTS—Jell-O and other gelatin desserts; Italian water ices and other water ices; sherbets if you are sure they contain no milk; puddings if made with skim milk.

DRINKS—skim milk drinks, with fruit flavors, coffee, vanilla flavors, (but not chocolate); 7-Up, cola drinks, beer, wine, liquor.

SWEETS—gum drops and other gum candies, marshmallows, jams, jellies, preserves.

NUTS—English walnuts are well recommended, pecans, almonds, peanuts (but not coconut or coconut products).

CONDIMENTS, ETC.—salt, pepper, herbs, relishes—and also conserves of all kinds that have not been marinated or made with animal fat (olive oil is permitted in moderation because its fat is rather "neutral," but safflower, corn, peanut, soybean and cottonseed oil are clearly preferred).

There are some items on the above list which do not fit into other factors you may have to watch—beer, for example, is not acceptable on a low calorie diet, salad greens are to be avoided on the bland diet. So, if you have a multiple problem, bear this in mind; this section deals primarily with foods which fit into the low fat—low cholesterol diet.

Dieters in general have a special source of concern—a psychological problem in cutting down the SIZE of portions. You cannot blame a dieter for having an inner resentment that other people can eat freely and he can't. This resentment often comes out in eating larger quantities, even though the dieter may hold fairly close to the diet restrictions. He stays with the idea but not the ideal.

It is not necessary to tell you here how to broil meats or fish, which you will have to depend upon frequently when on this diet. Your experience or any basic cook book will guide you there. But frying is out and baking has to be done without benefit of butter pats or ordinary margarine.

WHEN THE RECIPE CALLS FOR OIL

Whenever oil is mentioned in our recipes, just take it for granted we refer to the polyunsaturated oils, which are highly satisfactory and easy to handle and do not change the flavor of foods. The best of these oils are made from a plant named safflower; it is a light oil and can be bought at so-called health food stores. Corn oil, soybean oil, cottonseed oil, peanut oil, sesame oil, and sunflower oil are all acceptable. You can now buy corn oil in most supermarkets; the bottles are usually labeled "polyunsaturated." Olive oil, while a vegetable oil, is not polyunsaturated but, being rather neutral in its fat nature, can be used on occasion, in moderation. Coconut oil is out.

DIET MARGARINES

There are a number of "diet margarines" in the supermarkets and they contain half the fat of regular margarine or butter. For purely technical reasons, these must be labeled "imitation oleomargarine" or "imitation margarine," but they taste like, look like, spread like regular margarine. We accept them and recommend them for use in moderation, despite the fact that they do contain "partially hydrogenated soybean oil" or "partially hardened corn oil," which makes them saturated oils and would ordinarily be undesirable. However, we are not seeking to eliminate saturated oils entirely but to correct the *balance* between the two kinds of oil, polyunsaturated and saturated. The doctor wants to modify your diet so that instead of your eating four times as much of the saturated fats as you eat polyunsaturates, the proportion will turn almost the other way—more of the "polys" and less of the "sats."

Diet Chiffon is slightly preferable, but only slightly so, to Diet Mazola or other corn oil diet margarines because it contains liquid safflower oil. Diet Chiffon is made by Anderson, Clayton & Co., whose main address is P.O. Box 35, Dallas, Texas 75221. If you can get Diet Chiffon in your food store, fine, but if not you can accept Fleischmann's, Imperial, Mazola or other *diet* margarines. In using these margarines for sautéing, simply cover the skillet because the water content causes spattering; the acceptable (polyunsaturated) vegetable cooking oils are better for this purpose.

SALAD DRESSINGS

There is a good selection of diet salad dressings available in food stores. All or most of the usual oil is replaced in these dressings by non-caloric, non-fat gums. They can be used quite freely on this low fat–low cholesterol diet. Our own preference is the Frenchette line of salad dressings, which we know have been taste-tested and often win out for flavor over many oil-rich products. One of these dressings has no oil in it at all; this is Frenchette French-style dressing. The other current variations contain comparatively small amounts of vegetable oil and are all excellent for this diet. You have a selection of Frenchette Gourmet, Green Goddess, Thousand Island, Garlic, and Italianette dressings. In the recipes, where we say "Frenchette dressing," choose any one of these.

There is also a product called Mayonette, which is a find for those on this restricted diet. It does contain a tiny amount of egg yolk but the principal ingredients are cottonseed oil, cornstarch, vinegars and seasonings. A tablespoonful contains only 20 calories compared with 110 calories for regular mayonnaise. Use it *mit verstand,* that is, temperately, for salads, sandwiches, snacks and dips.

ON CHEESES

All ordinary cheeses are off the low fat–low cholesterol diet because they contain so much butterfat. The one freely permitted cheese is one labeled skim milk cottage cheese. Failing this, accept the carton or package labeled just plain cottage cheese, or dry pot cheese or farmer cheese. These are all low in fat, high in protein. Avoid the "creamed" cottage cheeses because they lack the very advantage which the uncreamed cottage cheese gives you. It isn't always easy to find uncreamed cottage cheese, so you may have to buy the creamed kind, put it in a colander, and run cold water through it to wash away the cream. You can then, if you wish, mix in some skim milk and a few dashes of salt. In some stores you may find "hoop" cheese, a desirable type of cottage cheese made entirely with skim milk.

To prepare something like cream cheese, try to get farmer cheese, which is dry, pressed cottage cheese, and soften it to spreading consistency with skim milk. This makes a satisfactory substitute for cream cheese in canapés and for plain or mixed sandwiches (with peanut butter, chives, cucumbers, watercress, jelly, etc.). Going a step further, for dips you may lighten the mixture with more skim milk (mushroom dip, anchovy, chick pea, smoked salmon, etc.).

As to milk—when fresh skim milk is not available, the reliquefied dry powder is an acceptable substitute. The powder can also be used in many recipes as a thickening agent. Add 2 tablespoons of non-fat dry milk powder to one cup of skim milk, for making "creamed" soups, sauces, puddings, etc.

Fat-free buttermilk and skim milk evaporated milk are available in some food stores and are worth looking for.

A CHEESE FOR TOPPINGS AND AU GRATIN DISHES

Since all but skim milk cheeses are taboo on the low fat–low cholesterol diet, the familiar grated Parmesan cheese cannot be used, except in the smallest amounts. There is a cheese called Sap Sago (or sapsago), which is made of partly skimmed milk and new-mown clover, and can be used over hamburgers to make cheeseburgers, or over spaghetti, macaroni, lasagne, soup, and au gratin dishes generally.

Sap Sago comes in sage-green 3-ounce cones, ready for grating, and you should grate it as you need it. This cheese is also called Green Cheese, Herb Cheese, and sometimes Schabzieger; it has a pleasant hay-like aroma. If you wish, mix a tablespoon of grated Parmesan to each 2 tablespoons of grated Sap Sago. You can sometimes buy Sap Sago already grated, but the cones you buy for home-grating are better. You must keep this cheese under refrigeration, but let it come to room temperature before using.

In New York, the food department of B. Altman & Co. carries Sap Sago; address: 5th Avenue at 34th Street, New York, N.Y. 10016. Or write to the cheese distributor, Otto Roth & Co., 179 Duane Street, New York, N.Y. 10013. (phone [212] 925-0818) to ask for the nearest place to buy it. Cheese stores seem to be springing up all over and there may be one near you which sells Sap Sago.

The chances are more than two to one that, directly or indirectly, the adult male American will die of heart disease. And the odds against him have been rising year by year. The rate of increase is even greater among younger men. Nowhere in the world has heart disease (among women as well as men) skyrocketed as it has in America. It is no wonder then that physicians are more and more frequently advising patients to alter their eating habits in order to reduce their blood cholesterol levels, and, hopefully, their risk from heart disease.

This book is performing a useful function if it does nothing more than give you a sense of direction on how to make the most of what you can eat so you don't miss the foods you can't eat. It is mighty frustrating to look into the ordinary cook book, only to find recipe upon recipe calling for gobs of butter, cream, whipped cream, sour cream, bacon, beef dripping, chicken fat, milk, evaporated milk, eggs, cheese, shortening, ice cream and other forbidden foods. As a test, I went through the 180 recipes in Peg Bracken's *I Hate to Cook Book* and, while it is most gay and helpful for people on eat-anything diets, there is just about one recipe in the entire book which can be used by those on a low fat–low cholesterol diet, and that one is in the form of a note recalling the English custom of ending a meal with walnuts and port wine. This paucity of usable recipes is more or less true of every other popular cook book. So, if we can help you to avoid frustration, and help to guide you to interesting if not exciting meals, we shall be happy to have served.

FAT-FREE WHOLE WHEAT BREAD

Most packaged breads and rolls today contain saturated fats because they are made with hydrogenated shortening, whole milk or milk solids, egg yolks, and occasionally butter. Also, most white breads shortchange you on nutrition because their flour is so highly refined. In many sections of the country, good home-style whole wheat bread is fortunately available. If you understand what you may and may not have on this diet, you will quickly be able to tell from the label whether the bread is for you. When an acceptable bread is not available, this recipe will produce a loaf you can safely eat.

3½ cups whole wheat flour	2 teaspoons salt
1 yeast cake	Dash of nutmeg or mace
2 tablespoons brown sugar	½ cup raisins (optional)

1. Soak yeast and sugar in ¼ cup lukewarm water until dissolved, and foam appears. Add the salt, and bring to a boil. Let cool to lukewarm. **2.** Mix the nutmeg or mace into the whole wheat flour, which must not be cold. Unless the flour has been at room temperature for at least 1 hour, put it in the oven, in a Pyrex dish for few minutes. **3.** Since this bread is dry and crumbly, ½ cup of raisins mixed into the flour at this point gives a more moist texture. **4.** Combine the yeast-water mixture with the flour and stir well with wooden spoon. Add a little lukewarm water if needed; dough should be stiff, yet soft. Place the mixing bowl in dishpan of warm but not boiling water and cover with towel. Rising takes 1½ to 2 hours. If dough does not rise easily and seems too stiff add a little lukewarm water. **5.** Stir vigorously with spoon for 1 minute. Grease and flour a large bread pan, turn in the dough, and let rise again 45 minutes to 1 hour. **6.** Place in cold oven and bake 45 to 50 minutes in moderate oven (350°F.). Turn down heat if baking is too fast. When done, turn out bread on its side, on a bread-board, and cover with thin cloth, for 4 to 5 hours.

WHOLE WHEAT MOLASSES BREAD

1⅔ cups skim milk, butter-milk, or strained buttermilk	½ cup molasses
2½ cups whole wheat flour	1½ teaspoons soda
½ cup cornmeal	1 teaspoon salt

1. Mix flour, cornmeal, soda and salt. Blend well. **2.** Combine buttermilk and molasses. Mix with dry ingredients. **3.** Bake in slow oven (275°F.) for 1 hour.

FOODS LOW OR COMPARATIVELY LOW
IN BOTH FAT AND CHOLESTEROL

ALL CEREALS	**ALL FRUITS**	**ALL VEGETABLES**
BAKED GOODS without milk, cream or butter	**BOUILLON CUBES** and **TABLETS**	**BREAD** and **CRACKERS** without milk, cream or butter
CANDIED FRUITS and **PEELS**	**CLAMS** and **SCALLOPS**	**CODFISH, PERCH** and **HADDOCK**
COFFEE and **TEA**	**COTTAGE CHEESE,** dry curd	**EGG WHITE,** fresh or dried

FOODS LOW OR COMPARATIVELY LOW
IN BOTH FAT AND CHOLESTEROL

FLOUNDER, BASS, gray PIKE	GELATIN	GLUTEN STEAKS, GLUTENBURGERS
HARD CANDY, MINTS, MARSHMALLOWS, GUM DROPS	JAMS, JELLIES, HONEY	LEGUMES
MACARONI and SPAGHETTI	MUSTARD, CATSUP, HORSERADISH, PICKLES, etc. in moderate amounts	SALT, HERBS and SPICES
SUGAR, MOLASSES, CORN SYRUP or MAPLE SYRUP	SKIM MILK, fresh or powdered	TUNA FISH, Dietetic Pack

FOODS TO AVOID in the **LOW FAT, LOW CHOLESTEROL DIET**	**BAKED GOODS** containing eggs, butter, etc.	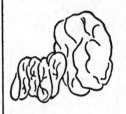 **BRAINS and SWEETBREADS**
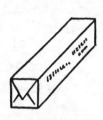 **BUTTER** and **MARGARINE**	 **ALL FATS**	 Many **CAKE, WAFFLE** and **PANCAKE MIXES** or whole milk powder
 **CANNED SOUPS** containing eggs, cream, etc.	 **CHEESES** with milk or cream	Many **CHOCOLATE DRINK POWDERS** with whole milk
 **COD** or **HALIBUT LIVER OIL**	 Creamed **COTTAGE CHEESE**	 **NUTS, OLIVES, PEANUT BUTTER, AVOCADOS, COCONUTS**

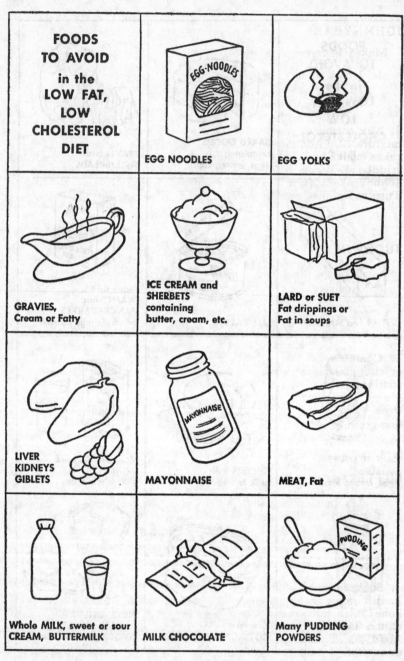

FOODS
TO AVOID
in the
LOW FAT,
LOW
CHOLESTEROL
DIET

EGG NOODLES

EGG YOLKS

GRAVIES,
Cream or Fatty

ICE CREAM and
SHERBETS
containing
butter, cream, etc.

LARD or SUET
Fat drippings or
Fat in soups

LIVER
KIDNEYS
GIBLETS

MAYONNAISE

MEAT, Fat

Whole MILK, sweet or sour
CREAM, BUTTERMILK

MILK CHOCOLATE

Many PUDDING
POWDERS

JOHNNYCAKE

Makes 4 servings.

2 cups white cornmeal | 1 teaspoon salt
1¼ cups non-fat milk | Vegetable oil
1 tablespoon brown sugar

1. Mix cornmeal, sugar and salt. Pour 2 cups boiling water over mixture. 2. Heat the griddle. 3. Add milk to mixture and form cakes which will stay in shape when dropped from spoon onto griddle. 4. When griddle is hot, grease with vegetable oil, put on Johnnycakes. Turn down heat after a minute, and cook slowly. Turn cakes once, when crust is brown. 5. Serve with sirup.

BUCKWHEAT BREAD

1¾ cups skim milk, butter-milk, or strained buttermilk | ½ cup brown sugar
2⅓ cups buckwheat flour | 1½ teaspoons soda
½ cup raisins, or soaked and chopped prunes | 1 teaspoon salt
| ½ teaspoon baking powder
| Vegetable oil or margarine

1. Combine dry ingredients and mix thoroughly. Stir in raisins or chopped prunes. 2. Add the sugar to the buttermilk, stir, and combine with dry ingredients. 3. Grease a bread pan with vegetable oil or margarine and turn in the mixture. 4. Bake in very slow oven (275°F.) for 50 minutes. A very high oven will burn this fine-grain bread.

BUTTERMILK RYE BREAD

1⅔ cups skim milk, butter-milk, or strained buttermilk | 2 teaspoons caraway seeds
2½ cups rye flour | 1½ teaspoons soda
½ cup cornmeal | 1 teaspoon salt
¼ cup honey | Vegetable oil or margarine

1. Soak caraway seeds in ¼ cup water for several hours; drain. 2. Sift flour, cornmeal, soda and salt. Add caraway seeds. 3. Mix honey with buttermilk. Combine with flour mixture. 4. Turn into a pan lightly greased with vegetable oil or margarine, and let stand 20 minutes. 5. Bake in very slow oven (275°F.) for 50 minutes to 1 hour.

CHAPATI—EAST INDIAN BREAD

Whole wheat flour   Salt

1. Put flour into bowl and make a little well in the center. Add just enough water to make a very dry dough; add a little salt in the process. **2.** Knead well with fingers, and divide dough into lumps the size of an egg. **3.** Roll out lumps on floured board, to the size and shape of very thin pancake. **4.** Heat a griddle and brown the pancakes on ungreased griddle. Press with a cloth before removing each pancake from the griddle, to expel the air and let the pancake puncture itself. Eat hot.

OATMEAL BREAD

2 cups rolled oats
1 cup oatmeal flour
2⅓ cups whole wheat flour
½ cup molasses

1 yeast cake
1 tablespoon margarine or vegetable oil
2 teaspoons salt

1. Combine rolled oats, salt, molasses, margarine or oil, and 2 cups boiling water. Stir very well, then add 1 cup whole wheat flour and the oatmeal flour. **2.** Melt yeast in ¼ cup lukewarm water. **3.** When oats mixture is lukewarm, add the yeast mixture. Then add remaining 1⅓ cups whole wheat flour and stir very actively for 1 minute. **4.** Set in pan of warm, but not boiling, water. Cover with towel and let rise 2 to 3 hours. Then stir with wooden spoon for 1 minute and turn into 2 small, greased bread pans. **5.** Cover with towel and let rise 1 hour, in a warm place. Finish rising in oven. When oven reaches 375°F., turn down to 350°F., then to 325°F. Let bake at this temperature. Total baking time, from start to finish, should be about ¾ hour.

CREAM OF MUSHROOM SOUP

Makes 2 eight-ounce servings (176 calories). Calories in 1 serving: 88.

¼ cup finely diced onion
¼ cup finely diced celery
3-ounce can chopped broiled mushrooms

1 Souplet
⅓ cup skim milk powder (nonfat dry milk solids)
Dash of pepper

1. Place onion, celery, contents of can of mushrooms, Souplet and ½ cup water in saucepan. Cover and bring to boil. **2.** Let cook over low heat until vegetables are barely tender and Souplet dissolved, about 5 minutes. **3.** Blend together skim milk powder (non-fat dry milk solids) and 1 cup water. **4.** Add to cooked vegetables and heat thoroughly. Season to taste with a dash of pepper.

"CREAM" SOUPS

Makes 4 servings.

3 cups non-fat fresh milk or reliquefied Starlac

2 tablespoons skim milk powder (dry Starlac)

1 to 2 cups vegetable purée or cooked chopped vegetables— asparagus, carrots, celery, potatoes, corn, peas, onions, spinach, lettuce, beans, etc.

2 tablespoons flour

1 crushed Souplet vegetable broth tablet

½ teaspoon salt

Beaten egg white

Pepper to taste

Paprika

1 tablespoon finely chopped onions (optional)

1. Shake together in a jar, or blender, the flour and skim milk powder, with 1 cup of the milk. **2.** Cook this slowly in a saucepan, until thickened and smooth. **3.** Dissolve the vegetable Souplet tablet in a little boiling water and add to the saucepan. Add the milk, vegetables, salt and pepper. Add chopped onions if desired. **4.** When heated through, serve with topping of beaten egg white and dash of paprika.

HODGE PODGE SOUP

This is one of those rainy day, or lazy Sunday, dishes. Cooking time is over 6 hours, but if you expect to be around the house anyhow, why not try it?

Makes 12 servings (3000 calories). Calories in 1 serving: 250.

1 pound lean beef

1 pound lean mutton

1 pound veal

1 ounce barley

2 parsnips

3 leaves lettuce

1 large carrot

Salt and pepper

Muslin bag containing:

1 chopped onion

3 cloves

8 peppercorns

1 bunch celery, chopped

1 bunch fresh herbs or 1 teaspoon dried thyme and 1 bay leaf

1. Cut meat into small pieces, put in large pot with 2½ quarts water. Start cooking, and add barley. **2.** Add muslin sack of seasoning vegetables and spices. **3.** Peel and quarter parsnips. Peel carrot and slice thickly. Cut lettuce into small pieces. Add all vegetables to soup pot. **4.** Cover, and simmer over very low flame for 6 hours. Skim off fat several times. **5.** Remove muslin bag, season with salt and pepper, and serve.

VICHYSSOISE

Makes 2 or 3 servings.

1 cup diced raw potatoes (6 ounces)
3 tablespoons finely diced onion
1 tablespoon minced parsley

1 Souplet vegetable bouillon tablet
1½ cups skim milk
Salt and pepper

1. Place potatoes, 1 cup water, onion, parsley and Souplet in saucepan. Cover and bring to boil. **2.** Cook over low heat until potatoes are tender, about 15 minutes. **3.** Put cooked vegetables through sieve or food mill, or blend in an electric blender. **4.** Add milk. Season to taste with salt and pepper. Chill thoroughly.

JELLIED CONSOMMÉ

Makes 3 or 4 servings.

1 tablespoon unflavored gelatin (1 envelope Knox's)

3 Souplets or other vegetable bouillon tablets
1 tablespoon lemon juice

1. Soften gelatin in ½ cup cold water, then dissolve over low heat or hot water. **2.** Pour 1 cup boiling water over the 3 Souplets and let stand until Souplets are dissolved. **3.** Combine Souplets broth with the dissolved gelatin. Add the 1½ cups cold water and the lemon juice. **4.** Chill until the consistency of egg-white, then stir well and chill until just set. Serve in chilled bouillon cups.

DILL PICKLE SOUP

Makes 4 servings.

2 dill pickles, diced
5 dried mushrooms
2 medium potatoes, diced
1 parsnip
1 onion

1 carrot
6 sprigs parsley
1 clove garlic
1 bay leaf

1. Put mushrooms in large soup pot and cover well with cold water. Bring to a slow boil, then simmer for 50 minutes. **2.** Slice the parsnip, carrot and onion, and add to the pot. Add garlic, parsley and bay leaf. **3.** Simmer until vegetables are soft, then rub all vegetables, except mushrooms, through a strainer. **4.** Slice the mushrooms and return to the pot, together with the soup, pickles and potatoes. **5.** Simmer until potatoes are quite soft, but not mushy.

CELERY CHOWDER

Makes 4 servings.

1½ cups chopped celery	1 medium-large potato
2 cups skim milk	Salt and pepper
1 Nestlé bouillon cube	Pinch of marjoram

1. Peel potato, cut into ½-inch cubes, and place in saucepan with 1½ cups boiling water. Add chopped celery, salt and pepper. **2.** Cook slowly for 30 minutes, or until potato is almost mushy. Add boiling water if necessary. Mash potato with fork, in the saucepan. **3.** Add milk, marjoram and vegetable or beef tablet dissolved in a little boiling water. **4.** Bring to a boil, simmer briefly and serve.

SPANISH GADITANA SOUP

This is a lively fish soup from Cadiz, Spain, and is a meal in itself.

Makes 6 servings.

1½ pounds assorted small fish (porgies, crappies, butterfish, smelts, well-drained sardines)	¼ cup Spanish brandy (Fundador)
	3 tablespoons oil
1½ pounds assorted large fish (cod, haddock, mullet, hake, etc.)	3 cloves garlic, lightly crushed
	1 large onion, finely minced
⅔ cup fresh white bread crumbs	1 large bay leaf
¼ cup orange juice	6 peppercorns
¼ cup lemon juice	Salt

1. Mash together the bread crumbs and the orange and lemon juices; mix with the brandy and set aside. **2.** Salt the fish lightly and refrigerate in glass or plastic bowl for 1½ hours. **3.** Drain fish. Heat oil in 6-quart kettle and sauté garlic until nut-brown; avoid burning it. **4.** Remove garlic and throw it away. In kettle, sauté onion until it begins to color. Add 8 cups boiling water. Add bay leaf and peppercorns. **5.** Cook 5 minutes at a rolling boil. Reduce heat and add fish. Cover and simmer 15 minutes. Remove the fish. **6.** Strain the broth and salt if necessary. Return broth to pot and stir in breadcrumb mixture. Remove fish skins and return fish to pot. Reheat to just under boiling.

STONE SOUP

The fable of stone soup, for which I am indebted to my daughter Nina, goes something like this: A stranger knocks at the cottage door of a poor woodcutter and asks for a meal. The inhabitants offer him hospitality, but say they have no food in the house and nothing with which to make him even a bowl of soup. The stranger produces a stone, saying, "This is a magic soup stone. Put it in a pot of boiling water, cook it for a while, and you will have enough soup to feed us all." After the stone is placed in the pot, the stranger says, "Now this stone makes very good soup by itself but if you happen to have an onion lying around, it will be that much better." And a little later, "If you can manage to scrape up a bit of meat, it will be still better." And so on. Likewise with this recipe, you can add whatever you happen to have around that comes within the diet. It all only improves the flavor of the soup. Here is a starter:

Makes 4 to 5 servings.

1-2 ounces dried mushrooms, rinsed	Salt
to remove grit	Pepper
2 medium carrots	Accent or MSG
2 medium onions	If you have cauliflower on hand,
½-1 cup chopped cabbage	toss it and any other such
2 stalks celery	items in the pot
2 tablespoons uncooked barley	
2 beef bouillon cubes (or 1 cube	
and 1-2 hamburgers' worth of	
lean chopped beef)	

PRESSURE COOKER—If you can use a 4-quart pressure cooker, place 4 cups of water and all the ingredients except the salt, pepper and Accent in the cooker and very gradually raise the pressure to 30 pounds. This slow increase in pressure is to avoid clogging that might be caused by the barley. Cook 30 minutes, then allow to cool. Add seasonings.

NO PRESSURE COOKER—If you cook in a plain pot, you will have to lengthen the time to about 2½ hours.

The soup, in either case, will be somewhat thin, despite the barley. On the second day, reheated, it will be thicker.

PETITE MARMITE

Petite marmite, which means little kettle, is one of the most satisfactory culinary achievements. It is a soup, but far more than a soup. It can be a main dish, along with some good French bread and a green salad, or it can be a tasty introduction to a larger meal. The broth and meat can be served together or separately, with the addition of rice, spaghetti or noodles (not egg noodles) to either. And, incidentally, it is one of the best buys on the menu of such restaurants as Longchamps in New York.

Makes 6 servings.

1½ pounds lean beef, cut in 1-inch	1 tablespoon salt
cubes	1 cup diced carrots

2 veal knuckles with some meat on them	1 cup diced turnips
1 small chicken, cut up	¾ cup chopped onion
3 tablespoons oil	½ cup chopped leeks, white part only
1 bay leaf	½ cup diced celery
2 cloves	Croutons made of unbuttered toast
4 peppercorns	Grated Sap Sago cheese
¼ teaspoon thyme	

1. Heat oil in skillet, add beef and cook until browned. 2. Tie beef in muslin or cheesecloth bag and place this, with veal knuckles and chicken, in a kettle. 3. Add 3½ quarts cold water and seasonings. Bring to a boil slowly, removing scum. 4. Cover and simmer gently about 3 hours. Strain, setting meat and bones aside. Return stock to kettle. 5. Add vegetables and adjust seasoning, possibly adding some MSG. Boil gently until vegetables are tender, about 20 minutes. 6. Remove meat from veal knuckles and chicken. Dice and return with beef to the hot soup. Discard bones and chicken skin. Skim off all fat and serve in soup bowls, preferably earthenware. Add croutons and grated Sap Sago cheese.

VERSION 2

There are probably as many variations on petite marmite as there are French cooks. My East Hampton, Long Island, townsman, Craig Claiborne, would throw up his hands at the recipe above. He uses no veal bones, the chicken must be cut exactly right—leg and thigh each cut into 3 pieces, each breast-half into four—and the vegetables cut into precise 2-inch lengths. The beef and chicken are cooked first for 5 minutes; the vegetables are cooked 15 minutes; then 7 cups of chicken stock are added to the combined meat and vegetables. After an hour or more of slow simmering, the broth is ready. You may prefer this or some other petite marmite recipe, but we do advise that you make this dish one of your diet mainstays.

BROILED FLANK STEAK WITH TOMATO SAUCE

Makes 4 servings.

1½ pounds lean flank steak (you may have to buy 2 pounds and trim off the fat)	Powdered cloves or mace
	Salt and pepper
	1 cup tomato purée

1. Score or cut surface of meat crosswise about every 3 inches. Sprinkle lightly with cloves or mace, salt and pepper. 2. Put steak in broiler, 5 to 6 inches from tip of flame. Broil 10 minutes on one side and 7 minutes on the other. 3. Heat tomato purée. 4. Carve meat on the bias with sharp knife, in 8 slices not more than ¼-inch thick. Serve tomato sauce over 2 slices meat.

BOHEMIAN STYLE BEEF WITH KALE

Makes 6 servings.

2 pounds leanest possible brisket of beef
2 pounds kale

½ cup dry rice
2 onions, chopped or sliced
1 teaspoon salt

1. Cut meat into 6 serving portions. Wash, drain and chop the kale. Wash and drain the rice. 2. Combine all ingredients, including the chopped onion and salt. Cook in covered pot over moderate heat 1½ hours. Do not add water unless necessary to prevent scorching, as the water that clings to the kale is usually enough. 3. Shake the pot occasionally to prevent sticking—do not stir. Carefully skim off fat. Serve when meat is tender and rice is soft.

BAKED VEAL

Makes 4 servings.

1½ pounds veal cutlet
3 onions
4 tomatoes

Wine vinegar
Salt and pepper
Small amount vegetable oil

1. Place veal in deep bowl; season with salt and pepper. Add vinegar to cover and marinate for 1 hour. 2. Remove meat from vinegar, dry with cloth, and place in a greased roasting pan. 3. Place in very hot oven (450°F.) until meat browns. Slice onions and tomatoes and add to meat. 4. Reduce oven to slow (300°F.), add stock or water to cover, and continue to bake 30 to 45 minutes.

SHASHLIK

Makes 8 servings.

1 leg lamb, about 6 pounds
Juice of 5 lemons
2 cloves garlic, chopped

1 bunch dill
1 bunch parsley
Salt and pepper

1. Cut meat off lamb leg, into cubes about 1½ inches square. Remove tendons in the process. 2. Place in a deep dish or crock

and pour the lemon juice over the lamb cubes. **3.** Add parsley, dill, garlic, salt and pepper, and mix up well, so that each cube is seasoned. Cover and put in cool place for 3 or 4 hours. **4.** Run skewers through meat and cook under a clear flame, in broiler pan—or cook over hot coals.

JELLIED VEAL

Makes 6 servings.

2-pound veal shank, with bone in
1 stalk celery
1 small onion
1 small carrot
Salt and pepper

1. Salt and pepper meat and place in kettle with 2 quarts cold water. Add the other ingredients. **2.** Bring to a boil, reduce heat, cover pot, and simmer very slowly until meat falls away from bone. **3.** Strain broth, remove bone, and cut meat into small uniform pieces. Boil broth until it is reduced to half its volume. **4.** Rinse a mold in cold water, and place meat and vegetables in it. Pour in liquid, and chill. Stir mixture several times before it sets, to keep meat and vegetables from dropping to the bottom. **5.** When firm, cut into slices and serve.

STUFFED CABBAGE

Makes 4 servings (920 calories). Calories in 1 serving: 230.

¾ pound ground beef round
8 large cabbage leaves
⅓ cup cooked rice
2 cups tomatoes
Juice of 1 small onion
1 onion, finely chopped
1½ tablespoons vinegar
1½ tablespoons sugar
Salt and pepper

1. Soak cabbage leaves in hot water for few minutes, until soft enough to handle. **2.** Season meat well, with salt and pepper. Add onion juice and rice. **3.** Fill cabbage leaves with meat mixture by laying leaves out flat and placing a portion of the mixture about an inch above the heavy stem end. Roll this end over the mixture once, then fold in each side of the leaf and continue rolling. Hold together with toothpicks if necessary. **4.** Place the 8 rolls in a kettle with the rest of the ingredients, add a little water, and let simmer until the cabbage is tender and well browned.

BROILED SKINNED DUCKLING

An average serving of duck has half the cholesterol of an equal weight of egg yolk, but a good deal more than a breast of chicken. But since white meat of chicken or turkey can become tiring, and since 3½ ounces (a normal serving) of skinned, defatted duckling meat contains only about 7% hidden fat, its occasional use is permitted.

Makes 4 servings.

4–5 pound Long Island duckling, ready-to-cook
2 teaspoons lemon juice
1½ teaspoons Kitchen Bouquet

½ teaspoon salt
¼ teaspoon onion salt
½ teaspoon ginger

1. Cut wing tips from duckling. With sharp knife score duck skin from neck to vent along center of breast. Peel back layer of skin and fat with one hand, running knife underneath to help cut connective tissue but keeping flesh intact. **2.** Cut the skinned duckling in quarters with a cleaver or kitchen shears. Cut wings from breast quarters. These may be broiled or cooked with wing tips to make duck broth for soup. **3.** Place the pieces of skinned duckling in a bowl and sprinkle with lemon juice, Kitchen Bouquet, salt, onion salt, and ginger. Toss pieces gently with a fork in order to coat evenly. Let stand half an hour to season. **4.** Arrange pieces of duckling on rack in preheated broiling compartment, with the bony, or inside, up to start. **5.** Broil 4 to 5 inches from moderate heat for 15 minutes. Turn pieces and continue broiling for another 15 minutes. Serve immediately.

HERBED POT ROAST

Makes 6 to 8 servings.

3½ pounds sirloin roast
Salt
Freshly ground black pepper
¼ cup + 2 tablespoons flour
3 tablespoons peanut oil
1 cup finely chopped onion
¼ cup vinegar
1 tablespoon finely chopped anchovy fillets

2 tablespoons dark honey
½ tablespoon thyme
1 bay leaf
2 sprigs parsley
2 cups clear beef broth
2 tablespoons diet margarine

1. Preheat oven to 350°F. Sprinkle meat with salt, pepper and ¼ cup flour. **2.** In skillet, in 2 tablespoons of the peanut oil, brown meat on all sides. Then transfer meat to Dutch oven and pour off all fat from skillet. **3.** In remaining tablespoon of oil, cook onion until wilted. **4.** Add to skillet the vinegar and all other ingredients, except margarine and remaining flour; bring to boil. **5.** Pour mixture over the beef in Dutch oven, cover and bring to a boil on top of stove. **6.** Bake until meat is tender, about 2½ hours. Strain pan juices and heat with remaining flour and margarine to make gravy.

SAUERBRATEN

Makes 6 servings.

2-3 pounds lean beef—chuck, eye round, top or bottom round	½ teaspoon salt
1 cup vinegar	10 peppercorns
2 large onions, chopped	⅛ teaspoon powdered clove
2 large carrots, sliced	3 bay leaves

1. Trim off all the fat the butcher has left on the meat. Place meat in a bowl. **2.** Place all the other ingredients in a pot. Add 1 cup water. Bring to a boil to make a marinade. Pour this over the meat. **3.** Refrigerate 2 to 3 days, turning frequently. **4.** Drain the meat and save the marinade. Place the meat in a very hot Teflon (nonstick) pot; reduce to low heat and brown the meat carefully. If you don't have a Teflon pot, use an iron pot and brown the meat in a minimum of oil. **5.** Add the marinade, cover the pot, and cook over low heat 2 to 3 hours. Skim off any fat as it appears.

GINGERED BEEF

You can obtain the ginger root for this recipe at Chinese, Japanese, and many Spanish food shops. As to the 48 calories in a tablespoon of sugar, remember this is spread over 4 to 6 servings. Although you can try Sucaryl or other noncaloric substitutes, some people are taste-sensitive to artificial sweeteners, and the substitution may hardly be worthwhile.

Makes 4 to 6 servings.

1 pound fat-trimmed beef, cubed	¼ cup soy sauce
2 tablespoons peanut or corn oil	2 tablespoons sherry
2 slices fresh ginger root	1 tablespoon sugar
1 scallion or shallot cut into 2-inch pieces	

1. Place oil, ginger and scallion in saucepan and heat over high heat. **2.** Add beef cubes and cook, stirring, until meat is lightly browned. **3.** Add soy sauce, sherry and sugar. Cook 5 minutes, stirring. **4.** Add 1 cup water, cover, and cook 30 minutes over medium heat, stirring occasionally. Continue cooking for 30 more minutes.

SWISS STEAK

Makes 6 servings.

2 pounds fat-trimmed beef—round, rump or chuck—cut 1 to 1½ inches thick
⅓ cup flour
½ teaspoon salt
Freshly ground black pepper
2 tablespoons oil
1 onion, sliced
2 carrots, sliced
1½ cups canned or stewed tomatoes

1. Wipe meat with a cloth. Rub in salt and pepper. Dredge with flour and pound in seasonings and flour with mallet. 2. Brown meat on all sides in the oil in a heavy skillet or Dutch oven. 3. Add onions, carrots and tomatoes. Cover, and simmer gently about 1½ to 2 hours, or until meat is tender.

ARMENIAN BEEF STEW

Makes 6 servings.

2 pounds fat-trimmed beef—chuck, neck or shin—cut in 1-inch cubes
⅓ cup flour
½ teaspoon salt
⅛ teaspoon freshly ground black pepper
2 tablespoons oil
2 medium onions, sliced
1 No. 2 can tomatoes
1 cup green beans, in ½-inch lengths

1. Mix flour, salt and pepper and dredge meat cubes. 2. Heat oil in heavy skillet or Dutch oven; avoid smoking. Add onions and cook until yellow. 3. Add meat and brown on all sides. Add tomatoes. 4. Cover, and simmer over low heat about 1½ hours. 5. Add beans and continue cooking until meat and beans are tender. Remove to hot platter and, if desired, thicken gravy with a little additional flour.

HAM AND SAUERKRAUT

Makes 6 servings.

2 cups diced lean ham
1 1-pound 11-ounce can sauerkraut
2 apples, pared and thinly sliced
4 tablespoons firmly packed brown sugar
¼ teaspoon cinnamon
Oil for greasing baking dish

1. Drain liquid from sauerkraut. In large mixing bowl, combine the sauerkraut with ham, half of the sliced apple, and 2 tablespoons of the sugar. 2. Spoon mixture into greased 6-cup baking dish. 3. Top the mixture with the remaining apple slices, overlapping them. 4. Mix cinnamon with the remaining 2 tablespoons sugar, sprinkle over apple slices, and cover. 5. Bake in moderate, 350°F. oven for 1 hour, or until bubbly hot.

TARTAR STEAK

Makes 4 or more servings.

1 pound prime lean sirloin,
    ground three times
3 anchovies, mashed
1 medium onion, grated
¼ teaspoon freshly ground
    black pepper

2 egg whites
Anchovy fillets for garnish
Watercress sprigs or lettuce
Pumpernickel bread

1. Combine meat, mashed anchovies, onion and pepper. 2. Add egg whites as a binder. 3. Form into a rectangle or square and crisscross the top with the dull edge of a knife to form small diamond shapes. 4. Press ½ anchovy fillet into each diamond. Chill thoroughly. 5. Cut out the diamonds and serve on pumpernickel cut into similar shapes, placing small pieces of lettuce or sprigs of watercress between meat and bread.

SWEDISH MEAT BALLS

Makes 6 servings as main dish, 12 as an hors d'oeuvre.

1 pound very lean ground veal
½ pound very lean round ground
    beef
1 small onion, grated
1 clove garlic, minced
¼ teaspoon nutmeg
1 carrot, finely grated

1 teaspoon salt
¼ teaspoon paprika
Freshly ground black pepper
3 slices white bread, crusts
    removed
½ cup skim milk
4 tablespoons oil

1. Combine the veal and beef. Add grated onion, garlic, nutmeg, carrot, salt, paprika and pepper. Mix well together. 2. Soak bread in skim milk, then beat together until fluffy. Add to meat mixture. 3. Blend or beat well and work mixture with your hands until smooth and light. 4. Form into balls, using wet hands. For hors d'oeuvres roll to 1-inch size; for main dish make larger. Place in refrigerator for an hour. 5. When ready to cook, heat oil in heavy skillet and cook meat balls until golden brown. Leave oil in the skillet for the sauce. There should be about 2 tablespoons oil left; add more if needed.

Sauce: 2 tablespoons flour
    ¾ tablespoon salt
    Black pepper

2 cups skim milk
1 teaspoon Kitchen Bouquet

1. Scrape the crust from the bottom of the skillet and leave it in the oil. Add flour, salt and pepper; mix well. 2. Over low flame, add milk slowly, stirring constantly until mixture thickens and bubbles. Add Kitchen Bouquet and cook for a minute more. 3. Return meat balls to skillet, cover, and let simmer over low flame 20 to 25 minutes.

ROAST LAMB MARINATED WITH HERBS

Makes 8 servings.

1 6 pound leg of lamb, fat-trimmed but unskinned	¼ teaspoon dried rosemary (or 2 sprigs fresh rosemary)
¾ teaspoon dried sage (or fresh sage branches)	Salt
	Pepper

1. If you can obtain fresh herbs from a herb garden, wrap them around the lamb. But if not, rub the lamb lightly with the powdered sage. Cut 2 gashes in the meat with a sharp knife and insert ⅛ teaspoon dried rosemary into each gash. 2. Cover well with aluminum foil or wax paper and place in refrigerator overnight. 3. Remove herbs when ready to roast. Sprinkle meat lightly with salt and pepper and place on rack in roasting pan. 4. Preheat oven and roast meat at 400°F. for 15 minutes. Remove fat and pour in a cup of hot water. 5. Reduce heat to 330°F. and roast 30 minutes per pound for medium-done and 35 minutes per pound for well-done meat.

LAMB CURRY

To put some zest into the diet when it is running in low gear, try this one.

Makes 4 servings.

1 pound lean lamb, cut in 1-inch cubes	1 teaspoon paprika
2½ tablespoons oil	½ teaspoon powdered ginger
1 onion, finely chopped	¼ teaspoon chili powder
1 clove garlic, finely minced	¼ teaspoon sugar
1 tart apple, chopped	Salt
1 tablespoon curry powder	2 tablespoons tomato paste

1. Brown the lamb cubes in the oil in a skillet. 2. Transfer the lamb to a casserole and sauté the onion, garlic and apple in the skillet. Cook until onion is golden. 3. Add all the seasonings except tomato paste and salt, and cook briefly until blended. Salt to taste. 4. Spoon mixture over the lamb and add the tomato paste. 5. Add a little water to the skillet and pour this gravy over the lamb; add extra water to cover. 6. Cover the casserole and cook on top of stove until meat is tender, about 1 to 1½ hours.

CHICKEN BRAZIL

Makes 2 servings.

1 chicken breast	3 tablespoons chopped onion
1 tablespoon oil	3 tablespoons coarsely chopped
Salt	mushrooms
Pepper	6 walnut halves, coarsely
MSG (Accent)	broken up
3 tablespoons barbecue sauce	

1. Remove skin and fat from chicken breast. Place, topside up, in small roasting pan. 2. Brush with oil. Sprinkle generously with salt, pepper, and some MSG. 3. Preheat oven and bake at 375°F. When chicken is golden brown, remove and brush on barbecue sauce. Replace in oven and bake 5 minutes more. 4. Place onions, mushrooms and walnuts in saucepan. Cook in remaining oil until onions are transparent, stirring constantly. 5. Pour mixture over the chicken and cook 5 more minutes.

CHICKEN BREAST AND MACARONI

Some day, when you have a ham bone left over from a baked ham, think of this recipe. And do leave a little meat on the bone.

Makes 6 servings.

1 chicken breast (about ¾ pound)	¼ teaspoon pepper
2 tablespoons oil	1 teaspoon mixed salad herbs
1 cup chopped onion	1 8-ounce package elbow macaroni
1 ham bone	Chopped parsley for garnishing
2 teaspoons salt	

1. Brown chicken breast in oil in an iron kettle; push to one side. 2. Stir in onion and sauté until soft. 3. Add ham bone, 8 cups water, salt, pepper and salad herbs. Simmer for 1 hour. 4. Remove chicken and ham bone. Heat liquid to boiling and stir in macaroni. Cook 20 minutes or until macaroni is tender. 5. Skin the cooked chicken and dice the meat. Strip the ham bone of any bits of meat (no fat). Stir these into the soup. Serve in soup bowls; garnish with parsley.

RICED MEAT BALLS

Makes 4 servings (1304 calories). Calories in 1 serving: 326.

1 pound ground beef round	¼ teaspoon garlic salt
⅓ cup raw rice	⅛ teaspoon basil
3 tablespoons chopped onion	½ bay leaf
2 tablespoons chopped parsley	Salt and pepper
1 can Campbell's tomato soup	

1. Combine beef, rice, onion, parsley, garlic salt and basil. Season with salt and pepper, mix thoroughly and shape into 1-inch balls. **2.** Place in 1-quart casserole. Combine ½ cup water with the soup and pour over meat balls. Crush ½ bay leaf and add. **3.** For 30 minutes bake *covered* in moderate oven (350°F.). Then uncover and bake 20 to 30 minutes more, until brown.

BANANA MEAT LOAF

Makes 4 to 6 servings.

1 pound lean ground beef	2 teaspoons salt
1 cup soft bread crumbs	½ teaspoon dry mustard
¾ cup mashed ripe bananas	¼ teaspoon pepper
1 tablespoon chopped onion	

1. Blend mustard through the mashed bananas. In a separate bowl mix the meat, onion, crumbs, salt, and pepper. **2.** Combine banana and meat mixtures. Mix well. **3.** Shape into a loaf and place in a baking dish lined with aluminum foil. **4.** Bake in moderate oven (350°F.), about 1 hour.

FISH PUREÉ

Makes 8 servings.

4 pounds non-fatty fresh-water fish	1 leek
1 carrot	3 bay leaves
1 stalk celery	1 tablespoon lemon juice
1 onion	10 peppercorns
1 parsnip	Salt to taste

1. Bring 12 cups water to a boil; add all ingredients except fish and lemon juice. **2.** Simmer 15 minutes and add half the fish. Cook until it begins to fall apart. Slice the remaining 2 pounds of fish. **3.** Force cooked fish through a sieve. Return to pot, bring to a boil and add the sliced raw fish. **4.** Cook about 15 minutes. Serve hot, add lemon juice before serving.

FISH STEW

Makes 6 servings.

1 pound pike	½ lemon
1 pound white fish	1 bay leaf
6 potatoes, in ¾-inch cubes	1 tablespoon salt
3 large onions, sliced	⅓ teaspoon pepper
2 carrots, quartered	Paprika

1. Wash and slice fish, squeeze lemon juice over it. Place in refrigerator for several hours. 2. Wash lightly and cook in 8 cups water. Bring to a boil, add all other ingredients, then simmer for 1 hour. 3. Serve very hot.

SWEET AND SOUR FISH

Makes 4 to 6 servings.

3 to 3½ pounds pike (or pickerel)	½ cup honey
2 medium onions, sliced	⅓ cup white raisins
1 teaspoon salt	½ teaspoon ground ginger
5 tablespoons lemon juice	

1. Put 3 cups of water, the onions and salt in 4-quart pot and bring to a boil. Lower the heat and simmer 15 minutes. 2. Wrap fish in cheesecloth for easy handling and place in the pot. Simmer 20 minutes or until fish is flaky. Remove fish to a baking dish. 3. Strain 1 cup of the fish liquid and place in saucepan with the lemon juice, honey, raisins and ginger. Simmer for about 10 minutes. 4. Pour over fish and place in 400°F. oven for 10 minutes.

FLOUNDER AND SALMON ROLL

Helen Latson, our housekeeper, joined the Weight Watchers and came back with this simple and successful recipe.

Makes 4 servings.

4 fillets of flounder rolled around	Salt
4 small pieces of fresh salmon,	Pepper
well-anchored with toothpicks	Lemon juice or white wine

1. Season with salt and pepper. 2. Set the fish on a baking pan or broiler with the opening up. Bake or broil for 20 minutes in moderate 350°F. oven. 3. Serve on a warm platter and pour on lemon juice or wine.

SWORDFISH ITALIANETTE

Makes 4 servings.

1½-1¾ pounds swordfish steak   ½ cup Italianette low calorie
                                    Italian dressing

1. Cut swordfish into serving pieces. 2. Place fish in a disposable aluminum foil broiling pan. Pour dressing over fish pieces, turning them to coat well with the dressing. 3. Refrigerate about 1 hour, turning pieces occasionally. 4. Broil fish right in the pan for about 15 minutes or until done.

POACHED BASS IN WHITE WINE

Makes 6 servings.

1 6-pound striped bass   1 teaspoon dried tarragon (or 4
2 onions, coarsely chopped   sprigs fresh tarragon)
3 carrots, coarsely chopped   3 cloves garlic, peeled
2 leeks, split and cut into 1-inch 2 tablespoons peppercorns
  cubes   1 bottle dry white wine
4 bay leaves   Salt
1 teaspoon dried thyme (or 2 sprigs
  fresh thyme)

1. Use a fish cooker with an inner rack, if possible. Otherwise use a large pot with handles on which to hang the fish in a sling of cheesecloth. 2. Simmer all the ingredients, except the fish, in 1 gallon of water for 10 minutes. 3. Set the fish in this bouillon and simmer for 20 minutes. 4. Let stand in liquid until ready to serve, then gently transfer fish to warm serving platter. Garnish with the carrots, leeks and onions. 5. Serve with mock cream sauce or just lemon.

FISH IN LEMON ASPIC

Makes 4 to 6 servings.

2 tablespoons (2 envelopes)   1 cup of any non-fatty cooked
  gelatin   or canned fish, flaked
½ teaspoon salt   2 tablespoons chopped pi-
1 tablespoon sugar   miento
½ cup Sunkist lemon juice   1 cup chopped celery

1. Sprinkle gelatin on top of ¼ cup cold water. 2. Add 1½ cups hot water; add salt, sugar, and lemon juice. 3. Cool, and add flaked fish, pimiento, and celery. 4. Chill in individual molds. Unmold on crisp salad greens. 5. With scissors cut interestingly-shaped garnishes out of lemon slices. Accompany with tartar sauce in baskets made from lemons.

DELUXE POTATO OR MACARONI SALAD

Makes 6 servings.

4 cups cooked, diced potatoes
or macaroni
1 cup Lowmay mayonnaise
substitute
1½ cups diced celery, or 1 cup
diced celery and ½ cup
diced green pepper or cu-
cumber
½ cup sliced scallions

¼ cup sliced radishes
2 tablespoons finely chopped
parsley
1 tablespoon vinegar
2 teaspoons prepared mustard
1½ teaspoons salt
½ teaspoon celery seeds
⅛ teaspoon pepper

1. Combine all ingredients several hours before serving. Chill in
refrigerator. 2. Serve on shredded lettuce or cabbage. 3. Garnish
with grated carrots, tomato wedges or sweet pickles.

COUNTRY CHICKEN SALAD

Makes 8 servings.

6 cups cooked or canned chick-
en (or turkey or duck) in
large fat-free pieces
4 cups thinly sliced celery
½ cup Lowmay mayonnaise
substitute

¼ cup Frenchette dressing
(cholesterol-and-fat-free)
2 tablespoons lemon juice
1 teaspoon salt
¼ teaspoon pepper

1. Toss all ingredients together one hour or more before serving.
Chill in refrigerator. 2. Serve on lettuce, with jellied cranberry
sauce slices, carrot curls, tomato wedges or radishes.

LASAGNE (Vegetarian)

This won't taste as good as lasagne with meatballs between some
of the layers, but it makes a fairly acceptable substitute. If you wish,
follow the Swedish Meatballs recipe and add crushed meatballs
when you spread the sauce.

Makes 6 servings.

1 package ribbed lasagne
1 onion, diced
1 clove garlic
½ cup oil
1 No. 2½ can tomatoes
1 tablespoon chopped parsley
3 basil leaves (or 1 tablespoon
crushed basil)

1 12-ounce can tomato paste
Salt to taste
Pepper to taste
3 tablespoons salt
2 8-ounce cartons skim milk
cottage cheese
Grated Sap Sago cheese

1. In a saucepan brown the diced onion and garlic clove in the oil. 2. Add the tomatoes, parsley, basil, tomato paste and dashes of salt and pepper to taste. Simmer for 15 minutes. 3. While sauce is simmering, boil 6 quarts of water, adding the 3 tablespoons salt. 4. When water boils briskly, slowly add the lasagne. Cook for 10 minutes and drain well. 5. Into a casserole place several spoonfuls of sauce, a layer of lasagne, 4 tablespoons cottage cheese, another layer of lasagne and a layer of sauce. Repeat. End with a layer of lasagne, sauce, and a topping of grated Sap Sago cheese. 6. Bake 20 minutes in moderate 350°F. oven.

STUFFED PEPPERS GEORGIA STYLE

Makes 4 servings.

2 green peppers	3 tablespoons fine dry bread
2 cups homemade hash mixture, free of fat	crumbs
	2 cans tomato sauce
1 teaspoon horseradish	Salt

1. Cut peppers in half, lengthwise, remove seeds, and cook in boiling salted water 5 minutes. Remove from water. Drain. 2. Mix hash, bread crumbs and horseradish. Fill into pepper shells. 3. Pour tomato sauce into greased shallow baking dish. 4. Place peppers in dish. Bake in hot oven (400°F.) 30 minutes, or until browned. 5. Five minutes before removing from oven, baste peppers with sauce.

RIZ BOUILLI

Makes 6 servings.

1 cup uncooked rice	1 tablespoon grated Parmesan
3 teaspoons salt	cheese
1 slice bacon	⅛ teaspoon pepper
Pinch of saffron	

1. Add salt, bacon and saffron to 2 quarts boiling water, and boil 5 minutes. 2. Wash and drain rice; add slowly to boiling water and continue cooking 15 to 20 minutes, or until a grain, when pressed between the thumb and forefinger, is entirely soft. 3. Drain and remove bacon. Stir lightly into rice, Parmesan cheese, and pepper. Serve hot.

BAR HARBOR SALAD

Makes 4 servings.

4 firm tomatoes
1 cup codfish flakes or other similar fish flakes (7½-ounce can)
2 tablespoons capers

½ cup minced celery
2 teaspoons prepared horse-radish
½ cup chili sauce
Water cress

1. Quarter tomatoes without cutting through bottoms; scoop out. 2. Combine fish flakes, capers, celery, horseradish and chili sauce; chill. 3. Fill tomatoes with fish mixture. Serve on water cress. If desired garnish with pickled onions.

TUNA STUFFED TOMATO SALAD

Makes 6 servings.

6 ripe tomatoes
1 tin dietetic pack fancy tuna (7½ ounces)
3 or 4 tablespoons Lowmay mayonnaise substitute

2 tablespoons chopped celery
6 tablespoons dry farmer cheese or pot cheese
Salt and pepper
Lettuce leaves

1. Scald and peel tomatoes. Cut segments halfway down; pull back to form petals. 2. Remove pulp, add well-drained tuna, salt, pepper, and celery. 3. Replace in shells, top with Lowmay, chill and serve on crisp lettuce leaves. Sprinkle cheese on each salad.

TOMATO AND CARROT SALAD

With so many of the larger tomatoes being picked before ripe and packed under cellophane, you will get a taste improvement with the following combination.

Serves 2.

2 plum tomatoes (or 4 grape tomatoes)
1 carrot (the sweeter the better)
Few pieces diced celery
Bit of sliced mild Spanish onion (optional)

Squirt of lemon juice or Frenchette dressing
Salt
Pepper

1. Quarter or halve the tomatoes into a bowl. Grate in the carrot. Add the celery and onion. 2. Squirt on the lemon juice or dressing and plenty of salt and pepper. Mix and serve.

CHEF'S SALAD

When you crave something light yet filling and satisfying, a chef's salad can just hit the spot. I once found myself in a fine restaurant in Paris, quite surfeited by a constant round of gourmet meals, when I was inspired to ask for a chef's salad. After the *maitre d'* recovered from the shock, they made a presentable combination, and I was flattered to find "Chef's Salad" among the restaurant's specialties when next I visited.

Any variety of mixed greens you like—lettuces (bibb, iceberg, Boston, romaine), chickory, fennel, raw spinach, endive. If you wish, include very thinly sliced cucumber and watercress.

Frenchette low calorie dressing—any variety: plain, Gourmet, Green Goddess, Thousand Island, Garlic or Italianette. Some of these contain egg yolk, but the amount is negligible. The Blue Cheese variety of Frenchette is also permissible because of the very small amount of cheese.

Long, very thin slivers of absolutely fatless cold roast veal, turkey and/or chicken white meat, plus a smaller amount of slivers of ham and roast beef or roast lamb. And, if you've been good and held to your diet all week, you can toss in just about 3 slivers of Swiss or American cheese per serving.

1. Shred the greens into bite-size pieces and mix thoroughly in a large bowl. 2. Add the meats and toss. 3. From a good height, to make a thin stream, pour on the dressing of your choice, mixing with the other hand if you can manage it. Judge the amount you use somewhat by the calorie count on the bottle. 4. Chill before serving. Top off each serving with a green pepper ring or a slice of tomato.

CELERY ROOT REMOULADE

If you are not familiar with celery root (or celeriac), it's a good vegetable to know. Popular in France as an hors d'oeuvre or first course, it can also be one of the dishes for a buffet supper.
Makes about 2 ½ cups.

2 cups celery root (celeriac), cut in julienne strips	Chopped parsley
	1 sour pickle, finely chopped
Frenchette French-style dressing	1 tablespoon capers, finely chopped
Mayonette imitation mayonnaise	
Prepared hot mustard	

1. Cover the celery root strips with boiling water and cook 1 minute. 2. Drain, cover with Frenchette dressing and refrigerate at least 6 hours. 3. Mix 2 to 3 tablespoons Mayonette with enough hot mustard to give it a good sharp tang; mix in the chopped parsley. 4. Drain the celery root and moisten it with the Mayonette mixture. 5. Mix in the chopped pickle and capers.

TOMATO SALAD

On your first trip to Paris, when you're not quite sure of even your restaurant French, *Salade des Tomates* on a *carte* looks friendly—easy to say and to eat—so you order it and find it's just sliced tomatoes with oil, vinegar and a touch of seasoning. Nonetheless, it's a good way to start a meal. Let the tomatoes marinate in the dressing for a bit, and add a sprinkle of oregano, chives or watercress. Use a minimum of oil or Frenchette Gourmet dressing.

HOLIDAY SALAD

Makes 6 servings.

2 cups cranberries	½ cup seedless grapes
1 whole orange, sliced	1 cup diced celery
¾ cup sugar	Lettuce
1 tablespoon unflavored gelatin	Lowmay or Frenchette dressing

1. Cook cranberries, orange, sugar and 1 cup water, until all the cranberry skins pop open. Put through fine sieve. 2. Soften gelatin in 2 tablespoons cold water and dissolve in hot cranberry mixture. Chill until slightly thickened. 3. Pour a thin layer of gelatin mixture into bottom of ring mold and arrange grapes in circle to form topping. Chill. 4. Fold celery into remaining mixture and add to ring mold. Chill until firm. 5. Unmold and fill center with lettuce. Serve with Lowmay mayonnaise substitute, or Frenchette dressing.

WAGON WHEEL SALAD

Makes 1 large serving.

1 ripe banana	Berries or cherries
2 slices canned pineapple	Frenchette dressing (cholesterol-and-fat-free) or Lowmay
Crisp salad greens—chicory, water cress, etc.	

1. Enlarge pineapple center holes if necessary, and fit one slice onto each end of the peeled banana, to form 2 wheels on 1 axle. 2. In between, arrange salad greens, with strawberries or other berries or cherries. 3. Serve with Frenchette dressing or Lowmay.

GRAPEFRUIT JUICE DRESSING

Grapefruit juice alone or with a sprinkling of salt and paprika makes an excellent dressing for a sliced tomato or lettuce salad, in a low-fat, low-cholesterol menu.

Grapefruit juice may also be used to bring out flavor and to keep certain other fruits, such as bananas, apples, pears, peaches, light in color. Dip or sprinkle fruit with juice.

FLOATING SALAD

Onions thinly sliced
Cucumbers thinly sliced
Green pepper rings
Tomatoes, thickly sliced

Flavored vinegar (herb vinegar,
garlic vinegar, wine vinegar,
etc.)
Salt and pepper

1. Arrange vegetable slices in layers, in a bowl. 2. Sprinkle each layer lightly with salt and pepper. 3. Dilute vinegar with equal quantity of cold water, to cover vegetables. Chill and serve.

PEACH BANANA FAN SALAD

Makes 1 large serving.

½ fresh or canned peach
1 ripe banana
Lettuce leaf
Cherry or berry

Water cress or other salad
greens
Frenchette dressing (cholesterol-and-fat-free)

1. Cut banana in 3 lengthwise slices. On one side of plate, arrange banana slices like a fan—together at one end, spread out at the other. 2. Next to the banana fan, place peach half on lettuce leaf, round side down. Put cherry or berry in peach cavity. 3. Garnish with greens and serve with Frenchette dressing.

CHINESE STEAMED RICE

1 cup rice

1. Wash rice and drain off water. 2. Add 2 to 3 cups clear water if rice is long-grained; 3 to 4 cups if oval-grained. 3. Bring to a boil and boil 5 minutes. Drain off the "rice soup" and place the rice in individual serving bowls (no more than ¾ full). 4. Set in pan of water and steam over medium heat for 1 to 1½ hours. Be sure to have enough water in pan, but do not let water get into the bowls.

APRICOT MUSTARD SAUCE

(For rice)

1½ cups apricot purée
3 tablespoons honey
2 tablespoons dry mustard
2 or 3 tablespoons sherry wine
or sweet vermouth

1 tablespoon ginger
1½ teaspoons curry powder
1 teaspoon almond or vanilla
extract

1. Mix apricot purée with all other ingredients, using mixer, or electric blender. 2. Pour over rice, or first add chopped scallions to rice, then pour on sauce.

BROWN RICE COOKED IN MILK

Makes 2½ cups—about 3 servings.

½ cup brown rice   ¾ teaspoon salt
2 cups non-fat milk

1. Boil milk, and place in double boiler top with washed rice, and salt. 2. Cover tightly and cook 1 hour over boiling water. Stir several times. Add more hot milk if necessary. (Or cook in covered casserole in the oven.) 3. Turn into a Pyrex dish, and place in warm oven for few minutes to fluff up the rice. 4. Serve as vegetable or with honey, jam, raisins, etc., as a dessert.

RICE WITH ORANGES

Makes 6 servings.

1½ cups rice   ⅔ cup sugar
3 medium oranges   6 cloves

1. Steam the rice, so kernels are dry and separate. 2. Dissolve ⅓ cup sugar in ⅔ cup warm water and stir into the cooked rice; set aside. 3. To the grated rind of 1½ oranges, add cloves, ¾ cup water, ⅓ cup sugar and cook this into a sauce in a shallow pan. Let it cool. 4. Peel oranges carefully, to remove white skin as well as remaining rind. Separate orange segments, remove seeds. 5. Place orange segments on a platter with the rice; pour the cooled orange sirup over all.

FRUITS AND VEGETABLES

There is not much point in burdening these pages with an excessive number of recipes or remarks on fruits and vegetables. You can eat these freely on this diet and other cook books supply many interesting recipes. By now you know what foods to stay away from— whole milk, cream, butter, ordinary margarine, egg yolk, shortening, etc. Give preference to fresh fruits and vegetables. Try to avoid canned vegetables packed with added salt, canned fruits packed with added sugar, and frozen fruits or juices with added sugar.

ABOUT POTATOES

The potato is a good food nutritionally—it supplies a number of vitamins, minerals and other nutrients. When eaten plain—without butter or sour cream which are taboo on this diet—there are only about 83 calories in a medium-size potato. To preserve the comparatively high amount of Vitamin C which potatoes contain, cook them in their skins as quickly as possible; use a small amount of water and cover the pot tightly.

For a surprisingly tasty hors d'oeuvre, pick the tiniest fresh new potatoes, as small as marbles if you can get them, boil till tender but not soft, and serve in their skins.

Instant mashed potato (we use the one made by R.T. French Company) turns out fairly well when made with skim milk and diet margarine.

Ordinary baked potatoes, pan-browned potatoes, parsleyed potatoes, potato casserole, and many other styles of potatoes fit into this diet. Diet margarine, skim milk cottage cheese, Lawry's or McCormick's seasoning salts, paprika, parsley, dill or chives can all be used in connection with potatoes. The following recipe for stuffed baked potatoes gives a little added interest and can be prepared ahead and kept in the refrigerator until you are ready to bake.

STUFFED BAKED POTATOES

Makes 6 servings.

6 medium potatoes	1 tablespoon chopped chives
2 tablespoons oil, plus oil to coat potatoes	1 egg white, stiffly beaten
	Paprika
4 tablespoons non-fat dry milk	Chopped parsley
1 teaspoon salt	
Freshly ground pepper	

1. Preheat oven to 400°F. Scrub potatoes well, dry, and prick with fork to let steam escape during baking. 2. Oil the potatoes and bake until they squeeze soft, 45 minutes to an hour. 3. Cut a large slice off the top of each potato, scoop out the insides, and mash. Add the oil, milk powder, salt, pepper and about 3 tablespoons to ¼ cup hot water. 4. Mix well until potatoes are light and fluffy. Add the chives and fold in the beaten egg white. Check the seasonings. Add a dash of Lawry's salt or MSG if desired. 5. Fill the potato skins with the mixture and sprinkle lightly with paprika and chopped parsley. Replace in 350°F. oven and bake until tops are brown, about 20 to 25 minutes.

LYONNAISE POTATOES

Potatoes are often avoided in restricted diets because they have the reputation for being extra-high in calories. The truth is that a medium-size potato contains but few more calories than half a grapefruit, which is considered a low calorie food. And a potato matches the half-grapefruit in supplying bulk—that is, it is equally filling. Elsewhere we mention the good nutrients in potatoes.

Makes 6 servings.

6 medium potatoes, peeled and sliced	Pepper
	Nutmeg
4 tablespoons oil	Grated rind of ½ lemon
1 cup finely chopped onions	1 teaspoon lemon juice
1 clove garlic, very finely minced	1 tablespoon finely chopped
1 teaspoon salt	parsley

1. Heat oil in skillet and very lightly sauté onions and garlic. 2. Add potatoes and mix well. Add salt, a dash of pepper, a dash of nutmeg, and the lemon rind. Cook, covered, over low heat for 15 minutes. 3. Remove cover and stir gently to avoid mashing potatoes. Recover and cook until potatoes are tender, about 20 to 30 minutes. 4. Add lemon juice and stir gently. Cook just a little longer, uncovered, if potatoes appear too moist. Sprinkle on parsley and serve.

BAKED WHOLE ONIONS

This recipe makes use of the herb savory, which is also excellent in bean dishes, chilled vegetable juices, and meat loaf.

Makes 6 servings.

6 large onions	1 tablespoon chopped fresh savory (or 1 teaspoon ground
2 tablespoons diet margarine	savory)
	¼ teaspoon salt

1. Wipe the onions without peeling. Bake in a 350°F. oven until tender, about 1 to 1¼ hours. 2. Remove from oven, peel off skins, and season with margarine, savory and salt.

CELERY WITH DILL

Nature packs a lot of water into such vegetables as celery, string beans, carrots, and asparagus, so they are filling without being fattening.

Makes 4 servings.

3 cups chopped celery	Freshly ground black pepper
½ teaspoon dill seed	1 tablespoon diet margarine
½ teaspoon salt	

1. Put celery in a quart pot; rinse and drain. 2. Cover and set over medium-high heat. When cover becomes hot to the touch, turn heat to low and cook 10 minutes. 3. Add remaining ingredients, stir and serve.

SNOW PEAS AND WATER CHESTNUTS

To habitués of Chinese restaurants, neither of these vegetables is a stranger. Their popularity is growing and both are now available, if not in every supermarket, at least in the better food shops.

Makes 6 servings.

3 10-ounce packages of frozen snow peas	4 tablespoons peanut oil
3 bunches scallions or shallots	2 teaspoons salt
1 5-ounce can water chestnuts, sliced	1 teaspoon MSG (Accent)

1. Thaw peas and spread out on paper towels to dry. 2. Slice scallions or shallots into 1-inch pieces. 3. Heat oil in large skillet. Add scallions and cook over medium heat for 1 minute, stirring constantly. 4. Add the other ingredients and continue cooking and stirring for 2 or 3 minutes, until snow peas are very hot and slightly browned.

ACORN SQUASH WITH APPLESAUCE

There are two deserving vegetables that are often underrated. One is the parsnip, which has a naturally sweet nutty taste and readily boils up and mashes like potatoes. The other is acorn squash, baked with brown sugar and margarine. Here is a variation:

Makes 4 servings.

2 acorn squash, cut in half	4 teaspoons diet margarine
1 cup unsweetened applesauce	Cinnamon
4 teaspoons brown sugar	

1. Place squash halves in shallow baking pan, cut side down. Cover bottom of pan with water. 2. Bake at 400°F. until tender, about 45 minutes to an hour. Then turn squash over. 3. Mix applesauce with the brown sugar and spoon one-quarter of the mixture into each squash. Dot with margarine and sprinkle with cinnamon. 4. Continue baking until applesauce is bubbly, about 15 to 20 minutes.

OVEN BAKED BEANS

This is a fine dish for a light buffet supper. Ordinarily, it should be made with pork-and-beans and topped with bacon slices, but here it has been accommodated to the diet. Serve with cold meats and a large green salad topped with one of the Frenchette dressings for the dieters.

Makes 10 servings.

4 cans vegetarian-style baked beans	½ cup good first-run maple syrup
½ cup catsup	4 slices Canadian bacon
½ cup molasses	

1. Preheat oven to 350°F. 2. Mix all ingredients except the Canadian bacon. Place in a large earthenware casserole. 3. Crisscross the Canadian bacon on top of the bean mixture and bake for 1 hour.

SLICED CUCUMBER WITH LEMON

Makes 4 to 6 servings.

2 cucumbers, peeled and thinly sliced	¼ cup lemon juice
Oil (optional)	Salt
2 tablespoons cut-up fresh dill	Freshly ground pepper

1. Brush cucumber slices lightly with oil (not essential but it does improve taste). 2. Mix the other ingredients together. Pour over cucumbers and toss. 3. Chill well before serving.

A WORD ABOUT CUCUMBERS

Some people can't eat cucumbers because they "disagree." I have found that putting thinly sliced unpeeled cucumbers in a bowl, salting them thoroughly, and pouring off the liquid frequently is the first step in making cucumbers enjoyable. Press down on the sliced cucumbers with a plate, put them in a muslin bag and squeeze for all you're worth; it makes no difference that you mess up the appearance—at least you're removing the arsenic or whatever it is in cucumbers that's disturbing. When the cucumbers are dry and limp, marinate them in white vinegar, a little oil, salt, pepper, mustard seed, and oregano if you like it.

TZIMMES (Compote of dried fruits and sweet potato)

Like so many recipes of foreign origin, there are many versions of Tzimmes, depending upon the area from which the immigrants brought them. Since Tzimmes is a good dish for this diet, we give you two versions.

Makes 8 servings.

1 pound prunes, pitted	2 tablespoons honey
½ pound dried apricots	3 tablespoons brown sugar
½ pound dried pears or apples	½ teaspoon cinnamon
½ pound sweet potatoes, peeled and sliced	¼ tablespoon salt

1. Soak the fruits until plump. 2. Place all the ingredients, with 2 cups of water, in a saucepan. 3. Bring to a boil and cook over low heat for 25 minutes or until the water is absorbed. Stir occasionally. Serve with meat or as a dessert.

VERSION 2

1 pound carrots (6 medium)	2 tablespoons lemon juice
1 pound sweet potatoes	1 tablespoon honey or sugar
(3 medium)	
2 tablespoons oil	

1. Cook carrots and unpeeled sweet potatoes in boiling water until tender. 2. Remove potato skins. Slice potatoes and carrots and mash them somewhat. 3. Add lemon juice, oil and sweetening. Simmer for about 10 minutes.

PICKLED BEETS

Makes 10 to 12 servings.

2 No. 2 cans whole beets	15 whole cloves
⅓ cup cider vinegar	3 tablespoons brown sugar
⅓ cup tarragon vinegar	½ teaspoon salt
1 stick cinnamon (2 inches)	

1. Boil together vinegar, 1⅓ cups beet juice from can of beets, cinnamon, cloves, sugar and salt. 2. Strain over beets and let stand overnight, or pour into jars and seal. 3. Drain beets. Serve hot or cold.

ITALIAN FENNEL (or ANISE)

Makes 4 servings.

3 heads fennel	1 onion, sliced
1 clove garlic, finely chopped	½ cup consommé or chicken
1 carrot, sliced, or ½ cup	broth
green peas	Salt

1. Cut off tops of fennel; remove any outer discolored stalks. Wash thoroughly. Cut each head into quarters or sixths, leaving stalks attached at root end. 2. Cook, covered, with the garlic, onion and carrot or peas in the consommé or broth; salt to taste. Cook 15 minutes, or until tender. 3. Drain or serve in broth.

CRANBERRY-QUINCE PRESERVES

Makes 1¼ quarts.

3 cups cranberries
2 cups peeled, chopped quince
2 cups peeled, chopped apples

¼ cup orange juice
Grated rind of 1 orange
4 cups sugar

1. Combine all ingredients in saucepan and cook slowly until thick—about 15 minutes. **2.** Stir frequently during cooking to prevent sticking. **3.** Pack in sterilized jars and seal with paraffin. Serve with toast.

RAW CUCUMBER RELISH

Makes about 1 cup.

1 large cucumber
1 tablespoon lemon juice or
vinegar
½ teaspoon salt

1 teaspoon finely chopped
onion
⅛ teaspoon paprika
Few grains cayenne pepper

1. Peel and seed the cucumber, and chop up until fine. **2.** Add other ingredients and mix well.

ONION RELISH

Makes about 2 cups.

3 medium onions
1 cucumber, peeled and seeded
1 tomato, peeled
1 green pepper, seeded and cored
½ cup wine vinegar

2 tablespoons oil
3 teaspoons sugar
Juice of 1 lemon
Tabasco sauce to taste

1. Thinly slice the onions, cucumber, tomato and pepper. 2. Combine all the ingredients and chill until ready to serve.

PEPPER RELISH

Makes 2 to 3 pints.

12 onions
12 red peppers
12 green peppers

3 cups vinegar
2 cups brown or white sugar
3 tablespoons salt

1. Finely chop onions and peppers. **2.** Cover with boiling water; let stand 10 minutes, then drain well. **3.** Add vinegar, sugar and salt, and boil 20 minutes. Bottle in sterile jars.

FRESH TOMATO RELISH

Makes about 2 cups.

2 cups peeled, diced tomatoes	1 teaspoon salt
¼ cup chopped onion	1 teaspoon sugar (optional)
1 tablespoon lemon juice	

1. Combine all ingredients, mix well, and chill for 2 hours. **2.** Serve in a relish dish or on lettuce in place of a salad.

MOCK CREAM SAUCES

Just in case you have not read the introduction to this section, we emphasize that whenever "oil" is listed in these recipes, it refers automatically to polyunsaturated oil—safflower, corn, soybean, sesame, peanut, cottonseed.

Makes about 1 cup.

1 tablespoon oil	1 cup skim milk (or part skim
1 tablespoon flour	milk and part bouillon,
½ teaspoon salt	consommé or wine)
Dash of white pepper	

1. Heat oil in small saucepan and blend in flour over a low flame. Do not let it brown. 2. Add salt and pepper. Over medium heat, stir in milk until mixture thickens and bubbles. Stir constantly. 3. Reduce heat and cook 1 minute more. For a thicker sauce, double the oil and flour. For a still thicker sauce, use 3 tablespoons of oil and 4 tablespoons flour.

BROWN SAUCE

Makes about 2 quarts. If you plan to freeze the sauce, place it in containers of usable size.

5 pounds cracked veal bones	¾ teaspoon thyme
5 carrots, cleaned and quartered	1 tablespoon salt
3 stalks celery, chopped	1 teaspoon coarsely ground
1 onion, quartered	peppercorns
3 cloves garlic, unpeeled	½ cup flour
4 bay leaves	1 10½-ounce can tomato puree
	3 sprigs parsley

1. Preheat oven to 475°F. 2. In a large baking pan combine veal bones, carrots, celery, onion, garlic, bay leaves, thyme, salt and pepper. Bake ¾ hour. The bones should be brown when cooked; if

they start to burn, reduce heat slightly. **3.** Sprinkle bones with flour, moving them around with tongs or fork to coat them evenly. Bake them ¼ hour longer in same pan. **4.** Transfer the ingredients to a large, heavy kettle. To get the benefit of all the particles clinging to the pan, add 3 cups water to the pan, place over moderate heat and scrape sides and bottom of pan. **5.** Empty pan liquid into kettle. Add tomato puree, parsley, and 2¼ quarts water. Bring to a boil, then simmer 2 hours. Skim occasionally to remove fat and scum. **6.** Strain the stock for immediate use or for freezing.

DEVIL'S SAUCE

Makes about 1 cup.

3 teaspoons dry mustard	1 teaspoon sugar (or
½ cup dry red wine	equivalent sugar substitute)
3 tablespoons oil	Juice of 1 lemon

1. In a blender or by hand, mix all ingredients together until smooth.

CUMBERLAND SAUCE

Makes about ½ cup.

2 oranges	1 tablespoon dry red wine
5 tablespoons currant jelly	1 teaspoon dry mustard

1. Peel oranges very thinly with a potato peeler and chop the peels coarsely. **2.** Squeeze juice from oranges and mix with jelly, wine and mustard. **3.** Blend well and add chopped orange rind. Chill before serving.

BLACK PEPPER STEAK SAUCE

No matter how well you trim a steak of its fat, there is usually enough fat marbled in between the fibres to put this meat on the Occasionally Only list. This sauce enlivens a fatless piece of meat.

Makes ⅔ cup.

½ cup soy sauce	½ teaspoon coarsely ground
2 pieces whole ginger	pepper
2 tablespoons oil	1/16 teaspoon cayenne pepper
1 tablespoon brown sugar	¼ teaspoon ground allspice

1. Combine all ingredients and store in a tightly covered jar. **2.** Marinate steaks in the mixture for 1 to 2 hours before broiling. **3.** Baste steaks with sauce during cooking as often as meat looks dry.

MEXICAN TOMATO SAUCE

Makes 4 to 5 cups.

1 medium onion	1 teaspoon vinegar
6 large fresh tomatoes (or 1½ No. 2 cans whole pack tomatoes)	1 can (6 ounces) green chili peppers
	1 teaspoon salt

1. Chop all ingredients together. **2.** Let stand for 20 minutes, pour off juice, add salt if needed. Place in refrigerator; serve cold.

HONEY BEET PRESERVE

Fresh beets	Ginger root
Honey	

1. Wash, peel and cut beets into ½-inch slices. Cook and drain. **2.** Add 1 cup honey for each cup of beets and cook until thick. Flavor with ginger root. Serve cold.

FRUIT SAUCES

For use over cottage cheese or beaten egg whites as a dessert, as a luncheon dish alone, or as part of a fruit platter. Calorie counters: Use sparingly.

Makes about 2½ cups.

1 quart fresh strawberries or raspberries
½-¾ cup sugar, confectioners' or finely granulated
2-3 tablespoons kirsch, cognac or lemon juice

1. Hull, wash and drain berries. **2.** Add sugar and whip in blender 2 or 3 minutes (or 10 minutes with electric beater). Add the kirsch, cognac or lemon juice during this process. **3.** If not sweet enough, add a few drops of Sucaryl, Sweeta or other sugar substitute.

PINEAPPLE–CRANBERRY SAUCE

Makes 1¼ quarts.

1½ cups sugar	4 cups cranberries
½ cup canned pineapple juice	2 tablespoons chopped preserved ginger
1 cup canned, drained, shredded pineapple	

1. Boil sugar, pineapple juice and ½ cup water, for 5 minutes. **2.** Add cranberries and cook, without stirring, until all the skins pop open. **3.** Add pineapple and ginger and let stand in saucepan until cool.

CRANBERRY MILK DRINK

Makes about 1⅓ cups.

1 cup non-fat fresh milk, or reliquefied skim milk powder

⅓ cup chilled, beaten, jellied, prepared cranberry sauce

1. Gradually stir milk into cranberry sauce, blending well. Serve at once.

LEMON MINT SAUCE

Makes 1½ cups.

1 cup sugar
½ cup lemon juice

¼ cup finely minced mint leaves

1. Dissolve sugar in lemon juice. 2. Combine with mint leaves and let stand about ½ hour. Goes very well with lamb and veal.

MAPLE MARSHMALLOW SAUCE

Makes 1½ cups.

8 marshmallows

¾ cup maple sirup

1. Heat maple sirup to a boil. 2. Quarter the marshmallows and add to boiling sirup. Stir until marshmallows are partially melted. Serve hot.

ANGEL FOOD LOAF

½ cup sifted cake flour
¾ cup sifted sugar
⅔ cup (5 or 6) egg whites, at room temperature

⅛ teaspoon salt
½ teaspoon cream of tartar
½ teaspoon vanilla
¼ teaspoon almond extract

1. Sift flour once, measure, add ¼ cup of the sugar, and sift together four times. 2. Beat egg whites and salt with flat wire whisk or rotary egg beater until foamy. Sprinkle in cream of tartar and continue beating until egg whites are stiff enough to hold up in soft peaks, but are still moist and glossy. 3. Sprinkle remaining sugar on egg whites, 2 tablespoons at a time, and beat after each addition to blend (25 strokes). Beat in flavoring (10 strokes). 4. Sift about half of flour over mixture and fold in lightly (15 fold-over strokes), turning bowl gradually. Add last of flour and fold in well (25 strokes). 5. Turn into ungreased 10 x 5 x 3-inch loaf pan. Bake in moderately hot oven (375°F.) 25 minutes, or until done. Remove from oven, invert pan on rack, and let stand 1 hour, or until cake is cool.

WHOLE WHEAT ANGEL FOOD CAKE

½ cup whole wheat flour,
measured after 4 siftings
¼ cup rice flour, measured
after sifting
1¼ cups sifted light yellow, or
white, sugar

1⅓ cups egg whites
1¼ teaspoons cream of tartar
1 teaspoon vanilla extract
1 teaspoon almond extract
⅛ teaspoon salt

1. Add salt to egg whites and beat with wire whisk until half stiff. Add cream of tartar, and beat until stiff but not dry. 2. Add sifted sugar very slowly beating continuously. Fold in vanilla extract and almond extract. 3. Sift the flours together (after whole wheat flour has been sifted 4 times before measuring, and rice flour once before measuring). Fold flour mixture gradually into egg and sugar mixture. 4. Bake in ungreased tube pan in very slow oven (275°F.) for 1 hour and 10 minutes. 5. Turn over onto cake plate and allow to cool. Then cover with icing, if desired.

FRUITED ANGEL FOOD CAKE

Makes 6 to 8 servings.

1 cup sifted cake flour
¼ teaspoon salt
1½ cups sugar
1⅓ cups egg whites
1⅓ teaspoons cream of tartar

1 teaspoon lemon extract
¼ cup each candied pineapple and candied cherries,
finely chopped

1. Sift together flour, salt and ½ cup sugar. 2. Beat egg whites until frothy; add cream of tartar and lemon flavoring and beat until mixture is stiff but not dry. 3. Beat remaining 1 cup of sugar into egg whites, a little at a time. When meringue is thick and feathery, sift few tablespoons flour over top and fold in gently. Continue in this manner until all flour mixture is used. 4. Spread part of batter in ungreased 10-inch tube pan; sprinkle with chopped fruit. Alternate batter and fruit, finishing with chopped fruit on top. 5. Bake in moderately slow oven (325°F.) 50 minutes to 1 hour. Invert on cake rack and loosen with spatula when cool. 6. Serve plain or ice with thin fruit-flavored frosting.

CHERRY–BERRY KISEL

Makes 4 servings.

1½ pounds mixed cherries and
raspberries (or cranberries
and strawberries, or combinations of other berries)

1¼ cups sugar
3 teaspoons grated lemon rind
Cornstarch

1. Wash and pick over fruit, pit cherries, hull berries. **2.** Add just enough water to cover, and simmer 10 minutes. Put fruit and juice through sieve. **3.** Add sugar and lemon rind. Bring to a boil. **4.** Measure, and for each 2 cups of the mixture, allow (but do not add) 1 tablespoon cornstarch, or more if a thicker result is desired. **5.** Moisten the cornstarch with cold water and mix well. Then stir in 1 cup of fruit mixture. Add this to the remaining fruit mixture and bring to a boil. Cool, then chill and serve.

CHOCOLATE MERINGUE COOKIES

Makes about 2 dozen 2½-inch cookies.

2 cups sifted confectioners' sugar
1 tablespoon flour
¼ teaspoon salt
3 egg whites

2 or 3 squares Baker's unsweetened chocolate, melted and cooled
1 teaspoon vanilla

1. Sift together sugar, flour and salt. **2.** Beat egg whites until stiff. Add sugar mixture, 2 tablespoons at a time, beating after each addition until blended. Fold in chocolate and vanilla. **3.** Drop from teaspoon on lightly greased baking sheet. **4.** Bake in moderately hot oven (375°F.) about 10 minutes. (For best results, start cookies on lower shelf of oven and move to upper shelf after 5 minutes, to complete baking.) **5.** Remove from baking sheet immediately, using knife or spatula. Cool. Store in airtight container.

WHITE BOILED ICING

½ cup light yellow, or white, sugar
¼ cup white corn sirup

¼ cup egg whites
½ teaspoon cream of tartar

1. Boil sugar, corn sirup, 2 tablespoons water and cream of tartar. Boil until sirup drops off spoon in heavy threads. **2.** Beat egg whites to stiffness. Beat boiled sirup into the stiff egg whites, until icing is spreadable.

MAPLE ICING

½ cup maple sirup
¼ cup white corn sirup

¼ cup egg whites
½ teaspoon cream of tartar

1. Boil sirups and cream of tartar, until sufficiently thick to drop off a spoon in large, heavy threads. **2.** Beat egg whites to stiffness. Beat the sirup mixture into the stiff egg whites, until icing is thick enough to spread on cool cake.

MOCHA SPONGE

Makes 4 to 6 servings.

1 tablespoon unflavored gelatin (1 envelope Knox's)
1½ cups very strong hot coffee
¾ cup sugar

1 teaspoon vanilla or maple
flavoring
3 egg whites, beaten stiff

1. Soak gelatin in ¼ cup cold water and stir into hot coffee until dissolved. Add sugar and flavoring. **2.** Chill mixture until thick and sirupy; beat until light and fold in egg whites. **3.** Turn into mold and chill until set.

RYE HONEY CAKES

Makes 2 dozen cakes.

2 cups honey
1 cup sifted rye meal

1 cup sifted cake flour
Vegetable oil or margarine

1. Heat honey in saucepan until thin. Mix rye meal and cake flour, and heat in separate pan, shaking constantly. **2.** Remove honey from stove and add flour mixture gradually. Beat constantly with large spoon, until dough comes off easily. **3.** Cut with round cutter or shape as desired. Bake until well browned, in moderate oven (350°F.) on lightly greased cookie sheet. These honey cakes will keep indefinitely.

MARSHMALLOW CREAM CAKE FILLING

¾ cup sugar
⅓ cup light corn sirup
2 egg whites, stiffly beaten

16 marshmallows, cut into
quarters

1. Cook sugar and sirup with ¼ cup water. Cook until a long thread is spun when dropped from fork or spoon. **2.** Remove from stove and add quartered marshmallows at once. **3.** Beat until thoroughly blended, then pour gradually over stiffly beaten egg whites. Beat constantly until mixture is smooth. **4.** Use immediately or pour into pint jar and store in refrigerator until needed. Will keep several weeks.

CREAMY RICE PUDDING

Makes 4 or 5 servings.

1 package Jell-O Rice Pudding

2½ cups non-fat milk

1. Combine Jell-O Rice Pudding with milk, in saucepan. **2.** Bring to a full boil, stirring constantly. **3.** Reduce flame and boil gently 10 minutes, stirring occasionally. **4.** Cool, and stir after 15 minutes. Serve warm or cold.

Variations: Add before cooking: ⅛ teaspoon cinnamon or nutmeg, and ¼ cup raisins.

Fold in while warm: ¼ cup pitted and cut dates.

Fold in before serving: ½ cup diced apricots, diced peaches, crushed pineapple or sliced berries.

APRICOT WHIP
(Dessert or Salad)

Makes 6 servings.

1 cup well-cooked stewed apricots, pitted	2 teaspoons lemon juice
⅓ cup sugar	⅛ teaspoon salt
3 egg whites	Liqueur to flavor—Triple Sec,
¼ cup sirup from apricots	Cointreau or other

1. Beat egg whites lightly. Whip in other ingredients at moderate beating speed. **2.** Add liqueur when whip is nearly firm. Continue beating until firm. **3.** Serve at once in sherbet glasses or serve on salad greens, ringed by canned or fresh apricot halves.

CORNMEAL MUSH

1 cup cornmeal	3½ to 4 cups non-fat milk (or
2 teaspoons salt	water, or a mixture of both)

1. Mix cornmeal with 1 cup cold milk (or water). Scald the remaining milk, or boil balance of water and add into cornmeal mix. Add salt. **2.** Cook 30 minutes in double boiler top, stirring occasionally. Serve with milk and sugar or sirup.

BAKED APPLES WITH RED WINE

Makes 6 servings.

6 tart apples	½ cup brown sugar
1 cup red wine	¼ teaspoon cinnamon

1. Wash, wipe and core apples. Mix sugar with cinnamon and fill apple centers. **2.** Place in baking dish and cover bottom of dish with boiling water. Bake in hot oven (400°F.) until soft. Baste frequently with sirup from dish. **3.** When apples are partly soft, add wine and continue baking. Baste with the wine sirup.

BANANA GELATIN DESSERT

Makes 4 servings.

1 package Jell-O, or 4 envelopes Glow low-calorie gelatin, any flavor

2 ripe bananas
Fruit sauce or other topping

1. Mix gelatin according to package directions. Chill only until slightly thickened. 2. Partly fill pint-sized mold with gelatin. Peel bananas, slice crosswise onto gelatin in mold. 3. Fill mold with remaining gelatin. Chill until firm. 4. Unmold and garnish with additional slices of ripe banana or other fruit, if desired. Serve plain or with fruit sauce or low-fat milk.

APPLE-GINGER SHERBET

Makes 6 servings.

½ tablespoon unflavored gelatin
2½ cups applesauce

1 tablespoon preserved ginger or ⅛ teaspoon dry ginger
2 tablespoons lemon juice

1. Soak gelatin in 4 tablespoons cold water and dissolve in double boiler over hot water. 2. Place applesauce, ginger and lemon juice in Waring Blendor (or other electric blender); add the gelatin mixture. 3. Run Blendor about 2 minutes. 4. Place in refrigerator tray and freeze, stirring occasionally.

BAKED PEARS IN MAPLE SIRUP

Makes 6 servings.

6 large cooking pears
¾ cup maple sirup

1 tablespoon lemon juice

1. Peel and halve the pears. 2. Put in baking dish and sprinkle lemon juice over them. Cover pears with maple sirup. 3. Cover dish and bake in very slow oven (250° to 275°F.) for 4 hours.

BAKED SPICED ORANGES

Makes 6 servings.

6 large navel oranges
½ grapefruit
12 dates, cut in small pieces
¼ cup molasses
3 teaspoons margarine

3 teaspoons brown sugar
4 whole cloves
Cinnamon, nutmeg, Angostura bitters

1. Combine molasses, whole cloves and ½ cup water; boil 5 minutes. 2. Cut a slice from blossom end of oranges. Cut around the pulp and scoop out, keeping pieces as firm as possible. 3. Peel and section grapefruit and cut in medium-size pieces. Combine orange, grapefruit and dates, and fill orange shells. 4. Sprinkle each with cinnamon and nutmeg, 2 dashes Angostura bitters, and top with ½ teaspoon each brown sugar and margarine. 5. Place in baking dish, add sirup and bake in moderate oven (350°F.) about 30 minutes, basting occasionally. Serve hot.

PRUNE WHIP

1 cup prune purée (rub cooked prunes through fine sieve)
2 egg whites, beaten stiff
½ cup powdered sugar

1 teaspoon lemon juice (if prunes are not flavored with lemon)

1. Chill all ingredients in refrigerator. 2. Fold the prune pulp, powdered sugar and lemon juice into stiffly beaten egg whites. 3. Pile lightly into a serving bowl or individual dishes. Chill again.

Variations: Pour prune whip, made with egg whites, into ungreased baking dish. Bake in moderate oven (350°F.) for 35 to 40 minutes, or until light and delicately browned. Serve with non-fat milk.

Other fruit whips may be made by using 1 cup of thick fruit pulp from any of the following cooked fruits: apples, peaches, plums, rhubarb, apricots.

BRANDIED PEACHES

4 pounds ripe peaches
2 pounds sugar

Brandy

1. Scald and peel peaches. Pit fruit or not, as preferred. 2. Place sugar and peaches in alternate layers in jars. 3. Fill with brandy, and cover tightly.

CRANBERRY LEMON CUPS

2 to 3 large lemons
1 cup sugar

2 cups fresh cranberries

1. Halve lemons and scoop out pulp. Save pulp for other uses. 2. Combine sugar with 1 cup water, bring to boil and add cranberries. Cook until cranberries pop—about 5 minutes. 3. Fill lemon cups with cranberry sauce. Serve as garnish around chicken.

GRILLED PEACHES WITH JELLY SAUCE

Peach halves, fresh or canned   Brown sugar
Whole cloves   Jelly
Cinnamon

1. Place a peach half in custard cup. **2.** Fill cavity with teaspoon each brown sugar and jelly. **3.** Top with second peach half to look like whole peach, stud with cloves; sprinkle with cinnamon and brown sugar. **4.** Broil under medium heat until sugar melts and peach begins to brown. **5.** Serve hot with melted jelly spooned over peach.

CRANBERRY SHERBET

Makes 4 servings.

½ pound cranberries   ½ tablespoon unflavored gela-
1 cup sugar   tin
⅓ cup lemon juice

1. Cook cranberries in 1½ cups water, until soft. **2.** Place cooked cranberries in Waring Blendor container, and run Blendor 2 minutes. Strain cranberries and return to container. **3.** Soak gelatin in 4 tablespoons cold water and dissolve in double boiler, over hot water. **4.** Add gelatin, sugar and lemon juice to cranberries in container. Run Blendor until contents are thoroughly blended, about 10 seconds. **5.** Cool, place in refrigerator tray and freeze, stirring occasionally.

CORNSTARCH PUDDING

Makes 4 to 6 servings.

2¼ cups skim milk   ¼ teaspoon salt
3 tablespoons cornstarch   1 teaspoon vanilla
⅓ cup sugar   2 egg whites

1. Scald 2 cups milk in double boiler. Set aside. **2.** Mix cornstarch, sugar and salt; add ¼ cup cold milk and stir until smooth. **3.** Add mixture to scalded milk and cook 15 minutes over hot water. Stir constantly until mixture thickens, then stir occasionally. Cool slightly and add the vanilla. **4.** Beat egg whites until stiff and fold into finished pudding.

SNOW PUDDING

Makes 6 servings.

1 envelope (1 tablespoon) gelatin	¼ cup lemon juice
1 cup sugar	3 egg whites
¼ teaspoon salt	Crushed fruit

1. Mix the gelatin, sugar and salt. Add 1½ cups boiling water and stir until gelatin dissolves. 2. Add the lemon juice and chill until semi-thick, not too runny. 3. Add the egg whites and beat until mixture is thick enough to hold its shape. Mold and chill until firm. 4. Top with crushed fruit or fruit cocktail, and serve.

WARM FRUIT CASSEROLE

Makes 4 servings.

1 1-pound 1 ounce jar or can of fruit cocktail	⅓ cup slivered almonds
	½ teaspoon mace
2 bananas, cut in half lengthwise and then cut into 1-inch pieces	2 tablespoons brown sugar
¼ cup lemon juice	

1. Drain fruit cocktail, mix fruit and bananas and place in baking dish. Add lemon juice. 2. Sprinkle with almonds, mace and brown sugar. Stir to mix. Preheat oven. 3. Cover dish and bake in 375°F. oven 30 minutes. Serve warm or cold.

FRUIT SOUFFLE

Makes 4 servings.

¾ cup fruit pulp (preferably made with fresh peaches, apricots, pitted cherries, pears, quinces —but drained canned fruit is acceptable)	Salt
	Sugar
	3 egg whites
	Diet margarine
1 tablespoon lemon juice	

1. Press the fresh or canned fruit through a sieve to make the ¾ cup pulp or puree. Heat this with the lemon juice, a few grains of salt and a little sugar to your taste. 2. Beat egg whites stiff and add the hot fruit mixture. Continue beating until well blended. 3. Grease 4 individual molds with diet margarine (or oil) and sprinkle lightly with sugar. 4. Fill ¾ full with the mixture and bake at 325°F. until firm, about 20 to 25 minutes.

INDIAN PUDDING

Here is where we use up one of the few eggs permitted on this diet, but, since the recipe makes a number of servings, the amount of egg yolk in each is small.

Makes 4 to 6 servings.

2 cups skim milk, scalded	⅓ cup molasses
1 tablespoon diet margarine	¼ cup black raisins
¼ teaspoon salt	¼ teaspoon cinnamon
¼ cup cornmeal	Oil for greasing baking dish
1 egg, beaten	

1. In a double boiler, combine the scalded milk, margarine and salt. 2. Gradually stir in cornmeal and cook about 20 minutes. 3. When thickened, add the beaten egg, molasses, raisins and cinnamon. If mixture hasn't thickened, add some skim milk powder. Preheat oven. 4. Pour mixture into well-oiled baking dish and bake at 350°F. for about 1 hour. Serve hot or cold.

APPLE TAPIOCA

Makes 4 to 6 servings.

3 cups peeled and sliced tart apples	⅓ cup quick tapioca
½ cup brown sugar	¼ cup white sugar
½ teaspoon cinnamon	⅛ teaspoon salt

1. Place the apples in a baking dish. Set oven at 350°F. 2. Mix the brown sugar and cinnamon and sprinkle over apples. Bake 15 minutes. 3. In the meantime, put the tapioca, white sugar, salt and 2 cups boiling water into a saucepan and cook, stirring, over moderate heat 5 to 10 minutes or until tapioca is transparent. 4. Pour over the apples and continue baking until apples are tender.

CHERRY-NUT PUDDING

Makes 4 to 6 servings.

¾ cup canned pitted cherries	¼ cup lemon juice
1 cup liquid from canned cherries	2 egg whites
1 package cherry gelatin	½ cup coarsely chopped walnuts

1. Heat cherry liquid to boiling and dissolve the gelatin in it. 2. Stir in the lemon juice. Cool for 1 hour. 3. Beat the egg whites until stiff and fold them into the mixture. 4. Chill in refrigerator for ½ hour, then beat the mixture with electric mixer, and fold in cherries and nuts. 5. Pour into a rinsed mold and chill 4 hours or until firm.

ANOTHER CHERRY-WALNUT MOLD

Since walnuts are particularly suitable for the low cholesterol diet, we give you this combination, which is slightly simpler than the previous recipe.

Makes 4 to 6 servings.

1 No. 2 can pitted Bing cherries	1 envelope (1 tablespoon)
Shelled walnuts	gelatin

1. Stuff each cherry with a piece of walnut. 2. Drain the cherry juice into a measuring cup and add enough cold water to make 2 cups of liquid. 3. Place the stuffed cherries in a mold. Put ½ cup of liquid into a saucepan. 4. Sprinkle on the gelatin and stir over low heat until gelatin dissolves. Add the rest of the liquid. 5. Pour this over the cherries, chill until firm, and unmold. Serve on lettuce with watercress garnish, with meat, or as a dessert.

BAKED APPLE WITH NO-CAL

This recipe makes one of the easiest and best desserts for most special diets—or nondiets. It can also be used as a breakfast or luncheon filler-upper.

Large, red baking apples	No-Cal or other noncaloric
Cinnamon or nutmeg	drink (black cherry or
1 teaspoon confectioners' sugar	raspberry flavor)
or equivalent in powdered	
sugar substitute per apple	

1. Core apples; remove the top ⅓ of the peel. 2. Set each apple in individual casserole dish. 3. Combine a generous dash of cinnamon or nutmeg per apple, sugar or sweetener, and enough No-Cal to reach halfway up apple. 4. Bake at 375°F. until apples are tender, about ¾ hour. Serve warm or cold.

COFFEE JELL—Plain or with brandy

Makes 4 servings.

1 envelope (1 tablespoon) gelatin	¼ cup brandy or sherry if
¼ cup sugar	desired
2 cups strong hot coffee	

1. Mix the gelatin and sugar. Add the hot coffee and stir until gelatin dissolves. Mold and chill. 2. For brandied coffee jell, reduce the hot coffee to 1¾ cups and add the ¼ cup brandy when the gelatin is dissolved. Or, if you prefer sherry to brandy, reduce the hot coffee to 1½ cups and use ½ cup sherry.

WINE JELLY

Here is a delicious and colorful addition to a plate of cold chicken or turkey.

Makes 10 to 12 servings as a meat accompaniment, or 6 as a dessert.

2 envelopes (2 tablespoons) gelatin	3 tablespoons lemon juice
1 cup sugar	1 cup Madeira or sherry wine
⅓ cup orange juice	

1. Mix the gelatin and sugar. Add 2 cups boiling water. 2. Stir until gelatin dissolves, then add the fruit juices and wine. 3. Mold and chill.

DIVINITY FUDGE

There are times when one just has to have a piece of candy, and while Divinity Fudge isn't exactly low in calories, it is low in fat and cholesterol.

Makes about 1 pound.

1½ cups light brown sugar	½ cup chopped walnuts,
1 teaspoon vinegar	almonds, pecans, or a mixture
1 egg white	½ teaspoon vanilla

1. In a saucepan, cook the brown sugar, vinegar and ½ cup water until a firm but not hard ball is made by dropping a little of the syrup into cold water. (Take the syrup off the heat while you make this test.) 2. In the meantime, beat the egg white stiff but not dry. 3. Slowly pour the syrup over the egg white, beating until creamy. 4. Add the nuts and vanilla. 5. Drop by teaspoonfuls on waxed paper, or spread into a greased 8-inch square pan and cut into pieces.

VIENNA WAFERS

Makes 18.

1 egg white	¼ cup finely chopped almonds
½ teaspoon vanilla	Diet margarine or oil
½ teaspoon lemon juice	Flour
¼ cup powdered sugar	

1. Grease and flour a cookie sheet. Set oven at 350°F. 2. Mix together the egg white, vanilla and lemon juice. 3. Stir in the powdered

sugar and almonds. **4.** Place on cookie sheet by small teaspoonfuls.
5. Bake about 10-15 minutes, or until dry. Top with orange or lemon
frosting if desired.

ORANGE OR LEMON FROSTING

¼ cup cool orange or lemon juice   Confectioners' sugar

1. Place juice in bowl and stir in confectioners' sugar until thick
enough to spread. Preferably use electric beater, but wooden spoon
will do. Frosting should be creamy.

PECAN CHEWS

Make these on a dry day; when the day is damp, they don't turn
out firm enough to chew.

Makes 24.

1 egg white	1 cup finely chopped pecan
1 cup light brown sugar	meats
¼ teaspoon salt	Oil
½ teaspoon vanilla	Flour

1. Grease and flour 2 cookie sheets. Set oven at 325°F. **2.** Beat the
egg white until very stiff and, beating constantly, gradually add the
sugar. **3.** Add the salt and vanilla and fold in the chopped pecans.
4. Place teaspoonfuls on the cookie sheets. Bake 8 to 10 minutes, or
until dry on top. The pecan chews will firm up when cold.

DEVILLED NUTS

Walnuts and pecans are desirable items on this diet. You can
easily give them a piquant touch this way. Serve as a snack or to top
hors d'oeuvres of cottage cheese on Melba toast or thin bread.

Shelled walnuts or pecans	Salt
Oil	Curry powder

1. Place nuts in a well-oiled shallow baking dish. **2.** Bake at 350°F.
about 10 minutes. **3.** Drain and sprinkle with salt and curry powder.

DATE PUDDING

1 cup pitted and chopped
dates
½ cup non-fat milk
⅔ cup whole wheat flour
1 cup brown sugar

½ cup yellow or white sugar
1 tablespoon margarine
2 teaspoons vanilla
2 teaspoons baking powder

1. Sift together the flour, baking powder and yellow or white sugar. 2. Mix in the chopped dates, then add milk and turn into a greased baking dish. 3. Mix brown sugar with 2 cups boiling water; add margarine and vanilla. Stir until sugar dissolves and margarine is melted. 4. Pour this over the date mixture and bake in moderate oven (350°F.) 45 minutes. 5. Serve hot, without extra sauce.

FROZEN TROPICAL WHIP

Makes 1 quart.

2 cups cranberries
¼ pound marshmallows
1 cup pineapple juice
2 tablespoons lemon juice

½ cup sugar
⅛ teaspoon salt
2 egg whites, whipped stiff

1. Cook cranberries in 1 cup water until all the skins pop open; put through fine sieve. 2. Heat marshmallows in pineapple juice until melted; combine with sieved cranberries, lemon juice, sugar and salt. 3. Transfer to freezing tray of refrigerator; freeze to a mush. 4. Remove and fold in whipped egg whites. 5. Return to tray; freeze until firm—about 4 hours.

GINGER FRUIT COCKTAIL

Makes 8 servings.

½ cup sugar
½ cup light corn sirup
1 orange
½ pound (2¼ cups) red
skinned apples

½ pound (1½ cups) red
grapes
⅓ cup candied or preserved
ginger, cut fine

1. Boil sugar, corn sirup and 1 cup water for 5 minutes. Chill. 2. Dice apples and cut grapes in halves, removing seeds. Cut orange in cubes, saving juice to prevent apples from turning dark. 3. Chill thoroughly and place in cocktail glasses. Pour over some sirup. Add diced ginger to each cocktail.

PEARS IN KIRSCH

Makes 8 servings.

8 firm pears
1 cup dark brown sugar

½ cup Kirsch

1. Combine sugar and 1 cup water; heat until sugar is dissolved. 2. Peel pears, leaving stem on, and add to sirup. Baste frequently while cooking and turn pears around when about half done. 3. When soft, but still perfect in shape, dip each pear in the Kirsch and set aside to cool in serving dish. 4. Add the remaining liqueur to sirup; continue cooking about 10 minutes longer and pour over pears. Serve very cold.

LEMON MILK SHERBET

Makes about 4½ cups.

1½ teaspoons unflavored gelatin
¾ cup Starlac non-fat milk powder

¾ cup sugar
½ cup lemon juice
¼ teaspoon lemon rind
1 egg white, stiffly beaten

1. Set refrigerator control at coldest point. 2. Soak gelatin in 2 tablespoons water in a cup for 5 minutes. 3. Sprinkle Starlac over 1⅞ cups water in mixing bowl; let stand 5 minutes, then beat with egg beater until milk powder is dissolved in water, about 1 minute. 4. Put in top of double boiler and stir in sugar; place over boiling water and heat for 3 minutes. Remove from stove; add gelatin and stir until dissolved. Chill. 5. Gradually stir in lemon juice and lemon rind. Pour into freezing tray of refrigerator and cover top with waxed paper. Freeze until half frozen. 6. Turn into chilled bowl and beat well with chilled egg beater until fluffy but not melted. Fold in stiffly beaten egg white. Quickly return to tray; cover with waxed paper. Return to freezing unit. Freeze firm.

RASPBERRY SHERBET

Makes 4 servings.

2 cups cooked and sieved (or canned) raspberries
⅓ cup sugar

2 teaspoons unflavored gelatin
2 tablespoons lemon juice
Few grains salt

1. Soften gelatin in 2 tablespoons cold water. Add sugar to ½ cup water and boil this. 2. Add gelatin mix to sugar sirup and stir until dissolved. Add berries, lemon juice and salt. Cool. 3. Pour into freezing tray and set refrigerator to freezing point. 4. Freeze mixture to a mush, then place in chilled bowl and beat with rotary mixer until smooth. 5. Return to tray. Freeze firm, stirring several times during process.

LIME SHERBET

Makes 4 servings.

1½ teaspoons unflavored gelatin
¾ cup sugar
¼ cup lime juice
2 egg whites

⅓ cup orange juice
2 tablespoons lemon juice
Green food coloring
Few grains salt

1. Soften gelatin in 2 tablespoons cold water. Combine 1½ cups water and sugar, and boil 2 minutes. Add gelatin; stir until dissolved. **2.** Add lime, orange and lemon juices and salt; cool. **3.** Tint light green. Pour into freezing tray of refrigerator with cold control set at point for freezing ice cream. Freeze to mush. **4.** Place in chilled bowl. Beat with rotary beater until smooth. **5.** Beat egg whites stiff; fold in. Return to tray. Freeze firm, stirring several times.

ORANGE ICE

Makes 4 servings.

1 teaspoon unflavored gelatin
½ cup sugar
1 tablespoon grated orange rind

1½ cups orange juice
1 tablespoon lemon juice
Few grains salt

1. Soften gelatin in 2 tablespoons cold water. Combine ½ cup water and sugar; boil 2 minutes. **2.** Add orange rind and gelatin; stir until gelatin is dissolved. **3.** Cool; combine with orange and lemon juices and salt. Strain. **4.** Pour into freezing tray of refrigerator with cold control set for freezing ice cream. Freeze to mush. **5.** Place in chilled bowl. Beat with rotary beater until smooth. Return to tray. Freeze firm, stirring several times.

LEMON SHERBET

Makes 4 servings.

1¼ cups sugar
1 egg white

½ cup lemon juice
Few grains salt

1. Combine ½ cup water and sugar; boil 5 minutes. **2.** Beat egg white stiff; slowly add sugar sirup, beating constantly. **3.** Combine lemon juice, ½ cup water and salt. Add slowly to egg white mixture. Cool. **4.** Pour into freezing tray of refrigerator. Set at freezing point. Freeze to mush. **5.** Place in chilled bowl. Beat with rotary beater until smooth. Return to tray. Freeze firm, stirring several times.

MERINGUE KISSES

Makes about 48 meringues.

4 egg whites
1 cup sugar
⅛ teaspoon cream of tartar

⅛ teaspoon vinegar
⅛ teaspoon salt

1. Beat egg whites until stiff, then add sugar and salt gradually, beating continuously. 2. Add cream of tartar and vinegar, and beat until egg whites stand in peaks. 3. Drop on a cookie sheet covered with waxed paper. 4. Bake in moderately slow oven (325°F.) for 1 hour.

CANDIED MINT LEAVES

½ cup granulated sugar
Fresh mint leaves

Egg white
6 drops peppermint oil

1. Remove mint leaves from stems and coat both sides with egg white. 2. Combine sugar and peppermint oil. Dip mint leaves in this sugar. Cover both sides. 3. Place on waxed paper to dry, or place in a very slow oven (275°F.). 4. Use as garnish for fruit cocktail, fruit salads, or eat as a confection.

SUGARED POPCORN

1 cup sugar (or ½ cup maple
sirup and ½ cup sugar)

½ cup popping corn

1. Pop corn in wire popper. Remove the unpopped kernels. 2. Make sirup by boiling sugar with ½ cup water (or if maple sirup and sugar mixture is used, cut to ¼ cup water). 3. Boil sirup until a fairly hard ball is formed when a little is dropped off spoon into cup of cold water. 4. Pour sirup over popcorn and stir until all kernels are covered.

SPANISH CANDIED ORANGE PEEL

Peel of 4 oranges
2 cups sugar

8 drops peppermint oil
Green food coloring

1. Cut orange peel into thin strips with scissors. Place in a saucepan, cover with 2 cups cold water and let come to a boil. 2. Drain, cover again with cold water, and bring to a boil again. 3. Drain, add sugar and water. Bring to a boil, add food coloring and oil of peppermint. Continue to cook slowly until all but one tablespoon of sirup has boiled away. 4. Turn strips out on a plate or pan, sprinkle with granulated sugar and roll until each piece is well coated with sugar. Store in lightly covered container.

THE DIABETES DIET

There is no doubt that the discovery of insulin has prolonged the lives of millions of diabetics. But insulin alone has never been able to keep a diabetic patient under control—a special diet must always be used even when the regular injections of that lifegiving hormone are given. In fact, once proper treatment has been started, many of the milder cases will get along very well with just dietary restrictions.

The big problem for the diabetic has always been keeping to the diet which his physician has prescribed. Learning to give himself "shots," to test his urine, to avoid the proffered piece of candy, are all simple compared with what, until recently, has been the complex task of calculating the carbohydrates, proteins and fats of every single item of food, and balancing them into a satisfying and enjoyable menu.

In order to lighten this burden for the diabetic patient, and to give him a wider scope of foods without constant calculation and measuring, a simplified plan has been devised through the cooperation of the American Dietetic Association, the American Diabetes Association and the Diabetic Branch of the U. S. Public Health Service.

Through this plan, "Food Exchanges" have been established in 6 different divisions of daily food requirements. Each food in these divisions is measured in advance, by dietitians, and is called an "Exchange."

When the doctor says that you may have five "Meat Exchanges," he means that you may select any five units in the Meat Exchange list. One Meat Exchange unit could be an egg, or a certain size slice of roast beef, or an ounce of Cheddar cheese—or other units of your selection. Your physician will also give you a meal plan, so that you can divide your Food Exchange selections to your best advantage.

The purpose of this section is to help brighten the diet and lighten the burden of the diabetic patient, through handy reference charts of "Food Exchanges," and calculated recipes covering a wide variety of tasty dishes. If it does nothing more, this book should supply a few new recipes to add to your repertoire, and bring greater interest and anticipation to your daily meals.

The American Diabetes Association, seeking to cooperate to the fullest extent in increasing the range of recipes available to the diabetic, has graciously given permission to publish all the recipes from its magazine, *The Forecast*. All such recipes used are indicated by a superior numeral, as [1].

Sister Maude Behrman, dietitian of the Lankenau Hospital in Philadelphia, whose great interest in diabetic diet improvement is well known, has also contributed many recipes from her files. Such recipes are indicated by a superior numeral, as [2].

The calorie calculations for all recipes in this section have been made by the CHx4, Px4, Fx9 formula, and therefore may vary slightly from the calorie counts for similar recipes in the Low Calorie section of this book. The Low Calorie and Low Sodium sections contain many recipes which the diabetic patient may be able to use as given, or with a little adjustment. Calories are shown above the recipes in both these sections; through reference to the following books, the content of carbohydrates, protein and fat may be calculated without difficulty:

Food Values of Portions Commonly Used, by Bowes and Church. Available from Anna dePlanter Bowes, 7th and Delancey Streets, Philadelphia 6, Pa. Price $2.25.

U. S. Department of Agriculture Handbook No. 8—*Composition of Foods.* Available from Department of Agriculture, Washington 25, D. C. Price 35c.

FOOD LISTS

		C gms.	P gms.	F gms.	Calories
List 1. Milk Exchanges	1 cup whole milk	12	8	10	170
List 2. "A" Vegetables	As desired	neg.	neg.	neg.	neg.
Vegetable "B" Exchanges	1/2 cup	7	2	—	36
List 3. Fruit Exchanges	See list for size of serving	10	—	—	40
List 4. Bread Exchanges	1 slice bread	15	2	—	68
List 5. Meat Exchanges	1 ounce meat (lean)	—	7	5	73
List 6. Fat Exchanges	1 teaspoon butter	—	—	5	45

LIST 1—MILK EXCHANGES—Carbohydrate—12 gms.; Protein—8 gms.; Fat—10 gms.; Calories—170.

Milk, whole .... 1 cup
Milk, evaporated .... 1/2 cup
Milk, powdered whole .... 1/4 cup
Buttermilk .... 1 cup
Skim milk .... 1 cup (add 2 Fat Exchanges)

LIST 2—VEGETABLE EXCHANGES

"A" Vegetables—may be used as desired in ordinary amounts.

Asparagus	Escarole*	Lettuce
Beans, string	Greens:*	Mushrooms
Broccoli*	Beet	Okra
Brussels sprouts	Chard	Pepper, green*
Cabbage	Collard	Radish
Cauliflower	Dandelion	Rhubarb
Celery	Kale	Sauerkraut
Chicory*	Mustard	Summer squash
Cucumber	Spinach	Tomatoes*
Eggplant	Turnip	

"B" Vegetables—Carbohydrate—7 gms.; Protein—2 gms.; Calories—36. One serving equals 1/2 cup or 100 gms.

Beets	Peas, small green	Squash, winter*
Carrots*	Pumpkin*	Turnip
Onions	Rutabagas	

*These vegetables have a high vitamin A value. At least one serving should be included in the diet each day

LIST 3—FRUIT EXCHANGES—Carbohydrate—10 gms.; Calories—40.

Water packed canned fruits contain no added sugar and may be used in the same amount as listed for the fresh fruit. Canned or frozen fruits and fruit juices containing added sugar are not included in this list.

		Grams
Apple, 1 small 2-inch diameter or 1/2 medium		80
Applesauce	1/2 cup	100
Apricots, fresh	2 medium	100
Banana	1/2 small	50
Blueberries	2/3 cup	100
Cantaloupe†	1/4-6-inch diameter	200
Cherries	10 large	75
Dates	2	15
Figs, dried	1 small	15
Figs, fresh	2 large	50
Grape juice	1/4 cup	60
Grapefruit†	1/2 small	125
Grapefruit juice†	1/2 cup	100
Grapes	12	75

Honeydew melon ....1/8—6-inch diameter 100
Mango ....1/2 small 75
Orange† ....1 small 100
Orange juice† ....1/2 cup 100
Papaya ....1/2 medium 100
Peach ....1 medium 100
Pear ....1 small 100
Pineapple ....1/2 cup 80
Pineapple juice ....1/3 cup 80
Plums ....2 medium 100
Prunes, dried ....2 small 25
Raisins ....2 tablespoons 15
Strawberries,† raspberries
  and blackberries ....1 cup 150
Tangerines ....1 large 100
Watermelon ....1 cup 175

†These fruits are excellent sources of vitamin C. One serving should be included in the diet each day.

LIST 4—BREAD EXCHANGES—Carbohydrate—15 gms.; Protein—2 gms.; Calories—68.

Grams

Bread ....1 slice 25
    Bread, corn ....1-1/2-inch cube 35
    Biscuit, roll (2-inch diameter)........1 30
    Muffin 2-inch ....1 medium 35

Cereal, cooked ....1/2 cup 120
Cereal, dry ....3/4 cup 20
Grits, rice, noodles, spaghetti,
  macaroni, etc. ....1/2 cup 100

Crackers, Graham 2 20
    Oyster ....1/2 cup 20
    Saltines 5 20
    Soda 3 20
    Round, 1-1/2-inch, thin 6–8 20

Vegetables, beans, peas, lima,
  navy, cowpeas, etc. ....1/2 cup 90
    Corn ....1/3 cup 80
    Parsnips ....2/3 cup 125
    Potatoes, white ....1 small 100
    Potatoes, baked ....2-inch diameter 100
    Potatoes, mashed, boiled ....1/2 cup 100
    Potatoes, sweet ....1/4 cup 50

Sponge cake ....1-1/2-inch cube 25

Vanilla ice cream (Omit 2
  Fat Exchanges) ....1/8 of 1 quart 70

LIST 5—MEAT EXCHANGES—Protein—7 gms.; Fat—5 gms.; Calories—73.

		Grams
Meat and Fowl (medium fat) (beef, lamb, pork, liver, etc.)	1 ounce	30
Cold cuts	1 slice	45
Frankfurter	1	50
Fish, cod, herring, etc.	1 ounce	30
Salmon, tuna, crab	1/4 cup	30
Oysters, shrimps, clams	5	45
Sardines	3	30
Cheese, cheddar and American	1 ounce	30
Cottage	1/4 cup	45
Egg	1	50
Peanut Butter (Limit use or adjust carbohydrate	2 tablespoons	30

LIST 6—FAT EXCHANGES—Fat—5 gms.; Calories—45.

		Grams
Avocado	1/8—4-inch diameter	25
Bacon, crisp	1 slice	10
Butter or margarine	1 teaspoon	5
Cream, heavy	1 tablespoon	15
Cream, light	2 tablespoons	30
Cream cheese	1 tablespoon	15
French dressing	1 tablespoon	15
Mayonnaise	1 teaspoon	5
Nuts	6 small	5
Oil or cooking fat	1 teaspoon	5
Olives	5 small	50

The following may be taken as desired:

Gelatin sweetened with saccharin	Broth
Spices, such as nutmeg, cinnamon, bay leaves, cloves, etc.	Tea
	Coffee

The selection of food depends on the diet prescription given by the physician. Following is a diet which contains all the foods which are considered essential and are sometimes referred to as the Basic 7. The total amount of carbohydrate, protein, and fat in this can be a guide in your selection. Compare your figures with those of this diet. If, for example, your diet calls for 15 grams less of carbohydrate, then omit one slice of bread from this diet. If your diet calls for 15 grams more, then add 1 slice of bread or any food equivalent which will bring the total up or down to compare with your own figures. The same with protein and fat.

SAMPLE DIET

Breakfast:	No. of Exchanges	C Gms.	P Gms.	F Gms.
Fruit Exchange	1	10	—	—
Bread Exchange	2	30	4	—
Meat Exchange	1	—	7	5
Fat Exchange	1	—	—	5
Milk Exchange	1	12	8	10
		52	19	20

Lunch:				
Meat Exchange	2	—	14	10
Bread Exchange	1	15	2	—
"A" Vegetable	as desired	—	—	—
Vegetable "B" Exchange	1	7	2	—
Fat Exchange	1	—	—	5
Fruit Exchange	1	10	—	—
Milk Exchange	1	12	8	10
		44	26	25

Dinner:				
Meat Exchange	3	—	21	15
Bread Exchange	1	15	2	—
"A" Vegetable	as desired	—	—	—
Vegetable "B" Exchange	—	—	—	—
Fat Exchange	1	—	—	5
Fruit Exchange	1	10	—	—
Milk Exchange	1	12	8	10
		37	31	30

Bedtime Snack:				
Milk Exchange	1	12	8	10
Total for day		145	84	85

SAMPLE MENUS FOR ONE WEEK

On the following pages are sample menus for one week. These menus can be used for almost any diet calculation. Simply use the number of Exchanges which total up to the amount prescribed for your own diet. The totals of the menus are given with the number of Exchanges. Compare your total with this total and make subtractions or additions accordingly. The recipes in this book are combinations of these Exchanges and may be used wherever the Exchanges fit into your diet.

MONDAY	EXCHANGES	Carbo-hydrate Gms.	Protein Gms.	Fat Gms.
Breakfast:				
Applesauce—½ cup	1 Fruit Exchange	10	—	—
Puffed rice—¾ cup	1 Bread Exchange	15	2	—
Soft-cooked egg—1	1 Meat Exchange	—	7	5
Bread and butter—1 slice —1 teaspoon	1 Bread Exchange 1 Fat Exchange	15 —	2 —	— 5
Milk—1 cup	1 Milk Exchange	12	8	10
		52	19	20
Dinner:				
Hamburgers—2 ounces	2 Meat Exchanges	—	14	10
Parsleyed potatoes—1 small	1 Bread Exchange	15	2	—
Peas—½ cup	1 Vegetable B	7	2	—
Bread and butter—1 slice —1 teaspoon	1 Bread Exchange 1 Fat Exchange	15 —	2 —	— 5
Apricots—2 medium	1 Fruit Exchange	10	—	—
Milk—1 cup	1 Milk Exchange	12	8	10
		59	28	25
Supper:				
Noodles—½ cup	1 Bread Exchange	15	2	—
Green peppers stuffed with cottage cheese—1 pepper plus ½ cup cheese	1 Vegetable A 2 Meat Exchanges	— —	— 14	— 10
Wedged tomatoes	1 Vegetable A	—	—	—
Bread and butter—1 slice —1 teaspoon	1 Bread Exchange 1 Fat Exchange	15 —	2 —	— 5
Pears—1 medium	1 Fruit Exchange	10	—	—
Milk—1 cup	1 Milk Exchange	12	8	10
		52	26	25
9 P. M.				
Milk—1 cup	1 Milk Exchange	12	8	10
Graham crackers—2	1 Bread Exchange	15	2	—
		27	10	10
	Total for day	190	83	80

TUESDAY	EXCHANGES	Carbohydrate Gms.	Protein Gms.	Fat Gms.
Breakfast:				
Orange juice—½ cup	1 Fruit Exchange	10	—	—
Wheatena—½ cup	1 Bread Exchange	15	2	—
Soft-cooked egg—1	1 Meat Exchange	—	7	5
Bread and butter—1 slice	1 Bread Exchange	15	2	—
—1 teaspoon	1 Fat Exchange	—	—	5
Milk—1 cup	1 Milk Exchange	12	8	10
		52	19	20
Dinner:				
Pork chop—1 large	3 Meat Exchanges	—	21	15
Mashed potatoes—½ cup	1 Bread Exchange	15	2	—
Brussels sprouts	1 Vegetable A	—	—	—
Bread and butter—1 slice	1 Bread Exchange	15	2	—
—1 teaspoon	1 Fat Exchange	—	—	5
Peach—1 medium	1 Fruit Exchange	10	—	—
Milk—1 cup	1 Milk Exchange	12	8	10
		52	33	30
Supper:				
Dried beef and stewed tomatoes —2 ounces dried beef; ½ cup tomatoes	2 Meat Exchanges 1 Vegetable A	— —	14 —	10 —
Radishes	1 Vegetable A	—	—	—
Bread and butter—1 slice	1 Bread Exchange	15	2	—
—1 teaspoon	1 Fat Exchange	—	—	5
Milk—1 cup	1 Milk Exchange	12	8	10
Grapes—12	1 Fruit Exchange	10	—	—
		37	24	25
9 P. M.				
Milk—1 cup	1 Milk Exchange	12	8	10
Graham crackers—2	1 Bread Exchange	15	2	—
		27	10	10
	Total for day	168	86	85

WEDNESDAY	EXCHANGES	Carbo-hydrate Gms.	Protein Gms.	Fat Gms.
Breakfast:				
Grapefruit juice—½ cup	1 Fruit Exchange	10	—	—
Wheaties—¾ cup	1 Bread Exchange	15	2	—
Soft-cooked egg—1	1 Meat Exchange	—	7	5
Bread and butter—1 slice	1 Bread Exchange	15	2	—
—1 teaspoon	1 Fat Exchange	—	—	5
Milk—1 cup	1 Milk Exchange	12	8	10
		52	19	20
Dinner:				
Stewed meat cubes with pota-toes and carrots—2 ounces meat; 1 small potato; ½ cup carrots	2 Meat Exchanges 1 Bread Exchange 1 Vegetable B	— 15 7	14 2 2	10 — —
Bread and butter—1 slice	1 Bread Exchange	15	2	—
—1 teaspoon	1 Fat Exchange	—	—	5
Fruit cocktail—½ cup	1 Fruit Exchange	10	—	—
Milk—1 cup	1 Milk Exchange	12	8	10
		59	28	25
Supper:				
Tomato juice	1 Vegetable A	—	—	—
Cold cuts—2 slices	2 Meat Exchanges	—	14	10
Mixed salad—½ cup	1 Vegetable B	7	2	—
Bread and butter—1 slice	1 Bread Exchange	15	2	—
—1 teaspoon	1 Fat Exchange	—	—	5
Plums—2 medium	1 Fruit Exchange	10	—	—
Milk—1 cup	1 Milk Exchange	12	8	10
		44	26	25
9 P. M.				
Milk—1 cup	1 Milk Exchange	12	8	10
Graham crackers—2	1 Bread Exchange	15	2	—
		27	10	10
	Total for day	182	83	80

THURSDAY	EXCHANGES	Carbo-hydrate Gms.	Protein Gms.	Fat Gms.
Breakfast:				
Cantaloupe—¼ of 6-inch diameter	1 Fruit Exchange	10	—	—
Oatmeal—½ cup	1 Bread Exchange	15	2	—
Soft-cooked egg—1	1 Meat Exchange	—	7	5
Bread and butter—1 slice　—1 teaspoon	1 Bread Exchange 1 Fat Exchange	15 —	2 —	— 5
Milk—1 cup	1 Milk Exchange	12	8	10
		52	19	20
Dinner:				
Baked ham—3 ounces	3 Meat Exchanges	—	21	15
Potatoes, baked—1 small	1 Bread Exchange	15	2	—
Beets—½ cup	1 Vegetable B	7	2	—
Bread and butter—1 slice　—1 teaspoon	1 Bread Exchange 1 Fat Exchange	15 —	2 —	— 5
Sliced orange—1 small	1 Fruit Exchange	10	—	—
Milk—1 cup	1 Milk Exchange	12	8	10
		59	35	30
Supper:				
Macaroni and cheese—½ cup of macaroni; 2 ounces cheese	1 Bread Exchange 2 Meat Exchanges	15 —	2 14	— 10
Sliced tomatoes	1 Vegetable A	—	—	—
Bread and butter—1 slice　—1 teaspoon	1 Bread Exchange 1 Fat Exchange	15 —	2 —	— 5
Pineapple—½ cup	1 Fruit Exchange	10	—	—
Milk—1 cup	1 Milk Exchange	12	8	10
		52	26	25
9 P. M.				
Milk—1 cup	1 Milk Exchange	12	8	10
Graham crackers—2	1 Bread Exchange	15	2	—
		27	10	10
	Total for day	190	90	85

FRIDAY	EXCHANGES	Carbo-hydrate Gms.	Protein Gms.	Fat Gms.
Breakfast:				
Grapefruit—½	1 Fruit Exchange	10	—	—
Puffed wheat—¾ cup	1 Bread Exchange	15	2	—
Soft-cooked egg—1	1 Meat Exchange	—	7	5
Bread and butter—1 slice	1 Bread Exchange	15	2	—
—1 teaspoon	1 Fat Exchange	—	—	5
Milk—1 cup	1 Milk Exchange	12	8	10
		52	19	20
Dinner:				
Baked tuna fish—2 ounces or ½ cup	2 Meat Exchanges	—	14	10
Potatoes—1 small	1 Bread Exchange	15	2	—
Spinach	1 Vegetable A	—	—	—
Bread and butter—1 slice	1 Bread Exchange	15	2	—
—1 teaspoon	1 Fat Exchange	—	—	5
Banana in D-Zerta—½ small	1 Fruit Exchange	10	—	—
Milk—1 cup	1 Milk Exchange	12	8	10
		52	26	25
Supper:				
Baked beans—½ cup	1 Bread Exchange	15	2	—
Sliced cheese—2 slices	2 Meat Exchanges	—	14	10
Celery hearts	1 Vegetable A	—	—	—
Bread and butter—1 slice	1 Bread Exchange	15	2	—
—1 teaspoon	1 Fat Exchange	—	—	5
Apple—1—2-inch diameter	1 Fruit Exchange	10	—	—
Milk—1 cup	1 Milk Exchange	12	8	10
		52	26	25
9 P. M.				
Milk—1 cup	1 Milk Exchange	12	8	10
Graham crackers—2	1 Bread Exchange	15	2	—
		27	10	10
	Total for day	183	81	80

SATURDAY	EXCHANGES	Carbo-hydrate Gms.	Protein Gms.	Fat Gms.
Breakfast:				
Grapefruit and orange slices— ½ cup	1 Fruit Exchange	10	—	—
Shredded Wheat—1 biscuit	1 Bread Exchange	15	2	—
Soft-cooked egg—1	1 Meat Exchange	—	7	5
Bread and butter—1 slice —1 teaspoon	1 Bread Exchange 1 Fat Exchange	15 —	2 —	— 5
Milk—1 cup	1 Milk Exchange	12	8	10
		52	19	20
Dinner:				
Broiled liver—3 ounces	3 Meat Exchanges	—	21	15
Mashed potatoes—½ cup	1 Bread Exchange	15	2	—
Onions—½ cup	1 Vegetable B	7	2	—
Bread and butter—1 slice —1 teaspoon	1 Bread Exchange 1 Fat Exchange	15 —	2 —	— 5
Pear—1 medium	1 Fruit Exchange	10	—	—
Milk—1 cup	1 Milk Exchange	12	8	10
		59	35	30
Supper:				
Chicken salad—2 ounces chicken; 1 teaspoon mayonnaise	2 Meat Exchanges 1 Fat Exchange	— —	14 —	15 5
Baked potato—1 small	1 Bread Exchange	15	2	—
Asparagus salad	1 Vegetable A	—	—	—
Bread and butter—1 slice —1 teaspoon	1 Bread Exchange 1 Fat Exchange	15 —	2 —	— 5
Cherries—10 large	1 Fruit Exchange	10	—	—
Milk—1 cup	1 Milk Exchange	12	8	10
		52	26	35
9 P. M.				
1 serving of fruit	1 Fruit Exchange	10	—	—
		10	—	—
	Total for day	173	80	85

SUNDAY	EXCHANGES	Carbo-hydrate Gms.	Protein Gms.	Fat Gms.
Breakfast:				
Orange juice—½ cup	1 Fruit Exchange	10	—	—
Farina—½ cup	1 Bread Exchange	15	2	—
Soft-cooked egg—1	1 Meat Exchange	—	7	5
Bread and butter—1 slice	1 Bread Exchange	15	2	—
—1 teaspoon	1 Fat Exchange	—	—	5
Milk—1 cup	1 Milk Exchange	12	8	10
		52	19	20
Dinner:				
Roast beef—2 slices	2 Meat Exchanges	—	14	10
Peas—½ cup	1 Vegetable B	7	2	—
Potatoes—1 small	1 Bread Exchange	15	2	—
Bread and butter—1 slice	1 Bread Exchange	15	2	—
—1 teaspoon	1 Fat Exchange	—	—	5
Ice cream—⅛ cup	1 Bread Exchange	15	2	10
	2 Fat Exchanges	—	—	—
Milk—1 cup	1 Milk Exchange	12	8	10
		64	30	35
Supper:				
Cold cuts—2 slices	2 Meat Exchanges	—	14	10
Potatoes—1 small	1 Bread Exchange	15	2	—
Sliced cucumbers in vinegar	Vegetable A	—	—	—
Bread and butter—1 slice	1 Bread Exchange	15	2	—
—1 teaspoon	1 Fat Exchange	—	—	5
Blueberries—⅔ cup	1 Fruit Exchange	10	—	—
Milk—1 cup	1 Milk Exchange	12	8	10
		52	26	25
9 P. M.				
Milk—1 cup	1 Milk Exchange	12	8	10
Graham crackers—2	1 Bread Exchange	15	2	—
		27	10	10
	Total for day	195	85	90

MILK EXCHANGES

Each Milk Exchange contains: Carbohydrate — 12 gm.;
Protein — 8 gm.; Fat — 10 gm.; Calories — 166.

WHOLE MILK	EVAPORATED MILK
Amt.: 1 cup (8 oz.) Wt.: 240 gm.	Amt.: 1/2 cup Wt.: 120 gm.
SKIM MILK*	BUTTERMILK*
Amt.: 1 cup (8 oz.) Wt.: 240 gm.	Amt.: 1 cup (8 oz.) Wt.: 240 gm.
POWDERED WHOLE MILK	POWDERED SKIM MILK*
Amt.: 1/4 cup Wt.: 35 gm.	Amt.: 1/4 cup Wt.: 35 gm.

*Since skim milk does not have the 10 gm. fat in whole milk, you are entitled to 2 additional Fat Exchanges in your meal if you use 1 cup skim milk. Most buttermilk is skimmed also. Ask your local dairy.

413

VEGETABLE "B" EXCHANGES

Each Vegetable "B" Exchange contains: Carbohydrate—7 gm.;
Protein—2 gm.; Fat—negligible; Calories—35.

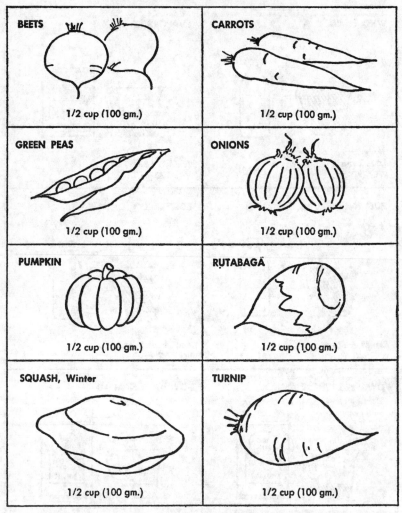

BEETS 1/2 cup (100 gm.)	**CARROTS** 1/2 cup (100 gm.)
GREEN PEAS 1/2 cup (100 gm.)	**ONIONS** 1/2 cup (100 gm.)
PUMPKIN 1/2 cup (100 gm.)	**RUTABAGA** 1/2 cup (100 gm.)
SQUASH, Winter 1/2 cup (100 gm.)	**TURNIP** 1/2 cup (100 gm.)

NOTE: See text for complete list of "A" Vegetables. These "A" Vegetables contain a negligible amount of carbohydrate, protein and fat in ordinary amounts used. However, if you use more than one cup of cooked "A" Vegetables at a meal, it should be counted as one Vegetable "B" Exchange.

The following vegetables (from both the "A" and "B" lists) are high in vitamin A: broccoli, chicory, escarole, parsley, green peppers, tomatoes, watercress, greens (such as beet or turnip greens), carrots and squash. Eat a serving of one of these vegetables every day.

414

FRUIT EXCHANGES

Each Fruit Exchange contains: Carbohydrate — 10 gm.;
Protein — negligible; Fat — negligible; Calories — 40.
See Index for complete list of Fruit Exchanges.

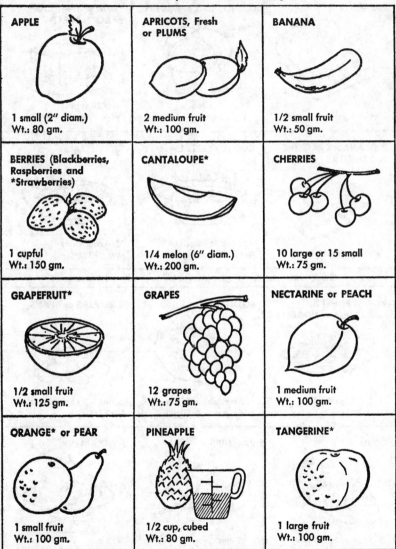

APPLE	**APRICOTS, Fresh or PLUMS**	**BANANA**
1 small (2" diam.) Wt.: 80 gm.	2 medium fruit Wt.: 100 gm.	1/2 small fruit Wt.: 50 gm.
BERRIES (Blackberries, Raspberries and *Strawberries)	**CANTALOUPE***	**CHERRIES**
1 cupful Wt.: 150 gm.	1/4 melon (6" diam.) Wt.: 200 gm.	10 large or 15 small Wt.: 75 gm.
GRAPEFRUIT*	**GRAPES**	**NECTARINE or PEACH**
1/2 small fruit Wt.: 125 gm.	12 grapes Wt.: 75 gm.	1 medium fruit Wt.: 100 gm.
ORANGE* or PEAR	**PINEAPPLE**	**TANGERINE***
1 small fruit Wt.: 100 gm.	1/2 cup, cubed Wt.: 80 gm.	1 large fruit Wt.: 100 gm.

* These fruits, and their juices, are high in vitamin C.
Eat a serving of one of these fruits every day.

BREAD EXCHANGES

Each Bread Exchange contains: Carbohydrate — 15 gm.;
Protein — 2 gm.; Fat — negligible; Calories — 65.

BREAD	BISCUIT, ROLL or MUFFIN	PLAIN SPONGE CAKE or CORN BREAD
1 slice Wt.: 25 gm.	1 roll, 2" diam. Wt.: 35 gm.	1-1/2" cube Wt.: 25 gm.
2 GRAHAM CRACKERS or 5 SALTINES	COOKED CEREALS	DRY CEREALS
Wt.: 20 gm.	1/2 cup, cooked Wt.: 100 gm.	3/4 cup, scant Wt.: 20 gm.

The following foods may also be counted as one Bread Exchange:

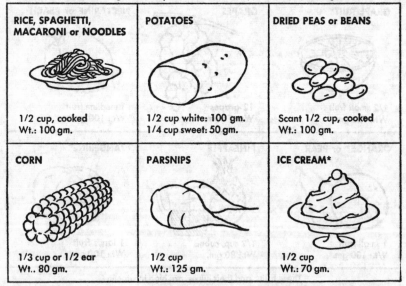

RICE, SPAGHETTI, MACARONI or NOODLES	POTATOES	DRIED PEAS or BEANS
1/2 cup, cooked Wt.: 100 gm.	1/2 cup white: 100 gm. 1/4 cup sweet: 50 gm.	Scant 1/2 cup, cooked Wt.: 100 gm.
CORN	PARSNIPS	ICE CREAM*
1/3 cup or 1/2 ear Wt.. 80 gm.	1/2 cup Wt.: 125 gm.	1/2 cup Wt.: 70 gm.

*1/2 cup of ice cream uses up 2 Fat Exchanges in addition to one Bread Exchange.

MEAT EXCHANGES

Each Meat Exchange contains: Carbohydrate — negligible;
Protein — 7 gm.; Fat — 5 gm.; Calories — 75.

BEEF, LAMB, VEAL or LIVER	HAM (LEAN) or PORK	POULTRY
Amt.: 1 oz. Wt.: 30 gm.	Amt.: 1 oz. Wt.: 30 gm.	Amt.: 1 oz. Wt.: 30 gm.
COLD CUTS (1 slice) or 1 FRANKFURTER	COD, HADDOCK, HALIBUT, HERRING, ETC.	SALMON, TUNA, CRAB, or LOBSTER
Wt.: 50 gm.	Amt.: 1 oz. Wt.: 30 gm.	Amt.: 1/4 cup Wt.: 30 gm.
SHRIMP, CLAMS, OYSTERS (Medium size)	SARDINES	CHEDDAR TYPE CHEESE
Amt.: 5 shellfish Wt.: 45 gm.	Amt.: 3 medium fish Wt.: 30 gm.	Amt.: 1 oz. Wt.: 30 gm.
COTTAGE CHEESE	EGG	PEANUT BUTTER (Limit to 1 serving per day)
Amt.: 3 level tablespoons. Wt.: 45 gm.	Amt.: 1 egg Wt.: 50 gm.	Amt.: 2 scant tablespoons. Wt.: 50 gm.

417

FAT EXCHANGES

Each Fat Exchange contains: Carbohydrate — negligible;
Protein — negligible; Fat — 5 gm.; Calories — 45.

BUTTER or MARGARINE	**CRISP BACON**	**LIGHT CREAM, SWEET or SOUR**
Amt.: 1 level teaspoon Wt.: 5 gm.	Amt.: 1 slice Wt.: 10 gm.	Amt.: 2 level tablespoons Wt.: 30
HEAVY CREAM	**CREAM CHEESE**	**FRENCH DRESSING**
Amt.: 1 level tablespoon Wt.: 15 gm.	Amt.: 1 level tablespoon Wt.: 15 gm.	Amt.: 1 level tablespoon Wt.: 15 gm.
MAYONNAISE	**OIL or COOKING FAT**	**OLIVES**
Amt.: 1 level tablespoon Wt.: 5 gm.	Amt.: 1 level tablespoon Wt.: 5 gm.	Amt.: 5 small olives Wt.: 50 gm.

SOUPS

The diabetic should limit varieties of soup to those prepared only for him. Canned soups may have many things in them which are not on the diet. Soup for the diabetic is simply prepared. Broths are always allowed. If these are prepared for the family a little broth can be set aside for the diabetic. Bouillon cubes may be used as the basis for a variety of soups.

Broth variations:

1. One-half cup of rice, noodles, barley may be used as a Bread Exchange. These may be added to beef broth, chicken broth or lamb broth. A teaspoon of celery may be added with the seasonings.

2. An assortment of "A" vegetables, such as tomato, asparagus, string beans, cabbage, celery and cauliflower may be added to broth to make a delicious vegetable soup.

3. Milk allowed on the diet as a beverage can be heated and mixed with strained, allowed vegetables and served as a cream soup.

4. Hot tomato juice and a slice of bread toasted and cut up into croutons makes a delicious dish on a cold day.

To eat with soup:

Saltines: 5 Saltines equal 1 Bread Exchange.
Rice Krispies: 3/4 cup equals 1 Bread Exchange.
Croutons: 1 slice of bread, toasted and cut into 1-inch squares, equals 1 Bread Exchange.

MEAT BROTH[2]

1 pound beef, veal, chicken or lamb, or 1 pint of clams should make one quart of broth. Let cool and skim off all fat before serving.

Variations:

1. One cup of assorted "A" vegetables, such as tomatoes, celery, cabbage, cauliflower, string beans. Add these vegetables to the broth and prepare a thick vegetable soup which may be eaten in place of a serving of "A" vegetable.

2. One-half cup rice, barley, noodles, tapioca or farina (cooked) may be placed in broth for soup and used in exchange for one slice of bread.

3. Five clams chopped and added to the clam broth will be the base for a clam chowder. One medium-sized potato, diced, may be added and 1/2 cup of milk. This will be an exchange for 1/2 cup of milk, 1 Bread Exchange and 1 Meat Exchange.

MUTTON BROTH[2]

2 pounds lean mutton cut from forequarter with bones
2 pinches salt

1. Wipe the meat, remove skin and fat and put through a meat chopper. Add 1 quart water and salt. **2.** Simmer down to one pint (do not boil) for 3 to 4 hours over a slow fire, adding more water if necessary. **3.** Strain, and when cold remove the fat. **4.** Serve hot, or cold in the form of jelly.

Note: Some of allowed milk may be added to this broth.

MANHATTAN CLAM CHOWDER[2]

INGREDIENTS	AMOUNT Household Measure	Grams	C Gm.	P Gm.	F Gm.
clams, minced	5	45	—	7	5
boiling water	1/2 cup	120	—	—	—
canned tomatoes	1/2 cup	100	—	—	—
salt and pepper	to taste	—	—	—	—
onions, chopped	1 teaspoon	5	—	—	—
carrots, chopped	1 teaspoon	5	—	—	—
celery, chopped	1 teaspoon	5	—	—	—
thyme	sprinkle	—	—	—	—
celery seed	sprinkle	—	—	—	—
Calories: 73.			—	7	5

1. Combine all the ingredients in a saucepan. **2.** Allow to simmer for 30 to 40 minutes.

Exchanges: 1 Meat; 2 A Vegetables.

CLAM BROTH[2]

INGREDIENTS	AMOUNT Household Measure	Grams	C Gm.	P Gm.	F Gm.
clams	5	45	—	7	5
salt and pepper	few grains	—	—	—	—
Calories: 73.			—	7	5

1. Scrub clam shells. Place in water to cover well and heat until the shells open. **2.** Remove clams from the shells, saving the water. **3.** Cut clams into small slices and return to water. Cook fifteen minutes. **4.** Season with salt and pepper. Strain and serve.

Note: Part of your allowance of milk and butter may be added. If you are allowed a potato, this may be diced and added.

Exchange: 1 Meat.

VEGETABLE SOUP[1]

INGREDIENTS	AMOUNT Household Measure	Grams	C Gm.	P Gm.	F Gm.
carrots...................					
peas......................					
string beans..............	1/2 cup	100	7	2	—
tomatoes.................					
celery....................					
bouillon cube.............1		—	—	—	—
boiling water.............1 cup		—	—	—	—
Calories: 36.			7	2	—

1. Place the bouillon cube in a saucepan and cover with 1 cup of boiling water. (Any broth may be used.) **2.** Place the vegetables into the broth and heat through. If raw vegetables are used they will have to be cooked longer. (If necessary it is better to cook the vegetables separately in water otherwise the broth will boil away while the vegetables are cooking.)

Exchange: 1 B Vegetable.

TOMATO SOUP[1]

INGREDIENTS	AMOUNT Household Measure	Grams	C Gm.	P Gm.	F Gm.
tomato juice.................1/2 cup		100	—	—	—
broth, clear................. 1/2 cup		100	—	—	—
Calories: 0.			—	—	—

1. Mix the tomato juice and the broth together. Season to taste.

Exchange: 1 A Vegetable.

TOMATO BOUILLON[2]

INGREDIENTS	AMOUNT Household Measure	Grams	C Gm.	P Gm.	F Gm.
tomatoes, stewed............1/2 cup		100	—	—	—
broth.......................1 cup		240	—	—	—
onion extract................1/2 teaspoon		3	—	—	—
bay leaf.....................1		—	—	—	—
clove........................1		—	—	—	—
celery salt.................. 1/4 teaspoon		—	—	—	—
Calories: negligible.			—	—	—

1. Mix all ingredients and boil 20 minutes. **2.** Strain and serve.

CREAM SOUP[2]

INGREDIENTS	AMOUNT Household Measure	Grams	C Gm.	P Gm.	F Gm.
milk, whole..................	1/2 cup	120	6	4	5
strained vegetable...........	1/2 cup	100	7	2	—
butter......................	1 teaspoon	5	—	—	5
salt and pepper..............	to taste	—	—	—	—
Calories: 166.			13	6	10

1. Heat milk in top of double boiler. **2.** Strain the vegetable or use canned strained vegetable. **3.** Add strained vegetable to the milk with butter, salt and pepper.

Exchanges: 1/2 cup Whole Milk; 1 B Vegetable; 1 Fat.

CREAM OF PEA SOUP[2]

INGREDIENTS	AMOUNT Household Measure	Grams	C Gm.	P Gm.	F Gm.
peas (cooked)................	1/2 cup	100	7	2	—
milk........................	1 cup	240	12	8	10
butter......................	1 teaspoon	5	—	—	5
salt........................	few grains	—	—	—	—
pepper......................	few grains	—	—	—	—
Calories: 251.			19	10	15

1. Mash cooked peas and put through a strainer. **2.** Add hot milk, salt, pepper and butter. **3.** Bring to a boil and serve at once.

Exchanges: 1 cup Milk; 1/2 cup B Vegetable; 1 Fat.

MOCK LOBSTER SOUP[2]

INGREDIENTS	AMOUNT Household Measure	Grams	C Gm.	P Gm.	F Gm.
flaked cooked codfish........	1 ounce	30	—	7	5
canned tomatoes.............	1/2 cup	100	—	—	—
milk........................	1/2 cup	120	6	4	5
Calories: 158.			6	11	10

1. Break the codfish into very small pieces. **2.** Add the fish to 1/2 cup of stewed tomatoes and bring to a boil in a saucepan. **3.** Scald the 1/2 cup of milk and add to the codfish and tomatoes. **4.** Serve at once. (Do not reheat.)

Exchanges: 1/2 Milk; 1 Meat; 1 A Vegetable.

COLD BUTTERMILK SOUP[2]

INGREDIENTS	AMOUNT Household Measure	Grams	C Gm.	P Gm.	F Gm.
buttermilk................1 cup		240	12	8	10
shrimps (medium)............5		30	—	7	5
diced cucumber..............1/8 cup		25	—	—	—
chopped dill pickle..........1 teaspoon		10	—	—	—
mustard, prepared...........1/2 teaspoon		3	—	—	—
salt.......................few grains		—	—	—	—
Sacrose....................8 drops		—	—	—	—
Calories: 243.			12	15	15

1. Chop the cooked shrimps and mix with diced cucumber and dill pickle. **2.** Add the salt, mustard and Sacrose to the cold buttermilk. **3.** Mix all the ingredients together, chill and serve.
Exchanges: 1 Milk; 1 Meat.

OYSTER STEW[2]

INGREDIENTS	AMOUNT Household Measure	Grams	C Gm.	P Gm.	F Gm.
milk......................1 cup		240	12	8	10
oysters....................5		45	—	7	5
butter....................1 teaspoon		5	—	—	5
salt and pepper...........to taste		—	—	—	—
Calories: 288.			12	15	20

1. Heat milk. In a pan, melt the butter, and cook oysters until edges curl. **2.** Add salt and pepper to taste. **3.** When ready to serve, add oysters to hot milk. **4.** Crackers may be served as an exchange for bread.
Exchanges: 1 cup Milk; 1 Meat; 1 Fat.

GREEN PEA SOUP[1]

INGREDIENTS	AMOUNT Household Measure	Grams	C Gm.	P Gm.	F Gm.
peas......................1/2 cup		100	7	2	—
broth.....................1/2 cup		—	—	—	—
milk......................1/2 cup		120	6	4	5
salt and pepper............to taste		—	—	—	—
bread, toasted..............1 slice		25	15	2	—
Calories: 189.			28	8	5

1. Mash the cooked peas and put them through a coarse strainer. **2.** Heat the milk, add to hot broth and season. **3.** Stir in the strained peas and reheat. **4.** Toast the bread and cut up into croutons, or for a holiday the toast can be cut into various shapes, as a flag for Fourth of July. The remaining pieces of toast can be cubed and used as croutons.

Exchanges: 1/2 cup Milk; 1 B Vegetable; 1 Bread.

SCALLOP BROTH[2]

INGREDIENTS	AMOUNT Household Measure	Grams	C Gm.	P Gm.	F Gm.
scallops	1 ounce	30	—	7	5
lemon juice	1 teaspoon	5	—	—	—
milk, scalded	1 cup	240	12	8	10
salt	few grains	—	—	—	—
pepper	few grains	—	—	—	—
nutmeg	few grains	—	—	—	—
butter	1 teaspoon	5	—	—	5
Calories: 288.			12	15	20

1. Sprinkle the scallops with lemon juice. Let stand for 15 minutes. **2.** Add 1/4 cup cold water and slowly bring to the boiling point. **3.** Add the salt, pepper, nutmeg, butter and milk. Always keep below the boiling point after the milk is added, and serve as quickly as possible.

Exchanges: 1 Milk; 1 Meat; 1 Fat.

APPETIZERS AND LUNCHEON DISHES

CREAM CHEESE STUFFED CELERY[2]

INGREDIENTS	AMOUNT Household Measure	Grams	C Gm.	P Gm.	F Gm.
celery	2 small stalks	—	—	—	—
cream cheese	1 tablespoon	15	—	—	5
pimiento (chopped fine)	1 teaspoon	—	—	—	—
salt	few grains	—	—	—	—
lemon	1 slice	—	—	—	—
Calories: 45.			—	—	5

1. Use inside, clean stalks. Wash well and chill in ice water with the lemon slice. **2.** Mash cheese, pimiento and salt to a paste. Fill stalks.

Exchange: 1 Fat.

CELERY CURLS[2]

INGREDIENTS	AMOUNT Household Measure	Grams	C Gm.	P Gm.	F Gm.
celery..........................	1 celery heart	—	—	—	—
Calories: 0.			—	—	—

1. Cut celery in 3-inch lengths. Shred both ends almost to center. **2.** Keep in ice water until ends curl. Serve in celery dish with little chopped ice.

Exchange: 1 A Vegetable.

PEANUT BUTTER STUFFED CELERY[2]

INGREDIENTS	AMOUNT Household Measure	Grams	C Gm.	P Gm.	F Gm.
celery.........................	1 stalk	—	—	—	—
peanut butter...............	2 tablespoons	30	—	7	5
Calories: 73.			—	7	5

1. Cut celery lengthwise into 6 pieces. **2.** Fill peanut butter into cavity of celery. **3.** Serve in celery dish on crushed ice.

Exchange: 1 Meat.

SEAFOOD COCKTAIL[2]

INGREDIENTS	AMOUNT Household Measure	Grams	C Gm.	P Gm.	F Gm.
shrimps......................	5	45	—	7	5
crab meat...................	1/4 cup	30	—	7	5
lobster meat................	1/4 cup	30	—	7	5
cocktail sauce..............	2 tablespoons	—	—	—	—
lemon.......................	1 slice	—	—	—	—
Calories: 219.			—	21	15

COCKTAIL SAUCE

chili sauce..................	1 tablespoon	—	—	—	—
horseradish.................	1 tablespoon	—	—	—	—
			—	21	15

1. Quarter shrimps and break lobster and crab meat into large lumps. **2.** Mix with shrimps. **3.** Serve meat in a cocktail glass mixed with cocktail sauce.

Exchange: 3 Meat.

CELERY AND OLIVES[2]

INGREDIENTS	AMOUNT Household Measure	Grams	C Gm.	P Gm.	F Gm.
celery.....................3 center stalks		—	—	—	—
olives (green)...............5		50	—	—	5
Calories: 45.			—	—	5

1. Serve on a small platter on ice.

Exchange: 1 Fat.

GRATED CUCUMBER COCKTAIL[2]

INGREDIENTS	AMOUNT Household Measure	Grams	C Gm.	P Gm.	F Gm.
cucumber.....................1/2 small		—	—	—	—
onion juice..................1/2 teaspoon		—	—	—	—
tomato juice.................1/2 cup		—	—	—	—
salt.........................few grains		—	—	—	—
pepper.......................few grains		—	—	—	—
horseradish..................1 teaspoon		—	—	—	—
Calories: 35.			—	—	—

1. Grate washed, unpeeled cucumber. **2.** Combine with onion juice, salt, pepper, horseradish and tomato juice. **3.** Chill and serve in small cocktail glass.

Exchange: 1 A Vegetable.

CHOPPED BEEF AND BACON CURLS[2]

INGREDIENTS	AMOUNT Household Measure	Grams	C Gm.	P Gm.	F Gm.
bacon.......................2 strips		10	—	—	10
chopped beef................1 ounce		30	—	7	5
salt........................few grains		—	—	—	—
egg.........................1		—	—	7	5
paprika.....................few grains		—	—	—	—
water cress.................1 small bunch		—	—	—	—
Calories: 236.			—	14	20

1. Mix chopped beef with salt and raw egg. **2.** Form meat into 4 small balls. **3.** Wrap each in 1/2 slice of bacon. Hold together with a toothpick and sprinkle with paprika. **4.** Broil under hot broiler. **5.** Serve with a small sprig of water cress.

Exchanges: 2 Fat; 2 Meat.

CLAM COCKTAIL²

INGREDIENTS	AMOUNT		C	P	F
	Household Measure	Grams	Gm.	Gm.	Gm.
cherrystone clams............5 (chilled)		45	—	7	5
cocktail sauce...............2 tablespoons			—	—	—
lemon.....................1/8 section			—	—	—
Calories: 73.			—	7	5

1. Serve clams on chopped ice in a soup plate. **2.** In center set the glass of cocktail sauce (see Seafood Cocktail). **3.** Garnish with lemon.

Exchange: 1 Meat.

CRAB MEAT COCKTAIL²

INGREDIENTS	AMOUNT		C	P	F
	Household Measure	Grams	Gm.	Gm.	Gm.
lettuce......................1 leaf			—	—	—
crab meat (fresh)...........1/4 cup		30	—	7	5
lemon.....................1/8 section			—	—	—
cocktail sauce..............2 tablespoons			—	—	—
Calories: 73.			—	7	5

1. Flake crab meat with a fork. **2.** Chill and serve on a crisp lettuce leaf, in cocktail glass. **3.** Pour sauce over (see Seafood Cocktail) and garnish with lemon.

Exchange: 1 Meat.

LOBSTER COCKTAIL²

INGREDIENTS	AMOUNT		C	P	F
	Household Measure	Grams	Gm.	Gm.	Gm.
lettuce......................1 leaf			—	—	—
lobster meat (cooked and chilled)..................1/4 cup		30	—	7	5
cocktail sauce..............2 tablespoons			—	—	—
lemon.....................1/8 section			—	—	—
Calories: 73.			—	7	5

1. Flake lobster meat with a fork and chill. **2.** Serve on crisp lettuce leaf in a cocktail glass. **3.** Pour sauce over (see Seafood Cocktail) and garnish with lemon.

Exchange: 1 Meat.

SHRIMP COCKTAIL[2]

INGREDIENTS	AMOUNT Household Measure	Grams	C Gm.	P Gm.	F Gm.
lettuce heart................	1 small piece	—	—	—	—
shrimps....................	5 whole	45	—	7	5
cocktail sauce..............	2 tablespoons	—	—	—	—
lemon......................	1/8 piece	—	—	—	—
oyster crackers.............	1/2 cup	20	15	2	—
Calories: 141.			15	9	5

1. Place piece of lettuce and whole shrimps in cocktail glass. **2.** Cover with cocktail sauce (see Seafood Cocktail) and place lemon on side of glass. **3.** Serve with oyster crackers.

Exchanges: 1 Bread; 1 Meat.

SARDINE COCKTAIL[2]

INGREDIENTS	AMOUNT Household Measure	Grams	C Gm.	P Gm.	F Gm.
sardines.....................	3	30	—	7	5
tomato catchup..............	1 tablespoon	—	—	—	—
Worcestershire sauce.........	few drops	—	—	—	—
tabasco sauce...............	1 drop	—	—	—	—
lemon juice.................	few drops	—	—	—	—
lettuce.....................	1 leaf	—	—	—	—
Calories: 73.			—	7	5

1. Skin and bone sardines and separate into small pieces. **2.** Mix with catchup, lemon juice, Worcestershire sauce and tabasco sauce. **3.** Serve mixture on a lettuce leaf on a small plate.

Exchange: 1 Meat.

CURRIED OYSTERS[2]

INGREDIENTS	AMOUNT Household Measure	Grams	C Gm.	P Gm.	F Gm.
oysters (cooked).............	5	45	—	7	5
pimiento (chopped)..........	1 teaspoon	—	—	—	—
curry powder................	1/4 teaspoon	—	—	—	—
mayonnaise.................	1 teaspoon	5	—	—	5
lemon juice.................	1/2 teaspoon	—	—	—	—
lettuce.....................	1 leaf	—	—	—	—
Calories: 118.			—	7	10

1. Place curry powder in a cup with pimiento. **2.** Mix well, add mayonnaise and lemon juice. **3.** Serve oysters in celery dish with lettuce leaf on bottom, and top with sauce.

Exchanges: 1 Meat; 1 Fat.

EPICUREAN OYSTER COCKTAIL[2]

INGREDIENTS	AMOUNT Household Measure	Grams	C Gm.	P Gm.	F Gm.
oysters (loose)..............5		45	—	7	5
celery (chopped).............1/2	tablespoon		—	—	—
pimiento (chopped)...........1/2	tablespoon		—	—	—
lemon......................1	slice		—	—	—
lemon juice.................3/4	tablespoon		—	—	—
catsup.....................1	teaspoon		—	—	—
shallot or onion (chopped)....1/2	teaspoon		—	—	—
tabasco sauce..............3	drops		—	—	—
horseradish (grated).........1	teaspoon		—	—	—
Calories: 73.			—	7	5

1. Mix lemon juice, catchup, shallot, tabasco sauce and horseradish together. **2.** Serve oysters in fruit cocktail glass, with celery and pimiento on bottom. **3.** Cover liberally with sauce and serve slice of lemon on side.

Exchange: 1 Meat.

BAKED LYNNHAVEN OYSTERS[2]

INGREDIENTS	AMOUNT Household Measure	Grams	C Gm.	P Gm.	F Gm.
oysters.....................5		45	—	7	5
horseradish.................1	teaspoon		—	—	—
lemon juice.................1/2	teaspoon		—	—	—
bacon......................1	slice	10	—	—	5
lemon......................1	slice		—	—	—
parsley.....................1	sprig		—	—	—
tartar sauce................1	tablespoon	5	—	—	5
Calories: 208.			—	7	15

1. Place oysters on rock salt, with some horseradish on top of each oyster. **2.** Sprinkle with lemon juice. **3.** Cover each with small piece of bacon. **4.** Bake until oysters ruffle and bacon is brown. **5.** Serve very hot with slice of lemon, sprig of parsley, and small shell of tartar sauce on side.

Exchanges: 1 Meat; 2 Fat.

STUFFED TOMATOES

Here are three ways to prepare stuffed tomatoes. Thoroughly wash each tomato first.

1. Cut in fifths, sixths or eighths almost to the bottom without severing the sections completely.

2. Scald in boiling water, peel and then cut as in 1.

3. Cut off the stem end, scoop out center, season inside well and let soak upright for 15 minutes. Then turn upside down to drain for another 15 minutes.

In each method, the tomato and all ingredients should be thoroughly chilled before serving.

STUFFED TOMATO WITH LOBSTER[2]

INGREDIENTS	AMOUNT Household Measure	Grams	C Gm.	P Gm.	F Gm.
tomato (peeled).............	1 medium	—	—	—	—
lobster meat................	1/4 cup	30	—	7	5
celery (chopped).............	1 tablespoon	—	—	—	—
salt.......................	few grains	—	—	—	—
mayonnaise.................	1 teaspoon	—	—	—	5
lettuce....................	1 leaf	—	—	—	—
stuffed olive..............	1/2	—	—	—	—
Calories: 118.			—	7	10

1. Cut tomato in half and scoop center out. **2.** Cut lobster meat in small cubes and mix with celery. Add mayonnaise and salt. **3.** Fill each half of tomato with mixture, and place half stuffed olive on top. Chill. **4.** Serve on lettuce leaf.

Exchange: 1 Meat.

STUFFED TOMATO WITH CHICKEN[3]

INGREDIENTS	AMOUNT Household Measure	Grams	C Gm.	P Gm.	F Gm.
tomato (peeled).............	1 small	100	—	—	—
chicken (diced).............	1 ounce	30	—	7	5
celery (chopped).............	1 teaspoon	5	—	—	—
mayonnaise.................	1 teaspoon	5	—	—	5
lemon section..............	1/8 section	—	—	—	—
lettuce....................	1 leaf	—	—	—	—
Calories: 118.			—	7	10

1. Cut top off the tomato and scoop out center. **2.** Mix together chicken, celery and mayonnaise, and stuff tomato. **3.** Serve on lettuce leaf on cold plate with slice of lemon.

Exchanges: 1 A Vegetable; 1 Meat; 1 Fat.

STUFFED TOMATO WITH CRAB MEAT[2]

INGREDIENTS	AMOUNT Household Measure	Grams	C Gm.	P Gm.	F Gm.
tomato (peeled)............1 medium		—	—	—	—
crab meat..................1/4 cup		30	—	7	5
salt......................few grains		—	—	—	—
lemon juice................1 teaspoon		—	—	—	—
mayonnaise................1 teaspoon		5	—	—	5
pimiento..................1/4		—	—	—	—
lettuce....................1 leaf		—	—	—	—
Calories: 118.			—	7	10

1. Mix crab meat, mayonnaise, salt and lemon juice. 2. Cut top off tomato and scoop out center. 3. Fill with crab meat mixture, and replace top. 4. Chill thoroughly. 5. Serve on lettuce leaf on a cold plate. Garnish with pimiento.

Exchanges: 1 Meat; 1 Fat.

EGGS

There is a variety of ways in which eggs can be simply prepared:

fried (if butter allowance permits)
soft-cooked
scrambled with onions, chives and
  parsley
omelet, plain or with vegetables
baked
hard-cooked with spinach
hard-cooked, on lettuce

scrambled with tomato
baked in tomato, with cheese on
  top
stuffed
dropped
ham omelet
egg and dried beef
Spanish omelet

Following are some interesting omelets and other egg dishes.

BAKED EGGS[2]

INGREDIENTS	AMOUNT Household Measure	Grams	C Gm.	P Gm.	F Gm.
egg........................1		50	—	7	5
butter.....................1 teaspoon		5	—	—	5
milk.......................1 teaspoon		—	—	—	—
corn flakes................2 teaspoons		—	—	—	—
Calories: 118.			—	7	10

1. Place milk in a shirred egg dish. 2. Break the egg on top of milk. 3. Sprinkle corn flakes over top of egg. 4. Place butter on top and bake in moderately slow oven (325°F.) until white is set. (About 8 minutes.)

Exchanges: 1 Meat; 1 Fat.

BAKED EGG WITH CHEESE[2]

INGREDIENTS	AMOUNT Household Measure	Grams	C Gm.	P Gm.	F Gm.
egg................	1	50	—	7	5
milk...............	1 teaspoon	—	—	—	—
cheese, grated......	1 ounce	30	—	7	5
butter.............	1 teaspoon	5	—	—	5
Calories: 191.			—	14	15

1. Using a small pinch of the teaspoon of butter, grease an individual Pyrex baking dish. 2. Break an egg into the Pyrex baking dish. 3. Taking 1 teaspoon of milk from regular allowance, place this over the egg. 4. Sprinkle the grated cheese over the egg, and place the remaining butter on top. 5. Place the casserole in a pan and surround the baking dish with water. Bake in a moderate oven (350°F.) until the cheese is melted and brown.

Exchanges: 2 Meat; 1 Fat.

DEVILED EGG[2]

INGREDIENTS	AMOUNT Household Measure	Grams	C Gm.	P Gm.	F Gm.
egg, hard-cooked.....	1	50	—	7	5
vinegar.............	1 teaspoon	—	—	—	—
mayonnaise..........	1 teaspoon	5	—	—	5
mustard.............	few grains	—	—	—	—
paprika.............	few grains	—	—	—	—
salt and pepper......	few grains	—	—	—	—
lettuce.............	1 leaf	—	—	—	—
Calories: 118.			—	7	10

1. Cut the egg in half lengthwise. 2. Remove the yolk and mix thoroughly with seasonings and mayonnaise. 3. Refill the white. 4. Serve on lettuce leaf.

Exchanges: 1 Meat; 1 Fat.

FOAMY OMELET[2]

INGREDIENTS	AMOUNT Household Measure	Grams	C Gm.	P Gm.	F Gm.
eggs...............	2	100	—	14	10
butter.............	1 teaspoon	5	—	—	5
salt...............	few grains	—	—	—	—
pepper.............	few grains	—	—	—	—
Calories: 191.			—	14	15

1. Wash eggs. Separate the yolks from the whites. 2. Beat the

whites until they are very stiff. Beat the yolks until creamy. **3.** Add salt and pepper to yolks. **4.** Fold the yellow into the white with a spatula. This must be done gently. **5.** Melt the butter in a small frying pan. Place the mixture in the pan and cook until bottom browns. The mixture will rise as it cooks. **6.** When nice and brown underneath, place in a broiler to brown the top. Remove and serve.

Exchanges: 2 Meat; 1 Fat.

EGG IN NEST[1]

INGREDIENTS	AMOUNT Household Measure	Grams	C Gm.	P Gm.	F Gm.
egg......................	1	50	—	7	5
salt and pepper.............	to taste	—	—	—	—
Calories: 73.			—	7	5

1. Separate the white of the egg from the yolk. Do not break the yolk. **2.** Beat the white of the egg until it is stiff and stands up in peaks when the beater is removed. **3.** Moisten a Pyrex baking dish with cold water, and place the beaten egg white in the baking dish. Sprinkle with a little salt and pepper. **4.** Make a small depression in the center of the white and slide the yolk into the depression. This looks like an egg in a nest. **5.** Place the Pyrex baking dish in a pan of warm water and place in moderate oven (350°F.) to bake. When the white begins to brown remove it from the oven and serve at once.

Exchange: 1 Meat.

COTTAGE CHEESE OMELET[2]

INGREDIENTS	AMOUNT Household Measure	Grams	C Gm.	P Gm.	F Gm.
egg......................	1	50	—	7	5
cottage cheese..............	1/4 cup	45	—	7	5
butter.....................	1 teaspoon	5	—	—	5
salt and pepper.............	few grains	—	—	—	—
Calories: 191.			—	14	15

1. Add 2 teaspoons water to the egg yolk, after separation of egg. **2.** Beat until thick and lemon-colored. **3.** Mix in the cottage cheese, salt and pepper, and fold yolk mixture into stiffly beaten egg white. **4.** Cook as an ordinary omelet, using the butter in the pan for browning.

Exchanges: 2 Meat; 1 Fat.

ASPARAGUS OMELET[2]

INGREDIENTS	AMOUNT Household Measure	Grams	C Gm.	P Gm.	F Gm.
eggs........................1 (or 2)		50	—	7	5
milk........................3 teaspoons		—	—	—	—
butter......................1 teaspoon		5	—	—	5
asparagus tips..............8		—	—	—	—
salt and pepper ....few grains		—	—	—	—
Calories: 118. (With 2 eggs, calories: 191.)			—	7	10

1. Heat cooked and seasoned asparagus in the butter. **2.** Make a plain omelet and fold asparagus tips in, letting tips protrude. Exchanges: 1 Meat (or 2, if 2 eggs used); 1 Fat; 1 A Vegetable.

FISH OMELET[2]

INGREDIENTS	AMOUNT Household Measure	Grams	C Gm.	P Gm.	F Gm.
eggs........................2		100	—	14	10
milk........................3 teaspoons		—	—	—	—
butter......................1 teaspoon		5	—	—	5
flaked fish.................1 ounce		30	—	7	5
salt........................few grains		—	—	—	—
Calories: 264.			—	21	20

1. Heat fish with the butter in saucepan. **2.** Make plain omelet and place fish in center. Then roll together. **3.** Serve on a hot plate.

Exchanges: 3 Meat; 1 Fat.

SPANISH OMELET[1]

INGREDIENTS	AMOUNT Household Measure	Grams	C Gm.	P Gm.	F Gm.
eggs........................2		100	—	14	10
butter......................1 teaspoon		5	—	—	5
onion, chopped..............1 teaspoon		5	—	—	—
salt and pepper.............to taste		—	—	—	—
green pepper, chopped.......1 teaspoon		5	—	—	—
Calories: 191.			—	14	15

1. Beat the eggs well and add 1 tablespoon water, salt, pepper, green pepper and onion. **2.** Melt the butter in a small frying pan. **3.** Add the mixture and allow to cook for a few seconds, and then stir. **4.** When brown remove from the pan and serve at once.

Exchanges: 2 Meat; 1 Fat.

EGGS FLORENTINE[2]

INGREDIENTS	AMOUNT Household Measure	Grams	C Gm.	P Gm.	F Gm.
cooked spinach	1/2 cup	100	—	—	—
egg	1	50	—	7	5
salt	to taste	—	—	—	—
evaporated milk	1/2 cup	120	12	8	10
American cheese	1 slice	30	—	7	5
corn flakes	1 tablespoon	—	—	—	—
Calories: 316.			12	22	20

1. Drain the cooked spinach and place it in a shallow individual baking dish. **2.** Make a depression for the egg. Break the egg into the depression and sprinkle with a little salt. **3.** Prepare a cheese sauce by melting the cheese and milk over boiling water, heating only until the cheese is melted. **4.** Pour this cheese sauce over the egg and spinach. **5.** Save 1 tablespoon corn flakes from your breakfast cereal for topping this mixture. Crumble corn flakes over the top and bake in a moderate oven (350°F.) until crumbs are brown and egg is set.

Exchanges: 1 A Vegetable; 2 Meat; 1 cup Milk.

SAVORY EGG ON TOAST[2]

INGREDIENTS	AMOUNT Household Measure	Grams	C Gm.	P Gm.	F Gm.
egg	1 ounce	30	—	7	5
chopped meat (chicken, tongue or ham)	1/2 teaspoon few grains	—	—	—	—
parsley, finely chopped	few grains	—	—	—	—
salt	1 teaspoon	5	—	—	5
pepper	1 slice	25	15	2	—
butter	1	50	—	7	5
bread, toasted					
Calories: 259.			15	16	15

1. Butter a small mold with 1/2 teaspoon of butter. **2.** Mix together chopped meat, parsley and seasonings. **3.** Sprinkle mixture into mold and shake around to stick on sides. **4.** Break an egg in carefully. Dot with remaining butter. **5.** Bake 10 minutes in moderately slow oven (325°F.) until set, and serve with toast on a hot plate.

Exchanges: 2 Meat; 1 Fat; 1 Bread.

SALADS

SUGGESTIONS FOR SALAD COMBINATIONS

FRUIT SALADS:

1. apple and celery.
2. apple, celery and pineapple.
3. grapefruit and lettuce.
4. orange and water cress.
5. pineapple with cottage cheese balls.
6. pineapple, orange and pears (water-pack).
7. pears.
8. orange and apple.

In every case the amount of fruit allowed on the diet should be used. If only one serving of fruit is allowed and the salad calls for two kinds of fruit, then the size of portions should be cut accordingly.

VEGETABLE SALADS:

1. asparagus on lettuce with hard-cooked eggs.
2. cabbage, shredded.
3. diced celery with radish.
4. cucumbers and green peppers.
5. tomatoes with other vegetables.
6. grated carrot and cabbage.
7. beets.
8. greens, such as lettuce, romaine, escarole, tossed with cubed tomatoes, radishes, celery, string beans.

TO STORE LETTUCE:

1. Wash lettuce. 2. Remove outside leaves. 3. Wrap in a damp towel and put into refrigerator until ready to use.

BLACK-EYED SUSAN[2]

INGREDIENTS	AMOUNT		C	P	F
	Household Measure	Grams	Gm.	Gm.	Gm.
orange.......................1		100	10	—	—
cream cheese................1 tablespoon		15	—	—	5
salt........................few grains		—	—	—	—
egg yolk (hard-cooked).......1 (see note below)		—	—	7	5
lettuce.....................1 leaf		—	—	—	—
French dressing.............1 tablespoon		15	—	—	5
Calories: 203.			10	7	15

1. Mash cheese and roll into ball. Add salt. 2. Peel orange and separate sections, removing all white membranes. 3. Grate the egg yolk. 4. Arrange lettuce leaf on cold plate. Place orange sections in center like petals of a flower. 5. Put cream cheese ball in center of orange sections. 6. Sprinkle with grated egg yolk. 7. Serve with French dressing.

Note: Do not discard the white of the egg—mix it in with fruit juice or milk used some other time during the day.

Exchanges: 1 Fruit; 1 Meat; 2 Fat.

LETTUCE SALAD²

INGREDIENTS	AMOUNT Household Measure	Grams	C Gm.	P Gm.	F Gm.
wedge of lettuce.............1		100	—	—	—
mayonnaise.................1 teaspoon		5	—	—	5
chili sauce..................1 teaspoon		5	—	—	—
Calories: 45.			—	—	5

1. Cut lettuce into wedge-shaped pieces (4 to 6 to a head). **2.** Use 1/2 lettuce leaf to garnish plates. Place wedge of lettuce on leaf, and cut each wedge twice. **3.** Mix mayonnaise with chili sauce, and serve.

Exchange: 1 Fat.

PICKLED BEETS²

INGREDIENTS	AMOUNT Household Measure	Grams	C Gm.	P Gm.	F Gm.
beets.......................1/2 cup		100	7	2	—
Sucaryl tablet...............1		—	—	—	—
cider vinegar...............1/2 cup		—	—	—	—
pickling spices...............1 tablespoon		—	—	—	—
(wrap in cheesecloth)					
salt.......................1/2 teaspoon		—	—	—	—
Calories: 36.			7	2	—

1. Slice beets. **2.** Bring vinegar and seasonings to a boil. Let simmer 5 minutes. **3.** Pour over beets and let stand in a cool place overnight.

Exchange: 1 B Vegetable.

CAULIFLOWER SALAD²

INGREDIENTS	AMOUNT Household Measure	Grams	C Gm.	P Gm.	F Gm.
cauliflower flowerets..........3		100	—	—	—
curry powder................1 teaspoon		5	—	—	—
mustard....................1/4 teaspoon		—	—	—	—
lemon juice.................1 teaspoon		—	—	—	—
Calories: negligible.			—	—	—

1. Cook the cauliflower, drain and cool. **2.** Serve on lettuce with a dressing of curry, mustard and lemon juice mixed well together.

Exchange: 1 A Vegetable.

CRAB MEAT AND CELERY SALAD[2]

INGREDIENTS	AMOUNT Household Measure	Grams	C Gm.	P Gm.	F Gm.
crab meat....................	1/4 cup	30	—	7	5
celery (chopped).............	1/4 cup	50	—	—	—
mayonnaise..................	1 teaspoon	5	—	—	5
lettuce......................	1 leaf	—	—	—	—
lemon juice.................	few drops	—	—	—	—
salt.........................	few grains	—	—	—	—
lemon.......................	1 slice	—	—	—	—
stuffed olive................	1	—	—	—	—
Calories: 118.			—	7	10

1. Drain the crab meat, take out fins and break up fine. 2. Add the celery, lemon juice and salt. 3. Mix and let stand for 10 minutes. 4. Add the mayonnaise and mix well. 5. Place lettuce leaf in salad bowl. 6. Place salad mixture on center of lettuce leaf. 7. Garnish with stuffed olive and a slice of lemon.

Exchanges: 1/2 A Vegetable; 1 Meat; 1 Fat.

BEET AND STRING BEAN SALAD[2]

INGREDIENTS	AMOUNT Household Measure	Grams	C Gm.	P Gm.	F Gm.
sliced beets.................	1/2 cup	100	7	2	—
string beans.................	1/2 cup	100	—	—	—
vinegar.....................	1/4 cup	—	—	—	—
Calories: 36.			7	2	—

1. Mix the sliced beets with the string beans. A few rings of onion and a teaspoon of diced celery may be added. 2. Mix with the vinegar and allow to stand until flavors blend. 3. Serve on a lettuce leaf.

Exchange: 1 B Vegetable.

CARROT AND RAISIN SALAD[2]

INGREDIENTS	AMOUNT Household Measure	Grams	C Gm.	P Gm.	F Gm.
carrot......................	1 small	100	7	2	—
raisins......................	2 tablespoons	15	10	—	—
mayonnaise..................	1 teaspoon	5	—	—	5
Calories: 121.			17	2	5

1. Grate the carrot and mix with washed raisins. 2. Mix carrot and raisins with mayonnaise. 3. Serve on lettuce leaf.

Exchanges: 1 B Vegetable; 1 Fruit; 1 Fat.

TOMATO ASPIC[2]

INGREDIENTS	AMOUNT Household Measure	Grams	C Gm.	P Gm.	F Gm.
gelatin, unflavored...........	1 teaspoon	5	—	—	—
tomatoes, canned............	1/2 cup	—	—	—	—
onion, chopped..............	1 teaspoon	—	—	—	—
cayenne....................	few grains	—	—	—	—
bay leaf...................	1	—	—	—	—
salt.......................	to taste	—	—	—	—
whole cloves................	2	—	—	—	—
celery, diced...............	1 teaspoon	—	—	—	—
vinegar....................	1 tablespoon	—	—	—	—
Calories: negligible.			—	—	—

1. Stir gelatin into 1/2 cup cold water. Let stand 15 minutes. 2. Combine diced onion, cayenne, bay leaf, salt, whole cloves, celery and tomatoes and boil until well flavored. 3. Strain. Add soaked gelatin and stir until dissolved. Let cool and add vinegar. 4. Put into individual mold. 5. If desired, celery and grated cabbage can be put into the aspic when it is partially set.

Exchange: 1 A Vegetable.

SALMON, CABBAGE, CELERY AND PICKLE SALAD[2]

INGREDIENTS	AMOUNT Household Measure	Grams	C Gm.	P Gm.	F Gm.
lettuce......................	3 leaves	—	—	—	—
salmon......................	1/4 cup	30	—	7	5
cabbage (shredded)..........	1/2 cup	100	—	—	—
tomato......................	1	100	—	—	—
celery (diced)...............	1 tablespoon	—	—	—	—
pickle (chopped).............	1 tablespoon	—	—	—	—
mayonnaise.................	1 teaspoon	5	—	—	5
Calories: 118.			—	7	10

1. Shred salmon. Mix together all ingredients, except lettuce and tomato, with mayonnaise. 2. Line a plate with three lettuce leaves and place salad thereon. 3. Garnish with tomato slices.

Exchanges: 2 A Vegetables (may be exchanged for 1 B Vegetable); 1 Meat; 1 Fat.

FRESH SHRIMP SALAD[2]

INGREDIENTS	AMOUNT Household Measure	Grams	C Gm.	P Gm.	F Gm.
lettuce.....................3 leaves		—	—	—	—
shrimps....................5 medium		45	—	7	5
French dressing.............1 tablespoon		15	—	—	5
olive.......................1		—	—	—	—
celery (chopped)............1 tablespoon		—	—	—	—
cocktail sauce (see recipe)....2 tablespoons		—	—	—	—
green pepper (chopped).......1 teaspoon		—	—	—	—
Calories: 118.			—	7	10

1. Shortly before serving, marinate separately shrimps and celery with French dressing. 2. Line a plate with crisp lettuce and place shrimps around edge of the plate. 3. Serve cocktail sauce in center and surround with the chopped celery. 4. Use olive and chopped pepper for garnish.

Exchanges: 1 Meat; 1 Fat.

TOMATO ASPIC WITH TUNA[2]

INGREDIENTS	AMOUNT Household Measure	Grams	C Gm.	P Gm.	F Gm.
gelatin, unflavored...........1 teaspoon		5	—	—	—
tomatoes, canned.............1/2 cup		100	—	—	—
Worcestershire sauce.........1/2 teaspoon		—	—	—	—
vinegar.....................2 tablespoons		—	—	—	—
paprika.....................few grains		—	—	—	—
salt........................few grains		—	—	—	—
onion juice..................1/2 teaspoon		—	—	—	—
lemon juice..................1/2 teaspoon		—	—	—	—
tuna fish....................1/4 cup		30	—	7	5
celery......................1 teaspoon		—	—	—	—
green pepper................1 teaspoon		—	—	—	—
lettuce.....................1 leaf		—	—	—	—
egg, hard-cooked.. 1		50	—	7	5
Calories: 146.			—	14	10

1. Stir the gelatin into 1/2 cup cold water. Let stand until gelatin swells. 2. Strain the tomatoes. Heat the juice and pour in the dissolved gelatin. 3. Add Worcestershire sauce, vinegar, paprika, salt, onion, and lemon juice. 4. Cool. When the mixture begins to thicken, add the flaked tuna. 5. Dice the celery. Chop green pepper fine and add to the gelatin mixture. Fill individual molds and chill. When firm serve on a lettuce leaf and garnish with sliced egg.

Exchange: 2 Meat.

HAM SALAD[2]

INGREDIENTS	AMOUNT Household Measure	Grams	C Gm.	P Gm.	F Gm.
ham, (cooked and chopped)...2 ounces		60	—	14	10
celery (chopped)..............1/4 cup		50	—	—	—
pickle relish.................1 tablespoon		—	—	—	—
mayonnaise.................1 teaspoon		5	—	—	5
Calories: 191.			—	14	15

1. Use leftover pieces of ham. Grind meat fine. 2. Combine all ingredients thoroughly. 3. Serve on lettuce leaf.

Exchanges: 2 Meat; 1 Fat.

EGG SALAD[2]

INGREDIENTS	AMOUNT Household Measure	Grams	C Gm.	P Gm.	F Gm.
eggs (hard-cooked)..........2		—	—	14	10
lettuce (crisp)..............3 leaves		—	—	—	—
mayonnaise.................1 teaspoon		5	—	—	5
olive (stuffed)..............1		—	—	—	—
Calories: 191.			—	14	15

1. Line a salad bowl with the lettuce. 2. Cut the eggs into quarters. 3. Place eggs in the bowl, flower fashion. 4. Place the mayonnaise in the center and garnish with an olive.

Exchanges: 2 Meat; 1 Fat.

BEEF SALAD[2]

INGREDIENTS	AMOUNT Household Measure	Grams	C Gm.	P Gm.	F Gm.
beef (chopped, cooked).......1 ounce		30	—	7	5
horseradish..................1/2 tablespoon		—	—	—	—
celery (chopped)............2 tablespoons		—	—	—	—
mayonnaise.................1 teaspoon		5	—	—	5
green pepper (chopped)......1/2 tablespoon		—	—	—	—
pickle relish.................1 tablespoon		—	—	—	—
Calories: 118.			—	7	10

1. Use leftover beef, ground fine. 2. Combine all ingredients well. 3. Serve on lettuce leaf.

Exchanges: 1 Meat; 1 Fat.

GOLDENROD EGG SALAD[1]

INGREDIENTS	AMOUNT Household Measure	Grams	C Gm.	P Gm.	F Gm.
egg..........................1		50	—	7	5
lettuce leaves...............2		—	—	—	—
Calories: 73.			—	7	5

1. Cook the egg until it is hard. Peel and separate the egg white from the yolk. **2.** Chop the white very fine and mash up the yolk. Use a fork to break up the yolk—it makes it more fluffy. **3.** Place the chopped white on a lettuce leaf and then sprinkle the yolk over the white. Garnish with a sprig of parsley.

If mayonnaise is desired for this salad, 1 teaspoon of mayonnaise or 1 tablespoon of French dressing can be used in exchange for 1 teaspoon of butter. This will add 45 calories.

Exchange: 1 Meat; 1 Fat, if mayonnaise or French dressing is used.

CHOPPED EGG AND CELERY SALAD[2]

INGREDIENTS	AMOUNT Household Measure	Grams	C Gm.	P Gm.	F Gm.
egg (hard-cooked)...........1		50	—	7	5
mayonnaise..................1 teaspoon		5	—	—	5
salt........................few grains		—	—	—	—
pepper......................few grains		—	—	—	—
celery (finely chopped).......1/4 cup		50	—	—	—
Calories: 118.			—	7	10

1. Chop egg and mix all ingredients together well. **2.** Serve on lettuce leaf.

Exchanges: 1/2 A Vegetable; 1 Meat; 1 Fat.

EGG AND BEET SALAD WITH FRESH GREENS[2]

INGREDIENTS	AMOUNT Household Measure	Grams	C Gm.	P Gm.	F Gm.
egg (hard-cooked)...........1		50	—	7	5
beets (cooked and diced).....1/2 cup		100	7	2	—
lettuce.....................1 leaf		—	—	—	—
mayonnaise..................1 teaspoon		5	—	—	5
water cress.................1 sprig		—	—	—	—
Calories: 154.			7	9	10

1. Dice egg and beets in 1/2-inch cubes. Mix together with 1 teaspoon mayonnaise. 2. Arrange lettuce leaf on a cold plate with salad in center. 3. Garnish with water cress.

Exchanges: 1 B Vegetable; 1 Meat; 1 Fat.

PICTURE SALAD[2]

INGREDIENTS	AMOUNT Household Measure	Grams	C Gm.	P Gm.	F Gm.
sliced tomato...............	1	—	—	—	—
cottage cheese..............	1/4 cup	45	—	7	5
egg, hard-cooked............	1	50	—	7	5
grapefruit slices............	1/2 of grapefruit	100	10	—	—
iceberg lettuce..............	2-3 leaves	—	—	—	—
water cress.................	1 sprig	—	—	—	—
French dressing.............	1 tablespoon	5	—	—	5
Calories: 231.			10	14	15

A medley of cottage cheese served on a slice of tomato, with slices of hard-cooked egg on lettuce leaf, grapefruit slices on lettuce leaf and garnished with water cress. Serve the French dressing in a small lettuce cup.

Exchanges: 1 A Vegetable; 1 Fruit; 2 Meat; 1 Fat.

FLORIDA LUNCHEON[2]

INGREDIENTS	AMOUNT Household Measure	Grams	C Gm.	P Gm.	F Gm.
grapefruit sections...........	1/2 of grapefruit	100	10	—	—
cottage cheese with chives....	1/4 cup	45	—	7	5
tomato.....................	1 small	100	—	—	—
egg, hard-cooked............	1	50	—	7	5
bread......................	1 slice	25	15	2	—
pimiento...................	1 teaspoon	—	—	—	—
Calories: 254.			25	16	10

1. Arrange on lettuce leaves, grapefruit sections, a mound of cottage cheese with chopped chives, and a small tomato cut into 4 wedges. 2. Chop the hard-cooked egg fine and mix with chopped pimiento. Use this as a spread on the bread. Make a half sandwich and then cut into 2 strips. Place these finger sandwiches on the platter.

Exchanges: 1 Fruit; 2 Meat; 1 Bread.

AMERICAN CHEESE AND TOMATO SALAD[2]

INGREDIENTS	AMOUNT Household Measure	Grams	C Gm.	P Gm.	F Gm.
American cheese (grated)......1	ounce	30	—	7	5
egg, hard-cooked (chopped)...1		50	—	7	5
tomato....................1	medium	—	—	—	—
French dressing..............1	tablespoon	15	—	—	5
mustard....................few grains		—	—	—	—
lettuce....................1	leaf	—	—	—	—
Calories: 191.			—	14	15

1. Combine cheese, egg, mustard and French dressing. **2.** Blend well and form into balls. Chill. **3.** Arrange lettuce leaf on a small, cold plate. **4.** Place tomato slices and cheese balls on the lettuce.

Exchanges: 1 A Vegetable; 2 Meat; 1 Fat.

WALDORF SALAD[2]

INGREDIENTS	AMOUNT Household Measure	Grams	C Gm.	P Gm.	F Gm.
apple......................1	medium	80	10	—	—
celery, diced................1/4	cup	20	—	—	—
lettuce....................few leaves		—	—	—	—
mayonnaise.................1	teaspoon	5	—	—	5
Calories: 85.			10	—	5

1. Cube apple and celery. Mix and add the mayonnaise. **2.** Serve on lettuce and garnish with 1/2 walnut meat.

Exchanges: 1 Fruit; 1 Fat.

ORANGE AND APPLE SALAD[1]

INGREDIENTS	AMOUNT Household Measure	Grams	C Gm.	P Gm.	F Gm.
orange....................1/2 small		50	5	—	—
apple, medium size..........1/2		40	5	—	—
Calories: 40.			10	—	—

1. Slice the apple and section the orange. Try to get as many slices of apple as you have sections of orange. **2.** Place alternate slices of orange and apple on a lettuce leaf.

Exchange: 1 Fruit.

ROQUEFORT CHEESE AND HEART OF LETTUCE SALAD WITH CHILI SAUCE[2]

INGREDIENTS	AMOUNT		C	P	F
	Household Measure	Grams	Gm.	Gm.	Gm.
lettuce...................	1/4 small head	—	—	—	—
Roquefort cheese............	1 ounce	30	—	7	5
chili sauce.................	1 ounce	—	—	—	—
French dressing............	1 tablespoon	15	—	—	5
Calories: 118.			—	7	10

1. Break cheese into crumbs. Combine with chili sauce and French dressing. **2.** Arrange lettuce on a cold plate and pour the cheese mixture over.

Exchanges: 1 Meat; 1 Fat.

POINSETTIA SALAD[2]

INGREDIENTS	AMOUNT		C	P	F
	Household Measure	Grams	Gm.	Gm.	Gm.
lettuce...................	3 leaves	—	—	—	—
tomato...................	1 medium	—	—	—	—
cottage cheese..............	1/4 cup	45	—	7	5
French dressing............	1 tablespoon	15	—	—	5
salt...................	few grains	—	—	—	—
pepper...................	few grains	—	—	—	—
paprika...................	few grains	—	—	—	—
Calories: 118.			—	7	10

1. Scald, peel and chill tomato. Cut into fifths from top to bottom, but do not sever from base. **2.** Fold back the five petals about one inch to form a flower, but leave the center pulp intact. **3.** Combine the cheese, salt and pepper and work into a cream. **4.** Put cheese on center pulp and top with paprika. **5.** On a cold plate arrange lettuce leaves with tomato in center. **6.** Serve with French dressing.

Exchanges: 1 Meat; 1 Fat.

STUFFED GREEN PEPPERS[2]

INGREDIENTS	AMOUNT		C	P	F
	Household Measure	Grams	Gm.	Gm.	Gm.
green pepper................	1	—	—	—	—
cottage cheese..............	1/4 cup	45	—	7	5
French dressing............	1 tablespoon	15	—	—	5
Calories: 118.			—	7	10

1. Select a smooth well-shaped green pepper. Cut a slice from the top. **2.** Remove pith and seeds and pack tightly with cottage cheese which has been seasoned to taste. Chill. **3.** Slice crosswise into 1/4-inch slices and place the slices on a lettuce leaf. **4.** Use a tablespoon of French dressing over the top.

Exchanges: 1 Meat; 1 Fat.

COTTAGE CHEESE, CRESS, DATE AND ENDIVE SALAD[2]

INGREDIENTS	AMOUNT		C	P	F
	Household Measure	Grams	Gm.	Gm.	Gm.
cottage cheese..............1/4 cup		45	—	7	5
dates......................2		15	10	—	—
French dressing.............1 tablespoon		15	—	—	5
endive.....................2 pieces		—	—	—	—
cress......................1 ounce		—	—	—	—
pimiento...................4 small pieces		—	—	—	—
Calories: 158.			10	7	10

1. Wash and pit dates. Stuff with cheese. Arrange on endive and garnish with cress. **2.** Top each date with a small piece of pimiento. Serve with French dressing, and extra cottage cheese on the side.

Exchanges: 1 Fruit; 1 Meat; 1 Fat.

PINEAPPLE-LIME SALAD[2]

INGREDIENTS	AMOUNT		C	P	F
	Household Measure	Grams	Gm.	Gm.	Gm.
pineapple, cubed.............1/2 cup		80	10	—	—
celery, diced................ 1 teaspoon		5	—	—	—
pimiento, chopped...........1 teaspoon		5	—	—	—
salt.......................to taste		—	—	—	—
vinegar....................1 tablespoon		—	—	—	—
lime saccharin-sweetened gelatin (Glow or D-Zerta brands)..................1 envelope		—	—	2	—
Calories: 48.			10	2	—

1. Cut the pineapple into cubes. Clean and dice celery, and pimiento. Measure out other ingredients. **2.** Dissolve the gelatin in 1/2 cup hot water. When the gelatin begins to set, add the fruit, celery and pimiento, which have been marinated in the vinegar and salt. **3.** Put into individual mold and let stand until set. **4.** Unmold and serve on crisp lettuce leaf.

Exchange: 1 Fruit.

	COFFEE, black
THESE FOODS MAY BE USED QUITE FREELY ON THE DIABETES DIET almost without measuring Carbohydrate or Calorie Content	

CLEAR BROTH or BOUILLON	TEA, plain or with lemon	VINEGAR or LEMON JUICE

GUM CANDY and other candy substitutes having little or no food value	NON-CALORIC CHEWING GUM	LOW CALORIE gelatin desserts

SPICES and HERBS	LOW CALORIE substitutes for JAM, JELLY and MARMALADE	CRANBERRIES or RHUBARB (sweetened with Saccharin or Sucaryl)
 Caution: Always measure Worcestershire sauce, catsup, etc.		

MAIN DISHES FOR LUNCH OR DINNER

BEEF STEW[2]

INGREDIENTS	AMOUNT Household Measure	Grams	C Gm.	P Gm.	F Gm.
beef (cubed)................ 2 ounces		60	—	14	10
peas........................1/4 cup		50	4	1	—
carrots....................1/4 cup		50	3	1	—
bay leaf....................1		—	—	—	—
salt.......................few grains		—	—	—	—
pepper.....................few grains		—	—	—	—
Calories: 182.			7	16	10

1. Brown the beef in frying pan. **2.** Add enough water to cover. **3.** Add bay leaf, pepper, and salt. **4.** Simmer until tender. **5.** Add cooked peas and carrots. (Other vegetables may be used if desired.)

Exchanges: 2 Meat; 1 B Vegetable.

CHICKEN AND SPAGHETTI[2]

INGREDIENTS	AMOUNT Household Measure	Grams	C Gm.	P Gm.	F Gm.
spaghetti, cooked............1/2 cup		100	15	2	—
diced chicken, cooked........2 ounces		60	—	14	10
Calories: 214.			15	16	10

1. The spaghetti should be cooked in chicken broth. This gives it extra flavor. **2.** Take the chicken from the breast of a chicken which has been cooked for the family. **3.** Mix the two and heat through. **4.** A little tomato juice may be added, to flavor.

Exchanges: 1 Bread; 2 Meat.

BEEF AND NOODLES[2]

INGREDIENTS	AMOUNT Household Measure	Grams	C Gm.	P Gm.	F Gm.
noodles, cooked..............1/2 cup		100	15	2	—
beef broth..................1 cup		240	—	—	—
onion.......................1, chopped		—	—	—	—
salt, pepper................to taste		—	—	—	—
celery salt.................to taste		—	—	—	—
beef, diced.................2 ounces		60	—	14	10
Calories: 214.			15	16	10

1. Cook noodles in hot beef broth to which the chopped onion, salt, pepper and celery salt have been added. 2. Cut pieces of beef from roast. Pieces should be about 1/2-inch cubes. 3. When the noodles are tender, add the diced meat. Cook together for a few minutes. 4. If desired the vegetable which is allowed for this meal may be added to this mixture. Carrots, peas, lima beans, diced celery are all good.

Exchanges: 1 Bread; 2 Meat.

CASSEROLE CHOP SUEY[2]

| INGREDIENTS | AMOUNT | | C | P | F |
	Household Measure	Grams	Gm.	Gm.	Gm.
veal, cut in fine strips.......	2 ounces	60	—	14	10
celery, cut in fine pieces.....	1 piece	10	—	—	—
salt.......................	to taste	—	—	—	—
meat stock (or bouillon made with 1 cup water and 1 cube)........	3/4 cup	180	—	—	—
onion.......................	1 slice	5	—	—	—
green pepper, chopped........	1 teaspoon	5	—	—	—
soy sauce...................	1/2 teaspoon	—	—	—	—
Calories: 146.			—	14	10

1. Place all the ingredients in an individual casserole and bake for about 3/4 hour in moderate oven (350°F.). 2. Uncover during last quarter of cooking to evaporate excess moisture.

Exchange: 2 Meat.

INDIVIDUAL MEAT LOAF[2]

| INGREDIENTS | AMOUNT | | C | P | F |
	Household Measure	Grams	Gm.	Gm.	Gm.
ground beef, veal and lamb...	3 ounces	90	—	21	15
salt and pepper.............	to taste	—	—	—	—
poultry seasoning...........	few grains	—	—	—	—
minced onion................	1 teaspoon	5	—	—	—
minced parsley..............	1/2 teaspoon	3	—	—	—
celery tops.................	1/8 cup	—	—	—	—
carrots, shredded...........	1/2 cup	100	7	2	—
Calories: 255.			7	23	15

1. Grease the bottom of a small individual baking pan (toy bread pan). 2. Pack the mixture made from all the above ingredients into the pan and smooth the top. 3. Bake in moderately slow oven (325°F.) until it is done in the center and nice and brown on top.

Exchanges: 3 Meat; 1 B Vegetable.

SWEDISH MEAT CAKES[2]

INGREDIENTS	AMOUNT Household Measure	Grams	C Gm.	P Gm.	F Gm.
ground beef, top round.......3 ounces		90	—	21	15
egg......................... 1		50	—	7	5
grated onion................ 1 teaspoon		5	—	—	—
carrot and turnips, diced and cooked................ 1/2 cup		100	7	2	—
caper, chopped.............. 1		—	—	—	—
evaporated milk............. 1 teaspoon		—	—	—	—
horseradish................. 1 teaspoon		—	—	—	—
salt and pepper............. to taste		—	—	—	—
Calories: 328.			7	30	20

1. Mix the chopped beef and unbeaten egg together. **2.** Add the remaining ingredients and mix well. **3.** Form into two patties. **4.** Chill thoroughly in refrigerator until ready to cook. **5.** Cook the meat cakes in a preheated broiler until brown on both sides.

Exchanges: 4 Meat; 1 B Vegetable.

SKEWERED LAMB

INGREDIENTS	AMOUNT Household Measure	Grams	C Gm.	P Gm.	F Gm.
lamb chop, lean............. 1		60	—	14	10
onion....................... 4 slices		50	4	1	—
salt and pepper............. to taste		—	—	—	—
Calories: 166.			4	15	10

1. Remove the bone from the chop and cut the meat into 4 pieces. **2.** Alternate pieces of lamb and slices of the onion on a skewer. **3.** Place in a shallow baking pan and place under the broiler. **4.** When brown on one side, turn and continue to broil until the meat is done. **5.** Season to taste and serve on the skewer if desired.

Exchanges: 1/2 B Vegetable; 2 Meat.

ROAST PORK[2]

INGREDIENTS	AMOUNT Household Measure	Grams	C Gm.	P Gm.	F Gm.
sliced pork or pork chop................ 2 ounces or small chop		60	—	14	10
apple, sliced................ small		80	10	—	—
butter...................... 1 teaspoon		5	—	—	5
Calories: 231.			10	14	15

1. Salt the meat to taste. **2.** Place the pork in a pan and cover with apple slices. **3.** Add the butter and a small amount of water. **4.** Cover the pan and bake 20 minutes in a moderate oven (350°F.).

Exchanges: 1 Fat; 1 Fruit; 2 Meat.

HUNGARIAN GOULASH[2]

INGREDIENTS	AMOUNT Household Measure	Grams	C Gm.	P Gm.	F Gm.
beef, top round (or any beef free from fat) cut in inch squares	3 ounces	90	—	21	15
pepper, diced	1 teaspoon	5	—	—	—
soup stock	1/4 cup	60	—	—	—
tomato juice	1/4 cup	60	—	—	—
carrots cut in inch lengths	1/2 cup	100	7	2	—
bay leaf	1	—	—	—	—
garlic	1/2 clove	—	—	—	—
salt and pepper	to taste	—	—	—	—
paprika	sprinkle	—	—	—	—
Calories: 255.			7	23	15

1. Place all ingredients except carrots in a small iron frying pan and cover. Let simmer for 2 hours. **2.** Add more soup stock or tomato juice if needed, and the carrots. **3.** Simmer 15 minutes longer.

Exchanges: 1 B Vegetable; 3 Meat.

CHICKEN WITH MUSHROOMS[2]

INGREDIENTS	AMOUNT Household Measure	Grams	C Gm.	P Gm.	F Gm.
chicken (broiler)	1/2 average	120	—	28	20
onion	2 teaspoons	—	—	—	—
butter	1 teaspoon	5	—	—	5
mushrooms	4	—	—	—	—
salt	few grains	—	—	—	—
pepper	few grains	—	—	—	—
Calories: 336.			—	28	25

1. Melt the butter. **2.** Place chicken and onion in pan and fry until golden brown. Add salt and pepper. **3.** Cover and cook slowly until done. **4.** Cook the mushrooms in boiling water. **5.** Drain and add to the chicken while it is still cooking.

Exchanges: 4 Meat; 1 Fat.

OVEN-FRIED CHICKEN[2]

INGREDIENTS	AMOUNT Household Measure	Grams	C Gm.	P Gm.	F Gm.
chicken, fryer................	1/4 of a 3-lb. fryer	90	—	21	15
corn flakes.................	3/4 cup	20	15	2	—
Calories: 287.			15	23	15

1. Wash the chicken and allow to remain damp. **2.** Crush the corn flakes and dip the chicken into the corn flakes until they are entirely used up. **3.** Place chicken in shallow baking dish, and bake in moderate oven (350°F.) for 3/4 hour or until golden brown and well done.

Exchanges: 3 Meat; 1 Bread.

CHICKEN SUPREME[2]

INGREDIENTS	AMOUNT Household Measure	Grams	C Gm.	P Gm.	F Gm.
canned, boned chicken.......	2 ounces	60	—	14	10
egg.........................	1	50	—	7	5
milk........................	1/4 cup	60	3	2	3
celery......................	1 stalk	25	—	—	—
salt and pepper.............	to taste	—	—	—	—
Calories: 266.			3	23	18

1. Beat the egg slightly. **2.** Add the chicken and celery, cut in small pieces. **3.** Add the milk, salt and pepper. **4.** Place in a mold or custard cup and set in pan of hot water. **5.** Bake in moderate oven (350°F.) until firm.

Exchanges: 3 Meat; 1/4 cup Milk from allowance.

HALIBUT CREOLE[1]

INGREDIENTS	AMOUNT Household Measure	Grams	C Gm.	P Gm.	F Gm.
tomatoes....................	1/2 cup	100	—	—	—
minced onion................	1 teaspoon	—	—	—	—
salt and pepper	pinch	—	—	—	—
butter......................	1 teaspoon	5	—	—	5
paprika.....................	sprinkle	—	—	—	—
halibut.....................	3 ounces (approximately 2-1/2 x 2-1/2 x 1 inch)	90	—	21	15
Calories: 264.			—	21	20

1. Cook the tomatoes, onion, pepper, salt and paprika together for about five minutes. **2.** Melt the butter, and add to the tomato mixture, stirring constantly. Cook for a few minutes more. **3.** Place the fish in a greased, shallow pan and pour the sauce over it. **4.** Bake in moderately hot oven (375°F.) for about 15 to 20 minutes, until the fish is cooked through. If the fish becomes dry add a small amount of water or tomato juice.

Exchanges: 1 A Vegetable; 1 Fat; 3 Meat. (If the diet calls for only 2 ounces of meat this same recipe can be prepared with only 2 ounces of halibut.)

SALMON LOAF[2]

INGREDIENTS	AMOUNT Household Measure	Grams	C Gm.	P Gm.	F Gm.
canned salmon...............	1/4 cup	30	—	7	5
egg........................	1	50	—	7	5
butter.....................	1 teaspoon	5	—	—	5
milk, skim	1/4 cup	60	3	2	—
vinegar....................	2 teaspoons	—	—	—	—
gelatin....................	1/2 teaspoon	—	—	—	—
salt.......................	to taste	—	—	—	—
cucumber..................	several slices	—	—	—	—
Calories: 238.			3	16	15

1. Flake the salmon. **2.** Add the beaten egg, melted butter, milk, vinegar and salt. **3.** Cook in the top of a double boiler stirring constantly until the mixture thickens. **4.** Soak gelatin in 1 tablespoon cold water and add to the salmon. **5.** Fill the mold or custard cup, chill and serve with sliced cucumbers.

Exchanges: 2 Meat; 1 Fat; 1/4 cup Skim Milk from allowance.

MACARONI AND CHEESE[2]

INGREDIENTS	AMOUNT Household Measure	Grams	C Gm.	P Gm.	F Gm.
macaroni (cooked)...........	1/2 cup	100	15	2	—
cheese (cheddar).............	1 ounce	30	—	7	5
milk.......................	1/2 cup	120	6	4	5
salt and pepper.............	to taste	—	—	—	—
Calories: 226.			21	13	10

1. Heat the milk. **2.** Cut the cheese into small pieces and place in the hot milk. **3.** Place the cooked macaroni in an individual casserole. **4.** Pour the milk and cheese mixture over the macaroni. Season. **5.** Place in a moderate oven (350°F.) to cook and brown.

Exchanges: 1 Bread; 1 Meat; 1/2 cup Milk.

FINNAN HADDIE CALEDONIA[2]

INGREDIENTS	AMOUNT Household Measure	Grams	C Gm.	P Gm.	F Gm.
finnan haddie...............	3 ounces	90	—	21	15
milk.......................	1 cup	240	12	8	10
bay leaf....................	1	—	—	—	—
thyme.....................	pinch	—	—	—	—
peppercorns................	2-3	—	—	—	—
paprika....................	sprinkle	—	—	—	—
Calories: 389.			12	29	25

1. Soak the finnan haddie with bone and skin in cold water for one hour. **2.** Lay skin side down on baking dish. **3.** Cover with cold milk. Add bay leaf, pinch of thyme and the peppercorns. **4.** Heat very slowly for about 30 minutes without letting the milk boil. **5.** Drain off the milk and reserve it. **6.** Bake the fish in a moderate oven (350°F.) for about 25 minutes, pouring the milk back over the fish about 10 minutes before it leaves the oven. **7.** Sprinkle with paprika and serve.

Exchanges: 3 Meat; 1 Milk.

BOILED BEEF PLATE[2]

INGREDIENTS	AMOUNT Household Measure	Grams	C Gm.	P Gm.	F Gm.
boiled beef..................	2 ounces	60	—	14	10
horseradish.................	1 tablespoon	—	—	—	—
potato......................	1 medium	100	15	2	—
spinach greens..............	1/2 cup	100	—	—	—
Calories: 214.			15	16	10

1. Arrange on dinner plate.

Exchanges: 2 Meat; 1 Bread; 1 A Vegetable.

COLD HAM PLATE[2]

INGREDIENTS	AMOUNT Household Measure	Grams	C Gm.	P Gm.	F Gm.
cold ham...................	1 ounce	30	—	7	5
deviled egg.................	1	50	—	7	5
tomato, sliced..............	1 small	100	—	—	—
Calories: 146.			—	14	10

1. Arrange on cold dinner plate.

Exchange: 2 Meat.

COLD PLATE FOR HOT DAY[2]

INGREDIENTS	AMOUNT Household Measure	Grams	C Gm.	P Gm.	F Gm.
cold cut.....................	1 slice	45	—	7	5
cottage cheese...............	1/4 cup	45	—	7	5
radish roses.................	3	—	—	—	—
celery heart.................	1	—	—	—	—
pear, canned................	1 medium	100	10	—	—
bread.......................	1 slice	25	15	2	—
peanut butter...............	2 tablespoons	30	—	7	5
Calories: 327.			25	23	15

1. After salad greens are prepared they should be allowed to stand in the refrigerator until crisp. **2.** Take two halves of the pear and place 1 tablespoon of peanut butter in the hollow, and place pear halves together. **3.** Cut the slice of bread in half and spread 1 tablespoon of peanut butter on one half. Place the other half on top and then cut the half sandwich into 2 strips or fingers. **4.** Arrange the stuffed pear on a crisp lettuce leaf and garnish with a sprig of mint. Place this in center of plate. Around the side place slice of bologna, cottage cheese in cup of lettuce, celery heart and radish rose with finger sandwiches.

Exchanges: 3 Meat; 1 Fruit; 1 Bread.

CABBAGE BUNDLE[2]

INGREDIENTS	AMOUNT Household Measure	Grams	C Gm.	P Gm.	F Gm.
cabbage leaf.................	1 large	—	—	—	—
ground cooked ham..........	2 slices	60	—	14	10
cooked rice.................	1/2 cup	100	15	2	—
cheddar cheese, shredded.....	1 slice	30	—	7	5
chopped onion..............	1 teaspoon	5	—	—	—
chopped green pepper........	1 teaspoon	5	—	—	—
salt, pepper.................	to taste	—	—	—	—
tomato purée...............	1/4 cup	50	—	—	—
Calories: 287.			15	23	15

1. Cook cabbage leaf in boiling salted water until almost tender. Drain well. **2.** Combine the ground cooked ham with the cooked rice, shredded cheese, onion, green pepper and seasonings. **3.** Place the mixture in the center of the cabbage leaf and wrap the leaf around it. **4.** Place the bundle in a shallow baking dish and pour over it the tomato purée and 1/4 cup water. Bake for about 10 minutes until heated through.

Exchanges: 3 Meat; 1 Bread.

RICE AND FRANKFURTER SPECIAL[2]

INGREDIENTS	AMOUNT Household Measure	Grams	C Gm.	P Gm.	F Gm.
V-8 vegetable juice	1/2 cup	100	3	1	—
rice, cooked	1/2 cup	100	15	2	—
green pepper, chopped	1 teaspoon	5	—	—	—
cooked frankfurter	1	50	—	7	5
Italian-type cheese	1 slice	30	—	7	5
Calories: 230.			18	17	10

1. Cook rice, V-8 and green pepper together for a few minutes until the rice is well done. Add salt and pepper to taste. **2.** Slice the frankfurter and add to the mixture. **3.** Place the mixture in a casserole and sprinkle the cheese, which has been grated, over the top. **4.** Serve hot in the casserole.

Exchanges: 1 A Vegetable; 1 Bread; 2 Meat.

SCALLOPED OYSTERS[2]

INGREDIENTS	AMOUNT Household Measure	Grams	C Gm.	P Gm.	F Gm.
oysters	5	45	—	7	5
corn flakes	3/4 cup	20	15	2	—
butter	1 teaspoon	5	—	—	5
oyster liquor	2 tablespoons	—	—	—	—
salt and pepper	to taste	—	—	—	—
Calories: 186.			15	9	10

1. Wash the oysters. **2.** Mix the melted butter with crushed corn flakes. **3.** Place some of corn flakes in an individual baking dish. **4.** Put in oysters and sprinkle with salt and pepper. **5.** Cover with a layer of corn flakes, and moisten with oyster liquor. **6.** Bake in a hot oven (400°F.) until the oysters are plump, and the corn flakes brown. A little nutmeg sprinkled over the top may improve the flavor.

Exchanges: 1 Meat; 1 Bread; 1 Fat.

SPAM AND SCRAMBLED EGGS[2]

INGREDIENTS	AMOUNT Household Measure	Grams	C Gm.	P Gm.	F Gm.
Spam	2 slices	60	—	14	10
egg	1	50	—	7	5
Calories: 219.			—	21	15

1. Scramble the egg and serve on side of 2 slices of hot Spam. Garnish with sprigs of parsley. 2. Tomato juice served as first course is a suggestion. 3. Bread may be toasted and served under the scrambled eggs if so desired.

Exchange: 3 Meat.

CORN PUDDING[2]

INGREDIENTS	AMOUNT Household Measure	Grams	C Gm.	P Gm.	F Gm.
corn (crushed)	1/4 cup	80	15	2	—
butter	1 teaspoon	5	—	—	5
egg	1	50	—	7	5
salt	few grains	—	—	—	—
pepper	few grains	—	—	—	—
Calories: 186.			15	9	10

1. Beat egg. Mix with corn, pepper and salt. 2. Pour the mixture into an individual baking dish. Place butter on top. 3. Place in baking pan, surrounded by water. Bake in moderate oven (350°F.) for about 20 minutes. 4. Pudding is done when an inserted silver knife comes out clean. (You may use more butter if it is allowed on your diet.)

Exchanges: 1 Bread; 1 Meat; 1 Fat.

VEGETABLES

Vegetables for the diabetic are determined by the diet. The vegetables may be combined with the meat as one will see by glancing over the luncheon and dinner recipes. Varieties of soup may be prepared by using the allowed vegetables in broth or with the allowed milk. Vegetables may be served plain by steaming, baking or boiling. Raw vegetables are also welcome, and may be combined in salads of various descriptions. Following are some suggestions for the use of the "A" and "B" vegetables on the diet for the diabetic.

THE "A" VEGETABLES

ASPARAGUS may be served hot or cold. When served hot it may be served plain or in broth or hot milk. When served cold, asparagus may be combined in salads with egg, tuna fish or pineapple.

STRING BEANS may also be served hot or cold. When served hot they are tasty with bacon. A Fat Exchange may be used for one slice of bacon. As a salad string beans are good with sliced onion and vinegar dressing.

BROCCOLI served hot with a slice of lemon is delicious. Be very careful when cooking not to break up the stalks.

BRUSSELS SPROUTS carefully cooked so the leaves don't turn brown are very tasty served plain, well seasoned with salt and pepper.

CABBAGE lends itself well to a variety of dishes. Hot quarters of cabbage are delicious with corned beef or ham. Do not cook cabbage until it is overdone. Golden yellow leaves taste so good. Cabbage is also good chopped up with green pepper.

CAULIFLOWER may be served hot or cold. Steam cauliflower until tender, but not overdone. Sprinkle with a little paprika to give color. Cold flowerets of cauliflower are good with salads.

CELERY can be served as a side dish, chopped fine in salads or as a vegetable itself.

CHICORY makes a nice salad base. The leaves of chicory may be cup up fine and mixed with vinegar and Sacrose liquid sweetener or a Sucaryl tablet, and served as a salad. Chicory may also be mixed with cut-up tomatoes, celery, cabbage, peppers and other "A" vegetables as a tossed salad. Always season well with salt and pepper.

CUCUMBERS may be peeled, diced, boiled and served hot with a little vinegar. They are delicious sliced with the green skin on and served with onion and vinegar. Grated, they taste good with fish.

EGGPLANT may be diced, and then boiled or baked. If fried, the diabetic may have to use some Fat Exchanges and Bread Exchanges. A suggestion is that the eggplant be peeled and sliced; then, using 3/4 cup of corn flakes as a Bread Exchange, the eggplant slices can be dipped into the corn flakes and baked with dabs of Fat Exchanges. Season with salt and pepper.

ESCAROLE is a salad vegetable and works in well with all sorts of tossed salad combinations.

"GREENS" are good as salad bases or they may be served hot, seasoned well.

MUSHROOMS may be cooked and mashed and mixed with hot milk to make mushroom soup, or they may be browned in a Fat Exchange and served with chicken or steak.

OKRA diced and served in soups is well liked.

PEPPER, GREEN can be stuffed with chopped ham, egg, or cottage cheese and baked or served cold on lettuce. Peppers also add flavor to cooked meats, and, served raw, add flavor to salads.

RADISHES are attractive as garnishes and also mixed into tossed salads.

SAUERKRAUT, hot and steaming, served with a pork chop as the Meat Exchange, or frankfurters, is always a good dish on a cold day. The juice is good, too.

SUMMER SQUASH steamed and strained with salt and pepper is very good.

TOMATOES, cooked or cold, lend themselves to many varieties of recipes which will be found in other pages of the book. The juice of the tomato is good hot or cold.

THE "B" VEGETABLES

The B vegetables must be measured carefully and 1 serving is usually equal to 1/2 cup measure.

BEETS may be diced or sliced and served hot or cold. Vinegar and cloves make them taste better. Combined with eggs, beets make good salads.

CARROTS lend color and can be used in many ways: carrot sticks raw or cooked; carrot circles raw or cooked; combined with peas as a hot vegetable; strained and combined with milk for carrot soup; raw, grated and mixed with raisins as the Fruit Exchange and mayonnaise as the Fat Exchange.

ONIONS are flavorful. They are excellent in salads, and are also good served as a boiled vegetable.

PEAS are usually served as a hot vegetable. They may also be served cold in salads.

PUMPKIN is a nice change and is best baked and mashed, and then seasoned well with salt and pepper.

RUTABAGAS and TURNIPS, especially yellow turnips, have a delicious flavor. Dice them or mash them, season with salt and pepper. Try them with turkey as the Meat Exchange.

WINTER SQUASH is good baked, steamed or boiled.

VEGETABLES CONSIDERED AS BREAD EXCHANGES

Vegetables which are higher in carbohydrate than the "A" or "B" vegetables are considered as Bread Exchanges. These include:

Beans and Peas, dried, such as lima, navy, cowpeas, split peas, etc.	Corn Parsnips Potatoes, white or sweet

CORN can be served on the cob or off, plain. It may also be combined with egg and milk, and made into a corn custard.

POTATOES may be baked or boiled. If they are mashed, the milk and butter used in the mashing must be taken from the allowance for the meal.

For potato salad, cube boiled potatoes and mix with some celery and mayonnaise (as a Fat Exchange). Serve on a lettuce leaf with hard-cooked egg (as a Meat Exchange). Use only the amount your diet permits. For variety sprinkle vegetable dishes with grated cheese and brown in the broiler.

GREEN BEANS HONGROISE

INGREDIENTS	AMOUNT Household Measure	Grams	C Gm.	P Gm.	F Gm.
mushrooms...............	1/2 cup	100	—	—	—
butter or margarine.........	1 teaspoon	5	—	—	5
green beans, cooked.........	1/2 cup	100	—	—	—
Yogurt, Dannon's...........	1/4 cup	60	3	2	3
salt......................	to taste	—	—	—	—
pepper...................	to taste	—	—	—	—
nutmeg..................	few grains	—	—	—	—
Calories: 92.			3	2	8

1. Brown the mushrooms in the butter. 2. Add the green beans, yogurt and seasonings. 3. Heat thoroughly and serve.

Exchanges: 2 A Vegetables; 1 Fat; 1/4 cup milk.

BAKED STUFFED POTATO[1]

INGREDIENTS	AMOUNT Household Measure	Grams	C Gm.	P Gm.	F Gm.
potato....................	1 small—2-inch	100	15	2	—
butter...................	1 teaspoon	5	—	—	5
cheese, grated............	1 ounce	30	—	7	5
Calories: 186.			15	9	10

1. Wash and bake the potato. 2. Take from the oven and cut a small piece off the top. Scoop out the potato, trying not to break the shell. 3. Mash the potato, using the butter allowed. 4. Mix the grated cheese with the mashed potato, and replace the mixture in the shell. 5. Return to the oven and bake until the top is a golden brown. Sprinkle with paprika if desired.

Exchanges: 1 Bread; 1 Meat; 1 Fat.

STEAMED CARROT PUDDING

INGREDIENTS	AMOUNT Household Measure	Grams	C Gm.	P Gm.	F Gm.
carrot, finely shredded.......	1/2 cup	100	7	2	—
grated lemon peel..........	2 teaspoons	—	—	—	—
Wheat Krumbles or Wheaties..	3/4 cup, scant	20	15	2	—
egg......................	1	50	—	7	5
lemon juice................	1 tablespoon	—	—	—	—
Sacrose..................	1 teaspoon	—	—	—	—
Calories: 177.			22	11	5

1. Place the carrot, lemon peel and Wheat Krumbles or Wheaties in a mixing bowl. 2. Beat the egg, lemon juice and Sacrose together until thoroughly mixed. Add to the carrot and mix well. 3. Place pudding mixture in an individual greased Pyrex baking dish. Cover tightly with waxed paper or aluminum foil. 4. Place on a rack in a kettle. Add boiling water to depth of 1 inch in kettle. Cover tightly and steam for one hour. 5. Serve the pudding hot. If exchange permits, use Imitation "Whipped Cream" to garnish.

Exchanges: 1 B Vegetable; 1 Bread; 1 Meat.

SANDWICHES

The diabetic often does not have an allowance of two pieces of bread for a sandwich. However, if the diet is liberal there are many varieties of sandwiches. Sandwich combinations must be foods on the Exchange lists.

Mayonnaise must be used only if the individual has enough Fat Exchanges.

Sandwiches for diabetics can be made up of luncheon meats, cheese, sardines and cold roast meat as well as chicken and turkey. Eggs lend themselves to a variety of sandwich mixes combined with peppers, pickles or olives.

Since 1 tablespoon of cream cheese is an Exchange for 1 teaspoon of butter, one has more to work with if cream cheese is used in place of butter.

CHOPPED BOLOGNA SANDWICH[1]

INGREDIENTS	AMOUNT Household Measure	Grams	C Gm.	P Gm.	F Gm.
margarine or butter	1 teaspoon	5	—	—	5
bologna	1 slice 4¼ x ⅛-inch thick	45	—	7	5
salt	few grains	—	—	—	—
horseradish	1/4 teaspoon	—	—	—	—
onion, grated	1 teaspoon	5	—	—	—
green pepper, chopped	1 teaspoon	5	—	—	—
egg	1	50	—	7	5
Calories in filling: 191, plus 68 for each slice of bread.			—	14	15

1. Melt the butter in the top of a double boiler. 2. Add the chopped pepper, onion, horseradish and salt. 3. Chop the sliced bologna and mix with the other ingredients. 4. Beat the egg well and add to the mixture. Cook slowly until the pepper and onion are soft. This can be spread between two slices of bread or on a split 1-ounce sandwich roll.

Exchanges: 2 Meat; 1 Fat; 1 or 2 Bread, depending on choice.

HAMBURGER ROLL²

INGREDIENTS	AMOUNT Household Measure	Grams	C Gm.	P Gm.	F Gm.
roll.........................	1—2-inch diam.	30	15	2	—
beef, chopped...............	1 ounce	30	—	7	5
onion, chopped fine..........	1 teaspoon	—	—	—	—
Calories: 141.			15	9	5

1. Make small flat cake of ground meat and pan broil. **2.** Serve on roll, topped with onion and thin slice of pickle if desired.

Exchanges: 1 Bread; 1 Meat.

HAMBURGER CHEESE BUN²

INGREDIENTS	AMOUNT Household Measure	Grams	C Gm.	P Gm.	F Gm.
ground beef patty............	2 ounces	60	—	14	10
old English cheese............	1 slice	30	—	7	5
round bun....................	2-inch diam.	25	15	2	—
dill pickle...................	1 strip	—	—	—	—
mayonnaise..................	1 teaspoon	5	—	—	5
Calories: 332.			15	23	20

1. Shape the beef into a patty, and broil. **2.** Split and toast the bun. Cover the lower half with a slice of cheese. **3.** Place bun under a slow broiler until the cheese is melted. **4.** Place hot hamburger in bun and top with dill pickle. **5.** Spread with mayonnaise, and serve at once. These sandwiches can be prepared for the whole family.

Exchanges: 3 Meat; 1 Bread; 1 Fat.

PIMIENTO, CHEESE, EGG, GREEN PEPPER SANDWICH¹

INGREDIENTS	AMOUNT Household Measure	Grams	C Gm.	P Gm.	F Gm.
pimiento cream cheese.......	1 tablespoon	15	—	—	5
egg, hard-cooked............	1	50	—	7	5
mustard....................	1/4 teaspoon	—	—	—	—
green pepper, chopped.......	1 teaspoon	5	—	—	—
Calories: 118, plus 68 for each slice of bread.			—	7	10

1. Chop the egg and mix with cream cheese, mustard and pepper. **2.** Spread on the amount of bread allowed for the meal.

Exchanges: 1 Meat; 1 Fat; 1 or more Bread, depending on diet.

SALMON SANDWICH DELUXE[2]

INGREDIENTS	AMOUNT Household Measure	Grams	C Gm.	P Gm.	F Gm.
salmon	1/4 cup	30	—	7	5
horseradish	1 teaspoon	5	—	—	—
lemon juice	few drops	—	—	—	—
mayonnaise	1 teaspoon	5	—	—	5
salt, pepper	to taste	—	—	—	—
bread, enriched white	2 slices	50	30	4	—
cheese	1 slice	30	—	7	5
milk, whole	1/2 cup	120	6	4	5
Calories: 412.			36	22	20

1. Flake the salmon and remove the bones. **2.** Mix the salmon with the horseradish, lemon juice, mayonnaise and seasonings. **3.** Spread between the two slices of bread, place in the broiler and toast on both sides. **4.** Place milk in top of double boiler and heat. Add cheese and allow to melt. **5.** Place the sandwich on a hot plate, and pour over it the cheese mixture.

Exchanges: 2 Meat; 2 Bread; 1 Fat; 1/2 cup Whole Milk, from allowed amount.

BEEF OR CHICKEN AND CELERY SANDWICH[1]

INGREDIENTS	AMOUNT Household Measure	Grams	C Gm.	P Gm.	F Gm.
cooked beef or chicken	1 ounce	30	—	7	5
celery, chopped	1 teaspoon	5	—	—	—
pickle relish	1 teaspoon	5	—	—	—
mayonnaise	1 teaspoon	5	—	—	5
Calories: 118, plus 68 for each slice of bread.			—	7	10

1. Combine chopped beef or chicken with the celery, pickle relish and mayonnaise. **2.** Spread on the amount of bread allowed.

Exchanges: 1 Meat; 1 Fat; 1 or 2 Bread, depending on diet.

VEGETABLE SANDWICH[1]

INGREDIENTS	AMOUNT Household Measure	Grams	C Gm.	P Gm.	F Gm.
carrot, raw, grated	1/2 cup	100	7	2	—
celery, chopped fine	1 teaspoon	5	—	—	—
cabbage, grated	1 teaspoon	5	—	—	—
chili sauce	1/2 teaspoon	—	—	—	—
mayonnaise	1 teaspoon	5	—	—	5
Calories: 81, plus 68 for each slice of bread.			7	2	5

1. Combine all the ingredients and use with the allowed amount of bread.

Exchanges: 1 B Vegetable; 1 Fat; 1 or 2 Bread, depending on diet.

EGG AND CHICKEN LIVER SANDWICH[2]

INGREDIENTS	AMOUNT Household Measure	Grams	C Gm.	P Gm.	F Gm.
chicken liver	1 ounce	30	—	7	5
egg	1	50	—	7	5
bread	2 slices	50	30	4	—
butter	1 teaspoon	5	—	—	5
olive, stuffed	1	—	—	—	—
Calories: 327.			30	18	15

1. Cook liver and chop it fine. **2.** Beat egg and add liver. **3.** Fry in one teaspoon of butter. **4.** Serve on bread with olive slices.

Exchanges: 2 Meat; 2 Bread; 1 Fat.

LUSCIOUS SANDWICH[2]

INGREDIENTS	AMOUNT Household Measure	Grams	C Gm.	P Gm.	F Gm.
egg, hard-cooked	1	50	—	7	5
cream cheese	1 teaspoon	5	—	—	5
green pepper, chopped	1 teaspoon	5	—	—	—
onion, chopped	½ teaspoon	3	—	—	—
lettuce	1 leaf	—	—	—	—
bread, whole wheat	2 slices	50	30	4	—
Calories: 254.			30	11	10

1. Chop the egg. Combine with the cream cheese, chopped pepper and onion. **2.** Season to taste with a little salt. **3.** Spread on one slice of bread with lettuce, and cover.

Exchanges: 1 Meat; 1 Fat; 2 Bread.

SAUCES AND RELISHES

CUCUMBER RELISH[2]

This is particularly good with fish. Grate 1/2 cucumber and mix in a small piece of red pepper which has been finely chopped. Season with salt, pepper and vinegar.

Calories: negligible.

Exchange: 1 A Vegetable.

UNCOOKED TOMATO PICKLE[1]

(By Mrs. N. Maxwell, Toronto, Canada)

INGREDIENTS	AMOUNT Household Measure	Grams	C Gm.	P Gm.	F Gm.
ripe tomatoes...............	4 quarts	3,000	120	30	8
chopped onions..............	1-1/2 cups	240	24	2	—
diced celery.................	4 cups	400	15	5	—
sweet red pepper, chopped....	1/4 cup	—	—	—	—
cider vinegar................	2-1/2 cups	600	30	—	—
salt........................	1/2 cup	—	—	—	—
mustard seed................	2 tablespoons	—	—	—	—
Sacrose (liquid sweetener).....	to taste, if desired	—	—	—	—
Makes 5 pints. Calories in 1 pint: 195. The fuel value of this pickle is very low, and it may be eaten in moderation as desired.			189	37	8

1. Chop onions and tomatoes fine and place in separate containers. Add 1/4 cup salt to each and let stand 3 hours. 2. Drain overnight. 3. Add remaining ingredients and pack in sterile jars. Seal airtight. This pickle has kept for as long as three years.

MUSTARD SAUCE

INGREDIENTS	AMOUNT Household Measure	Grams	C Gm.	P Gm.	F Gm.
cornstarch..................	2 tablespoons	16	14	—	—
dry mustard................	3 tablespoons		—	—	—
cold water.................	1/4 cup	60	—	—	—
Worcestershire sauce........	1 teaspoon		—	—	—
Kitchen Bouquet.............	1/4 teaspoon		—	—	—
vinegar....................	2 tablespoons		—	—	—
boiling water...............	3/4 cup	180	—	—	—
Sacrose (liquid sweetener).....	1 teaspoon		—	—	—
	1 cup		14	—	—
	1 tablespoon		1	—	—

Makes 1 cup (56 calories). Calories in 1 tablespoon: 4.

1. Blend cornstarch, mustard, cold water, Worcestershire sauce, Kitchen Bouquet and vinegar in a small saucepan, until smooth. 2. Add boiling water and cook, stirring constantly until the sauce thickens and boils. 3. Remove from the heat and add Sacrose. Serve on meat, fish or salad.

Exchange: If only 1 tablespoon is used this contains negligible carbohydrate. Only when more is used at a time should an Exchange be made.

HOLIDAY RELISH[2]

INGREDIENTS	AMOUNT Household Measure	Grams	C Gm.	P Gm.	F Gm.
green pepper.................1		50	—	—	—
red pepper..................1		50	—	—	—
onion.......................1/2 small		25	—	—	—
vinegar....................1 tablespoon		—	—	—	—
Sucaryl or saccharin..........1 tablet		—	—	—	—
Calories: negligible.			—	—	—

1. Place ingredients in a saucepan and cover with water. Salt to taste. Boil till tender.

Exchange: 1 A Vegetable.

LOW-CALORIE CATSUP

INGREDIENTS	AMOUNT Household Measure	Grams	C Gm.	P Gm.	F Gm.
tomato purée.................1 cup		249	18	5	1
lemon juice..................1 tablespoon		—	—	—	—
dry mustard.................1/2 teaspoon		—	—	—	—
allspice.....................1/8 teaspoon		—	—	—	—
Sacrose saccharin solution ...1 teaspoon		—	—	—	—
	8 Tablespoons		18	5	1
	1 Tablespoon		2.3	0.6	—

Makes 1/2 cup (101 calories). Calories in 1 tablespoon: 13.

1. Place the tomato purée in a saucepan. **2.** Add the lemon juice, mustard and allspice. Bring to a boil. **3.** Let simmer over low heat until of desired consistency, about 10 minutes. **4.** Remove from the heat and stir in the Sacrose. **5.** Use as dressing for cooked vegetables, meat or fish, or add horseradish and use as cocktail sauce on seafoods.

Exchange: 1 tablespoon for 1 serving of A Vegetable.

SWEET AND PUNGENT SAUCE

INGREDIENTS	AMOUNT Household Measure	Grams	C Gm.	P Gm.	F Gm.
chicken broth...............1/2 cup		120	—	—	—
vinegar....................2 tablespoons		—	—	—	—
cornstarch.................2 teaspoons		6	5	—	—
Sacrose (liquid sweetener).....1 teaspoon		—	—	—	—
Calories: 20.			5	—	—

1. Blend together in a saucepan the chicken broth, vinegar, and cornstarch. **2.** Bring to a boil and cook over moderate heat, stirring constantly, about 1 minute, until the sauce thickens. **3.** Remove from the heat and stir in Sacrose. Serve as a sauce with cooked vegetables, poached fish, tongue, eggplant or any seafood. Exchange: None.

COOKED SALAD DRESSING

| INGREDIENTS | AMOUNT | | C | P | F |
	Household Measure	Grams	Gm.	Gm.	Gm.
non-fat milk powder.........	5 tablespoons	50	24	16	—
flour.......................	2 tablespoons	14	10	1	—
salt.......................	1 teaspoon	—	—	—	—
dry mustard................	1 teaspoon	—	—	—	—
egg, beaten................	1	50	—	7	5
oil........................	2 tablespoons	30	—	—	30
lemon juice................	1/4 cup	50	5	—	—
Sacrose (liquid sweetener).....	1 teaspoon	—	—	—	—
	8 servings		39	24	35
	1 serving		5	3	4

Makes 8 servings (567 calories). Calories in 1 serving: 70.

1. Place milk solids, flour, salt, mustard and 1 cup water in a jar with a tight-fitting cover. Shake until well blended. **2.** Pour into a saucepan and cook over moderate heat, stirring constantly until the mixture thickens. **3.** Blend together the egg, oil and lemon juice. Add the cooked mixture to the beaten egg gradually, to prevent curdling. **4.** Return to the saucepan and cook over very low heat 5 minutes more, stirring constantly. **5.** Remove from the heat and stir in the Sacrose. Cool and store in a refrigerator.

Exchange: 1 serving may be exchanged for 1/2 cup Milk. (It is important that this mixture be divided into 8 equal portions.)

RHUBARB SAUCE[2]

| INGREDIENTS | AMOUNT | | C | P | F |
	Household Measure	Grams	Gm.	Gm.	Gm.
rhubarb....................	1/2 cup	100	—	—	—
Sacrose liquid sweetener......	8 drops	—	—	—	—
Calories: negligible.			—	—	—

1. Wash the rhubarb and cut into 1-inch pieces without removing the skin. This gives a pretty pink color to the juice. **2.** Put into double boiler and add Sacrose. Steam until soft.
Exchange: 1 A Vegetable.

DESSERTS

JUNKET[2]

INGREDIENTS	AMOUNT Household Measure	Grams	C Gm.	P Gm.	F Gm.
milk.......................	1/2 cup	120	6	4	5
liquid rennet (or 1/2 junket tablet)...................	1/2 teaspoon	—	—	—	—
vanilla.....................	few drops	—	—	—	—
nutmeg....................	few grains	—	—	—	—
Calories: 85.			6	4	5

1. Heat the milk to body temperature. 2. Add the vanilla and the rennet. 3. Stir quickly and pour into glass dish. 4. Do not disturb until set. 5. Chill in the refrigerator. 6. Sprinkle nutmeg on top.

Exchange: 1/2 cup Milk.

FRUIT CUP[2]

INGREDIENTS	AMOUNT Household Measure	Grams	C Gm.	P Gm.	F Gm.
honeydew melon balls........6		75	5	—	—
grapes, seedless..............6		37	5	—	—
Calories: 40.			10	—	—

1. Mix the grapes and honeydew melon balls in a sherbet dish and garnish with a sprig of mint. If desired these pieces of fruit may be frosted in the refrigerator.

Exchange: 1 Fruit.

DATE BON-BONS[2]

INGREDIENTS	AMOUNT Household Measure	Grams	C Gm.	P Gm.	F Gm.
dates.......................2		15	10	—	—
nuts, small.................6		5	—	—	5
Calories: 85.			10	—	5

1. Chop dates after stone is removed. Chop nuts. 2. Mix and roll into small balls.

Exchanges: 1 Fruit; 1 Fat.

BREAD PUDDING WITH APPLE[1]

INGREDIENTS	AMOUNT Household Measure	Grams	C Gm.	P Gm.	F Gm.
bread......................	1 slice	25	15	2	—
apple......................	1, medium-size	150	10	—	—
milk.......................	1/4 cup	60	3	2	3
corn flakes..................	1 tablespoon	—	—	—	—
egg........................	1	50	—	7	5
vanilla.....................	few drops	—	—	—	—
cinnamon...................	sprinkle	—	—	—	—
Calories: 228.			28	11	8

1. Wash the apple and cut into small cubes. 2. Toast the bread and cut into 1/2-inch squares. 3. Place alternate layers of apple and bread in small baking dish. 4. Beat the egg. Combine with milk and add the vanilla. Pour mixture over the apple and bread. 5. Sprinkle cinnamon and corn flakes on top. Bake in moderate oven (350°F.) until a silver knife inserted comes out clean. 6. May be served hot or cold.

Exchanges: 1 Bread; 1 Fruit; 1 Meat; 1/4 cup Milk.

BAKED CUSTARD

INGREDIENTS	AMOUNT Household Measure	Grams	C Gm.	P Gm.	F Gm.
skim milk...................	1-1/2 cups	360	18	12	—
eggs.......................	2 medium	100	—	14	10
Sacrose (liquid sweetener).....	1/2 teaspoon	—	—	—	—
salt........................	dash	—	—	—	—
vanilla.....................	1/4 teaspoon	—	—	—	—
nutmeg....................	dash	—	—	—	—
Makes 4 servings (266 calories). Calories in 1 serving: 67.	4 servings 1 serving		18 5	26 7	10 3

1. Scald the milk. Beat the eggs slightly. 2. Add Sacrose, salt and vanilla to beaten eggs and stir until well mixed. 3. Add the scalded milk gradually, while stirring. 4. Pour the custard into four 5-ounce custard cups. Sprinkle with nutmeg. 5. Place in a shallow pan with hot water to the level of custard mixture in the cups. 6. Bake in a moderately slow oven (325°F.) for 45 minutes, or until the tip of a sharp knife comes out clean when inserted in the center of the custard. 7. Chill and serve.

Exchanges: (4 servings) 2 Meat; 1½ Milk. (Since skim milk contains no fat, add 3 Fat Exchanges to the diet for this recipe.) One serving: ½ Meat; ⅜ Milk.

FRENCH TOAST[1]

INGREDIENTS	AMOUNT Household Measure	Grams	C Gm.	P Gm.	F Gm.
egg......................1		50	—	7	5
butter....................2	teaspoons	10	—	—	10
bread....................1	slice	25	15	2	—
milk.....................1	tablespoon	—	—	—	—
vanilla extract..............4	drops	—	—	—	—
salt......................	dash	—	—	—	—
Calories: 231.			15	9	15

1. Break the egg into a shallow dish and beat until frothy. **2.** Add one tablespoon milk, 1/4 grain crushed saccharin (if desired), 4 drops of vanilla extract, and a dash of salt. Beat again until frothy. **3.** Dip a slice of bread into egg mixture until all is absorbed. **4.** Using a small frying pan, melt the butter and heat until slightly brown. **5.** Drop into hot browned butter and allow to brown for 1 minute. Then turn over and brown the other side for 1 minute.

Exchanges: 1 Bread; 1 Meat; 2 Fat.

SLICED BANANA IN ORANGE JUICE[1]

INGREDIENTS	AMOUNT Household Measure	Grams	C Gm.	P Gm.	F Gm.
banana, small...............1/2		50	10	—	—
orange juice.................1/2	cup	100	10	—	—
Calories: 80.			20	—	—

1. Peel and slice the banana into an attractive sherbet dish. **2.** Pour the orange juice over the banana and chill. **3.** Garnish with a quarter of a maraschino cherry.

Exchange: 2 Fruit.

MACAROONS[1]

INGREDIENTS	AMOUNT Household Measure	Grams	C Gm.	P Gm.	F Gm.
egg white...................1		30	—	4	—
walnuts or blanched almonds..5		5	—	—	5
saccharin or Sucaryl tablet...1		—	—	—	—
Calories: 61.			—	4	5

1. Mash the saccharin or Sucaryl tablet and place in the egg white. 2. After it has dissolved, beat the egg white stiff. 3. Chop the nuts very fine and fold into the egg white. 4. Drop spoonfuls of the mixture onto waxed paper. 5. Brown in a moderate oven (350°F.).

Exchanges: 1 Fat; 1 Meat. (Use the yolk in some other part of the meal. It may be beaten and stirred into some hot broth.)

DEEP DISH APPLE PIE

INGREDIENTS	AMOUNT Household Measure	Grams	C Gm.	P Gm.	F Gm.
apples..........................	3—2-inch diam.	240	30	—	—
cake flour....................	1/3 cup	36	28	4	—
Sacrose (liquid sweetener).....	2 teaspoons	—	—	—	—
margarine or lard............	4 teaspoons	20	—	—	20
nutmeg......................	1/8 teaspoon	—	—	—	—
cinnamon....................	1/16 teaspoon	—	—	—	—
salt........................	dash	—	—	—	—
Makes 2 servings.					
	2 servings		58	4	20
Calories in 1 serving: 209.	1 serving		29	2	10

1. Peel and dice the apples. Sprinkle with Sacrose, nutmeg and cinnamon. 2. Divide the apple mixture into two 4-inch casserole dishes. 3. Place the flour and salt in a mixing bowl. With a fork, work in the fat and 1 tablespoon cold water until mixture is dry enough to roll out. 4. Roll out on a lightly floured board. Cut into two pieces and place over the apple mixture in the casserole dishes. 5. Slash to allow steam to escape. 6. Bake in a hot oven (400°F.) about 30 minutes until the pastry is lightly browned and the apples are tender. 7. Cool to room temperature and serve.

Exchanges (1 serving): 1 Fruit; 1 Bread; 2 Fat.

FRUIT DESSERT[1]

INGREDIENTS	AMOUNT Household Measure	Grams	C Gm.	P Gm.	F Gm.
grapes, seedless..............	12	75	10	—	—
lime flavor gelatin, saccharin sweetened (Glow or D-Zerta brand)....................	1 envelope	—	—	—	—
Calories: 40.			10	—	—

1. Place the grapes in a sherbet dish. 2. Place the gelatin in the dessert dish also and pour over it 1/2 cup of hot boiling water. 3. Let cool and place in the refrigerator to set.

Exchange: 1 Fruit.

SPONGE CAKE

INGREDIENTS	AMOUNT Household Measure	Grams	C Gm.	P Gm.	F Gm.
egg whites................ } 5		250	—	35	25
egg yolks................ }					
cake flour, sifted............1 cup		110	84	12	1
sugar......................1/2 cup		100	100	—	—
Sacrose liquid sweetener .....1 tablespoon		—	—	—	—
lemon juice.................1 tablespoon		—	—	—	—
cold water.................2 tablespoons		—	—	—	—
cream of tartar.............1/4 teaspoon		—	—	—	—
salt......................1/4 teaspoon		—	—	—	—
Calories in whole cake: 1158. 1—9-inch cake			184	47	26
Calories in 1/12 piece: 96. 1/12 of the cake			15	4	2

1. Beat the egg whites, salt and cream of tartar together until frothy. Use a rotary beater. Continue beating until the whites stand up in peaks, and then gradually add the sugar. 2. Place cold water, Sacrose, lemon juice and egg yolks in another mixing bowl and beat until frothy. Then beat in the flour until the mixture is smooth. 3. Fold the yolk mixture gently into the beaten egg whites until no streaks remain. 4. Pour the mixture into ungreased 9-inch tube pan. 5. Bake in a moderate oven (350°F.) until the cake springs back into shape after being pressed lightly with the fingers. This takes about 45 minutes. Invert the cake on drying rack immediately after it is taken from the oven and allow to cool before removing from the pan.

(It is very necessary for the diabetic who uses this recipe to follow the instructions for the size of serving so that a very accurate exchange may be made. If the exchange used below is followed, this cake must be cut into 12 pieces of the same size.)

Exchanges (1/12 of the cake): 1 Bread; 1/2 Fat.

CUSTARD SAUCE

INGREDIENTS	AMOUNT Household Measure	Grams	C Gm.	P Gm.	F Gm.
skim milk...................2/3 cup		160	8	5	—
egg yolks...................2		—	—	7	10
salt........................dash		—	—	—	—
mace.......................dash		—	—	—	—
vanilla extract..............1/4 teaspoon		—	—	—	—
Sacrose (liquid sweetener).....1/2 teaspoon		—	—	—	—
Makes 2/3 cup (170 calories).			8	12	10

1. Scald the milk in a double boiler. 2. Beat the egg yolks, salt and mace together. 3. Add the milk, a little at a time, stirring constantly. 4. Return to the double boiler and cook over hot (not boiling) water, stirring constantly until the mixture coats the spoon. 5. Remove from hot water, stir in Sacrose and vanilla. Chill quickly.

Exchange: 2 Meat.

Suggestion: Try 1/2 Fruit Exchange with the 1/3 cup of custard sauce as a dessert.

SOUTHERN SNOWBALLS[2]

INGREDIENTS	AMOUNT		C	P	F
	Household Measure	Grams	Gm.	Gm.	Gm.
rice, cooked................	1/2 cup	100	15	2	—
milk.......................	1/2 cup	120	6	4	5
strawberries, cooked.........	1 cup	150	10	—	—
Calories: 193.			31	6	5

1. Cook the rice and milk together until all the milk has been absorbed. 2. Dip egg cup in cold water and carefully pack the rice into it, as tightly as possible. 3. Turn out on a deep serving dish and cover with cooked strawberries.

Exchanges: 1 Bread; 1 Fruit; 1/2 cup Milk from allowance.

BISCUIT TORTONI

INGREDIENTS	AMOUNT		C	P	F
	Household Measure	Grams	Gm.	Gm.	Gm.
water, cold................	1/2 cup	120	—	—	—
lemon juice................	2 tablespoons	—	—	—	—
non-fat milk powder........	5 tablespoons	50	24	16	—
Sacrose (liquid sweetener).....	2 teaspoons	—	—	—	—
almond flavoring............	1/4 teaspoon	—	—	—	—
Makes 4 servings (160 calories). Calories in 1 serving: 40.			24	16	—

1. Place the water and lemon juice in a mixing bowl. Add the milk solids and beat with a rotary beater until stiff. 2. Add Sacrose and almond flavoring and beat until thoroughly mixed in. 3. Pour the mixture into a freezing tray or small custard cups. 4. Save 1 teaspoon of corn flakes from breakfast cereal. Crush this very fine and use for topping. 5. Freeze as quickly as possible with refrigerator turned to coldest setting. Serve when just frozen.

Exchanges: Entire recipe (4 servings) is an exchange for 2 cups Skim Milk. 1 serving is an exchange for 1/2 cup Skim Milk.

VANILLA ICE CREAM[2]

INGREDIENTS	AMOUNT Household Measure	Grams	C Gm.	P Gm.	F Gm.
skim milk.................1 cup		240	12	8	—
Sacrose liquid sweetener......2 teaspoons		—	—	—	—
egg, small, separated.........1		50	—	7	5
gelatin, unflavored...........1 teaspoon		—	—	—	—
vanilla.....................1-1/2 teaspoons		—	—	—	—
salt.......................few grains		—	—	—	—
Calories: 153.			12	15	5

1. Scald 1/2 cup of the skim milk. Add the Sacrose to the milk and then pour over the beaten egg yolk. **2.** Sprinkle the gelatin over the remaining half cup of skim milk. **3.** Stir together the 2 milk mixtures until all the gelatin is dissolved. **4.** Heat over a low flame, adding the vanilla and salt. **5.** Pour into freezing tray; freeze firm. **6.** Remove from tray to chilled bowl and break up with a wooden spoon. **7.** Beat with electric beater or rotary egg beater until free from lumps, but crumbly. **8.** Fold in the stiffly beaten egg white and return to tray and again freeze firm.

Exchanges: 1 cup Skim Milk from allowance; 1 Meat.

PUMPKIN TART

INGREDIENTS	AMOUNT Household Measure	Grams	C Gm.	P Gm.	F Gm.
water......................3/4 cup		180	—	—	—
non-fat milk powder.........2-1/2 tablespoons		25	12	8	—
egg, medium................1		50	—	7	5
Sacrose (liquid sweetener).....2 teaspoons		—	—	—	—
pumpkin, canned or cooked...1/2 cup		100	7	2	—
salt.......................1/4 teaspoon		—	—	—	—
ginger.....................1/8 teaspoon		—	—	—	—
nutmeg....................1/8 teaspoon		—	—	—	—
orange rind, grated.........1 teaspoon		—	—	—	—
Calories in two tarts: 189.			19	17	5

1. Place water and milk powder in a bowl. Beat with a rotary beater until smooth. **2.** Add the remaining ingredients, beating smooth. **3.** Pour into 2 individual baking dishes. Divide evenly (*important*). **4.** Bake in a moderate oven (350°F.) for 30 minutes. **5.** Remove from oven. Sprinkle with 2 teaspoons of corn flakes which have been crumbled very fine. (Save these 2 teaspoons of corn flakes from your morning cereal.) Serve hot or cold.

Exchanges: If the two tarts are eaten during one day this recipe is an exchange for: 1 Skim Milk; 1 Meat; 1 B Vegetable. If only one tart is taken then divide each exchange in half.

RICE PUDDING[2]

| INGREDIENTS | AMOUNT | | C | P | F |
	Household Measure	Grams	Gm.	Gm.	Gm.
cooked rice................	1/2 cup	100	15	2	—
milk.......................	1/2 cup	120	6	4	5
Sacrose (liquid sweetener).....	8 drops if desired	—	—	—	—
raisins.....................	2 tablespoons	15	10	—	—
Calories: 193.			31	6	5

1. Add hot milk to 1/2 cup of cooked rice and place in individual baking dish. **2.** Mix in the raisins and Sacrose if desired. **3.** Bake in moderate oven (350°F.) until brown.

Exchanges: 1 Bread; 1 Fruit; 1/2 cup Milk from allowance.

FLOATING ISLAND[2]

| INGREDIENTS | AMOUNT | | C | P | F |
	Household Measure	Grams	Gm.	Gm.	Gm.
egg........................	1	50	—	7	5
milk.......................	1 cup	240	12	8	10
vanilla....................	1/2 teaspoon	—	—	—	—
Sacrose (liquid sweetener).....	to taste	—	—	—	—
Calories: 243.			12	15	15

1. Separate the egg. Beat the white very stiff. **2.** Beat the yolk and mix it with the milk, vanilla and Sacrose. **3.** Pour into the top of a double boiler and cook until it coats a silver spoon. **4.** Pour into an attractive serving dish and allow it to cool. **5.** Place the beaten egg white on top and garnish with a tiny piece of red cherry. **6.** If one desires this may be browned under the broiler.

Exchanges: 1 Meat; 1 cup Milk.

MIXED FRUIT CUP[2]

Assorted fruits can be used by the diabetic to make varied desserts. Suggested combinations:

Banana and Orange: Use 1/4 banana, sliced, and sections of 1/2 of an orange. This equals 1 Fruit Exchange.

Grapes and Pineapple: Cut the grapes in two and remove the seed. Dice the pineapple. Use 6 grapes and 1/4 cup of diced pineapple to equal 1 Fruit Exchange.

Watermelon Balls and Honeydew Melon Balls: Use 1/2 cup of Watermelon balls and 1/2 cup of Honeydew melon balls. This equals 1 Fruit Exchange.

Blueberries and Honeydew Melon Balls: Use 1/2 cup of each for 1 Fruit Exchange.

PLAIN BAVARIAN CREAM[2]

INGREDIENTS	AMOUNT Household Measure	Grams	C Gm.	P Gm.	F Gm.
egg, beaten................1		50	—	7	5
milk........................1/2 cup		120	6	4	5
gelatin, unflavored...........1 teaspoon		5	—	—	—
Sacrose (liquid sweetener).....1 drop		—	—	—	—
vanilla extract..............1/2 teaspoon		—	—	—	—
Calories: 158.			6	11	10

1. Soak the gelatin in 2 tablespoons of cold water. **2.** Scald the milk in the top part of a double boiler. Add the beaten egg. **3.** When the mixture begins to coat a spoon remove from the fire. **4.** Add the gelatin and stir until it is completely dissolved. **5.** Add the Sacrose and vanilla. Pour into a serving dish. **6.** When cool, place in the refrigerator to set.

Exchanges: 1/2 cup Milk; 1 Meat.

BAKED APPLE

INGREDIENTS	AMOUNT Household Measure	Grams	C Gm.	P Gm.	F Gm.
apple, small................1—2-inch diam.		80	10	—	—
water......................1/4 cup		60	—	—	—
Sacrose (liquid sweetener).....1 teaspoon		—	—	—	—
cinnamon..................sprinkle		—	—	—	—
Calories: 40.			10	—	—

1. Wash and core apple. Peel off the skin about a third of the way down from the top. **2.** Place apple in an individual casserole or shallow custard cup. **3.** Combine the remaining ingredients and pour over the apple. **4.** Bake in a moderately hot oven (375°F.) until the apple is tender and juicy. This takes about 45 minutes, depending on the kind of apple. **5.** Serve warm or cold.

Exchange: 1 Fruit.

GINGER BAKED PEAR

INGREDIENTS	AMOUNT Household Measure	Grams	C Gm.	P Gm.	F Gm.
ripe pear...................1 small		100	10	—	—
water......................3 tablespoons		—	—	—	—
ginger.....................1/16 teaspoon		—	—	—	—
Sacrose (liquid sweetener).....1 teaspoon		—	—	—	—
Calories: 40.			10	—	—

1. Wash the pear. Cut in half and remove the core. 2. Stand two pear halves in a custard cup or individual baking dish. 3. Combine the remaining ingredients and pour over the pear halves. 4. Bake in a moderately hot oven (375°F.) until tender and juicy, about 30 minutes. 5. Serve warm or cold.

Exchange: 1 Fruit.

BANANA SPECIAL[1]

INGREDIENTS	AMOUNT Household Measure	Grams	C Gm.	P Gm.	F Gm.
banana....................	1/2 medium	50	10	—	—
peanut butter...............	2 tablespoons, scant	30	—	7	5
milk......................	1/2 cup	120	6	4	5
Calories: 198.			16	11	10

1. Skin a banana and cut it in half. 2. Slice one of the halves in two, lengthwise. 3. Spread one of these sections with the peanut butter and put the two halves together as you would a sandwich. 4. Place in a dessert dish and serve with 1/2 cup of milk.

Exchanges: 1 Meat; 1 Fruit; 1/2 cup Milk.

CHOCOLATE PUDDING

INGREDIENTS	AMOUNT Household Measure	Grams	C Gm.	P Gm.	F Gm.
cornstarch..................	1 tablespoon	10	9	1	—
cocoa......................	1 tablespoon	7	4	1	2
salt.......................	few grains	—	—	—	—
milk, whole.................	2/3 cup	160	8	5	6
vanilla extract..............	1/3 teaspoon	—	—	—	—
cinnamon...................	dash	—	—	—	—
Sacrose (liquid sweetener)....	1/2 teaspoon	—	—	—	—
Calories: 184.			21	7	8

1. Mix the cornstarch, cocoa and salt with 1/3 of milk until smooth. 2. Meanwhile scald the remaining milk in a double boiler. 3. Pour a little of the scalded milk into the cornstarch mixture and blend until smooth. 4. Stir this slowly into remaining scalded milk, then cook, stirring constantly until the pudding is thick and smooth. 5. Cover the double boiler and cook 20 minutes, stirring occasionally. 6. Cool slightly, then add Sacrose, cinnamon and vanilla, stirring well. 7. Pour the pudding into a serving dish and chill before serving.

Exchanges: ¾ Milk; 1 Bread.

CRISPY COOKIES

INGREDIENTS	AMOUNT Household Measure	Grams	C Gm.	P Gm.	F Gm.
egg white.................1		30	—	4	—
Sacrose (liquid sweetener).....1/2 teaspoon		—	—	—	—
almond extract..............1/8 teaspoon		—	—	—	—
corn soya cereal............1 cup		50	38	9	—
Makes 12 cookies (204 calories). Calories in 1 cookie: 17.			38	13	—

1. Place egg white, Sacrose and almond extract in a mixing bowl. Beat until stiff. **2.** Fold in soya shreds. **3.** Drop, by teaspoonful, one inch apart on lightly greased cookie sheet. (It is most important that every cookie weigh the same.) **4.** Bake in a moderately hot oven (375°F.) about 10 minutes until lightly browned and crisp.

Exchange: 5 Cookies—1 Bread.

BEVERAGES

DIABETIC MILK DRINK

INGREDIENTS	AMOUNT Household Measure	Grams	C Gm.	P Gm.	F Gm.
rennet tablet...............1/2 tablet		—	—	—	—
Sacrose (liquid sweetener).....1 drop					
milk, warm..................2/3 cup		—	—	—	—
milk, cold..................1/3 cup		240	12	8	10
vanilla......................1/3 teaspoon		—	—	—	—
nutmeg.....................sprinkle		—	—	—	—
Calories: 170.			12	8	10

Method:

1. Dissolve the piece of rennet tablet in 1/2 tablespoon cold water. **2.** Place 1 drop of Sacrose into the cold milk. **3.** When the rest of the milk is COMFORTABLY WARM (110°F.) remove from the heat. Add the dissolved rennet tablet and vanilla. Stir quickly for a few seconds only. **4.** Pour at once into a serving pitcher. Allow to set. This will take about 10 minutes. **5.** Chill, and just before serving, add the cold milk which has been mixed with the Sacrose. Beat well with a rotary egg beater. **6.** Sprinkle with the nutmeg and serve.

Variations: Omit the vanilla and substitute lemon flavoring, orange flavoring or root beer or maple extract. Use only a few drops of these.

Exchange: 1 cup Whole Milk.

APRICOT MILK SHAKE

INGREDIENTS	AMOUNT Household Measure	Grams	C Gm.	P Gm.	F Gm.
dried apricots, stewed........4 halves		20	10	—	—
cold water..................1 cup		240	—	—	—
non-fat dry milk.............2-1/2 tablespoons		25	12	8	—
Sacrose (liquid sweetener).....1 teaspoon		—	—	—	—
lemon juice..................1 teaspoon		—	—	—	—
Makes 1 large serving. Calories: 120.			22	8	—

1. Place all the ingredients in a deep bowl. Beat until smooth with a rotary egg beater. 2. Pour over ice cubes in a tall glass and serve immediately.

Exchanges: 1 Fruit; 1 Skim Milk. (If diet calls for whole milk, add 2 Fat Exchanges since this recipe uses skim milk.)

COFFEE MILK SHAKE

INGREDIENTS	AMOUNT Household Measure	Grams	C Gm.	P Gm.	F Gm.
coffee, cold..................1 cup		240	—	—	—
Sacrose (liquid sweetener).....1/2 teaspoon		—	—	—	—
non-fat milk solids...........2-1/2 tablespoons		25	12	8	—
Calories: 80.			12	8	—

1. Place all ingredients in a glass jar or cocktail shaker. 2. Shake until milk solids are smoothly blended in. 3. Pour over ice cubes and let stand two or three minutes, then serve.

Exchange: 1 Skim Milk.

PINEAPPLE TEA PUNCH

INGREDIENTS	AMOUNT Household Measure	Grams	C Gm.	P Gm.	F Gm.
cold tea....................3/4 cup		—	—	—	—
pineapple juice..............3 tablespoons		40	5	—	—
lemon juice..................1 tablespoon		—	—	—	—
Sacrose (liquid sweetener).....1 teaspoon		—	—	—	—
Makes 1 large glass. Calories: 20.			5	—	—

1. Combine all the ingredients. 2. Pour over ice cubes in tall glass. 3. Let stand two or three minutes, then serve.

Exchange: 1/2 Fruit.

HOT COCOA

INGREDIENTS	AMOUNT Household Measure	Grams	C Gm.	P Gm.	F Gm.
skim milk................1 cup		240	12	8	—
cocoa....................1 tablespoon		7	4	1	2
cinnamon.................dash		—	—	—	—
Sacrose (liquid sweetener).....1/4 teaspoon		—	—	—	—
Calories: 118.			16	9	2

1. Place skim milk (fresh or made from dry skim milk and water), cocoa and cinnamon in a covered glass jar. **2.** Shake until smoothly mixed. **3.** Pour into a saucepan and bring to a boil. Let boil for about one minute. **4.** Remove from heat and add the Sacrose.

Exchange: 1 Milk. (Add 2 Fat Exchanges to Diet.)

MISCELLANEOUS

IMITATION "WHIPPED CREAM"

INGREDIENTS	AMOUNT Household Measure	Grams	C Gm.	P Gm.	F Gm.
cold water.................1/2 cup		120	—	—	—
lemon juice.................1 tablespoon		—	—	—	—
Sacrose (liquid sweetener).....2 teaspoons		—	—	—	—
non-fat milk powder.........5 tablespoons		50	24	16	—
Calories: 160.			24	16	—

1. Place water in bowl. Add the lemon juice, Sacrose and milk solids. **2.** Beat with a rotary beater or electric mixer until as thick as marshmallow cream. This topping will stay light and fluffy for about 30 minutes.

Exchange: Only when the amount used exceeds 1/4 cup at a time, need an equivalent amount of skim milk be exchanged.

CREAM CHEESE EASTER EGGS[1]

INGREDIENTS	AMOUNT Household Measure	Grams	C Gm.	P Gm.	F Gm.
cream cheese.................2 tablespoons		30	—	—	10
vegetable colors.............			—	—	—
Calories: 90.			—	—	10

1. Using small amount of vegetable coloring, color the cream cheese as desired. 2. Make small balls of the cream cheese. These may be served in the center of fruit salad or may be used to garnish the meat.

Exchange: 2 Fat.

LEMON VEGETABLE JELLY[1]

INGREDIENTS	AMOUNT		C	P	F
	Household Measure	Grams	Gm.	Gm.	Gm.
carrots, raw................1/2 cup		100	7	2	—
cabbage and celery, raw......1/2 cup		100	—	—	—
lemon saccharin-sweetened gelatin (Glow or D-Zerta)...1 envelope		—	—	—	—
Calories: 36.			7	2	—

1. Chop the vegetables up very fine and mix. 2. Dissolve the gelatin in 1/2 cup hot water. 3. Place the chopped vegetables and liquid gelatin in a mold and cool. Chill in refrigerator until firm. 4. When ready to serve, unmold onto lettuce leaf.

Note: If mayonnaise is desired, 1 Fat Exchange may be used as 1 teaspoon of mayonnaise, or 1 tablespoon of French dressing. This will increase the calories to 81.

Exchanges: 1 B Vegetable; 1 A Vegetable.

CRACKER GRUEL[2]

INGREDIENTS	AMOUNT		C	P	F
	Household Measure	Grams	Gm.	Gm.	Gm.
crushed saltines.............5		20	15	2	—
scalded milk.................1 cup		240	12	8	10
Calories: 238.			27	10	10

1. Pour hot milk gradually over the cracker crumbs, stirring constantly. 2. Cook 5 minutes in a double boiler, or 2 minutes over direct heat. (2 graham crackers may be used in place of 5 saltines.)

Exchanges: 1 Bread; 1 Whole Milk.

CHINESE BOILED RICE

See recipe in Low Calorie Diet section, page 223.
Exchange (1/2 cup cooked rice): 1 slice of Bread.

THE HIGH CALORIE OR HIGH ENERGY DIET

To increase the source of energy, to help correct underweight

No one but the person who is underweight or run down is able to realize how difficult it can be to put on good firm flesh, overcome chronic fatigue, and build up strength. The "skinny," underweight man or woman is often irritable, and is more susceptible to colds and other infections, than one who is well nourished and of the proper weight.

There can be many causes of underweight and chronic fatigue, including infected teeth, bad tonsils or other hidden diseases. Steady loss of weight for no apparent reason calls for a visit to your doctor, as this can often be the first sign of some illness which requires prompt treatment. Usually, however, the causes of underweight are twofold. One is too-intense living—the inability to relax, competition in business or social life, and other psychological strains. The other common cause of underweight is excessive physical stress—always on the go and never getting enough rest. But no matter what other factors may contribute to underweight or malnutrition, the immediate cause is not getting as many calories in your diet as you require . . . with the result that your body burns its own tissues for energy.

Just as too-fat people frequently forget to count the little extras which they eat, so too-thin people often suffer from the delusion that they eat as well as others . . . which is usually not so. Many times, underweight men and women have a long list of foods which they "hate"; so while they do eat certain favored foods, they avoid many others. They may also skimp on portions; while the normal or overweight individual eats a full, well-buttered slice of bread, the underweight person eats half a slice and spreads his butter thinly. You cannot fool your body—it cannot make use of calories it does not receive.

To build up your weight, gain new energy and achieve physical well-being, your doctor usually works with you in two ways—first, to help you relax, and second, to give you a special diet.

482

Relaxation should be cultivated particularly before, during and after meals, because nervous tension will reduce your stomach capacity and interfere with your appetite. You must get eight to ten hours of sleep a night. Do not hesitate to talk over your emotional problems with your family physician.

The special diet requires concentration on the high energy foods. Food is the body's only source of energy. Some foods contain a great deal more energy value, or calories, than do other foods, and it is these higher sources of energy which the doctor places in the diet of the person who is underweight, or who has been weakened by malnutrition, fever, infection or other illness.

There are five good rules for you to follow if you would fill out your figure and raise your weight to the desirable level, as shown in the weight charts at the beginning of this book.

1. Eat an adequate breakfast. When you wake up, you have gone without food for ten to fourteen hours, your available sources of energy have been depleted, and you need food to renew your supply of energy.

2. Guard your appetite. Do not eat candy or drink sweet beverages shortly before meals. Do not fill up on bulky, low calorie foods. Increase your meal-time calories gradually, since a too sudden addition of concentrated foods may overtax your digestive system and ruin your appetite. Smoke after meals if you wish, but not on an empty stomach.

3. Get in some nourishment between meals. Drink a glass of good, rich milk or an eggnog every day in the middle of the morning and afternoon, and at bedtime, together with some crackers, cookies, cake or fruit.

4. Be certain to get some of each of the Seven Basic Foods each day: milk, eggs; meat or fish; green or yellow vegetables; citrus fruit or tomato; whole grain or enriched bread or cereal; butter or other fats; and additional vegetables (potatoes, beets, etc.) and fruit (apples, peaches, etc.).

5. Do not feel discouraged if the scales fail to show the results of your efforts right away. Weight changes do not always occur immediately. If you eat 600 to 1,000 more calories of food each day than you did formerly, and if you give your body systematic rest, you should start to gain one to two pounds weekly, within the first three or four weeks.

A BASIC "3000 CALORIE" MENU (Approximate)

BREAKFAST	1/2 GRAPEFRUIT SOFT-BOILED EGG 2 SLICES BUTTERED TOAST OATMEAL WITH MILK AND SUGAR COFFEE WITH CREAM AND SUGAR
MID-MORNING	EGGNOG OR MALTED MILK
LUNCHEON	CHEESE SOUFFLÉ 2 SLICES BUTTERED BREAD FRUIT COCKTAIL BAKED POTATO and TOMATO SALAD WITH MAYONNAISE MILK (8-ounce glass)
MID-AFTERNOON	ORANGE JUICE (8-ounce glass) *and* 2 tablespoons GLUCOSE
DINNER	1 SLICE BUTTERED BREAD CHOCOLATE LAYER CAKE MEAT, FISH OR POULTRY (1/4 pound) CANDIED SWEET POTATO BUTTERED LIMA BEANS MILK (8-ounce glass) OR COFFEE OR TEA WITH SUGAR AND CREAM
BEDTIME	WARM OR COOL MILK (8-ounce glass) *AND* 2 SLICES LIGHTLY BUTTERED BREAD

FOODS PARTICULARLY SUITABLE FOR
THE HIGH CALORIE (Weight-Gaining) DIET

BREADS and CEREALS	BREAD · OATMEAL · WAFFLES AND PANCAKES · ROLLS · FARINA
BUTTER, FATS, OILS, CREAM	CREAM · MAYONNAISE · MARGARINE · BUTTER · OLIVE OIL
SUGAR, GLUCOSE, JAMS	SUGAR · JELLY · PRESERVES · JAM · GLUCOSE · MARMALADE
HIGH CALORIE DESSERTS	PUDDINGS WITH WHIPPED CREAM · BANANA SPLIT · CREAM PIES

QUICK AND EASY SANDWICH IDEAS

Olive Nut: Combine ½ cup chopped ripe olives with ½ cup finely chopped nuts, ¼ cup mayonnaise and salt to taste. Add finely chopped celery if desired.

Total calories: 900.

Broiler Treat: Spread olive nut filling on 5 slices toast and top each with a thin slice processed cheese. Broil until cheese melts. Serve at once.

Total calories: 1750. Calories in 1 slice: 350.

Tuna Favorite: Combine ¾ cup flaked canned tuna or salmon with ½ cup mayonnaise, ½ cup chopped nuts, ⅔ cup chopped ripe olives, 1 chopped canned pimiento and tabasco sauce to taste.

Total calories: 1640.

Crisp Cruster: Blend together 1 cup grated sharp American cheese with ⅔ cup coarsely chopped ripe olives, ⅓ cup mayonnaise, 1 teaspoon grated onion, ¼ teaspoon salt and pepper and tabasco sauce to taste. Spread on 5 slices buttered bread and cut into triangles. Dip into egg-milk mixture as for French toast and fry to golden brown in hot fat.

Total calories: 2200.

Stuffed Rolls: Blend 1 cup grated cheese, 1 (3-ounce) can deviled ham, ¼ cup mayonnaise, 1 teaspoon prepared horseradish and 1 teaspoon Worcestershire sauce. Stir in 1 cup chopped pitted ripe olives or whole olives cut from pits. Gently spread open 12 fantan rolls leaving sections together at bottom. Spread filling between sections. Place on baking sheet and bake in moderate oven (350°F.) 15 minutes.

Total calories: 2600. Calories in 1 stuffed roll: 217.

OLIVE HORS D'OEUVRES AND CANAPÉ TIDBITS

Garlic Olives: Drain olives and roll or let stand in olive oil flavored with a crushed clove of garlic. Or, heat liquid from olives with crushed clove of garlic, pour over the olives and let stand several hours. Roll in olive oil to keep shiny.

Calories in 1 Garlic Olive: about 10.

Bacon Broiled: Stuff pitted ripe olives with anchovy fillets or cheese. Wrap with strip of bacon, fasten with a pick and broil. Serve hot.

Calories in 1 Bacon Broiled Olive: about 60.

Pastry Bites: Combine equal parts coarsely cut ripe olives and cheese spread with chili powder to taste. Roll pastry thin and cut into 2-inch squares. Place spoonful of olive mixture in center and fold corners of pastry over it. Bake in hot oven (400°F.) 10 minutes or until browned.

Calories in 1 Pastry Bite: about 80.

Cheese Dip: Blend a 3-ounce package of cream cheese with a little milk. Stir in ⅛ teaspoon curry powder, ¼ teaspoon grated onion, ½ cup chopped ripe olives, dash of paprika and pepper. Serve with potato chips or crackers.

Total calories in spread: 440. Calories in 1 Ritz cracker: 16. Calories in 1 average potato chip: 10. Calories in 1 saltine: 17.

CHICKEN IN PAPRIKA CREAM

Makes 4 servings (3032 calories). Calories in 1 serving: 758.

1 fowl, 5 pounds	½ cup sour cream
1 cup tomato purée or tomato sauce	1 tablespoon paprika
	Salt and pepper
½ pound onions, finely chopped	Butter to grease pan

1. Cut up fowl as for fricassee; season with salt and pepper. 2. Sauté onions in butter, with paprika until light yellow. Add tomato purée and simmer for few minutes. Add sour cream. 3. Put fowl in deep baking dish and add the sauce. Cover and bake in moderate oven (350°F.) for 2 hours or more. Shake occasionally. 4. Strain sauce before serving. If too thick, add a little chicken broth or other stock.

BEEF STROGANOFF

Makes 4 servings (3440 calories). Calories in 1 serving: 860.

1½ pounds tenderloin of beef, cut in small strips, size of French fried potatoes	½ cup sour cream
	3 onions, cut small
	2 tablespoons tomato sauce
½ pound mushrooms, cut small	2 tablespoons flour
1 cup heavy sweet cream	Butter
1 cup beef bouillon	Worcestershire sauce

1. Sauté the cut-up onions in butter, until golden color. Add tomato sauce. 2. Stir in flour, then stir in bouillon gradually. Simmer together until mixture thickens, stirring constantly. Add the cut-up mushrooms and simmer 10 minutes longer. 3. Fry the pieces of beef tenderloin in hot butter, over a high flame. As soon as beef starts to fry, add it to the vegetable mixture. 4. Add sour cream, sweet cream and enough Worcestershire sauce to give desired flavor, and heat thoroughly.

CHICKEN WITH RICE

Makes 6 servings (4530 calories). Calories in 1 serving: 755.

1 fowl, 5 pounds	3 carrots
1½ cups rice	3 stalks celery
1 cup sour cream	½ bunch parsley
2 tablespoons flour	Juice of ½ lemon
2 tablespoons butter	Salt and pepper
3 onions	

1. Cover celery, onions, carrots and parsley with 1 quart water; bring to a boil. **2.** Add the whole fowl and cook quickly for 15 minutes. Cover, reduce heat and simmer for 1 to 1½ hours, or until tender. **3.** Boil rice separately; drain. Heat butter in saucepan, stir in the flour and slowly add chicken stock. Add lemon juice; season with salt and pepper. **4.** Simmer 15 minutes. One minute before serving, add the sour cream. Arrange chicken on one side of large warm platter, with large mound of hot rice on other side. Pour sauce over rice.

POZHARSKY KOTLETY (Cutlets)

Makes 4 servings (2980 calories). Calories in 1 serving: 745.

1 fowl, 3½ pounds	1 egg
8 slices enriched white bread, with crusts removed	4 tablespoons butter
	Coarse bread crumbs
1 egg beaten with a little water	Milk
	Salt

1. Cut all meat from uncooked fowl, and put through meat chopper twice. **2.** Soak bread in milk; squeeze almost dry. Combine chicken, bread and 1 egg. Mix well, then force through sieve. Add salt to taste. **3.** Cream the butter and add to mixture. Mix with hands until ingredients are well blended. **4.** Form into small thick cutlets; use 2 tablespoons of mixture for each cutlet. Dip into egg beaten with a little water. Roll in bread crumbs. **5.** Fry in a liberal amount of butter until cutlets are well browned on all sides.

PHILADELPHIA HASH

Makes 4 servings (1900 calories). Calories in 1 serving: 475.

4 cups meat leftovers from roasts, steaks or stews	1 tablespoon butter
	2 hard-boiled eggs
1 onion	Salt and pepper

1. Chop the meat very fine. **2.** Chop the onion and hard-boiled eggs very fine, then put them with the meat into the stewingpan. Add butter, salt and pepper. **3.** Stew and stir over a very slow fire for 15 minutes.

BREAST OF VEAL IN CREAM

Makes 4 servings (2352 calories). Calories in 1 serving: 588.

2 pounds breast of veal	¼ pound mushrooms
1 cup heavy cream	3 stalks celery
2 cups stock	2 onions
3 tablespoons butter	3 sprigs parsley
2 tablespoons flour	Salt and pepper

1. Place veal in pot and cover with boiling water. Boil 7 minutes, remove meat, rinse it in cold water, and set aside. 2. To the stock add onions, celery, parsley, and salt and pepper to taste. Simmer 30 minutes, then add meat. Cover and simmer until veal is done. 3. Wash and peel mushrooms and lightly brown them in 1 tablespoon butter. 4. Heat 2 tablespoons butter in saucepan, stir in flour, 2 cups of veal stock and sautéed mushrooms. Simmer 10 minutes, stirring often. Add cream. 5. Remove veal and cut into uniform cubes. Add to cream sauce and cook over boiling water for 15 minutes.

LIVER IN CREAM

Makes 4 servings (2460 calories). Calories in 1 serving: 615.

2 pounds calf's liver	Butter
2 cups milk	Salt
2 onions, chopped	Flour
1 cup cream	

1. Slice liver, place in shallow dish, and add milk. Cover and place in refrigerator for 12 hours. 2. Remove liver; drain. Season and roll lightly in flour. 3. Brown onions in butter. Remove, and fry liver on both sides quickly in the same butter. 4. Reduce the heat, add onions and cream to cover, and simmer 15 minutes.

HUNGARIAN VEAL WITH NOODLES

Makes 4 servings (1780 calories). Calories in 1 serving: 445.

2 tablespoons fat	⅛ teaspoon pepper
1½ cups chopped onions	2 tablespoons catsup
1 pound veal, cut in cubes	1 cup sour cream
1 cup sliced fresh mushrooms	3 cups cooked noodles (4
1½ teaspoons salt	ounces uncooked)

1. Heat fat in skillet. Add onions, veal and mushrooms, and sauté until lightly browned, stirring constantly. 2. Add salt, pepper, catsup and 1 cup water. 3. Cover and cook over low heat 45 minutes, or until veal is tender. 4. Add sour cream and noodles and heat thoroughly.

HAM-BANANA ROLLS WITH CHEESE SAUCE

Makes 4 servings (1850 calories, including cheese sauce). Calories in 1 serving: 462.

4 thin slices boiled ham
4 firm bananas
Prepared mustard

1½ tablespoons melted butter
or margarine
Cheese sauce

1. Spread each slice of ham lightly with mustard. Peel bananas. Wrap a slice of the prepared ham around each banana. 2. Brush tips of bananas with butter or margarine. Place in a greased shallow baking dish, and pour cheese sauce over them. 3. Bake in a moderate oven (350°F.) 30 minutes, or until bananas are tender—easily pierced with a fork. 4. Serve hot with the cheese sauce from the baking dish.

CHEESE SAUCE

Makes about 1 cup sauce (1000 calories).

1½ tablespoons butter or margarine
1½ tablespoons flour

¾ cup milk
1½ cups grated sharp American cheese

1. Melt butter or margarine in saucepan; add flour and stir until smooth. Stir in milk slowly. 2. Add cheese and cook, stirring constantly until sauce is smooth and thickened.

SCHNITZEL BEANS AND BACON WITH POTATOES

Makes 6 servings (960 calories). Calories in 1 serving: 160.

1½ quarts string beans, cut
into small pieces
2 tablespoons diced bacon
1 tablespoon lard

3 large onions, sliced
4 medium potatoes, diced
1 teaspoon salt
Dash of pepper

1. Fry the bacon until crisp, add to string beans and 1½ cups hot water. 2. Cook about 20 minutes. Add the potatoes and other ingredients and cook until potatoes are soft.

HAM AND CHEESE TOSTADA

Makes 1 serving (300 calories).

1 Mexican tortilla (can be purchased in cans)

1 slice boiled ham
1 slice American cheese

1. Place in oven until cheese is melted.

CHICKEN FORSHMAK

Makes 4 servings (1700 calories). Calories in 1 serving: 425.

1 cup cubed cooked chicken	1 cup light cream
½ cup cubed cooked ham	¼ pound mushrooms, sliced
¾ cup cubed boiled potatoes	1 onion, chopped
⅓ cup grated cheese, cheddar or sharp	Butter
	Salt and pepper

1. Fry onion in butter; remove and keep hot. Brown mushrooms in same pan. 2. Return onion to pan and add cubes of chicken, ham and potatoes. Mix and add cream. Season with salt and pepper. Add a little hot water if necessary. 3. Simmer gently, shaking pan often, but do not stir. 4. When smooth and slightly moist, turn into buttered casserole. Cover with grated cheese. 5. Bake in moderate oven (350°F.) about 25 minutes, until top is brown.

CHOPPED BEEF SCRAMBLE

Makes 3 servings (708 calories). Calories in 1 serving, including ½ picnic bun: 236.

2 teaspoons fat	1 teaspoon cornstarch
1 small clove garlic, minced	1 tablespoon pickle relish
½ pound chopped beef round	2 picnic buns
1 Souplet	Salt and pepper

1. Melt fat in saucepan. Add garlic and let cook 1 minute over moderate heat. 2. Add chopped beef molded into small portions. Cook until lightly browned and done. 3. Dissolve Souplet in ½ cup boiling water and add to beef. Blend together and add cornstarch, ½ cup cold water and pickle relish. 4. Cook, stirring constantly, until mixture thickens. Season to taste with salt and pepper. Serve over a toasted half of a picnic bun.

SALMON AND MUSHROOMS ON SKEWERS

Each serving contains about 700 to 800 calories.

Fresh salmon	Sour cream
Mushrooms	Hard boiled eggs, chopped
Butter	Lemon juice
Fresh bread crumbs	Salt and pepper

1. Clean salmon, wipe dry, and cut in pieces 2 inches by 1 inch. 2. Season salmon with salt and pepper and sprinkle with lemon juice. Use only caps of mushrooms; peel and sauté lightly in butter. 3. Roll salmon in bread crumbs. Alternately place salmon and mushroom caps on skewers. 4. Grill slowly over, or under, a clear flame. 5. Serve with sour cream and chopped egg.

HAWAIIAN PORK AND PINEAPPLE

Makes 2 servings (552 calories). Calories in 1 serving: 276.

¼ pound lean pork	½ cup slivered green pepper
1 teaspoon fat	2 small slices unsweetened
1 tablespoon minced onion	canned pineapple
1 Souplet or Nestlé bouillon	2 teaspoons cornstarch
cube	1 tablespoon pineapple juice
1 teaspoon sugar	1 teaspoon vinegar

1. Cut pork in strips the diameter of a pencil. Melt fat in saucepan. Add pork and onion and let cook over moderate heat for about 5 minutes, stirring occasionally. **2.** Add ½ cup water, Souplet and sugar. Cover and bring to boil. **3.** Let cook about 15 minutes over low heat. Cut pineapple into chunks. **4.** Add pineapple and green pepper. Cover and continue cooking 5 minutes. **5.** Blend together and stir in the cornstarch, pineapple juice and vinegar. Serve immediately.

FISH CUTLETS

Makes 3 servings (1200 calories). Calories in 1 serving: 400.

1 pound boned whitefish	½ teaspoon salt
2 slices bread, crust removed	¼ teaspoon pepper
4 tablespoons cream	Dry bread crumbs
1 egg white	Butter for frying
1 tablespoon melted butter	Tartar sauce or lemon wedges
1 tablespoon chopped dill	

1. Soak bread in cream. Put fish through chopper and mash fish with the soaked bread; add salt, pepper, melted butter, dill and unbeaten white of egg. **2.** Mix thoroughly, then place in refrigerator for several hours. **3.** Sift dry bread crumbs on waxed paper and roll out fish mixture into cakes 3 inches long and 1½ inches wide. Roll well in the crumbs. **4.** Fry in plenty of butter, turning as needed, to give a good browning. Serve very hot with tartar sauce or lemon wedges.

CRAB MEAT SALAD

Makes 4 servings (1040 calories). Calories in 1 serving: 260.

1 cup flaked crab meat	1½ tablespoons catsup
1 cup ripe olives	1 teaspoon lemon juice
1½ cups thinly sliced celery	Lettuce cups
⅓ cup mayonnaise	

1. Cut ripe olives into wedges and combine with celery and crab meat. **2.** Toss lightly with mayonnaise, catsup and lemon juice. **3.** Serve in lettuce cups.

DEVILED CLAMS

Makes 4 servings (1080 calories). Calories in 1 serving: 270.

1 pint hard clams, with their juice
½ cup cream
½ cup fine buttered bread crumbs
2 tablespoons butter
2 tablespoons flour

1 tablespoon lemon juice
1 tablespoon finely chopped green pepper
1 tablespoon finely chopped parsley
½ teaspoon Worcestershire sauce

1. Put clams through meat chopper, using medium cutter. Strain juice and combine ½ to ¾ cup juice with the cream. 2. Melt butter, add flour, and stir until smooth. Gradually add the cream-juice mix and continue cooking until thick and smooth, stirring constantly. 3. Add clams, lemon juice, green pepper, parsley and Worcestershire sauce. Turn into greased scallop shells or shallow ramekins. 4. Top with buttered crumbs and bake in moderately hot oven (375°F.) 20 minutes or until well browned.

SHAD ROE SALAD

Makes 4 servings (2700 calories). Calories in 1 serving: 675.

2 shad roes
1 teaspoon salt
1 slice onion

1 cup mayonnaise
Lettuce leaves

1. Wash shad roes, put them in a saucepan, cover them with boiling water, add a teaspoonful of salt. Put lid on saucepan and simmer gently 20 minutes. 2. When done, lift roes carefully away from water and place in refrigerator until cold. 3. Remove skin from outside of roes and cut them into thin slices. 4. Place one slice of onion in center of salad dish, arrange around it crisp lettuce leaves, heap shad roe in center, pour cup of cold mayonnaise over it, and serve.

VEGETABLE SALAD WITH SOFT EGGS

Makes 6 servings (2100 calories). Calories in 1 serving: 350.

6 eggs
1 cup chopped celery
1 cup cooked corn
1 cup cooked green peas
½ cup cooked string beans
2 young carrots, grated

2 young boiled beets, sliced
2 scallions, chopped
1 tablespoon chopped green pepper
¾ cup mayonnaise
Salt and black pepper

1. Place eggs in saucepan, cover with boiling water, and add 1 teaspoon salt. Simmer, covered, 4 minutes. **2.** Mix all vegetables together, blend in the mayonnaise, and season liberally with salt and black pepper. Arrange nicely into a flattened shape, on cold platter. **3.** Drain eggs, crack shells very slightly and place in bowl. Let cold water run into bowl; peel eggs when cold. **4.** Arrange eggs on top of vegetables.

MEXICAN RICE

Recipe from Señora Alonzo de Aguillar, whose beauty conquered Mexico . . . and who in turn was conquered by it.

Makes 6 servings (1490 calories). Calories in 1 serving: 248.

1 cup raw rice
Fat for frying
1 clove garlic

1 cup tomatoes
Salt

1. Soak rice in cold water for about 15 minutes. **2.** Put fat in pan, about ½ inch high. Drain water from rice and fry with garlic, until golden brown. **3.** Remove garlic and remains of fat; add tomatoes and salt. Let simmer for few minutes, then add 2 cups water. **4.** Bring to a slow boil, then lower flame and let cook until all water has evaporated.

EGGS WITH CHESTNUTS

Makes 3 servings (852 calories). Calories in 1 serving: 284.

6 eggs
8 roasted chestnuts
¼ cup light cream
½ tablespoon Madeira wine

Cayenne
Grated nutmeg
Salt
Butter

1. Peel and cook the chestnuts in 1 cup water, in a covered saucepan, 20 minutes. **2.** Drain, rub through a sieve. Stir in by degrees the wine and cream. Pour into a saucepan. Season to taste with cayenne, grated nutmeg and salt. **3.** Divide between six buttered ramekins. Break an egg into each. Season to taste. **4.** Bake in a hot oven (425° to 450°F.) for 3 minutes.

CHICKEN SALAD

Makes 4 servings (1200 calories). Calories in 1 serving: 300.

1½ cups cubed cooked
   chicken
1½ cups diced celery
¾ cup sliced olives
3 tablespoons heavy cream

3 tablespoons mayonnaise
Juice of 1 lemon
½ teaspoon prepared horseradish
Salt and pepper to taste

1. Combine chicken, celery and olives. Sprinkle with lemon juice.
2. Blend together mayonnaise, cream and horseradish. Toss with chicken mixture. Season to taste with salt and pepper.

LIME SALAD

Makes 4 servings (1260 calories). Calories in 1 serving: 315.

1 package lime flavor gelatin
1 cup grapefruit sections
½ cup mayonnaise
¾ cup grated carrot
⅓ cup sliced ripe olives
1 tablespoon lemon juice
½ teaspoon grated lemon rind

1. Dissolve gelatin in 1½ cups hot water or fruit juice. 2. Blend in grapefruit sections, grated lemon rind and lemon juice. Cool until slightly thickened. 3. Fold in sliced olives and grated carrot. Chill until firm. Top each serving with 2 tablespoons mayonnaise.

YERBA BUENA SALAD

Makes 4 servings (452 calories). Calories in 1 serving: 113.

½ cup ripe olives
1 tablespoon chopped green sweet pepper
1 tablespoon chopped green onion
1 cup creamed cottage cheese
4 medium tomatoes
Salad greens
4 sprigs parsley
Salt

1. Cut olives from pits, into large pieces. Stir olives, chopped pepper and chopped onion into cottage cheese. Add salt to taste. 2. Peel and core tomatoes. Cut in halves crosswise. 3. Put halves together with filling of cheese mixture. Serve on salad greens. Top with parsley sprig.

VEGETABLE SALAD

Makes 4 servings (600 calories). Calories in 1 serving: 150.

2 cups finely shredded cabbage or grated carrot
½ cup sliced ripe olives
¼ cup thinly sliced green onion
2 tablespoons diced green pepper
¼ cup mayonnaise
1 teaspoon Worcestershire sauce
½ teaspoon salt
¼ teaspoon dill seed
Pepper

1. Toss vegetables together lightly with mixture of mayonnaise and seasonings.

EGG AND VEGETABLE CASSEROLE

Makes 4 servings (1920 calories). Calories in 1 serving: 480.

6 eggs, hard cooked
¼ cup butter or margarine
1 teaspoon Worcestershire sauce
1 teaspoon prepared mustard
1 tablespoon grated onion
1 tablespoon minced parsley

2 cups hot cooked peas, green beans or broccoli
1 can Heinz cream of mushroom soup
1 teaspoon salt
½ cup milk
1 cup grated cheese

1. Cut eggs in half lengthwise; remove yolks. **2.** Cream butter and yolks with ½ teaspoon salt and other seasonings. Fill each egg half with mixture and place in shallow buttered casserole. **3.** Arrange green vegetables around eggs. Combine mushroom soup, ½ teaspoon salt and milk. Heat and pour over eggs and vegetable. **4.** Sprinkle with cheese and heat in moderately hot oven (375°F.) from 10 to 15 minutes.

PATIO SUPPER SALAD

Makes 6 servings (2490 calories). Calories in 1 serving: 415.

2 cups cooked salad macaroni
2 chopped hard-boiled eggs
⅔ cup sliced ripe olives
1½ cups sliced celery
⅔ cup mayonnaise
¼ cup chopped pimiento

¼ cup chopped sweet pickle
¼ cup chopped green pepper
1 tablespoon grated onion
1 tablespoon vinegar
¾ teaspoon salt

1. In a large salad bowl combine macaroni, chopped eggs, sliced olives, celery, pimiento, pickle and green pepper. **2.** In a separate bowl blend together mayonnaise, grated onion, vinegar and salt. Toss with salad mixture and serve at once.

MOLDED FRUIT SALAD

Makes 6 servings (1320 calories). Calories in 1 serving: 220.

1 package lemon flavor gelatin
1 No. 1 flat can crushed pineapple (including liquid)
1½ cups sour cream
¾ cup canned apricot halves

1 diced apple
½ cup sliced ripe olives
2 tablespoons lemon juice
Salad greens

1. Dissolve gelatin in 1½ cups hot water. Blend in pineapple and lemon juice. Cool until slightly thickened. **2.** Fold in apricot halves, cut in two, diced apple and sliced olives. **3.** Turn into 6 individual molds and chill until firm. Unmold onto salad greens. Top each salad with ¼ cup sour cream.

RICE AND CHEESE CASSEROLE

Makes 6 servings (2040 calories). Calories in 1 serving: 340.

1⅓ cups (5-ounce package)
Minute Rice
½ teaspoon salt
½ cup grated Parmesan
cheese

1½ cups cottage cheese
4 eggs, beaten
2 cups milk
1½ tablespoons butter
1½ teaspoons salt
Dash of pepper

1. Combine Minute Rice, 1½ cups water and salt in saucepan. Mix just until all rice is moistened. 2. Bring quickly to a boil over high heat, uncovered, fluffing rice gently once or twice with a fork. (Do *not* stir.) Cover and remove from heat. Let stand 10 minutes. 3. Add cottage and Parmesan cheese to eggs, blending thoroughly. Add milk, butter, salt and pepper; mix well. 4. Add hot cooked rice; blend. Turn mixture into buttered shallow 1½-quart casserole. 5. Place in pan of hot water and bake in moderate oven (350°F.) 30 minutes; stir and bake 30 minutes longer, or until a knife inserted comes out clean.

STUFFED FRUIT SALAD

Makes 4 servings (760 calories). Calories in 1 serving: 190.

8 halves canned pears or
peaches
½ cup cottage cheese
⅓ cup chopped ripe olives

⅓ cup chopped nuts
1 tablespoon lemon juice
Salad greens

1. Combine cottage cheese with olives, nuts and lemon juice. 2. Arrange 2 pear or peach halves on each plate with salad greens. Top fruit with mound of cheese mixture.

DUTCH POTATO SALAD

Makes 8 servings (1760 calories). Calories in 1 serving: 220.

6 frankfurters, cooked and cut
in ½-inch slices
4 cups hot diced potatoes
1 medium-sized onion,
chopped
½ cup celery, chopped
1 tablespoon parsley, chopped

1½ teaspoons salt
1 tablespoon flour
2 tablespoons fat (bacon drippings are good)
⅓ cup sugar
⅓ cup vinegar
¼ teaspoon pepper

1. Fry chopped onion in hot fat until light brown. Add flour and blend, browning flour lightly. 2. Add sugar, salt, vinegar and ⅔ cup water. Bring to a boil, stirring constantly. 3. Pour dressing over the diced potatoes, chopped celery and sliced frankfurters. Sprinkle with pepper and parsley. Serve hot.

MEXICAN GUACAMOLE

Makes 4 servings (1178 calories). Calories in 1 serving: 294.

2 ripe avocados
3 tablespoons chopped sweet onions
3 tablespoons lime juice

½ clove garlic finely chopped
2 canned green chili peppers
½ teaspoon salt
Pinch of pepper

1. Mash avocados to a pulp. Cut chili peppers into ½-inch pieces.
2. Mix all ingredients thoroughly. Serve on tortillas, Fritos, bread or crackers—or serve plain with cold cuts.

CELERY ROOT (CELERIAC) AU GRATIN

Makes 4 servings (860 calories). Calories in 1 serving: 215.

2 cups celery root, peeled and cubed, or sliced
4 tablespoons butter
1½ tablespoons flour
¾ cup consommé or strong chicken broth
Salt and pepper

1 teaspoon grated onion (optional)
¾ cup soft bread crumbs or cubes
⅓ to ½ cup grated Swiss cheese

1. Boil celery root, covered, in a small amount of salted water about 20 minutes or until tender. Drain, reserving broth. Turn into a shallow baking dish. 2. Melt half the butter, blend in flour and cook, stirring, till browned. 3. Add consommé, ¼ of the cup reserved broth and onion, and cook, stirring till thickened. Season to taste with salt and pepper. 4. Pour sauce over celery root. Cover with crumbs and grated cheese. Dot with bits of butter. Bake in a moderately hot oven (375°F.) until crumbs are browned, about 20 minutes.

SQUASH BAKED WITH MARSHMALLOWS

Makes 4 servings (632 calories). Calories in 1 serving: 158.

8 marshmallows
1 box (1 pound) frozen cooked squash
3 tablespoons melted butter

1 egg yolk, slightly beaten
1 teaspoon salt
⅛ teaspoon cinnamon
Dash of nutmeg

1. Thaw squash and combine with butter, seasonings and egg yolk.
2. Turn into greased shallow baking dish. Arrange marshmallows on top. 3. Place in pan of hot water and bake in moderately hot oven (375°F.) 20 minutes, or until marshmallows are browned and partially melted.

CREAMED GREENS, FRENCH STYLE

Makes 4 servings (568 calories). Calories in 1 serving: 142.

1½ pounds spinach or other tender leafy greens
¾ cup chicken stock
¼ cup light cream
1 tablespoon finely chopped onion
2 tablespoons butter
2 tablespoons flour
Pinch of thyme
Pinch of nutmeg
Dash of cayenne pepper
1 teaspoon salt

1. Remove roots and any tough stems from greens and wash thoroughly. 2. Cook, covered, in water that clings to the leaves, about 5 minutes, or until tender, adding ½ teaspoon salt after greens are half done. 3. Drain well and chop or force through a food mill or coarse sieve. 4. Heat butter, add onion and cook, stirring, till lightly browned. Blend in flour. Add stock, cream, remaining salt, thyme, nutmeg and cayenne and cook till thickened. 5. Add chopped greens to the sauce and boil, stirring until well blended.

ORANGE CANDIED YAMS

Makes 4 servings (1452 calories). Calories in 1 serving: 363.

4 medium-sized yams
1 cup orange juice
1 tablespoon grated orange peel
½ cup granulated sugar
1 tablespoon cornstarch
2 tablespoons melted butter

1. Wash yams and boil until tender. Peel and cut in halves lengthwise. 2. Place in buttered baking dish. Mix remaining ingredients and pour over yams. 3. Bake about 1 hour in slow oven (300°F.). Baste several times during baking with sirup in dish. 4. Garnish with slices of unpeeled oranges.

CUCUMBER IN CREAM DRESSING

Total calories: 324.

1 large cucumber
1 large onion, sliced
½ cup sour cream
1 tablespoon vinegar
Paprika
Salt

1. Peel cucumber and slice very thin. Put in bowl, add salt and place in refrigerator. 2. When thoroughly cold, press the cucumber slices between the hands to remove salt. 3. Now add sliced onion and add following dressing: Combine the sour cream with the vinegar and paprika. Mix well.

BASIC WHITE SAUCE
Total calories: 420.

1 cup milk	¼ teaspoon salt
2 tablespoons flour	Few grains pepper
2 tablespoons butter	

1. Melt butter in small flat-bottom saucepan or double boiler top. Add flour and seasoning, and stir until well blended. Use wire whisk, to obtain smoothness. **2.** Pour on milk gradually; stir constantly. **3.** Bring to a boil; boil 2 minutes. **4.** Cook in double boiler top for 15 minutes. Stir well. If sauce becomes too thick, thin out with a little more milk. Taste, and add seasoning if needed.

Variations: THIN WHITE SAUCE: Use 1 tablespoon butter and 1 tablespoon flour, instead of 2.

THICK WHITE SAUCE: Use 4 tablespoons butter and 4 tablespoons flour (to thicken croquette mixtures and canapés).

CREAM SAUCE: Use cream instead of milk. If too thick, thin out with cream or milk. Season to taste.

SAVORY CREAM SAUCE: Add ¼ teaspoon dry mustard with flour, or prepared mustard to taste; add few drops onion juice and ¼ to ½ teaspoon paprika.

CHEESE SAUCE: Add ¾ cup mild cheese, grated or cut into small cubes. Reheat in double boiler until cheese melts.

WHITE SAUCE WITH EGG: Stir in slightly beaten egg yolk, just before serving.

LOBSTER SAUCE: To white sauce made with cream, add 1 teaspoon meat extract, ½ cup diced lobster and the coral from 1 lobster.

PARSLEY CREAM SAUCE: Add 2 to 4 tablespoons finely chopped parsley.

CURRIED CREAM SAUCE: To white sauce made with cream, add 1 teaspoon curry powder and ¼ teaspoon ground ginger which have been mixed into a little flour. Season to taste with a good amount of onion juice and paprika.

HAM SAUCE
Makes 1 cup (450 calories).

½ cup heavy cream, whipped	4 teaspoons prepared horse-
3 tablespoons chili sauce	radish

1. Fold chili sauce and horseradish into whipped cream. Chill. **2.** Serve with baked ham or boiled tongue.

HOLLANDAISE SAUCE

Total calories: 930.

3 fresh egg yolks
¼ pound best butter, preferably sweet butter

Salt
Lemon juice, if desired

1. Place egg yolks in a small bowl; add 1 tablespoon water. 2. Place bowl over hot water—not boiling. Whisk with a wire whisk until creamy. 3. Add the butter bit by bit, whisking gently but constantly. 4. Add salt to taste (add a squeeze of lemon juice if desired) and strain through cheesecloth.

MOUSSELINE SAUCE

Total calories: 1300.

2 tablespoons (or more)
whipped cream

1 cup Hollandaise sauce

1. Mix Hollandaise with whipped cream. 2. Heat carefully in double boiler top, whipping constantly, but gently, until heated through.

VELOUTÉ SAUCE

Total calories: 540.

¼ cup butter
¼ cup flour

2 cups chicken broth
Salt

1. Make a *roux* by cooking butter and flour together. 2. Add chicken broth, and salt to taste. 3. Cook over low flame 1 hour. Skim off butter which has risen to the top. 4. Strain through cheesecloth.

SOUBISE, or FRENCH ONION SAUCE

Total calories: 850.

4 onions, finely chopped
Butter

¾ cup Velouté sauce

1. Stew onions in butter, but do not let them brown. 2. Add Velouté sauce and finish cooking onions. 3. Rub through a fine-mesh sieve. Correct the seasoning before serving.

MUSHROOM CREAM SAUCE

Total calories: 900.

½ pound small mushrooms
2 tablespoons butter, preferably sweet

1 cup light cream
2 tablespoons cream sauce
Salt

1. Clean mushrooms and stew lightly in saucepan, with the butter.
2. Add cream and cook 7 or 8 minutes. 3. Thicken with cream
sauce and season with salt.

RÉMOULADE SAUCE

Total calories: 4400.

3 cups mayonnaise
4 finely chopped gherkins
2 tablespoons chopped chives

Handful of spinach
Handful of water cress

1. Grind spinach and water cress in a mortar, until a fine paste
is made. 2. Place in a cloth and press out the juice into the mayonnaise. 3. Add chopped gherkins and chives, and mix thoroughly.

TARTARE SAUCE

Total calories: 1650.

1 cup mayonnaise
2 small sour pickles, finely
chopped
10 olives, chopped
1 tablespoon capers
1 tablespoon chopped chives

1 tablespoon chopped parsley
Salt
Freshly ground pepper
1 tablespoon lemon juice or
vinegar

1. Mix together all ingredients except lemon juice or vinegar. 2.
Add the lemon juice or vinegar when the sauce has been well
mixed.

HOT SALAD DRESSING

This is a famous Pennsylvania Dutch salad dressing which is
good on lettuce, dandelion greens, endive, garden salad and
potatoes.

Total calories: 230.

3 slices bacon
1 teaspoon flour
½ cup vinegar
½ teaspoon dry mustard

½ teaspoon salt
⅛ teaspoon pepper
1 egg yolk
¼ teaspoon sugar

1. Cut bacon in small cubes and fry crisp. Remove bacon cubes
from grease and set them aside. 2. Blend the flour into the grease
and brown it. Remove from the stove and add the vinegar; stir
until flour mix thickens. 3. Mix together the sugar, mustard, salt
and pepper and add to the mixture. Pour over the beaten egg
yolk and mix well. 4. Return the dressing to the heat again and
cook 1 minute longer. 5. Add bacon cubes when ready to use.

MEAT SOUP

Makes 8 servings (2160 calories). Calories in 1 serving: 270.

1 pound brisket of beef
1 beef bone, about 1 pound
1 veal bone, about 1 pound
1½ cups canned tomatoes
2 carrots
¼ pound string beans

1 small onion
1 stalk celery, with leaves
½ bunch parsley
1 teaspoon salt
½ cup egg noodles

1. Place meat, bones, tomatoes, and salt in soup pot, with 2 quarts water. 2. Cover pot tightly and simmer for 3½ hours. Cut up the vegetables and add to soup after 3½ hours. 3. Simmer soup an additional ½ hour, remove the meat and run soup through purée strainer. 4. Chill soup and remove all fat. 5. Boil gluten noodles in separate saucepan for 10 minutes to tenderize. Then add to the soup and simmer soup for 10 minutes, or until noodles are completely tender.

CREAMED ONION SOUP

Makes 4 servings (1000 calories). Calories in 1 serving: 250.

3 large onions, peeled
3 tablespoons flour
3 tablespoons butter

2 cups milk
Salt and pepper
Buttered croutons

1. Cook peeled onions with 2 cups cold water until tender. Press through sieve. 2. Blend flour in hot melted butter, and stir in the milk, for a smooth white sauce. 3. Add sauce to onions, season, beat 2 minutes in the pot, with rotary beater. Add croutons.

PORTUGUESE EGG SOUP

Makes 4 servings (920 calories). Calories in 1 serving: 230.

4 eggs
2 tablespoons olive oil
1 clove garlic, chopped or crushed
3 beef bouillon cubes or 2 teaspoons beef extract

1 cup chopped onions
2 teaspoons salt
1 teaspoon thyme
1 teaspoon celery salt
⅓ teaspoon pepper
About ¼ of a French bread

1. Use 1 large frying pan throughout. Fry onions and garlic in olive oil, until light brown. 2. Add 5 cups water, bouillon cubes or beef extract, and seasonings. Boil for 5 minutes. 3. Reduce heat as low as possible. Slip in the 4 eggs and poach very gently for 5 minutes or so, or until definitely cooked through. 4. Tear up some of the French bread into 1-inch bits and place in oven for few minutes until hot and dry. 5. Put bread in large soup bowls and pour soup over. See that 1 egg goes into each bowl.

GIBLET SOUP

The song is full of pity for the sorrowful soul who gets the neck of the chicken, but lots of us love it . . . love to lift it up out of giblet soup and pick every particle. Then there are some who prefer wings, gizzards, and even chicken feet. This soup is for all chicken parts lovers—a good homey meal in itself.

Makes 12 servings (2500 calories). Calories in 1 serving: 209.

4 pounds chicken parts—necks, wings, and gizzards (and feet if desired)
4 tablespoons flour
3 ounces egg noodles
3 onions, quartered or sliced

2 carrots
1 parsnip
3 tablespoons chopped fresh parsley
1 teaspoon salt
½ teaspoon pepper

1. Clean giblets thoroughly; remove inner lining from gizzards. 2. Combine all ingredients except flour, noodles, and parsley. 3. Cook over low heat 1 to 1½ hours, then blend some of the liquid with the flour, and add to the soup. 4. Cook gluten noodles or spaghetti curls, for 15 minutes, then add to soup. Remove carrots and parsnip, slice them, and return to the pot. 5. Cook 15 minutes longer and serve at once, with sprinkling of chopped parsley.

TOMATO SHERBET COCKTAIL

Makes 4 servings (340 calories). Calories in 1 serving: 85.

2 cups peeled and seeded fresh tomatoes
½ cup light cream

½ teaspoon salt
Pepper
Chives or parsley

1. Place all ingredients except garnishing herbs in electric blender. 2. Blend quickly, and chill. Serve with chives or parsley.

HUSH PUPPIES

Makes 3 servings (1200 calories). Calories in 1 serving: 400.

1 cup cornmeal
1 egg
1 medium onion, finely chopped

¼ cup milk
2 teaspoons baking powder
½ teaspoon salt
Hot fat

1. Combine cornmeal, baking powder, salt and chopped onion. 2. Add egg and beat vigorously. Mix in the milk. 3. Shape into small patties. Drop into deep smoking fat until patties are deep brown. Serve hot.

HIGH CALORIE FOOD-DRINK

Makes 1 serving (650 calories).

½ cup light cream
½ cup ice cream
1 heaping tablespoon choco-
late-flavored malted milk
powder

1 egg
1 medium banana (ripe)

1. Place all ingredients in Waring Blendor, in the order given above. 2. Cover container and run Blendor about 30 seconds.

HOT CHOCOLATE

Makes 6 servings (1722 calories). Calories in 1 serving: 287.

3 squares unsweetened chocolate
⅔ cup Karo sirup, red label

¼ teaspoon salt
4 cups milk
½ teaspoon vanilla

1. Place chocolate and ½ cup boiling water in top of double boiler. Cook over direct heat, stirring constantly, until chocolate is melted. 2. Add sirup and salt; blend well. 3. Boil 3 minutes, stirring constantly. Place over hot water. Gradually add milk. Add vanilla. 4. Just before serving, beat with rotary beater until frothy. Serve very hot, topped with whipped cream, if desired.

SUNNY BREAD PUDDING

Makes 4 servings (2840 calories including Orange Pudding Sauce). Calories in 1 serving: 710.

3 eggs, beaten
1⅓ cups sugar
¼ teaspoon salt
1½ cups orange juice

4 cups cubes from day-old
bread
¼ cup grated coconut
2 tablespoons raisins

1. Combine eggs, sugar, salt and orange juice. Pour over bread. Stir in raisins and coconut. 2. Bake in buttered baking dish in moderate oven (350°F.) about 30 minutes, or until set. 3. Increase heat (450°F.) to brown peaks. Serve with Orange Pudding Sauce.

ORANGE PUDDING SAUCE

1 tablespoon cornstarch
½ cup sugar
1 teaspoon grated orange peel

1 cup orange juice
1 tablespoon lemon juice
2 tablespoons butter

1. Mix cornstarch, sugar, peel and orange juice. Boil 5 minutes. 2. Remove from fire. Add lemon juice and butter. Serve hot.

WALDORF-ASTORIA ICE CREAM PRALINE

Makes 12 servings (6600 calories). Calories in 1 serving: 550.
Our thanks to Executive Chef Ernest Treyvaud, for his assistance in supplying a famous recipe of a famous hostelry, the great Waldorf-Astoria Hotel in New York City.

1 pint cream	8 ounces praline paste
6 ounces granulated sugar	Fresh strawberries
(¾ cupful)	Orange liqueur or "Cordial
8 egg yolks	Medoc Liqueur"
1 pint whipped cream	

1. Mix the cream with sugar and egg yolks, over medium heat; stir while cooking. 2. Remove from stove before mixture boils. When cool, add the previously prepared praline paste. Strain the mixture, add whipped cream and set in a paper-collared mold. 3. Freeze for 1½ hours, then remove paper and serve on fancy ice cream form. Have very ripe fresh strawberries already macerated in liqueur; serve as a garnish.

RECIPE FOR PRALINE PASTE

1 pound powdered sugar	20 ounces dry unpeeled almonds

1. Melt sugar in small saucepan until it acquires a golden color.
2. Add the dry unpeeled almonds. Pour over an oiled platter and let cool. 3. When cool, pound or put through a fine meat grinder.

MELTING MOMENT COOKIES

Makes about 2 dozen cookies (2496 calories). Calories in 1 cookie: 104.

½ cup cornstarch	1 cup sifted all-purpose flour
½ cup confectioners' sugar	1 cup butter or margarine

1. Sift together cornstarch, confectioners' sugar and flour into bowl. 2. Have butter or margarine at room temperature. Blend butter into dry ingredients with a spoon until a soft dough is formed. Shape into balls about 1 inch in diameter. 3. Place on ungreased cookie sheet about 1½ inches apart. Flatten cookies with fork. To prevent sticking immerse tines of fork in hot water. Shake off excess moisture before pressing cookies. 4. Bake in slow oven (300°F.) 20 to 25 minutes or until edges of cookies are lightly browned.

Note: If dough is too soft to handle, cover and chill in refrigerator about 1 hour.

APPLE PANDOWDY

Makes 6 servings (1900 calories). Calories in 1 serving: 317.

1 can Musselman's sliced apples
⅓ cup brown sugar, firmly packed
¼ teaspoon nutmeg
¼ teaspoon cinnamon
¼ cup shortening

⅓ cup granulated sugar
1 egg
¾ cup sifted flour
¾ teaspoon baking powder
¼ teaspoon salt
⅓ cup milk

1. Cream shortening; add sugar gradually and beat until fluffy. Add egg and beat well. 2. Add sifted dry ingredients alternately with milk, and beat until smooth. Spread the brown sugar and spices over the sliced apples. 3. Spread the other mixture over the apples. Bake about 30 minutes in moderately hot oven (375°F.). 4. Serve warm with foamy sauce, hard sauce or whipped cream.

RICH PIE CRUST

Total calories: 2220.

2 cups cake flour
½ cup butter
⅓ cup lard

⅓ teaspoon baking powder
⅓ teaspoon salt

1. Sift the dry ingredients together and work in lard with knife or pastry mixer. Add enough ice water to make a stiff dough. 2. Roll out and dot with one-third of the butter. Roll up like a jelly roll and chill in refrigerator 20 minutes. 3. Repeat this rolling process twice, using one-third of the butter each time. Then wrap in waxed paper and chill 1 hour. 4. Divide into 2 pieces and roll out to ⅛-inch thickness and use either for two-crust pie, or for 2 open pies.

PINEAPPLE CREAM PIE

Makes 6 servings (2880 calories). Calories in 1 serving: 480.

1 baked 9-inch pie shell
½ cup flour
1 cup sugar
1 No. 2 can crushed pineapple

1 tablespoon butter
3 eggs
¼ teaspoon salt
1 cup whipped cream

1. Mix sugar, flour, salt. Add pineapple and 1 cup hot water. Boil until thick, stirring frequently. 2. Add butter and eggs, mix well with a little of the hot mixture, and cool. 3. Pour into baked shell. Place in refrigerator and when ready to serve, spread with whipped cream.

BANANA SPLIT

Makes 1 full-sized Banana Split (1000 calories).

1 ripe banana
3 balls or scoops ice cream (one, two or three flavors)
3 tablespoons chocolate sauce, butterscotch sauce or marshmallow sauce

6 tablespoons fruit sauce, crushed fruit or preserves
Whipped cream
Finely chopped nuts
Cherry or berry

1. Peel banana and cut lengthwise into halves. Place halves cut side up, side by side, in a shallow dish. 2. Place balls or scoops of ice cream, side by side, in center on top of banana halves. 3. Pour chocolate sauce, or other sauce, over 1 portion of ice cream. Cover other 2 portions of ice cream with fruit sauce, crushed fruit or preserves. 4. Garnish with whipped cream, nuts and cherry or berry, if desired.

RHUBARB PIE

Makes 6 servings (3150 calories). Calories in 1 serving: 525.

1 recipe Rich Pie Crust
2 cups peeled and cut rhubarb (1-inch pieces)
1 egg
1 tablespoon sifted flour

1 cup sugar, more or less, depending on sourness of rhubarb
Cold milk

1. Line 9-inch pie tin with Rich Pie Crust. 2. Plunge the rhubarb into boiling water. Cook 1 minute; drain thoroughly. 3. Mix sugar and egg well; add flour. Stir into rhubarb. 4. Fill pie crust with rhubarb mixture. Across the top, run lattice strips of pie crust dough. Brush with milk or ice water. 5. Bake on bottom shelf of very hot oven (450°F.) for 10 minutes. Then move to middle shelf and reduce oven to moderate heat (350°F.). Bake 35 minutes longer, or until rhubarb is tender.

CALIFORNIA RICE

Makes 6 servings (1880 calories). Calories in 1 serving: 313.

2 cups fluffy, cooked rice
½ pint whipping cream
1 cup orange juice

¾ cup sugar
1 tablespoon grated orange peel

1. Sprinkle 1 teaspoon of the grated peel over the rice. When cold fold the rice into the whipped cream. 2. Serve with sauce made by combining the orange juice, sugar and remaining grated peel. Stir to dissolve sugar.

ORANGE-FLAVORED PIE CRUST

Makes 1 pie crust (1500 calories).

1½ cups sifted flour	1 teaspoon grated orange peel
1 tablespoon sugar	½ cup shortening
½ teaspoon salt	¼ cup orange juice (about)

1. Sift dry ingredients and add orange peel. Cut in shortening until pieces are about the size of small peas. **2.** Add orange juice, a small amount at a time, mixing lightly with fork only enough to make the particles hold together. **3.** Continue until all ingredients are mixed and there are neither sticky nor crumbly portions. Handle as little as possible. Wrap in waxed paper and chill thoroughly. **4.** Roll out on lightly floured board. Fit into 9-inch pie plate, prick bottom and sides; or fit second pie plate inside on crust to hold crust in shape. **5.** Bake in very hot oven (450°F.) 15 minutes, or until browned.

ORANGE MERINGUE PIE

Makes 1 pie, 6 servings (3240 calories). Calories in 1 serving: 540.

1 baked 9-inch Orange Pastry shell	2 cups orange juice
	3 egg yolks
1 cup sugar	1 tablespoon butter
5 tablespoons cornstarch	2 tablespoons lemon juice
¼ teaspoon salt	3 egg whites
1 tablespoon grated orange peel	6 tablespoons sugar

1. Mix 1 cup of sugar with the cornstarch, salt and grated peel in double boiler top. **2.** Add the orange juice and cook over boiling water about 15 minutes, or until thickened, stirring frequently. **3.** Stir in beaten egg yolks and cook 2 minutes. Remove from stove. Add butter and lemon juice. Cool slightly. **4.** Pour into baked 9-inch Orange-Flavored Pie Crust. Cover with meringue made by beating 3 egg whites until frothy, and gradually beating in the 6 tablespoons sugar. **5.** Place in moderate oven (350°F.) about 15 minutes, or until delicately browned.

BLANC MANGE

Makes 4 servings (2880 calories). Calories in 1 serving: 320.

1 quart milk	8 tablespoonsful cornstarch
½ cup sugar	¼ teaspoonful salt

1. Put milk on to boil. Moisten the cornstarch with a little cold milk, then add to the boiling milk, and stir until it thickens; add the sugar and salt. **2.** Take away from fire, pour it into custard cups, and put in refrigerator to harden. **3.** Serve with cream sauce.

BANANA FRITTERS

Makes 9 fritters (3200 calories). Calories in 1 fritter: 355.

Melted fat or salad oil	¼ cup flour
3 firm bananas	Fritter batter

1. To deep-fry, have deep kettle ½ to ⅔ full of melted fat or oil. To shallow-fry, have 1½ to 2 inches of melted fat or oil in frying pan. 2. Heat fat to 375°F., or until a 1-inch cube of bread will brown in about 40 seconds. 3. Peel bananas and cut each crosswise into 3 diagonal pieces. Roll in flour. Dip into fritter batter, completely coating the banana pieces with the batter. 4. Deep-fry or shallow-fry in the hot fat about 6 minutes, or until well browned. Turn fritters frequently to brown evenly. Drain on a rack. 5. Serve hot with the main course, or serve as a dessert with a hot fruit sauce, sirup or sweetened whipped cream.

FRITTER BATTER

1 cup sifted flour	1 egg, well beaten
2 teaspoons baking powder	⅓ cup milk
1¼ teaspoons salt	2 teaspoons melted shortening
¼ cup sugar	

1. Sift together flour, baking powder, salt and sugar into mixing bowl. 2. Combine egg, milk and shortening. Add to dry ingredients and mix until batter is smooth.

Important: Have fat at correct temperature (375°F.) before frying. This is a stiff batter and it makes a crisp fritter which will stay crisp for 15 to 20 minutes. This batter should not be "thinned down."

FRENCH TOAST WITH SLICED BANANAS

Makes 4 servings (1800 calories). Calories in 1 serving: 450.

3 eggs, slightly beaten	Butter or margarine
1 cup milk	8 slices bread
1½ teaspoons sugar	2 ripe bananas
¼ teaspoon nutmeg	

1. Combine eggs, milk, sugar and nutmeg in mixing bowl. Melt butter or margarine in large frying pan. 2. Dip bread slices, one at a time, into egg mixture. Remove immediately and place into frying pan. 3. Fry over low heat until bread is browned on both sides, turning once. 4. Peel bananas. Slice the bananas over half of the pieces of French toast. Cover each piece quickly with another piece of French toast, making a sandwich. 5. Serve hot, with sirup or confectioners' sugar if desired.

SHOO-FLY PIE

Makes 1 pie, 6 servings (2160 calories). Calories in 1 serving: 360.

1 unbaked 9-inch pastry shell	2 tablespoons shortening
½ tablespoon soda	¼ teaspoon salt
½ cup molasses	½ teaspoon cinnamon
1 egg yolk (beaten well)	⅛ teaspoon nutmeg
¾ cup flour	⅛ teaspoon ginger
½ cup dark brown sugar	

1. Dissolve the soda in ¾ cup boiling water, add the molasses and beaten egg yolk. 2. Mix the dry ingredients together, then work in the shortening, to make crumbs. 3. Line a pie pan with pastry. Fill pastry with alternate layers of liquid and crumbs. 4. Put crumbs on top and bake in very hot oven (450°F.) until edges of crust start to brown. 5. Reduce heat to moderate (350°F.) and bake about 20 minutes more or until firm.

CHOCOLATE PECAN PIE

Makes 6 servings (4200 calories). Calories in 1 serving: 700.

Pastry for one-crust pie	3 eggs, slightly beaten
2 squares Baker's unsweetened chocolate	1 teaspoon vanilla
	1 cup coarsely chopped pecan meats
3 tablespoons butter	
1 cup light corn sirup	½ cup heavy cream, whipped
¾ cup sugar	

1. Line a 9-inch pie plate with pastry rolled ⅛-inch thick, allowing pastry to extend 1 inch beyond edge. 2. Fold edge back to form standing rim and flute with fingers. 3. Melt chocolate and butter over hot water. Boil sirup and sugar together 2 minutes. 4. Add chocolate mixture. Pour slowly over eggs, stirring constantly. Add vanilla and nuts. Turn into pie shell. 5. Bake in moderately hot oven (375°F.) 45 to 50 minutes, or until pie is completely puffed across top. Cool. Top with whipped cream.

TART CHERRY CREAM

Makes 4 servings (1072 calories). Calories in 1 serving: 268.

1 package Cherry Jell-O	¾ cup sour cream
½ cup evaporated milk	¼ cup chopped walnuts

1. Dissolve Jell-O in 1 cup *hot* water. Add ¾ cup cold water and evaporated milk. 2. Chill until slightly thickened. Then fold in sour cream and walnuts. 3. Turn into sherbet glasses. Chill until firm.

COFFEE CHARLOTTE SQUARES

Makes 8 servings (2150 calories). Calories in 1 serving: 268.

2 tablespoons Instant Maxwell House or Instant Sanka coffee

1 cup heavy cream, whipped

½ pound (32) marshmallows, cut in small pieces

18 double ladyfingers

1. Dissolve instant coffee in 1 cup hot water. Add marshmallows. Place over low heat and stir until marshmallows are completely melted. 2. Chill until slightly thickened. Fold in whipped cream. 3. Separate ladyfingers and line bottom of shallow oblong serving dish. Top with half of the coffee mixture. 4. Cover with another layer of ladyfingers and top with remaining coffee mixture. 5. Chill in refrigerator 8 hours or overnight. Serve in squares.

JELLY ROLL

Makes 8 servings (2400 calories). Calories in 1 serving: 300.

1 cup tart jelly
3 eggs
1 cup sugar
3 tablespoons milk

1⅓ cups cake flour
½ teaspoon salt
1½ teaspoons baking powder
1 teaspoon vanilla

1. Beat eggs well. Add sifted sugar gradually and continue beating. 2. Add liquid and vanilla, and beat. Sift flour, measure and add salt and baking powder. Sift again. 3. Sift slowly over egg mixture, fold in with a wire whisk. Cover a shallow pan 12 x 16 x ½ inch with waxed paper. Pour dough in pan. 4. Bake in hot oven (400°F.) for 12 to 14 minutes. Turn out on a damp cloth that has been sprinkled with powdered sugar. Remove paper, cut off hard crusts. Allow to cool. 5. Spread with tart jelly—a good one is Musselman's apple blackberry. Roll up, jelly-roll fashion.

FRUIT TAPIOCA

Makes 4 servings (800 calories). Calories in 1 serving: 200.

1 package Jell-O Tapioca Pudding; vanilla or orange-coconut flavor

1¾ cups fruit juice and water

1 cup well-drained cut or crushed canned or fresh fruit, sweetened if necessary

1 to 2 tablespoons lemon juice

1. Place pudding powder in saucepan. Add fruit juice and water and mix well. 2. Cook and stir over medium heat until mixture comes to a boil and is slightly thickened. (Do not overcook—pudding thickens as it cools.) 3. Add fruit and lemon juice as needed for tartness. Cool, stirring once after 15 to 20 minutes. 4. Turn into sherbet glasses or serving bowl. Chill. Serve plain or with cream.

CARAMEL RICE

Makes 6 servings (2070 calories). Calories in 1 serving: 345.

1 cup sugar	¼ cup sugar
⅔ cup Minute Rice	½ teaspoon vanilla
2 cups milk	⅓ cup raisins
2 tablespoons butter	2 egg whites, stiffly beaten
2 egg yolks	⅓ cup light cream, whipped

1. Combine Minute Rice and milk in saucepan. Cook, covered, over low heat 15 minutes, fluffing rice occasionally with a fork. Add butter and cool to lukewarm. **2.** Cook 1 cup sugar in skillet over low heat until lightly browned, stirring constantly with wooden spoon. **3.** Pour half of this caramelized sugar into 1-quart baking dish, spreading to coat sides of dish. Add ¼ cup water to remaining caramel. Cook slowly 2 or 3 minutes, stirring until blended. Chill. **4.** Beat egg yolks with ¼ cup sugar until light. Add to rice. Add vanilla and raisins. Fold in egg whites. Turn into the caramel-coated baking dish. Cover. Place in pan of hot water. **5.** Bake in moderate oven (350°F.) 50 minutes. Serve warm. Fold chilled caramel into whipped cream and serve with the pudding.

INDIAN PUDDING

Makes 6 servings (1590 calories). Calories in 1 serving: 265.

4 cups milk	½ teaspoon salt
⅓ cup cornmeal	½ cup molasses
¼ cup sugar	2 tablespoons melted butter or
½ teaspoon cinnamon	margarine
¼ teaspoon nutmeg	

1. Scald 3 cups of the milk in the top of double boiler. **2.** Add cornmeal, sugar, spices, salt, molasses and butter. Cook over boiling water, stirring constantly until the mixture thickens or for about 20 minutes. **3.** Pour into a greased baking pan. **4.** Add the remaining cup of milk, without stirring. **5.** Bake in a slow oven (300°F.) for about 2½ hours. Serve warm with milk or cream or ice cream.

QUICK APPLE DESSERT

Makes 3 servings (720 calories). Calories in 1 serving: 240.

1 jar Musselman's Pennsylvania Dutch "Applpie" filling	½ teaspoon cinnamon
	Blanched almonds
1 tablespoon butter or margarine	Light cream

1. Pour contents of jar of Applpie into a baking dish, add butter or margarine, cinnamon. **2.** Slice almonds in strips and stick halfway into apple slices. **3.** Place in moderate oven (350°F.) until nuts are brown. Cool. Serve with cream.

BANANA WHIPPED CREAM PIE

Makes 1 pie, 6 servings (2100 calories). Calories in 1 serving: 350.

5 ripe bananas	Toasted coconut, or finely
1 baked 9-inch pie shell	chopped nuts, grated semi-
1 cup heavy cream	sweet chocolate, or finely
2 tablespoons sugar	chopped candied fruit peel
Few drops vanilla or almond	Dash of salt
flavoring	

1. Add salt to cream and beat with rotary egg beater or electric mixer until stiff enough to hold its shape. **2.** Fold in sugar and vanilla or almond flavoring. Cover bottom of pie shell with small amount of whipped cream. **3.** Peel bananas and slice into pie shell. Cover immediately with remaining whipped cream. **4.** Garnish with toasted coconut or other topping.

STICKY CINNAMON BUNS

Makes about 2 dozen buns (2700 calories). Calories in 1 bun: 112.

1 cup scalded milk	3 tablespoons sugar
2 tablespoons dried currants	3 cups flour
½ cup chopped raisins	½ teaspoon salt
½ teaspoon cinnamon	3 tablespoons butter
2 tablespoons chopped citron	Brown sugar
½ yeast cake	

1. Dissolve yeast in ¼ cup warm water and add to milk, which should be lukewarm. **2.** Add 3 tablespoons of sugar, salt and flour and knead thoroughly until it becomes a soft dough. **3.** Put the dough in a buttered bowl and also butter the top of the dough. Cover bowl and put in a warm place. **4.** Let stand until dough becomes three times its original size. Then roll until it is ¼ inch in thickness, brush with butter and spread with the raisins, currants, citron, brown sugar and cinnamon. **5.** Roll as a jelly roll and cut into slices ¾-inch thick. Place slices in buttered pans, spread well with brown sugar, and bake in hot oven (400°F.) for 20 minutes.

APPLE BUTTER CAKE

Makes 8 servings (3680 calories). Calories in 1 serving: 460.

1 cup Musselman's or other apple butter	½ teaspoon salt
½ cup shortening	1½ teaspoons soda
4 eggs, beaten	1 teaspoon cinnamon
1 cup sugar	½ teaspoon nutmeg
2½ cups all-purpose flour	½ teaspoon cloves
	1 cup sour milk or buttermilk

1. Cream the shortening. Add sugar gradually and continue to cream until fluffy. 2. Add well-beaten eggs and mix thoroughly. Sift flour, measure, and sift again with soda, spices and salt. 3. Add dry ingredients alternately with sour milk. Add apple butter and blend well into mixture. 4. Pour into a greased loaf pan 5 x 9 x 4 inches. Bake 50 minutes in moderate oven (350°F.).

ALMOND BREAD

Makes about 3 dozen pieces (4130 calories). Calories in 1 piece: 115.

1 cup sugar	3 teaspoons baking powder
3 eggs	½ teaspoon salt
½ cup shortening	1 cup blanched almonds, finely
3 cups sifted all-purpose flour	chopped

1. Mix and sift flour, baking powder and salt. 2. Cream shortening. Add eggs gradually, one at a time, beating well after each addition. 3. Stir in dry ingredients and chopped almonds. Shape into two loaves, place on greased baking sheet and bake in moderate oven (350°F.) 30 to 35 minutes. 4. Remove to board, cut into ½-inch slices. Place on baking sheet and put under broiler until golden brown. Turn and brown on other side.

WHIPPED CREAM WITH BERRIES OR PINEAPPLE

Makes 6 servings (1200 calories). Calories in 1 serving: 200.

2 cups diced or crushed pineapple, or berries, sweetened to taste	1 cup chilled heavy cream
	¼ cup vanilla sugar

1. Beat cream, and add sugar gradually 2. Add fruit to the whipped cream and serve in dessert dishes or sherbet glasses. If desired, use some of the fruit as a garnish.

BANANA OATMEAL COOKIES

Makes about 40 cookies (4000 calories). Calories in 1 cookie: 100.

1½ cups sifted flour	¾ cup shortening
1 cup sugar	1 egg, well beaten
½ teaspoon baking soda	1 cup mashed ripe bananas
1 teaspoon salt	(2 to 3 bananas)
¼ teaspoon nutmeg	1¾ cups rolled quick oats
¾ teaspoon cinnamon	½ cup chopped nuts

1. Sift together flour, sugar, soda, salt, nutmeg and cinnamon into mixing bowl. Cut in shortening. **2.** Add egg, bananas, rolled oats and nuts. Beat until thoroughly blended. Drop by teaspoonfuls, about 1½ inches apart, onto ungreased cookie pans. **3.** Bake in a hot oven (400°F.) about 15 minutes, or until cookies are done. Remove from pan immediately.

CHEESE FRITTERS

Makes 1 serving (640 calories).

1 egg yolk	1 tablespoon dry mustard
3 ounces cheddar cheese	Pinch of cayenne
2 tablespoons butter	Butter for frying
2 tablespoons bread crumbs	

1. Mix all the ingredients to a smooth paste; roll out to ½-inch thickness. Cut into strips three inches by one inch. **2.** Coat in butter and fry to a golden brown. Drain on paper and serve very hot.

COCONUT PRALINE SAUCE

Makes 1⅓ cups (1660 calories).

⅓ cup butter	2 tablespoons light corn sirup
1 cup Baker's coconut, cut	¾ cup evaporated milk
½ cup brown sugar, firmly	½ teaspoon vanilla
packed	Dash of salt

1. Melt butter in saucepan. Add coconut and sauté until golden brown, stirring constantly. **2.** Remove coconut. Add sugar, corn sirup and salt. Place over low heat until mixture bubbles vigorously, stirring constantly. **3.** Add milk gradually, bring to a boil, and boil gently 1½ minutes. **4.** Remove from stove. Add vanilla and coconut. **5.** Serve warm or cold on plain cake, ice cream, or pudding.

CHOCOLATE DIXIE WAFFLES

Makes about five 7-inch waffles (2360 calories). Calories in 1 waffle plain: 472. Calories in 1 waffle with 1 ball of ice cream and 2 tablespoons sirup: 672.

2 squares Baker's unsweetened chocolate, melted
2 cups sifted flour
2½ teaspoons Calumet baking powder
¾ teaspoon salt
⅓ cup sugar

2 eggs, well beaten
1½ cups milk
5 tablespoons shortening, melted
Ice cream
Sirup

1. Sift flour once, measure, add baking powder, salt, and sugar, and sift again. **2.** Combine eggs and milk. Add to flour mixture, add shortening, then mix *only* until smooth. **3.** Add chocolate and blend. Bake in hot waffle iron. **4.** Top hot waffle quarters with ice cream and serve with sirup.

QUAKER-JACK

Total calories: 1680.

1 cup sugar
1 teaspoon vinegar
½ package Quaker Puffed Rice

3 tablespoons molasses
1 tablespoon butter
½ teaspoon salt

1. Combine sugar, vinegar and ½ cup water. Bring to a boil and cook 5 minutes. **2.** Add molasses, butter and salt and cook until a few drops in cold water become hard and brittle. **3.** Crisp the puffed rice in a moderate oven (350°F.) 10 minutes. **4.** Pour hot sirup over the puffed rice, stirring quickly and spread in greased pan to cool.

CHEESE SNACKS

Total calories: 1050.

6 cups Puffed Rice
⅓ cup butter or margarine
½ teaspoon paprika

6 drops tabasco sauce (optional)
¼ cup grated American cheese

1. Measure puffed rice into a shallow pan; heat in a moderate oven (350°F.) 10 minutes. Place in a large bowl. **2.** Melt butter; cool, and then add tabasco sauce, paprika and grated cheese. **3.** Slowly pour over puffed rice, mixing so all kernels are coated.

CALORIE CONTENT OF MORE THAN 400 FOODS

The handy lists on this and the following pages show graphically the number of calories in many common foods. Generally speaking, the low calorie dieter will look to the lower portion of the lists for menu suggestions, and the high calorie dieter will tend to make selections from the top of the lists.

FISH

	Average Serving	Calories	
Smelts (fried)	4 to 5 smelts	448	
Scallops (fried)	5 to 6 medium	427	
Frog Legs (fried)	6 large legs	418	
Oysters (fried)	6 oysters	412	
Lake Trout (broiled)	1 serving (1/5 pound)	290	
Bass (baked)	1 serving 3″ x 3″ x ½″	287	
Porgy (fried)	1 medium serving	279	
Mackerel (broiled)	1 piece, 4″ x 2″ x ¾″	273	
Bluefish (broiled)	1 serving, ½ fish	269	
Shad Roe (baked)	½ medium roe	262	
Shad (broiled)	1 serving (1/5 pound)	250	
Tuna (canned)	¾ cup	240	
Herring (pickled)	2 small fish	223	
Brook Trout (broiled)	1 serving (1/5 pound)	216	
Haddock (fried)	1 fillet, 3″ x 3″ x ½″	214	
Butterfish (fried)	1 fish, 6¼″ long	211	
Halibut Steak	1 serving (¼ pound)	205	
Flounder or Sole (baked)	1 serving (¼ pound)	204	
Codfish Cakes	2 balls or 1 large cake	202	
Herring	1 small fish	190	
Eel (fresh)	1 serving (¼ pound)	180	
Cod Steak (baked)	1 piece, 4 oz. (raw)	170	
Perch (fried)	1 serving	162	
Whitefish	1 piece, 3″ x 3″ x ⅞″	156	
Salmon	1 serving, ⅔ cup	150	
Lobster (broiled)	1 lobster, ¾ pound	108	
Sardines	1 fish, 3″ x 1½″ x 1″	107	
Crab	⅝ cup flakes	104	
Smoked Salmon	2 to 3 small slices	90	
Clams, long, round	5 to 10 clams	81	
Shrimp (canned)	4 to 6 shrimps	64	
Anchovies	5 thin fillets	35	

518

MEATS

	Average Serving		Calories
Porterhouse Steak	1	large steak (⅓ pound)	513
Beef Rump (pot roasted)	1	slice, 5″ x 3½″ x ¼″	320
Roast Beef	3	slices, 3″ x 2¼″ x ¼″	287
Roast Pork Loin	2	slices, 3½″ x 3″ x ¼″	266
Salami	2	slices, 3¾″ diam. x ¼″	260
Sirloin Steak	1	piece, 4″ x 2¼″ x 1″	252
Beef Flank (cooked)	1	piece, 4″ x 2½″ x ½″	251
Frankfurter	2	average, 5½″ long	248
Hamburger (ground beef)	1	medium patty	246
Roast Leg of Lamb	3	slices, 3″ x 2¾″ x ⅛″	246
Roast Pork Spareribs	6	average ribs	246
Chicken (hen, stewed)	3	slices, 3½″ x 2⅝″ x ¼″	246
Fresh Ham (cooked)	2	slices, 4″ x 2½″ x ⅛″	240
Bologna	4	slices, 4½″ diam. x ⅛″	240
Liverwurst	3	slices, 3″ diam. x ¼″	240
Smoked Ham (cooked)	2	slices, 4″ x 2½″ x ⅛″	238
Pork Chop (loin)	1	medium chop, fried	233
Chicken (broiler)	¼	bird, fried	232
Chicken (fryer)	½	breast, fried	232
Breast of Veal (raw)	4	pieces, 2½″ x 1″ x 1″	223
Veal Cutlet (breaded)	1	average serving	217
Corned Beef (canned)	3	slices, 3″ x 2½″ x ¼″	216
Lamb Chops (shoulder)	1	chop	215
Round of Beef (cubed)	1	piece, 4″ x 3″ x ⅜″	214
Dried Chipped Beef	6	slices, 4″ x 5″	210
Turkey (roasted)	3	slices, 3½″ x 2¼″ x ¼″	200
Pork Sausage	2	links, 3″ long x ½″	188
Beef Liver (cooked)	2	slices, 3″ x 2¼″ x ⅜″	172
Beef Shank (soup meat)	1	piece, 3″ x 2½″ x ⅝″	168
Beef Tongue	3	slices, 3″ x 2″ x ⅛″	160
Hamburger (round only)	1	medium patty	160
Calf Liver (cooked)	2	slices, 3″ x 2¼″ x ⅜″	148
Beef Kidney	3	slices, 3″ x 2½″ x ¼″	141
Corned Beef Hash	½	cup serving	141
Lamb Chops (rib)	1	chop	128
Chicken (fryer)	2	small legs, fried	126
Brains	2	pieces, 2½″ x 1½″ x ⅞″	125
Bacon	2	strips	100

CEREALS AND FLOURS

	Average Serving	Calories	
Bisquick	1 cup	490	
Aunt Jemima Pancake Mix	1 cup	432	
Bread Flour (wheat)	1 cup	408	
All-purpose Flour (wheat)	1 cup	401	
Self-rising Flour (wheat)	1 cup	385	
Softasilk Cake Flour	1 cup	325	
Rye Flour	1 cup	285	
Soy Flour (full fat)	1 cup	250	
Spaghetti	1 cup, cooked	218	
Macaroni	1 cup, cooked	209	
Rice	1 cup, cooked	201	
Oatmeal	1 cup, cooked	148	
Corn Grits (Hominy)	1 cup, cooked	122	
Cornmeal	1 cup, cooked	119	
Post's Sugar Crisps	1 ounce	110	
Rice Krispies	1 cup	108	
Egg Noodles	1 cup, cooked	107	
Kellogg's Pep	1 cup	107	
Puffed Rice	1 cup	107	
Pablum	¾ cup	105	
Shredded Ralston	½ cup	105	
Wheaties	1 cup	105	
Shredded Wheat	1 large biscuit	102	
Wheatena	⅔ cup, cooked	101	
Cream of Wheat	¾ cup, cooked	100	
Grape-Nuts	¼ cup	100	
Grape-Nuts Flakes	1 cup	100	
Kix	1 cup	100	
Post Toasties or Ralston	scant ¾ cup, cooked	100	
Barley	2 tablespoons	99	
Pettijohn's Wheat	⅔ cup, cooked	99	
40% Bran Flakes	¾ cup	97	
Cheerios	1 cup	92	
Kellogg's All-Bran	½ cup	89	
Corn Flakes	1 cup	80	
Wheat Germ	2 tablespoons	72	
Popcorn, popped	1 cup	54	
Puffed Wheat	1 cup	44	
Tapioca, granulated	1 tablespoon	36	
Cornstarch	1 tablespoon	29	

CRACKERS, CAKES, BREADSTUFFS

	Average Serving	Calories
Chocolate Layer Cake	1 piece, 1/12 cake	356
Bread Crumbs, dry	1 cup, grated	339
Waffle	1 small, 5½" diam.	232
Cup Cake, iced	1 medium	230
Plain Cake	1 piece, 2" x 3"	228
Gingerbread	2" x 2" x 2"	206
Coffee Cake, iced	1 cake, 4½" diam.	196
Cinnamon Bun	1 bun	158
Angel Cake	1 piece, 1/10 cake	145
Brownies	1 piece, 2" square	141
Danish Pastry	1 small	140
Cornbread	1 piece, 2" square	139
Doughnut	1 plain	135
Muffin	1 average	120
Oatmeal Cookies	1 large cookie	114
Biscuit	1 biscuit, 2" diam.	109
Macaroons	1 large	108
Hard Roll	1 roll	95
Popover	1 average	90
Roll (Parker House)	1 roll	81
Matzoh	1 tea matzoh	78
Pretzel	1 medium	72
Boston Brown Bread	1 slice, ½" thick	71
Pancake	1 pancake, 4" diam.	68
Raisin Bread	1 slice	65
White Bread	1 slice	63
Oreo Crackers	1 sandwich	62
Rye Bread	1 slice	57
Fig Newton	1 small, average	56
Whole Wheat Bread	1 slice	55
French Bread	1 slice	54
Lady Fingers	1 large	37
Cracker Meal	1 tablespoon	34
Zwieback	1 piece	32
Pretzel Sticks	5 thin sticks	25
Oysterettes	5 crackers	21
Ry-Krisp	1 double square wafer	21
Saltines	1 cracker	17
Ritz Crackers	1 cracker	16
Graham Crackers	1 cracker	13
Animal Crackers	1 cracker	9
Cheese Tid-Bits	5 crackers	7

DAIRY PRODUCTS

	Average Serving	Calories	
Condensed Milk	½ cup	490	
Evaporated Milk	½ cup	173	
Milk, Whole	½ pint, 8 oz.	166	
Yogurt	½ pint, 8 oz.	160	
Ice Cream	½ cup	154	
Cheddar Cheese	1 ounce	113	
Parmesan Cheese	1 ounce	112	
Cottage Cheese	½ cup	108	
Cream Cheese	1 ounce	106	
Swiss Cheese	1 ounce	105	
Bleu Cheese	1 ounce	104	
Butter	1 tablespoon	100	
Limburger Cheese	1 ounce	97	
Velveeta Cheese	1 ounce	92	
Edam Cheese	1 ounce	87	
Skim Milk	½ pint, 8 oz.	87	
Buttermilk	½ pint, 8 oz.	86	
Camembert Cheese	1 ounce	85	
Eggs, Whole	1 medium egg	77	
Cream, Light (sweet or sour)	1 ounce, 2 tbsp	61	
Egg Yolk	1 average	61	
Cream, Whipped	1 heaping tbsp	50	
Cream, Heavy	1 tablespoon	49	
Egg White	1 average	16	

NUTS

		Calories	
Brazil Nuts	1 nut	48	
Shredded Coconut	1 tablespoon	42	
Coconut	1 piece, 1″ x ½″ x ½″	35	
Butter Nuts	1 nut	19	
Cashew Nuts	1 nut	11	
Chestnuts	1 nut	10	
Pecans	1 nut	9	
Filberts	1 nut	8	
Walnuts	1 nut	8	
Hickory Nuts	1 nut	7.	
Litchi Nuts	1 nut	7	
Almonds	1 nut	6	
Peanuts	1 nut	5	
Pistachio Nuts	1 nut	3	

FRUITS

	Average Serving	Calories	
Avocado	½ small pear	245	
Raisins (dried)	½ cup	215	
Rhubarb (cooked)	½ cup, sweetened	137	
Prunes (dried)	5 large	134	
Banana	1 medium or 1 cup slices	132	
Dates (dried, pitted)	¼ cup	126	
Cherries (canned)	½ cup, sirup pack	105	
Fruit Cocktail (canned)	½ cup	94	
Blueberries (fresh)	1 cup	85	
Blackberries (fresh)	1 cup	82	
Figs (dried)	2 small	81	
Apricots (canned)	4 halves, 2 tablespoons sirup	80	
Apricots (dried)	4 to 6 halves	79	
Figs (raw)	2 large	79	
Pineapple (canned)	1 slice, 1 tablespoon sirup	78	
Apple	1 medium, 2½″ diam.	76	
Plums (canned)	2 medium, 1 tablespoon sirup	76	
Grapefruit (fresh)	½ medium grapefruit	72	
Seedless Grapes	1 bunch (¼ pound)	70	
Oranges	1 medium, 3″ diam.	68	
Peaches (canned)	2 halves, 1 tablespoon sirup	68	
Pears (canned)	2 halves, 1 tablespoon sirup	68	
Honeydew Melon	½ of 5″ melon	64	
Pears (fresh)	1 medium pear	63	
Cherries (fresh)	15 large	60	
Watermelon	1 cup cubes	56	
Apricots (fresh)	2 to 3 medium	51	
Applesauce	½ cup, unsweetened	50	
Cranberries (fresh)	1 cup	50	
Plums (fresh)	2 medium plums	50	
Peaches (fresh)	1 medium large	46	
Loganberries (fresh)	½ cup	45	
Pineapple (fresh)	1 slice, ¾″ thick	44	
Tangerines	1 large	44	
Cranberry Sauce	1 rounded tablespoon	40	
Red Raspberries (fresh)	½ cup	39	
Limes	1 large	37	
Lemons	1 medium	32	
Nectarines	1 medium	30	
Strawberries (fresh)	½ cup	27	
Cantaloupe	½ cup, diced	24	

VEGETABLES

	Average Serving	Calories	
Sweet Potatoes	1 medium, baked	183	▬▬▬
Yams	½ cup, cooked	120	▬▬
Pinto Beans	½ cup, cooked	120	▬▬
Red Kidney Beans	½ cup, cooked	115	▬▬
Lentils	½ cup, cooked	101	▬▬
Corn	½ cup or 1 ear 5″ long	85	▬▬
White Potatoes	1 potato, 2¼″ diam.	83	▬▬
Lima Beans	½ cup, cooked	76	▬
Green Peas	½ cup, cooked	56	▬
Artichokes	1 large bud	51	▬
Brussels Sprouts	9 medium	47	▬
Parsnips	½ cup, cooked	47	▬
Winter Squash	½ cup, baked	47	▬
Onions	1 raw, 2¼″ diam.	45	▬
Rutabagas	½ cup, cooked	42	▬
Collards	½ cup, cooked	40	▬
Leeks	3 to 4	40	▬
Onions	½ cup, cooked	38	▬
Green Beans	1 cup	35	▬
Pumpkin	½ cup, canned	35	▬
Beets	½ cup, diced	34	▬
Bean Sprouts	1 cup	30	▬
Tomatoes	1 medium, raw	30	▬
Broccoli	1 large stalk	29	▬
Okra	8 pods, cooked	28	▬
Greens (Beet, Turnip, etc.)	½ cup, cooked	27	▮
Bamboo Shoots	¾ cup	25	▮
Eggplant	2 slices or ½ cup	24	▮
Carrots	½ cup, diced	23	▮
Kohlrabi	½ cup, cooked	23	▮
Spinach	½ cup, cooked	23	▮
Tomatoes	½ cup, canned	23	▮
Kale	½ cup	22	▮
Sauerkraut	⅔ cup, canned	22	▮
Asparagus	⅔ cup pieces	20	▮
Cabbage	½ cup, cooked	20	▮
Green Peppers	1 medium shell	19	▮
Summer Squash	½ cup, cooked	18	▮
Mushrooms	10 small or 4 large	16	▮
Cauliflower	½ cup, cooked	15	▮

(continued)

VEGETABLES (continued)

Chard	½ cup, cooked	15
Shredded Cabbage	½ cup, raw	12
Celery	½ cup, cooked	12
Pickles	1 large dill	11
Chicory or Curly Endive	15 to 20 inner leaves	10
Pimientos	1 medium, canned	9
Celery	1 large stalk	7
Cucumber	½ medium	6
Lettuce	3 small leaves	5
Garlic	2 cloves	4
Radishes	2 small, raw	4
Watercress	10 sprigs	2
Parsley	2 sprigs	1

SOUPS

	Average Serving	Calories
Homemade Oyster Stew	1 serving containing ½ cup milk, 4 oysters	321
Homemade Split Pea	¾ cup	201
Homemade Cream of Tomato	¾ cup	196
Homemade Bean	¾ cup	195
Heinz Cream of Mushroom	1 serving*	183
Homemade Cream of Celery	¾ cup scant	157
Campbell's Tomato	1 serving*	146
Campbell's Cream of Asparagus	1 serving*	132
Campbell's Green Pea	1 serving*	102
Campbell's Beef	1 serving*	94
Heinz Vegetable-Beef	1 serving*	81
Heinz Vegetable—No Meat	1 serving*	81
Campbell's Ox Tail	1 serving*	77
Heinz Clam Chowder	1 serving*	70
Campbell's Vegetable	1 serving*	68
Heinz Beef Noodle	1 serving*	68
Heinz Chicken with Rice	1 serving*	39
Campbell's Consommé	1 serving*	29
Campbell's Bouillon	1 serving*	27

*3 from 1 can

See Index for additional calorie counts of Campbell's and Heinz soups.

BEVERAGES

	Average Serving	Calories	
Chocolate Malted Milk	1 regular (8 oz. milk)	502	
Chocolate Milk Shake	1 regular (8 oz. milk)	421	
Ice Cream Soda	1 regular	255	
Ovaltine	1 glass (8 oz. milk)	235	
Eggnog (without liquor)	1 glass (6 oz. milk)	233	
Hot Chocolate	1 teacup (6 oz. milk)	208	
Chocolate Milk	½ pint, 8 oz.	185	
Cocoa	1 teacup (6 oz. milk)	174	
Milk, whole	½ pint, 8 oz.	166	
Hot Chocolate	1 teacup (3 oz. milk)	146	
Beer	1 large glass, 8 oz.	114	
Cocoa	1 teacup (3 oz. milk)	112	
Cordials	1 oz.	110	
Lemonade	1 large glass, 8 oz.	104	
Cider or Apple Juice	1 glass, 6 oz.	94	
Skim Milk	½ pint, 8 oz.	87	
Buttermilk	½ pint, 8 oz.	86	
White Wine	1 wine glass	85	
Prune Juice	4 oz.	84	
Orange Juice (fresh or unsweetened canned)	1 glass, 6 oz.	81	
Carbonated Drinks (Cola, Ginger Ale, etc.)	1 bottle, 6 oz.	78	
Coffee (1 teaspoon sugar, 2 tablespoons light cream)	1 teacup	76	
Tea (1 teaspoon sugar, 2 tablespoons light cream)	1 teacup	76	
Red Wine	1 wine glass	73	
Grape Juice	3 oz.	67	
Coconut Milk	1 large glass, 8 oz.	60	
Pineapple Juice	4 oz.	60	
Grapefruit Juice (fresh or unsweetened canned)	4 oz.	47	
Postum, black	1 teacup	34	
Tomato Juice	4 oz.	25	
Tea (1 teaspoon sugar, 1 lemon slice)	1 teacup	20	
Coffee, black		0	
Tea, clear		0	
Water or Carbonated Water		0	

FATS AND OILS

		Calories
Bacon Fat	1 tablespoon	126
Chicken Fat	1 tablespoon	126
Lard	1 tablespoon	126
Olive Oil	1 tablespoon	124
Peanut Oil	1 tablespoon	124
Corn Oil	1 tablespoon	124
Suet, rendered	1 tablespoon	118
Vegetable Shortenings	1 tablespoon	110
Margarine	1 tablespoon	101
Butter	1 tablespoon	100
Mayonnaise (average)	1 tablespoon	92
Peanut Butter	1 tablespoon	90
French Dressing (homemade)	1 tablespoon	86
French Dressing (commercial)	1 tablespoon	59
Boiled Dressing (homemade)	1 tablespoon	30
Lowmay mayonnaise substitute	1 tablespoon	25
Frenchette Dressing	1 tablespoon	9

CONDIMENTS

	Average Serving	Calories
Green Olives	6 olives	48
Mission Olives, ripe	4 olives	42
Chili Sauce	2 tablespoons	34
Tomato Catsup	2 tablespoons	34
Leeks	2 stalks 5 inches long	24
Dill Pickles	1 pickle 4 inches long	15
Mixed Pickles, chopped	1 tablespoon	14
Horseradish, prepared	1 tablespoon	8
Capers	1 tablespoon	8
Vanilla Extract	½ teaspoon	3
Garlic	1 clove garlic	2
Cider Vinegar	1 tablespoon	2
Salt	¼ teaspoon	0
Pepper	⅛ teaspoon	0
Paprika	⅛ teaspoon	0
Herbs and Spices	⅛ teaspoon	0

SWEETSTUFFS

	Average Serving		Calories
Puddings (Chocolate, etc.)	½ cup	200	
Ice Cream	½ cup	154	
Chocolate Bars	1 regular small bar	154	
Fudge	1 piece, 1¼" square	118	
Peanut Brittle	1 piece, 2½" x 2½" x ⅜"	110	
Lollipops	1 medium, 2¼" diam.	108	
Chocolate Mints	1 medium	87	
Jelly Beans	10 jelly beans	66	
Honey (strained)	1 tablespoon	62	
Jam or Jelly	1 tablespoon	55	
Popcorn (popped)	1 cup	54	
Corn Sirup	1 tablespoon	52	
Sorghum	1 tablespoon	52	
Brown Sugar	1 tablespoon	52	
Maple Sugar	1 piece, 1" x 1¼" x ½"	52	
Chocolate Creams	1 average	51	
Maple Sirup	1 tablespoon	50	
Granulated Sugar	1 tablespoon	48	
Molasses	1 tablespoon	46	
Chocolate Marshmallow	1 average	45	
Powdered Sugar	1 tablespoon	42	
Caramels	1 medium	42	
Fondant	1 average	39	
Hard Candy	2 pieces	38	
Apple Butter	1 tablespoon	37	
Gum Drops	1 large or 8 small	33	
Candied Orange Peel	1 large piece	32	
Marshmallows	1 average	25	
Butterscotch	1 average piece	21	
Saccharin		0	
Sucaryl sweetener		0	

MEASURES (always LEVEL)

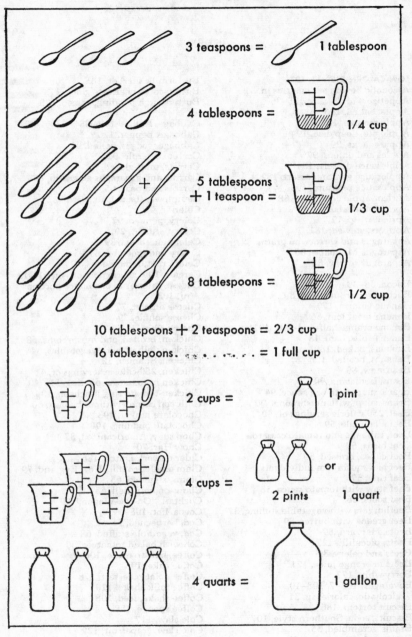

3 teaspoons = 1 tablespoon

4 tablespoons = 1/4 cup

5 tablespoons + 1 teaspoon = 1/3 cup

8 tablespoons = 1/2 cup

10 tablespoons + 2 teaspoons = 2/3 cup

16 tablespoons . . . . = 1 full cup

2 cups = 1 pint

4 cups = 2 pints or 1 quart

4 quarts = 1 gallon

INDEX